Nova Scotia

the Bradt Travel Guide

David Orkin

edition 2

www.bradtguides.com

Bradt Travel Guides Ltd, UK
The Globe Pequot Press Inc, USA

KEY
Capital city
Other city
Main town
Airport
Main road
Other road
Railway
Province boundary
National park/provincial park/
wilderness area/game sanctuary
PRINCE
EDWARD
ISLAND
NEW
BRUNSWICK
Northumberland Strait
See the 'Three Sisters' sea stacks and go hiking in Cape Chignecto Provincial Park
page 267
Visit the quaint town of Annapolis Royal (population 500)
page 208
Digby Neck – one of the best places in the world for whale watching
page 200
Visit the imposing lighthouse at Peggy's Cove
page 132
Lunenburg – a UNESCO World Heritage Site
page 149
Take a tour of Lunenburg Harbour on Bluenose II, a replica 1920s fishing schooner
page 153
Amherst Shore
Fort Lawrence
AMHERST
Pugwash
Wallace
Upper Nappan
Oxford
Tatamagouche
SPRINGHILL
Wentworth
Chignecto Bay
Chignecto Game Sanctuary
Cape Chignecto Provincial Park
Parrsboro
Cape Chignecto
Cape d'Or
Cape Split
Cape Blomidon
Blomidon Provincial Park
Cobequid Bay
Sheffield Mills
KENTVILLE
Wolfville
Bay of Fundy
North Mountain
South Mountain
Middleton
Windsor
Bridgetown
Musquodoboit Harbour
Victoria Beach
Annapolis Royal
BEDFORD
Digby
DARTMOUTH
Digby Neck
HALIFAX
East Ferry
St Mary's Bay
Maitland Bridge
Chester
Long Island
Weymouth
LaHave
Mahone Bay
Peggy's Cove
Pennant Point
Lunenburg
Kejimkujik National Park
Bridgewater
Freeport
Brier Island
Tobeatic Wilderness Area
Meteghan
Lake Rossignol
Cape St Mary
Liverpool
Jordan
YARMOUTH
Argyle
SHELBURNE
Tusket Islands
Barrington Head
Shag Harbour
Clark's Harbour
Cape Sable Island

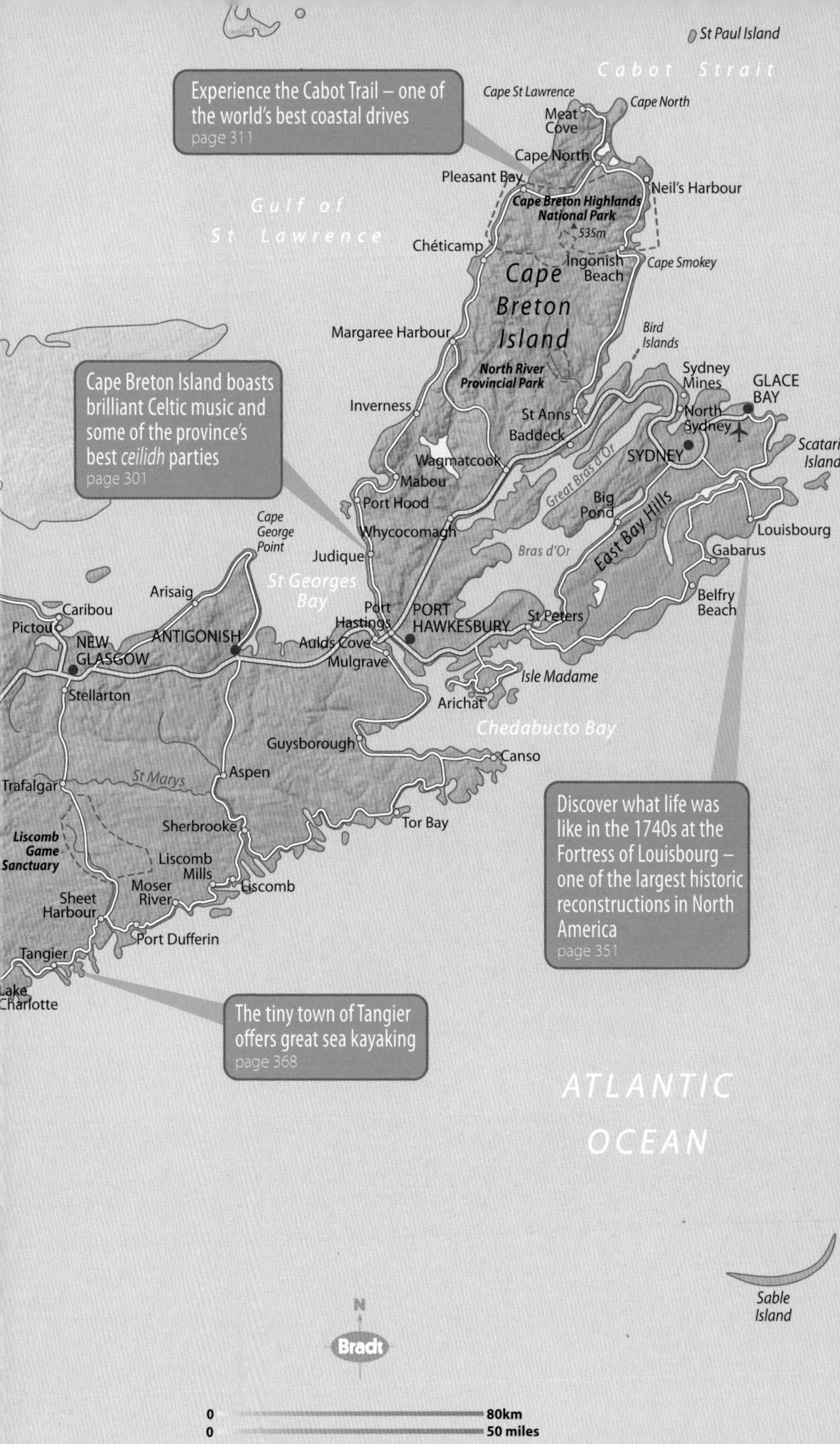

St Paul Island
Cabot Strait
Experience the Cabot Trail – one of the world's best coastal drives
page 311
Cape St Lawrence
Cape North
Meat Cove
Cape North
Pleasant Bay
Neil's Harbour
Cape Breton Highlands National Park
535m
Gulf of St Lawrence
Chéticamp
Ingonish Beach
Cape Smokey
Cape Breton Island
Bird Islands
Margaree Harbour
North River Provincial Park
Sydney Mines
GLACE BAY
Cape Breton Island boasts brilliant Celtic music and some of the province's best *ceilidh* parties
page 301
Inverness
St Anns
North Sydney
Baddeck
Scatarie Island
Wagmatcook
SYDNEY
Mabou
Great Bras d'Or
Port Hood
Big Pond
East Bay Hills
Louisbourg
Whycocomagh
Cape George Point
Bras d'Or
Gabarus
Judique
St Georges Bay
Arisaig
Belfry Beach
Caribou
Port Hastings
PORT HAWKESBURY
St Peters
Pictou
ANTIGONISH
NEW GLASGOW
Aulds Cove
Mulgrave
Isle Madame
Stellarton
Arichat
Chedabucto Bay
Guysborough
Canso
Trafalgar
St Marys
Aspen
Discover what life was like in the 1740s at the Fortress of Louisbourg – one of the largest historic reconstructions in North America
page 351
Tor Bay
Sherbrooke
Liscomb Game Sanctuary
Liscomb Mills
Moser River
Liscomb
Sheet Harbour
Port Dufferin
Tangier
Lake Charlotte
The tiny town of Tangier offers great sea kayaking
page 368
ATLANTIC OCEAN
Sable Island
N
Bradt
0
80km
0
50 miles

Nova Scotia

Don't miss...

Historic colonial architecture

The Fortress of Louisbourg, the largest reconstructed 18th-century French fortified town in North America, is just one example of Nova Scotia's colonial past

(NSTA) page 351

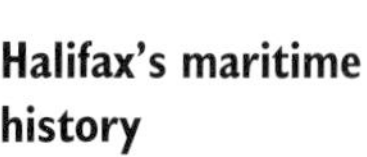

Halifax's maritime history

The province's most important metropolis is a testament to its strong links to the sea: the bustling waterfront is home to a range of museums and festivals, such as the Tall Ships festival held every four years in July

(MJ/S) page 86

Stunning geological sites
Locations such as the UNESCO-designated Joggins Fossil Cliffs – a paleontological site with extensive deposits of 300 million-year-old fossils are a geologist's and fossil hunter's dream (NSTA) page 268

Spectacular whale watching
Digby Neck is one of the best places in the world for sightings – spot smaller finback and minke whales early in the season and enormous humpbacks in the summer
(NSTA) page 200

Drives along the coast
One of the finest coastal drives in the world, the Cabot Trail weaves through miles of untouched wilderness, perfect for spotting moose, bald eagle and whale
(c) page 311

Nova Scotia in colour

top left The Old Town Clock in downtown Halifax, near Citadel Hill (CKPI/D) page 113

left Halifax Public Gardens are perfect for an afternoon stroll (NSTA) page 111

below Traditional architecture on a Halifax street (NSTA) page 32

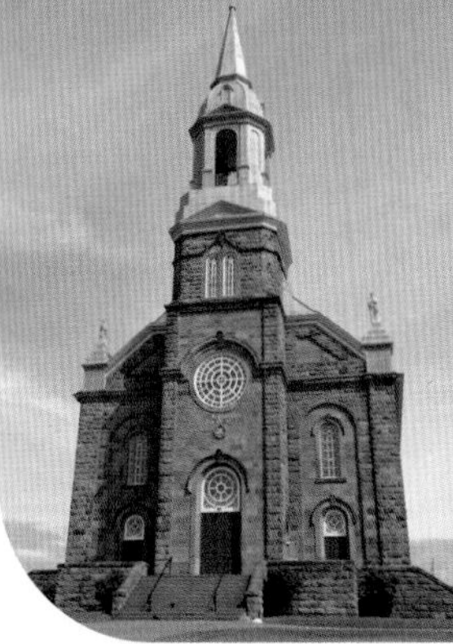

above left The Acadian church of Saint-Pierre sits in the village of Cheticamp (PM/S) page 312

above right Fort Anne National Historic Site in Annapolis Royal (NSTA) page 213

right Peggy's Cove is a popular, picturesque fishing village with a c1914 white octagonal lighthouse (A) page 132

below The colourful town of Lunenburg – the Old Town is one of the province's three UNESCO World Heritage Sites (GY/S) page 149

above Autumn is a perfect time to visit Nova Scotia for the explosion of colours. On Cape Breton Island, time your visit to coincide with the Celtic Colours Festival (NSTA) page 5

below Beautiful forest walks are a highlight of Kejimkujik National Park (SS) page 214

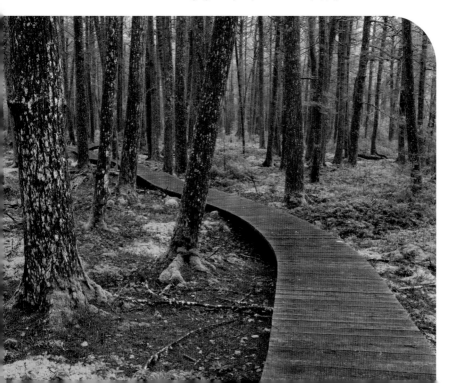

AUTHOR

David Orkin is a freelance travel writer whose work appears regularly in leading UK publications such as *The Independent*, *Wanderlust* and *Condé Nast Traveller*. He began writing about travel in 2000 after working in the travel industry for over 15 years, including eight years co-running his own successful company. He has travelled extensively since the mid 1970s and first visited Nova Scotia in 2004. Since then he has returned several times, exploring every corner of the province and (when not globetrotting) now spends the majority of the year in Nova Scotia.

AUTHOR'S STORY

When I visited Nova Scotia for the first time I looked for a guidebook to help enhance my experience there, but found that most of them lumped the province with its neighbours, Prince Edward Island and New Brunswick, some also including Newfoundland and Labrador. Fine for an overview of the entire region, but of limited use to anyone wanting to focus solely on Nova Scotia. I turned to Nova Scotia's tourism authorities who produced (and still do) *Doers' & Dreamers'*, a thorough listing of all the province's museums and attractions and virtually all accommodation choices from campgrounds to deluxe resorts, but these are unedited lists.

Each time that I went back to Nova Scotia and explored places – some wonderful, others missable – it became increasingly obvious that there was a need for a more comprehensive, subjective guide. Something to cater to those who wanted to do, those who wanted to dream, and those who wanted to discover the province's highlights, as well as its virtually unknown nooks and crannies. I put a proposal to write a book to the publisher that I thought would be most appropriate for such a guide. Bradt agreed.

Research took place on foot, in canoe and kayak, by ferry, by bike, by coach, and tens of thousands of kilometres by car – and I tried to return everywhere at a different time of year to see if my impressions changed. Now, my (Canadian) Permanent Resident status allows me to spend even more time exploring the province and enjoying long conversations with waiters, fishermen, B&B owners, shopkeepers, park rangers, artists, tourists, birders, musicians and many more – in Nova Scotia it is hard to find someone who doesn't like talking about their fascinating homeland. This guidebook is the collective result of those discussions and explorations.

PUBLISHER'S FOREWORD

Adrian Phillips, Publishing Director

Bradt has built a reputation around publishing guides to destinations off the tourist trail. That can mean places like Rwanda and Ethiopia, of course, but we mustn't forget that there are still areas of mystery and romance in the developed world. As author David Orkin says, despite many visits to Canada over the years, he knew very little about Nova Scotia before going there for the first time – just that it was probably 'cold, wet and windy'. Well, what a land of colour awaited. Who could fail to be enchanted by rugged cliffs, mist-veiled lighthouses and legends of pirates' derring-do? And who could fail to relax in a province where time marches to a slower beat? Nova Scotia – and David's excellent book – is very much in the Bradt mould.

Second edition published April 2013 First published December 2009

Bradt Travel Guides Ltd
IDC House, The Vale, Chalfont St Peter, Bucks SL9 9RZ, England
www.bradtguides.com
Print edition published in the USA by The Globe Pequot Press Inc,
PO Box 480, Guilford, Connecticut 06437-0480

Project Managers: Anna Moores and Kelly Randell
Cover research: Pepi Bluck

ISBN: 978 1 84162 454 9 (print)
e-ISBN: 978 1 84162 763 2 (e-pub)
e-ISBN: 978 1 84162 665 9 (mobi)

British Library Cataloguing in Publication Data
A catalogue record for this book is available from the British Library

Photographs Aconcagua (A); Alamy: Chris Cheadle (CC/A); chensiyuan (c); David Orkin (DO); Dreamstime: Charles Knox Photo Inc (CKPI/D); FLPA: Tony Hamblin (TH/FLPA); Justin Russell (JR); Maureen Newman (MN); Mike Baird (MB); Nova Scotia Tourism Agency (NSTA); Qias (Q); Shutterstock: Gary Yim (GY/S), Matthew Jacques (MJ/S), matthewsinger (m/S), Paul McKinnon (PM/S); Sherman Hines (SH); SuperStock (SS)
Front cover Lobster pots at Peggy's Cove (CC/A)
Back cover Autumn colours in Cape Breton Highlands National Park (NSTA); Cyclists along the LaHave River in Lunenburg County, near Riverport (NSTA)
Title page Brightly coloured houses in Lunenburg (GY/S); Lupins blooming along the roadside (NSTA); Scottish heritage lives on in modern-day Nova Scotia (NSTA)

Maps David McCutcheon FBCart.S; colour map base by Nick Rowland FRGS; the Nova Scotia map published by ITMB Publishing (*www.itmb.ca*) was used to produce many of the maps in this book. A map published by All 4 One Graphics was used to produce the maps of Shelburne.

Typeset from the author's disc by Wakewing, High Wycombe
Production managed by Jellyfish Print Solutions; printed in India
Digital conversion by the Firsty Group

Acknowledgements

The list could fill a chapter, so I'll try to concentrate on those who have gone way beyond the call of duty. My thanks go to (those I've omitted and) Doug Anweiler, Alain Belliveau, Ed Bottrell, Louise Breton, Susan Budd, Lindsay Champion, Angela Chartier, Scott Cunningham, Sebelle Deese, Dennis Doyon, Ray Fraser, Bev Gabriel, Laena Garrison, Lee George, Emily Gratton, Leslie Langille, Sue MacIsaac, Mike Mackenzie, Blake Maybank, Bill Monk, Oralee O'Byrne, Dorothy Outhouse, Danny Paul, Roger Savage, Jonathan Sheppard, Lillian Stewart, and Andrea Young.

(I didn't meet him, and didn't know him, but) Raymond Taavel helped with the book's first edition: tragically he was in the wrong place at the wrong time and was killed in April 2012 trying to break up a fight outside a Halifax bar.

Thanks to everyone at Bradt, particularly Anna Moores, Kelly Randell and Rachel Fielding, and to David McCutcheon for his sterling work in converting my barely legible scribbles into such good maps. Last, but by no means least, special thanks to Vanessa, Oliver and Eleanor for their patience and support.

FEEDBACK REQUEST

Whilst much seems timeless in Nova Scotia, many things relevant to the visitor change frequently. Cafés, restaurants and B&Bs seem to close down, open up or change owners more often than elsewhere. Museums move or expand, new tours start up, etc. Even more common are changes to opening hours, days and dates. I will do my best to keep up with all the changes, but welcome your help. In addition, your tips, ideas, personal reflections – and criticism – will help improve the next edition. Contact me by email at **e** info@bradtguides.com or by post c/o Bradt Travel Guides, First Floor, IDC House, The Vale, Chalfont St Peter, Bucks SL9 9RZ. You can also visit the Bradt website at www.bradtguides.com/guidebook-updates for updates to information in this guide. Alternatively you can add a review of the book to www.bradtguides.com or Amazon. Thanks! David

Contents

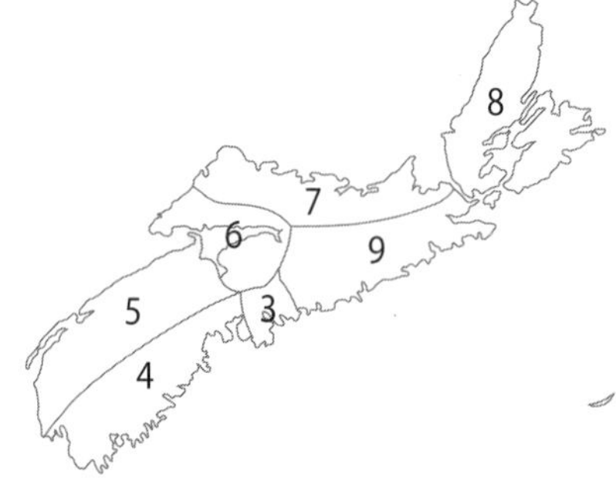

LIST OF MAPS

Introduction

By the time I first visited Nova Scotia I had worked in the travel industry for close to 20 years and considered myself well travelled. I had made numerous long trips to Canada, but other than the fact that its airport (and presumably biggest city) was Halifax, I knew very little about Nova Scotia. If pressed, I would have said that I imagined it was cold, wet and windy.

Since then, I've learnt much about the province. Although it always seemed to be lumped in with its maritime neighbours (New Brunswick, Prince Edward Island and Newfoundland and Labrador), it is large enough (55,300km^2) and varied enough (dense forest, countless remote lakes and waterways, a vibrant capital, fabulous music, photogenic fishing villages, towering cliffs and beautiful sandy beaches) to be a popular destination in its own right. Wrapped in 7,400km of coastline and virtually an island, Nova Scotia's culture and heartbeat has always been shaped by the sea. Stories of pirates, buried treasure and ghost-ships abound, and there are stunningly located lighthouses to photograph.

Compared with the UK, it may have relatively cold winters with a fair amount of snow, but Nova Scotia is hardly 'the Frozen North' – the provincial capital, Halifax, is on the same latitude as Bordeaux, France.

When in Nova Scotia, my partner and I liked the contrast of the simple, slow rural lifestyle versus the buzz of Halifax; we were enchanted by the character, comfort (and breakfasts) at the B&Bs; we delighted in the heritage architecture, the music, the seafood, the orchards and the wild flowers; and chatting to the locals – humorous, welcoming and proud of their province – was always entertaining.

We wondered how the kids would enjoy it. Nova Scotia's theme parks are few and far between, and the province's biggest, Upper Clements Theme Park (see page 207), isn't exactly Disneyland. There are only a few cinemas and, with a couple of exceptions, the museums aren't exactly hi-tech. Apart from the Northumberland Strait (and a few other hotspots) the sea isn't warm enough for swimming.

But they loved watching a blacksmith at work and wool being spun at the living museums, taking a boat trip in search of whales, paddling a canoe, and gorging themselves on berries at a U-pick (pick-your-own) farm. On Cape Breton Island we had moose-spotting competitions, sailed on the Bras d'Or Lake, explored the fortress at Louisbourg and swapped four wheels for two on Isle Madame.

The kids played soldiers at the Halifax Citadel, and rolled down the grassy ramparts at Annapolis Royal's Fort Anne. Ice creams made up for the disappointment of failing to find any fossils or gemstones on the beach at Scots Bay.

After several visits we decided to save the time and expense of crossing and re-crossing the Atlantic. We bought a big souvenir – a house overlooking the sea – and now call Nova Scotia home.

Bradt Travel Guides

Claim 20% discount on your next Bradt book when you order from www.bradtguides.com quoting the code BRADT20

Africa

Africa Overland £16.99
Algeria £15.99
Angola £18.99
Botswana £16.99
Burkina Faso £17.99
Cameroon £15.99
Cape Verde £15.99
Congo £16.99
Eritrea £15.99
Ethiopia £17.99
Ethiopia Highlights £15.99
Ghana £15.99
Kenya Highlights £15.99
Madagascar £16.99
Madagascar Highlights £15.99
Malawi £15.99
Mali £14.99
Mauritius, Rodrigues & Réunion £16.99
Mozambique £15.99
Namibia £15.99
Nigeria £17.99
North Africa: Roman Coast £15.99
Rwanda £16.99
São Tomé & Príncipe £14.99
Seychelles £16.99
Sierra Leone £16.99
Somaliland £15.99
South Africa Highlights £15.99
Sudan £16.99
Swaziland £15.99
Tanzania Safari Guide £17.99
Tanzania, Northern £14.99
Uganda £16.99
Zambia £18.99
Zanzibar £15.99
Zimbabwe £15.99

The Americas and the Caribbean

Alaska £15.99
Amazon Highlights £15.99
Argentina £16.99
Bahia £14.99
Cayman Islands £14.99
Chile Highlights £15.99
Colombia £17.99
Dominica £15.99
Grenada, Carriacou & Petite Martinique £15.99
Guyana £15.99
Haiti £16.99
Nova Scotia £15.99
Panama £14.99
Paraguay £15.99
Peru Highlights £15.99
Turks & Caicos Islands £14.99
Uruguay £15.99
USA by Rail £15.99
Venezuela £16.99
Yukon £14.99

British Isles

Britain from the Rails £14.99
Bus-Pass Britain £15.99
Eccentric Britain £16.99
Eccentric Cambridge £9.99
Eccentric London £14.99
Eccentric Oxford £9.99
Sacred Britain £16.99
Slow: Cornwall £14.99
Slow: Cotswolds £14.99
Slow: Devon & Exmoor £14.99
Slow: Dorset £14.99
Slow: New Forest £9.99
Slow: Norfolk & Suffolk £14.99
Slow: North Yorkshire £14.99
Slow: Northumberland £14.99
Slow: Sussex & South Downs National Park £14.99

Europe

Abruzzo £16.99
Albania £16.99
Armenia £15.99
Azores £14.99
Belarus £15.99
Bosnia & Herzegovina £15.99
Bratislava £9.99
Budapest £9.99
Croatia £15.99
Cross-Channel France: Nord-Pas de Calais £13.99
Cyprus see *North Cyprus*
Estonia £14.99
Faroe Islands £16.99
Flanders £15.99
Georgia £15.99
Greece: The Peloponnese £14.99
Hungary £15.99
Iceland £15.99
Istria £13.99
Kosovo £15.99
Lapland £15.99
Liguria £15.99
Lille £9.99
Lithuania £14.99
Luxembourg £14.99
Macedonia £16.99
Malta & Gozo £14.99
Montenegro £14.99
North Cyprus £13.99
Serbia £15.99
Slovakia £14.99
Slovenia £13.99
Svalbard: Spitsbergen, Jan Mayen, Franz Jozef Land £17.99
Switzerland Without a Car £15.99
Transylvania £15.99
Ukraine £16.99

Middle East, Asia and Australasia

Bangladesh £17.99
Borneo £17.99
Eastern Turkey £16.99
Iran £15.99
Israel £15.99
Jordan £16.99
Kazakhstan £16.99
Kyrgyzstan £16.99
Lake Baikal £15.99
Lebanon £15.99
Maldives £15.99
Mongolia £16.99
North Korea £14.99
Oman £15.99
Palestine £15.99
Shangri-La: A Travel Guide to the Himalayan Dream £14.99
Sri Lanka £15.99
Syria £15.99
Taiwan £16.99
Tajikistan £15.99
Tibet £17.99
Yemen £14.99

Wildlife

Antarctica: A Guide to the Wildlife £15.99
Arctic: A Guide to Coastal Wildlife £16.99
Australian Wildlife £14.99
East African Wildlife £19.99
Galápagos Wildlife £16.99
Madagascar Wildlife £16.99
Pantanal Wildlife £16.99
Southern African Wildlife £19.99
Sri Lankan Wildlife £15.99

Pictorials and other guides

100 Alien Invaders £16.99
100 Animals to See Before They Die £16.99
100 Bizarre Animals £16.99
Eccentric Australia £12.99
Northern Lights £6.99
Swimming with Dolphins, Tracking Gorillas £15.99
The Northwest Passage £14.99
Tips on Tipping £6.99
Total Solar Eclipse 2012 & 2013 £6.99
Wildlife & Conservation Volunteering: The Complete Guide £13.99

Travel literature

A Glimpse of Eternal Snows £11.99
A Tourist in the Arab Spring £9.99
Connemara Mollie £9.99
Fakirs, Feluccas and Femmes Fatales £9.99
Madagascar: The Eighth Continent £11.99
The Marsh Lions £9.99
The Two-Year Mountain £9.99
The Urban Circus £9.99
Up the Creek £9.99

Part One

GENERAL INFORMATION

NOVA SCOTIA AT A GLANCE

Name of province Nova Scotia
Country name Canada
Languages English, French
Population 922,000 (2011 census)
People Scottish 29%, English 27%, Irish 19%, French/Acadian 12%, German 8%, Mi'kmaq 2%, others 3%
Religion Roman Catholic 37%, United Church 16%, Anglican 13%, Baptist 11%, Presbyterian 3%, Lutheran 1%, Pentecostal 1%, other or no religious affiliation 18%
Canadian Prime Minister Stephen Harper
Nova Scotia Premier Darrell Dexter
Nova Scotia ruling political party New Democratic Party (NDP)
Neighbouring provinces and states Land border with New Brunswick, Canada; nearby Canadian provinces Prince Edward Island and Newfoundland and Labrador. Nearest US state: Maine.
Area 55,300km^2
Time Atlantic Standard Time Zone (AST). Winter GMT -4; summer GMT -3 (clocks adjusted second Sunday in March and first Sunday in November).
Currency Canadian dollar (CAN$ or CAD)
Exchange rate £1=CAN$1.58, US$1=CAN$0.99, €1=CAN$1.33 (January 2013)
Flag An extended blue cross on a white background superimposed with a shield bearing the Royal Arms of Scotland
Telephone codes Canada +1 (international code); Nova Scotia 902 (also 782 from late 2014 – see box, page 75)
Electricity supply 110v 60Hz
Public holidays 1 January (New Year's Day), March/April (Good Friday), March/April (Easter Monday), May (Victoria Day; first Monday after 25 May), 1 July (Canada Day), August (Natal Day; first Monday in August), September (Labour Day; first Monday in September), October (Thanksgiving Day; second Monday in October), 11 November (Remembrance Day), 25 December (Christmas Day), 26 December (Boxing Day)

1

Background Information

GEOGRAPHY

With an area of 55,300km^2, Nova Scotia is the second smallest of Canada's 13 provinces and territories – only nearby Prince Edward Island (at 5,660km^2) is smaller. For a European comparison Nova Scotia is larger than Denmark (approximately 43,000km^2) but much smaller than Scotland (approximately 79,000km^2).

Connected to mainland Canada only by a narrow isthmus, it is almost surrounded by the sea. To the south and east is the Atlantic Ocean; to the northeast is the Cabot Strait; to the north the Northumberland Strait; and to the northwest the Bay of Fundy. Although it measures over 550km in length, with an average width of 130km, Nova Scotia has 7,400km of coastline. No point of land is more than 60km from the sea. The shape of the province has been likened to that of a lobster, with Cape Breton Island to the northeast forming the claws.

Halifax is Nova Scotia's capital and is situated at the head of a huge natural harbour on the southeastern coast of the province. In terms of latitude, Halifax is further south than both Paris and Vienna. In fact, the province lies halfway between the North Pole and the Equator, straddling the 45th parallel.

Thick forests – with pine, spruce, fir, hemlock, birch and maple dominating – dotted with lakes cover 80% of the land, but there are also blossom-covered orchards, blueberry fields, and rolling farmland. Much of the best farmland is found in the Annapolis Valley, sheltered by hills to both the north and south.

In general, elevations do not exceed 200m. The main exception is on Cape Breton Island, where 535m-high White Hill forms the province's highest point.

CLIMATE

Nova Scotia lies within the Northern Temperate Zone. The climate is more typically continental than maritime, although the sea has an attenuating effect on the temperature highs and lows. Cape Breton Island experiences much more extreme weather patterns than mainland Nova Scotia. In general, sea temperatures are too low for enjoyable swimming: the main exceptions to this are the coastal waters of the Northumberland Strait and northwest Cape Breton Island, particularly in August.

Annual precipitation averages 1,200mm, falling mainly as rain during autumn and as snow in winter. Boosting the average are the highlands of Cape Breton Island (an average of over 1,600mm of precipitation per year) and the southwest (1,500mm): in comparison, the Northumberland Strait receives less than 1,000mm a year.

The merging of warm, moisture-laden air above the Gulf Stream with the far cooler air above the Labrador Current results in a lot of fog: this can often blanket coastal regions, particularly in the morning between mid spring and early summer. The good news is that the fog is often localised, and more often than not dissipates by late morning. Some of the foggiest parts of the province are Halifax, Yarmouth, Canso, Sydney and Sable Island.

Although most fizzle out before they reach Nova Scotia, some hurricanes and tropical storms do stay the distance and sweep across the province, uprooting trees, knocking down power lines and washing away bridges. The worst in recent years was Hurricane Juan (September 2003) which caused vast amounts of damage.

Environment Canada's website (*www.weatheroffice.gc.ca/canada_e.html*) offers weather forecasts for over 40 towns across the province. Current weather forecasts can also be obtained by phone (☏ *426 9090*).

WINTER (*early November–mid April*) Winter is moderately cold with high temperatures ranging from an average of -4°C to 5°C. At this time of year, freezing rain is a Nova Scotia speciality. There are a fair number of bright, sunny (albeit cold) days. The Northumberland Strait and Gulf of St Lawrence are ice-covered during much of the winter, cooling down nearby coastal areas.

SPRING (*mid April–mid June*) During spring average high temperatures range from 4°C to 14°C inland, and a couple of degrees cooler in coastal areas.

SUMMER (*mid June–mid September*) Summer temperatures range from daytime highs of 18°C to 25°C (occasionally reaching 30°C) to evening lows of 9°C to 14°C. Further inland, the air is typically about 5°C warmer.

AUTUMN (*mid September–early November*) Early autumn is often mild, and the warm Gulf Stream extends the season, but days become cooler as winter approaches.

NATURAL HISTORY

FLORA The province offers a range of habitats from the Atlantic Coastal Plain to the high plateaux of Cape Breton's northern highlands, and these support a wide variety of flora – including over 1,650 vascular plants. Trees cover close to 80% of Nova Scotia, but aren't just evergreen conifers, something that becomes even more apparent if you visit in the autumn. At this time, hardwoods such as maple, birch, oak, aspen and mountain ash burst into an explosion of brilliant colour. It is a conifer, however, the red spruce (*Picea rubens*), which has been designated Nova Scotia's provincial tree.

In exposed coastal areas, stunted trees such as black spruce, often bent by the wind, are common as are shrubs like creeping juniper, common juniper and black crowberry. Sand dunes are usually covered with marram grass (also known as American beach grass). You're also likely to see seaside plantain, beach pea, sea rocket and seaside goldenrod: look out too for the aromatic northern bayberry and beautiful wild roses.

Nova Scotia's provincial flower is the mayflower, or trailing arbutus, which blooms (with delicately scented pink flowers) in the forest glades in early spring, often amid the last remaining snows of winter. From then until early autumn a range of species will be in bloom – the visitor will often see carpets of colour by the roadside. Stands of lupins, for example, are stunning in June. Some of the more common summer-flowering species include Queen Anne's lace, ox-eye daisy,

AUTUMN COLOURS

As summer begins to give way to autumn, days become shorter and nights become cooler. The colour of the leaves of deciduous trees and shrubs, dark green with chlorophyll in summer, also begins to change. Chlorophyll production declines, and the green colour fades. Whilst the leaves of many species turn yellow, the colour pigmentation of red oak, mountain ash, blueberry and huckleberry leaves, for example, turn red, whilst the colour of sugar and red maple leaves runs the range from yellow to purple.

When contrasted with the dark green of the evergreens and the blue (hopefully) of the sky, the result is one of nature's most stunning displays.

In a typical year, the 'leaf-peeping' season runs from the end of September until late October, and is at its height in the second week of October. Nature being nature, not all years are typical: summer 2012, for example, was sunnier and far drier than the norm, confusing the leaves into turning weeks earlier. In season, there's a regularly updated leaf-watch map and blog on the official Tourism Nova Scotia website (*www.novascotia.com/leaf*).

Where are the best viewing areas? A free booklet available from tourist offices lists over 80 possibilities. Personal favourites (if you time it right) are Milton (see page 168), Kejimkujik National Park (if it is open – see page 214), Bear River (page 204), Wentworth (page 281) and Cape George (page 299). There are many wonderful areas on Cape Breton Island, too – try to time your visit to coincide with the wonderful Celtic Colours Festival (see box, page 306).

pearly everlasting and yarrow. Purple loosestrife may be an aggressive weed, but still contributes to the floral colour show.

Bog plants typically include various mosses, cranberries and liverwort. Many types of orchid can also be seen. Some bogs are also home to insectivorous plants such as sundew, butterwort, pitcher plant and bladderwort.

Seaweeds Many of the algae found on the beaches and shores are put to good use. Rockweed is the dominant brown seaweed found intertidally along the province's coast. Hand-harvested, its main use is as a fertiliser. Irish moss has long been harvested for use as a food source: it contains high amounts of carrageenan, used in the manufacture of dairy products, cosmetics and more.

Dulse has reddish-purple, somewhat leathery fronds. Rich in minerals and vitamins and with a high protein content, it is often dried and sold as a snack food (something of an acquired taste which I am yet to acquire!).

SLIMY SUCCESS STORY

Dartmouth-based Acadian Seaplants (*468 2840; www.acadianseaplants.com*) has come a long way in a couple of decades. Based near Lower East Pubnico (see page 181), it operates the largest land-based commercial seaweed cultivation facility in the world, and has expanded into the neighbouring provinces of New Brunswick and Prince Edward Island. Rockweed, Irish moss, kelp, bladderwrack and other algae are collected, processed, and used to produce a range of agricultural, beauty and brewing products, including an 'instant seaweed salad' which is very popular in Japan.

FAUNA

Mammals You're too late for the woodland caribou (hunted to extinction here by the 1920s), but Nova Scotia is home to almost 70 different land mammals. The most common large mammal is the white-tailed deer, which, when disturbed, will 'flash' the white underside of its distinctive tail. The deer are often seen prancing across the road in wooded rural areas, particularly early or late in the day. Other species include mink, river otter, red fox, coyote (similar to a large, grey-brown fox), red squirrel, seven types of bat, eastern chipmunk (reddish-brown in colour with five distinct black stripes down its back and a member of the squirrel family), and various members of the weasel family including the American marten.

Mammals with which visitors from the UK may be less familiar include the porcupine, common on the mainland. The porcupine – the province's second-largest rodent after the beaver – is an excellent climber. It has strong, short legs with powerful claws and is covered with thousands of sharp quills. Porcupines feed on twigs, leaves, buds and the inner bark of trees and are nocturnal (so I was surprised to find two up one of my apple trees recently). If you travel off the major highways, you're likely to see porcupines, but sadly they will almost always be roadkill (killed by traffic). Kejimkujik National Park is a good place to try and spot a live one.

Another common species is the eastern striped skunk, easily recognised by its long, black fur, long, bushy tail, and two white strips that run along its back. It can grow up to 1m in length. If a skunk turns its back on you and raises its tail, run – or at least cover your eyes: it is about to squirt from its anal glands a particularly malodorous and long-lasting spray. Racoons are found throughout the province: excellent climbers and generally nocturnal, they have small pointed ears, greyish fur, a black mask around the eyes and black rings around a long, bushy tail.

Also known as a groundhog, the woodchuck is the largest member of the squirrel family and grows up to 40–50cm in length. It has a stocky build with a flattened head and short tail. The muskrat is a large (40–50cm) rodent with brown to black fur, webbed feet and a long, scaly tail flattened on both sides. It is an excellent swimmer. The northern flying squirrel is common throughout the forests of Nova Scotia; the smaller and much rarer southern flying squirrel is thought to be limited to parts of the Gaspereau Valley and Kejimkujik National Park. The squirrels have a pair of skin membranes which enable them to glide (rather than fly) up to 35m.

Approximately 100–500 lynx live on Cape Breton Island, the majority in remote areas of the island's northern highlands. Sometimes mistaken for a bobcat, the lynx has larger paws, longer ear tufts and a totally black-tipped tail. Bobcats have stumpy tails, with a dark tip on top. Their hind legs are noticeably longer than the forelegs, and their coats tend to be more patterned than the lynx.

Having survived the days when their pelts were the mainstay of Nova Scotia's economy, the beaver is common throughout the province, and is Nova Scotia's

MYSTERY CAT

Although (supposedly) hunted to extinction in the province over a century ago, no-one is too sure whether cougars (known elsewhere in North America as mountain lions) exist in Nova Scotia. There are about 100 reported sightings a year (one man alone has claimed five separate sightings between 1991 and 2009), but as yet no physical evidence. The Department of Natural Resources sits on the fence: apparently the animal has been included on the Department's 'protected' list 'just in case'.

largest rodent. It is known for its habit of building dams (and dome-shaped lodges) on streams to form ponds.

There are not thought to be any wolves in Nova Scotia, and the first reports of coyotes in the province date from the late 1970s. Now they are a common feature of the environment. In recent years, there have been a handful of high-profile interactions between coyotes and humans, culminating in a tragedy on Cape Breton Island in October 2009 when two coyotes attacked and killed a 19-year-old lone female hiker. That was only North America's second reported fatal coyote attack on a human (the other victim was a three year old in California in 1981).

The type of coyote (*Canis latrans var.*) found in the region is said to be more of a coyote/wolf hybrid, and is approximately 20% larger and heavier than its counterpart in western Canada. Male coyotes in Nova Scotia average 15kg but can weigh over 20kg. They generally eat deer, squirrels, rabbits, hares and fruit, and are excellent scavengers. The coyote population in Nova Scotia is estimated to be around 8,000. In 2010, the provincial government introduced a CAN$20 per pelt bounty to encourage hunters to 'harvest' coyotes during the hunting season.

In the unlikely event that you encounter a coyote at close range, official advice includes 'don't try to feed or photograph the coyote(s)' and 'remain calm and remove yourself from the area by backing away slowly – do not turn and run'.

With the possible exception of the black bear, the land mammal that most visitors want to see is the largest member of the deer family, the moose. Dark brown and awkward-looking, moose have humped shoulders, spindly legs, a drooping muzzle, and a bell – a flap of skin hanging from the throat. An adult male (bull) moose stands approximately 2m tall at the shoulder and weighs around 500kg. In spring, bulls grow (often huge) antlers that are shed late in winter. Moose can be dangerous if approached too closely, especially during mating season (September–October) or calving season (late May–early June). There are two moose sub-species in the province: the mainland moose and the Cape Breton moose. Approximately 5,000 moose live on Cape Breton Island, which offers the highest chance of a sighting, whereas fewer than 1,000 individuals are thought to survive in isolated areas of the mainland.

The black bear is usually (but not necessarily) black, and is the only type of bear found in Nova Scotia. Though widespread, it is not often seen by visitors. Although not true hibernators, bears tend to stay in their dens from mid November to early spring. During this period, their metabolism slows and they are unconscious but will wake and respond to danger. Adult males stand at about 1m high at the shoulder and can weigh 200kg. They are said to be nocturnal, but I have seen black bears crossing backroads and walking along the edge of woodland in the middle of the day. Whilst undoubtedly dangerous, there have been no records of anyone even being scratched by a bear in Nova Scotia. Don't be the first, though – be aware.

Finally, the only wild horses to be found in Nova Scotia are Sable Island horses (see box, page 383, for further information).

Reptiles and amphibians Nova Scotia has no poisonous snakes: the largest (rarely over 1m in length) and most widespread is the maritime garter snake.

Seven species of turtle can be found off Nova Scotia's shores at different periods of the year. During summer, there are sightings of the Atlantic leatherback, Ridley and loggerhead turtles.

Four species of (harmless) salamander live in the province, the rarest of which is the four-toed salamander, which is orange to reddish brown with black spots and is the only white-bellied salamander. In addition, there's just one type of toad (the eastern American) and seven frog species – the largest of which is the bullfrog.

Birds *with Blake Maybank, author of* Birding Sites of Nova Scotia.

Nova Scotia is a superb birdwatching (we call it 'birding') destination. Despite being the second-smallest province in Canada, it boasts the country's third-highest bird species' total; only British Columbia and Ontario – Canada's largest provinces – have more.

While there are no species endemic to Nova Scotia, the province is a reliable and logistically friendly base to seek out certain sought-after birds, including boreal forest specialities (spruce grouse, boreal chickadee, black-backed woodpecker and white-winged crossbill), winter birds from the high arctic (dovekie and black-headed gull), seabirds (Manx shearwater and great skua), and regional specialities (Bicknell's thrush that breeds in the Cape Breton Highlands, and the Ipswich race of savanna sparrow, that breeds only on Sable Island).

The province is well situated in all seasons. The surrounding ocean moderates the climate, and the cooler summers mean that northern species can breed – among the 150-plus breeding species are 22 warblers, nine flycatchers and 20 sparrows and finches. The ocean also moderates the winter, with nearly 200 species sighted each year between December and February (see *http://tinyurl.com/nswinter*). And because Nova Scotia lies at the eastern end of the continent, halfway between the Pole and the Equator, many waifs and rarities have visited, comprising more than 35% of the province's impressive total of 470 species.

Visitors are also drawn to the province's birding spectacles. From June to October the Bay of Fundy offers superb whale-watching, and the abundant food that attracts the whales also lures large numbers of seabirds, making Nova Scotia the most affordable and reliable spot in eastern North America to see thousands of shearwaters (great, sooty and Manx), storm petrels (both Wilson's and Leach's),

NOTABLE BIRDING SITES

During the breeding season the best sites are in the interior, where the diversity of breeding birds is the greatest. The two national parks, Kejimkujik (page 214) in the south, and Cape Breton Highlands (page 317) in the north are both rewarding, with extensive trail systems, visitor facilities, and informed staff. Elsewhere there are dozens of smaller provincial and regional parks, trails, and freshwater marshes. Try, for example, the Uniacke Estate (page 121), Annapolis Royal's French Basin Trail (page 212), Amherst Point (page 277), the Fairmont Ridge Trail (page 299) and the Musquodoboit Trailway (page 364). For spring and autumn land bird migration the best sites are the Canso Peninsula (page 301), Hartlen Point (page 81), Cape Sable Island (page 179) and Long and Brier islands (page 203).

Autumn shorebirds are best viewed at Cherry Hill Beach (page 165), Cape Sable Island (page 179) and inner Cole Harbour (page 361). The finest autumn hawk-watching site is on Brier Island (page 203).

Winter birding (see *tinyurl.com/nswinter*) is primarily a coastal experience, with popular areas including Halifax Harbour (page 82) and the Eastern Shore, Pictou Harbour (page 285), Cape Sable Island (page 179), Canso Harbour (page 301), Brier Island (page 203), and Sydney Harbour (page 301).

If you want to go birding with a guide, try Blake Maybank (*852 2077;* e *bmaybank@gmail.com; www.blakemaybank.com*). Alternatively, consider going out with a local birdwatcher: two or three are usually listed on http://birdingpal.org.

and phalaropes (red and red-necked), as well as numerous puffins, razorbills, fulmar, jaegers, and occasionally south polar skuas.

Nova Scotia has its own seabird colonies. Atlantic puffins, razorbills and black-legged kittiwakes reign over the Bird Islands in Cape Breton, accessible by daily guided boat tour, and Canada's largest roseate tern colony lies on The Brothers Islands, off the village of Lower West Pubnico in Yarmouth County. Another great avian display is the southward migration of arctic-nesting shorebirds. Millions of sandpipers refuel in the rich Bay of Fundy mudflats exposed by the world's highest tides. The largest flocks, primarily semi-palmated sandpipers and sometimes in excess of half a million birds, typically occur in the second and third weeks of August. Along the Atlantic coast shorebird flocks are smaller, but contain more species.

Winter offers its own spectacle, when nearly 1,000 bald eagles descend on the Annapolis Valley (see page 185).

The search for bird species and spectacles occurs against a backdrop of uncommon beauty – visiting birdwatchers, especially those from Europe or the urban United States, enjoy the absence of crowds, and the freedom to wander almost anywhere the urge takes them. The joy of watching shorebirds on a nearly deserted pristine beach, or listening to warblers sing along well-maintained and secure trails, is an experience rare or absent in much of the world.

MARINE WILDLIFE

Whales Whilst man has been instrumental in wiping out over 90% of the world's whale population in the last couple of centuries, the good news is that Nova Scotia is one of the best places in the world to go whale-watching, both in terms of quantity, and variety – 21 whale species cruise the province's coastal waters. Baleen whales (such as minke, humpback, fin and the critically endangered north Atlantic right whales) are drawn by huge amounts of plankton, krill and schools of small fish, particularly where the cold outflow of the Bay of Fundy meets the warm Gulf Stream waters. Toothed whales (such as pilot, killer (orca) and sperm whales) tend to eat fish and squid and are common in the Gulf of St Lawrence and Cabot Strait. Although it varies from species to species, whale numbers tend to be highest from late July to mid September.

For many visitors, a tour on a whale-watching boat is a must-do (and highlight) of a summer or early autumn visit to Nova Scotia. Seeing a huge humpback whale breaching at close quarters or watching a huge fluked tail disappear into the sea are memories that will last a lifetime. On many tours, porpoises, dolphins, seals and pelagic seabirds join in the action and are added bonuses.

Although trips are offered from various places in the province, two areas stand out. One is northern Cape Breton Island, but, for me, the best whale-watching trips depart from Westport (see page 202) on Brier Island, and Freeport and Tiverton (see page 202) on adjacent Long Island. Boat trips apart, it is not unusual to spot whales from the land, especially in the areas just mentioned.

Seals Two seal species are commonly found in the coastal waters of Nova Scotia: harbour, and grey seals. Harp and hooded seals are far rarer here. Don't be surprised to see a harbour seal pop its head out of the water in Halifax Harbour; otherwise good places to see seals include Kejimkujik Seaside (see page 170), Brier Island (see page 203), northeast Cape Breton Island (see page 301), and Sable Island (see page 382) – home to the world's largest breeding colony of grey seals. Most maritime fishermen blame seals for decimating fish stocks in the region.

Fish, shellfish and molluscs For centuries, incredible quantities of fish – particularly cod – drew fishermen from near and far to the region's waters. As recently as the last few decades, cod numbers have dropped alarmingly, largely because of overfishing. Dozens of other species live in the province's coastal waters, streams, rivers and lakes: these include Atlantic salmon, mackerel, pollock, haddock, flounder, hake, herring, monkfish, perch, pickerel, trout and eel. Bluefin tuna, porbeagle and blue shark are popular targets for deep-sea sport-fishing.

Despite the (near) death of groundfishing, shellfish and molluscs – particularly lobster, scallop, shrimp, clam and crab – are now the focus of the fishermen's attention, and grace many a table in the province's eateries.

NATIONAL PARKS Nova Scotia boasts three of Canada's 44 national parks: Kejimkujik National Park & National Historic Site, Cape Breton Highlands National Park, and the newly designated Sable Island National Park Reserve.

Kejimkujik National Park & National Historic Site 'Keji' – as it is more commonly known – is accessed by Highway 8 which connects Liverpool (see page 162) and Annapolis Royal (page 208). The largest inland national park in Atlantic Canada draws lovers of the outdoors for hiking, lake swimming, mountain biking, canoeing and kayaking. The park has another section (Kejimkujik Seaside), approximately 100km away on the coast. For more information, see pages 214 and 170 respectively.

Cape Breton Highlands National Park Completely different in character from Keji, this national park is situated in northern Cape Breton Island. Boasting magnificent coastal and mountain scenery and superb hiking, it is accessed by a dramatic scenic drive, the **Cabot Trail**, and is described on pages 311–12.

Sable Island National Park Reserve Those lucky enough to get to one of Canada's newest national parks, a narrow, windswept crescent and one of Canada's furthest offshore islands, will be rewarded with shifting sand dunes, seals and wild horses (see pages 382–5).

UNESCO BIOSPHERE RESERVES Nova Scotia is also home to two UNESCO biosphere reserves: such reserves are described as 'sites established... to promote sustainable development based on local community efforts and sound science'. One – the **Southwest Nova Biosphere Reserve** (*www.swnovabiosphere.ca*) encompasses (as you might have guessed) most of the province's southwest, and occupies over 1.5 million hectares. The other is Cape Breton Island's **Bras d'Or Lakes Biosphere Reserve** (*http://blbra.ca*).

PROVINCIAL PARKS Nova Scotia also has almost 130 provincial parks (*http://parks.gov.ns.ca*) administered by the Parks and Recreation section of the Department of Natural Resources. These vary from parks with a few picnic tables and interpretive panels, to magnificent stretches of coastal scenery peppered with hiking trails.

The majority of provincial parks are day-use only and are open between mid May and mid October: about 20 others have campgrounds – reservations can be made online or by phone (**t/f** *1 888 544 3434*) – and generally shorter seasons. Sadly, some are only open between late June and the beginning of September. When parks are closed for the season, barriers prevent vehicular entry: grounds, trails and roads are not maintained and no services are provided (water is turned off and

UNKIND CUTS

The 2012 federal budget hit hard at Parks Canada, which is responsible for the country's National Parks (NPs), National Historic Sites (NHSs), and more). The government said that 600 jobs would go at Parks Canada, with another 400 'at risk' (250–350 of those positions are in Nova Scotia). Since then, Parks Canada staff have spent countless hours trying to work out how to try and keep everyone (including visitors and staff) as happy as possible. The short-term solution seems to be to cut services and access in the long off-season to try to maintain the best possible experience for those that visit between Victoria Day (late May) and Thanksgiving (early–mid October). For example, whereas Kejimkujik NP (see page 214) has long been open year-round (albeit with limited services and facilities in the off-season), it will now be closed to the public for over seven months of the year. It is too early to tell whether other things – for example, the chance to interact with men, women and children (in character and in period costume), which was one of the highlights of a visit to Fortress of Louisbourg NHS (pages 351–3) – can still be maintained at previous levels.

toilets locked). However, it is almost always possible to park outside and enter the parks on foot – but be aware that you do so at your own risk.

Admission is charged at just two of the parks: Shubenacadie Provincial Wildlife Park (see page 251), and Cape Chignecto Provincial Park (page 267). For wonderful coastal hiking, try for example Cape Chignecto, Blomidon (page 228) or Taylor Head (page 369): beach fans will enjoy Rissers Beach (page 164), Summerville (page 169), Thomas Raddall (page 171), Mavillette Beach (page 192), the beach parks of the Northumberland Shore (pages 271–300), and Martinique Beach (page 365). Look for moose in the park at Cape Smokey (page 325).

CONSERVATION AND ENVIRONMENTAL ISSUES

Nova Scotia has a strong and enduring tradition of environmental activism. With its forests, lakes, and compelling intricate coastline of peninsulas, coves and harbours comes a history of human habitation that goes back over 10,000 years. The various settler groups (from the Mi'kmaq, through the 17th- and 18th-century French and English colonisers, to 'recent' immigrants from around the world) have found their livelihood in the natural abundance of the region. Forestry, hunting, fishing and trapping have provided shelter and food and a basis for trade and commerce that endure, to varying degrees, to this day.

The population grew and technological advances provided the means of sourcing, harvesting and exploiting the natural resources, but awareness of the systematic degradation of the environment and its natural species didn't really start surfacing until the 1970s. City sewage was being pumped into the harbours of Halifax and Sydney. The aggressive harvesting and destruction of the once vast cod fish populations; the clear-cutting of forests to produce pulp and paper; the accumulation of noxious by-products of steel manufacturing residue in Sydney's tar ponds (see page 340) are all examples of short-term economic gains at the expense of the environment and future generations.

In recent decades, Nova Scotians have increasingly come together in alliances and coalitions to fight for the protection of their environment and the reversal of environmentally damaging practices. The province has a waste diversion rate higher than any industrialised nation and has many other emerging success stories.

The tar ponds of Sydney are in the final stages of a CAN$400 million cleanup, which has taken years of fighting and false starts to get off the ground – and around six years to execute. Water quality in the once polluted Halifax Harbour has improved significantly, to the extent that some city beaches have reopened for swimming. Provincial law now requires that 40% of electricity sold by the monopoly provider, Nova Scotia Power, be generated from renewable resources by 2020. This is one of the most ambitious targets in North America and, with its abundant wind, tidal, biomass (and even solar resources), the target is achievable. However, some environmental advocates are concerned that to meet this target the government will include large-scale forest biomass. After years of overcutting to feed the (now failed) paper pulp mills, the controversy regarding clear-cutting, how it is defined, and how forest harvesting will be managed and monitored, will continue to cause tension between politicians and environmentalists.

Wind farms are more and more in evidence across the province. An additional potential source of renewable energy is the power generated by the Bay of Fundy tides (see page 23). The switch to renewables, energy efficiency programmes and the closure of at least one pulp mill has reduced demand for electricity and Nova Scotia has reduced its reliance on coal by 20%.

Nova Scotia has made good progress in meeting its target of protecting 12% of the provincial landmass by 2015. A deep decline in the global pulp and paper market has led to the closure of some of the largest paper mills in the province. In the case of one of the mills, this will trigger the sale of vast tracts of forest known as the Bowater-Mersey lands throughout Nova Scotia. Active campaigns are running in a co-ordinated effort by a coalition of citizens' groups, residents' associations, environmentalists and historians to reclaim these lands from private ownership, to be 'returned to the people of Nova Scotia' for sustainable commercial and recreational use and for the preservation of historical sites, with hopes that some of the land will be added to the other protected areas (see opposite). If this campaign succeeds Nova Scotia will become an even more highly accessible wilderness tourism destination, with a range of back-country experiences awaiting the fishing, canoeing, hiking and camping tourists of tomorrow.

Over the past several decades, the province has seen an increase in reliance on imported foods and consequently its food transport carbon footprint. To try to counter this, the environmental movement is actively engaged in protecting farmlands from development (300ha have been protected through working land conservation easements) and there are campaigns supporting organic farming and sustainable fishing practices, and experimentation with urban agriculture projects. There is growing public interest in home-grown foods, composting and community gardening, with environmentalists engaging schools and communities to build awareness and competence. The province now has over 40 farmers' markets.

Other ongoing environmental campaigns include the removal of lawn pesticides from the shelves of local stores. Green construction and renovation methods are on the increase. And though this is no Holland, there has been an increase in the number of cycle lanes; in 2010 the province introduced a 'one-metre rule' compelling drivers to give cyclists they were passing a wider berth.

The province's major environmental group is the **Ecology Action Centre** (*2705 Fern Lane, Halifax;* ☎ *429 2202; www.ecologyaction.ca*), established in 1971 and now with over 2,000 members, 400 volunteers and staff, and seven active teams and committees.

PROTECTED LAND Approximately 30% of land in Nova Scotia is Crown (or public) land. The province has close to 40 'Protected Areas' (the largest of which being the Tobeatic Wilderness Area, known as 'The Toby'; see box, page 176), over 20 nature reserves and two heritage rivers (the Margaree and the Shelburne).

Mining, forestry and the like are prohibited in Protected Areas (except where pre-existing commitments were made), which is all well and good. There are, however, many other areas of public land which concerned citizens believe should be protected from such things as industrial forestry and exploitative mining. In Nova Scotia, game sanctuaries don't protect habitat; they only curtail certain types of hunting activities. By contrast, protected wilderness areas protect habitat and prevent forest harvesting, mining, road building, and other types of development.

UNESCO WORLD HERITAGE SITES Three of Canada's 16 UNESCO World Heritage Sites are found in the province: Old Town Lunenburg (see page 150), the newly designated Grand Pré (page 235), and the Joggins Fossil Cliffs (page 269).

HISTORY

Note: Nova Scotia was not thus named until 1621, and was not declared a province until 1867. Nevertheless, I have used this designation for history before those dates to save repetition of the phrase 'what is now called'. Similarly, current place names have been used to describe events in areas that were at the time unnamed or known by a different name.

THE FIRST INHABITANTS The earliest evidence of human habitation found in Nova Scotia was discovered in 1948 at Debert, near Truro. Thousands of Paleo-Indian artefacts were later unearthed, and some were radiocarbon-dated to 8,600BC. Paleo-Indians are believed to have crossed to the North American continent from Siberia. Over the years, as temperatures in the region waxed and

NEW SCOTLAND

Sir William Alexander, a member of the court of King James I, proposed establishing a New Scotland in North America and put his idea to HRH in 1621. In a generous mood, the king granted Sir William most of the northeast American continent. The land was to be named 'Nova Scotia' and in return, Sir William had to pay 'one penny of Scottish money'.

After failed attempts to get shiploads of immigrants to his land in both 1622 and 1623, he came up with another scheme. In 1624, Sir William persuaded the king to create 150 Baronets of the Kingdom of New Scotland: in return for a substantial amount of money, those so honoured would receive a land grant in the new kingdom, a knighthood, and several other privileges. Barons did not even have to cross the Atlantic to receive their titles – a small patch of Edinburgh Castle's parade ground was declared to be part of Nova Scotia and set aside for the purpose (to this day a little bit of Nova Scotia lies under Edinburgh Castle's Esplanade). Finally, in 1628, he sent his (Baronet) son in command of four vessels to Port-Royal, but soon after, King Charles, who had succeeded James, instructed Sir William to demolish all New Scotland's buildings and remove all his people from it. Sir William complied, but never received the £10,000 compensation promised. He died bankrupt in 1640.

THE MI'KMAQ

Pre-colonisation, Mi'kmaq territory included all of Nova Scotia and Prince Edward Island, and parts of Quebec, New Brunswick and Maine.

The Mi'kmaq practised a religion based on Mother Nature, deeply tied to the land. Mythology also played an important part in spiritual life. They lived in conical birch-bark wigwams; birch bark was also used to make canoes in which to travel the waterways. The Mi'kmaq were also at home on the sea, travelling in ocean-going versions of their light canoes.

For centuries, they lived along the shoreline in summer, fishing, gathering shellfish, and hunting seals and whales. In the winter, most moved inland, setting up settlements in sheltered forested areas. Moose, bear, caribou, and smaller game provided food and clothing, supplemented by wild berries: plants and herbs were used for teas and medicinal purposes.

They respected their environment and only killed, took or used what they needed. When Europeans first settled Nova Scotia, the natural resources were virtually untouched. They befriended the first French settlers, acting as guides, teaching them to live off the land and showing them how to make fish-weirs and eel-traps, how to ice-fish, which wild berries were safe to eat and how to prepare them, how to cure and prevent scurvy, and more.

The Mi'kmaq began to convert to Christianity in 1610, and their way of life underwent other major changes as they abandoned many traditional customs and focused on gathering furs and hides for trade purposes. The French gave them weapons, and both French and English passed on diseases such as smallpox which killed hundreds – if not thousands. Distrustful and fearful, the English and New Englanders saw the Mi'kmaq not as allies but hostile savages, and decided that forceful subjugation and assimilation would be the best course of action. In 1749, Governor Cornwallis put a bounty on the head (or scalp) of every Mi'kmaq, man, woman or child. The amount of the bounty was increased the following year.

Although a proclamation by King George III in 1763 promised protection for the Mi'kmaq and their hunting grounds, they suffered a similar fate to that of First Nations people and Native Americans across the continent. Often caught between the French and the English/British power struggle for North America, they were robbed of their land, persecuted, forced to live with virtually no rights, and herded onto reserves. For decades, the federal government actively suppressed Mi'kmaq traditions. For example, in 1885, religious ceremonies were prohibited. In 1927, Canadian government legislation forbade aboriginals in Canada from forming political organisations, as well as practising their traditional culture and language.

In the 19th century, the Mi'kmaq were confined to about 60 locations, both on and off reserves, dotted about the province. In the 1940s, the Canadians implemented a Centralisation Policy, which mandated that they be moved against their will to just two reserves. Young Mi'kmaq children were taken away from their families and taught the 'white-man's ways', to integrate them into mainstream society – and rapidly lose the culture and heritage of their ancient way of life.

See also box, page 25.

waned, the inhabitants of the area are likely to have retreated south, returning perhaps a few centuries later: this cycle was probably repeated a few times. The native people living in Nova Scotia were the Mi'kmaq, members of the Algonquian-speaking Abenaki Confederacy.

EARLY VISITORS? There is much speculation – and the occasional shred of evidence – to suggest that various outsiders visited Nova Scotia well before French settlement.

Irish-born St Brendan the Navigator may have stopped by early in the 6th century. Vikings almost certainly visited nearby Newfoundland very early in the 11th century, and there have been several claims that Iceland-born Leif Ericsson stopped at several places on Nova Scotia's southwest coast in 1007.

Some say Prince Henry Sinclair from Scotland landed in 1398, and the Venetian Zeno brothers may have visited soon after. One man claimed to have found ruins of a 15th-century Chinese settlement on Cape Breton Island.

Basque fishermen are certain to have made landfall in Nova Scotia during whaling and cod-fishing trips in the province's waters, possibly as early as the 15th century.

In 1497, John Cabot crossed the Atlantic from England. None of Cabot's own records has survived, but a map drawn 45 years later by his son suggests that Cabot landed at northern Cape Breton Island.

In the early 1520s, the Portuguese probably had a seasonal fishing colony at the site of present-day Ingonish.

THE FRENCH AND ENGLISH In 1603, the French were looking to plant Gallic seeds in the New World. French nobleman Pierre du Gua, Sieur de Mons (sometimes written as 'de Monts'), was awarded a monopoly to trade fur across a vast swathe of North America on the condition that he would establish a colony there. In 1604, he and Samuel de Champlain established the first permanent European settlement north of St Augustine, Florida, at Port-Royal (see page 219). They were befriended by Mi'kmaq in the area. The French named the entire region 'Acadie', anglicised as Acadia.

At roughly the same time, England began to colonise some of the eastern parts of the United States of America. For over 150 years the English and these settlers were allies: English ships under Samuel Argall from Virginia destroyed the Port-Royal settlement in 1614. A 1632 treaty returned Acadia to the French who made another attempt to colonise, establishing a settlement on the LaHave River (see page 164), and re-establishing Port-Royal close to its original site. As French presence in – and colonisation of – Acadia grew slowly, one man in particular, **Nicolas Denys** (see page 335) was instrumental in establishing settlements both on mainland Nova Scotia and on Cape Breton Island.

Treaties between the English and French continued to pass Nova Scotia back and forth, and in the late 1680s, the French in Quebec attacked New England. This prompted the New Englanders to attack the Acadians, who were far more interested in farming than fighting. Each time the French attacked New England from Quebec or New Brunswick, the New Englanders ransacked a few more Acadian villages in misguided revenge. The Treaty of Utrecht in 1713 gave most of Acadia to the British, but left Cape Breton Island in French hands. Nova Scotia became an official colony, and Annapolis Royal (see page 208) its capital.

LOUISBOURG AND HALIFAX The French decided that they had to build a mighty fort on Cape Breton Island, to protect their fishing interests and help guard Quebec from prospective attacks by the British navy. The chosen site was Louisbourg (see page 349), named for Louis XV.

War broke out again in 1744, and the French attacked Canso (see page 376). Effectively, they now controlled the region's highly lucrative fishing industry. This was not good for the New Englanders who attacked and took the fortress of Louisbourg in 1745: in 1748, a treaty returned it and Cape Breton Island to the French.

Halifax was founded by **General Edward Cornwallis** in 1749, partly as a secure base from which the British could attack the French. It was declared Nova Scotia's capital. Attempts to increase the population went into overdrive: land, rations, equipment, support and military protection were all promised to those prepared to start a new life in Nova Scotia.

Beyond Halifax Shiploads of new immigrants began to arrive in Halifax, the vast majority foreign Protestants predominantly from German-speaking parts of modern-day France, Switzerland and Germany.

When they reached Halifax, they found that land grants were far smaller than had been advertised, rations and supplies were meagre, and wages were set so low that paying off passages would take a lifetime. The British kept them quiet and created another base by shipping many of the German-speakers to Lunenburg (see page 149).

Oaths of allegiance In general, the Acadians had tried to get on with their lives (whether the land was called Acadia or Nova Scotia), building dykes in order to reclaim the marshlands and wetlands around tidal river estuaries, and farming the fertile results. They planted orchards and the odd vineyard. However, they spoke French, were friendly with the Mi'kmaq – with whom the French were still closely allied – and were not trusted by the British.

Governor Cornwallis had demanded an oath of allegiance from them, but terms were not agreed. When Charles Lawrence became lieutenant-governor in 1753, approximately 10,000 Acadians lived in Nova Scotia. In 1755, they were asked to sign another oath of allegiance to the British, this one even stronger, stating that in the case of war, the Acadians could be told to fight with the British against the French. Again, they refused to sign.

***LE GRAND DERANGEMENT* – THE GREAT UPHEAVAL** On 28 July 1755, Lawrence and the rest of the governing council in Halifax called for the deportation of 'French inhabitants'. Orders were sent to the major British forts, and the operation began in mid August. The Acadians were to be sent off on ships and could take with them only what they could carry: land and livestock would become the property of the Crown.

Almost 3,000 Acadians were deported from one area alone – Grand Pré (see page 235) – and in all around 10,000 were herded onto ships and banished to colonies along the eastern American seaboard, to French colonies in the Caribbean, some even to Europe. In many cases, families became separated in the huge operation. Troops burned all the Acadians' buildings so that they would have nothing to return to.

Some Acadians adapted to their new lives. Some drifted south and reached Louisiana, then under French control. Many others never lost their attachment to their former homeland, and survived from day to day, hoping for an opportunity to return from Expulsion. Another British–French war started in 1756, and the supposedly invincible French fortress at Louisbourg fell again in 1758.

FILLING THE VACUUM The flow of immigrants increased significantly with the signing of the Treaty of Paris in 1763, after which the French were no longer seen as a threat in Nova Scotia.

The Planters In its efforts to re-populate Nova Scotia – and increase and improve the food supply – the government attempted to attract New Englanders with free grants of rich farmland (stolen from the Acadians) and other benefits. The first such land grants were in two dykeland areas near modern-day Wolfville (see page 229) and the first Planters – as these immigrants were called – arrived from Connecticut, Rhode Island and Massachusetts in 1760.

Returning Acadians From 1763, the British allowed exiled Acadians to return to Nova Scotia. Unable to pay for passage by sea, hundreds returned on foot to find that their old lands had been given away to other immigrants. They walked on and settled eventually in less desirable areas with poor-quality soil, such as the Bay of Fundy coast between Yarmouth and Digby, part of which is still known as the French Shore (see page 191). Many former farmers turned to fishing.

The Scots After the Battle of Culloden in 1746, the British authorities began to stamp out all aspects of Scottish Highland culture. Those that could afford to do so moved away, and many headed for the New World. The major influx to Nova Scotia began in 1763 when the *Hector* sailed into Pictou (see page 285).

Back home, the Highland Clearances forced tens of thousands off the land they had long called home: many followed in the wake of the *Hector* and headed for Pictou. On arrival, they dispersed along the Northumberland Strait shore (by 1830 there were around 50,000 Scots in Pictou and Antigonish counties) and on to Cape Breton Island, which became part of Nova Scotia in 1820.

The Irish By 1760, the Irish (mostly Catholics) made up about 20–25% of the population of Halifax. This was thanks in large part to Alexander McNutt – born in Londonderry, Northern Ireland – who emigrated to America in the early 1750s, and was stationed in Nova Scotia whilst in the army. Simply by applying to the governor, he received generous (free) land grants on both sides of the Minas Basin, and on the South Shore. He dreamt of turning Nova Scotia into 'New Ireland' and invited primarily Presbyterians from the country of his birth to come over and buy

SHIPBUILDING – THEN

With Halifax beginning to grow, Governor Cornwallis (see opposite) introduced a bounty for every new vessel built. Vessels were needed for trade, transport, and – in times of war – as privateers (see box, page 18).

Between 1800 and 1875, thousands of vessels were built in hundreds of shipyards all around the province. Nova Scotia had safe harbours and river mouths, plentiful timber and sawmills, and some of the world's best ship designers, craftsmen and shipwrights. However, from the late 1870s onward the demand for wooden ships began to slow down, not helped by the use of the new railways and the increasing use of steel in shipbuilding. The Golden Age of Sail was over.

Over the years, nature, time and recycling of building materials have removed most traces of those shipyards.

their own plot of land from him. Almost 300 arrived in Halifax from Londonderry in 1761, and another 150 or so followed. The Irish Privy Council didn't want a mass exodus of its citizens and stopped McNutt from emptying (old) Ireland. (Incidentally, McNutt then turned his attention to building a New Jerusalem on the South Shore – but that's another story.)

Economic conditions were not good in Ireland even before the devastation resulting from failed potato crops in the 1840s. North America offered hope, possibilities, dreams, and (sometimes) work. A fair share of the hundreds of thousands of Irish who emigrated across the Atlantic in the 19th century made Nova Scotia their new home.

Loyalists When the American Revolution started in 1775, a good chunk of the population of the colonies preferred to remain loyal to the British Crown, but understandably were far from popular in the United States. From 1783, tens of thousands of 'Loyalists' emigrated, with around 20,000 going to Nova Scotia. Some 10,000 went to Shelburne (see page 172), instantly creating (what was then) North America's fourth-largest city.

Comparatively wealthy – even aristocratic – and well educated, many Loyalists were not best suited to pioneer life and moved on to pastures new. The remainder persevered and, in general, adapted well to Nova Scotia.

Germans The first wave of German immigrants arrived in the early 1750s: after the American Revolution, there was a second wave when soldiers in German regiments hired to fight by the British Crown were offered land and provisions to start a new life in Nova Scotia. These men were mostly from Hesse, Brunswick, Anspach-Bayreuth and Waldeck; many settled between Digby and Annapolis Royal.

PRIVATEERS – OR PIRATES?

War, particularly sea battles, dominated much of Nova Scotia's early history, with almost constant conflict between the colony's 'Anglo' settlers and either (sometimes both) the French and the Americans.

Privateers – privately owned vessels which would attack the enemy's merchant ships, allowing the navies to concentrate on fighting each other – took to the seas. This form of 'legalised piracy', which reached a peak between 1760 and 1815, had strict rules: captains (usually backed by private investors) had to register full details of their vessel and its owners, and a bond was payable. The captain would then receive a *letter of marque*, an official licence to set out to harass the enemy, and capture every enemy vessel ('prize') he could. Privateers often strayed far from Nova Scotia's coastal waters, hunting American ships along the eastern seaboard and seeking out French vessels trading in the Caribbean.

When a prize was captured, it and at least one member of its crew would be taken to naval officials. Nova Scotia's privateers were required to take prizes to Halifax's Privateers Wharf where they would be inspected. Legally captured prizes – no enemy men were to be killed in cold blood or inhumanely treated, and the prize had to be an enemy, rather than a neutral, ship – were sold at auction and the money was split between (in descending order) the authorities, the privateer's owners, the captain and his officers, and perhaps a few coins for the rest of the crew. The highest bidders were privateer investors who bought the captured ships to put back to use in their own privateer fleets. Consequently, some vessels changed sides frequently.

Black immigration There were three significant tranches of black immigration to Nova Scotia.

When the Loyalists left the United States in the aftermath of the American Revolution, they were joined by their slaves and former slaves who had fought on the Loyalist side in return for their freedom. About 3,000 blacks came to Nova Scotia, many settling at Burchtown (later Birchtown – see box, page 175). Some went to Halifax, settling near Dartmouth in Preston – which to this day has a sizeable black population.

In 1796, over 500 Trelawny Maroons (maroons were runaway slaves and/or their descendants) were sent to Halifax from Jamaica.

Another wave of black immigration came during the 1812–15 Anglo-American War: American slaves who deserted to the British side were offered the opportunity to serve with the British military service or go as free settlers to a British colony. In this time, approximately 1,500 former slaves settled in Nova Scotia.

It is recorded that in the 1820s, Halifax had at least one black policeman, a Constable Septemus Hawkins.

PEACE AND CONFEDERATION After so much conflict, from 1815 Nova Scotia enjoyed a rare long period of peace. In the 1820s, a British company, the **General Mining Association (GMA)**, won control of mining leases in the colonies – and a monopoly over coal mining in Nova Scotia. It invested large sums of money into the mines and the mining infrastructure.

Having been stung by its American colonies, the British government was reluctant to let colonies have too much power, and did its best to ensure that major decisions were always along the lines of what London (rather than the colonists) might want.

Privateers didn't restrict themselves to the sea when seeking bounty, often putting in to feebly defended ports and harbours where armed raiders would rush ashore and strip the settlement of anything of value. Louisbourg (see page 349) was a haven for French privateers, but the Nova Scotia port most associated with privateers was Liverpool (see page 162).

At an auction in 1811, Liverpool-born Enos Collins purchased a captured slave-smuggling schooner, to convert and use as a privateer vessel: he named her the *Liverpool Packet*, and put her under the command of Joseph Barss. The *Liverpool Packet* wreaked havoc on American shipping between 1812 and 1814 and by the end of the conflict had taken over 50 prizes. When he died in 1871, Collins, who had been a shrewd banker, merchant and investor, was said to be the richest man in Canada. Most of those who invested in privateers, however, made little or no money at all.

Privateering was abolished in 1856 by the Declaration of Paris, but its memory lives on – each July Liverpool celebrates 'Privateer Days'.

Nova Scotia is incredibly rich in pirate folklore and it seems that there is a tale of buried treasure for almost every one of the province's multitude of beaches, coves and islands. Most pirate activity took place between the late 17th and mid 18th centuries, but the vast majority of pirate tales told these days are probably better filed under 'fiction' than 'fact'.

However, during the 1830s and 1840s, **Joseph Howe**, a newspaper owner and politician, led a group of political reformers. Through his efforts, Nova Scotia became the first colony in the British Empire to become self-governing and to achieve responsible government based on parliamentary accountability. Howe later became premier of Nova Scotia from 1860 to 1862.

Nova Scotia had long been only too happy to stand alone politically, but the idea of joining together with neighbouring New Brunswick and Prince Edward Island had begun to sound a lot more attractive. As it turned out, within a few years the Dominion of Canada was created (see box, below).

Many people in Nova Scotia were anti-Confederation, but it did bring the province benefits – including a railway connection with the rest of Canada. Steel was first produced commercially in 1883, and many more coal mines were opening, particularly in Pictou and Cumberland counties, and on Cape Breton Island.

THE 20TH CENTURY AND BEYOND The new century brought two tragic events which put Halifax in the news: the aftermath of the sinking of the *Titanic* in 1912 (see box, page 89), and 1917's Halifax Explosion (see box, page 90). The latter (in particular) left a big grey cloud over the province, and for many years the people's mood remained sombre. Times continued to be hard, and worsened as Nova Scotia suffered its own elongated Great Depression.

One of the few bright lights shining through those gloomy times came in the unlikely form of a fishing vessel, the *Bluenose* (see box, page 153). Through a long and difficult period, this racing champion's successes gave the people a reason to be proud, and lifted the spirits of many.

Halifax was a very important port during World War I. In World War II, it was again a crucial part of the Allied war effort as a gathering point for convoys heading across the Atlantic, a 'holding area' for neutral ships, and the departure point for Canadian forces heading out by sea.

The post-war years brought the opening of the **Canso Causeway** (see box, page 304) providing a land link between mainland Nova Scotia and Cape Breton Island. In general, though, the economy was in poor shape, and thousands left the province to seek greener grass elsewhere.

In the late 1950s and 1960s, workers left farming and fishing for new jobs in manufacturing and there was a big population shift from rural to urban areas. Coal mining – long a mainstay of the economy – began to die as the cost of obtaining the coal made it uncompetitive compared with oil and gas. Just a few small mines hung on, but most were closed.

FATHERS OF CONFEDERATION

In the mid 1860s, conferences were held in Charlottetown (Prince Edward Island), Quebec City and London, England. These gave birth to the British North America Act to which Queen Victoria gave royal assent. The act, which united the Province of Canada with New Brunswick and Nova Scotia to form the Dominion of Canada, came into effect on 1 July 1867: 1 July is still celebrated as Canada Day. The 36 attendees at the historic conferences, six of whom were from Nova Scotia, are known as the Fathers of Confederation.

In 1982, the British Parliament passed the Canada Act which left Canada as part of the Commonwealth, but finally severed all Canada's remaining legislative dependence on the United Kingdom.

RUM RUNNING

As the 19th century progressed, the temperance movement had been gaining strength across North America. Prohibition laws were introduced in Canada in 1878, but individual areas could choose to opt out of the legislation.

When the US government introduced (stricter) Prohibition in 1920, Canadian distillers were permitted to export to non-Prohibition nations, the nearest being the French-owned islands of St Pierre and Miquelon (off the southeast coast of Newfoundland), and vast quantities of alcohol were sent there.

Nova Scotia's coastal waters were the perfect secret sea route between the islands and the east coast of the US, and many fishing-boat owners adapted their vessels to carry liquid contraband. When the US authorities began to use faster craft, the province's boatbuilders designed more efficient purpose-built vessels in which to evade their pursuers.

Ports such as Mahone Bay, Lunenburg, Liverpool, Yarmouth and Meteghan were home to dozens of 'rum-running' vessels. Rum, in fact, was very rarely part of the cargo but was used as a generic term for the alcoholic drinks that were carried.

Sometimes vessels failed to evade the American or Canadian authorities and the boat's captain would normally be jailed, but – until 1933 when prohibition was repealed in the US – Nova Scotia's skilled seafarers enjoyed a very profitable, albeit illegal, period.

Then the fishing industry – a major contributor to Nova Scotia's economy for centuries – hit serious problems. Overfishing had resulted in massive drops in catch sizes, and by the early 1990s, tens of thousands of jobs were lost – not just by those who fished for cod and flat-fish, but in the processing plants, boatbuilders, and those who serviced them.

Natural gas was discovered off Sable Island in 1968, but at that time, developing costs were prohibitive. However, oil was discovered in the same region and was drilled from 1992 to 1999 – Canada's first offshore oil project. The first gas was finally shipped to market in December 1999 via the Sable Offshore Energy Project, and production is still going (see page 23).

The consequences of Nova Scotia's economic woes through much of the 20th century haven't all been bad. Outside a few urban areas, there has been precious little development. Forests still cover the majority of the land, and – in the main – the coastline is generally unspoilt. Another positive trend is just beginning as former fishermen are beginning to look at tourism as a way to make use of their boats.

The economy was given (what should turn out to be) a huge economic boost when a Halifax shipyard won a huge naval contract late in 2011 (see box, page 24); the mood stayed positive even with the closure of some of the province's largest paper mills a few weeks later.

GOVERNMENT AND POLITICS

A member of the Commonwealth, Canada is a constitutional monarchy, with Queen Elizabeth II the sovereign and head of state. The queen appoints a governor-general to represent her for a five-year term. Canada's federation of ten provinces and three territories operates under a parliamentary democracy in which power is shared between the federal government, based in Ottawa, and the provincial governments.

THE FEDERAL GOVERNMENT The head of government is the prime minister, who is the leader of the majority party or party coalition in the House of Commons.

The Canadian Parliament comprises two houses: the House of Commons, with 308 members (11 from Nova Scotia), is apportioned by provincial population and elected by plurality from the country's districts; the Senate comprises 105 members (ten from Nova Scotia) appointed by the governor-general on the advice of the prime minister. Legislation must be passed by both houses and signed by the governor-general to become law.

The federal government has authority over defence, criminal law, trade, banking, and other affairs of national interest.

PROVINCIAL GOVERNMENT Responsible for civil services, health, education, natural resources and local government, Nova Scotia's Legislative Assembly consists of a one-house legislative body with members elected every four years. Although there is a nominal head of government (the lieutenant-governor, appointed by the Governor-General of Canada), executive power rests with the 52-member Halifax-based Nova Scotia House of Assembly, headed by a premier, the leader of the majority party. At the time of writing, the lieutenant-governor is Brigadier-General The Honourable J J Grant, CMM, ONS, CD (Ret'd).

For many years, the people of Nova Scotia have been ruled by a minority government. In May 2009, the Nova Scotia Progressive Conservative Party ('Tories') under Rodney MacDonald (who took office in February 2006) lost a vote of confidence over financial policy.

Elections the following month saw a huge swing to the left, with the New Democratic Party (NDP) led by Darrell Dexter sweeping to power and winning 31 of the province's 52 ridings. The Liberals ('Grits') became the official Opposition with 11 seats, and the Tories were reduced to just ten seats.

The NDP win ended ten years of Tory rule.

In an effort to reduce bureaucracy, the government did away with incorporated cities in the 1990s forming the Halifax Regional Municipality (HRM) through the amalgamation of the former cities of Halifax and Dartmouth and the town of Bedford and the municipality of Halifax County, and the Cape Breton Regional Municipality (CBRM) by amalgamating the former city of Sydney, six towns and the municipality of the county of Cape Breton.

ECONOMY

Traditionally, Nova Scotia's economy has been based on natural resources. Fishing has been important since the days of pre-European settlement, and the profusion of forest was the basis for a strong lumber industry and shipbuilding. Coal mining took off in the mid 19th century, and flourished for a century – it is said that the province contains more coal fields for its area than any other part of the world. Iron mines were in operation between 1825 and 1920, and the province had a gold rush in the 1860s, though gold mining's best years proved to be from 1885 to 1903.

Gypsum has been mined since the 1770s (the province is now the leading Canadian producer), salt since 1918, first at Malagash (see page 281), then at Pugwash (see page 278), and barytes, primarily around the Minas Basin, since the 1860s.

In the main, the economy continues to undergo the slow transition from industrial to more service-oriented, and the **service industries** now employ the largest number of workers in the province.

Overfishing and poor resource management from the 1970s to early 1990s had devastating effects on the region's cod-fishing industry. Fishing bans, quotas and other attempts to turn things around seem to be having little effect. More important to the sector today are shellfish: shrimps, crabs and scallops – oh, and lobster: Nova Scotia is the world's largest exporter of the crustacean.

The waters off Sable Island (see page 382) are the site of offshore **natural gas-drilling platforms**. The Sable Offshore Energy Project (SOEP) started production in 1999, and at its height was pumping around 500 million cubic feet of gas per day. In 2011, production had dropped to around 275 million cubic feet per day, and some industry experts say that they wouldn't be surprised if production ceases around 2015. ExxonMobil Canada is the majority shareholder. Encana's gas production at Deep Panuke, a little bit further to the southwest, is scheduled to have started production by the time you read this, and the site is estimated to be productive until around 2025.

Although less than 10% of Nova Scotia's land is arable, **agriculture** contributes heavily to the economy. Significant crops include apples, cranberries and wild blueberries; and poultry and dairy products figure strongly. Over two-thirds of the province is covered by productive forest, some of which is harvested for lumber and pulp. Nova Scotia is the world's largest exporter of wild blueberries and Christmas trees. Acadian Seaplants, based in the province (see box, page 5), is the world's largest manufacturer of seaweed-based speciality products.

There are both hydro-electric and – harnessing the power of the sea – tidal-power generating plants (see page 208). Manufacturing is also a major contributor, but it is small businesses that make up over 90% of the province's economy. Tourism has also been a growing contributor, but the world economic situation and the strength of the Canadian dollar against the US dollar, sterling and the euro have meant reduced visitor numbers in the last few years.

HIGH TIDES, GREEN ENERGY

The power of the Bay of Fundy tides is so amazing that scientific experts and engineers are still not all that close to harnessing it to produce energy efficiently.

The power-generating energy of this resource is a subject under intensive study involving the Nova Scotia Department of Energy, major universities in the province, the Fundy Ocean Research Centre for Energy (FORCE), and various commercial companies.

The Annapolis Tidal Power Plant (see page 208) came online in 1984. Currently the only such plant in the western hemisphere, it has a capacity of 20 megawatts and a daily output of roughly 80–100 megawatt hours, depending on the tides. A test site for a second tidal energy plant in Nova Scotia is located near Parrsboro (see page 260).

In September 2012 it was announced that another CAN$10 million would be invested in (what is believed to be) the world's first underwater monitoring platform, scheduled to be in place in 2015. The hope is that this will help bring commercially viable tidal power closer to reality.

Don't hold your breath, though: in 2009 Nova Scotia Power tested a CAN$10 million turbine (from an Irish company) which the tides soon made mincemeat out of – and sent designers from three other companies (one Nova Scotian, one French and one English) back to their drawing boards.

SHIPBUILDING – NOW

In 2011, the federal government decided that new vessels would be required for the Canadian navy for the coming decades. Once the programme had been announced, bids (for a contract said to be worth CAN$25 billion) were invited from interested parties. In the end, there was a three-horse race between a shipyard in British Columbia, one in Quebec, and Nova Scotia's Halifax Shipyard. In addition to the contract itself, spin-offs were estimated to include close to 12,000 new jobs.

Committees examined every aspect of each bid with fine-toothed combs, deliberated for ages, and you can barely imagine the wave of euphoria that swept through Halifax and beyond on that fateful October day when the winner was declared.

But joy, hopes and dreams are often tempered by reality: the following summer the federal government was having concerns about defence spending, and a date for the first steel to be cut had not yet been agreed. Doubts began to creep in.

Will 19 October 2011 turn out to be one of the most important days in the province's history? 'Fair winds and following seas', as they say.

In 2010, Nova Scotia's per-capita GDP was $38,475 (the average across Canada was $47,605). The province's economic output has been lower than the national average for most years of the past decade. Nova Scotia did improve on the national average during the 2008–09 financial crisis and recession, but prior to that, it was only during the construction and initial (peak) production of the Sable Offshore Energy Project that the province's real GDP growth exceeded the national average.

At the time of writing, the latest private sector consensus for Nova Scotia's growth for 2012 is +1.6%, though the private sector is more optimistic about the outlook for 2013, with the expectation of +2.2% for that year.

In 2010, Nova Scotia's (nominal) gross domestic product (GDP) was CAN$36.352 billion (real GDP CAN$29.951 billion). These figures may well be boosted by the new shipbuilding contract (see box, above), and initial production from the Deep Panuke gas site (see page 23).

PEOPLE

Nova Scotia is home to approximately 922,000 people: the majority live in urban centres, with approximately 40% living in the Halifax Regional Municipality. This means the province's population density is 18 people/km^2 (England's is approximately 390 people/km^2).

Almost 80% of the population can trace their ancestry to Scotland, England or Ireland; France and Germany are next on the list. Although the highest number of immigrants continue to arrive from the UK and Ireland, arrival numbers from eastern Europe, the Middle East, and southeast Asia and the Far East are not insignificant. Recent years have also seen many Canadians move here from the provinces of Ontario, Alberta and British Columbia: many sold their homes and realised that – in terms of buying property – their dollars will go much further in Nova Scotia.

As is generally the case, life in the big urban centres is lived at a much faster pace than in small towns and rural areas: if you've been exploring the province for a few days, coming back to Halifax can seem like jumping forward a few decades.

THE MI'KMAQ IN THE 21ST CENTURY

Today, approximately 16,000 Mi'kmaq (see box, page 14) live in the province. They are divided into 13 Mi'kmaq First Nation Bands, whose members have usufructuary rights (rights to enjoy and benefit from property that belongs to someone else) to approximately 11,200ha of mostly unproductive land (the title of Reserve Land is held by the Canadian Crown). About 60% live on 32 widely scattered Indian reserves. In recent years, in a few cases the Mi'kmaq have used their Aboriginal Rights, supported by the Royal Proclamation of 1763, to try to reclaim their hunting and fishing rights – albeit to the annoyance of some in the province's heavily regulated mainstream fishing industry.

After centuries of suffering suppression, persecution and attempted genocide, there are attempts to put the historical record straight. Daniel N Paul's *We Were Not the Savages* (*www.danielnpaul.com*) is a must-read for anyone interested in the history of the province from a Mi'kmaq perspective. The author is also behind a petition (*www.petitiononline.com/01101749/petition.html*) to rename all of the province's public entities named in honour of Governor Edward Cornwallis who founded Halifax in 1749 and who offered bounties for the scalps of Mi'kmaq men, women and children. A hopeful sign for the future is that many younger Mi'kmaq are rediscovering their language, culture and heritage.

The population has a median age of 44.6, but the number of younger people in the big urban centres means that in less built-up areas, there is a far higher proportion of senior citizens. Visitors will find most locals approachable, friendly and helpful – 'old timers' in particular love to talk, so if you ask one for directions you may also get their (usually fascinating) life histories.

GENEALOGY There is far more interest in genealogy in Nova Scotia (and North America in general) than in Europe. The Mi'kmaq apart, everyone is – or descends from – an immigrant, and perhaps because people's ancestors only started arriving

CANADIAN ENGLISH

Just occasionally, the visitor may be thrown by an unusual word or expression. A resident of Nova Scotia is a Bluenose (or Bluenoser). There are different versions of the origin: these include the coloured marks left on their noses by fishermen wearing (poorly dyed) blue mittens, and a variety of knobbly potato, blueish in colour, grown in (and exported from) the province early in the 19th century. Nova Scotia's most famous sailing vessel (see box, page 153) was named the *Bluenose*.

Someone from elsewhere who now lives in the province is a Come-From-Away (CFA). All over Canada a 'looney' (or 'loonie') is a Canadian one-dollar coin (a bird, the loon, has for many years appeared on the tails side of the coin) and a 'twoonie' (or 'tooney' or 'toonie') is a two-dollar coin. Furthermore, a take-away is referred to as a 'take-out'; and a look-out is called a 'look-off'. Finally, dates are written numerically (MM/DD/YY), so 18 March 2010 would be written 03/18/10. 'Quite nice', when used by your average British person, equates to a Nova Scotian saying something is 'awesome'.

here in the last four centuries, tracing roots is more manageable. You'll find genealogical research facilities and archives all over the province.

LANGUAGE

Canada is bilingual (English and French) by constitution, but less than 7% of Nova Scotia's residents are bilingual. English is the language of choice for almost 93% of the population, while just under 4% call French their mother tongue. In some places (Pugwash and Antigonish, for example; see pages 278 and 295, respectively) street signs are in Scottish Gaelic (Gáidhlig), the language brought over by the Scottish Highlanders: in recent years many community name signs on Cape Breton Island have been replaced with signs showing both the English and Scottish Gaelic names.

RELIGION

Church affiliation in Nova Scotia is higher than elsewhere in Canada. Roman Catholics are the largest group, making up almost 37% of the population. Next (in descending order) are the United Church of Canada, Anglicans and Baptists. There are smaller percentages of Lutheran, Presbyterian, Greek Orthodox and other Christian denominations. The province has a fast-growing Muslim population, and small populations of Hindus, Buddhists and Jews. Pockets of (Protestant) Mennonites are dotted about rural areas.

MAN ON A MISSION

At Port-Royal (see page 185) in 1607, Frenchman Marc Lescarbot taught the Mi'kmaq about Christianity, and is credited with establishing Canada's first Sunday School.

EDUCATION

Nova Scotia has more than 440 public (state) schools. These are under the auspices of seven regional school boards, and one school board which is responsible for the province's 20 French-language schools. Private schools include Halifax Grammar and Windsor's Kings Edgehill, and there are Montessori schools (where tuition is based on the child-development theories of Maria Montessori, who advocated that

THE POWER OF THE LORD

It is told that a few decades back, the Pentecostal pastor at the Bethel Mission near Mahone Bay (on the province's South Shore) decided to hold a Divine Healing service. Preacher Burton Shupe led the prayers, and called for those in need of more curative medical treatment than the health services had managed to provide to come forward. One Letitia Sawler, mother of 14 and dependent on crutches, was helped onto the dais by some of the faithful. Preacher Shupe spoke in tongues, and then ordered Lettie to throw away her crutches. There was an audible gasp as two walking aids were cast away. Lettie teetered for a moment, then lost her balance and fell to the ground, prompting another gasp. Some members of the congregation rushed to try and help her, but Preacher Shupe – who had had a moment to gather his thoughts – commanded 'Leave r 'er layin' where Jesus flang 'er'.

the teacher's role is to introduce children to materials and then remain a silent presence in the classroom, whilst the children direct their own learning) in Halifax, Windsor, Wolfville and Sydney.

Children normally begin school in September if their fifth birthday is before 31 December. Parents are allowed to home school if they wish. The first year is called Primary and the next year is Grade 1 and so on to Grade 12, the final year of high school. There are no equivalents to the UK's Ofsted reports or school 'league tables'. In addition to 11 universities, the Nova Scotia Community College (NSCC) has 13 campuses around the province.

CULTURE

LITERATURE Although the Mi'kmaq have a long history of oral storytelling, the first recorded written work in the province was scribed by the French at Port-Royal (see page 185) in the first years of the 17th century. Since then, much of the best literature to come out of the province has been historical fiction. Perhaps the most prolific author of this genre was Thomas H Raddall (1903–94), who was born in England but came to Nova Scotia in 1913. He later worked as a wireless operator on Sable Island (see page 382), and in 1923, settled in Liverpool. He wrote a number of historical novels and tales, and history books. *Halifax, Warden of the North*, for example, is an excellent history of the province's capital from its founding to the mid 20th century.

Evelyn Eaton's third novel, *Quietly My Captain Waits* (1940) was set in Port-Royal (see page 185) between 1690 and 1706. Eaton wrote the book, which became a great commercial success, whilst staying at her summer home in Victoria Beach (see page 219). Set in the Annapolis Valley, and highly regarded, is Ernest Buckler's *The Mountain and the Valley* (1952), the story of a young man's artistic and spiritual awakening. Around the same time, Will R Bird wrote *This is Nova Scotia* (1950) and *Off-Trail in Nova Scotia* (1956), both sets of tales about motoring around the province.

Most historical fiction (and history) books were written in eras when nobody batted an eyelid when the Mi'kmaq were portrayed as treacherous savages. Daniel Paul (b1938) is a journalist, activist and lecturer. His First Nations History, *We Were Not the Savages*, offers a Mi'kmaq perspective on the province's history.

Although a man of many talents, in literary terms Thomas Chandler Haliburton (1796–1865) is best known for his political satire – and creating Sam Slick, protagonist of his humorous 'Clockmaker' books (see box, page 241). Rita Joe (1932–2007) was born on Cape Breton Island and started writing poetry in her late thirties. *The Poems of Rita Joe* was published in 1978, and other books followed. Known as 'the Poet Laureate of the Mi'kmaq', she was awarded the Order of Canada, the country's highest civilian honour, in 1989.

Born in Massachusetts, poet and writer Elizabeth Bishop (1911–79) spent some of her childhood in Great Village (see page 256). Much of her work was inspired by her time in Nova Scotia. She later became Poet Laureate of the United States and a Pulitzer Prize winner. Contemporary literary stars include Alistair MacLeod (try *No Great Mischief* or *The Lost Salt Gift of Blood*) and Hugh MacLennan (eg: *Barometer Rising* and *Two Solitudes*).

ART Nova Scotia has a vibrant artistic community with artists and creators of fine art, folk art, and crafts to be found in countless nooks and crannies.

The province has been home to some impressive fine artists such as Helsinki-born William deGarthe (1907–83) who lived in Peggy's Cove (see page 132) for almost 30 years: much of his work had a marine theme. His home is now a gallery.

MAUD LEWIS

Born in rural Yarmouth County in 1903, Maud Dowley suffered birth defects that gave her hunched shoulders and pressed her chin into her chest. She was very small and developed rheumatoid arthritis in childhood. Maud had no formal art training and dropped out of school (where she had been teased incessantly) at 14. When her parents died in the late 1930s, their 'estate' was left to their son, and he made no provision for his sister. She answered an advert for a housekeeper and moved to the home of Everett Lewis, a door-to-door fish seller. The two lived in his simple one-room home in Marshalltown (near Digby), and were married soon afterwards. Here, despite worsening arthritis, Maud painted and painted. Every surface in the house became her canvas, as did any scraps of cardboard or wallpaper. Everett sold Maud's paintings of colourful scenes of rural Nova Scotia whilst on his fish rounds, and later to tourists in the area. Most sold for a dollar or two.

In 1965, still living in the tiny hut – Everett didn't want to waste money on running water or electricity – Maud was featured on a television documentary, and soon after, in a Toronto paper. Her fame began to spread rapidly: in 1969, a White House aide commissioned two of her paintings for Richard Nixon (Maud asked for payment in advance). Sadly, her arthritis prevented her from being able to fulfil most of the orders that fame had finally brought.

She died of pneumonia in 1970 and was buried in a pauper's grave. Everett tried forging a few paintings and died in 1979: the Lewis shack was acquired by the Art Gallery of Nova Scotia (see *Halifax*, page 114) where it is now on display.

Willard M Mitchell (1881–1955) lived in Amherst (see page 271) for about 20 years and is best known for his miniature landscape watercolours. Much of the work by Robert Pope (1956–92) who died aged just 35 was inspired by his experience of healthcare and life as a cancer patient. One of Canada's greatest contemporary artists, Alex Colville (b1920) has spent most of his life in Nova Scotia and has lived in Wolfville (see page 229) for the last three decades.

The province has produced some renowned folk artists including Maud Lewis (see box, above) and Joe Norris (1924–96), both of whose work can be seen at the Art Gallery of Nova Scotia (see page 114). In the 21st century, the tradition continues. Dotted around the province, you'll find some excellent folk art galleries, and the genre is celebrated with an annual festival in Lunenburg (see page 149).

Aboriginal art is also well worth seeking out: Alan Syliboy is the best-known contemporary Mi'kmaq artist. Up-and-coming, edgier Mi'kmaq artists include Charles Doucette of Potlotek (see page 337).

MUSIC Music has always been an important part of life in Nova Scotia, particularly since the Scots began to pour into Pictou in the 1770s (see page 285). Whilst a wide variety of musical genres has begun to take off, this has not been at the expense of the popularity of Celtic music: whether traditional or fused with other styles, Celtic music is very much alive, well, and thriving in 21st-century Nova Scotia. Some visitors come primarily for the music; others look back on their time in Nova Scotia and realise what a highlight the music was.

Celtic music The Scottish Highlanders who arrived in the late 18th and early 19th centuries brought their music with them, and all these years later the highest concentration of Celtic music and dancing is to be found in the region where so many of those immigrants settled: Cape Breton Island.

The term 'Celtic music' covers a broad spectrum. Pure traditional tunes are still played, virtually unchanged from when they were learnt in Scotland, but the music has evolved its own identity, too, in forms such as Cape Breton fiddle music. Some musicians add a dollop of other musical influences into the Celtic mix.

You can hear wonderful Celtic music throughout the year on Cape Breton Island, but opportunities increase dramatically in the summer, when there's a kitchen party or *ceilidh* (pronounced 'kay-lee' – a Gaelic word which refers to a traditional dance or music gathering) almost every evening somewhere in easy reach. That is definitely the case during October's joyous Celtic Colours Festival (see box, page 306), timed to coincide with nature's brilliant autumn leaf display. Celtic music aficionados should not miss this festival. Look out for ceilidhs all over the province – they aren't exclusive to Cape Breton Island.

So who are the people to watch out for? Top names include former members of the Rankin Family, particularly Jimmy Rankin: in October 2012, cancer accounted for his sister (and fellow group founder) Raylene. Gordie Sampson is a multi-award-winning singer-songwriter. Natalie MacMaster is Cape Breton Island's best-known fiddler – one of her cousins is Ashley MacIsaac, also a master of the instrument. Other big names include The Cottars and The Barra MacNeils.

Those well-established, but less well-known on the international circuit include Mary Jane Lamond who fuses Gaelic music and contemporary pop, fiddler Andrea Beaton, Troy MacGillivray, stringed-instrument maestro Dave MacIsaac, Celtic harpist Alys Howe, and a band, Celtic Rant. Sadly, Cape Breton guitar maestro Dave McKeough was killed in a car crash in 2012. He was just 46. But don't just look for those who have made it – in general, the standard of playing is so high that you're unlikely to be disappointed whoever you see. And where there's music, feet start tapping: step dancing, square dancing, highland dancing – and 'enthusiastic-but-unco-ordinated-tourists-forgetting-inhibitions dancing'. Those interested in Celtic music should ensure that they visit the Celtic Music Interpretive Centre in Judique (see page 304).

Classical and choral Nova Scotia has produced one of the greatest contraltos in Canadian music history. Portia White (1911–68) was born in Truro and received international acclaim in the 1950s and 1960s. She was also an inspiration for the province's black community.

Established over a quarter of a century ago, Halifax-based Symphony Nova Scotia (*www.symphonynovascotia.ca*) is the province's top chamber orchestra. Peter Allen is the province's leading classical pianist. Comprising coal miners from Cape Breton Island, male choral ensemble The Men of the Deeps has been entertaining audiences for over four decades (see *Around Sydney*, page 346).

Country, folk, pop and rock The province has produced some country megastars including Hank Snow (see *Liverpool*, page 162), Wilf Carter and more recently Anne Murray (see *Springhill*, page 269). Born in 1944, folk/country singer Rita MacNeil has been wowing audiences since the 1970s. Folk legend Stan Rogers (who died in a plane crash in 1983, aged just 33) spent many summers in Nova Scotia and is commemorated in an annual festival (see *Canso*, page 376). Sarah McLachlan was born in Halifax in 1968 and spent almost 20 years in the province before moving to Vancouver.

Country music is alive today with the flag flown by artists and bands such as George Canyon, Joyce Seamone, RyLee Madison and Jesse Beck, but is often blended with roots, folk and rock by bands such as the Moonshine Ramblers. Yarmouth's Ryan Cook is more country than folk. Old Man Luedecke sings fun songs and plays the banjo, and Truro's James Hill is a ukulele maestro. Probably the closest thing that Nova Scotia has to an international rock star is Joel Plaskett (either solo or with band). However, there is a whole host of individuals and bands who are well worth seeing and/or listening to.

In no particular order, and often crossing genres, here are some names to look out for: In-flight Safety, Wintersleep, roots singer-songwriters Dave Gunning, Jenn Grant and Christina Martin, J P Cormier (who plays guitar and dobro mixing genres including Celtic, folk and bluegrass), and Lennie Gallant. Carmen Townsend rocks, Andrew Hunter & the Gatherers play power-pop and rock, The Stanfields blend heavy rock, bluegrass and Celtic music. Quiet Parade cover the range from gentle acoustic pop to more anthemic rock. John Campbelljohn is quite bluesy, Crowdis Bridge are very easy on the ear, Breagh MacKinnon plays folk-pop, and Rich Aucoin is definitely worth seeing (you'll love him or hate him). Keith Mullins describes his music as 'Folk Soul', there's the Django Rheinhardt-style gypsy swing Swingology, Matt Minglewood also crosses several genres, and The Town Heroes are a drum and guitar duo. Dog Day is an indie-rock duo, Gloryhound an old-fashioned rock band, The Trews play hard rock, and Last Call Chernobyl's music tends to be metal (often with a lighter touch). Oh, and I nearly forgot to mention Charlie A'Court, Dali Van Gogh, Dylan Guthro, Steven Gates and Tim Crabtree's Paper Beat Scissors.

On the **jazz and blues** front, a sad loss was the passing in 2012 (at age 75) of Halifax saxophonist Bucky Adams. Other heroes from the past include 'The Prime Minister of the Blues', Dutch Mason (1938–2006) – his son, Garrett Mason, looked set to follow in his father's footsteps but has been out of the limelight for a while. Detroit-born blues guitarist Morgan Davis has played with all the greats and has been living in Nova Scotia for over a decade. Another guitarist, Roger Howse's music straddles the blues, roots and Americana genres, and Dan Doiron has many fans. Drumlin (see opposite) play folk-rock infused with 'Nova Scotia heritage music'. The Hupman Brothers play folky blues, and saxophonist and singer Shirley Jackson is worth seeing with or without 'Her Good Rockin' Daddys'. Steve Dooks plays smooth and easy piano, Thom Swift rootsy blues, and Shan Arsenault is an excellent jazz improv guitarist.

Halifax, in particular, has a powerful **hip-hop** scene. Important artists include Three Sheet, Something Good, Anonamyss, and Buck 65. Happy listening!

FOLKLORE Long before the Europeans arrived, the Mi'kmaq had their customs, tales – most of which involved Glooscap (sometimes written as 'Kluscap'), a mythical demi-god who slept using Nova Scotia as a bed and Prince Edward Island as a pillow – beliefs and sayings. As a consequence of the trials and tribulations of having to share their land for over four centuries, some of their folklore was lost for ever. The work of people such as **Silas Tertius Rand** (see box, opposite) has helped to stop even more being forgotten.

The Europeans – particularly those of Celtic origin – brought their own folklore with them, and over time this has been shaped by their lives and surroundings in Nova Scotia, with the sea perhaps the biggest influence. Most early immigrants from Scotland and Ireland in particular arrived with a belief in God and the supernatural: they were no strangers to stories of mysterious unworldly creatures inhabiting hills, valleys and dark forests (of which Nova Scotia has many). Sprinkle into the mix the (supposedly hostile) local people who lived in tepees, spoke a strange language and had strange customs. Then add the sea: fog and sea mists,

SILAS TERTIUS RAND

Born in 1810, Silas Tertius Rand became a Baptist missionary largely by self-education. Rather than go overseas, he lived with the local Mi'kmaq for over 40 years, attempting to show them the way to heaven. He had to master their language and in thus doing, compiled a dictionary and wrote a grammar, and recorded a collection of 80 Mi'kmaq stories and legends. These actions are said to have saved the Mi'kmaq language (and some more of their tales) from oblivion. Much of what we know today about Mi'kmaq traditions is a direct result of his work.

huge tides, howling wind, pirates. The result is an incredibly rich folklore of sea shanties, songs and ballads, proverbs, tales of buried treasure, witches, all manner of superstitions – and so much more.

Much of this has been lost, but Nova Scotia has benefited from the work of some forward-thinking folklorists who realised that records had to be made before it was too late. The province's best-known folklorist was Dartmouth-native **Helen Creighton** (1899–1989) who collected folk songs and tales across the province and further afield for over 50 years. She wrote 13 books on the subject and recorded over 15,000 songs and ballads. In 2008, Bridgewater-based family band Drumlin (*http://drumlin.ca*) released *Mackerel Skies*, an excellent CD of 12 of the heritage songs collected by Helen Creighton.

Many of her books are collections of tales of ghostly (or at least unexplained) happenings. These tell of 'forerunners' (see box, page 32), phantom ships, ghosts guarding buried treasure, and non-threatening spectres who just pass by. And her material didn't just come from the Scots and Irish: she collected many stories from

THE BEGINNING AND THE END

According to Mi'kmaq tradition, there were seven stages in the creation of the world (seven is an important recurring number in Mi'kmaq mythology). First there was Kisu'lkw, the Giver of Life, followed by Na'ku'set, the Sun (also called Grandfather). Created by bolts of lightning were both Sitgamu'k, Mother Earth, and the fourth stage of creation, Glooscap, who was later charged with passing on his knowledge to the Mi'kmaq people. He was followed by his Grandmother, Nokami (or Nugumi), with Glooscap's nephew, Netaoansum, and mother, Ni'kanaptekewi'sqw, completing the set.

When it was time for Glooscap to leave his people, he chanted and called for a whale to carry him to a land far to the west. The first whale to respond was rejected as being too small, but one of the desired proportions was the next to appear. Glooscap climbed onto its huge back, and the pair headed off through the sea.

When they reached their destination, Glooscap bade farewell to the whale, and offered the creature a pipe to smoke. The whale put the pipe in its huge mouth and swam off back towards its distant home: Glooscap climbed a hill and watched its progress, smiling as he saw the whale puffing out plumes of smoke at intervals.

Glooscap still lives away to the west: it is hoped that he will return to ease his people's troubles when the time is right.

FORERUNNERS

In Nova Scotia, supernatural warnings of approaching (generally bad) events are most commonly known as 'forerunners'. There are several types, including unexplained knocks-on-doors or walls (typically of bedrooms), or pictures or mirrors suddenly falling down and smashing. There was, for example, a man who lived alone in a fishing shack and regularly complained of hearing screams and moans. Eventually these bothered the man so much that he moved away. Shortly afterwards, a ship was blown onto the rocks near the shack, and despite attempts to rescue those on board, they were thrown from the vessel and dashed against the rocks, their screams of pain and terror being carried on the howling wind to the onlookers. Whilst graves were dug the victims' bodies were placed in a temporary morgue – the very hut where the screams had previously been heard.

Forerunners mostly deal with sound, but visual signs are labelled foresight too. In a typical example, someone would have a vision of a funeral for a particular person before the 'deceased-to-be' had even fallen sick.

Even those who proclaim themselves non-believers in ghosts having no time for that 'stuff-and-nonsense' seem to find it acceptable to believe in forerunners and foresight.

those of German, Acadian (in the 1830s, a French missionary recorded that some of the Acadians in Yarmouth County used books of spells regularly), Mi'kmaq and English origin.

ARCHITECTURE The history of Nova Scotia's early architecture and town planning is more varied (and complex) than you find in any other Canadian province, with strong French, British, German/European, pre- and post-revolution American, and Scottish influences. Through time – and British thoroughness in razing everything Acadian to the ground in the 1750s – no Acadian buildings remain from pre-Expulsion, although the Habitation (see *Granville Ferry*, page 218) is a pretty accurate reconstruction of the original (1605) French fur-trading post.

Most of the earliest-surviving edifices were built by Loyalists (see *History*, page 18) from New England. In some cases, timber frames for the houses were cut in Boston, Massachusetts, and shipped to Nova Scotia where local materials were used to complete the structure: such was the case with St Paul's Church in Halifax (see page 88). The Loyalists also introduced the popular Cape Cod design, a simple wood-frame house with a gabled roof and shingle siding.

Fine mansions were later built from the profits of shipbuilding and shipping. Be sure to visit Lunenburg (see page 149), the best-surviving example of a planned

A BUNCH OF FAMOUS NOVA SCOTIANS

Those born (or who lived) in Nova Scotia include: shipping magnate Sir Samuel Cunard, Alexander Graham Bell, actor Donald Sutherland, Pulitzer Prize-winning poet Elizabeth Bishop, singers Anne Murray, Hank Snow, Denny Doherty (of the Mamas & the Papas), Sarah McLachlan, Sara Vaughan, Rita MacNeil, the Rankin Family, fiddler Natalie MacMaster and ice hockey star Sidney Crosby.

British colonial settlement in North America – though the buildings themselves show a strong European influence. A particular feature to look out for is the Lunenburg 'bump' (see page 152). Liverpool (see page 162), Shelburne (page 172), Yarmouth (page 186) and Annapolis Royal (page 208) should all be included in your itinerary.

Prescott House (see *Wolfville*, page 235), Province House in Halifax (page 116) and Uniacke House (page 121) are all excellent examples of Georgian architecture. Other styles frequently occurring include Queen Anne Revival, Second Empire, Gothic Revival and Victorian Italianate. Amherst (see page 271) has numerous impressive 19th- and early 20th-century public buildings constructed from local sandstone in a variety of styles. You often hear the term 'century house' in Nova Scotia – this tends to be used when describing houses constructed in the late 1800s (presumably because they are more than 100 years old).

SHIPWRECKS For centuries, attempting to navigate round the coastal waters, rocky shores and islands of Nova Scotia – especially in darkness, fog, blinding blizzards and/or raging seas – proved too much for countless vessels. Almost 5,000 wrecks have been recorded (you wonder how many more haven't made it onto the lists).

Some areas in particular have seen alarming numbers of wrecks. Sable Island (see page 382) has long been known as the 'Graveyard of the Atlantic'. St Paul Island (see page 322) the 'Graveyard of the Gulf'. Dozens of vessels have gone down in the Cape Sable Island (see page 179) area, and, in truth, there are few parts of the province's coastline that haven't seen a shipwreck. Lighthouses, their foghorns and technological improvements were great navigational steps forward, but the boom in the quantity of shipping, particularly in the second half of the 19th century, kept wreck numbers high. The good news was that on many occasions, a higher proportion of those on board survived.

The RMS *Titanic* (see box, page 89) is closely associated with Nova Scotia, but actually went down over 900km east–southeast of the province. Almost 40 years earlier, however, another White Star Line ship, the SS *Atlantic* (see box, page 132) met her end near Lower Prospect, with over 560 lives lost: it was at the time the world's worst merchant shipwreck.

In many cases, a ship's unfortunate end brought some good to local residents: valuable cargo was often washed ashore, and salvaging wreckage provided a living in some areas. So much so that there were several cases where ships were lured deliberately onto rocks by those hoping to reap reward from the resulting wrecks. Many of the wrecks now attract recreational divers (see *Sports and activities*, page 69), and there are still those who seek treasure – though legislation was introduced in the 1960s to prohibit salvage work on old shipwrecks without a permit. Late in 2011, the 225m-long MV *Miner* – under tow, and Turkey-bound – was shipwrecked off the southeast coast of Cape Breton Island.

NOVA SCOTIA'S BLACK HOLE?

Although there have been many cases of ships 'disappearing', they are almost always found in pieces, run aground, damaged but still afloat – or, like the *Mary Celeste* (see box, page 265) empty and off-course – at a later date. The largest vessel to disappear without trace in Nova Scotia's waters was the SS *City of Boston* which left Halifax for Liverpool, England, late in January 1870 but wasn't seen again. No trace of the Inman Line's ship – or the 207 people on board – has yet been found.

2

Practical Information

WHEN TO VISIT

Whilst there are reasons to visit Nova Scotia in the winter – a few festivals, some wildlife-spotting opportunities, and some minor ski resorts – there can be a lot of snow and it can get very cold. Most attractions, many eateries and places to stay outside the biggest urban centres are closed. More doors begin to open after Canadian Mothers' Day (the second Sunday in May).

Realistically, those considering a visit to the province should concentrate on the period between May and late October. May is quiet, though the days are long and the weather is warming up. Later in the month apple blossom covers much of the Annapolis Valley, and flowers begin to bloom. By the beginning of June the weather is generally good for outdoor activities such as hiking, cycling, swimming, kayaking, etc, though late spring and early summer can be foggy. The golf courses and most provincial parks are open, more attractions are opening by the day, the festival season is well underway, and by the middle of June whale-watching trips have begun.

July, August and early September are relatively busy; everything is open, though high-season pricing is in effect. Those who enjoy swimming in the sea will find that August and early September offer the warmest air and water temperatures. If you will be visiting at these times, book your accommodation well in advance, and bear in mind that things will be busier. You can still find uncrowded beaches – though you'll have to walk away from the parking areas – but bear in mind that a crowded beach by Nova Scotia standards would seem relatively quiet in many other places.

WHY THE 'CLOSED' SIGN?

If you are visiting outside July, August or early September, a consequence of the worldwide economic downturn seems to be some B&Bs, restaurants, parks and attractions opening later in the (day or) year, and closing earlier. This can also be true of tourist information offices – lack of volunteers (or funds for staff and premises) can mean that communities forsake these centres for the season. Decisions can also be weather-dependent: a good spring (for example) can mean things opening earlier in the year but a quiet, wet summer may mean people shut up shop earlier in the year than usual. Similarly, the staff at a café or restaurant due to be open until (say) 20.00 may make an ad-hoc decision to close an hour or two early if traffic has been slow. If you are making a special journey – or, for example, depending on a restaurant to be open for supper – it may be prudent to call ahead to be sure.

By the second week of September things quiet down: many attractions have already started to close (their first trigger is Labour Day, the first Monday in September), and kids are back at school. Having said that, if your travel is not restricted to school holidays, it is a good time to visit. The daytime weather generally remains good, though night-time temperatures begin to drop. Another wave of visitors then arrives to enjoy the magnificent autumn colours – and to attend the Celtic Colours Festival (see box, page 306) on Cape Breton Island.

HIGHLIGHTS

'Something for everyone' is a much-used phrase in guidebooks and destination-based travel articles. Does it apply to Nova Scotia? Almost. But don't come for nightlife (limited) or hi-tech theme parks (the one major theme park doesn't have state-of-the-art rides), and don't come for bustling resorts with beach bars and lines of sun-lounger chairs and parasols on the sand.

CULTURE Nova Scotia is proud of its cultural heritage. Numerous centres and festivals have been established to educate and celebrate Celtic, Gaelic, Acadian and Mi'kmaq (aboriginal) cultures. In all, there are over 500 festivals, most of which are held during the summer, celebrating everything from rhubarb to the roseate tern, black flies to blueberries. Celtic music fans should make a beeline for Cape Breton Island Celtic Colours Festival, but a wide variety of musical genres can be heard at music festivals held all over the province (see individual chapters). Halifax has a particularly strong live music scene, which spans the range from rap to classical.

FOLKLORE Dozens of locations, including a university, schools, inns, B&Bs and restaurants, are said to be haunted, and several towns host ghost walk tours – even candlelit graveyard tours – in case you fancy rubbing shoulders with ghouls. Shag Harbour (see box, page 180) was the site of an as yet unexplained UFO crash in 1967. Several places are associated with tales of buried treasure too – none more so than Oak Island.

FOOD AND DRINK Long known for sublime seafood – particularly scallops, clams and lobster – the province has developed a good little wine industry. Tour its wineries and sample their produce.

ACCOMMODATION WITH CHARACTER There are a few high-rise hotels in the biggest urban centres, but far better are the delightful B&Bs and inns, many of which occupy beautifully restored century-old houses and mansions.

HISTORICAL SITES Nova Scotia is very rich in historical sites compared with much of North America. The most important sites include: Halifax Citadel, one of the largest British fortresses on the North American continent (page 111); Port-Royal, the earliest European settlement in North America north of Florida (page 185); Fort Anne, which contains the oldest building in any Canadian National Historic Site (page 213); the Alexander Graham Bell National Historic Site (page 333); and the Fortress of Louisbourg, one of the largest historic reconstructions in North America (page 351). There are numerous lighthouses (including Canada's first), and countless examples of well-preserved Victorian and Georgian architecture. Old Town Lunenburg is a UNESCO World Heritage Site, as is the Grand Pré region (see pages 150 and 235, respectively).

NATURAL HISTORY Geologists and fossil fans will want to visit the Joggins Fossil Cliffs – designated a UNESCO World Natural Heritage Site in 2008 – a world-renowned paleontological site with extensive deposits of 300 million-year-old fossils (see page 269). There are a number of other major fossil sites in Nova Scotia (note: unless you have a Heritage Research Permit – for details see http://museum.gov.ns.ca/fossils/protect/permits.htm – you're not allowed to take the fossils away with you). In addition, Parrsboro is home to the Fundy Geological Museum. Some beaches on the Bay of Fundy's shores can be good hunting grounds for those in search of semi-precious stones.

OUTDOOR ACTIVITIES For outdoor types, there is superb hiking, particularly on Cape Breton Island. Waterways in remote parts of the province such as the Tobeatic Wilderness Area and Kejimkujik National Park attract adventurous get-away-from-it-all canoeists.

There are numerous golf courses; two on Cape Breton Island are rated amongst Canada's best.

Choose from over 100 beaches, many beautiful, most almost deserted and with virtually no development, or cool off in one of the multitude of lakes. Water-based activities include world-class sea kayaking, sailing and tidal-bore rafting. Surfing and scuba diving (primarily wreck diving) are also popular. Fish numbers have dropped, but both deep-sea sport-fishing and freshwater angling continue to be popular, as does (rightly or wrongly) hunting.

The terrain in many parts of Nova Scotia, including the Yarmouth area and Cape Breton Island's Isle Madame, lends itself to cycling holidays. If you prefer four wheels, the province offers several lovely drives, the majority overlooking the sea. One – the Cabot Trail – ranks amongst the world's best coastal drives.

WILDLIFE AND NATURE For wildlife enthusiasts, the Digby Neck in particular offers some of the world's best whale-watching opportunities. In addition, there are several seal colonies just off Brier Island (see page 203). From the few roads which pass through the province's densely forested interior you may be lucky to spot black bear. If you want to see moose, head for the Cape Breton Highlands National Park (see page 317).

Birdwatchers are spoilt for choice: bald eagles can be seen around the Bras d'Or Lake in summer and autumn, and in huge numbers near Sheffield Mills in the winter. August is the best time to see the southward migration of arctic-nesting shorebirds.

New England might be better known for its autumn colours, but they can be pretty impressive here, too. Combine leaf-peeping with some of the world's best Celtic music at Cape Breton Island's annual Celtic Colours Festival in October.

SUGGESTED ITINERARIES

As everyone has their likes and dislikes and their own preferred way of travel, use these basic itineraries as starting points and tailor them to your own preferences. Personally, I prefer to spend more time in fewer places, but I appreciate that others may wish to pack as much of the province as possible into their trip. Keep your fingers crossed for good weather: like many other places, too many grey, wet days can easily take the gloss off a holiday.

A WEEKEND Stay in Halifax and take a day trip out to Mahone Bay and Lunenburg.

A WEEK Stay a couple of nights in Halifax, a couple of nights in Lunenburg (visiting Chester and Mahone Bay *en route*), relax on one of the beaches near Liverpool or explore Kejimkujik National Park *en route* to Annapolis Royal: spend two nights there, taking a whale-watching tour from Brier Island, then a night in Wolfville (visiting Grand Pré). Or, stay a couple of nights in Halifax, a night in Antigonish, head to Cape Breton Island and start driving the Cabot Trail clockwise, stay a couple of nights in the Ingonishes, a night in Sydney or Louisbourg and a night on Isle Madame.

TWO WEEKS Combine the two one-week suggestions, replacing two of the Halifax nights with a night in Parrsboro (between Wolfville and Antigonish) and a night in Guysborough (after Isle Madame).

Any extra days will allow you to include Shelburne, Yarmouth, Cape Chignecto, and more of the Eastern Shore. Ideally, take longer and cover less distance. Don't rush Nova Scotia!

TOUR OPERATORS

Any decent travel agent in the UK should be able to book you a flight to Nova Scotia, book rooms at the big hotels and arrange car (or motor-home) hire. There isn't a company that focuses solely on the province, but some know it better than others.

Some of the **UK operators** mentioned below offer suggested self-drive itineraries around the province, and should also be able to organise a tailor-made itinerary to suit your needs. Note that UK operators don't offer multi-day escorted trips just around Nova Scotia – most combine a few days exploring the province with time also in New Brunswick and Prince Edward Island. The operators starred below (*) – all of whom will tailor-make itineraries for you – are those with good Nova Scotia content in their programmes. The rest are strong on Canada, but have more limited Nova Scotia product.

The companies listed under **Europe** (see page 38) specialise in holidays in North America and can advise on and arrange Nova Scotia itineraries. Few **Australian tour operators** know Nova Scotia well, or even include much about the province in their brochures. Your best bet is listed on page 38.

You're unlikely to save much money, but you can of course **tailor-make your own trip** by booking flights through an operator or direct with the airline and hiring a vehicle through an operator, car-hire broker or direct with the car-hire (or motorhome) company. Larger hotels can be booked through a travel company or direct with the hotel, but for most inns and B&Bs you'll need to contact the property directly.

UK

1st Class Holidays ☎ 0845 644 3939; www.1stclassholidays.com

Audley Travel New Mill, New Mill Lane, Witney, Oxfordshire OX29 9SX; ☎ 01993 838700; www.audleytravel.com

Bridge & Wickers* 3 The Courtyard, 44 Gloucester Av, London NW1 8JD; ☎ 020 3642 9221; www.bridgeandwickers.co.uk. 6- & 7-night self-drive Nova Scotia itineraries, plus longer trips combining the maritime provinces.

Canadian Affair* ☎ 0843 955 2807; www.canadianaffair.com. Especially good for flights on Air Transat. 7-night self-drive Nova Scotia itinerary.

Frontier Canada* ☎ 020 8776 8709; www.frontier-canada.co.uk. Tailor-made holidays to Canada. 6-night walking holidays in Nova Scotia, 8- & 14-night self-drive holidays in the province.

Independent Traveller Devonshire Hse, Devonshire Lane, Loughborough, Leicestershire

LE11 3DF; 01509 618800; www.itiscanada.co.uk
Inn Travel* Whitwell Grange, near Castle Howard, North Yorkshire YO60 7JU; 01653 617001; www.inntravel.co.uk. 11-night Nova Scotia self-drive tours using selected inns & B&Bs in Nova Scotia.
North America Travel Service 0113 243 0000; www.northamericatravelservice.co.uk
Tailor Made Travel 0800 988 5887; www.tailor-made.co.uk
Titan 0800 988 5823; www.titantravel.co.uk. Focuses on escorted coach tours.
Trailfinders* 020 7368 1200; www.trailfinders.com. 13-night Nova Scotia self-drive tours.
Travel 2 Bookable only through travel agents.
Travelbag 0871 703 4698; www.travelbag.co.uk
World Discovery 01306 888799; www.worlddiscovery.co.uk. Offers self-drive tours.

US

Backroads 801 Cedar St, Berkeley, CA; **t/f** 1 800 462 2848; www.backroads.com. Offers hiking & biking tours.
Caravan **t/f** 1 800 227 2826; www.caravan.com
Field Guides **t/f** 1 800 728 4953; http://fieldguides.com. Offers tours for birdwatchers, combining Nova Scotia & Newfoundland.
Grand Circle Travel **t/f** 1 800 221 2610; www.gct.com. Offers escorted tours with good Nova Scotia content.
Road Scholar **t/f** 1 800 454 5768; www.elderhostel.org. A Boston-based non-profit organisation offering 'learning adventures' & educational tour programmes for those aged 55 or over. Formerly branded as 'Elderhostel'.
Tauck **t/f** 1 800 788 7885; www.tauck.com. Offers escorted tours with good Nova Scotia content.

EUROPE

Germany

America Unlimited Hanover; +49 (0) 511 3744 4750; www.america-unlimited.de
Canusa Touristik Hamburg; +49 (0) 180 530 4131; www.canusa.de

Netherlands

Jan Doets America Tours Heerhugowaard; +31 (0) 7257 53333; www.jandoets.nl

AUSTRALIA

Fresh Tracks Canada +61 (0) 808 149 2580; www.freshtrackscanada.com

SPECIALIST TOUR OPERATORS

CYCLING AND SEA KAYAKING TOURS Excellent cycle-tour companies offer both guided small group trips and self-guided tours through some of Nova Scotia's prettiest countryside. And you won't be roughing it at night – the companies tend to use some of the province's wonderful B&Bs and inns for overnight accommodation. Some tours are accompanied by a support vehicle to carry luggage (and saddle-weary tour participants). Bike hire is included, or you can use your own. With the exception of Eastwind, all the following companies also offer sea kayaking holidays.

Coastal Adventures 772 2774; www.coastaladventures.com
Eastwind Cycle 471 4424; www.eastwindcycle.com
Freewheeling Adventures 857 3600, **t/f** 1 800 672 0775; www.freewheeling.ca
Pedal & Sea Adventures **t/f** 1 877 777 5699; www.pedalandseaadventures.com

WINE TOURS A variety of vineyard and winery tours are offered by:

Go North 352 2552, **t/f** 1 877 365 2552; www.gonorthtours.com
Grape Escapes 446 9463, **t/f** 1 855 850 9463; www.novascotiawinetours.com

NOVA SCOTIA AND CANADA

Ambassatours Gray Line ☎ 423 6242, **t/f** 1 800 565 9662; www.ambassatours.com. Offers day & multi-day coach tours.
Atlantic Tours ☎ 423 7172, **t/f** 1 800 565 7173; www.atlantictours.com. One of the province's biggest tour operators: wide range of day, escorted & customised tours.
Great E.A.R.T.H Expeditions ☎ 223 2409; http://greatearthexpeditions.com. Offers eco-adventures, hiking, camping, kayaking & more to out-of-the-way areas.
Maxxim Vacations **t/f** 1 800 567 6666; www.maxximvacations.com. Offers guided & independent packages.
Nova Scotia Travel **t/f** 1 888 682 6449; http://novascotiatravel.ca. Offers packaged & custom tours.
Nova Scotia Vacations ☎ 405 4900; http://novascotiavacations.ca. Offers various packages in Nova Scotia & the maritimes.
Sea Spray Outdoor Adventures ☎ 383 2732; www.cabot-trail-outdoors.com. Offers a range of Cabot Trail tours, from trail running in summer to snow-shoeing in winter.
TayMac Tours ☎ 422 4861, **t/f** 1 800 565 8296; http://taymactours.com. Offers guided & independent packages.

TOURIST INFORMATION

OVERSEAS Nova Scotia tourism has representation in the UK and German-speaking markets and recently introduced a freephone number in the UK (☎ *0800 1565 0000*), which connects through to tourist information staff in the province. From elsewhere in the world (for North America, see *In Nova Scotia*, below) you'll need to ring this alternative number (☎ *425 5781*). You can also contact Nova Scotia's tourist information department by email (**e** *info@checkinnovascotia.com*).

The tourism website (*www.novascotia.com*) is also a good source of information and offers some free, useful brochures, maps and leaflets, including the annual *Doers' & Dreamers'* services guide published annually in the early spring. Canada has tourist offices in about a dozen of the world's major cities, but in my experience these offices provide pretty limited information on Nova Scotia.

IN NOVA SCOTIA Just three provincial visitor information centres are open year-round in Nova Scotia: one at Halifax Airport (see *Getting there and away*, page 43), one on Halifax's waterfront (see page 81), and the other at Amherst (see page 271), near the Nova Scotia–New Brunswick border. Between mid May and mid October (hitting a peak in July and August), many more locally operated tourist information offices open, and these are listed under the relevant towns later on in the book. Within North America (and, of course, Nova Scotia) you can obtain tourist information and assistance, make reservations and more by phoning (or faxing) **t/f** 1 800 565 0000.

RED TAPE

At the time of writing, citizens of the EU, Australia and New Zealand, and many other countries (visit *www.cic.gc.ca/english/visit/visas.asp* for an up-to-date list) do not require a visa to visit Canada. As long as they meet certain criteria (eg: good health, enough money for their stay, ability to satisfy the immigration officer that they will leave Canada at the end of their visit), most visitors are permitted to stay in Canada for up to six months. If you wish to extend your stay once in Canada, you must apply at least 30 days before the stamp in your passport expires. There is a form to complete (this can be done online), and a fee (currently CAN$75) to pay.

> **WILDE'S WIT**
>
> Touring North America in 1882, Oscar Wilde was asked by a customs official if he had anything of value to declare. 'Only my genius' was Wilde's reply.

Unless you are a citizen of the US (see below), you will need a valid passport to enter Canada and it should be valid for at least as long as your intended period of stay. If you are a citizen of the US, you do not need a passport to enter Canada (unless arriving in Canada from a third country), but you now need a passport to re-enter the US, and those travelling by land or sea need a passport, or other appropriate secure document like a NEXUS card. If you are a permanent resident of the United States, you must bring your permanent resident card (ie: Green Card) with you. The US Department of State website (*www.travel.state.gov/travel/*) will have the latest information.

Most visitors to Canada are not allowed to work or study in Canada without permission. You must apply for a work or study permit before coming to Canada. If you are visiting Canada and you want to apply to work or study, you must leave Canada and apply from your home country. The Canadian government's Citizenship and Immigration website (*www.cic.gc.ca*) should answer most questions. Note: This information is correct at the time of writing, but rules and practices change so do check the current situation before buying your ticket.

CUSTOMS REGULATIONS Visitors to Nova Scotia (and Canada in general) are permitted to bring in personal items such as clothing, camping and sports equipment, cameras and personal computers that will be used during a visit. Gifts (each valued at CAN$60 or less) for friends or family can be brought in duty- and tax-free, but alcohol and tobacco products are not classed as gifts.

Those aged over 18 (19 for alcohol) can bring in the following duty-free: either 1.5 litres of wine or 1.14 litres of liquor (maximum 1.14 litres if you're bringing wine and liquor) or 24 (355ml) cans (maximum 8.5 litres) of beer or ale. Despite the ban on smoking in public places, you can bring in 200 cigarettes, 50 cigars/cigarillos, and 200g of manufactured tobacco duty-free.

There are strict rules concerning the import of numerous things from food products to firearms, plants to prescription drugs. For full information, see the guide for 'Visitors to Canada' at www.cbsa-asfc.gc.ca.

EMBASSIES

CANADIAN EMBASSIES ABROAD

(website for all is www.canadainternational.gc.ca)

Australia Commonwealth Av, Canberra, 2600 ACT; +61 (0) 2 6270 4000; e cnbra@international.gc.ca. There is also a Consulate General in Sydney & consulates in Melbourne & Perth.

Austria Laurenzerberg 2 (3rd floor), A 1010, Vienna; +43 (0) 1 531 38 3000; e vienn-visa@international.gc.ca

France 35 Av Montaigne, 75008 Paris; +33 (0) 1 44 43 29 00

Germany Leipziger Platz 17, 10117 Berlin; +49 (0) 30 203 120. Visa & immigration matters are handled in Vienna (Wien), Austria.

Italy Via Zara 30, 00198 Rome; +39 (0) 6 854 44 3937; e romevisa@international.gc.ca

UK Macdonald Hse, 1 Grosvenor Sq, London W1K 4AB; +44 (0) 20 7258 6600. There are also consulates in Cardiff & Edinburgh.

US 501 Pennsylvania Av, NW, Washington, DC, 20001; 1 202 682 1740. There are also a number of Consulates General & consulates in the US – see website above.

AH, MR DELISLE. WE HAVE BEEN EXPECTING YOU

Born near Halifax in 1971, Jeffrey Delisle joined the Canadian forces reserves in 1996, and became a regular member of the Canadian army in 2001, working in intelligence. In 2007, dressed not in a tuxedo and bow tie but a red baseball cap and anorak, and rather than parachuting onto the roof, Delisle walked into the Russian Embassy in Ottawa and offered to sell secrets to that country's military intelligence agency.

Delisle worked at a secret super-high-security location in Halifax on an assignment called the *Stone Ghost*: the ultra-sensitive project involved the intelligence services of the 'Five Eyes' – Canada, the USA, the UK, Australia and New Zealand. Although the computer he worked on had highly elaborate security, apparently there was another computer alongside it that was totally un-monitored. It is said that Delisle simply copied reams of classified, top-secret information onto a disk, transferred it to the second computer, copied the data onto a memory stick and carried that out of the building to collate at home. Once a month – in return for a payment of CAN$3,000 per batch – he would send a package of *Stone Ghost* intelligence information to the Russians.

In 2009, Delisle contacted the Russians and told them that he wanted to stop the arrangement: shortly afterwards, he received an envelope in the mail containing a photo of his daughter walking to school in Halifax. Delisle was instructed to fly to Brazil to meet his Russian 'handler': alarm bells finally rang when he was stopped on his return by Canadian customs officials who were suspicious because he had been away only a few days and was carrying almost CAN$50,000. However, Delisle continued to pass secret data onto the Russians until his arrest in January 2012. Rather than being suspended over a shark pool and left to die (or escape and just manage to stop a timing device before it blew up the Western world), he was imprisoned. At his Halifax court appearance in October 2012, he pleaded guilty to breach of trust, and two counts of passing information to a foreign entity. He is due to be sentenced in January 2013.

CONSULATES IN NOVA SCOTIA

E Germany Suite 1100, Purdy's Wharf Tower 1, 1959 Upper Water St, Halifax B3J 3R7; 420 1599

E UK 1 Canal St, Dartmouth B2Y 3Y9; 461 1381; http://ukincanada.fco.gov.uk/en

E US Suite 904, Purdy's Wharf Tower 2, 1969 Upper Water St, Halifax B3J 3E5; 429 2480; http://halifax.usconsulate.gov

GETTING THERE AND AWAY

Most European visitors arrive into Nova Scotia by air, flying into Halifax Robert L Stanfield International Airport. For those coming from (or going to) other parts of Canada, there are a few other options: one rail connection, and two road crossings from the neighbouring province of New Brunswick (itself connected by road to the Canadian province of Quebec, and to Maine in the United States). There are also ferry connections with New Brunswick, Prince Edward Island and Newfoundland. A ferry connection with Maine is under discussion (see box, page 45) and there has been speculation about a sea connection linking Halifax with Boston, USA.

Travellers from the US have the choice of flying, driving to Saint John (New Brunswick) and taking the ferry from there, driving through New Brunswick to take the land route into Nova Scotia, or hoping that a ferry service (probably from Portland or Bar Harbor (both in Maine) to Yarmouth) gets the green light. By road, Portland, Maine, to Saint John (New Brunswick), is just over 480km by road: Portland to the New Brunswick–Nova Scotia border, near Amherst, is 750km.

BY AIR After improving for a few years, options for those looking to fly to Nova Scotia from Europe suffered a setback in 2008 when low-cost airline Zoom went into administration. Economic downturn has reduced the number of airlines offering flights between Europe and Halifax, and even Air Canada – which offers daily non-stop flights between Heathrow and Halifax for much of the year – has cut their direct flights to three- or four-times weekly out of season. A couple of other companies offer a direct flight once or twice weekly between late spring and early autumn. Flying time from London to Halifax is around 6½ hours (the Gulf Stream winds mean that the return journey is usually about 45 minutes quicker). If you are having problems finding seats at a competitive fare, try looking beyond direct flights – more options exist if you are prepared to change planes. However, it's worth comparing any savings in cost against the extra time and inconvenience the stopovers will incur. The most expensive time to fly is in July and August.

DAYS GONE BY

In 1936, an aircraft crash-landed in a bog near Main-a-Dieu (see page 348) in eastern Cape Breton Island. The shaken pilot climbed out of the cockpit and said 'I'm Mrs Markham: I've just flown from England'. Beryl Markham had just flown for 21 hours, completing the first-ever east-to-west solo flight between England and the American continent.

If you're coming from elsewhere in Canada, options also exist in the summer to fly direct to Sydney (on Cape Breton Island) from Toronto.

In addition to the daily (except where specified) direct **flights between US airports and Halifax**, if you are prepared to change planes, there are dozens more possibilities. Incidentally, if you are flying directly to the US, Halifax Airport has a US Customs pre-clearance facility allowing you to go through US Customs and Border Protection before your flight – saving quite a bit of time at the other end.

There are no direct **flights between Australia and Nova Scotia**. You will have to change planes at least twice. A couple of airlines offer through fares, for example **Air Canada** (☎ *1300 655 767; www.aircanada.com/au/en/home.html*) and **United** (☎ *131 777; www.unitedairlines.com.au*). It is often cheaper to buy a ticket to (say) New York, and a separate ticket New York–Halifax.

From the UK

✈ **Air Canada** ☎ 0871 220 1111; www.aircanada.co.uk. Daily flights between London Heathrow & Halifax (*Apr–Oct; 3–4-times weekly Nov–Mar*). In general, if direct flights are full or don't operate on a particular day, it is possible to change planes in Toronto or Montreal for the same fare.

✈ **Air Transat** ☎ 020 7616 9187; www.airtransat.co.uk. Direct weekly flights between London Gatwick & Halifax (*mid May–mid Sep*).

✈ **Icelandair** ☎ 0844 811 1190; www.icelandair.co.uk. No direct flights, but flights 2–3 times weekly (*early Jun–early Oct*) from Heathrow, Manchester & Glasgow with a plane change in Reykjavik.

From Europe

✈ **Air Canada** www.aircanada.com. Daily flights from Paris, Frankfurt, Munich, Rome & Zurich with a change in Toronto or Montreal.

Condor +49 (0) 6171 698 8920 (in Germany); www.condor.com. Twice-weekly direct flights between Frankfurt & Halifax (*mid May–late Oct*).

Icelandair www.icelandair.com. Flights via Reykjavik (*early Jun–early Oct*) – with a plane change – from various European cities including Madrid, Paris, Amsterdam, Milan, Munich, Frankfurt & Berlin.

From elsewhere in Canada

Air Canada & Air Canada Jazz t/f 1 888 247 2262; www.aircanada.com. Direct flights to Halifax from Calgary, Charlottetown, Deer Lake, Fredericton, Gander, Goose Bay, Montreal, Saint John, St John's, Toronto & Vancouver. Also a Toronto–Sydney service (*May–Oct*).

Air St Pierre t/f 1 877 277 7765; www.airsaintpierre.com. Flights between Saint Pierre (St Pierre & Miquelon islands, just south of Newfoundland) & Halifax year-round, & Sydney (*early Jul–early Sep*).

Porter Airlines t/f 1 888 619 8622; www.flyporter.com. Flights between Halifax, & both Montreal, Toronto, St John's & Ottawa.

Westjet t/f 1 888 937 8538; www.westjet.com. Flights to Halifax daily year-round from St John's, Toronto & Calgary, & in the summer to Halifax from Hamilton, Ottawa & Edmonton, & to Sydney from Toronto.

From the US

Air Canada t/f 1 888 247 2262; www.aircanada.com. Direct flights to Halifax from Boston.

Delta t/f 1 800 221 1212; www.delta.com. Direct summer flights between Atlanta, Detroit, New York (JFK & La Guardia) & Halifax.

Twin Cities Air Service t/f 1 800 564 3882; www.twincitiesairservice.com. Flights between Portland, Maine & Yarmouth 3 to 5 times a week.

United t/f 1 800 538 2929; www.united.com. Direct flights between Newark, Chicago & (seasonal) Washington, DC & Halifax.

Airports

Halifax Robert L Stanfield International Airport (873 4422; *www.flyhalifax.com*) Not surprisingly, this tends to be referred to as Halifax Airport or 'the airport': its IATA code is YHZ. Modern and efficient (though if a couple of international flights arrive at the same time, it can take a while to clear immigration) this airport processes some 3.5 million passengers annually. There's a well-stocked tourist information office just outside the arrivals hall (*09.00–21.00 daily*), as well as ATMs, bureaux de change, car hire and ground transportation desks, and shops and cafés. A 2,300-space multi-storey car park opened in spring 2009, and a new airport hotel is due to open in spring 2013. The airport is situated just off Exit 6 of Highway 102, approximately 35km from downtown Halifax. In general, the journey to or from the city should take 30–45 minutes, but traffic can be bad going into Halifax between 08.00 and 09.30, and leaving the city between 16.30 and 18.00, so allow perhaps 80 minutes at these times. Incidentally, between Exit 6 and the airport you'll pass a Tim Horton's (it's on your right if coming from the highway). Inside are (coffee, doughnuts and) flight departures and arrivals boards.

BAGGAGE (AND OTHER) HANDLING

In 2009, the Sons of Maxwell, a Halifax-based musical duo, hit the (relative) big-time when their song and video 'United Breaks Guitars' attracted much public and media attention. When one of the duo flew from Halifax (via Chicago) to Omaha (Nebraska, USA), his guitar was damaged *en route*. The song was inspired not just by the damage sustained, but also by the musician's dissatisfaction with the way the airline handled the resulting complaint. You can find the song (and a couple of sequels) at www.youtube.com. Contact details for United Airlines are detailed above.

Savvy drivers who don't want to overspend on airport parking often hang out here, for example when waiting to meet someone off an incoming flight. For details of transport to and from the airport, see *Getting there and away*, page 41. For listings of airport hotels, see page 91.

Sydney Airport (☎ *564 7720; www.sydneyairport.ca*) Sydney Airport is 9km from Sydney, Cape Breton Island. The airport's IATA code is YQY. Few flights come and go, but there's a restaurant, ATM and car-hire desks.

Yarmouth (International) Airport (*310 Forest St;* ☎ *742 6484; www.yarmouthairport.ca*) The airport's IATA code is YQI. Approximately 3.5km from downtown Yarmouth, this airport is not a great place from which to plane-spot – at the time of writing, only five scheduled aircraft per week were landing at and taking off from the airport.

BY CAR Whether driving from the US or Canada, (unless you take a ferry – see *By sea*, opposite), you'll pass through New Brunswick and cross into Nova Scotia near Amherst (see page 271). From there it is 215km/134 miles – about a 2½- to three-hour drive – to Halifax. Montreal is about 1,250km/777 miles from Halifax by road, and (again if you don't take a ferry) Boston is 1,120km/700 miles. For more on driving in Nova Scotia, see *Getting around*, page 53.

BY COACH **Maritime Bus** (**t/f** *1 800 575 1807; www.maritimebus.com*) took over long-distance coach services from Acadian Lines in December 2012. Their intention is to operate at least one daily service in each direction between Halifax (calling at various places in Nova Scotia including Dartmouth, Halifax Airport, Truro and Amherst) and Sackville and Moncton (both in New Brunswick). From Moncton there will be connecting services through New Brunswick to Quebec. Those wishing to connect to/from Prince Edward Island will change buses in Amherst. Many details are still to be finalised at the time of going to press, so check the Maritime bus website for details.

PEI Express Shuttle (**t/f** *1 877 877 1771; www.peishuttle.com*) operates 11-passenger air-conditioned vans daily between Nova Scotia and Prince Edward Island via the Confederation Bridge (which connects New Brunswick and Prince Edward Island). The route is Charlottetown–Summerside–Borden (all in Prince Edward Island)–Halifax Airport–Halifax City–Dartmouth. Journey time is approximately four to five hours and the trip costs CAN$65 one-way.

BY TRAIN **VIA Rail** (**t/f** *1 888 842 7245; www.viarail.ca*) operates an overnight train, *The Ocean*, three times a week between Montreal and Halifax. The train leaves Montreal in the evening, travels via Moncton and New Brunswick, arriving in Halifax mid-afternoon. In the other direction, afternoon departures from Halifax reach Montreal the next morning.

Year-round, the train offers standard economy class and sleeper class; the latter affords you a bed in private accommodation. Between mid June and mid October, you can also travel in sleeper touring class. Extra benefits, instead of standard sleeper class, include on-train presentations with cultural and historical insights to the Maritimes, exclusive access to the train's lounges and panoramic section of the luxurious Park Car, breakfast, lunch and a three-course dinner. Regular fares are CAN$263 each way in economy class, but early bookers may be able to secure 'supersaver' economy class fares, offering a discount of around CAN$100 (each way) off regular fares.

WHO PAYS THE FERRY MAN?

A few years ago, two passenger and vehicle sea connections existed between Yarmouth and Maine, USA. Yarmouth was connected by ferry with Portland, Maine, and by *The CAT* (a big high-speed catamaran) with Bar Harbor, Maine. Both of these services relied heavily on Nova Scotia provincial government subsidies, but in 2009 these were stopped – and so (a year later) were the services. Despite public outcry, job losses, reduced visitor numbers to the area, and a knock-on devastating impact on tourism in southwest Nova Scotia, campaigns, petitions and the like brought only talks about talks. In September 2012 some progress was made when the provincial government said it would commit millions of dollars to a marine service connecting Yarmouth with Maine – if the federal government would also play ball. In addition, a suitable ferry-operating partner would have to be found, and various other organisations expected to play their part in getting the service running again. A report suggested that the service would need to carry a minimum of 135,000 passengers a year to be profitable. Ominously, that is almost double the number of people who used *The CAT* in 2009, its last year on the run.

BY SEA **Bay Ferries** (**t/f** *1 888 249 7245; www.bayferries.com*) operates Digby–Saint John (New Brunswick) on the *Princess of Acadia* year-round, once or twice daily (*3hrs, passenger fares from CAN$30 one-way, vehicle cost from CAN$104*); and Caribou (near Pictou)–Wood Island (Prince Edward Island) on NFL Ferries MV *Confederation* and MV *Holiday Island* from May to mid December, three to eight times daily (*75mins; fares from CAN$17 round-trip for passengers, from CAN$71 round-trip – including passengers – for a vehicle*).

Marine Atlantic (**t/f** *1 800 341 7981; www.marine-atlantic.ca*) offers two connections between Nova Scotia's Cape Breton Island and the Canadian province of Newfoundland: North Sydney–Port aux Basques (Newfoundland) year-round (*6–7hrs; passenger fares from CAN$41, vehicle from CAN$105*); and North Sydney–Argentia (Newfoundland) three sailings a week from late June to late September (*14hrs; passenger fares from CAN$1,086, vehicle from CAN$217*). Fares shown are one-way. Note that the vehicle rate does not include driver or passengers.

PASSAGE FROM THE PAST

In 1877 the steamer *Scud* operated twice-weekly sailings between Annapolis Royal and Saint John (New Brunswick). The fare was CAN$2.

HEALTH *with Dr Felicity Nicholson*

The standard of public health in Canada is excellent, but very expensive for non-residents. If you become ill in Nova Scotia, for minor ailments, seek out a pharmacy. If it is something more serious, your next step is to go to one of the few walk-in clinics or to the emergency department of a hospital. You will have to pay at both to use the facilities and to see a doctor, and for any treatment and/or medicines that may be required. It is a similar story for emergency dental work. Consequently, it would be foolhardy to visit Nova Scotia (and anywhere in North America) without comprehensive medical insurance (check that your travel insurance policy includes adequate cover).

If you take prescription medicines to Nova Scotia, make sure that they are in their original packaging (with a label that specifies what they are and that they are being used under prescription). If that is not possible, carry a copy of the prescription or a letter from your doctor. Otherwise, they may be confiscated by customs officials. No vaccinations are legally required, but it is always wise to be up to date with routine vaccinations such as diphtheria, tetanus and polio. Tap water is safe to drink.

BLACK FLIES AND MOSQUITOES Tiny, biting black flies appear in the spring and (though everyone says that they go by early to mid June) may hang around into July. They cannot bite through clothing, but sometimes bite above the hairline, or below the collar line. They don't bite after dark. In rural areas in May and early June, it is not uncommon to see locals who are working outside wearing head nets.

Just before the black flies start to die down for the year, mosquitoes make their appearance, and buzz around until late summer – even longer in swampy areas. Whereas in many places mosquitoes are creatures of the night, in Nova Scotia they are just as evident in the daytime. In theory, coastal areas are less badly affected, but I've seen plenty of evidence to the contrary. Mosquitoes here do not carry malaria, but there is said to be a tiny risk of West Nile virus. However, as of January 2009, no humans have ever been recorded as having acquired West Nile virus in the province.

Help protect against black flies and mosquitoes by covering up: wear light-coloured long-sleeved shirts and trousers and cover exposed skin with a DEET-based insect repellent.

TICKS Forests and areas with long grass can be home to ticks, particularly in spring and early summer. In certain parts of the province – Bedford, Gunning Cove (near Shelburne) and the Lunenburg area – some black-legged ticks carry the bacteria which could cause **Lyme disease**. Both black-legged and dog (or wood) ticks are found in other parts of Nova Scotia. If you go walking in tick country, try to avoid tall grasses and shrubby areas. Wear long trousers tucked into socks, a long-sleeved shirt and a hat, and spray a DEET-based insect repellent on outer clothing. After leaving the area, carefully examine yourself all over as soon as it is practical. If you find a tick they should be removed with special tick tweezers that can be bought in good travel shops. Failing that you can use your fingernails: grasp the tick as close to your body as possible and pull steadily and firmly away at right angles to your skin. The tick will then come away complete, as long as you do not jerk or twist. If possible douse the wound with alcohol (any spirit will do) or iodine. Irritants (eg: Olbas oil) or lit cigarettes are to be discouraged since they can cause the ticks to regurgitate and therefore increase the risk of disease. It is best to get a travelling companion to check you for ticks; if you are travelling with small children, remember to check their heads, and particularly behind the ears. Spreading redness around the bite and/or fever and/or aching joints after a tick bite imply that you have an infection that requires antibiotic treatment, so seek advice.

EMERGENCY

Owing to a shortage of funds, not all hospital departments are open 24/7: in the case of a medical emergency, phone 911 – the ambulance crew will know where to take you. Do make sure that you have adequate travel/medical insurance as an ambulance trip to the nearest hospital will cost over CAN$650.

LEECHES Leeches can occur in still or slow-moving water, such as the shallow edges of lakes. Many locals carry salt shakers with them when going on swimming (or paddling) trips to a lake, and if a leech attaches itself, a sprinkle of salt will usually make the creature dislodge. Leeches do not carry disease but do inject an anti-coagulant agent into the wound, so try to clean the wound, put on a dab of antiseptic cream, and cover with a plaster.

RABIES Rabies is spread through the saliva of an infected animal. It is usually transmitted through a bite or a scratch but can be transmitted by licks over broken skin or saliva getting into the eyes or mouth. The risk in terrestrial animals in Canada is low but not non-existent, so it is always wise to seek medical advice if you have a potential exposure from any warm-blooded mammal, including bats. However, the first thing to do before you seek advice is to thoroughly wash the wound with soap and water for a good ten to 15 minutes.

POISON IVY This toxic plant is found here and there in Nova Scotia (and in most of North America): it produces urushiol, an irritant which causes an allergic reaction to most of those who come in contact with it. The reaction takes the form of itching and inflammation and can be severe. I've only seen poison ivy once in Nova Scotia, and there were several big 'Warning! Poison Ivy' signs all around.

SUN Especially with cooling coastal breezes or thin layers of cloud, it is easy to get sunburned in Nova Scotia. Cover up and use sun cream.

SAFETY

Canada is politically stable and one of the world's safer places, and – Halifax and Dartmouth apart – Nova Scotia's crime rates are about average for the country (they have been on a downward trend for the last few years). Halifax (including Dartmouth) is second to Winnipeg as the Canadian city with the highest murder rate, and violent crime figures in the city are bucking the national trend and are on the increase. Having said that, you would have to be exceedingly unlucky to be in the wrong place at the wrong time.

Crimes tend to be a different story outside the city. Rightly or wrongly, many people in rural areas still don't lock their doors. I don't suggest that you follow their example, however romantic the notion might be.

Violent crimes are infrequent; far more common is petty theft. Some parts of the big urban areas are troubled by youth crime, often drug- or drink-inspired, but probably to a lesser degree than in equivalent cities in Europe or the US.

Outside the urban centres, things seem so laid-back that it is easy to forget common sense. For instance, if you must leave valuable items in your car unattended, keep them out of sight, preferably locked in the vehicle's boot. And wherever you are in the world, carrying large amounts of cash around isn't a great idea.

THE LAW If you steer clear of drugs, you are unlikely to have unsolicited contact with the police in Nova Scotia. Pedestrians should be aware that although in the UK, crossing the road safely is considered a personal responsibility, in Canada and the US jaywalking (crossing a road without regard to traffic regulations) is a crime – albeit one that dozens of people in the province commit regularly, often in view of the police. Once behind a wheel, your chances of attracting the attention of local law enforcers do increase (see *By car*, page 44)

THE POLICE You won't see red-jacketed, horseriding Mounties in Nova Scotia – here the Royal Canadian Mounted Police (RCMP) dress less garishly and travel in police cars.

Municipal governments around the province are responsible for policing, and can choose if they want policing to be done by the RCMP or their own force. There are municipal forces in the two major urban centres (the central core of the Halifax

NOTES FOR DISABLED TRAVELLERS

Lieke Scheewe (with advice from Gordon Rattray; www.able-travel.com)
Canada, including Nova Scotia, has relatively high accessibility standards. There has been an increasing awareness that many people need special services, from various diet requirements to accessibility arrangements and protection from animal allergies. As such, its beach resorts as well as its wilderness are becoming a joy for everyone.

GETTING THERE AND AROUND Access to Travel (*www.accesstotravel.gc.ca*) is a comprehensive resource that emerged from a co-operative effort between federal and local governments as well as the private and non-profit sectors. It provides up-to-date information on accessible transportation services across Canada, including information on transportation by bus, rail, air and ferry, local public and private transportation. A few essential services:

By air Halifax International Airport is fully accessible for wheelchair users (including availability of narrow-aisle chairs, adapted washrooms, etc) and way-finding is accessible for those with visual impairments (eg: signs have contrasting colours and lifts have tactile markers). A Volunteer Host Program, called the Tartan Team, provides personal assistance. **Need-A-Lift** (☎ *222 5438*) is one of the wheelchair-accessible transportation services providing airport transfer.

By ferry Marine Atlantic (**t/f** *1 800 341 7981; www.marine-atlantic.ca*) operates all its ferries in full compliance with Canadian accessibility legislation. It has, for example, an adapted cabin for persons with limited mobility and appropriate informational signage for those with visual impairments. Make reservations in advance and mention required services. For some of these services proof of disability is required.

BY ROAD AND RAIL Whilst neither of the province's new long-distance coach operators offer accessible vehicles, I'm told that they hope to address the issue. Short-distance transit services are much more accessibility-friendly (see *By Coach*, page 57 for contact details).

VIA Rail Canada (**t/f** *1 888 842 7245; www.viarail.ca*) offers a wide variety of services to those with limited mobility or other disabilities. The services may vary from one region to another. Book your ticket at least 48 hours in advance and specify which services you will require.

ACCOMMODATION Accessible accommodation is not very difficult to find, although the number of accessible rooms is usually very limited. Travellers with special needs are urged to make their reservations in advance of arrival and to mention any specific arrangements they may require at the time of booking. A few useful resources:

Regional Municipality and Cape Breton Regional Municipality) and ten other towns, while the RCMP provides policing elsewhere in the province and in rural areas. It also performs the vast majority of highway policing. Some communities have their own local numbers on which to contact the police for non-emergencies. These can be found in the phone directory, or online at www.411.ca. The standard number to call for police assistance (and the fire or ambulance service) is 911.

Access Advisor (566 3501; *http://accessadvisor.ca*) collates accessible (four levels of designation) accommodation, eateries, attractions and shops in Nova Scotia.

Check In (t/f *1 800 565 0000*) can help you locate (partially) accessible, smoke-free and pet-free properties.

The website of **Cottage Portal™** (*www.cottageportal.com*) is very useful in finding wheelchair-accessible accommodation.

Mersey River Chalets and Nature Retreat (*682 2443; www.merseyriverchalets.ns.ca*) is a wilderness resort which provides fully accessible accommodation for wheelchair users. In addition, they offer specially designed nature trails and wharfs to allow access to swimming, canoeing and kayaking.

The 'Plan Your Trip' section of Nova Scotia's official tourism website (*www.novascotia.com*) has a page of frequently asked questions about accessibility in the province.

ACTIVITIES Besides Access Guide Canada (see *Further information* later in this box), other interesting websites for recreational activities are:

www.acadventures.ca Accessible Canadian Adventures designs, co-ordinates and arranges hunting, fishing and wildlife-photography trips for disabled sportsmen and women.
www.ns.edining.ca eDining.ca provides listings of restaurants and specifies their wheelchair accessibility.
www.pc.gc.ca The Parks Canada website has accessibility information on national parks, historic sites and marine conservation areas.

TRAVEL INSURANCE Most insurance companies will cater for disabled travellers, but it is essential that they are made aware of your disability. Examples of specialised companies in the UK that cover pre-existing medical conditions are **Free Spirit** (*0845 230 5000; www.freespirittravelinsurance.com*) and **Age UK** (*0845 601 2234; www.ageuk.org.uk*), who have no upper age limit.

FURTHER INFORMATION The most comprehensive accessibility information website is offered by **Access Guide Canada**, a voluntary programme compiling information on a wide variety of services, from transportation to lodgings and entertainment venues. Start your search by entering your destination province and community within Canada at www.abilities.ca/agc/. Contact the **Nova Scotia League for Equal Opportunities** (*5251 Duke St, Suite 1211, Halifax B3K 4E1; 455 6942; e nsleo@eastlink.ca; www.novascotialeo.org*) with enquiries regarding transportation services, access to recreational facilities, or other services and referrals.

TERRORISM No recent terrorism events have occurred in the province (unlike in 1883 – see adjacent box), and Canada as a whole has had few problems with terrorists in the last couple of decades.

WOMEN TRAVELLERS Women using their common sense are unlikely to have any problems in Nova Scotia, even if travelling alone. There have been claims that immigration officials give solo female travellers more of a grilling than others. Other than that it's just a case of being sensible: don't wander in dodgy areas at night, hitchhike alone, etc.

POWER BEATS TERRORISTS

In 1883, Chief Constable Nicholas Power arrested two men in possession of explosives suspected of planning to blow up the HMS *Canada* in Halifax Harbour. At the time, Prince George, who would later become King George V, was serving on that very ship. Power was awarded the King's Police Medal (the police equivalent of the Armed Forces' Victoria Cross) in 1915.

GAY AND LESBIAN TRAVELLERS Attitudes to gays and lesbians vary across the province. The Halifax Pride Festival (*www.halifaxpride.com*), for example, is Atlantic Canada's largest Pride celebration. On the other hand, in 2007, Truro's mayor and council refused requests to raise the Gay Pride flag at the town hall and opposed a local Gay Pride parade. It is said that attitudes in the town are unaltered – it takes time for embedded conservative beliefs to change. Truro's officials apart, in general there is greater acceptance in the big urban centres and more tourist-orientated and/or arts-focused communities.

Look out for *Wayves* magazine (*www.wayves.ca*), published 11-times yearly in Halifax for gays across the Atlantic Canada region.

WHAT TO TAKE

Choose your clothes on the basis that temperatures and weather conditions can change quickly and dramatically even in summer. A sudden sea mist can block out the sun and cause the temperature to drop a number of degrees – dress in layers.

Rain- and wind-proof gear is useful at any time of year, and a sturdy, fold-up umbrella (which doesn't blow inside-out at the first hint of a breeze) can be useful for summer showers, or if the sun gets too strong. In addition to comfortable walking shoes, hiking boots or shoes (with a good grip) will enable you to better enjoy the many beautiful trails.

Long-sleeved shirts and blouses can help protect against mosquitoes and tiny black flies: insect repellent can be a necessity in some areas at some times of the year, though it can be purchased locally. Binoculars can be useful for wildlife spotting, and if you're taking electrical goods, or those that operate on rechargeable batteries.

Take out comprehensive travel insurance when you book your travel arrangements – this should cover cancellation, lost or stolen baggage, and – most importantly – medical emergencies.

ELECTRICITY Canada's electrical sockets are the same as those found in the US, ie: two flat-pin plugs. Occasionally, some have a third round earth pin. The electrical supply is 110 volts and 60 hertz (cycles per second).

Many, but not all, electrical appliances sold in the UK have dual voltage power supplies and will work happily in Canada once you attach a UK–US/Canada adaptor. If the appliance rating plate on your device does not say something like 'input 100–240V', you may need a transformer or converter and an adaptor: check with an electrical shop to be sure.

UK–US/Canada **adaptors** are surprisingly difficult to find in Nova Scotia, so take what you'll need with you.

MONEY

CASH The Canadian dollar (CAN$) is Canada's official unit of currency. One dollar equals 100 cents. Dollars are issued in banknote denominations of 5, 10, 20, 50 and 100 and coins of 1 (often called a 'looney'; see box, page 25) and 2 dollars (a 'toonie'). Cent coin denominations are 1 (penny), 5 (nickel), 10 (dime), 25 (quarter) and 50.

US dollars are widely accepted, but change (if any) will be given in Canadian dollars, and the exchange rate will almost always be worse than that offered by banks. In recent years, the Canadian dollar exchange rate has strengthened significantly against both the pound and the US dollar. The current exchange rates are £1=CAN$1.58, US$1=CAN$0.99 and €1=CAN$1.33 (January 2013).

CREDIT AND DEBIT CARDS Virtually all major credit and debit cards are quite widely accepted in Nova Scotia, but some businesses are still cash only. Although you can use your credit card to withdraw cash from an ATM, charges are significantly higher than using a debit card. As is the case in the UK, at some ATMs (for example, those in petrol stations or general stores) there may be a charge for using the machine, in addition to the fee charged by most UK banks each time that a debit card is used abroad. Check with your bank as other fees (for example, exchange-rate loading) may also apply. Using a credit card for purchases and a debit card for getting cash is now the most popular combination for those visiting the province. An ever-increasing number of businesses now use chip and pin credit/debit card machines. More than once I've had a UK card that just wouldn't work in any of these machines, but was fortunate that another of my chip and pin cards (attached to another account) did work.

I find the 'Cheap Travel Money' section at Martin Lewis's www.moneysavingexpert.com to be a very useful resource for the latest and best ways of getting the best rates whilst incurring the least charges.

It is worth notifying your bank where you will be going and for how long at least a week or so before you leave home: at the same time, make a note of the phone numbers to use if your card(s) are lost or stolen whilst in Nova Scotia.

HARMONISED SALES TAX (HST)

Harmonised Sales Tax (HST) of 15% (though the current provincial government has promised to cut HST to 13% by 2015) is added to the price of most goods and services in Nova Scotia. Exceptions include basic groceries (milk, bread, vegetables) and items bought at farmers' markets and yard sales. But in most cases whenever you see a price in Nova Scotia – on a menu, in a shop, for a hotel room, etc – expect an extra 15% to be added. Occasionally, something is listed as 'taxes in', which means the tax has already been added. Until recently, visitors could claim back some (or all) of the HST they had paid when in Nova Scotia, but no longer. Unless stated otherwise, prices shown in this book include HST.

EXCHANGING CURRENCY AND TRAVELLERS' CHEQUES Currency can be exchanged in banks, credit unions, trust companies, larger hotels and at currency-exchange bureaux. Check not only the exchange rate, but also any commission charges. Most travellers to Nova Scotia now rely on credit cards, and ATMs (often referred to as ABMs in Nova Scotia) for cash withdrawals with debit cards.

Many businesses in the province will accept travellers' cheques for payment (you're likely to need photo ID such as a passport in support) and give change in cash dollars. Travellers' cheques can only be used by the person who purchased them, and lost or stolen travellers' cheques can be replaced. I'd recommend getting American Express Canadian dollar travellers' cheques. In the UK these can be purchased from the Post Office (*www.postoffice.co.uk*).

PRE-PAID TRAVEL MONEY CARDS These are a relatively recent phenomenon and are designed to give the security of travellers' cheques with the convenience of a plastic debit card. You apply for a card, load it up with funds before you go, and use your card to withdraw cash at the province's ATMs, or to pay at most businesses that accept credit cards. You can even top the card up whilst you are away.

The downside is that again there are fees to watch out for. Some providers charge for card applications, ATM withdrawals and top-ups. However, as more players come into the market, it is likely that these cards will become more competitive and user-friendly. Once again, check the 'Cheap Travel Money' section at www.moneysavingexpert.com for current best buys (and their pros and cons).

BANKS Banking hours vary, but in general are 10.00–16.00 Monday–Friday. Some banks stay open later on Fridays, and a few may open on Saturday mornings. In terms of their networks, the province's main banks are **Scotiabank** (*www.scotiabank.com*) and **Royal Bank** (*www.rbcroyalbank.com*). Twenty-four-hour ATMs (often called ABMs) are commonplace (see *Credit and debit cards*, page 51). Larger supermarkets almost always have ATMs, and many offer some banking services. Some bigger stores offer 'cash-back'.

BUDGETING

So how expensive is a holiday in Nova Scotia going to be? Some things are easy to work out – air fares (including all the taxes), car hire (if you pre-pay), whilst others are of course more variable. A lot, too, depends on the vagaries of fluctuating exchange rates.

In general, you'll find grocery prices higher than both the UK and the US. Grocery bills can be reduced by taking advantage of the range of goods on special offer each week – these are listed in newspaper-like flyers which come out every Thursday. Eating out in most cafés and restaurants tends to be slightly more expensive than in the UK, less so for shellfish (eg: lobster, mussels, clams, etc).

DISCOUNT CARDS

If you have an International Student Card (ISIC), or International Youth Travel Card (IYTC), or are a 'senior', it is always worth asking for a discount at attractions, for tours, even for accommodation. Students, youths and seniors (60+) are entitled to reduced rates on VIA Rail.

SAMPLE PRICES (JANUARY 2013) INCLUDING TAX WHERE RELEVANT

A litre of (regular) petrol	CAN$1.35
A litre of milk	CAN$2.10
A (473ml) can of beer (Keith's IPA)	CAN$3.17
A dinner main course (including vegetables) at a reasonable restaurant	CAN$18–28
A bus (or ferry) ticket in Halifax	CAN$2.25
A three- to five-hour whale-watching trip from Brier Island (see box, page 202)	CAN$45–50
A dormitory bed in a backpackers' hostel	CAN$25–30
A daily newspaper (the *Chronicle Herald*)	CAN$1.60

Petrol (gas) prices have fluctuated a lot of late, but are usually significantly cheaper than the UK (see *www.novascotiagasprices.com*). Compared with provinces (and American states) on the west of the continent, Nova Scotia is quite compact, so driving distances tend to be shorter too.

Although there aren't many youth (or backpacker) hostels, there are plenty of cheap motels, and most B&Bs are very well priced (especially when you take the quality breakfasts into account), and tend to be cheaper than in many other Canadian provinces. A range of accommodation is available for those who are happy to spend more for more space, better facilities, etc.

GETTING AROUND

It is easy to travel around Nova Scotia – if you have a vehicle. Sadly, public transport is extremely limited, and virtually non-existent in many areas.

BY AIR **Air Canada** (**t/f** *1 888 247 2262; www.aircanada.com*) offers a few flights a day between Halifax and Sydney, Cape Breton Island.

BY CAR For the freedom it gives you, the (generally) good roads, and – compared with much of Europe and urban North America – the (generally) very light traffic, driving is by far the best way to get around the province. British motorists, used to driving on the left, will quickly adapt to driving on the right. Most drivers in Nova Scotia are courteous, patient and observant of speed limits. Outside downtown Halifax, parking is rarely a problem.

Traffic jams are not unheard of, particularly during rush hour on the approaches to and from Halifax and Dartmouth, and the motorway (Highway 102) which links them with the airport.

Everywhere is well within a day's drive of Halifax. You could easily reach Yarmouth in three–four hours, and Sydney (on the east coast of Cape Breton Island) in four–five hours. But Nova Scotia is not about rushing from A to B: in fact, quite the opposite. Where possible, try to avoid the motorways and aim instead for the smaller, often much more scenic – albeit slower – alternatives. Try to allow far more time than distances on the map might suggest. One of the joys of touring the province is discovering what lies beyond the main roads: making side trips down virtually uninhabited peninsulas, trying to spot whales from a headland, stopping to pick your own strawberries, to wander deserted beaches, take in the view from a look-out, or to watch boats bobbing in the harbour at tiny fishing villages.

DRIVING THROUGH HISTORY

In September 1899, The *Halifax Echo* reported the arrival (from Liverpool, England) of a ship carrying the first car ever seen in Nova Scotia.

Until 14 April 1923, driving was on the left-hand side of the road. At that time, teams of oxen (pulling wagons) were common on the province's roads, but it proved almost impossible to retrain them to walk on the other side of the road. So many redundant oxen were sent to the slaughterhouse as a result that there was a dramatic reduction in the price of beef. Horses proved a bit more adaptable: almost nine decades later, it is only the occasional absent-minded driver visiting from the UK who gets it wrong.

If you're a member of an automobile association such as the AAA, AA or RAC, you should be able to take advantage of the services of the **Canadian Automobile Association (Atlantic)** (*www.caa.ca: note that this is the 'national' CAA site – you may need to link on to the CAA Atlantic site*) which has offices in Halifax (*443 5530*) and Dartmouth (*468 6306*). Members of related overseas associations can enjoy many benefits including free maps and guides, travel agency services, and emergency road services.

Roads Nova Scotia has some 23,000km of roads, and 4,100 road bridges. Officially, all named roads in Nova Scotia are 'highways' whether they are (what we would call) motorways or narrow country roads. Limited-access motorways (usually blue or green on road maps, and numbered 100–199) are usually two lanes in each direction, sometimes dual carriageways, but sometimes just a single lane in each direction.

The vast majority of those entering the province by road will do so near Amherst (see page 271) on the Trans Canada Highway (TCH), Highway 104. Between Exits 8 and 10, a toll (from CAN$4) is levied. The TCH heads east to Cape Breton Island (*en route* a short spur, Highway 106, leads to the Caribou ferry terminal, see page 45) where it connects with Highway 105. Highway 104 continues to St Peter's (see page 337), whereas Highway 105 leads to North Sydney (see page 342).

For those renting a car at Halifax Airport, the airport is off Highway 102, which connects Halifax with the Trans Canada Highway, meeting it near Truro.

Highway 101 runs between Halifax and Yarmouth via the Annapolis Valley, and Highway 103 connects the same end points via the South Shore.

The old (pre-motorway) single-digit main roads tend to run almost parallel with their motorway counterparts (eg: Highway 1 and 101, 2 and 102, etc).

Most other roads are one lane in each direction, with soft (gravel) shoulders. Be prepared for some rough surfaces and pot-holes – a combination of winter weather and the cost of maintaining thousands of kilometres of backroads. In rural areas (much of the province!) watch out for wildlife (eg: deer, racoons, porcupine) particularly if driving at dusk or after dark.

Petrol (gas) is sold by the litre. Small discounts are sometimes offered to those paying in cash or by debit card. You should bear in mind that few rural petrol stations are open 24/7. Similarly, not all rural petrol stations open on Sundays or holidays. The (self-explanatory) website www.novascotiagasprices.com may also be of interest.

Licences Full national driving licences from most major countries of the world, including the UK, Australia and the US, are valid in Nova Scotia. If your licence is not in English or French, I'd recommend obtaining an International Driving Permit. UK drivers with two-part (photocard and paper) licences should take both parts with them, though the paper part is rarely asked for. Those who are staying long-term and working in Nova Scotia, or whose children will be attending school in the province, should check at what stage they need to exchange their 'foreign' licence for a Nova Scotia licence (Nova Scotia has a licence reciprocity agreement with the UK).

Driving laws Wearing of safety belts is compulsory for all passengers, and motorcyclists and any pillion passengers must wear helmets. Infants weighing under 10kg must be strapped into a rear-facing secured approved seat: toddlers weighing 10–18kg must be strapped into an appropriate forward-facing child's seat. Children over 18kg, but under 145cm, must use a booster seat. Those hiring cars can request these seats to be included at extra cost: I've found it easier to take them with me from the UK.

Speed limits are generally 100km/h on the Trans Canada Highway and 100-series roads, 80km/h on other highways, 50km/h in cities and towns, and 30km/h when children are present.

The province's highways are patrolled by the Royal Canadian Mounted Police (RCMP) and by air patrol: substantial fines are imposed for violating speed limits.

Be very careful around yellow, old-fashioned school buses: you must stop at least 20m from a school bus, on either side of the road, which is loading or unloading passengers (this will be indicated by flashing red lights, or 'stop flags' on the side of the bus). Do not proceed until the lights are switched off, or flags lifted.

When driving in towns and cities, take great care when you see pedestrians anywhere near the kerb: it is compulsory to stop for pedestrians at a crosswalk (like a zebra crossing but without the Belisha beacons), and some pedestrians have become so used to courteous local drivers stopping and waving them across the road that they may step out into the road without looking.

You must stop completely at a stop sign (traffic police aren't impressed by 'rolling stops'), but – unless signs say otherwise – you are permitted to turn right at a red traffic light, having first stopped and checked that it is safe to do so. When turning left at a junction, turn in front of a car coming from the opposite direction which is also turning left.

When overtaking (passing), you are supposed to sound your horn (though almost nobody does).

In an emergency, pull as far away from the driving lanes as possible, and switch on your hazard lights. If you are involved in a collision, within 24 hours you must notify the RCMP, local police, or the Registry of Motor Vehicles if the accident involves injury, death or damage of more than CAN$1,000.

Authorities in Nova Scotia regard drinking and driving (with a blood-alcohol level of 0.08% or higher), or driving whilst under the influence of drugs, as very serious offences. You could be imprisoned for up to five years even on a first offence.

For further information, see the provincial government-produced *Nova Scotia Driver's Handbook*, at www.gov.ns.ca/snsmr/rmv/safe/handbook.asp.

Insurance for US drivers If you are driving your vehicle in Nova Scotia, proof of auto insurance is required. US auto insurance is accepted as long as you are visiting as a tourist. US insurance firms will issue a Canadian insurance card, which should be obtained prior to departure from the US and carried with you when driving in Nova Scotia. You may also be asked to prove vehicle ownership, so it is wise to carry your vehicle registration form.

Car hire Most visitors driving in Nova Scotia will need to hire (or rent) a vehicle. You will need to be 21 or over: most rental companies apply a Young Driver Surcharge for under 25s, present a passport, full driving licence, and – even if you have pre-paid for your vehicle hire – will be asked for a credit card to cover any incidental charges.

All major car-hire companies have outlets at Halifax International Airport and in (or close to) downtown Halifax. For other locations, see below. Most companies will allow you to pick-up in downtown Halifax and drop-off at Halifax International Airport at no extra cost. If, however, you want to pick-up in Halifax and drop-off in, say, Sydney, check for one-way rental surcharges.

When comparing prices, there are numerous factors to take into consideration: check inclusions and exclusions, extra driver charges if more than one of you will take the wheel, taxes and more. All-inclusive pre-paid rates, especially when booked via the internet, are often the best value. Using an internet car broker (eg: www.carhireexpress.co.uk or www.carhire4less.co.uk) can save a lot of searching time. Major rental companies (and locations of their depots) include:

Avis 0844 581 0147; www.avis.co.uk. Halifax & airport, Dartmouth, New Glasgow, Sydney, Bridgewater & Yarmouth.

Budget 0844 544 3439; www.budget.co.uk. Halifax & airport, Dartmouth, Sydney, Truro & Yarmouth.

Dollar 020 3468 7685; www.dollar.co.uk. Halifax & airport.

Enterprise 0800 800 227; www.enterprise.co.uk. Halifax & airport, Dartmouth, Falmouth, New Glasgow, Sydney, Bridgewater, Yarmouth, Amherst, Antigonish, Barrington, Digby, Lower Sackville, Middleton & New Minas.

Hertz 0843 309 3099; www.hertz.co.uk. Halifax & airport, Bridgewater.

National 0870 599 4000; www.nationalcar.co.uk. Halifax Airport.

Tour operators are also worth checking: I've found **netflights.com** (*0844 692 6792; www.netflights.com*), **Expedia** (*0800 783 2384; www.expedia.co.uk*) and **Canadian Affair** (*0843 955 2807; www.canadianaffair.com*) to be competitive.

Motorhome rental Another option is to hire a motorhome (campervan) or RV (recreational vehicle) as they're often known in North America. You can then reduce costs by sleeping (comfortably) and even cooking in your vehicle. Prices aren't particularly cheap, and there are extras to add. Personally, I think western Canada is better suited to motorhome holidays, but it is something to consider.

Canadream 435 3276, **t/f** 1 800 461 7368; www.canadream.com. Bookable through Canadian Affair (see above) & based in Dartmouth.

Cruise Canada 865 0639, **t/f** 1 800 671 8042; www.cruisecanada.com. Bookable in the UK through North America Travel Service (see page 38) & based in Upper Sackville.

KEEPING UP APPEARANCES

By the 1840s there was a regular stagecoach service between Halifax and Truro. On leaving Halifax, the coach was pulled by six grey horses. However, this was mainly for show: just a few miles after leaving Halifax, the handsome horses were changed and replaced with (less eye-catching) heavier and more powerful beasts. Strength was needed – the road was often axle-deep in mud.

BY COACH With the exceptions of one section of railway line (serving just four stations thrice-weekly – see page 58), a few local public bus services (see page 58) and private shuttle companies (see below), from December 2012 Nova Scotia's primary public transport network is due to consist of coach services offered by **Maritime Bus** (**t/f** *1 800 575 1807; www.maritimebus.com*) and its mother company **Trius Tours** (**t/f** *1 877 566 1567; www.peisland.com/trius tours*).

The Maritime Bus network should include a daily (or more frequent) service in each direction between Halifax and Kentville stopping at Dartmouth, Lower Sackville, Falmouth (for Windsor), Wolfville and New Minas.

Halifax will also be connected a few times daily with Dartmouth, Halifax Airport, Truro, Amherst and Moncton, New Brunswick.

Maritime Bus stops on once- or twice-daily services between Halifax and Sydney (Cape Breton Island) should include Dartmouth, Halifax Airport, Elmsdale, Stewiacke, Truro, New Glasgow, Antigonish, Port Hawkesbury, Whycocomagh, Baddeck and North Sydney. On this route, passengers will probably have to transfer buses in Truro in each direction.

Trius Tours also plans to operate a service three to four days per week in each direction connecting Halifax with Chester, Mahone Bay, Lunenburg and Bridgewater.

Once the routes have been up and running for a few months, I would not be surprised to see changes, tweaks and updates to the services promised. Consequently, be sure to check with the relevant company before making too many plans. Full, up-to-date details of public transport in Nova Scotia can be found on the website of the author of this guide (*www.davidorkin.info*).

BY SHUTTLE Shuttle services, usually in comfortable minivans, are another option. Most shuttle operators will also do pick-ups/drop-offs at Halifax International Airport. For services between Halifax International Airport and downtown Halifax/Dartmouth, see page 82.

Shuttle services and operators

Between Halifax and Yarmouth

Daily service; approx CAN$75–85 one-way.

Bernie's Shuttle Service 742 6101, **t/f** 1 800 742 6101; http://berniesshuttle.com. Via the South Shore.

Cloud Nine Shuttle 742 3992, **t/f** 1 888 805 3335; www.thecloudnineshuttle.com. Via the South Shore or Annapolis Valley.

Mariner Shuttle **t/f** 1 855 586 6140; www.marinershuttle.co. Via the French Shore, Digby & the Annapolis Valley.

Nelson's Shuttle 532 0441, 526 2989; http://nelsonsshuttle.com. Between Halifax & Digby via the Annapolis Valley.

Between Halifax and Mahone Bay, Lunenburg and Bridgewater

Daily service by advance reservation.

Kiwi Kaboodle 531 5494, **t/f** 1 866 549 4522; www.novascotiatoursandtravel.com. Halifax Airport–Mahone Bay or Lunenburg.

Try Town Transit 521 0855

Between Digby, Yarmouth and Halifax

Daily service by advance reservation.

Kathleen's Shuttle and Tours 834 2024; www.freewebs.com/digbytoursandshuttle/

Between Halifax and Cape Breton Island

Daily service; approx CAN$60–80 one-way.

Bay Luxury Shuttle 849 8083, **t/f** 1 855 673 8083; www.capebretonshuttle.ca

Cape Shuttle Service 539 8585, **t/f** 1 800 349 1698; www.capeshuttleservice.com

Flying Scotsman Shuttle 404 5300, **t/f** 1 855 404 5300; www.flyingscotsmanshuttle.ca

BUSES STOP

For a few years, Acadian Lines (owned by Orleans Express of Quebec) operated over 20 daily coach services in and through Nova Scotia. But it announced in August 2012 that less than four months later it would cease operations in the region. It was said that the company had lost close to CAN$12 million in eight years, with dropping passenger numbers (apparently the average number of passengers on each 51-seat coach trip was 12), and over-regulation by provincial governments among the reasons put forward. Trius Tours (which had been operating a daily service in each direction between Halifax and Yarmouth for some years) set up a daughter company known as Maritime Bus. Maritime Bus has taken over many of the old Acadian routes, but some sections (such as Kentville to Digby, and Bridgewater to Yarmouth) have been left coach-less. Would-be passengers in those areas will have to cadge lifts or rely on shuttle services.

Most services between Halifax and Cape Breton Island will allow pick-ups and drop-offs at Dartmouth, Halifax Airport, Truro, New Glasgow, Antigonish, Port Hastings, Whycocomagh and Baddeck. Various shuttle operators/guides will customise tours for you: try for example Digby-based **Kathleen's Shuttle and Tours** (see page 57).

BY BUS Local public bus services cover the most populated parts of the Halifax Regional Municipality (see page 84), the Cape Breton Regional Municipality (see page 342), and the stretch of the Annapolis Valley and environs between Weymouth and Brooklyn (see page 195).

BY TRAIN Passenger rail travel is very limited, but possible: three days a week, **VIA Rail** (**t/f** *1 888 842 7245; www.viarail.ca*) runs a service between Montreal, Quebec and Halifax, and this stops at Amherst, Springhill Junction and Truro.

BY BIKE Cyclists are permitted on all Nova Scotia's roads, including motorways. Helmets must be worn. When riding at night you must use a white front light and a red rear reflector (a rear-facing, flashing red light is acceptable). Reflectors and reflective clothing are also advisable. Most airlines allow bikes as checked baggage, but will have rules as to how the bike should be packed: a handling fee may apply. Check and re-check before booking your ticket. For more on cycling, see page 69.

HITCHHIKING Hitchhiking is not allowed on 100-series major (controlled-access) motorways. Whilst chances are that all will go well and that you'll meet some interesting people, climbing into a stranger's vehicle always carries some degree of risk. Police may also pull over and chat to hitchers to check that they are not missing persons or runaways. As in much of the world, hitching isn't as easy (or as safe) as it used to be – and the release in 2007 of a remake of a 1986 film, *The Hitcher*, hasn't helped. Storylines of psychopathic, murderous hitchhikers don't exactly encourage drivers to pick up strangers.

ACCOMMODATION

The province offers a range of places to stay, from wilderness campsites through to deluxe hotels and resorts. Virtually all of these are listed on Nova Scotia's official

SALTY BEAR

Salty Bear (☎ *404 3636,* **t/f** *1 888 425 2327; www.saltybear.ca*) offers tours geared towards the backpacker – similar in many ways to Australia's OZ Experience bus service, although the network is very limited and there are few departures. Accommodation is usually in dorms, but upgrades to private rooms can normally be arranged.

The three-day tour goes via Antigonish to Cape Breton Island (there's also a five-day option which squashes in a quick visit to the neighbouring province of Prince Edward Island before returning to Halifax). Departures are weekly, and you're permitted to get off somewhere *en route* and then get back on a week, fortnight, etc, later at no extra cost (apart from accommodation for the extra nights). Trips include free (or optional at extra cost) excursions. Bearing in mind the paucity of public transport in the province, Salty Bear's trips are worth considering both as tours and as a method of transport for the car-less.

tourism website (*www.novascotia.com*), and appear in the official annual *Doers' & Dreamers'* guide (see page i). Outside the biggest urban centres, relatively few properties are open year-round: for most, the season runs mid May to early October.

High season (with the highest prices) is July and early to mid September, but advance reservations are recommended for stays between late June and the end of September, and during the Celtic Colours Festival in Cape Breton in October (see page 306). Outside these dates, festivals apart, you should be able to find something in the area. If you're stuck, **Check In Nova Scotia** (**t/f** *1 800 565 0000; www.checkinnovascotia.com*) is the government-run accommodation reservation service that provides access to over 700 hotels, motels, inns, B&Bs and campgrounds throughout the province. Unless stated otherwise, the prices quoted in this book are high-season rates for a single night's stay in a room for two people. Many properties offer significantly cheaper rates out of season: others may give discounts for stays of more than a couple of nights. In my opinion, it is always worth asking about discounts – they are sometimes given to students, seniors, Automobile Association members, those wanting more than one room, etc – but don't expect reductions in high season.

HOTELS Halifax and Sydney are home to the big-name (relatively) high-rise hotels. Dotted about the province's shoreline are resorts offering everything from standard rooms to three- or four-bedroom private chalets, and numerous activities, which often include a golf course.

MOTELS Motels range from traditional family-owned single-storey buildings (some have seen better days) where you can park right outside the door of your room, to brand-new international chains, often with heated indoor swimming pools.

B&BS For me, one of the joys of travelling around Nova Scotia is its B&Bs and small inns. Several are housed in beautifully renovated historic buildings, many of which are heritage properties, and are tastefully decorated with period(ish) antiques. Despite the historical surroundings, amenities are modern and the plumbing works well. Each property is unique and full of character, and good hosts can quickly recognise whether you want your own space, or whether you'd like to sit, chat and perhaps benefit from their local knowledge. Breakfasts are generally superb. A good place to start looking is the website of the **Nova Scotia Association of Unique Country Inns** (*www.uniquecountryinns.com* or *www.bbcanada.com/nova_scotia*).

Bathrooms can be shared, private or en suite. Occasionally, the terminology can cause confusion: where a property has a shared bathroom, that bathroom is for the use of the occupants of more than one guestroom; a private bathroom is solely for the use of guests in a particular room, but guests will have to go out of their room and across the corridor or down the hall to the bathroom; if a bathroom is en suite, you will be able to access your own bathroom by opening a door in your guestroom. All (non-camping) accommodation listed in this book offers en-suite or private bathrooms unless otherwise noted.

Also be aware that some inns and B&B owners have pets and there may be dogs or cats on the premises: check before booking if that might bother you.

HOSTELS AND BACKPACKERS These are somewhat limited. There are Hostelling International (HI) hostels in Halifax (see page 95), at South Milford near Kejimkujik National Park (page 216), at Wentworth (page 281), on Cape Breton Island at Pleasant Bay (page 317), and Aberdeen (page 336). There are also private hostels in Halifax, near Lunenburg/Mahone Bay (page 146), at Port Mouton (page 170), just outside Kejimkujik National Park in Digby (page 197), on Brier Island (page 204), at Five Islands (page 259), and at surfers' mecca Lawrencetown (page 361). If there are two (or more) of you, a cheap room in a motel or simple B&B often won't cost much more than a couple of dormitory beds would.

CAMPING If you're looking to spend your nights under canvas – well, nylon – Nova Scotia has both province-run and privately owned campgrounds. The former are in

RATING THE RATINGS

In the absence of a standard international rating system for hotels, inns, B&Bs and other accommodation, Canada uses a star system under the auspices of **Canada Select** (*www.canadaselect.com*), administered in Nova Scotia by **Quality Visitor Services** (☎ *406 4747; www.qvs.ca*). The programme is voluntary in Nova Scotia. Accommodations are divided into five categories (Hotel/Motel, Inn, Resort, B&B/Tourist Home, Cottage/Vacation Home) – plus camping. Several of these categories have further subdivisions. Properties are evaluated by an inspector who takes several factors (including facilities, services and amenities provided) into account, and a star rating from 1 to 5, in ½-star increments is awarded.

This works fine for many types of accommodation, but doesn't work very well for B&Bs and inns. Under the rating system for B&Bs, an establishment that chooses to have a television in a lounge (rather than in each guestroom) drops one star. If it decides not to have a phone in every guestroom, another star disappears. Many people spend a couple of nights at a five-star-rated B&B or inn, then transfer to a three-star and are surprised to find it a lot better. For me, the system focuses too heavily on facilities/amenities offered, too lightly on individuality, ambience, charm, service and quality, and not at all on comfort or the hospitality offered. A number of inn and B&B owners agree, and – rather than receive a lower star rating based on a checklist of amenities – have withdrawn from the Canada Select programme. Don't rush to select or omit a property based just on its star rating (or lack thereof).

ACCOMMODATION TERMINOLOGY

At a B&B between one and four guestrooms are rented out in a private home; full or continental breakfast is included in the room rate. No other meals are offered.

A 'guesthouse' or 'guesthome' is like a B&B but doesn't necessarily serve breakfast. An 'inn' must offer breakfast and an evening meal on the premises. A 'resort' must have at least one full-service dining room, and offer recreational facilities on the premises. A 'housekeeping' unit will be equipped with cooking and eating utensils, stove and/or microwave, refrigerator, sink, etc.

the two mainland national parks (see page 10) and over 20 provincial parks (see *www.novascotiaparks.ca*) – but note that many provincial parks close in early September. There are about 120 privately owned campgrounds, over 70 of which are listed on the **Campground Owners Association of Nova Scotia** website (*www.campingnovascotia.com*). In addition to standard sites, many campgrounds have serviced sites where those with motorhomes can hook up to water, electricity and a sewer. Many private sites have sliding costs depending on site location – in other words, seafront sites, for example, may cost a lot more than those a few rows back. At the other end of the scale, there are also opportunities for wilderness or back-country camping.

RENTALS Those looking for more space will find a variety of places to rent, from studio apartments to large multi-bedroom houses. Confusingly, these are often referred to as housekeeping units, vacation homes or cottages. They will have equipped kitchens or kitchenettes, and towels and bedding will be provided. How well equipped they are varies from place to place. Often a minimum rental of three or more nights applies, and in summer a minimum of a week is the norm, usually starting on a Saturday.

Many are marketed by **Cottage Connection** (*634 7274,* **t/f** *1 800 780 3682; www.stayinnovascotia.com*). Also try **Sandy Lane Vacations** (*875 2729,* **t/f** *1 800 646 1577; www.sandylanevacations.com*), who focus on the South Shore west of Bridgewater. Rentals of all shapes and sizes are offered through **For Rent By Owner** (*www.frbo.ca*).

HOMESTAYS WITH THE MI'KMAQ As yet, there are no organised programmes for those who wish to stay overnight (or longer) with a Mi'kmaq family. However, it may be possible to arrange homestays on an ad hoc basis by contacting either the **Glooscap Heritage Centre** (see page 256), the **Wagmatcook Culture and Heritage Centre** (page 335), or **Eskasoni Cultural Journeys** (page 339).

ACCOMMODATION PRICE CODES

Accommodation listings are laid out in decreasing price order, under the following categories: Luxury, Upmarket, Mid range and Budget. The following key (also on the inside-front cover) gives an indication of prices. Prices are based on a double room (including tax) per night.

$$$$	CAN$250+	**$$**	CAN$100–174
$$$	CAN$175–249	**$**	<CAN$100

EATING AND DRINKING

> William Deer, who lives here, keeps the best of wine and beer, brandy, and cider, and other good cheer. Fish, and ducks, and moose and deer, caught or shot in the woods near here, with cutlets, or steaks, as will appear; If you will stop you need not fear But you will be well treated by William Deer, And by Mrs Deer, his dearest, deary dear!
>
> Sign outside an inn in Preston, Nova Scotia, in the 1850s

FOOD Visitors who enjoy **seafood** will be in gastronomic nirvana everywhere in Nova Scotia. The price may have crept up over the years, but fish (usually haddock) and chips is almost always done well, freshly cooked and not too greasy. You'll also see a lot of flounder, halibut and salmon: plank (or planked) salmon – where the fish is slow-cooked on a wood plank (usually cedar) – is a highlight.

Then there's the **shellfish**. Top of the pile is lobster – Nova Scotia is the world's largest exporter of the crustacean, but more than enough remains to grace menus throughout the province. It is usually steamed or boiled in seawater, then served with butter – fancier methods of presentation, such as lobster thermidor or lobster Newburg, are seen less often. The larger supermarkets often have glass lobster tanks – at Sobeys stores (see page 67) you can choose a lobster and have it cooked whilst you wait, at no extra cost.

But the province's waters offer other treats, too. Enjoy some of the world's most delicious scallops, plus tasty mussels, oysters, crab and clams. Seafood chowder (a thick, chunky creamy seafood soup) can be a meal in itself.

Those who choose not to eat, or want a change from, seafood need not worry. You will usually find a reasonable selection of chicken, turkey, beef and (to a lesser degree) lamb dishes. Upmarket steak restaurants tend to use beef flown in from Alberta, Canada, or the US.

ACADIAN CUISINE AND OTHER LOCAL SPECIALITIES

The province's earliest European settlers left a gastronomic legacy that still lives on. Order Solomon Gundy and you'll be presented with pickled herring; fiddleheads are the unfurled fronds of ostrich ferns, delicious steamed and served with a squeeze of lemon juice and a dab of butter. Dulse is dried, purple seaweed, usually nibbled as a snack. Lunenburg pudding is a kind of meat-based pâté. Blueberry grunt is a much-loved summer dessert. Although many dishes focus on seafood, there are several to look out for which are land-based: *chicken fricot* (stew), *tourtiere* (meat pie), *pâte à la rapure* (often called 'rappie pie'), and butterscotch pie. Particularly popular with the junk-food crowd are *donair* (a Nova Scotia version of the doner kebab) and *poutine* – chips (fries) topped with cheese curds and brown gravy. Taste buds tingling yet?

SOLOMON GUNDY

Ingredients

Six salt herring (heads and tails removed, cleaned, skinned and deboned)
Three medium onions, thinly sliced
Two cups vinegar
Two tablespoons pickling spice
Half a cup caster sugar

SHORN OF SHEEP

With a few exceptions (notably Pictou County), sheep are pretty scarce in Nova Scotia. There are a number of reasons for this: for example, much of the land is forested, the difficulty in protecting flocks from coyote predation, and higher returns from using pasture for cattle. It is also said that – unlike coyotes – most Nova Scotians just aren't all that keen on the taste of lamb.

In the summer and autumn, **fruit** is fresh and plentiful, and apples and blueberries in particular make their way onto many menus, and not just in the dessert section. For example, apple sauce is a perfect accompaniment to roast pork, whilst blueberry sauce works well with red meat.

Outside Halifax and Dartmouth, the university towns of Wolfville and Antigonish, and places that attract a high number of visitors, the majority of restaurateurs still seem to care little about their restaurant's aesthetics or their food's cholesterol levels. Less than a decade ago, those who wanted to avoid deep-fried food were looked upon with bewilderment.

The good news is that recent years have seen some changes. Driven by a combination of factors – the theory of healthy eating slowly filtering through to Nova Scotia, the culinary wishes expressed by visitors, and an increase in new restaurateurs from outside the province – many more establishments have learnt to use cooking methods other than the deep-fryer and use fresh, often organic, locally grown produce. Thought is given to the look of the establishment's interior, and food presentation, and the menus themselves are more varied and creative. Many of the old-style eateries have begun to join the revolution and will now grill (or at least) pan-fry fish for you – although this may add a dollar or two to the price. More

Directions Cut the herring into approximately 2cm pieces and soak for 24 hours in cold water. Squeeze the water from the herring. Place in jar with slices of onion, in alternate layers. Heat vinegar, pickling spice and sugar, stirring. Allow to cool, pour into jar. Seal jar and keep in fridge for eight–ten days.

BLUEBERRY GRUNT

Fruit mix ingredients

Four cups blueberries
Two-thirds of a cup caster sugar
Half a cup water
One tablespoon lemon juice

Dumpling ingredients

Two cups plain flour
Four teaspoons baking powder
One tablespoon caster sugar
Half a teaspoon salt
Two tablespoons butter
Milk

Directions Combine fruit mix ingredients and bring to a boil in a large saucepan. Reduce heat and simmer until berries are soft and sauce begins to thicken, about five minutes. Sift flour, baking powder, sugar and salt into a bowl. Cut in butter and stir in just enough milk to make a soft dough. Mix well, then drop spoonfuls of batter onto the simmering berry sauce. Immediately cover saucepan and simmer without removing cover for 15 minutes. Serve warm with whipped cream.

RESTAURANT PRICE CODES

Restaurant listings are laid out in decreasing price order, under the following categories: Luxury, Upmarket, Mid range and Budget. The following key (also on the inside front cover) gives an indication of prices. Prices are based on the cost of a main meal (including tax) per person.

$$$$	CAN$36+	$$	CAN$13–23
$$$	CAN$24–35	$	< CAN$13

sophisticated cuisine also tends to mean slightly smaller portions.

If you prefer fast and/or junk food, you need not worry: McDonald's (where the summer menu usually includes a McLobster roll!), KFC, Subway, Dairy Queen, Taco Bell and many other burger chains (eg: A&W) are well represented, and there are numerous pizza joints and take-aways.

Look, too, beyond traditional restaurants, cafés, dining rooms and bistros: community breakfasts and suppers may not offer *haute cuisine* but are almost always excellent value (breakfasts around CAN$6, dinners CAN$10–12), and a great way to meet (and chat to) the locals. Farmers' markets and supermarket deli counters are good places to put a picnic together, and – in season – you can pick your own fresh berries for dessert.

Bear in mind, too, that away from the capital, some of the province's best eateries are actually inn restaurants.

Vegetarians Whilst vegetarian restaurants are few and far between, vegetarian choices are usually offered, although they may not be more exciting than pasta or pizza. In general, the new-wave, more sophisticated cafés, bistros and restaurants will be more vegetarian-friendly.

Gluten-intolerants The types of cafés and restaurants who recognise that not everyone wants to eat meat, plus supermarkets, delis, and some bakeries have become aware of the boom in the number of people looking to avoid gluten. You may not find gluten-free products everywhere, but you shouldn't have to go too far.

BEER AND BEANS

Recent years have seen a rapid growth in both microbreweries and coffee roasteries. Coffee aficionados should look out for names such as Just Us!, Laughing Whale, Sissiboo, Java Blend, T.A.N., Full Steam and Puddle Jump.

Independent beer producers are dotted about the province and include Halifax-based **Bridge Brewing Co** (*www.bridgebeer.ca*), which makes Yardstick Ale, and the **Garrison Brewing Co** (*www.garrisonbrewing.com*), and **Propeller Brewing Co** (*www.drinkpropeller.ca*). The capital is also home to the **Granite Brewery** (*www.granitebreweryhalifax.ca*), **Hart & Thistle** (*www.hartandthistle.com*) and **Rogue's Roost** (*www.roguesroost.com*). Head to Guysborough for the **Chedabucto Bay Brewery** (*www.rarebirdpub.com/brewery/index.htm*), to Cherry Hill for **Hell Bay** (*www.hellbaybrewing.com*), to Yarmouth for **Rudder's** (*www.ruddersbrewpub.com*), and to Port Williams (near Wolfville) for **Sea Level Brewing** (*www.sealevelbrewing.com*).

THE NOBLE GRAPE

In recent years, Nova Scotian wines have begun to make their mark, both at home and on the international stage. The long-established wineries of Domaine de Grand Pré (see page 237) and Jost Vineyards (page 281) continue to deliver quality wines, whilst over a dozen other wineries scattered across the province are producing a variety of wines and wine styles. Nova Scotia excels at crisp, refreshing white wines made from L'Acadie Blanc, Seyval Blanc and Muscat grapes, all terrific with the local fresh seafood.

The province's wine industry was thrilled to introduce a new appellation wine called Tidal Bay. Stylistically, a wine bearing the 'Tidal Bay' appellation on its label is a fresh, crisp, off-dry, still, white wine that must meet a set of standards (like any established world-class wine-producing region).

Wineries such as L'Acadie Vineyards and Benjamin Bridge (the latter is not open to the public at the time of writing) are making world-class traditional-method sparkling wines that (some experts say) could be mistaken for French Champagne in a blind tasting.

Though Nova Scotia also makes red wines from (mainly) Marechal Foch, Leon Milot and Baco Noir grapes that range from light, fresh and juicy to full and earthy, the focus is clearly on their fresh whites and traditional method sparkling wines.

Oenophiles may wish to subscribe (free) to Canada's best wine e-newsletter (*www.nataliemaclean.com*). Its author, sommelier and award-winning wine writer Natalie MacLean, is particularly impressed by the province's sparkling wines and crisp whites, but adds that their production may still be too small for widespread national or international distribution.

A good time for wine aficionados to visit the province is mid September to mid October, to tie in with the month-long Nova Scotia Fall Wine Festival *492 9291*, **t/f** *1 800 281 5507*; *www.nsfallwinefestival.ca*). For the latest on what's what on the Nova Scotia wine scene, see the website www.winesofnovascotia.ca.

For companies offering wine tours in Nova Scotia, see page 38.

DRINK You'll find big-name Canadian and American beers everywhere, but even more popular are Nova Scotia-produced brands. Best known (and much-loved locally) is **Keith's**, and the love affair continues even though the brewery is now owned by Labatt's, a subsidiary of Anheuser-Busch InBev. Beer fans should also look out for Propeller (ESB and London-style porter are good), Granite (try Peculiar) and Garrison (try Irish Red Ale and Raspberry Wheat), all based in Halifax. There are also a few brewpubs dotted around both Halifax and the rest of the province (see box, below).

Another tipple that you should sample is Nova Scotia's **single malt whisky**, distilled on Cape Breton Island (see page 301).

With an abundance of delicious apples, you won't be surprised to hear that very good **cider** is produced locally. Visitors from the UK may get a surprise when they taste it though: unless called hard cider, it will be nothing stronger than sweet, refreshing apple juice.

The legal drinking age is 19 years. Accompanied children and those under 19 are allowed in licensed restaurants and pubs up to 21.00. Whilst it is generally not as bad as the US (where I – three decades over the minimum drinking age – have often been asked for photo ID to confirm I'm legal to drink), if you are (or look) young, you may be asked to prove your age.

With a few exceptions (eg: vineyard shops), alcohol is only sold at government-licensed liquor stores (see page 67).

A recent change in the provincial law means that licensed restaurants are allowed to operate a 'bring your own wine' policy: some have taken up the opportunity, but many of these charge outrageously for corkage – CAN$25 per bottle is not unknown. Licensed restaurants can serve alcoholic drinks from 10.00 to 02.00 daily.

PUBLIC HOLIDAYS AND FESTIVALS

Nova Scotia's calendar has long been packed with all manner of festivals (especially between late spring and autumn) celebrating the province's music, food, arts, heritage, history and more. In fact, Nova Scotia likes the tag 'Canada's Official Festival Province'. In recent years, more festivals have been added, and attempts have been made to hold some of these in traditional off-season periods.

Information on the best regional festivals and events is included under the relevant regional section. The following public holidays are celebrated annually (note that many businesses and shops may close on these days).

1 January	New Year's Day
March/April	Good Friday
March/April	Easter Monday
May	Victoria Day (the Monday preceding 25 May)
1 July	Canada Day
August	Natal Day (first Monday in August)
September	Labour Day (first Monday in September)
October	Thanksgiving Day (second Monday in October)
11 November	Remembrance Day
25 December	Christmas Day
26 December	Boxing Day

SHOPPING

Popular gifts or souvenirs include locally produced wine, especially ice wine (see page 282), whisky (page 309), maple syrup, Nova Scotia tartan, and all manner of arts and crafts. Recent years have seen a boom in the quantity and quality of artists and artisans in the province. So in addition to cuddly moose, whales and red plastic lobsters all mass-produced in factories on the other side of the world, visitors can take home a locally made individually crafted work of art.

ANTIQUES You'll also see plenty of antique shops – plus those that cross the line that divides antiques from junk. If you are interested in the former, you may find the website www.antiquesnovascotia.com of interest. Yard sales are very popular on weekends between spring and autumn: some are advertised in provincial papers, but in most cases just by hand-written fluorescent signs stuck up around the relevant town or village giving the address and time of the sale. These vary from a family clear-out held in an attempt to earn a few dollars for what they would otherwise throw out, to the disposal of the entire contents of an impressive, well-furnished old house. They can be rich hunting grounds or a waste of time. Get there early for the best stuff.

TARTAN TALE

In preparation for an agricultural show in 1953, Bessie Murray, a talented weaver (born in Crewe, England), was asked to make a wall panel depicting the history of sheep rearing in the province. She included a Scottish shepherd in her mural, and dreamt up a new tartan for his kilt. Inspiration came from her memories of the natural colours of the sea, forest and granite outcrops at the coastal community of Terence Bay (see page 131). So much interest was generated by the tiny kilt that Bessie and a friend started a company and began to produce the design on cloth in greater quantities. Her tartan was officially adopted by the province in 1955, the first provincial tartan in Canada: manufacture and sale of the tartan is now covered by the Nova Scotia Tartan Act and Nova Scotia tartan-makers must be licensed by the government.

FOOD SHOPPING For food shopping, self-caterers will probably look to stock up at the huge supermarkets, **Atlantic Superstore** (*www.superstore.ca/east/*) and **Sobeys** (*www.sobeys.com*). In general, these are open 07.30–22.00 Monday–Saturday and 10.00–17.00 Sunday, but check specific store hours for early mornings and late evenings. There are also smaller chains (Save Easy is a 'daughter' of Atlantic Superstore, Foodland of Sobey's), and a seemingly ever-decreasing number of general stores. **Farmers' markets** – usually held one morning a week – are well worth visiting, not just for fresh local produce and baked goods, but often too for arts and crafts. There are over 40 and some of the best include those at Halifax (see page 107), Hubbards (page 138), Wolfville (page 234) and Annapolis Royal (page 213).

The summer offers numerous **U-pick** ('pick-your-own') fruit possibilities. Prices are low and a certain amount of 'eating-as-you-pick' expected and tolerated.

With a few exceptions (eg: vineyard shops), alcohol is sold only at government-licensed liquor, beer and wine stores – and only to persons aged 19 and above. Expect to be asked for photo ID if you're under 40! A list of all Nova Scotia Liquor Commission (NSLC) stores and their opening hours – usually 10.00–21.00 Monday–Saturday, 12.00–17.00 Sunday – can be seen at the 'store information' section of the website www.mynslc.com.

SHOPPING MALLS Many people head out to the big malls to do their shopping. Apart from plenty of free parking and convenience, these tend to stay open later

HAPPY HOOKERS

Whilst experts continue to debate the origins of rug hooking – some say Yorkshire, England, in the early 1800s, others credit the Vikings several centuries earlier – there is no doubt that the craft is well established in Nova Scotia. Although more popular with women, a number of men (who wouldn't be seen dead knitting) are happy to show off their prowess at the whole rug-hooking process from design to pulling strips of yarn or material through a (typically) burlap cloth base, to finishing the raw edges. You'll find rug-hooking studios and galleries dotted about the province, and museums devoted to the activity in Hubbards (see page 138) and Cheticamp (page 316). You might even want to join the Rug Hooking Guild of Nova Scotia (*http://rhgns.com*).

than downtown shops. Alongside the malls you'll usually find big 'box' stores (such as Canadian Tire and Wal-Mart).

For the last few years, Sunday shopping has been legal, though in general it is mainly supermarkets and big mall stores that open on Sundays.

Remember that in most cases, 15% tax will be added to prices (see page 51).

SOUVENIR GOODS Studios and galleries are to be found all over the province, but some areas and communities, such as Bear River (see page 204) and North River on Cape Breton Island (see page 301) are particularly popular. Often you'll be able to watch artisans creating pottery, working glass, carving wood or painting. A piece of whimsical folk art, a stained glass sun-catcher, a handcrafted walking stick, or a hooked rug, all make excellent presents or keepsakes. In tourist offices, look out for the (free) Studio Map: produced annually, it lists art and craft studios and galleries all over the province and can also be viewed at www.studiorally.ca.

ARTS AND ENTERTAINMENT

CINEMA The province has just 14 cinemas, all owned by Empire Theatres (*www.empiretheatres.com*), many of which are in and around Halifax. In many towns, films are screened from time to time in theatres or community/cultural centres.

Before films can be screened, they have to be made: Halifax – home to the ten-day Atlantic Film Festival (see page 86) – is the hub of east-coast Canada's film industry. Film-making contributes about CAN$100 million annually to the province's economy and employs close to 2,000 people. **Film Nova Scotia** (☎ *424 7177*, **t/f** *1 888 360 2111; www.film.ns.ca*) is the starting point for those wanting to learn more.

Films shot in the province include *The Scarlet Letter* (1995), *Dolores Claiborne* (1995) and parts of *Titanic* (1997).

MUSEUMS Nova Scotia has well over 100 museums, ranging from little one-room schoolhouses to the Nova Scotia Museum of Industry (see page 293), one of the biggest museums in Atlantic Canada. Many are themed, with subjects covering for example fishing, mining, lighthouses, Acadian history, the Age of Sail, or individuals such as country singer Hank Snow. Popular too are the 'living museums', staffed by costumed interpreters who demonstrate the almost-forgotten skills of the blacksmith, the wool carder, the potter, the wooden boatbuilder and the lobster plug carver.

A total of 27 of the province's museums make up the diverse family of the **Nova Scotia Museum** (*museum.gov.ns.ca*): admission at each varies from CAN$2 to CAN$11. A pass is available covering admission to all 27 museums for CAN$43.

TITANIC TRIP

Various scenes from the 1997 blockbuster *Titanic* were shot on a Russian ship in Halifax's harbour in the summer of 1996. At the evening meal on the last day of filming, a disgruntled crew member (who is yet to be identified) added a strong dose of a hallucinogenic drug to one of the repast's first courses, lobster chowder. Around 80 crew and cast were affected, and over 50 taken to hospital. One – who had had seconds of the chowder – was still feeling the effects five days later. Apparently the director, James Cameron, was spared somewhat as he vomited before his digestive system absorbed too much of the hallucinogen.

At many other of the museums, often community-run and staffed by volunteers, entrance is free, but donations are encouraged. Consequently, if no admission price is shown in this guide, assume that entry is 'by donation'. These museums rely on the generosity of visitors – and volunteers giving up their time – to keep going, so try to chip in at least a couple of dollars a person where possible.

NIGHTLIFE Nightlife is best in Halifax and environs, and to a far lesser degree Sydney and the university towns of Wolfville and Antigonish. Other than that, you're probably looking at pubs and bars, a disco (if you're very lucky), or stargazing.

THEATRE During their time at Port-Royal (see page 185), one of the French party, lawyer, author and explorer Marc Lescarbot, wrote a play. *Le Théâtre de Neptune* had its world première when performed in the shallows between ships and shore in 1607. This was the first recorded dramatic production in Canada. Lescarbot was something of a poet, and in addition wrote at least once weekly on events at the little French Habitation. On this basis, it is said that Canadian drama, verse and prose were first created at Port-Royal.

Theatre still plays a big part in the province's arts scene: Halifax, Liverpool, Wolfville and Antigonish are some of the places with annual theatre festivals: calendars of events at theatres in many other communities mix performing arts with film screenings.

SPORTS AND ACTIVITIES

CANOEING AND RIVER KAYAKING An abundance of unspoilt (almost untouched) wilderness, lakes, ponds and rivers draw those wishing to explore the inland waters by canoe or kayak. In season, various commercial operators offer hourly rentals: to venture into the back country on a multi-day trip, it is worth consulting a specialist outfit such as **Hinterland Adventures** (*837 4092,* **t/f** *1 800 378 8177; www.kayakingnovascotia.com*).

CYCLING A good network of largely empty roads and (northern Cape Breton Island apart) low hills means wonderful cycling opportunities. In addition to magnificent and varied coastal scenery, there are fertile valleys and many historic towns to explore.

Either build an itinerary around one of the province's scenic trails or base yourself somewhere such as Hubbards, Lunenburg, Yarmouth or Wolfville for a few days, head out on day trips and return each evening to your accommodation.

Hundreds of old logging and mining roads and long-forgotten centuries-old footpaths cover much of rural Nova Scotia and provide excellent possibilities for mountain biking.

A few shops and companies around the province hire out road and mountain bikes for anything from an hour or two, allowing you to potter around the local area. These are listed in the following chapters. See also *Getting around, By bike*, page 58.

DIVING The waters around Nova Scotia offer some of the best cold-water wreck-diving places in the world (you'll need either a drysuit, or a warm wetsuit). Most diving is done in the summer months, when the winds are down and the water is at its warmest. A few hardy locals dive year-round.

The Atlantic Ocean and the Gulf of St Lawrence offer particularly good underwater visibility and the waters are home to a great variety of marine life and an incredible collection of shipwrecks.

There are a number of diving shops in Halifax/Dartmouth and elsewhere, of which the best is probably **Torpedo Rays** (*625 Windmill Rd, Dartmouth;* ☎ *481 0444,* **t/f** *1 877 255 3483; www.torpedorays.com*).

FISHING Deep-sea fishing tours in search of blue shark, or the increasingly rare bluefin tuna, are easily arranged on licensed charter boats berthed at many of the province's harbours. Try for example **Lunenburg Ocean Adventures** (☎ *634 4833; www.lunenburgoceanadventures.com*) in Lunenburg (see page 149) for shark and more. Based near Antigonish (page 295), **Zappa Charters** (☎ *386 2669; www.zappacharters.com*) specialise in bluefin tuna.

Freshwater anglers try for brook, rainbow and brown trout, Atlantic whitefish, yellow perch, shad, smallmouth bass and – the once-mighty – Atlantic salmon. For much of the past two decades, salmon numbers have been dropping towards critical levels. For more on Atlantic salmon and trout fishing in the province, see the **Nova Scotia Salmon Association's** website (*www.novascotiasalmon.ns.ca*).

If you are thinking of fishing whilst in the province, get clued up on the regulations via the **Department of Fisheries and Aquaculture** website (*www.gov.ns.ca/fish/*).

For fishing guides, try Hunt's Point-based Vinal Smith (☎ *356 2498; www.vinalsmith.com*), on the South Shore or Don MacLean (☎ *485 3472*), based in Pictou on the Northumberland Shore. Local general stores and outfitters are often good sources of advice. A list of fishing guides can be found on the Department of Fisheries and Aquaculture website.

SEA KAYAKING

with Dr Scott Cunningham

Sea kayaking has become increasingly popular in recent years and Nova Scotia, with its countless harbours and headlands, inlets and islands, offers a world-class destination. The meandering shoreline is extensive, access is easy and the contrasts are exceptional. There is something for paddlers of every taste and skill level. You will find protected day trips for the beginner as well as challenging multi-day routes, and everything in between. And thousands of kilometres of coastline means that you can explore all this in relative solitude.

My favourite realm, and my home, is along the rugged **Eastern Shore**, where an isolated band of islands stretches from Clam Harbour to Canso. This forgotten wilderness forms a compelling mix of natural and human history. Some of these outposts are just tiny specks, scarcely breathing air at high water, whilst others are huge forest-covered expanses that dominate the horizon, and beckon to the inquisitive traveller. Explore abandoned lighthouses and shipwrecks, uncover those vanishing signs of our own transient history, or camp on a deserted isle where your only companions are the seals and the seabirds, far from the summer bustle. Tangier is an ideal place from which to start. On the other side of Halifax, the **South Shore** offers dozens of places to put in and explore, especially the Kejimkujik Seaside, the LaHave Islands, Blue Rocks, and Prospect. Even Halifax, with its eclectic waterfront and harbour islands, merits a visit by kayak.

Further north, on **Cape Breton Island**, the majestic Highlands rising abruptly from the Gulf of St Lawrence are particularly imposing when viewed from the perspective of a sea kayak. Sea spires, caves and a colourful geology decorate the perimeter, while the Cabot Trail winds out of sight and sound far above. Rich deciduous valleys alternate with barren vertical cliffs, washed by waterfalls and you will certainly spot bald eagles and seals. If lucky you will also paddle with

GEOCACHING Geocaching (*www.geocachingnovascotia.ca*) – a type of treasure hunt game using a Global Positioning System (GPS) device – is quite popular in the province. The idea is to find a treasure or cache placed in a specific location using only GPS co-ordinates. Tales of buried treasure abound in the province, and there have been a handful of finds over the centuries. However, I have decided to leave 'metal detector' off the 'what to take' list.

GOLF Nova Scotia now has over 60 golf courses including world-renowned Highland Links (see page 325) and Bell Bay (page 333), both on Cape Breton Island. There's also a fabulous new links course, Cabot Links (see page 71). Depending on their location, and the weather, the season can start as early as April and run to the end of October. Standard high-season green fees (including tax) for 2012 are shown in this guide, although almost all courses offer discounts – often substantial – for early or late season, later tee offs, etc. Quite often courses work together with certain local accommodation to offer stay-and-play packages.

Golf Nova Scotia (**t/f** *1 800 565 0000; www.golfnovascotia.com*) markets over 20 of the province's well-regarded courses, publishes a guide to golf in Nova Scotia, and offers stay-and-play packages.

HIKING AND WALKING With fabulous varied coastal and mountain scenery, inland valleys, pristine rivers, dozens of lakes and waterfalls, wild flowers and abundant wildlife, Nova Scotia is a delight for the hiker.

the whales, as I have done many a time. By midsummer the water can warm up considerably, to 20°C, but this is an open coast and experience is advised.

The **Bay of Fundy** is perhaps the most distinctive region. The highest tides ever recorded on earth wash these shores, sculpting cliffs and inundating massive salt marshes and mud banks with surprising speed. Experience here is essential. Cape Chignecto's long and rich geological history has resulted in a striking melange of colours, textures and forms. The abrupt cliffs, numerous pinnacles and sea caves, combine with tides exceeding 12m to create a spectacular land/seascape.

If you arrive early in the season when the Atlantic coast may be draped in fog (the best times are early July to October), or if the Highlands and the Fundy are too exposed for your taste, you should try the province's **Northumberland Strait** shore where you will be treated to the warmest salt water north of the Carolinas. Fog has been banned, and the miles of sandy shores and salt-marsh estuaries offer protected paddling for the entire family. Kayakers are not the only ones who enjoy soaking up a few summer rays and this shore has become a mecca for the vacation crowd. However, secluded corners can still be found.

There are many other exciting areas of our coastline to entice you and your sea kayak. A comprehensive guide, *Sea Kayaking in Nova Scotia*, available at most bookshops, will help with detailed descriptions of over 40 routes. Bring your own boat and paddle on your own, or accompany a local outfit who can introduce you to the biology, geology and human history of this fascinating environment where the land meets the sea. Happy paddling!

For more information email **e** info@coastaladventures.com or visit www.coastaladventures.com.

The trails of the Cape Breton Highlands National Park (see page 317) are justifiably popular, but so many more areas are wonderful to explore on foot. Also on Cape Breton Island, there are a number of superb hikes in the Mabou area (see page 307), whilst on the 'mainland', Cape Chignecto Provincial Park (see page 267) and the Cape Split Trail (see page 228) are hiking highlights. Several sections of the province's old disused railway lines have been converted to multi-use trails.

RAFTING Whilst you won't find organised white-water rafting here, Nova Scotia offers a unique alternative. Several commercial operators take raftloads of (soft) adventure-seekers onto the Shubenacadie River to ride the tidal bore (see page 250).

ROCKHOUNDING The richest areas for rockhounding (looking for rocks, semi-precious stones and minerals in their natural environment) are the beaches of the Minas Basin and the Bay of Fundy. In fact, the annual Gem and Mineral Show, held in August in Parrsboro (page 260) used to be called the Rockhound Roundup. The region's extreme tides erode cliff faces that may contain jasper, amethyst, agates, zeolites and more, sometimes depositing the semi-precious stones in amongst other pebbles.

SAILING The waters of Nova Scotia are actively used by a 40,000-vessel fishery and a range of commercial and military vessels. However, the density of boats is low and few spots are busy or crowded. Even in relatively busy harbours and bays, sailors can quickly get away to pristine waters, uninhabited islands and secluded anchorages.

The vast Bras d'Or Lake of Cape Breton Island is a renowned cruising destination for larger sailboats and mega-yachts because of its beauty and its accessibility (north and south) from the ocean. Other noted cruising destinations include Mahone Bay, St Margaret's Bay and Halifax Harbour.

Nova Scotia is still one of the best-kept secrets for sailors, whether out for a day or a cruising adventure.

Whilst there are very few, if any, Nova Scotia businesses that offer bareboat (where you skipper and crew the yacht) charters, sailing and cruising training is readily available. A full range of courses with certified instructors is offered by the **Nova Scotia Yachting Association** (*www.nsya.ns.ca*) lasting from a few hours to a week. Try, for example, **Sou'Wester Adventures** (☎ *627 4004*, **t/f** *1 877 665 4004; www.souwesteradventures.com*).

TALLY-HO

Be aware that hunting is legal in Nova Scotia, and enjoyed by many. To avoid being mistaken for a black bear, moose or white-tailed deer, wear something brightly coloured if you go walking in the woods between September and mid December.

Hunting is regulated by the provincial government's Department of Natural Resources (*www.gov.ns.ca/natr/hunt/default.htm*). The following operators organise hunting trips:

Farmland Outfitters ☎ 899 3144; www.farmlandoutfitters.com. Based in Millbrook, near Truro.
Purcell's Hunting Excursions ☎ 483 1594; www.purcellshunting.com. Based near Halifax.

SKATING There are ice rinks all over the province, but the majority are only open between late autumn and early spring. Unfortunately, very few offer ice-skate hire. Many locals prefer outdoor skating (on frozen ponds and lakes) to arena rinks.

SKIING AND SNOWBOARDING Winter visitors do have some opportunities to strap on the skis (or a snowboard) and take to the slopes. Whilst vertical rises don't break any records, rentals and lift passes are cheap, and the resort staff – and other skiers – friendly.

The main downhill resorts are Ski Martock (see page 242) near Windsor, Ski Wentworth (page 282) between Truro and Amherst, and Cape Smokey (page 325) and Ski Ben Eoin (page 339), both on Cape Breton Island. Cross-country skiing is widespread, and snowmobiles are popular for whizzing across the white stuff.

STARGAZING Kejimkujik National Park (see page 214) is an official 'Dark Sky Preserve', but countless parts of the province have minimal light pollution. Incidentally, you may remember that the protagonist in Carly Simon's 1972 hit 'You're So Vain' flew to Nova Scotia to see the total eclipse of the sun (there were such eclipses in 1970 and 1972, and the next one is due in August 2017). Get an astronomy book or just look up and enjoy.

SURFING AND WINDSURFING Nova Scotia ain't Hawaii (at least in terms of weather), but adventure-loving locals – and a few visitors – love to slip into a wetsuit and climb onto a board year-round. The most popular base for surfers is Lawrencetown (see page 360) on the Eastern Shore, though you can find a couple of surf shops on the South Shore (see page 130). In general, the waves are best between September and May.

SWIMMING With over 7,000km of coastline, the province has a number of magnificent beaches. However, with a few exceptions (noted in the text) not all are ideal for swimming. Even when the air temperature rises, sea swimming can often be too nippy. Luckily, those wishing to cool off without freezing have numerous opportunities for freshwater dipping. Good lakes for a swim are dotted about the province and include Chocolate Lake (see page 119), Dollar Lake (page 366), Sandy Bottom Lake (page 216), Lake Midway (page 201), Bras d'Or Lake (page 301), and Porter's Lake Provincial Park (page 361).

Some hotels, and most resorts, have heated outdoor pools, and many towns have outdoor pools that may or may not be heated. Indoor pools are relatively rare.

ZIPLINING A recent addition to the province's outdoor adventure possibilities involves whizzing along whilst attached to an inclined cable high above the ground. You can zipline at OnTree Park (see page 242), Anchors Above (page 294), and – as part of a longer course – at Upper Clements Adventure Park (page 207).

TIME, MEDIA AND COMMUNICATIONS

TIME Nova Scotia is in the Atlantic Time Zone. This is four hours behind Greenwich Mean Time (GMT) but Daylight Saving Time is observed between the second Sunday in March and the first Sunday in November. During this period, the province is three hours behind GMT. The Atlantic Time Zone is one hour ahead of Eastern Standard Time and four hours ahead of Pacific Time.

PRINT The province's leading newspaper is the independently owned *Chronicle Herald*, which first appeared in 1875. Daily circulation is now close to 115,000, and the Sunday version, the *Sunday Herald*, sells about 100,000 copies. In general, editorial policy tends to be moderate conservative.

The TC Transcontinental media group publishes a number of regional weekly titles and four regional dailies: the *Amherst Daily News*, *Cape Breton Post*, *The News* (New Glasgow) and the *Truro Daily News*.

The free *Metro* is published on weekdays and distributed through much of the Halifax Regional Municipality (HRM).

The Coast (also free and available online; *www.thecoast.ca*) is published on Thursday and distributed in Halifax, Dartmouth, and some nearby communities: it focuses primarily on Halifax. There are excellent listings pages, and reviews, including restaurants, music, performing arts and more. Editorial policy tends to be slightly left-wing.

Almost 30 other local newspapers are published including one in French, *Le Courrier* (published monthly). Inspired by the UK's *Private Eye*, the fortnightly *Frank* magazine mixes humour, news and satire.

TELEVISION In addition to the Canadian Broadcasting Corporation's CBHT and French-language CBAFT, other terrestrial television stations include CJHC and CJCB (both parts of the CTV network) and CIHF Global Maritimes, owned by Shaw Communications. Catch up with the news on CBC at 06.00, midday or at 18.00.

Most tourist accommodations now offer cable/satellite television.

RADIO The Canadian Broadcasting Corporation offers five terrestrial networks: CBC Radio One, CBC Radio 2, CBC Radio 3, and two French-language networks, Première Chaîne and Espace Musique. You can tune in to a range of English and French radio stations in the province, though reception can be poor in some areas.

Some hire cars are equipped with satellite radio, opening up a host of other stations.

TELEPHONE Public telephones (pay phones) in Nova Scotia can be operated by phonecard. Some accept credit cards, and a decreasing number take coins. Sold at newsagents, general stores, petrol stations, post offices and many other places, phonecards come in various denominations (eg: CAN$5, CAN$10 or CAN$20). Some may be better than others depending on your requirements (for example, if you're likely to make a high proportion of calls to numbers outside the province). I've found the President's Choice cards sold at Atlantic Superstores to be a good all-rounder.

The area code for the whole of Nova Scotia is 902 (but see box opposite) and the international access code for Canada, like the US, is +1. If you're calling overseas from the province other than within Canada, to the US or Caribbean, the outgoing code is 011 followed by the relevant country code. Common country codes are: Australia +61, France +33, Germany +49, Ireland +353, UK +44. If you are calling the UK from Nova Scotia, prefix the number you are calling – less its initial zero – with 011 44.

Mobile phones Not all mobile (they are called 'cell' in Nova Scotia) phones are enabled for international roaming, and (more important), not all handsets work in Canada. If your phone is enabled and compatible with the Canadian mobile-phone providers, check with your provider for the charges for making and receiving calls and texts. Alternatively, you can buy a pay-as-you-go SIM card either in the UK before you go – try, for example, **0044** (*www.0044.co.uk*) – or once in Nova Scotia from **Rogers** (see the 'store locator' section of www.rogers.com for branches and phone numbers in the province). When I think how far we should've come since the days of Alexander Graham Bell, inventor of the telephone, who lived near Baddeck on Cape Breton Island, I must admit to getting frustrated when I lose mobile-phone contact when in some of the province's not all that far-flung areas.

Useful telephone numbers

Fire, police, medical ☎ 911
Operator ☎ 0
Local directory assistance ☎ 411
Long-distance directory assistance ☎ 1 + the area code, if you know it, + 555 1212 (directory assistance is free from a payphone)

POST OFFICES City and town post offices (**t/f** *1 866 607 6301*) are usually open 08.00–17.00 Monday–Friday, whilst rural outlets have varying hours (they may well close for lunch) and some may open on Saturday mornings. To confuse matters, in the biggest urban areas some larger shops have post office counters which operate different hours. Canada Post's website (*www.canadapost.ca*) has a 'find a post office' section which gives each office's location and opening hours.

Postage prices are determined by weight and size of the item, and destination: standard-size letters within Canada cost CAN$0.70, to send to the US it is CAN$1.21, and internationally CAN$2.07.

INTERNET A few internet cafés are to be found in some of the biggest urban centres, and the network of Wi-Fi hotspots is ever-growing. Many accommodations offer Wi-Fi for those travelling with a laptop, or have a computer terminal for guests' use.

Many public buildings, especially libraries and tourist offices, offer free public internet access: look for a sign saying C@P site or check www.nscap.ca.

NOVA SCOTIA PHONE NUMBERS

The vast majority of phone numbers listed in this guide are standard seven-digit numbers. If calling these numbers from anywhere in the province outside the immediate area, Canada or the USA, dial the provincial area code (902) first. You may hear a message telling you to redial, prefixing the 902 with a 1. If dialling from outside these areas, you'll also need to add the international code for North America (00). Numbers listed as **t/f** (which begin 1 8XX) are (in theory) toll-free. Some are toll-free from outside North America, but if you try to call others from abroad, you will be intercepted by a message telling you your call is not toll-free: you can proceed with the call and should be charged the normal tariff. To call these 1 8XX numbers from outside North America, dial 00 first (eg: 00 1 8XX, etc).

Nova Scotia shares the 902 code with the neighbouring province of Prince Edward Island, and in mid 2012 it was reported that there would not be enough seven-digit phone numbers left to handle new business by perhaps 2015.

From late 2014 there will be two major changes. Firstly, new numbers allocated will be prefixed by 782 rather than 902. Secondly, even if you are just making a local call, you will have to dial at least a ten-digit number, prefixing 'old' phone numbers (including all the seven-digit phone numbers in this book) with 902, and newly allocated numbers with 782.

Unfortunately, the federal government cut funding for C@P (Community Access Program) sites, so the list might not be up to date.

MAPS The provincial and regional tourist offices offer a range of free maps that might well be all you need on a holiday in the province. A range of simple regional and community maps can also be found online by looking at the 'Plan a Trip' section of www.novascotia.com and then selecting 'Maps' from the 'Travel Tools' box.

The provincial government's **Service Nova Scotia and Municipal Relations** department (☎ *667 7231,* **t/f** *1 800 798 0706; www.gov.ns.ca/snsmr/land/*) produces and sells a range of regional atlases, maps and guidebooks (including 98 1:50,000 topographic maps – with contours at 10m intervals – covering the entire province). These are available online, by phone, or at one of the province's six **Land Registration Offices**: for the Dartmouth address, see page 125; for the others, see the website www.gov.ns.ca/snsmr/offices.asp.

More detailed road atlases, often including New Brunswick and Prince Edward Island, can be purchased at bookshops and petrol stations for about CAN$10.

International Travel Maps (☎ *1 604 273 1400; www.itmb.ca*) publishes a good 1:400,000-scale map of Nova Scotia which has been used to produce several of the maps in this guide.

For shops selling specialised maps in Halifax, see page 107.

BUSINESS

Business etiquette is similar to that in western Europe and the US. Suits are common for men, but staff at many companies dress more casually. Business hours tend to be 08.00–09.00 to 16.00–17.00, with a break of 30–60 minutes at lunch. Many companies offer flexible working hours, and an increasing number of staff work from home. Halifax is a popular place for international business conferences and conventions, and several hotels and resorts around the province endeavour to attract the convention market.

Many global companies are represented in Nova Scotia including EADS (European Aeronautic Defence and Space Company), Composites Atlantic (ownership of which is shared by EADS and the provincial government) and Michelin. It is home to world-renowned research facilities such as the National Research Council's Institute for Marine Biosciences and the Bedford Institute of Oceanography. Defence, security and aerospace companies include Lockheed Martin, General Dynamics, IMP Group and Pratt and Whitney. The province is one of North America's leading emerging IT and business process outsourcing (BPO) destinations: Convergys, Research in Motion (RIM), Unisys and Xerox all have bases here.

A list of all the province's main Chambers of Commerce and Boards of Trade can be found at the Nova Scotia Chambers of Commerce website (*www.nschamber.ca*). The UK-based Canada–United Kingdom Chamber of Commerce (*38 Grosvenor St, London W1K 4DP;* ☎ *020 7258 6578; www.canada-uk.org*) might also be of use.

CULTURAL ETIQUETTE

TIPPING As in the US, tipping is a common practice in Canada. Taxi drivers are normally tipped 15% of the fare, hairdressers and barbers also 15%, airport/hotel porters CAN$1–2 per bag, and valet parkers CAN$1–2. Tour guides and bus drivers normally receive CAN$3–5 per day. Tipping your server, a dollar or two per round, whether at the bar or at your table, is common in bars.

In cafés and restaurants, you don't need to tip if eating at the counter (but of course you can do if the service is particularly good), but you are expected to tip 15–20% for meals.

SMOKING Smoking is not permitted in indoor public areas, bars and restaurants, or on restaurant and bar patios. It is illegal to smoke in a vehicle with passengers under the age of 19.

VISITING SOMEONE'S HOME Many people in Nova Scotia take their shoes off when they enter their homes: be aware of this, and perhaps ask your host if you should de-shoe.

TRAVELLING POSITIVELY

Canada has many worthy countrywide charities such as the **Canadian Society for the Prevention of Cruelty to Children** (*1 702 526 5647; www.parentingcourse.net*) and **Help the Aged Canada** (*1 613 232 0727,* **t/f** *1 800 648 1111; http://helpagecanada.ca*).

An increasing number of musicians and creative artists from the province work with the **ArtsCan Circle** (*www.artscancircle.ca*), travelling to remote northern Canadian First Nations communities to encourage self-esteem amongst indigenous youth through music and art workshops.

Specific to the province is **Feed Nova Scotia** (*213 Bedford Hwy, Halifax B3M 2J9; 457 1900; www.feednovascotia.ca*), which aims to feed hungry people by providing year-round food deliveries to a network of 150 food banks across the province. The organisation's ultimate aim is to eliminate chronic hunger and alleviate poverty.

For over 250 years, lighthouses helped reduce the high number of wrecked ships in the province's coastal waters. Unfortunately, the majority of the 350-plus lighthouses are now gone or in ruinous states. The **Nova Scotia Lighthouse Preservation Society** (*www.nslps.com*) does valiant work ploughing time, effort and money into preserving the province's lighthouse heritage. See box, page 350.

The **Nova Scotia Nature Trust** (*425 5263; www.nsnt.ca*) works to conserve the province's increasingly threatened ecologically significant lands.

There is a Nova Scotia chapter of the **Canadian Parks and Wilderness Society** (*5435 Portland Pl, Suite 101, Halifax B3K 6R7; 446 4155; www.cpawsns.org*), Canada's leading grass-roots non-government organisation for wilderness conservation.

Please remember that the majority of the province's museums are staffed by volunteers and offer free admission: they rely (in varying degrees) on donations from visitors.

Part Two

THE GUIDE

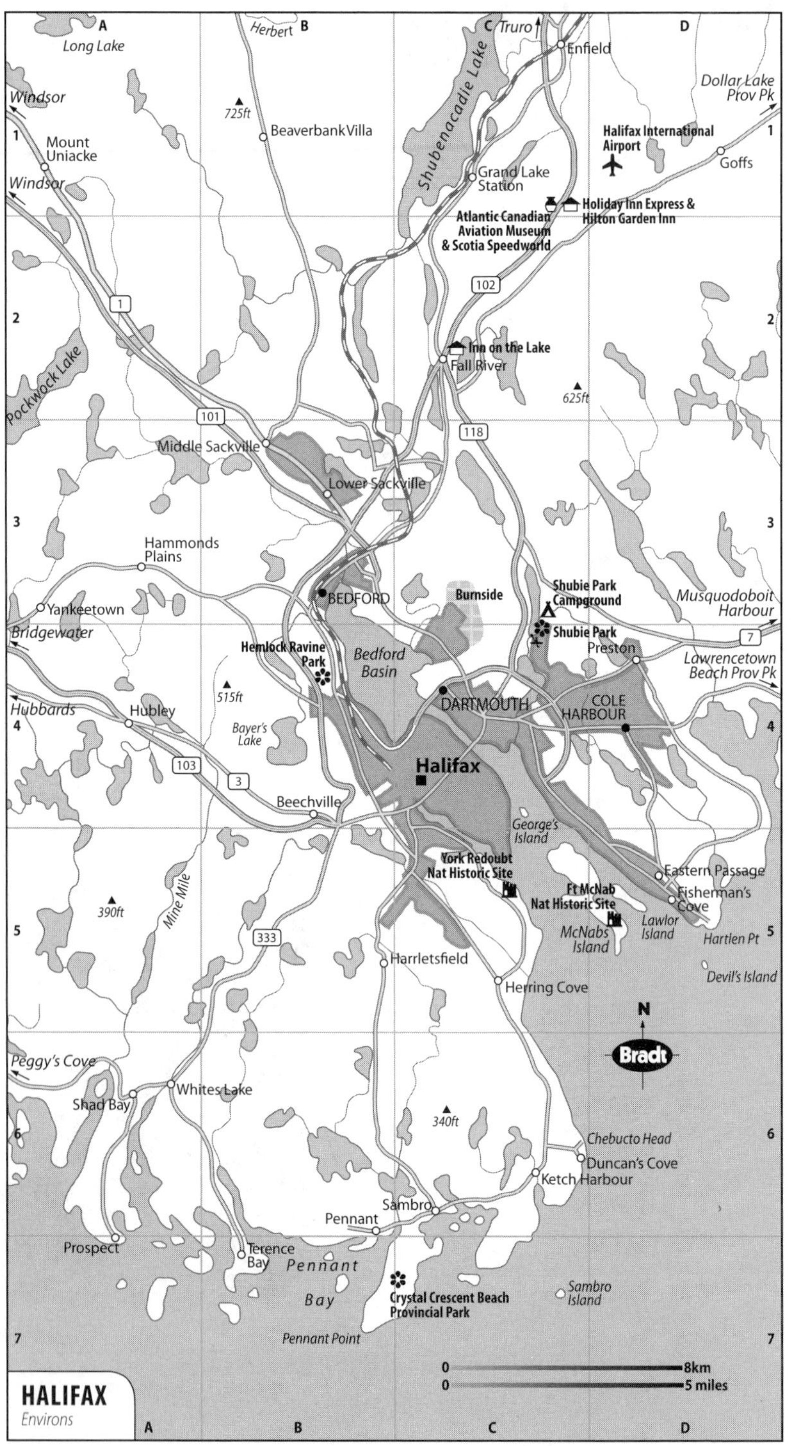

HALIFAX
Environs
Long Lake
Herbert
Truro
Enfield
Dollar Lake Prov Pk
Windsor
725ft
Beaverbank Villa
Halifax International Airport
Goffs
Mount Uniacke
Shubenacadie Lake
Grand Lake Station
Windsor
Holiday Inn Express & Hilton Garden Inn
Atlantic Canadian Aviation Museum & Scotia Speedworld
102
1
Pockwock Lake
Inn on the Lake
Fall River
625ft
101
118
Middle Sackville
Lower Sackville
Hammonds Plains
Shubie Park Campground
Musquodoboit Harbour
Yankeetown
BEDFORD
Burnside
Shubie Park
Bridgewater
Hemlock Ravine Park
Bedford Basin
Preston
7
Lawrencetown Beach Prov Pk
515ft
DARTMOUTH
COLE HARBOUR
Hubbards
Hubley
Bayer's Lake
103
3
Halifax
Beechville
George's Island
York Redoubt Nat Historic Site
Eastern Passage
Ft McNab Nat Historic Site
Fisherman's Cove
Mine Mile
390ft
McNabs Island
Lawlor Island
Hartlen Pt
333
Harrletsfield
Devil's Island
Herring Cove
N
Bradt
Peggy's Cove
Whites Lake
Shad Bay
340ft
Chebucto Head
Duncan's Cove
Ketch Harbour
Sambro
Pennant
Prospect
Terence Bay
Pennant Bay
Crystal Crescent Beach Provincial Park
Sambro Island
Pennant Point
0 8km
0 5 miles

3

Halifax, Dartmouth and Around

Nova Scotia's capital is not a city as such, but a municipality. The cities of Halifax and Dartmouth, the town of Bedford and the municipality of the county of Halifax were dissolved and amalgamated into the Halifax Regional Municipality (HRM) in 1996. The HRM has a population of close to 390,000 (of whom approximately 298,000 live in urban areas) and is home to over 40% of Nova Scotia's population. Despite the urban consolidation, virtually everyone still talks about the different entities as though nothing has changed.

Halifax – which has the largest component population (approximately 125,000) and is home to the majority of the government buildings and offices – sits at the heart of the HRM. It is here that you find the majority of the HRM's hotels, restaurants and best museums and attractions.

Dartmouth (with a population of approximately 72,000) is across the harbour from Halifax – a short ride by regular ferry.

At the head of the harbour is Bedford (population approaching 30,000). Compared with much of the rest of the province, the area to the north, northeast and northwest of Bedford is also quite densely populated, the major communities being the Sackvilles, Fall River and Waverley.

Visitors should try and head beyond the urban centres to explore areas such as the Northwest Arm (see page 119), the Eastern Passage (page 126) and the Uniacke estate (page 121).

Although its official boundaries stretch as far to the southwest as Hubbards (see page 137) and to the east as Ecum Secum (page 371), this chapter focuses on the heart of the HRM.

ORIENTATION

Halifax's *raison d'être* was its harbour, and the harbour is still a major part of life for Halifax, Dartmouth and Bedford. At the mouth of the harbour are Chebucto Head on the Halifax side and Hartlen Point on the Dartmouth side. Herring Cove Road and Purcell's Cove Road lead towards the downtown area from Chebucto Head, passing fjord-like Northwest Arm. On the Dartmouth side, Shore Road and Eastern Passage Road run close to the waterfront, with McNab's and Lawlor islands just offshore.

Connected by passenger ferry, downtown Halifax and downtown Dartmouth face each other across the harbour, which then narrows through a stretch called The Narrows, before opening up into the expanse of the 40km^2 Bedford Basin. Two toll bridges – the MacDonald to the south and MacKay slightly further north – cross the narrows, providing road links between the two communities. The MacDonald has cycle lanes, a pedestrian walkway, and great views.

Near Bedford, which is at the head of the Bedford Basin, two of the province's major motorways meet. Highway 102 leads southwest to Halifax and northeast to Halifax International Airport, approximately 38km from downtown, and Truro. Highway 101 leads southwest to Dartmouth, and northeast to Windsor, Wolfville and Yarmouth, via the Annapolis Valley.

The region's other major motorway, Highway 103, leads west from Halifax towards Liverpool, Bridgewater and Yarmouth, via the South Shore.

The layout of downtown Halifax is relatively simple, with a series of short streets rising up from the western side of Halifax Harbour towards Citadel Hill. On the waterfront itself, most of the tourist sites are between Casino Nova Scotia to the north, and the cruise ship dock to the south. Lower and Upper Water streets run parallel to the water, with Barrington Street two to three blocks inland.

En route up to Citadel Hill, grassy Grand Parade is bordered by Barrington, Argyle, Duke and Prince streets. Around Citadel Hill are large green areas with individual names, but collectively referred to as The Commons, and bordered by Robie Street. Cogswell Street runs from Barrington Street to Robie Street, continuing on as Quinpool Road before reaching the Armdale Rotary.

Locals tend to refer to everything south of The Commons as the South End, and everything to the north as the North End. The North End – much of which was flattened by the Halifax Explosion in 1917 (see box, page 90) – includes the Hydrostone district, bordered by Young, Agricola, Duffus and Gottingen streets. This European-style district was built in the aftermath of the Halifax Explosion using hydrostone, a special kind of masonry. Completed in 1920, the district includes a market with a collection of shops and eateries.

In the South End (the southernmost part of which is occupied by beautiful Point Pleasant Park) is the city's academic area, site of Dalhousie University, University of King's College, St Mary's University and the Nova Scotia College of Art & Design University.

GETTING THERE

For international and inter-provincial services, sees page 41–5.

BY AIR Flights connect Halifax with Sydney (see page 339).

Airport transfers

Taxi You can reach the centre of Halifax by taxi (CAN$53) or limousine (CAN$56). You'll see 'ground transportation' booths as you emerge from the arrivals hall.

Bus If you're not in a hurry and don't have much luggage, **MetroX** (see *By bus*, page 84) route 320 connects the airport with Dartmouth and Halifax (Albemarle Street, near the Metro Centre) with departures once or twice per hour between approximately 05.45 and midnight. The fare is CAN$3.25, and transfer onto Metro Transit bus/ferry is permitted. Note that this service is aimed at commuters so luggage space is limited. **Maritime Bus** (see *Chapter 2*, page 57) stops at the airport *en route* to and from some other destinations in the province.

Shuttle The **Maritime Bus** company intends to run a shuttle bus several times a day between the airport and downtown Halifax hotels for a fare of approximately CAN$22. Check with the company for details.

Several shuttle operators will pick up and drop off at the airport on their regular runs to destinations further afield. For details, see *Ground transportation* in the *Directions to airport* section of www.hiaa.ca.

BY CAR If you are travelling by car from the north and/or the airport, Highway 102 brings you into downtown Halifax via Bayers Road (avoiding the toll bridges). Coming from Dartmouth and/or the Eastern Shore, it makes most sense to take one of the toll bridges. If you are heading for Windsor or the Annapolis Valley, or the South Shore from the airport, head towards Halifax on Highway 102, then follow signs to Highways 101 or 103 respectively.

There are two toll bridges in the HRM: the A Murray MacKay Bridge and Angus L MacDonald Bridge; the latter has pedestrian and bicycle access. The toll is CAN$1 and some booths are designated for those without exact change.

Car hire Car-hire companies offer rentals at the airport and other locations including downtown Halifax and Dartmouth (see page 56 for further information).

BY BUS Long-distance bus services (see page 57) arrive and depart from the VIA Rail Station [98–9 G4] (*1161 Hollis St*), 1km south of downtown. **Maritime Bus** (see *Chapter 2*, page 44) offers departures from Halifax to various points throughout the province and beyond.

BY TRAIN Don't be fooled by the size and grandeur of the VIA Rail Station [98–9 G4] There's just one departure and arrival three days a week, a service which connects Halifax with Montreal, Quebec. Stops in Nova Scotia are at Truro, Springhill Junction and Amherst. For fares and times contact **VIA Rail** (**t/f** *1 888 842 7245; www.viarail.ca*).

GETTING AROUND

BY CAR The downtown core of Halifax is quite compact, and parking can be hard to find. If the meters or 'no parking' signs haven't gone up yet, there are a couple of (relatively central) streets allowing free one- or two-hour parking, for example Dresden Row [92–3 B6] and Birmingham Street, between Morris and Clyde streets [92–3 B8]. Failing that, colour-coded parking meters (*red: max 30mins; grey: max 1hr; green: max 2hrs; yellow: max 3–5hrs*) charge CAN$0.25/ten minutes and CAN$0.25/7.5 minutes at the waterfront meters. Downtown parking is strictly monitored by a very enthusiastic enforcement team. Downtown Dartmouth only has grey and green meters. Meters are in effect 08.00–18.00 Monday–Friday.

There are several underground or multi-storey garages (look for the blue 'P' sign) which charge from CAN$3/hour, for example at the Scotia Square Mall [92–3 E3], the Prince George Hotel [92–3 D4] or 1557 Granville Street [92–3 E6]. Hotels charge guests around CAN$20/day for parking.

By and large, Haligonians drive slowly and considerately: they will allow traffic to merge and often stop at the first sign of a pedestrian near a kerb (you are obliged to stop for pedestrians at crosswalks). There are several one-way streets to watch out for, and the Armdale Rotary – basically just a simple roundabout – often causes locals vast amounts of confusion.

BY TAXI Taxis are easiest to find outside major hotels, shopping malls and the VIA Rail Station [98–9 G4]. You may be able to flag down a cruising taxi. Fares start at CAN$3, with CAN$1.50/km added after that. Each extra passenger is charged CAN$0.50. A ride from the Halifax waterfront to Citadel Hill, for example, will cost about CAN$9.

Casino Taxi 429 6666
Yellow Cab 420 0000

BY BUS **Metro Transit** (*490 4000; www.halifax.ca/metrotransit*) operates public transport in Halifax, Dartmouth and to some other parts of the HRM. The website has schedules, route maps and more. Almost all tickets (including free transfers) cost: adult CAN$2.25, senior and child (aged five–15) CAN$1.50, and under fives free. A book of ten tickets costs CAN$18 (senior and child CAN$13). Conductors prefer exact change only. If you are changing buses, or will be travelling by both bus and ferry, ask for a (free) transfer ticket – valid for 90 minutes.

There are also a few **MetroX** express commuter routes on which the fare is CAN$3.25, or one transit ticket or transfer plus CAN$1.

If you're at a stop waiting for a bus, dial 480 followed by the four-digit bus stop number (marked in red at every stop) for real-time information on when the next bus will be arriving.

Many bus routes use accessible low-floor buses (ALF), and the ferries are also accessible. There is also an Access-A-Bus service providing door-to-door accessible transportation throughout the city. If you might use the service, contact Metro Transit in advance to register.

Need-A-Lift (*222 5438; www.needalift.ca*) offers a wheelchair-accessible bus and taxi service in many HRM areas. Prices start at CAN$34.

BY FERRY Metro Transit (*490 4000; www.halifax.ca/metrotransit*) also runs the Halifax–Dartmouth ferry (the oldest saltwater passenger service in North America) from the foot of George Street [98–9 G4] to Alderney Drive in Dartmouth [124 C4] (*06.30–22.15 Mon–Sat, 10.30–18.00 Sun*). Not that I want to take business away from Halifax's boat tour operators, but for CAN$2.25 each way, the eight- to ten-minute crossing (*departures every 15–30 mins*) makes an excellent, cheap harbour ride. There is also a similarly priced ferry service (*06.30–17.50 weekdays only*) between Halifax and Woodside (on the Dartmouth side). Municipal number-crunchers cut ferry hours in 2012 (they used to run to 23.30): it might be worth checking that more services (eg: on weekends) have not been affected.

BY BIKE In recent years, the HRM has made efforts to make the city more bike-friendly, and renting a bike (or riding your own) can be a good way to explore the area (with some steep hills to keep you fit). Best bet for rentals is **Idealbikes** [92–3 E5] (*1678 Barrington St; 444 7433; www.idealbikes.ca*) or **I Heart Bikes** [98–9 F3] (*1325 Lower Water St; 406 7774; www.iheartbikeshfx.com; seasonally*). **Pedal and Sea Adventures** (**t/f** *1 877 777 5699; www.pedalandseaadventures.com*) is based in Hubbards (see page 137) but offers free delivery to the Halifax area.

ON FOOT The downtown area is easily explored on foot, though Citadel Hill [92–3 B3] and the Public Gardens [92–3 A6] are a long way uphill from the waterfront. In the downtown area, many hotels and shops are connected by covered pedestrian walkways (pedways).

FESTIVALS AND EVENTS

Halifax, Dartmouth and the surrounding communities have an event-packed calendar. Although (not surprisingly) anything with an outdoor focus is held in the summer months, it seems that there is something going on throughout the year. Tickets for some of the bigger events are available through companies such as **Ticket Atlantic** (*451 1221*, **t/f** *1 877 451 1221; www.ticketatlantic.com*) and **Ticketpro** (**t/f** *1 888 311 9090; www.ticketpro.ca*) – phone or see websites for the nearest outlet.

JANUARY

In the Dead of Winter (*http://inthedeadofwinter.com*) Acoustic music festival held on the last weekend in January. Top singer-songwriter talent.

FEBRUARY

Savour Food and Wine (*429 5343*, **t/f** *1 800 665 3463; www.savourfoodandwine.com*) Month-long festival during which many of the city's best restaurants offer special fixed-price menus.

APRIL

Halifax Comedy Fest (*www.halifaxcomedyfest.ca*) A festival of laughs. Prices for shows range from free to CAN$40.

MAY

Bluenose Marathon (*www.bluenosemarathon.com*) Marathon, half-marathon and 5km and 10km events, plus a popular youth run.

SuperNova Theatre Festival (*www.easternfronttheatre.com*) Full-length and ten-minute plays at the Neptune Theatre [92–3 E6].

JUNE

Greek Festival (*www.greekfest.org*) Very popular even with those who don't have Hellenic roots. Held early to mid June.

The Nova Scotia Multi-cultural Festival (*www.multifest.ca*) A three-day Dartmouth waterfront event held in mid June. Take in the sights, sounds, smells and tastes.

The Scotia Festival of Music (*429 9467*, **t/f** *1 800 528 9883; www.scotiafestival.ns.ca*) A celebration of chamber music over two weeks in early June. Concert tickets CAN$30, discounted multi-concert tickets available.

JULY

AlFresco Film Festo (*www.atlanticfilm.com/alfresco/*) This outdoor film festival – held between late July and late August – hosts screenings on the Halifax waterfront [98–9 G3] with a range of films projected onto a special screen. CAN$5 donation per film suggested.

Halifax Jazz Festival (*www.halifaxjazzfestival.ca*) Held over eight days, this is the largest Canadian music festival east of Montreal, and one of North America's major jazz events. Performances are held in a range of venues – in a variety of music styles. Many of the world's big names come to play, but it is also a reminder of the breadth and depth of local talent. Some free shows. In general tickets are CAN$15 and up: day passes and festival passes available.

Halifax Pride (*www.halifaxpride.com*) In the words of the organisers: 'a Lesbian, Gay, Bisexual, Transgender and Queer (LGBTQ) Pride Week Festival … accessible to all.' Atlantic Canada's largest Pride celebration.

Maritime Fiddle Festival (*http://maritimefiddlefestival.ca*) Held in Dartmouth, Canada's longest running old-time fiddle festival also includes a step-dance competition and music workshops.

Nova Scotia International Tattoo (*420 1114,* **t/f** *1 800 563 1114; www.nstattoo.ca; tickets CAN$35–72*) Billing itself 'the world's largest annual indoor show', this is a fantastic eight-day mix of marching bands, gymnastics, pageantry, dance, military competitions, music and more held in early July. And the organisers keep trying to push the barriers further. Performers come from the world over, and previous tattoos have seen 20 Swiss Elvis impersonators performing on parallel bars, and regular favourites include the Gun Run. A great – and very popular – family event. Held at the Halifax Metro Centre [92–3 D4], there is one performance daily (either a matinee at 14.30, or in the evening at 19.30).

Shakespeare by the Sea (*422 0295; www.shakespearebythesea.ca; admission by donation – CAN$15 suggested*) Between July and early September a selection of the bard's (and other) works performed outdoors in an amphitheatre at an old gun battery in Point Pleasant Park [98–9 H6].

Tall Ships (*www.tallshipsnovascotia.com*) The bad news is that this event – where beautiful sailing ships from around the world join many of Canada's finest sailing vessels in Halifax Harbour – only takes place every three to five years and it was hosted here in 2012, so it may not be back until at least 2015.

AUGUST

International Busker Festival (*www.buskers.ca*) Those to whom a busker is just a one-man band covering a 1960s' Bob Dylan song (badly) will have their eyes opened at this ten-day celebration of 'street theatre'. See jugglers, mime artists and fire-eaters from all over the world – and a whole lot more – at six waterfront properties. Free and great fun.

Natal Day (*www.natalday.org*) The communities of Halifax and Dartmouth come together in early August to celebrate their birthdays with a civic holiday long known as Natal Day. The event is now sponsored by Alexander Keith's brewery, and is known as Alexander Keith's Natal Day Festival. It is held over five days: expect parades, running races, live entertainment, fireworks and more.

SEPTEMBER

Atlantic Film Festival (*422 3456,* **t/f** *1 877 611 4244; www.atlanticfilm.com*) This ten-day mid September celebration of film and video from the Atlantic Provinces, Canada and around the world offers screenings of more than 150 films. These are shown in cinemas in and around town. Tickets cost CAN$11.50 per screening (more on opening nights).

Atlantic Fringe Festival (☎ *422 7604; www.atlanticfringe.ca*) A week of 200 performing arts shows held at various downtown venues in early September. Tickets tend to be CAN$4–10 per show.

Word on the Street (*www.wordonthestreet.ca*) Literary festival – listen to readings, pitch to publishers.

OCTOBER

Halifax Pop Explosion (☎ *482 8176; www.halifaxpopexplosion.com*) A five-day festival featuring a range of music from folk-rock to hip-hop, with 150 bands over 18 venues.

Nocturne: Art at Night (*http://nocturnehalifax.ca*) Fab public art event held on one mid month evening.

NOVEMBER

Christmas at the Forum (*Halifax Forum, 2901 Windsor St;* **t/f** *1 866 995 7469; www.christmasattheforum.com*) A festival of crafts, antiques, art and food held over three days at the beginning of the month.

HALIFAX

The province's most important metropolis was once the major point of entry to Canada for over a million immigrants and refugees (see page 112), and the port remains a busy centre for shipping. Much attention focuses on the bustling waterfront, and traffic in the harbour is a mix of ferries, yachts, tugs, container ships, naval vessels and ocean cruisers.

Halifax and Nova Scotia's strong links to the sea are recognised at the absorbing Maritime Museum of the Atlantic [92–3 F5] (see page 112), whilst high up the hill is the impressive Halifax Citadel National Historic Site of Canada [92–3 B3] (see page 111).

A range of museums, galleries and indoor attractions – not to mention shopping, particularly on lively Spring Garden Road [92–3 D7] – will occupy you if the

LAME DUC

In an attempt to harass the British and the New Englanders who had taken Louisbourg (see page 349), in 1746, Louis XV sent a huge naval expedition to seek revenge. Under the command of the Duc d'Anville (who had little naval experience), a fleet of over 70 sailing vessels and thousands of men endured an awful ten-week crossing of the Atlantic – including losing ships off Sable Island (see page 382) – before reaching what is now Halifax Harbour. The Duc himself died within a week of the arrival and was buried on George's Island [98–9 H3] (see page 119). Typhoid continued to claim lives, and when the men went ashore to bury their dead, the disease was passed on to the local Mi'kmaq population with devastating results.

The battered French fleet limped out of the harbour with the intention of sailing round and attacking Annapolis Royal (see page 208) but turned back and headed for home. Less than a fifth of the original party reached France alive.

HANGING AROUND IN HALIFAX

In days long gone by, criminals were often flogged, then branded on the ball of a thumb. Second offenders often faced the noose. In Halifax, there were central gallows at the foot of George Street [92–3 G4] (near the modern-day ferry terminal) and military gallows in the middle of the Citadel Hill parade ground [92–3 B3].

At the mouth of Halifax Harbour, a small, open cove named Black Rock Beach was the site of one of Halifax's earliest public gallows. Years later, these gallows were dismantled, relocated to McNab's Island and reassembled on a beach there. To this day, that stretch of sand is known as Hangman's Beach.

weather isn't at its best, but when the sun comes out and the mercury rises you'll want to wander the beautiful Halifax Public Gardens [92–3 A6] (see page 111) and hike along the seafront at Point Pleasant Park [98–9 H6] (see page 115), take a boat on the harbour [92–3 G4], or go for a picnic. Summer is the time for an array of festivals, many of which are free.

Although hills may put some off, the downtown area is easily explored on foot – just as well bearing in mind that parking spots can be hard to find. Try to go beyond the downtown area to sample the shops and eateries of cosmopolitan Quinpool Road [98–9 C4], or the Hydrostone district [98–9 B1] (see page 82).

Halifax continues to evolve. Built for the 2011 Canada Winter Games, the Emera Oval [98–9 D3] (see page 109) is the largest outdoor, artificially refrigerated ice surface in Atlantic Canada. More major changes are underway: two complete city blocks (bordered by Prince, Argyle, Sackville and Market streets) are being transformed into the Nova Centre [92–3 D5] (*www.novacentre.ca*) which is set to house a financial centre, luxury hotel, residences, retail and entertainment amenities and a convention centre, parking, and public space: opening is scheduled for 2015–16. A new CAN$55 million Halifax Central Library [92–3 D7] should be open in 2014.

Whilst first impressions will suggest that Halifax is friendly, charming and relaxed, dig deeper and you'll also find a well-developed music scene, lively pubs, and restaurants and bars to suit most palates and budgets. The two universities keep the atmosphere youthful – but rarely rowdy.

HISTORY Late in the 1740s, the British were looking for a site for a garrison as a base from which to defeat the French at Louisbourg, now back in French hands. They saw the potential of the area known to the Mi'kmaq as Jipugtug ('the great long harbour'), which was later anglicised as Chebucto. On one side of the wonderful harbour was a drumlin on which a fortress could be built. In 1749, General Edward Cornwallis arrived with about 2,500 settlers on 13 ships, and founded a settlement. The Earl of Halifax, President of the Board of Trade and Plantations, had been instrumental in obtaining British government approval for the projected town, and it was named Halifax in his honour.

Immediately, the first fortress was built on the hilltop: this later developed into the Citadel [92–3 B3] (see page 111). St Paul's Church [92–3 E5] (see page 88), Canada's first Anglican sanctuary, was constructed in 1750: that year, more settlers arrived and founded Dartmouth across the harbour. By 1752, the two towns were linked by a ferry system, the oldest saltwater ferry system in North America.

Protestants were recruited from mainland Europe in an attempt to counter the French and Catholic presence in Nova Scotia and between 1776 and 1783, population in the settlement was further boosted with the arrival of thousands of Loyalists from America.

Realising Halifax's strategic importance, in the years that followed, fortifications went up along the harbour approaches: these included batteries at McNab's Island, a Martello tower at Point Pleasant [98–9 H6], and forts at George's Island [98–9 H3] and York Redoubt [80 C5].

St Mary's University [98–9 F5] was established in 1802 and Dalhousie University [98–9 D5] opened in 1818. Alexander Keith's brewing company [92–3 F7] (see page 115) opened in 1820. In 1834, a cholera epidemic killed over 600 people in Halifax.

Native Haligonian Samuel Cunard was the leading figure in the city's shipping business, and in 1840, the Cunard Steamship Company's *Britannia* became the first vessel to offer a regular passenger service between Liverpool, England, and Halifax.

The only North American city founded by the British government (as opposed to British merchants or individuals) was incorporated in 1841, and was connected by rail to Windsor (see page 237) and Truro (see page 252) in 1858.

After Canadian confederation in 1867, the city retained its British military garrison until British troops were replaced by the Canadian army in 1906. The British Royal Navy remained until 1910 when the newly created Royal Canadian Navy took over the Naval Dockyard.

The city leapt into the international spotlight in 1912 when the RMS *Titanic* sank northeast of Nova Scotia (see box, below).

The harbour, ice-free year-round, had long been recognised as one of the best deep-water ports in all of eastern North America. Opening into the expanse of Bedford Basin, this was a sanctuary where literally hundreds of ships could moor in safety.

During both World Wars, Halifax Harbour sheltered convoys from German U-boat attack before they headed out across the Atlantic. The port city was of great strategic importance both for this reason and as the departure point for Canadian soldiers heading overseas. The devastating Halifax Explosion (see box, page 90) occurred in December 1917.

Sir Winston Churchill visited Halifax twice during World War II. Having been shown the Public Gardens and Citadel Hill, he told the mayor: 'Now, sir, we know your city is something more than a shed on a wharf.'

By the 1960s, Halifax was looking more than a little run down. Just in time, there was massive investment from federal, provincial and private sectors: several old

RMS *TITANIC*

On 10 April 1912, the White Star Line's RMS *Titanic* – at that time the largest passenger steamship in the world – left Southampton, England, on her maiden voyage to New York, carrying over 1,300 passengers and 900 crew. Just before midnight on 14 April, she struck an iceberg south of Newfoundland, and sunk in less than three hours. Although 706 survivors were rescued, well over 1,500 men, women and children died. Some victims' bodies were recovered and buried at sea: 209 bodies were brought to Halifax. A temporary morgue was established in a curling rink (now an Army Surplus store): 150 victims were buried in three Halifax cemeteries between May and early June (121 in the Fairview Lawn Cemetery, 19 in the Mount Olivet Cemetery, and ten in the Baron de Hirsch Private Cemetery).

The Maritime Museum of the Atlantic (see page 112) has a special section devoted to the *Titanic* disaster and its aftermath.

THE HALIFAX EXPLOSION

In winter 1917, Halifax Harbour was alive with activity as heavily armed warships prepared to escort convoys carrying troops, munitions and supplies on the dangerous crossing of the Atlantic, neutral vessels waited at anchor, and the usual shipping traffic buzzed around.

On the morning of 6 December, the French ship *Mont-Blanc* left her anchorage outside the mouth of the harbour to join one of the convoys. She was loaded with hundreds of tons of TNT, picric acid, benzene and other explosives. At the same time, the *Imo*, a Norwegian ship in service of the Belgian Relief, was headed in the opposite direction. To cut a long story (and much speculation) short, the *Imo* struck the *Mont-Blanc* on the bow. Fire immediately broke out on board the *Mont-Blanc* and her terrified captain and crew took to the lifeboats and rowed for their lives to the Dartmouth shore.

The abandoned *Mont-Blanc* drifted toward the Halifax docks. At 09.05, what was at the time the largest manmade explosion in history – unrivalled until the detonation of the first atomic bomb – occurred. About 130ha of the city's North End was flattened, over 10,000 people were wounded (many blinded by glass from shattered windows), and almost 2,000 were killed. Around 8,000 people's homes were destroyed, and tens of millions of dollars of damage done. The shock wave of the blast was felt over 400km away in Sydney on Cape Breton Island.

Fort Needham Memorial Park on Needham Street is home to a memorial carillon dedicated in 1984 to the memory of those who died in the explosion.

Incidentally, in World War II, three other potentially huge explosions involving vessels carrying munitions were narrowly avoided.

buildings were renovated, the waterfront tastefully and imaginatively brought back to life, and many new hotels built. Care was taken to limit the height of high-rise buildings, and to preserve sight-lines.

Recent years saw another disaster, when huge amounts of damage were caused, but (thankfully) only eight people lost their lives. Tens of thousands of trees were knocked down, many in Point Pleasant Park: there was extensive damage to buildings, and many homes had no electricity for a fortnight. All this was a result of Hurricane Juan, which arrived in the early hours of 29 September 2003 and lashed Halifax with sustained wind gusts of over 180km/h. To date, this was the most damaging storm in modern history for Halifax.

TOURIST INFORMATION

Tourist information [92–3 G5] 1655 Lower Water St; 424 4248; Oct–mid May 09.00–17.00 daily; mid May–early Jun & mid Sep–mid Oct 08.00–18.00 daily; mid Jun–mid Sep 08.00–19.00 daily

LOCAL TOUR OPERATORS Biggest of the companies offering sightseeing tours in the HRM and further afield is **Ambassatours/Gray Line** (*423 6242*, **t/f** *1 800 565 7173; www.ambassatours.com*).

At 20.30 on certain dark evenings (see website for dates) between July and October, a guided two-hour **Halifax Ghost Walk** (*466 1060; www.thehalifaxghostwalk.com; CAN$10*) sets off from the Old Town clock. It's interesting – and fun.

Those who prefer to sightsee by less mainstream methods of transport should consider **Bluenose Sidecar Tours** (*579 7433; www.bluenosesidecartours.com*) who will let you take in the city sights and streets from a Russian-built motorbike sidecar. **Segway Tours** (*www.segwayns.com*) hope to be able to operate their tours (by two-wheeled self-balancing battery-powered scooter) from 2013.

A harbour tour is a must, and one company lets you combine land and sea: **Harbour Hopper Tours** [92–3 G5] (*490 8687; www.harbourhopper.com; early May–late Oct*) offers 55-minute tours in a brightly coloured amphibious vehicle.

Sailing the harbour in a historic tall ship is very popular. The beautiful ***Tall Ship Silva*** (*429 9463; www.tallshipsilva.com; mid Jun–mid Sep*) offers three 90-minute sailings daily, plus a two-hour 'Boat Party Cruise' on Friday and Saturday nights at 22.30. Do look out for the ***Bluenose II*** (*634 8483, or 634 4794, ext 221, **t/f** 1 866 579 4909, ext 221; http://bluenose.novascotia.ca*), see page 153. Though more often based in Lunenburg, she sometimes spends some of the summer season offering two-hour tours of Halifax Harbour. Check the schedule and call or make reservations online.

Murphy's [92–3 G5] (*420 1015; www.mtcw.ca; May–late Oct*) offers a wide range of tours on a variety of vessels including the tugboat *Theodore Too*, the Nova Scotia maritime equivalent of Thomas the Tank Engine.

LOCAL TRAVEL AGENTS

Flight Centre [92–3 E3] Scotia Sq, 5201 Duke St, Unit #180; **t/f** 1 866 788 5077; www.flightcentre.ca

Maritime Travel [98–9 A4] Halifax Shopping Centre, 7001 Mumford Rd; 455 7856, **t/f** 1 888 527 1444; www.maritimetravel.ca

WHERE TO STAY All too often, conventions or major events can fill all hotel beds in and close to downtown. Many of the bigger hotels are geared to business travellers and may offer cheaper rates on Friday and Saturday nights. It is always worth asking for a discount, especially if you're staying out of season or for more than a couple of nights. Many of the larger hotels are also bookable through internet travel companies such as Expedia (*www.expedia.co.uk*), which sometimes offers lower rates than the hotel itself. For the nearest camping to downtown, see page 123. All accommodation is open year-round unless stated otherwise.

For hotels close to the **airport**, see page 96. The Hilton and Holiday Inn both have indoor pools and offer 24-hour complimentary **airport shuttles**. Both are close to Exit 5A of Highway 102 and are less than 4km to the terminals. A new multi-storey (169-room) ALT hotel (*www.althotels.ca*) connected to the terminal by a walkway is due to open in spring 2013. The blurb says 'boutique-style', 'chic design and atmosphere', and 'sexy décor and decadent vibes' …

Waterfront and downtown

Luxury

Lord Nelson Hotel & Suites [92–3 A6] (262 rooms & suites) 1515 South Park St; 423 6331, **t/f** 1 800 565 2020; **e** ask@lordnelsonhotel.com; www.lordnelsonhotel.com. On the corner of Spring Garden Rd with many rooms overlooking the Public Gardens, the décor in this grandiose c1928 hotel is contemporary in style: bathrooms are spacious. There's a fitness room, & an on-site traditional-English style pub where food is served. Parking is CAN$20/day, valet parking CAN$25. **$$$$**

Prince George Hotel [92–3 D4] (189 rooms & 14 suites) 1725 Market St; 425 1986, **t/f** 1 800 565 1567; www.princegeorgehotel.com. Close to the Halifax Citadel (& uphill from the centre of downtown), this c1986 property is another good choice for those who like big, comfortable hotels. Good concierge service, plus business centre, fitness centre & indoor pool, & 2 fine eateries (Gio, see page 97, & Terrace). Underground parking CAN$20/day, valet parking offered. **$$$$**

Radisson Suite Hotel Halifax [92–3 F5] (104 suites) 1649 Hollis St; 429 7233, **t/f** 1 888

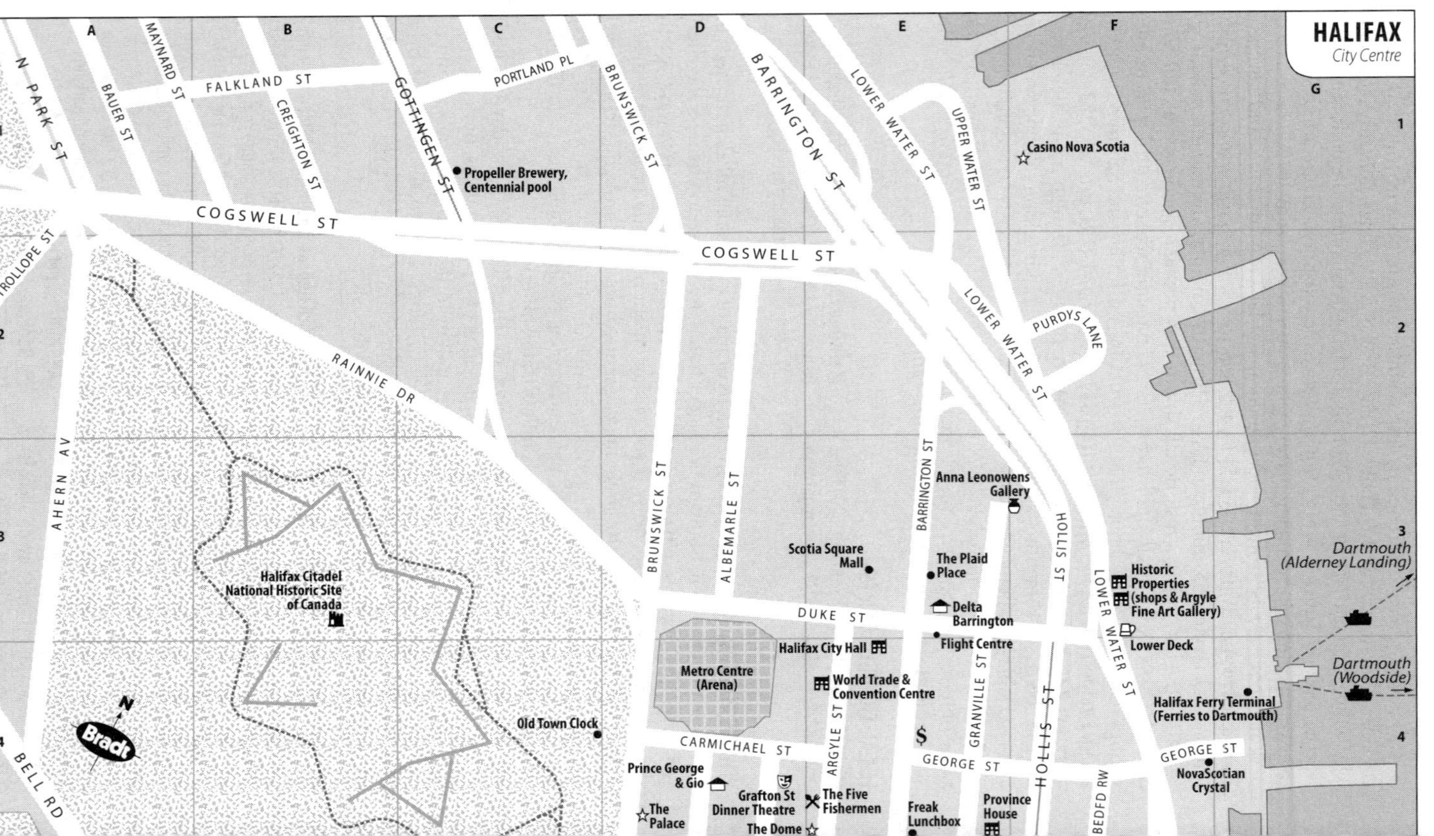

HALIFAX
City Centre
Casino Nova Scotia
Propeller Brewery, Centennial pool
Halifax Citadel National Historic Site of Canada
Scotia Square Mall
Anna Leonowens Gallery
The Plaid Place
Delta Barrington
Flight Centre
Historic Properties (shops & Argyle Fine Art Gallery)
Lower Deck
Dartmouth (Alderney Landing)
Dartmouth (Woodside)
Halifax Ferry Terminal (Ferries to Dartmouth)
NovaScotian Crystal
Halifax City Hall
World Trade & Convention Centre
Metro Centre (Arena)
Old Town Clock
Prince George & Gio
The Palace
Grafton St Dinner Theatre
The Five Fishermen
The Dome
Freak Lunchbox
Province House
N PARK ST
BAUER ST
MAYNARD ST
FALKLAND ST
CREIGHTON ST
GOTTINGEN ST
PORTLAND PL
BRUNSWICK ST
BARRINGTON ST
LOWER WATER ST
UPPER WATER ST
COGSWELL ST
TROLLOPE ST
PURDYS LANE
RAINNIE DR
AHERN AV
ALBEMARLE ST
HOLLIS ST
DUKE ST
CARMICHAEL ST
ARGYLE ST
GRANVILLE ST
GEORGE ST
BEDFD RW
BELL RD
Bradt

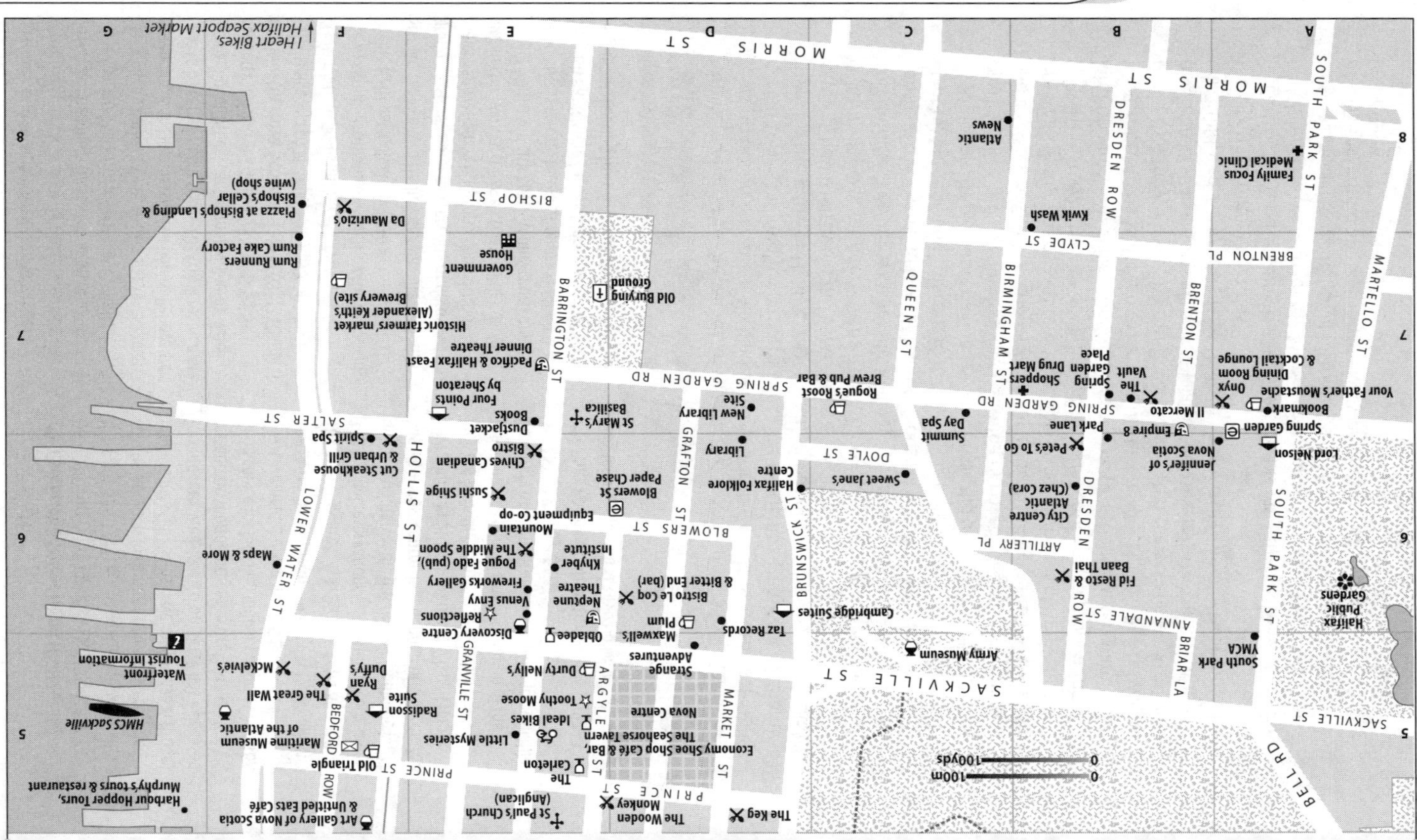
Harbour Hopper Tours, Murphy's tours & restaurant
HMCS Sackville
Waterfront Tourist Information
Art Gallery of Nova Scotia & Untitled Eats Café
Maritime Museum of the Atlantic
The Great Wall
McKelvie's
Maps & More
LOWER WATER ST
SALTER ST
Cut Steakhouse & Urban Grill
Spirit Spa
Old Triangle
BEDFORD ROW
Ryan Duffy's
Radisson Suite
PRINCE ST
HOLLIS ST
Rum Runners Rum Cake Factory
Piazza at Bishop's Landing & Bishop's Cellar (wine shop)
I Heart Bikes, Halifax Seaport Market
Da Maurizio's
Historic farmers' market (Alexander Keith's Brewery site)
Government House
BISHOP ST
St Paul's Church (Anglican)
The Carleton
Little Mysteries
Ideal Bikes
Toothy Moose
Durty Nelly's
GRANVILLE ST
Discovery Centre
Reflections
Venus Envy
Fireworks Gallery
Pogue Fado (pub), The Middle Spoon
Mountain Equipment Co-op
Sushi Shige
Chives Canadian Bistro
Dustjacket Books
Four Points by Sheraton
Pacifico & Halifax Feast Dinner Theatre
BARRINGTON ST
The Wooden Monkey
Economy Shoe Shop Café & Bar, The Seahorse Tavern
Nova Centre
Strange Adventures
ARGYLE ST
Obladee
Neptune Theatre
Khyber Institute
Maxwell's Plum
Bistro Le Coq & Bitter End (bar)
BLOWERS ST
Blowers St Paper Chase
St Mary's Basilica
Old Burying Ground
The Keg
MARKET ST
Taz Records
Cambridge Suites
GRAFTON ST
Halifax Folklore Centre
Library
New Library Site
BRUNSWICK ST
SPRING GARDEN RD
Rogue's Roost Brew Pub & Bar
Sweet Jane's
DOYLE ST
QUEEN ST
MORRIS ST
SACKVILLE ST
Army Museum
Summit Day Spa
ARTILLERY PL
City Centre Atlantic (Chez Cora)
Pete's To Go
Park Lane
BIRMINGHAM ST
Shoppers Drug Mart
Atlantic News
Kwik Wash
CLYDE ST
0 100m
0 100yds
Fid Resto & Baan Thai
DRESDEN ROW
ANNANDALE ST
The Spring Garden Place
The Vault
Empire 8
Il Mercato
BRENTON ST
BRIAR LA
Jennifer's of Nova Scotia
South Park YMCA
SOUTH PARK ST
Spring Garden
Lord Nelson
Bookmark
Onyx Dining Room & Cocktail Lounge
Your Father's Moustache
BRENTON PL
Family Focus Medical Clinic
BELL RD
Halifax Public Gardens
MARTELLO ST
A
B
C
D
E
F
G
5
6
7
8

664 1649; e reservations@radissonhalifax.com; www.radissonhalifax.com. Don't be put off by the downtown building's former life as an office block – the spacious 1-bedroom suites are comfortable, many have a harbour view, there's an exercise room, restaurant, & the indoor pool is a bonus. Renovations (due to be completed by early 2014) will mean more rooms & pool/fitness centre improvements. Valet parking is offered at CAN$18.95/day. **$$$$**

Westin Nova Scotian [98–9 G3] (310 units) 1181 Hollis St; 421 1000, **t/f** 1 877 993 7846; e reservations@westin.ns.ca; www.thewestinnovascotian.com. Built by the Canadian Pacific National Railway in 1930 as the Nova Scotian (adjacent to Halifax Railway Station), this grand 11-storey hotel has recently undergone major renovations & is looking good outside & 'urban chic' within. It has all the facilities you'd expect from a top city hotel (tennis court, indoor pool, fitness centre, business centre & more), a stylish bar & more casual, highly regarded restaurant. Parking from CAN$18/day. **$$$$**

Upmarket

Cambridge Suites Hotel Halifax [92–3 D6] (200 suites) 1583 Brunswick St; 420 0555, **t/f** 1 800 565 1263; www.cambridgesuiteshalifax.com. In addition to comfortable, well-equipped roomy suites (all rooms have microwave & fridge) this modern, well-located property has a licensed restaurant, rooftop fitness centre & sundeck. A good choice for families. Indoor parking CAN$16/day. Continental b/fast inc. **$$$**

Delta Barrington [92–3 E3] (200 rooms) 1875 Barrington St; 429 7410, **t/f** 1 800 268 1133; e hal.reservations@deltahotels.com; www.deltabarrington.com. This upscale boutique hotel has a business centre, indoor pool, fitness centre, new (summer 2012) restaurant & bar. It might look old from the Granville St side but that's just the result of a painstaking restoration of the building's original façade. Valet parking available at CAN$19.95/day. **$$$**

Four Points by Sheraton Halifax [92–3 E7] (159 rooms & 18 suites) 1496 Hollis St; 423 4444,

THE COMMUNITY THAT DISAPPEARED

Compared with the thousands of Acadians deported from Nova Scotia for refusing to sign an oath of allegiance to the British (see page 16), the eviction of 400 townsfolk might not seem a lot. The residents of Africville, a shanty town on the edge of Halifax, weren't turfed out of their homes in the 18th century, however, but in the 1960s.

Africville was founded in the 1840s by people living in very poor black communities seeking a better life. Railway lines were built right through the centre of the town and later a slaughterhouse, a fertiliser plant, and factories went up immediately adjacent to it.

Although the residents paid taxes, at no stage did the city of Halifax provide basic services such as running water, sewage or paved roads. The community had a school, post office, and its focus, the church. But in the 1950s, the large, open city dump was moved to within a few hundred metres of Africville.

Then in 1962, the city government announced it was expropriating the land on which Africville stood as part of an Urban Renewal programme. In 1964, rubbish trucks arrived to remove the first residents. Most had no way to prove that they owned the run-down houses that they occupied, and were given CAN$50 as a goodwill compensatory gesture. In 1970, the last property was bulldozed. Forty years later, Halifax's mayor issued an official apology for the city government's actions.

Part of the land on which Africville stood is now the Seaview Memorial Park (named in memory of the former community's demolished church), and this was designated a national historic site in 1996. A three-day picnic (*www.africville.ca*) is held annually on the last weekend in July to commemorate the community.

t/f 1 866 444 9494; www.starwoodhotels.com. This conveniently located modern c2002, 7-storey hotel is another good well-equipped choice. There's an indoor pool, fitness room & the Niche Restaurant. Underground parking at CAN$19.95/day. **$$$**

The Halliburton [98–9 F3] (25 rooms & 4 suites) 5184 Morris St; 420 0658, **t/f** 1 888 512 3344; www.thehalliburton.com. Occupying 3 adjoining c1809 properties, the beautifully restored Halliburton successfully blends B&B & boutique hotel. It is elegant & very comfortable, & when the sun comes out the courtyard garden is very pleasant. The on-site restaurant, Stories (see page 100), offers dinner every evening. There is also (limited) free parking. Light buffet b/fast inc. **$$$**

Waverley Inn [98–9 F3] (34 rooms) 1266 Barrington St; 423 9346, **t/f** 1 800 565 9346; www.waverleyinn.com. This delightful c1866 property has included Oscar Wilde amongst its guests. Expect hardwood floors & antiques. As the cheapest (Traditional) rooms are on the small side, you may want to consider upgrading. Rooms on 3 floors (no lifts). Free parking is a bonus. Hot b/fast buffet & snacks inc. **$$$**

Budget

HI-Halifax: Halifax Heritage House Hostel [98–9 F3] (75 beds) 1253 Barrington St; 422 3863; **e** halifax@hihostels.ca; www.hihostels.ca. The better located of the city's hostels is close to the waterfront in walking distance of many attractions & the bus/train station. In addition to dorm beds, there are a couple of private/family rooms with private baths & also shared bathrooms, a kitchen, common room & laundry. Discounts for YHA/HI members. *Dorm CAN$35, private room CAN$72.* **$**

Central Halifax

Mid range

Atlantica Hotel Halifax [98–9 D3] (230 units) 1980 Robie St; 423 1161, **t/f** 1 888 810 7288; **e** reservations@atlanticahalifax.com; www.atlanticahotelhalifax.com. Located at Robie St's junction with Quinpool Rd, directly across from the Halifax Commons. Restaurant & lounge, indoor pool, whirlpool, sauna, fitness equipment (seasonal) sundeck & business centre. Free Wi-Fi. On-site parking CAN$17/day. **$$–$$$**

Commons Inn [98–9 C2] (41 units) 5780 West St; 484 3466, **t/f** 1 877 797 7999; **e** commonsinn@hotmail.com; www.commonsinn.ca. Accommodation at this Edwardian building within a 15-min walk of many downtown attractions includes simple standard rooms, larger deluxe rooms with microwave & fridge, & a suite. There are also 2 rooftop patios. Free parking. Light b/fast inc. **$$**

Budget

Marigold B&B [98–9 C4] (2 rooms) 6318 Norwood St; 423 4798; www.marigoldbedandbreakfast.com. If you don't mind sharing a bathroom, this uncluttered c1893 house on a residential street approximately 25 mins' walk or a short bus ride from downtown – & well placed for shopping/dining on Quinpool Rd – is a good choice. Free off-road parking. Wi-Fi. Full b/fast inc. **$**

North Halifax

Budget

Halifax Backpackers Hostel [98–9 D2] (30 beds) 2193 Gottingen St; 431 3170, **t/f** 1 888 431 3170; **e** info@halifaxbackpackers.com; www.halifaxbackpackers.com. This friendly hostel is not far from things, but neither is it in the most salubrious part of town. An old building with dorms that are a little cramped. Communal kitchen, laundry, lounge & on-site organic fairtrade café. *Dorm CAN$23, private room CAN$58.* **$**

REDS IN THE BED

In 1917, during her husband's time in Amherst (see page 271), Mrs Trotsky and the boys stayed in Halifax, first at the home of the local man who had been assigned as Trotsky's interpreter when he first came ashore, and later at the Prince George Hotel which was on the corner of Sackville and Hollis streets. That hotel burned down a few months after the Trotskys checked out and is connected in name alone with today's Prince George Hotel on Market Street.

South Halifax

Mid range

At Robie's End B&B [98–9 F6] (2 rooms) 836 Robie St; 405 2424; e anna@robiesend.com; www.robiesend.com. Both of the guestrooms at this quiet B&B near St Mary's University & Point Pleasant Park have private entrances & mini fridges. Continental b/fast inc or, for a surcharge, an excellent full b/fast. **$$**

Budget

Dalhousie University [98–9 D5/E4] 494 8840, t/f 1 888 271 9222; e accommodations@dal.ca; www.conferenceservices.dal.ca; early May–late Aug. During the summer break, this university rents out sgl & twin rooms (shared facilities) at 2 locations: Howe Hall (*6230 Coburg Rd*) & Risley Hall (*1233 LeMarchant St*). Rates include use of the university recreation facilities. **$**

Near Northwest Arm

Mid range

The Pebble B&B [98–9 B5] (2 rooms) 1839 Armview Terrace; 423 3669, t/f 1 888 303 5056; www.thepebble.ca. On a quiet cul-de-sac a few mins' walk from the shops & eateries of Quinpool Rd. Bright, spacious rooms, tastefully furnished. Fine views over (& less than 100m from) the Northwest Arm. Pet-friendly. Rate inc gourmet b/fast. **$$–$$$**

Budget

Mumford B&B [98–9 A4] (2 rooms) 7015 Mumford Rd; 446 0766; www.mumfordbedandbreakfast.com; May–Oct. The 2 bedrooms share a bathroom at this friendly B&B conveniently located very near the Halifax Shopping Centre & Metro Transit Terminal. Specialists in relocation accommodation for anyone moving to Nova Scotia. Free off-street parking. Rate inc continental b/fast. **$**

Near the airport

Hilton Garden Inn Halifax Airport [80 C1] (145 rooms) 200 Pratt & Whitney Dr, Enfield; 873 1400; www.halifaxairport.stayhgi.com. Some rates inc b/fast. **$$**

Holiday Inn Express Halifax Hotel and Suites [80 C1] (96 rooms & 23 suites) 180 Pratt & Whitney Drive, Enfield; 576 7600; www.hiexpress.com. Hot b/fast buffet inc. **$$**

Inn on the Lake [80 C2] (39 units) 3009 Hwy 2, Fall River; 861 3480, t/f 1 800 463 6465; www.innonthelake.com. With 20 rooms & 19 executive rooms/suites (with whirlpool baths), this establishment just off Hwy 102 Exit 5 offers more than most airport hotels including an outdoor (seasonal) pool & sandy lakeside beach: guests can use canoes & pedal boats. A complimentary airport shuttle is offered 05.00–midnight daily. Olivers gastropub (*14.00–23.00 daily*) offers food, as does the rather good licensed Encore Restaurant (*07.00–22.00 daily*). **$$**

WHERE TO EAT In recent years, the food scene in Halifax has seen great and wondrous changes. A new breed of entrepreneur restaurateurs have already made their mark, transforming what wasn't (with the odd exception) a place with the most exciting dining choices in the world.

Today's Halifax (and environs) paints a different story, and one is almost spoilt for choice. Whether you choose to eat in a café, pub, old-style diner or zanily designed trendy upmarket restaurant, in general standards are high and prices reasonable. Hotel restaurants in particular have come forward in leaps and bounds. Multi-cultures also mean a wide range of ethnic restaurants – always a good thing for the adventurous eater. 'Fill yer boots' (as they say) here, as you won't find much ethnic food outside the HRM. Virtually all of the better restaurants accept reservations – some are so popular that these are a necessity.

Note that many restaurants charge significantly less for the same dish at lunch than in the evening.

Relatively new is **LocalTastingTours** [98–9 G3] (*818 9055; e info@localtastingtours.com; www.localtastingtours.com; mid Jun–mid Oct 13.30 Tue–Sun; CAN$30*), which offers 90-minute guided walking tours (including free tastings) of selected highlights of downtown and the waterfront's food shops and eateries. Tours depart from the Halifax Seaport Farmers' Market, and reservations are recommended. Occasional themed tours run in the off-season: check their website for details.

If you find downtown/waterfront prices too high, or fancy a wander past a varied selection of ethnic and/or budget eateries, head along **Quinpool Road**. A few highlights are listed on page 102.

Waterfront and downtown

Luxury

✗ **Cut Steakhouse & Urban Grill** [92–3 F6] 5120 Salter St; ☎ 429 5120; www.cutsteakhouse.ca; ⌚ (Grill) 12.00–15.00 daily, (Grill & Steakhouse) 17.00–22.00 daily. There are 2 different dining experiences here: the downstairs Grill is fun & funky with contemporary lighting & large comfortable booths; upstairs the atmosphere in the Steakhouse is relaxed yet luxurious. Both floors offer a fine view of the Halifax waterfront & alfresco dining. The Grill has a light, global menu of meat, fish, pasta, burgers, charcuterie & more: the lobster *poutine* is worth trying. Upstairs, carnivores prepared to pay for quality can choose from local (well, rural Nova Scotia), prime US, or Kobe beef steaks. There are several non-meat choices too, but this isn't a place for vegetarians. Grill $$; Steakhouse $$$$

✗ **Da Maurizio's** [92–3 F8] 1496 Lower Water St; ☎ 423 0859; www.damaurizio.ca; ⌚ 17.00–22.00 Mon–Sat. Before the new wave of exciting places to eat arrived in Halifax, there was da Maurizio's. Specialising in superb northern Italian cuisine, this elegant restaurant in the Alexander Keith's Brewery complex has more than held its own against some very good competition. Delightful fine-dining. $$$$

✗ **Ryan Duffy's** [92–3 F5] 1650 Bedford Row; ☎ 421 1116; www.ryanduffys.ca; ⌚ 06.30–22.00 Mon–Fri, 07.00–16.00 & 17.00–22.00 Sat/Sun. Settled in smoothly in a new location, this old-style upmarket steakhouse still draws discerning & well-heeled steak lovers. There are 2 eating areas, a lounge – which also features a tapas menu – & a more formal dining room: both are simple & elegant. Top-notch steak apart, seafood is strongly promoted too, but with slabs of (albeit high-quality) beef being carved table-side (before being wheeled away to be cooked over charcoal) it's probably not the first choice for vegetarians. $$$$

Upmarket

✗ **Chives Canadian Bistro** [92–3 E6] 1537 Barrington St; ☎ 420 9626; www.chives.ca; ⌚ 17.00–21.00 daily. Chefs Craig Flinn & Darren Lewis adjust their (relatively short) menus to take advantage of the best fresh local ingredients, dishing up Canadian cuisine with a unique twist. Housed in a former bank, the atmosphere is warm, casual & relaxed. Considering the quality of the food, presentation & service, prices are very reasonable. $$$

✗ **Fid Resto** [92–3 B6] 1569 Dresden Row; ☎ 422 9162; www.fidresto.ca; ⌚ 11.30–14.00 & 17.00–21.00 Tue–Sun (from 11.00 Sat/Sun). The frequently changing menu at this modern restaurant may be shorter than many in the city. But, oh, the food! Chef Dennis Johnston blends fresh, predominantly organic, ingredients simply but to stellar effect. On the lunch menu, *Pad Thai* might line up alongside smoked haddock with mash. In the evening, the mix of ingredients, for example beef cheek braised in espresso, might raise eyebrows, but works. Desserts keep up standards, too. $$$

✗ **The Five Fishermen** [92–3 E4] 1740 Argyle St; ☎ 422 4421; www.fivefishermen.com; ⌚ 17.00–21.00 daily. Housed in a historic c1816 building, once a funeral home. There are good non-fishy choices, but beautifully prepared fresh fish & shellfish – & the renowned wine cellar – are the focus. Main courses, such as The Five Fish, or lobster-stuffed Digby scallops, include unlimited mussels & salad bar. $$$

✗ **Gio** [92–3 D4] 1725 Market St; ☎ 425 1987; www.giohalifax.com; ⌚ 11.00–23.00 Mon–Fri, 17.00–23.00 Sat. The chef may change, but standards at this chic, modern, fine-dining – but casual – restaurant at the Prince George Hotel never seem to drop. Ingredients are high-quality & fresh, service & presentation delightful. The menu often includes more unusual meat & fish choices such as elk. Far from your average hotel restaurant. $$$

✗ **Onyx Dining Room & Cocktail Lounge** [92–3 A7] 5680 Spring Garden Rd; ☎ 428 5680; www.onyxdining.com; ⌚ 16.30–02.00 Mon–Sat. Elegant, sleek, with a magnificent translucent

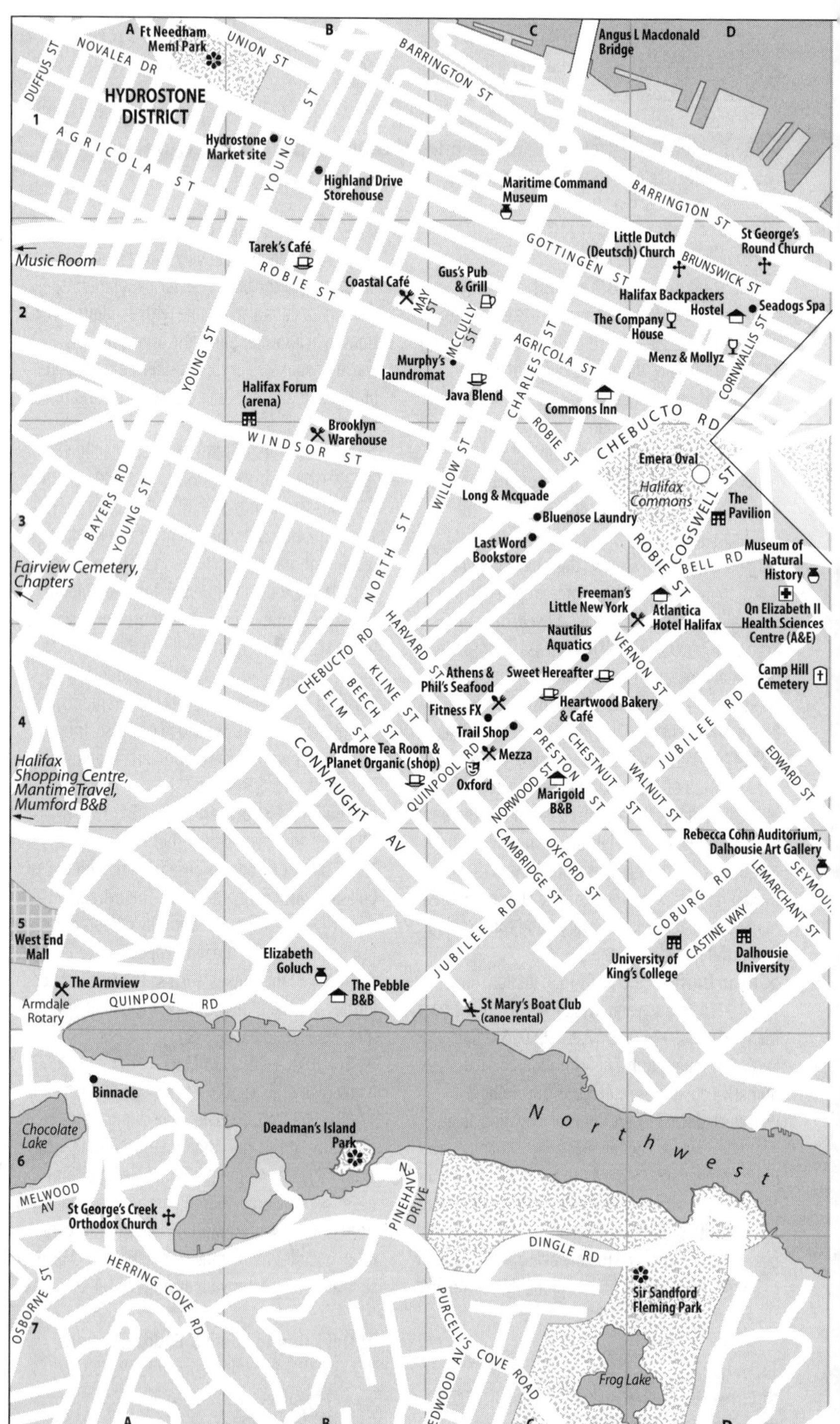

A
B
C
D
Ft Needham Meml Park
HYDROSTONE DISTRICT
Angus L Macdonald Bridge
Hydrostone Market site
Highland Drive Storehouse
Maritime Command Museum
Music Room
Tarek's Café
Coastal Café
Gus's Pub & Grill
Little Dutch (Deutsch) Church
St George's Round Church
Halifax Backpackers Hostel
Seadogs Spa
The Company House
Menz & Mollyz
Murphy's laundromat
Java Blend
Commons Inn
Halifax Forum (arena)
Brooklyn Warehouse
Emera Oval
Halifax Commons
The Pavilion
Long & Mcquade
Bluenose Laundry
Last Word Bookstore
Museum of Natural History
Fairview Cemetery, Chapters
Freeman's Little New York
Atlantica Hotel Halifax
Qn Elizabeth II Health Sciences Centre (A&E)
Nautilus Aquatics
Athens & Phil's Seafood
Sweet Hereafter
Camp Hill Cemetery
Heartwood Bakery & Café
Fitness FX
Trail Shop
Mezza
Ardmore Tea Room & Planet Organic (shop)
Oxford
Marigold B&B
Halifax Shopping Centre, Mantime Travel, Mumford B&B
Rebecca Cohn Auditorium, Dalhousie Art Gallery
West End Mall
Elizabeth Goluch
The Pebble B&B
University of King's College
Dalhousie University
The Armview
Armdale Rotary
St Mary's Boat Club (canoe rental)
Binnacle
Chocolate Lake
Deadman's Island Park
Northwest
St George's Creek Orthodox Church
Sir Sandford Fleming Park
Frog Lake
1
2
3
4
5
6
7
DUFFUS ST
NOVALEA DR
UNION ST
BARRINGTON ST
AGRICOLA ST
YOUNG ST
ROBIE ST
GOTTINGEN ST
BRUNSWICK ST
MAY ST
MCCULLY ST
CHARLES ST
CORNWALLIS ST
WINDSOR ST
WILLOW ST
CHEBUCTO RD
COGSWELL ST
BAYERS RD
NORTH ST
BELL RD
HARVARD ST
VERNON ST
KLINE ST
BEECH ST
ELM ST
JUBILEE RD
CONNAUGHT AV
QUINPOOL RD
PRESTON ST
CHESTNUT ST
WALNUT ST
EDWARD ST
NORWOOD ST
CAMBRIDGE ST
OXFORD ST
COBURG RD
CASTINE WAY
LEMARCHANT ST
SEYMOUR
MELWOOD AV
PINEHAVEN DRIVE
DINGLE RD
HERRING COVE RD
OSBORNE ST
PURCELL'S COVE ROAD
REDWOOD AV

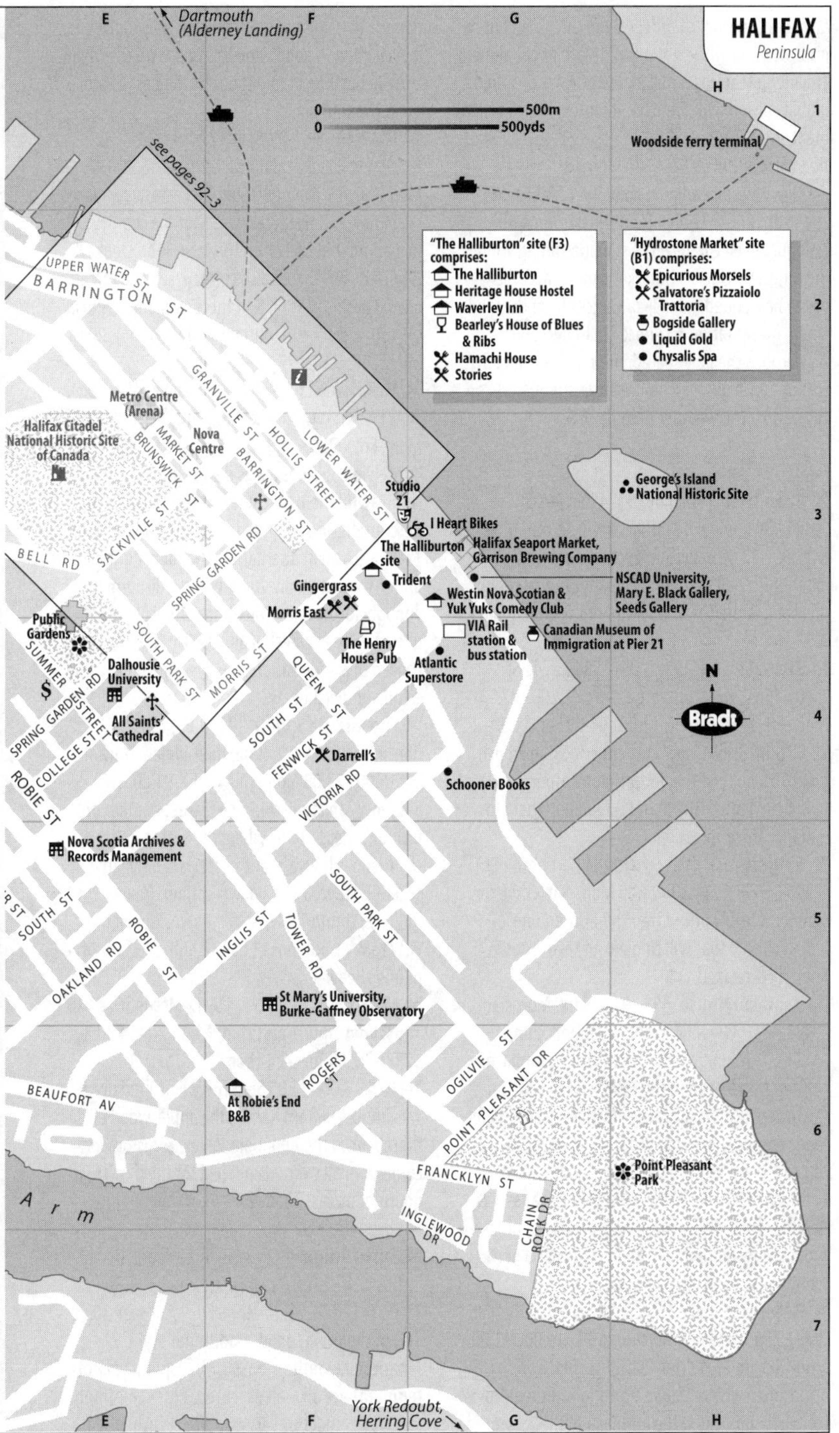

HALIFAX
Peninsula
Dartmouth (Alderney Landing)
0 500m
0 500yds
Woodside ferry terminal
see pages 92–3
"The Halliburton" site (F3) comprises:
The Halliburton
Heritage House Hostel
Waverley Inn
Bearley's House of Blues & Ribs
Hamachi House
Stories
"Hydrostone Market" site (B1) comprises:
Epicurious Morsels
Salvatore's Pizzaiolo Trattoria
Bogside Gallery
Liquid Gold
Chysalis Spa
UPPER WATER ST
BARRINGTON ST
GRANVILLE ST
HOLLIS STREET
LOWER WATER ST
Metro Centre (Arena)
Halifax Citadel National Historic Site of Canada
Nova Centre
MARKET ST
BRUNSWICK ST
BARRINGTON ST
Studio 21
I Heart Bikes
George's Island National Historic Site
SACKVILLE ST
BELL RD
SPRING GARDEN RD
The Halliburton site
Halifax Seaport Market, Garrison Brewing Company
Trident
NSCAD University, Mary E. Black Gallery, Seeds Gallery
Gingergrass
Morris East
Westin Nova Scotian & Yuk Yuks Comedy Club
Public Gardens
VIA Rail station & bus station
Canadian Museum of Immigration at Pier 21
The Henry House Pub
Atlantic Superstore
SOUTH PARK ST
MORRIS ST
QUEEN ST
Dalhousie University
SUMMER STREET
SPRING GARDEN RD
All Saints' Cathedral
COLLEGE ST
SOUTH ST
FENWICK ST
Darrell's
ROBIE ST
Schooner Books
VICTORIA RD
Bradt
N
Nova Scotia Archives & Records Management
SOUTH ST
SOUTH PARK ST
ROBIE ST
INGLIS ST
TOWER RD
OAKLAND RD
St Mary's University, Burke-Gaffney Observatory
ROGERS ST
OGILVIE ST
POINT PLEASANT DR
BEAUFORT AV
At Robie's End B&B
Point Pleasant Park
FRANCKLYN ST
Arm
INGLEWOOD DR
CHAIN ROCK DR
York Redoubt, Herring Cove
E F G H
1 2 3 4 5 6 7

onyx bar & crystal chandelier, you can't help but be impressed on entry: not a great place to eat alone. The menu features 'small plates' of Asian-inspired global cuisine with French influences. There's also a great cocktail menu. $$$

✕ **Stories** [98–9 F3] 5184 Morris St; ☎ 444 4400; www.storiesdining.com; ⏲ 17.30–21.00 Tue–Sun. Better known for its guestrooms, The Halliburton (see page 95) has a fine-dining winner in Stories. Cuisine is upmarket Canadian, & the menu has a good balance of choices from the land & sea. Presentation & service are impeccable: try perhaps the pan-seared, rice paper-wrapped scallops with ginger vinaigrette. In summer eat on the patio if the weather permits. $$$

Mid range

✕ **Baan Thai** [92–3 B6] 5324 Blowers St; ☎ 446 4301; www.baanthai.ca; ⏲ 12.00–14.30 & 17.00–22.00 daily, Sun evenings only). The exterior isn't all that promising, but the interior is pleasant, & the Thai food authentic & high quality. $$

✕ **Bistro Le Coq** [92–3 D6] 1584 Argyle St; ☎ 407 4564; www.bistrocoq.ca; ⏲ 12.00–22.00 Mon–Fri (to 01.00 Fri), 11.30–01.00 Sat, 11.30–22.00 Sun. Bright, new authentic-looking French bistro. It's not just the décor that transports you to la belle Paris – the menu & food both help to enhance the impression. $$–$$$

✕ **Gingergrass** [98–9 F3] 1284 Barrington St; ☎ 425 8555; ⏲ 11.30–21.00 Mon–Sat. Come for simple, sensibly priced traditional Vietnamese & Thai cuisine that will tingle your taste buds. Friendly & relaxed. $$

✕ **Hamachi House** [98–9 F3] 5190 Morris St; ☎ 425 7711; www.hamachirestaurants.com; ⏲ 11.00–midnight daily. The first of 5 Hamachi restaurants to open in the HRM (see website for the others), this is my favourite place in Halifax for Japanese food. The standards are there, of course, but so too are some brave 'fusion' additions. A bento box (Japanese take-away) makes a tasty & healthy lunch. Considering how expensive good Japanese restaurants can be in other parts of the world, treat yourself here! $$

✕ **Il Mercato** [92–3 B7] 5650 Spring Garden Rd; ☎ 422 2866; www.il-mercato.ca; ⏲ 11.00–22.00 Mon–Sat (to 23.00 Thu–Sat). The food & atmosphere shout 'Italian trattoria' but the décor is contemporary. From the antipasti to the *zucotto* (a dessert that will banish tiramisu from your mind), it is all good. A good wine list rounds off the menu. Usually bustling, it might not be the best bet for a quiet evening out. $$

✕ **The Keg** [92–3 D5] 1712 Market St; ☎ 425 8355; www.kegsteakhouse.com; ⏲ 16.30–22.00 Mon–Sat, 16.30–21.30 Sun. This Vancouver-based chain now has restaurants all over the country & in a number of US states. The focus is on steaks & prime rib, but there's also chicken, seafood, etc. Try a Keg Caesar cocktail, &, if there's still room, finish off with a wedge of (outrageously yummy) Billy Miner Pie. $$

✕ **McKelvie's** [92–3 F5] 1680 Lower Water St; ☎ 421 6161; www.mckelvies.com; ⏲ 11.00–21.30 Mon–Fri, 16.30–21.30 Sat/Sun. The full name is 'McKelvie's delishes fishes dishes' but this isn't some awful themed restaurant where the menu descriptions are peppered (ha) with bad puns. There are decent alternatives that didn't originate underwater, a family-friendly-but-still-formal-enough-for-business-meetings atmosphere, & a decent wine list. Best of all, the fish & shellfish – cooked in a wide variety of ways – are good value & indeed 'delishes'. $$

✕ **The Middle Spoon** [92–3 E6] 1559 Barrington St; ☎ 407 4002; themiddlespoon.ca; ⏲ 16.00–23.00 Mon–Thu, 16.00–01.00 Fri/Sat. How can a self-confessed sweet-toother not include a 'desserterie' where the vast majority of the menu is house-made desserts & innovative cocktails (there's also wine & coffee). Trendy, modern, comfortable, & (the downside) all too easy to walk out tens of dollars lighter & tens of pounds heavier. $$–$$$

✕ **Morris East** [98–9 F3] 5212 Morris St; ☎ 444 7663; www.morriseast.com; ⏲ 11.30–14.30 & 17.00–22.00 Tue–Sat (from 10.00 Sat), 10.00–14.30 & 17.00–21.00 Sun. The wood-fired oven was imported from Napoli, the apple-wood burned therein from the Annapolis Valley, & customers come from all over – & not just for the thin-crust gourmet pizzas. Good wine & cocktail list, nice atmosphere. $$

✕ **Sushi Shige** [92–3 E6] 1532 Granville St; ☎ 422 0740; http://sushishige.ca; ⏲ 11.30–14.00 & 17.00–21.30 Mon–Fri, 17.00–21.30 Sat. In the main, good, traditional-style Japanese favourites (eg: sushi, sashimi, yakitori, tempura) are all well executed. Plus something less traditional but very popular – sushi pizza (salmon, tuna or mixed seafood with toppings on a deep-fried rice cake). $$

✕ **Untitled Eats** [92–3 F5] 1723 Hollis St; ☎ 424 8708; www.untitledeats.com; 🕘 10.00–21.00 Mon–Sat. You don't need to be a culture-vulture to appreciate this excellent café in the Art Gallery of Nova Scotia. The menu is imaginative, & it is the kind of bright, vibrant but still laid-back place that is just as good for a coffee & scrumptious dessert as for something more substantial. $$

✕ **The Wooden Monkey** [92–3 E5] 1707 Grafton St; ☎ 444 3844; www.thewoodenmonkey.ca; 🕘 11.30–22.00 Sun–Thu, 11.30–23.00 Fri/Sat. Health- & environment-conscious diners will enjoy this eatery where just about everything is organic, macrobiotic, locally grown & very tasty. The sweet apple salad is a winner, & I'm told that Jerry Seinfeld loved the sesame-crusted haddock. The menu offers vegetarian – plus vegan & gluten-free – & meat options. As they have done since the 1960s, such places attract artists, musicians & other bohemians. And of course, Jerry Seinfeld. $$

Budget

✕ **Chez Cora** [92–3 B6] 1535 Dresden Row; ☎ 490 2672; www.chezcora.com; 🕘 06.00–15.00 Mon–Sat, 07.00–15.00 Sun. What started off in a former snack bar in Montreal has rapidly grown to become a chain of over 130 eateries countrywide. This one, just off Spring Garden Rd, is one of the most convenient. Expect bright, cheery décor, hearty servings of omelettes, waffles, pancakes & crêpes (balanced by lots of fresh fruit). $

✕ **Darrell's** [98–9 F4] 5576 Fenwick St; ☎ 492 2344; www.darrellsrestaurants.com; 🕘 11.00–22.00 daily. There are salads, very good pita bread wraps, sandwiches & more, but the burgers are hard to resist (except perhaps for the bizarrely popular, multi-award-winning peanut butter-smothered one). Attempt to wash it down with a super-thick milkshake. Close to the university & with a downstairs area where sport is shown on a large-screen TV, it is popular with students. $

✕ **The Great Wall** [92–3 F5] 1649 Bedford Row; ☎ 422 6153; www.thegreatwall.ca; 🕘 11.30–22.00 daily. Everything is made from scratch in this well-established Chinese restaurant. The dim sum session (*11.30–15.00 Sun*) is justifiably popular. Flavoursome & good value. $

✕ **Pete's** [92–3 B6] 1515 Dresden Row; ☎ 425 5700; www.petes.ca; 🕘 08.00–20.00 Mon–Fri, 08.00–18.00 Sat/Sun. Pete started his business life running a market stall in Nottingham, England. Although primarily a huge, upmarket deli, grocery & greengrocer's store, pop in to Pete's To Go or the Hot Bar Action Station for delectable healthy sandwiches & more. $

North End and Hydrostone

Mid range

✕ **Brooklyn Warehouse** [98–9 B3] 2795 Windsor St; ☎ 446 8181; www.brooklynwarehouse.ca; 🕘 11.30–15.30 & 16.30–closing Mon–Sat, 17.00–closing Sun. The Brooklyn has been a hit since opening in 2007 for its use of fresh, seasonal, local ingredients to create a varied & award-winning menu which blends & twists Canadian classics, hints of the Mediterranean, & Asia. $$

✕ **Coastal Café** [98–9 B2] 2731 Robie St; ☎ 405 4022; www.thecoastal.ca; 🕘 08.00–14.15 daily (from 10.00 Sun). This North End award-winner is 2 restaurants in 1. By day Mark Giffin dishes up exotic & exciting takes on b/fasts/diner food. Graeme Ruppel takes over for the evening shift, referred to as **Coastal@NIGHT** (*☎ 401 5307; www.facebook.com/coastal.night; 🕘 18.00–21.00 Thu–Sun*). Ruppel's themed menus are a blend of tantalisingly tasty dishes from around the globe; try, Persian roast lamb, pork arista or Thai green curry. Recommended at any time of day. $$

✕ **Epicurious Morsels** [98–9 B1] 5529 Young St; ☎ 455 0955; www.epicuriousmorsels.com; 🕘 11.30–15.00 & 17.00–20.00 Tue–Fri, 10.30–14.30 & 17.00–21.00 Sat, 10.30–14.30 & 17.00–20.00 Sun. Chef Jim Hanusiak has an interesting little place in the Hydrostone, tastefully decorated & comfortable – romantic even. Whether you're there for the excellent w/end brunch, or a dinner of French–Mediterranean-inspired dishes & a glass or 2 of wine, I think you'll be impressed. Be sure to try some in-house-smoked Atlantic salmon or *gravad lax* – oh, and leave room for dessert. Lunch/brunch $$; dinner $$–$$$

✕ **Salvatore's Pizzaiolo Trattoria** [98–9 B1] 5541 Young St; ☎ 455 1133; www.salvatorespizza.ca; 🕘 11.30–23.00 Tue–Sat, 16.00–22.00 Sun/Mon. It is hard for a pizzeria to stand out from a multitude of others without a gimmick or extreme toppings. The best in town shines bright for the thin-crust bases & quality of ingredients. With 20 toppings to choose from, build your own, or order from the menu – I like to keep it simple & stick to the roasted garlic & sautéed mushrooms. In the Hydrostone. $$

Budget

Tarek's Café [98–9 B2] 3045 Robie St; 454 8723; www.tarekscafe.ca; 11.30–19.30 Mon–Sat. Come for good, low-budget Lebanese/Greek food (dips, salads, pita sandwiches, etc), with some non-Mediterranean fillings (eg: Philly steak) & dishes (eg: curry ginger chicken). $–$$

Java Blend [98–9 C2] 6027 North St; 423 6944; www.javablendcoffee.com; 06.30–18.00 Mon–Fri, 07.30–17.00 Sat, 09.00–15.00 Sun. Great, well-established coffee roastery: wide selection of coffees & teas. $

Quinpool Road

Upmarket

Mezza [98–9 C4] 6386 Quinpool Rd; 444 3914; www.mezzarestaurant.com; 11.30–22.00 daily (to 23.00 Fri/Sat). Contemporary & stylish Lebanese fine-dining. For many, a selection of authentic hot & cold starters make a meal in themselves: others move on to grilled meat or seafood before an ambrosial dessert not often seen in the souks of Beirut – Bailey's cheesecake. $$$

Mid range

The Armview [98–9 A5] 7156 Chebucto Rd; 455 4395; www.thearmview.com; 11.00–22.00 Mon–Thu, 08.30–22.00 Fri–Sun. The décor is late 1950s, the menu long & varied, the service friendly, & the food – diner meets *haute cuisine* – very good. Near the Armdale Rotary. $$–$$$

Athens [98–9 C4] 6273 Quinpool Rd; 422 1595; www.athensrestaurant.com; 08.00–22.00 daily. Prices may have crept up by a few drachmas since Athens moved along the road, but the Greek food is usually very good & the portions generous. $$

Budget

Ardmore Tea Room [98–9 B4] 6499 Quinpool Rd; 423 7523; 05.00–20.00 daily. The Ardmore – going for over half a century – just keeps on dishing out the all-day b/fasts & more. Come for huge, cholesterol-packed portions & low prices – not décor or linen tablecloths. Small & ever-popular. $

Freeman's Little New York [98–9 D3] 6092 Quinpool Rd; 455 7000; www.freemanspizza.ca; 10.00–05.00 daily. Nightbirds who feel like something to eat in the wee small hours are best off at this Quinpool Rd institution. Pizzas, burgers, pastas, nachos & more. $

Heartwood Bakery & Café [98–9 C4] 6250 Quinpool Rd; 425 2808; www.heartwoodbakeryandcafe.ca; 11.00–21.00 Mon–Fri (to 22.00 Thu/Fri), 10.00–22.00 Sat, 10.00–15.00 Sun. Currently the only vegetarian/vegan restaurant in Halifax, food here is organic & made in-house. Pumphouse beer (from New Brunswick) is on tap. Pop in for a bite – try the Heartwood Bowl (brown rice or vermicelli noodles, topped with seasonal vegetables, mixed greens & sauce of your choice) – or just to grab a decadent-looking but apparently healthy hazelnut brownie or other treat. Outdoor patio. $–$$

BUCK STARS IN COFFEE SHOP – AND OTHER CERVINE CAPERS

On a Monday morning in June 2011, a young deer crashed through the window of the Uncommon Grounds coffee shop on Halifax's South Park Street. The poor creature thrashed around, jumping on tables and knocking over chairs before crashing out through another window pane. A year later, another deer explored the Dalhousie University campus, passed a few shops along Quinpool Road, and then walked up Citadel Hill. And, not to be outdone by its far more common cousins, a moose – very rarely seen in mainland Nova Scotia – was found wandering the streets not far from the Fairview Cemetery. Unfortunately for the glazier, officials reached the animal before it found a coffee shop. In all three cases, Department of Natural Resources staff tranquilised the animals and later released them back into woodland well outside the urban centre.

✕ **Phil's Seafood** [98–9 C4] 6285 Quinpool Rd; ☎ 431 3474; ⌚ 11.30–20.00 daily. A great fish & chip shop especially if you prefer lots of fish to lots of batter. There are scallops, shrimps & more, too – & it doesn't have to be fried. Good value, especially the large fish & chips. $

Sweet Hereafter [98–9 C4] 6148 Quinpool Rd; ☎ 404 8001; www.sweethereafter.ca; ⌚ 12.00–22.00 Mon–Sat (to 23.00 Thu–Sat). This striking, modern 'cheesecakery' (their description, not mine) offers decent beverages & all sorts of flavours of premium (you guessed it) cheesecake, including dozens of gluten-free & or vegan options. $

ENTERTAINMENT AND NIGHTLIFE It is often said that Halifax has more pubs/bars per capita than anywhere else in Canada. Several of the region's better **pubs** serve good-value, sometimes quite upmarket, pub food, and many of the following could also be listed in the *Where to eat* section.

Halifax's most famous brewery is Alexander Keith's (see page 115): within that complex is the Stag's Head Tavern. You'll visit it if you do the brewery tour, but can also just pop in for (for example) a glass of Keith's celebrated India Pale Ale. The atmosphere is friendly, but rarely raucous.

Currently, the HRM has just one out-and-out gay bar. But see also the gay-friendly **Reflections Cabaret** (page 104) and **The Company House** (page 104).

Far and away the best source of information for **live music** listings of all genres is the weekly free newspaper, *The Coast* (*www.thecoast.ca*), also available in an online format. Many of the eateries, pubs and bars already mentioned host live music, as does the casino (see page 105). Some options are listed on page 104.

Why not pay one price for a **meal and theatrical production**. We're not talking Shakespeare and Michelin-star cuisine but a fun evening with better than average food (see page 105 for dinner theatre options).

All of the HRM's main **cinemas** are part of the Empire (*www.empiretheatres.com*) group. In addition to the Oxford (see page 105) art-house films might be shown at venues such as the **Rebecca Cohn Auditorium** (see page 105).

Pubs

Durty Nelly's [92–3 E5] Corner Argyle & Sackville sts; ☎ 406 7640; www.durtynellys.ca; ⌚ 11.30–01.00 (or later) daily. This place prides itself so much on being authentic that it was designed & built in Ireland, shipped to Halifax & put together piece by piece.

The Henry House Pub [98–9 F4] 1222 Barrington St; ☎ 423 5660; www.henryhouse.ca; ⌚ 11.30–midnight Mon–Thu, 11.30–01.00 Fri/Sat, 11.30–23.30 Sun. In a lovely historic 1834 building, this is a must-visit for fans of traditional British pubs. The main dining area upstairs turns out well above average old-style dishes, supplemented by Maritime favourites. Amongst many other tipples, 6 locally brewed (Granite Brewery) British-style ales are offered – sample the Peculiar.

Lower Deck [92–3 F3] 1869 Upper Water St; ☎ 425 1501; ⌚ 11.30–01.00 daily. Another well-patronised place with regular generally high-quality live music & entertainment. Good food helps make this one of the waterfront's most popular venues.

Maxwell's Plum [92–3 D6] 1600 Grafton St; ☎ 423 5090; www.themaxwellsplum.com; ⌚ 11.00–01.00 daily. One of the largest selections of on-tap beers in the country, plus dozens of bottled varieties. A good place to try the produce of microbreweries, local & otherwise. 4 large-screen TVs, so often lively.

Old Triangle Irish Ale House [92–3 F5] 5136 Prince St; ☎ 492 4900; www.oldtriangle.com; ⌚ 11.00–midnight Sun–Tue, 11.00–01.00 Wed/Thu, 11.00–02.00 Fri/Sat. Equally good for a bite to eat, a drink, or live music. The sweet potato fries may be less authentic than, say, the steak & kidney pie, but boy are they good.

Pogue Fado [92–3 E6] 1581 Barrington St; ☎ 429 6222; www.poguefado.com; ⌚ 11.00–02.00 daily. Friendly, lively Irish pub with more than adequate food & live music.

Rogue's Roost Brew Pub & Grill [92–3 C7] 5435 Spring Garden Rd; 492 2337; www.roguesroost.ca; 11.30–01.00 Mon–Fri, 12.00–02.00 Sat, 16.00–midnight Sun. A brewpub, restaurant & live music venue. Try the Raspberry Wheat Ale. Service & food are both good.

Bars

Bitter End [92–3 D6] 1572 Argyle St; 425 3039; www.bitterend.ca; 16.00–02.00 daily. Warm & comfortable Martini bar & restaurant with wood floors, lots of exposed brickwork, table & booth seating. With 30 types of Martini, plus a wide range of cocktails & more.

Economy Shoe Shop Café and Bar [92–3 E5] 1661–3 Argyle St; 423 7463; 11.00–01.30 daily. Not the celeb hangout that it once was, but still a fun place to visit. Food standards seem to rise & drop (a couple of starters are usually a better bet than a main), but eating & drinking seem of secondary importance in this tangle of eclectically decorated rooms. Live jazz on Mon evenings.

Obladee, a Wine Bar [92–3 E5–6] 1600 Barrington St; 405 4505; obladee.ca; 16.00–midnight daily (to 02.00 Fri/Sat). Small, relaxed 'modern rustic' wine bar. Carefully chosen charcuterie & cheeses accompany a fantastic selection of wines, over 30 of which are available by the glass. Eat & drink alfresco in the summer.

Your Father's Moustache Pub & Eatery [92–3 A7] 5686 Spring Garden Rd; 423 6766; www.yourfathersmoustache.ca; 10.00–midnight Sun–Wed, 10.00–01.00 Thu–Sat. Restaurant, live music, bar & more. In good weather the rooftop patio overlooking the town is a delight.

Gay venues

Menz & Mollyz [98–9 D2] 2182 Gottingen St; 446 6969; www.menzbar.ca. Bar with live music, dancing, karaoke, etc. Proudly purveying MENZ Pale Ale, locally brewed & 'Atlantic Canada's first queer beer'.

Seadogs [98–9 D2] 2199 Gottingen St; 444 3647, t/f 1 888 837 1388; www.seadogs.ca. Very close by Menz & Mollyz (& under the same ownership) is this gay & bisexual sauna & spa. This part of town is known as Halifax's 'gay village'.

Live music

Bearly's House of Blues & Ribs [98–9 F3] 1269 Barrington St; 423 2526; www.bearlys.ca. The best of blues both from within the province & further afield.

The Carleton [92–3 E5] 1685 Argyle St; 422 6335; www.thecarleton.ca. Great venue showcasing some of the best local & national 'singer-songwriter style' music. Decent food & reasonably priced wine for a live music venue.

The Company House [98–9 D2] 2202 Gottingen St; 404 3050; www.thecompanyhouse.ca; 16.00–midnight (or later) Tue–Sat. Live music (singer-songwriter style), good beer selection, tasty snacks, etc. Between downtown & North End.

Gus's Pub and Grill [98–9 C2] 2605 Agricola St; 423 7786. Small & cramped, but a great rock venue (North End). Cheap food, good burgers.

The Pavilion [98–9 D3] 5816 Cogswell St; www.halifaxpavilion.com. Performances roughly once a week in this brick building near the pool & skate park on Halifax Common.

The Seahorse Tavern [92–3 E5] 1665 Argyle St; 423 7200; www.theeconomyshoeshopgroup.ca/seahorsetavern/. Located below the Economy Shoe Shop (see opposite), this great venue hosts everything from R&B to *klezmer* (Jewish folk/jazz).

Nightclubs

☆ **The Dome** [92–3 E4] 1726 Argyle St; 422 6907; www.thedome.ca; 22.00–03.30 Wed–Sun. Often referred to as the 'liquor dome' (or 'the dirty dome'), there are actually 4–5 adjoining club rooms under one roof. Can get very crowded with those just old enough to drink legally.

☆ **Pacifico** [92–3 E7] 1505 Barrington St; 422 3633; www.pacifico.ca; 21.00–02.00 Thu–Sat. Come here on a Fri/Sat & you'll feel out of place if you're not wearing something bright & shiny!

☆ **The Palace** [92–3 D4] 1721 Brunswick St; 420 0015; www.thenewpalace.com; 22.00–03.30 Wed–Sun. Live music, decent DJs, youthful crowd.

☆ **Reflections** [92–3 E6] 5184 Sackville St; 422 2957; http://reflectionscabaret.com; summer 20.00–04.00 daily; winter 20.00–04.00 Thu–Mon. Formerly known as an exclusively gay venue, now everyone comes here to dance & party.

☆ **The Toothy Moose** [92–3 E5] 1661 Argyle St; 417 3170; www.thetoothymoose.com. Plays rock & country music until late.

Theatre

Neptune Theatre [92–3 E6] 1593 Argyle St; 429 7070, t/f 1 800 565 7345; www.

neptunetheatre.com. Atlantic Canada's largest professional regional theatre incorporates the main auditorium of the Strand Theatre, built on this site (on the corner of Sackville Street) in 1915. Founded in 1962, the theatre group just celebrated its 50th anniversary. Normally, the season runs mid Sep–May: 6 mainstream productions are staged in the 485-seat Fountain Hall, whilst the intimate Studio Theatre is home to more innovative productions. Fountain Hall ticket prices tend to be CAN$30–45.

Dinner theatre

Grafton Street Dinner Theatre [92–3 D4] 1741 Grafton St; 425 1961; www.graftonstdinnertheatre.com; 18.45 Tue–Sun. A 3-act production & 3-course meal for CAN$50.

Halifax Feast Dinner Theatre [92–3 E7] 1505 Barrington St; % 420 1840; www.feastdinnertheatre.com; 18.30 daily. A 2-act musical comedy & 3-course meal for CAN$49.

Comedy

Yuk Yuks Comedy Club [98–9 G3] Westin Nova Scotian, 1181 Hollis St; 429 9857; www.yukyuks.com; 20.30 Tue–Thu, 19.30 & 22.30 Fri/Sat

Cinemas

Empire 8 [92–3 B7] Park Lane, 5657 Spring Garden Rd; 423 4860. 8-screen cinema.

Oxford [98–9 C4] 6408 Quinpool Rd; 423 7488. Although part of the Empire group, this lovely old Art Deco cinema with balcony has yet to be chopped up into a multi-screen. Generally, the programme sticks to art-house films, but sometimes new blockbusters slip in.

Classical music, ballet and opera **Symphony Nova Scotia** (*www.symphonynovascotia.ca*), one of Canada's finest chamber orchestras, is renowned for its versatility; it's equally at home performing anything from Baroque to jazz. The orchestra is based at the **Rebecca Cohn Auditorium** [98–9 D5] (*Dalhousie Arts Centre, 6101 University Av; 494 3820, t/f 1 800 874 1669; http://artscentre.dal.ca*). The same venue hosts ballet performances by such groups as the **Atlantic Ballet Theatre** (*www.atlanticballet.ca*), and big-name concerts. Opera and ballet are also performed at the Dalhousie University Arts Centre's **Sir James Dunn Theatre** [98–9 D5] (*Dalhousie Arts Centre, 6101 University Av; 494 3820, t/f 1 800 874 1669; http://artscentre.dal.ca*).

A great place to listen to chamber music is the **Music Room** [98–9 A2] (*6181 Lady Hammond Rd; 429 9467; www.scotiafestival.ns.ca*), a purpose-built 110-seat venue with superb acoustics.

The downtown **Halifax Metro Centre** [92–3 D4] (*1800 Argyle St; 421 8000; www.halifaxmetrocentre.com*) hosts major sporting events and concerts, and in the last year or two, the waterfront **Casino Nova Scotia** (see below) has begun to offer a stronger programme of regular entertainment.

Casino

Casino Nova Scotia [92–3 F1] (*1983 Upper Water St; 425 7777, t/f 1 888 642 6376; www.casinonovascotia.com; 10.00–04.00 daily*) Over 19s with money to burn can enjoy table games, slot machines and more at one of the province's two casinos – the other is in Sydney, Cape Breton Island (see page 301). There are a couple of dining options, the Trapeze Grille and Bar and Paradise Buffet, and a couple of entertainment venues, the Schooner Showroom and the smaller Harbourfront. If you don't gamble all your money away, Stay and Play packages (which include meal vouchers, parking and gaming lessons) can be good value.

SHOPPING **Spring Garden Road** [92–3 D7] is a good place to start, and now features a number of upmarket shopping arcades (such as City Centre Atlantic [92–3 B6], Spring Garden Place [92–3 B7] and Park Lane [92–3 B6]), housing most of Canada's best-known retail chains – and some good independents. The area also has a great selection of cafés and bistros. There are also boutiques, bars and restaurants in the **Historic Properties** [92–3 F3] on Upper Water Street, a group of restored warehouses. The adjoining Granville Mall [92–3 F3] is also worth a wander. **Barrington Place** [92–3 F3] is a collection of smaller, specialised stores and shops. Down on the waterfront, the upmarket **Piazza** at **Bishop's Landing** [92–3 F8] houses stylish shops and places to eat and drink.

Away from the centre, the **Hydrostone Market** [98–9 B1] is a European-style row of boutiques, independents, and mid- to high-range eateries: in contrast, nearby roads such as **Agricola Street** [98–9 A1] are home to many shops that tread that fine line between antique and junk.

The big shopping malls are outside the downtown area. In Halifax, near the Armdale Rotary are the **Halifax Shopping Centre** [98–9 A4] (*453 1752; www.halifaxshoppingcentre.com*) and, across the road, the **West End Mall** [98–9 A5] (*455 4101*). Many people head to Dartmouth and Bedford's malls, or up to Exit 2A of Highway 102 and the big stores of Bayer's Lake's Chain Lake Drive.

Arts and crafts

Bogside Gallery [98–9 B1] 5527 Young St, Hydrostone Market; 453 3063; 10.00–18.00 Mon–Fri, 10.00–17.00 Sat, 12.00–17.00 Sun. Intricate stained glass pieces & hand-crafted works.

Elizabeth Goluch [98–9 B5] 6913 Tupper Grove; 423 2102; www.elizabethgoluch.com; by chance or appointment. Ms Goluch creates amazing, detailed oversized insects from gemstones & metal. Near The Pebble B&B (see page 96).

Fireworks Gallery [92–3 E6] 1569 Barrington St; 420 1735, **t/f** 1 800 720 4367; www.fireworksgallery.com; 10.00–17.30 Mon–Sat. High-quality jewellery shop selling an extensive range by local & regional artisans.

Jennifer's of Nova Scotia [92–3 A6] 5635 Spring Garden Rd; 425 3119; jennifers.ns.ca; 09.30–17.30 (or later) Mon–Sat, 11.00–17.00 Sun. A range of quality crafts from all over the province plus a small selection of the best from other parts of the Maritimes.

Nova Scotia Art Gallery Shop [92–3 F5] 1723 Hollis St; 424 4303; www.artgalleryofnovascotia.ca; opening hours change seasonally – call/check website for current hours. A fine range of local art, crafts & folk art.

NovaScotian Crystal [92–3 F4] 5080 George St; 492 0416, **t/f** 1 888 977 2797; www.novascotiancrystal.com; call for hours. Was (& may still be) Canada's only crystal glass maker. Watch master craftspeople using techniques & tools that haven't changed for centuries.

The Plaid Place [92–3 E3] 1903 Barrington St; 429 6872, **t/f** 1 800 563 1749; www.plaidplace.com; 09.30–17.30 Mon–Fri, 10.00–17.00 Sat. Ideal for kilts & Celtic paraphernalia.

Seeds Gallery [98–9 G3] 1099 Marginal Rd, Suite 116; 494 8301; www.nscad.ca; 10.00–17.00 Tue–Fri, 10.00–16.00 Sat, 10.00–14.00 Sun. The gallery was thus named because it showcases & sells unique pieces created by students & alumni of NSCAD (Nova Scotia's College of Art & Design) University.

Studio 21 [98–9 G3] 1223 Lower Water St; 420 1852; www.studio21.ca; 11.00–18.00 Tue–Fri, 10.00–17.00 Sat (Sep–Jul also 12.00–17.00 Sun). Work from top contemporary artists from all over Canada.

The Vault [92–3 B7] 5640 Spring Garden Rd; 425 3624; 09.30–18.00 Mon–Wed, 09.30–21.00 Thu/Fri, 09.30–17.30 Sat, 12.00–17.00 Sun. Created by women for women, it displays designer jewellery collections from all over the world.

Books, magazines, maps, comics and more

Atlantic News [92–3 C8] 5560 Morris St; 429 5468; www.atlanticnews.ns.ca; daily. Huge selection of magazines & newspapers from around the world.

Binnacle [98–9 A6] 15 Purcell's Cove Rd; 423 6464, **t/f** 1 800 224 3937; www.binnacle.com; 09.00–18.00 Mon–Fri, 09.00–19.00 Sat. Nautical charts.

Bookmark [92–3 A7] 5686 Spring Garden Rd; 423 0419; www.bookmarkinc.ca; 09.00–22.00 Mon–Fri, 09.00–18.00 Sat, 11.00–18.00 Sun. Very good independent bookseller.

Chapters [98–9 A3] Bayers Lake Power Centre, 188 Chain Lake Dr; 450 1023; www.chapters.

indigo.ca; ⌚ 09.30–21.00 Mon–Sat, 12.00–21.00 Sun. Nova Scotia's biggest new book & music retailer.

Dustjacket Books [92–3 E7] 1505 Barrington St; ☎ 492 0666; www.dustjacket.ca; ⌚ 10.00–16.00 Mon–Fri. Easy to miss, in the Maritime Mall. Used books.

The Last Word Bookstore [98–9 C3] 2160 Windsor St; ☎ 423 2932; ⌚ 10.00–17.30 Mon–Sat, 12.00–17.00 Sun. Used books.

Maps and more [92–3 F6] 1601 Lower Water St; ☎ 422 7106; www.maps-and-ducks.com; ⌚ 10.00–18.00 Mon–Sat (Jun–Sep until 19.00). Should be your first stop for travel books & maps.

Schooner Books [98–9 G4] 5378 Inglis St; ☎ 423 8419; www.schoonerbooks.com; ⌚ 09.30–17.30 Mon–Thu, 09.30–18.00 Sat

Strange Adventures Comic Bookshops [92–3 D5] 5262 Sackville St; ☎ 425 2140; www.strangeadventures.com; ⌚ daily. An emporium for those who like pictures when they read.

Trident [98–9 F3] 1256 Hollis St; ☎ 423 7100; www.tridenthalifax.com; ⌚ 08.00–17.30 Mon–Fri, 08.30–17.00 Sat, 11.00–17.00 Sun. A fun used-book place which dishes up excellent coffee.

Venus Envy [92–3 E6] 1598 Barrington St; ☎ 422 0004; www.venusenvy.ca; ⌚ 10.00–18.00 Mon–Sat, 12.00–17.00 Sun. Erotica shop & adult bookstore for people of (almost) all imaginable kinds of sexual persuasion. Everything from DVDs to dildos – & more. Ironically (in that the HRM only has 1 vegetarian restaurant), vegan condoms are a big-seller. No doubt gluten-free ones also do well.

Food and wine

Bishop's Cellar [92–3 F8] 1477 Lower Water St; ☎ 490 2675; www.bishopscellar.com; ⌚ 10.00–22.00 Mon–Thu, 10.00–midnight Fri, 08.00–midnight Sat, 12.00–20.00 Sun. Knowledgeable staff & with a huge selection. One of the top wine stores in the country.

Freak Lunchbox [92–3 E4] 1723 Barrington St; ☎ 420 9151; www.freaklunchbox.com; ⌚ daily. Wacky & weird sweets/candy from around the globe.

Highland Drive Storehouse [98–9 B1] 5544 Kaye St; ☎ 454 0094. Upmarket Hydrostone butcher & produce shop.

Liquid Gold [98–9 B1] 5525 Young St; ☎ 406 8809; www.allthingsolive.ca; ⌚ 10.00–18.00 Mon–Sat (to 17.00 Sat), 12.00–17.00 Sun. Countless varieties & flavours of premium olive oil & balsamic vinegars, plus olive oil-based cosmetics.

Pete's [92–3 B6] (see page 101) An excellent upmarket food emporium.

Planet Organic [98–9 B4] 6487 Quinpool Rd; ☎ 425 7400; www.planetorganic.ca; ⌚ 09.00–21.00 daily. Friendly staff who understand organic/health foods & supplements.

Rum Runners Rum Cake Factory [92–3 F7] 1479 Lower Water St; ☎ 421 6079, **t/f** 1 866 440 7867; www.rumrunners.ca; ⌚ Jul–Sep 09.00–21.00 Mon–Sat, 10.00–18.00 Sun; Oct–Jun 10.00–18.00 daily. Delicious rum – & whisky – cakes which make great gifts.

Sweet Jane's [92–3 C6] 5431 Doyle St; ☎ 425 0168; www.sweetjanes.com; ⌚ daily. More sugarific treats for the sweet-toothed, plus fun stuff for round the house.

Music

Halifax Folklore Centre [92–3 D6]1528 Brunswick St; ☎ 423 7946; www.halifaxfolklorecentre.com; ⌚ 11.00–17.30 Mon–Wed, 11.00–19.00 Thu–Fri, 11.00–17.00 Sun. A good spot for Celtic music & instruments.

MARKETS

Halifax is blessed with two excellent farmers' markets: the **Halifax Seaport Farmers' Market** [98–9 G3] (*1209 Marginal Rd;* ☎ *492 6256; www.halifaxfarmersmarket.com;* ⌚ *10.00–17.00 Tue–Fri, 07.00–16.00 Sat, 08.00–16.00 Sun*), which includes food, produce, local crafts and much more, and the **Historic Farmers' Market** [92–3 F7] (*1496 Lower Water St;* ☎ *492 4043; www.historicfarmersmarket.ca;* ⌚ *07.00–13.00 Sat*), which is held in the old Alexander Keith's Brewery.

If flea markets are more your thing, head for the **Halifax Forum** [98–9 B2–3] (*2901 Windsor St;* ☎ *490 4614*) on a Sunday morning.

Long and Mcquade [98–9 B3] 6065 Cunard St; ☎ 496 6900; www.long-mcquade.com; ⏰ 10.00–18.00 Mon–Thu, 10.00–20.00 Fri, 10.00–17.00 Sun. If hearing all the wonderful Celtic music has inspired you to go & buy yourself a fiddle or other instrument, this is a good place to start.

Taz Records [92–3 D6] 1593 Market St; ☎ 422 5976; www.tazrecords.com; ⏰ 10.30–19.00 Mon–Fri, 10.30–18.00 Sat, 12.00–17.00 Sun. Ideal if you want to try to track down secondhand music.

New age

Little Mysteries Books [92–3 E5] 1663 Barrington St; ☎ 423 1313; www.littlemysteries.com; ⏰ 10.00–17.00 daily (from 12.00 Sun). No, not Agatha Christie or Sherlock Holmes. Books on spirituality, self-betterment, holistic health, etc, plus tarot cards, stones, crystals & other mumbo-jumbo (only joking) paraphernalia.

Outdoor and camping gear

Mountain Equipment Co-op [92–3 E6] 1550 Granville St; ☎ 421 2667; www.mec.ca; ⏰ Jun–Aug 09.30–21.00 Mon–Fri, 09.00–18.00 Sat, 11.00–17.00 Sun; Sep–May 09.30–19.00 Mon–Wed, 09.30–21.00 Thu–Fri, 09.30–18.00 Sat, 11.00–17.00 Sun. Outdoor gear emporium. Non-members pay a one-off CAN$5 fee when making their first purchase.

The Trail Shop [98–9 C4] 6210 Quinpool Rd; ☎ 423 8736, t/f 1 877 423 8736; www.trailshop.com; ⏰ 09.00–18.00 Mon–Wed & Sat, 09.00–21.00 Thu/Fri

SPORT For **spectator sports**, head to the Halifax Metro Centre to see the Halifax Mooseheads play ice hockey (September–March) and the Halifax Rainmen play basketball (January–March).

Tickets can be purchased from the **Ticket Atlantic Box Office** (☎ *451 1221; www.ticketatlantic.com*) at the Halifax Metro Centre (*1800 Argyle St*). Prices to see the Mooseheads start from CAN$14.50, and the Rainmen from CAN$18. Possibilities for those who wish to participate include:

Canoeing and kayaking **St Mary's Boat Club** [98–9 C5] (*1641 Fairfield Rd; ☎ 490 4688*) is located on the Northwest Arm. Hourly canoe rental on summer weekends is CAN$10/hour.

Diving The water isn't warm, but there are numerous shipwrecks to keep divers happy, and some good diving companies, both here and in Dartmouth (see page 125).

Divers World [off map] 11–12 Lakeside Park Dr, Lakeside; ☎ 876 0555; www.diversworld.ns.ca. 10 mins' drive from Armdale Rotary.

Nautilus Aquatics [98–9 C4] 6164 Quinpool Rd; ☎ 454 4296, t/f 1 866 423 0007; www.nautilusaquatichobbies.com

Go Karting Head out of the city centre to **Kartbahn Indoor Karting** [80 B4] (*66 Otter Lake Court, Bayers Lake; ☎ 455 5278; www.kartbahnracing.ca*).

Golf Golfers will find over a dozen nine- and 18-hole courses within easy reach of Halifax and Dartmouth. Here are four of the best full-length courses. **Granite Springs Golf Club** (see page 132) is another good option.

Eaglequest Grandview [off map] Golf & Country Club, 431 Crane Hill Rd, Westphal; ☎ 435 3767; www.eaglequestgolf.com. A challenging (particularly the forested back 9) 6,700yd course just outside Dartmouth off Hwy 7. Green fees CAN$59 Mon–Fri, CAN$69 Sat/Sun.

Glen Arbour [off map] 40 Clubhouse Lane, Hammonds Plains; ☎ 835 4653; glenarbour.com. A lovely, well-designed 6,800yd championship course with natural ponds, streams & mature trees. Not cheap in summer, but a great challenge for the serious golfer. Off Hammonds Plains Rd, 1km west of Bedford. Green fees CAN$121.

Hartlen Point Forces Golf Club [off map] Shore Rd; ☎ 465 4653; www.hartlenpoint.com. This 18-hole 5,862yd, par-71 course has beautiful views overlooking the eastern entrance to Halifax Harbour (& almost constant winds). Green fees CAN$59.

Lost Creek Golf Club [off map] 310 Kinsac Rd, Beaver Bank; ☎ 865 4653; www.lostcreek.ca. A beautiful, forested lakeside 5,876yd course. Reach it by taking Beaverbank Rd for 9km from Exit 2 of Hwy 101. Green fees CAN$51.

Gyms and fitness centres Many of the bigger hotels have some sort of fitness facilities for their guests, ranging from a small room with a few machines to large areas with state-of-the-art equipment. If your accommodation doesn't have suitable facilities, try the following:

Fitness FX [98–9 C4] 6330 Quinpool Rd; ☎ 422 1431; www.fitnessfx.ca. Day pass CAN$10.

SMUfit [98–9 F5] Saint Mary's University, The Homburg Centre, 920 Tower Rd; ☎ 420 5555; www.smuhuskies.ca. Excellent facilities plus squash courts. Day pass CAN$12 (photo ID required).

South Park YMCA [92–3 A5] 1565 South Park St; ☎ 423 9622; www.ymcahrm.ns.ca. By the Halifax Public Gardens. Day pass CAN$12.50.

Horseriding You'll have to head out of the city centre.

Hatfield Farms Adventures 840 Hammonds Plains Rd; ☎ 835 5676; www.hatfieldfarm.com. Offers trail rides for all levels, plus some 'dude ranch' type packages.

Isner Stables 1060 Old Sambro Rd, Harrietsfield; ☎ 477 5043; www.isnerstables.ca. Riding lessons, trail rides, pony rides, wagon rides & more.

Spas Spas offer a wide range of services. Expect to pay around CAN$100 for a 60-minute facial.

Chrysalis Spa & Skincare Centre [98–9 B1] 5521 Young St; ☎ 446 3929; http://chrysalisspa.com

The Summit Day Spa [92–3 C7] 5495 Spring Garden Rd; ☎ 423 3888; http://summitspa.ca

Spirit Spa [92–3 F6] 5150 Salter St #200; ☎ 431 8100; www.spiritspa.ca

Swimming Some hotels have pools, and hardy souls may like to brave the sea at one of the region's beaches. Freshwater swimming is popular, try **Chocolate Lake** [98–9 A6] (see page 119). Otherwise, try the **Centennial Pool** [92–3 C1] (*1970 Gottingen St; ☎ 490 7219; www.centennialpool.ca*), and the **South Park YMCA** [92–3 A5] (see *Gyms and fitness centres*, page 109).

Winter sports When the snow is on the ground, some of the HRM's walking trails are popular with **cross-country skiers**. The nearest downhill skiing is at Ski Martock (see page 242).

You can **ice-skate** indoors year-round in Dartmouth (see page 125) and in season (mid October–March) there are several possibilities in Halifax, including the **Halifax Forum** [98–9 B2] (*2901 Windsor St, ☎ 490 4500; e www.halifaxforum.ca; CAN$2.75/session*).

Best for outdoor skating is the new (2010–11) **Emera Oval** [98–9 D3] (☎ *490 2347; www.halifax.ca/skatehrm/*), the largest outdoor, artificially refrigerated ice surface in Atlantic Canada.

Several lakes in Halifax are great for skating, including Chocolate Lake, but you'll rarely find facilities, and skate rental is even harder to come by. It might be worth investing in a secondhand pair.

OTHER PRACTICALITIES

Banks You won't have a problem finding a bank or ABM (ATM) in Halifax or Dartmouth. Many hotels offer currency-exchange services – though the rate may be less competitive – as does the Casino Nova Scotia [92–3 F1] (see page 105).

$ Royal Bank [98–9 E4] 5855 Spring Garden Rd; ☎ 421 8177; ⏲ 09.30–17.00 Mon–Tue & Fri, 09.30–20.00 Wed–Thu, 10.00–15.00 Sat

$ TD Canada Trust [92–3 E4] 1785 Barrington St; ☎ 420 8040; ⏲ 08.00–18.00 Mon–Wed, 08.00–20.00 Thu–Fri, 08.00–16.00 Sat

Health The only medical emergency department in the HRM is located at the **Queen Elizabeth II Health Sciences Centre** [98–9 D3] (*1796 Summer St,; ☎ 473 3383*). The most central walk-in clinic is the **Family Focus Medical Clinic** [92–3 A8] (*5991 Spring Garden Rd; ☎ 420 6060; ⏲ 08.30–21.00 Mon–Fri, 11.00–17.00 Sat/Sun*).

Shoppers Drug Mart [92–3 B7] (*5524 Spring Garden Rd; ☎ 429 2400*) has a 24-hour pharmacy.

Internet Public internet access is free at libraries (see below) and for the last few years has been free at Community Access Program (C@P) sites. In 2012 it looked as though C@P site funding would be slashed. For the nearest C@P site, use the 'Find a C@P Site' facility on www.nscap.ca.

Internet cafés tend to come and go quite frequently, but the following have been around for a while:

Blowers St Paperchase News Café [92–3 D6] 5228 Blowers St; ☎ 423 0750; ⏲ 08.00–18.30 Mon–Sat, 09.00–17.00 Sun; closing times depend on how busy the café is. Has a good selection of newspapers & magazines downstairs, & rather good wholesome food. Internet costs CAN$0.13/min.

Spring Garden Internet Café [92–3 A6–7] 5681 Spring Garden Rd; ☎ 423 0785; ⏲ 06.00–23.30 daily. Internet CAN$2.30/20 mins, packages available.

Laundromats Coin-operated laundries in Halifax include:

Bluenose [98–9 C3] 2198 Windsor St; ☎ 422 7098

Kwik Wash [92–3 B8] 5506 Clyde St; ☎ 429 2023

Murphy's [92–3 C2] 6023 North St; ☎ 454 6294

Libraries **Halifax Public Libraries** (*www.halifaxpubliclibraries.ca*) has ten branches close to the downtown area; the largest and most central is the **Spring Garden Road Memorial Public Library** [92–3 D6] (*5381 Spring Garden Rd; ☎ 490 5700; ⏲ year-round 10.00–21.00 Tue–Thu, 10.00–17.00 Fri/Sat (winter only 14.00–17.00 Sun)*). All libraries offer internet-accessible computers.

Currently under construction on the corner of Spring Garden Road and Queen Street [92–3 D7] is a new Halifax Central Library, due to open in 2014.

Police For emergencies, ☎ 911; for non-emergency business, ☎ 490 5020.

Post offices The main post office is at 1680 Bedford Row [92–3 F5] (**t/f** *1 800 267 1177; ⏲ 08.00–17.00 Mon–Fri*). However, many standard post office services are now offered at a variety of other stores, such as some branches of Shoppers Drug Mart and Lawton Drugs, and these tend to be open on Saturdays and later in the evening.

WHAT TO SEE AND DO Halifax has something of a reputation for being foggy. In an average year, over 100 days will be foggy at some time or other. Mid spring to early summer tends to be particularly bad. Keep your fingers crossed because when the sun shines, the outdoor attractions, gardens, parks and waterfront are delightful, as is McNab's Island [80 C/D5].

The unmissables

Halifax Citadel National Historic Site of Canada [92–3 B3] (*5425 Sackville St; ☎ 426 5080; www.parkscanada.gc.ca/halifaxcitadel; ⏲ early May–Oct 09.00–17.00 daily (Jul/Aug to 18.00), grounds open year-round but no services available Nov–early May; admission Jun–mid Sep CAN$11.70, May & Oct CAN$7.80, Nov–Apr free, inc 45–60 min guided tour early May–Oct*) The first fortifications were constructed on what was then called Signal Hill in 1749. A three-storey octagonal blockhouse was added in 1776, and during the Duke of Kent's time in Halifax (1794–1800) he implemented major changes. In the 1820s, previous fortifications were levelled, and the height of the hill reduced – the earth moved was used to construct ramparts. The huge, star-shaped, Vauban-style Citadel that is seen today was constructed between 1828 and 1856. Officially known as Fort George and built to reduce the threat of a land attack by American forces, it was one of the largest British fortresses on the American continent, the hilltop setting providing a commanding view of the city and harbour. The Citadel continued its watch over Halifax until the end of World War II. For today's visitor, from below you get the impression of just a huge grassy mound. But once you've climbed the hill, crossed the plank bridge over the moat and gone through the arched entrance to the inner courtyard, you'll appreciate the full scale of the site. There are good audio-visual presentations, moats, barrack rooms, garrison cells, tunnels and ramparts to explore, and plenty of cannons – one of which is fired daily at noon. Throughout the summer, students dressed in the uniform of the 78th Highland Regiment (MacKenzie tartan kilts and bright-red doublets) enact the drills of 1869, marching to a bagpipe band. This is Halifax's major attraction and one of the most visited National Historic Sites in Canada.

Upstairs in the Cavalier Building is the **Army Museum** (*☎ 422 5979; www.parkscanada.gc.ca/lhn-nhs/ns/halifax/visit/visit11.aspx; ⏲ opening hours as above, admission inc in Citadel fee*), which presents hundreds of artefacts reflecting Atlantic Canada's military heritage and displays on military events in which Canadian forces played a significant role. There's a café downstairs.

To reach Citadel Hill on foot from the waterfront, follow George Street (which later becomes Carmichael Street) uphill.

Halifax Public Gardens [92–3 A6] (*Main entrance on the corner of South Park St & Spring Garden Rd; ☎ 490 4000; www.halifaxpublicgardens.ca; ⏲ early May–early Nov 08.00–dusk daily; admission free*) The Nova Scotia Horticultural Society was formed in 1836, and in the early 1840s began to lay out flower beds and vegetable plots. A civic garden opened in 1867 and has evolved into what many consider to be the finest original formal Victorian public garden in North America. In addition to magnificent floral displays (in late May and June, the tulips are stunning), there are beautiful fountains, ponds with ducks and geese, winding pathways, shady benches and an ornate, bronze-roofed bandstand which dates from Queen Victoria's Golden Jubilee and is the site of free Sunday afternoon concerts in July and August. The 7ha park, across Sackville Street from the Citadel grounds, is enclosed by a wrought-iron fence with a magnificent set of ornamental gates at the main entrance. Hurricane Juan wrought havoc on the trees in September 2003, but since then much sterling work has been done and the gardens are looking magnificent again.

Maritime Museum of the Atlantic [92–3 F5] (*1675 Lower Water St; ☎ 424 7490; http://museum.gov.ns.ca/mma; ⏲ Nov–Apr 09.30–20.00 Tue, 09.30–17.00 Wed–Sat, 13.00–17.00 Sun; May & Oct 09.30–17.30 Mon–Sat (to 20.00 Tue), 13.00–17.30 Sun; Jun–Sep 09.30–17.30 daily (to 20.00 Tue); admission May–Oct CAN$8.75, Nov–Feb & Apr CAN$4.75, Mar CAN$2.85*) Almost everything about Nova Scotia is linked to the sea, and if you only visit one museum in the province, make it Canada's oldest and largest maritime museum.

Housed in a well-designed purpose-built c1982 structure which incorporates an early 20th-century chandlery at the heart of the city's waterfront, the museum commemorates Nova Scotia's seafaring heritage, traditions and history. Many visitors come for an excellent collection of *Titanic*-abilia, and are not disappointed with the **Titanic: The Unsinkable Ship and Halifax Gallery**. But even more powerful is **Halifax Wrecked**, a gallery that recounts the devastating effects of the 1917 Halifax Explosion (see box, page 90). See, too, displays on three centuries of shipwrecks, the Golden Age of Sail and the Steam Age, some fabulous scale models of all manner of sea-going vessels, and much more, too.

Between May and October the admission charge will also allow you to board the CSS *Acadia*, moored on the waterfront by the museum. Built in Newcastle-upon-Tyne, England, in 1913, she was Canada's longest-serving survey vessel, and the only surviving ship to have served the Royal Canadian Navy during both World Wars.

Canadian Museum of Immigration at Pier 21 [98–9 G4] (*1055 Marginal Rd; ☎ 425 7770; www.pier21.ca; ⏲ May–late Nov 09.30–17.30 daily; late Nov–Mar 10.00–17.00 Tue–Sat; Apr 10.00–17.00 Mon–Sat; admission CAN$8.60*) Focusing on Canadian immigration and nation-building, this inspirational, award-winning interactive national museum is housed in the last remaining ocean immigration shed in Canada, through which – between 1928 and 1971 – nearly one million immigrants began new lives in Canada and 500,000 Canadians departed to World War II military service. For those who know New York, this is Canada's Ellis Island. Be sure to watch the poignant *Oceans of Hope*, a 30-minute multi-media presentation that tells the history of Pier 21 from the late 1920s, through the depression, war and post-war years. The family centre is popular with those whose ancestors passed through the building, and there's a café on site. The attraction has been recognised as one of the Seven Wonders of Canada by the Canadian Broadcasting Corporation (CBC).

Other museums

Discovery Centre [92–3 E6] (*1593 Barrington St; ☎ 492 4422; www.discoverycentre.ns.ca; ⏲ year-round 10.00–17.00 Mon–Sat, 13.00–17.00 Sun; admission CAN$10*) This hands-on interactive science centre tries to attract people of all ages, but will be of most worth to those with kids. Not a bad place to keep them happy if it is pouring outside. There are plans to move to a new location, perhaps in 2014.

Maritime Command Museum [98–9 C1] (*Admiralty Hse, 2725 Gottingen St; ☎ 721 8250; http://psphalifax.ca/marcom/; ⏲ early Jan–mid Dec 09.00–15.30 Mon–Fri; admission free*) Housed in a stately c1840s Georgian mansion on the grounds of Canadian Forces Base Halifax, this museum focuses on the history and development of the Canadian navy since its inception in 1910: there are also displays on almost two centuries of Royal Navy presence in – and influence on – Halifax. Photo ID is required for admission.

Museum of Natural History [98–9 D3] (*1747 Summer St; ☎ 424 7353; http://museum.gov.ns.ca/mnh/; ⌚ Jun–mid Oct 09.30–17.30 Mon–Sat (to 20.00 Wed), 13.00–17.30 Sun; mid Oct–May 09.00–17.00 Tue–Sat (to 20.00 Wed), 12.00–17.00 Sun; admission CAN$5.75*) Enter and you'll find not just the expected, galleries of botanical exhibits, stuffed animals and birds, whale skeletons – but plenty more, too. The Archaeology Gallery tells of 11,000 years of human life, the galleries feature 200 and 300 million-year-old fossils and centuries-old Mi'kmaq craftwork. Live exhibits can be seen in the Marine Gallery's tide tanks and the Nature Centre. There's also Science on a Sphere, a high-tech 360° digital experience. A good introduction to the natural wonders of the province.

Other historical sites

Government House [92–3 E7] (*1451 Barrington St; ☎ 424 7001*) The official residence of the Lieutenant-Governor of Nova Scotia was built between 1800 and 1805 for Governor Sir John Wentworth. It is not open to the public.

Historic Properties [92–3 F3] (*1869 Upper Water St; ☎ 429 0530; www.historicproperties.ca*) On the waterfront between the casino and the ferry terminal is a group of Canada's oldest surviving warehouses dating from the early 19th century. Nearly lost to 'urban renewal' in the early 1960s, the solid wood and stone structures – including the c1813 Privateers' Warehouse, built to store the privateers' booty (see page 18) – were painstakingly restored and now house pubs, bars, restaurants and boutiques.

HMCS Sackville: Canada's Naval Memorial [92–3 G5] (*Sackville Landing; ☎ 429 2132; www.hmcssackville-cnmt.ns.ca; ⌚ Jun–Oct 10.00–17.00 daily; admission CAN$4*) Explore the world's last surviving Flower-class corvette which saw much World War II action escorting convoys across the Atlantic, now restored to 1944 configuration as a memorial to all those who served in the Royal Canadian Navy. Between November and May, the vessel is usually moored in the naval dockyard: ☎ 427 2837 for location and opening hours.

Old Town Clock [92–3 C4] (*Citadel Hill just off Brunswick St*) Sometimes simply called the Town Clock, this three-tiered tower atop a rectangular building, which was originally used as a guard room and residence for the caretaker, is one of Halifax's most famous landmarks. Prince Edward, Duke of Kent, bothered by poor punctuality at the Halifax garrison, commissioned a clock before his return to England in 1800. The original mechanism, crafted in London, England, and wound twice a week, has been going strong since 1803. Unfortunately, when it originally arrived from England, there were no accompanying instructions, and it lay for some time unused and untouched near the (completed) clock building. Finally, a newly arrived soldier who had worked as a clock-maker did the trick.

Galleries and arts centres

Anna Leonowens Gallery [92–3 F3] (*NSCAD University, 1891 Granville St; ☎ 494 8223; www.nscad.ca/students/gallery_intro.php; ⌚ early Jan–late Aug & mid Sep–mid Dec 11.00–17.00 Tue–Fri, 12.00–16.00 Sat; admission free*) In an elegant Italianate building, the gallery displays contemporary art, craft and design: weekly exhibitions focus on the renowned Nova Scotia College of Art and Design (NSCAD) students' work. Occasional shows by visiting artists and curators. See box, page 114, for further information.

ANNA LEONOWENS

The building at 1740 Argyle Street once housed The Victoria College of Art and Design, founded and run by Anna Leonowens (1831–1915). Her time as governess and tutor to the King of Siam's 67 children was later filmed, first as *Anna and the King of Siam* (1946), then as a musical, *The King and I* (1951), and then again as *Anna and The King* (1999). Leonowens lived in Halifax for 19 years and was an active supporter of education and the arts. Her name and memory live on in an art gallery connected to the school she began.

Argyle Fine Art [92–3 F3] (*1559 Barrington St; ☎ 425 9456; http://argylefineart.com; ⌚ 12.00–17.00 Mon, 10.00–18.00 Tue–Sat; admission free*) One of Halifax's most progressive galleries, with an exciting range of contemporary art.

Art Gallery of Nova Scotia [92–3 F5] (*1723 Hollis St; ☎ 424 7542; www.artgalleryofnovascotia.ca; ⌚ May–Sep 10.00–21.00 Mon–Sat, 12.00–17.00 Sun; Oct 10.00–17.00 Mon–Sat (to 21.00 Thu), 12.00–17.00 Sun; Nov–Apr 10.00–17.00 Wed–Sat (to 21.00 Thu), 12.00–17.00 Sun; tours are offered at 14.30,& at 19.00 Thu; admission CAN$12*) Atlantic Canada's largest (and finest) art collection is divided between two mid 1860s buildings separated by a cobbled courtyard. The majority has been displayed in the Dominion Building (Gallery North) since 1988: ten years later the collection expanded onto two floors of the Provincial Building. The permanent collection includes contemporary and historic provincial, Canadian and international art: there's a wonderful folk-art section which includes the Maud Lewis House (see page 28). To round it off, the gallery has a good shop, and the excellent Untitled Eats (see *Where to eat*, page 101).

Dalhousie Art Gallery [98–9 D5] (*Dalhousie Arts Centre, 6101 University Av; ☎ 494 2403; www.artgallery.dal.ca; ⌚ year-round 11.00–17.00 Tue–Fri, 12.00–17.00 Sat/Sun; admission free*) Established in 1953, the oldest public art gallery in Halifax presents changing exhibitions of contemporary and historic art and a programme of lectures, films and artists' presentations. Guided tours offered.

Khyber Institute for Contemporary Arts [92–3 E6] (*1588 Barrington St; ☎ 422 9668; www.khyber.ca; ⌚ 12.00–17.00 Mon–Fri; admission free*) Housed in a splendid c1888 edifice, this artist-run centre presents exhibitions, concerts and film.

NSCAD University (Nova Scotia Centre for Craft and Design) [98–9 G3] (*1061 Marginal Rd; ☎ 492 2522; www.craft-design.ns.ca; ⌚ 09.00–17.00 Tue–Fri (to 20.00 Thu), 11.00–16.00 Sat; admission free*) Exhibitions of local, national and international fine crafts at the centre's Mary E Black Gallery. Also be sure to visit the Designer Craft Shop. Outside the summer months, the centre offers courses in pottery, jewellery, glass, metal- and woodworking, and textiles.

Brewery tours Only **Alexander Keith's** [92–3 F7] and the **Propeller Brewery** [92–3 C1] offer tours for individuals, couples or small groups. If there are ten or more of you, **Garrison Brewing** [98–9 G3] *(1149 Marginal Rd; ☎ 453 5343; www.garrisonbrewing.com*) will run special tours of its brewery for approximately CAN$12 per person.

Alexander Keith's Nova Scotia Brewery [92–3 F7] (*1496 Lower Water St; ☎ 455 1474, t/f 1 877 612 1820; www.keiths.ca; ⌚ tours Jun–Oct 12.00–20.00 Mon–Sat, 12.00–17.00 Sun; Nov–May 17.00–20.00 Fri, 12.00–20.00 Sat, 12.00–17.00 Sun; admission CAN$16.95*) Somewhat theatrical, but entertaining, 55-minute tours are offered of one of the oldest working breweries in North America, which opened in 1820 in this huge ironstone and granite building. Although most brewing operations were moved elsewhere years ago, the brewery still produces seasonal brews using traditional techniques. Costumed performers, dressed à la 1860s, tell of the brewery's history, often breaking into song (and dance). Fun, slightly camp, and a bit overpriced in my opinion, even with a couple of beers thrown in, rather than educational. Incidentally, Keith's India Pale Ale (IPA) is Nova Scotia's best-selling beer.

I'LL DRINK TO THAT

Born in Caithness, Scotland, Alexander Keith (1795–1873) emigrated to Canada and, having learned the art of brewing before leaving Britain, opened his eponymous brewing company in Halifax in 1820. A Freemason Grand Master, he served three times as mayor of the city. His birthday, 5 October, is not an official holiday, but there are celebrations in his honour on or around that day each year.

Propeller Brewery [92–3 C1] (*2015 Gottingen St; ☎ 422 7767; www.drinkpropeller.ca; ⌚ tours Jul–Sep 18.00 Wed; admission CAN$15, advance booking by credit card recommended*) Tour the brewery, then taste the beer and Propeller fizzy drinks.

Other sights

Burke-Gaffney Observatory [98–9 F5] (*Loyola Bldg, Saint Mary's University, Robie St; ☎ 496 8257; www.ap.smu.ca/bgo; free public tours on alternate Sat evenings, in summer every Sat*) The largest of the observatory's telescopes is 41cm in diameter.

Halifax City Hall [92–3 E4] (*1841 Argyle St; ☎ 490 4000; www.halifax.ca/community/HalifaxCityHall/; free guided tours Jul–Sep 10.00–12.00 & 14.00–16.00 Mon–Fri*) This c1888 Second Empire-style building at the opposite end of the Grand Parade from St Paul's Church is the seat of government for the Halifax Regional Municipality. In 1998, one of the clocks on the tower was set permanently to 09.04, the exact time of the Halifax Explosion (see box, page 90).

Point Pleasant Park [98–9 H6] (*Point Pleasant Dr; www.pointpleasantpark.ca; ⌚ 06.00–midnight daily*) This 75ha park at South End Halifax suffered devastation when Hurricane Juan struck in 2003 (see *History*, page 4). More than 75% of the 100,000 trees were destroyed: the cleanup closed the park for nine months. Over five years later, remnants of the destruction are still there, but so too are positive signs of the work done by Mother Nature (and the park authorities) to repair the damage.

The park is criss-crossed by tens of kilometres of walking and biking trails (bikes permitted Monday–Friday only, but not on statutory holidays), and a waterfront trail which is very popular with joggers leads along the Halifax Harbour side to the point, then back along the Northwest Arm shoreline (approximately 2km each way). In the park are ruins of several forts and fortifications, including the c1796–97 **Prince of Wales Martello Tower National Historic Site of Canada**

(☎ *426 5080; www.parkscanada.gc.ca/lhn-nhs/ns/prince/; ⌚ Jul–early Sep 10.00–18.00 daily; admission free*), built by order of Prince Edward, Duke of Kent, to help protect British gun batteries in Halifax. It was the first of its type in North America.

Park signage is plentiful but there is a paucity of maps: the only one that I've found is at the Tower Road entrance at Point Pleasant Drive. Smoking is not permitted in the park. Occupying such a strategically important position, the park is officially on British territory. In 1866, the (then) city of Halifax agreed to rent the site from the British government for one shilling (five pence, about ten cents Canadian) a year, on a 999-year lease.

To get to the park, take South Park Street south from Sackville Street: South Park becomes Young Avenue, and this leads to Point Pleasant Drive. Tower Road and Marginal Road also lead here. Those using public transport should take bus #9 from Barrington Street.

Province House [92–3 E4] (*1726 Hollis St;* ☎ *424 4661, 424 5982 (tours); www.gov.ns.ca/legislature/;* ⌚ *Jul/Aug 09.00–17.00 Mon–Fri, 10.00–16.00 Sat/Sun; Sep–Jun 09.00–16.00 Mon–Fri; admission free*) Opened in 1819 and constructed of Wallace sandstone (see page 280), this fine Palladian-style building is the seat of the Nova Scotia government, which was Canada's oldest provincial legislative assembly. Visiting Halifax in 1842, Charles Dickens called it 'a gem of Georgian architecture'. Call ahead to ask about guided tours.

Nova Scotia Archives and Records Management [98–9 E5] (*6016 University Av;* ☎ *424 6060; www.gov.ns.ca/nsarm/;* ⌚ *year-round 08.30–16.30 Mon–Fri (to 21.00 Wed), 09.00–17.00 Sat; admission free*) A splendid resource for genealogists.

CHURCHES AND CATHEDRALS

St Paul's Anglican Church [92–3 E5] (*1749 Argyle St;* ☎ *429 2240; www.stpaulshalifax.org;* ⌚ *09.00–16.00 Mon–Fri; tours offered Jun–Aug*) Built in 1750, white, wooden St Paul's is the oldest standing Anglican church in Canada and the oldest surviving building in Halifax. The church – at the edge of the Grand Parade – was modelled on St Peter's, a c1722 church in London, England's Vere Street: the timbers were cut in Boston, Massachusetts, and shipped to Halifax. A number of important colonial figures are buried in the crypt, including Bishop Charles Inglis (1734–1816) who was a driving force towards the construction of many of the province's churches. As a consequence of the Halifax Explosion (see page 90) a piece of window frame was embedded (and can still be seen) in the interior wall of the narthex (entry lobby area). The blast also damaged one of the windows, creating what looks a bit like the silhouette of a figure: it is said to resemble an early curate, Jean-Baptiste Moreau. The Explosion Window is on the upper level, and is the third from the back of the building.

Cathedral Church of All Saints [98–9 E4] (*1330 Martello St;* ☎ *423 6002; www.cathedralchurchofallsaints.com;* ⌚ *for services, plus year-round 09.00–16.00 Mon–Fri; guided tours mid Jun–mid Aug Mon–Fri*) Constructed from local stone, the church opened in 1910. There are beautiful stained glass windows, and fine woodcarvings.

Little Dutch (Deutsch) Church [98–9 D2] (*Brunswick St at Gerrish St;* ☎ *423 1059; www.roundchurch.ca;* ⌚ *for services, mid Jun–late Sep, check website for times; tours offered in the summer in conjunction with tours of St George's Round Church –*

see below) In 1756, some German Lutheran settlers moved a house to this location and adapted it to be Halifax's second church, after St Paul's. It was consecrated as an Anglican Church in 1761, but held on to its Lutheran roots and was, in practice in many ways, Lutheran until around 1811. Other locals confused 'Deutsch' ('German') with 'Dutch', and the church became known as the Little Dutch Church. Towards the end of the 19th century, the church attracted a growing non-Lutheran congregation – in numbers larger than it could cope with.

St George's Round Church [98–9 D2] (*2222 Brunswick St; ☎ 423 1059; www.roundchurch.ca; 🕘 to visit during services, tours offered in summer*) Built in 1799–1800 to accommodate the growing congregation of the Little Dutch Church (see opposite), this is an excellent example of a circular wooden Palladian church. Founded on a unique combination of German Lutheranism and Anglicanism, St George's became its own Anglican parish in 1827. In 1994, more than a third of the building – including the dome – was destroyed by fire. The church was restored using traditional 19th-century building techniques.

St Mary's Cathedral Basilica [92–3 E7] (*5521 Spring Garden Rd; ☎ 429 9800; www.stmarysbasilica.ns.ca; guided tours offered*) The Roman Catholic Church was not permitted to build a house of worship in Nova Scotia until 1784, when a small church was built on this site. Construction on what was to become the second Catholic cathedral in Canada began in 1820 and shipwrights were hired to build the roof. The first mass was celebrated in 1829 and St Peter's Church was renamed St Mary's Cathedral in 1833. Major renovations began in 1860, giving the building a far more Gothic appearance. The cathedral had beautiful stained glass windows, most of which were destroyed in the Halifax Explosion: these were replaced with equally impressive ones made in Munich, Germany. The title 'Basilica' was bestowed by Pope Pius XII who visited in 1950.

Cemeteries and burial grounds

Fairview Cemetery [98–9 A3] (*3720 Windsor St; ☎ 490 4883; 🕘 dawn–dusk daily*) Those fascinated by the story (and film) of the *Titanic* (see box, page 89) will want to visit this cemetery, the final resting place of 121 *Titanic* victims. Some graves just have numbers, but where identification was possible, a name accompanies the number.

Ah, the power of Hollywood: the most visited grave is that of J Dawson, #227. Leonardo DiCaprio played Jack Dawson in the 1997 film. Incidentally, the film's writer and director, James Cameron, said he had thought up the character's name and was not aware that there had been a J Dawson on board.

The cemetery also contains the graves of many victims of the Halifax Explosion (see box, page 90). Too far to walk from downtown for most people, to get here take Windsor Street north from Quinpool Road. The cemetery is near the junction with Connaught Avenue.

Old Burying Ground [92–3 E7] (*Barrington St & Spring Garden Rd; ☎ 429 2240; 🕘 Jun–Sep 09.00–17.00 daily*) The first burial ground in Halifax was in use from 1749 to 1844. Interpretive signs indicate gravestones of historic significance. Despite the busy surrounds, this graveyard is a tranquil place to wander and reflect.

Camp Hill Cemetery [98–9 D4] (*Robie & Sackville sts*) In 1844, this cemetery, located to the west of the Public Gardens (see page 111), replaced the Old Burying Ground: amongst provincial big names interred here are statesman Joseph Howe, privateer Enos Collins, Abraham Gesner (inventor of kerosene) and brewer Alexander Keith.

AROUND HALIFAX

MCNAB'S AND LAWLOR ISLANDS PROVINCIAL PARK Two islands lie at the mouth of Halifax Harbour. The smaller, Lawlor Island, is just off Fisherman's Cove (see page 127): an important bird nesting site, it is not currently open to the public.

McNab's Island, on the other hand, is not only easy to visit, but one of the HRM's hidden gems. Approximately 5km long and up to 1.5km wide, this 400ha island offers a combination of historical and natural features which will delight hikers, birdwatchers, and those with an interest in (particularly military) history.

Deer, coyote and other animals inhabit the island, and over 200 bird species, including nesting raptors such as osprey, have been documented here. Walk some of the many trails through the woods and past tidal pools, explore several former military installations and gun batteries, see some of the old residential houses, relax on sandy Mauger's Beach, and enjoy a wonderful view of the mouth of Halifax Harbour. If the weather is kind, this is a great place to spend a few hours or more.

History Evidence, including a 1,500-year-old shell midden, indicates a Mi'kmaq presence on McNab's Island long before the Europeans. The French used the island as a fishing camp during the 1690s, and in 1782, a Peter McNab purchased it. Around the turn of the 19th century, the British Admiralty built a gallows on what became known as Hangman's Beach, and used it to hang deserters. The bodies were left suspended as a warning to other sailors.

Fortifications were added, and in 1866 the island was forced into use as a makeshift quarantine area when a cholera epidemic struck on the *England*, a steamship *en route* from Liverpool to New York. Around 200 of the 1,200 on board are thought to have been buried on the island.

In the 1860s, the British Admiralty established defences including Ives Point Battery, Fort McNab and the Hugonin Battery.

Between the 1870s and 1920s, the island was a popular recreational destination for the people of Halifax and Dartmouth: thousands came to visit the fairgrounds, bath houses and tea rooms and for picnics or socials.

In both World Wars, defences and fortifications were enhanced, and the island anchored one end of a submarine net across the harbour. In 1974, the province began acquiring land for the creation of a provincial park: today, less than 3% of the island is privately owned.

Getting there **Great E.A.R.T.H. Expeditions** (see page 39) offers good four- to five-hour guided walking and history tours of the island. No services are available on McNab's Island, so remember to bring your own food and water. Be prepared too for changeable weather.

DEVIL'S ISLAND Approximately 12ha in size, Devil's Island is situated about 2km southeast of McNab's Island.

Originally granted to a Captain John Rous in 1752, the first permanent settlement was in 1830, and in 1900 there were about 20 families living on the island.

There are many explanations of how the island earned its current name. Historians say it was briefly owned and occupied by a man named 'Duval', and that with time his name was corrupted. Others say that some Haligonians visited the island for what was supposed to be a day trip, but – owing to a sudden weather deterioration – were stuck there for several days, describing it on their return as somewhere only the devil would live. There were many reports of shepherds (sheep were pastured on the island after the aforementioned fire) and passing sailors seeing ghosts there.

One of the most unusual stories is from the turn of the 20th century: a man reported that when out fishing, a halibut had popped its head out of the water, announced itself as the Devil, and told him that he would die the next day. On the morrow, the man was found dead in his boat near the spot where he claimed to have seen the satanic halibut: examinations showed that – even though he was found sitting in his boat, hands on oars and bone dry – he had drowned. Members of the dead man's family moved into his house on the island, and their baby died within a day or two with no obvious cause of death. There were also reports of the footsteps of a fisherman's boots walking the corridors.

Some claim that unexplainable lights and fires on the island are still seen from the mainland. A supposedly bottomless pit on the island is said to be either a hiding place for pirate treasure or a gateway to hell.

In 2006, psychic medium Alan Hatfield spent a night on the island with a camera crew filming a two-part television documentary entitled *The Ghosts of Devil's Island*. He claims to have recorded several clear and audible spirit voices on audio tape, and an apparition on infra-red video.

Devil's Island can be visited, but there are no scheduled boat services (try the McNab's Island operators). Only small vessels can safely navigate into the only landing area, and then only if sea conditions are perfect. If you get there, you'll find it hard to imagine that the island once boasted 18 houses and a small school.

GEORGE'S ISLAND (*☎ 426 5080; www.parkscanada.gc.ca/georgesisland*) For 200 years, George's Island was the scene of constant military activity, playing an integral role in harbour defence. For the past 40 years, however, the island has remained largely undisturbed, although tales of its secret tunnels abound. At this time Parks Canada has reported that the George's Island NHS will not be developed for public visitation, however the island will continue to be available for special events so it might be worth checking with Parks Canada for the latest news.

THE NORTHWEST ARM, HERRING COVE AND SAMBRO This is a fascinating excursion of less than 65km in total, especially for those who won't have time to explore much beyond the capital. It starts at the **Armdale Rotary** [98–9 A5], at the west end of Quinpool Road. From here, take Herring Cove Road, staying to the right when Purcell's Cove Road branches off to the left. Almost immediately, you'll see a sign for **Chocolate Lake Beach**, and a parking area on the right. Walk along a short path to a small, sandy beach, and one of the HRM's favourite swimming lakes.

After your dip, head back towards the roundabout (rotary), but take the first right and right again to join Highway 253, Purcell's Cove Road.

Look out for the impressive **St George's Greek Orthodox Church** [98–9 A6] (*38 Purcell's Cove Rd; ☎ 830 3377; ⏲ Sun morning for services, otherwise by appointment*): this and the adjacent community centre are the focus for Halifax's Greek community of approximately 400.

Pass the Armdale Yacht Club on Melville Island (formerly the site of a military prison), shortly after which a sign will indicate the turn-off (on the left) to

Deadman's Island Park [98–9 B6]. During the war of 1812, thousands of (mainly American) soldiers and sailors were held prisoner close by. Many died in captivity, and almost 200 were buried in unmarked graves on this site. In 2005, the US government erected a plaque to commemorate the men interred here.

You can walk from here to the **Sir Sandford Fleming Park** [98–9 D7] (*Dingle Rd; ☎ 490 4000; ⌚ 08.00–dusk daily*), but it is probably better to continue on Purcell's Cove Road, then follow Dingle Road to the car park. This 38ha largely forested park has extensive water frontage with lovely views over the yacht-dotted Northwest Arm, and two main trails. Always popular is the walk along the waterfront, but worthwhile too is the trail through the forest to Frog Pond.

SIR SANDFORD FLEMING

Born in Kirkcaldy, Fife, Scotland, Sandford Fleming (1827–1915) came to Canada in 1845. He designed Canada's first postage stamp, proposed, surveyed and engineered Canada's first railway line, and created Standard Time Zones (though these were not fully implemented until many years after his death). He was knighted by Queen Victoria in 1897, and – having lived in Halifax for a number of years – deeded his land (now the park that bears his name) to the city in 1908.

The park's distinctive c1912 ten-storey tower, The Dingle, was commissioned by Sir Sandford Fleming (see box above) to commemorate 150 years of representative government in Nova Scotia. In theory, the tower is open in summer and early autumn (if it is open, climb the winding staircase for fabulous views) but this seems a bit hit or miss.

Continuing on Purcell's Cove Road, you'll pass North America's oldest sailing club, the Royal Nova Scotia Yacht Squadron, which dates from 1837.

Originally built in 1793, most of the fortifications you see today at **York Redoubt** [80 C5] (*Purcell's Cove Rd; ☎ 426 5080; www.pc.gc.ca/lhn-nhs/ns/york/; ⌚ Nov–Mar 08.00–17.00 daily; Apr/mid May & Oct 08.00–18.00 daily; mid May–Aug 08.00–20.00 daily; Sep 08.00–19.00 daily; admission free*) date from more recent times, including tunnels, huge muzzle-loading guns, searchlights, and a Martello tower. The site was chosen for its commanding view over the entrance of Halifax Harbour, and has long been a key element in Halifax's defences. Paths lead downhill to the water, and if the weather is kind, the park makes a fine picnic spot.

York Redoubt is the terminus of bus #15 which runs hourly along Purcell's Cove Road from the terminal in the Halifax Shopping Centre on Mumford Road.

Next stop is the traditional fishing village of **Herring Cove** [80 C5], built on the rocks around a long narrow inlet. You won't find souvenir shops or restaurants, but places like this and Sambro (see page 119) are far closer to the real Nova Scotia than, for example, Fisherman's Cove (see page 127). Herring Cove is the terminus for bus #20 which runs every 30 minutes from downtown (Barrington Street and Duke Street).

From Herring Cove, turn left onto Highway 349, Ketch Harbour Road. Look for the sign to the left to **Chebucto Head** and Duncan's Cove. A paved, albeit not terribly well-maintained, road leads to a military communications complex at Chebucto Head. The car park is right by the c1967 lighthouse. Come here in August and September and you may be able to see whales from this spot high above the ocean.

Take a quick look at **Duncan's Cove** where houses are grouped around a small sandy cove, then return to Highway 359 and turn left.

Just before you reach **Sambro**, take Sandy Cove Road to the left. After 1.4km, stop just before the Agricultural Research Station. This spot offers the best views of Sambro Island and its lighthouse, the oldest standing and operating lighthouse in the Americas, commissioned in 1758.

Photogenic Sambro, at the head of the eponymous harbour, is the largest fishing village on this route. From here, follow signs to **Crystal Crescent Beach**. Short trails lead down from the car parks to three secluded coves with – if the sun's out – turquoise-blue water, white-sand beaches and beautiful natural surroundings. If such things offend you, be aware that the furthest beach is unofficially 'clothing optional'.

A gorgeous trail of approximately 11km return leads south along the shoreline, bending into the woods from time to time, to Pennant Point. Although this area can often be foggy, if it is clear you'll see plentiful seabirds, lovely coastal scenery, perhaps some seals, and views over to Sambro Island.

From here, head back to Sambro from where Highway 306 will whisk you back to Halifax via Harrietsfield (where – if you feel like swapping four wheels for four legs before you get back to the big, bad city – you can pop into the Isner Stables; see page 109).

NEAR THE AIRPORT

Atlantic Canada Aviation Museum (*20 Sky Bd; ☎ 873 3773; www.atlanticcanadaaviationmuseum.com; ⌚ mid May–end Sep 09.00–17.00 daily; admission free*) See over two-dozen aircraft, from 'home-builds' to supersonic jets, plus an extensive collection of artefacts and exhibits depicting Atlantic Canada's aviation history. There is also a good gift shop.

Scotia Speedworld (*Bell Bd; ☎ 873 2277; www.scotiaspeedworld.ca; ⌚ late May–early Sep, races Fri/Sat evenings; tickets CAN$12–40*) Watch the motors running at the premiere stock-car racing facility in eastern Canada.

Getting there Both attractions are on the other side of Highway 102 from the approach road to Halifax International Airport. Take Exit 6 from Highway 102, 38km/24 miles from Halifax.

THE UNIACKE ESTATE (*758 Hwy 1; ☎ 866 0032; http://museum.gov.ns.ca/uemp/; ⌚ Jun–mid Oct 09.30–17.30 Mon–Sat, 11.00–17.30 Sun; admission CAN$3.60*) Situated on a 930ha estate is a large colonial-style country home. Uniacke House was built between 1813 and 1815. Now a museum, the house is an all-too-rare example of a 19th-century Georgian estate intact with its original furniture. There are several kilometres of trails to wander – be sure to take the Lake Drumlin Field loop which offers a fantastic view of the main house. The grounds are open year-round but are not maintained out of season.

Uniacke is on Highway 1, approximately 35km/22 miles from Halifax.

DARTMOUTH

Directly opposite downtown Halifax, Dartmouth is a ten-minute ferry ride, or relatively quick drive over a toll bridge, across the harbour. Haligonians love to say that the best thing about Dartmouth is that it offers a great view of Halifax: Halifax may have been founded a year earlier and have the lion's share of attractions, but – views back across the water apart – there are some good (and diverse) reasons to visit this side of the harbour.

UNIACKE

Richard John Uniacke was born in Ireland, in 1753. He spent some time in New York and Nova Scotia before returning to Ireland to study law. He returned to Nova Scotia in 1781 and soon after was appointed solicitor-general for the province. His meteoric rise up the province's legal – and political – ladder continued. He received a 400ha land grant, expanded it and named it Mount Uniacke, and began building a fine house there in 1813. The house was completed two years later. The Uniackes hosted not just Halifax's elite, but international dignitaries too. In the summer, guests could take boat excursions on Lake Martha, named for Uniacke's wife (she died in 1803, having borne 11 children). Uniacke himself died in 1830, 49 of his 77 years having been spent in the public service of Nova Scotia. The oaks that ring the house are the result of a barrel of acorns brought over from Ireland and planted centuries ago.

While it continues to be a bedroom community for Halifax, Dartmouth also stands on its own feet. It is home to **Burnside** [80 C3–4], already the largest industrial/business park north of Boston and east of Montreal, and continuing to expand. Relatively new, too, is the much-loved Dartmouth Crossing shopping mall and entertainment complex. What is to be applauded is that development has shown some sensitivity to the environment: 23 bodies of water were reason enough for Dartmouth to be called the 'City of Lakes'. Although no longer a city (but part of the HRM), Dartmouth is still very popular with nature lovers and outdoor types for its trails, and kayaking, windsurfing, canoeing and swimming in places such as Lake Banook.

Waterfront boardwalks stretch out on both sides of the ferry terminal, providing visitors with excellent views of McNab's and George's islands, the harbour bridges – oh, and of course the Halifax skyline.

Right by the ferry terminal are the World Peace Pavilion (see page 126), and Alderney Landing, home to a Saturday morning farmers' market and a theatre. In easy walking distance are the Dartmouth Heritage Museum, the Quaker House, and the Christ Church.

Further afield are two contrasting don't-miss attractions: the Bedford Institute of Oceanography and the Black Cultural Centre for Nova Scotia (see page 125).

HISTORY Founded in 1750, a year after Halifax, Dartmouth later began to develop as a big whaling town. Many of the whalers were Quakers, originally from New England's Nantucket Island. At the end of the American Revolution, over 150 ships were engaged in the whaling business. Whale oil's uses included lighting and lubrication: whale bone – used in the manufacture of items including corsets and umbrellas – brought high prices. For several years, Dartmouth prospered with the profits of the whaling business, before the entire fleet moved to Milford Haven, Wales, in 1792. Soon after, Loyalists moved in and occupied the whalers' old homes.

Vehicle and passenger ferries regularly criss-crossed the water between Dartmouth and Halifax, but it was the opening of the Angus L MacDonald Bridge in 1955 which ushered in an unprecedented development boom in Dartmouth.

GETTING THERE To reach Dartmouth from Halifax, visitors can **drive** over the harbour on either the Angus L MacDonald Bridge [98–9 C1] or the A Murray

MacKay Bridge [off map]. Others may wish to take the longer scenic route around the harbour through Bedford, or – best of all – cross the harbour by **ferry**. For further details, see page 84.

WHERE TO STAY

Best Western Plus Dartmouth Hotel and Suites [124 C1] (121 units) 15 Spectacle Lake Dr; 463 2000; www.bestwestern.com/ca/. Decent facilities at this 4-storey property. Away from downtown but close to shopping malls. Good on-site restaurant & wine bar (see *Where to eat*, below), indoor pool, fitness centre & business centre. Rooms have fridges, some double whirlpool baths. Hot buffet b/fast inc. **$$**

Comfort Inn Dartmouth [124 A4] (80 rooms) 456 Windmill Rd; 463 9900, **t/f** 1 800 228 5150; www.choicehotels.ca. Large, well-maintained motel rooms at this 2-storey property near Hwy 111. Good continental b/fast inc. **$$**

Braeside Court B&B [124 C1] (1 unit) 34 Braeside Court; 462 3956, **t/f** 1 866 277 8138; **e** braeside@ns.sympatico.ca; www.braesidecourtbandb.ca. The spacious, 2-bedroom suite occupies the upstairs of an open-plan, spacious modern townhouse close to a lake & good for hiking trails. Away from downtown. Full b/fast inc. **$**

Blockhouse Hill B&B [124 B3] (2 rooms) 62 Wentworth St; 463 1811, **t/f** 1 866 873 1699; www.blockhousehillbedandbreakfast.com; mid Apr–Oct. The 2 spacious bedrooms share a nice bathroom in this lovely house on a quiet, residential street – but only 5 mins' walk to the Halifax ferry. Full b/fast inc. **$**

Further out

Shubie Park Campground (100 sites) [80 C3] Jaybee Dr, off Hwy 318; 435 8328, **t/f** 1 800 440 8450; www.shubiecampground.com; mid May–mid Oct. Open campground with lake access 3km from Exit 6A north of Hwy 111. Approx 6km to downtown Dartmouth, 10km to downtown Halifax.

WHERE TO EAT

La Perla [124 C4] 73 Alderney Dr; 469 3241; www.laperla.ca; 11.30–21.30 Mon–Fri, 17.00–21.30 Sat. Housed in a historic building in downtown Dartmouth, this upmarket north Italian restaurant has an intimate, romantic dining room with a lot of exposed brick, & views over the harbour to the Halifax skyline. If the weather's nice, try to eat on the patio. Lunches are good value. **$$$**

Nectar Social House [124 C3] 62 Octerloney St; 406 3363; www.nectardining.com; 11.30–14.00 & 17.00–21.00 Tue–Fri, 11.00–14.00 & 17.00–22.00 Sat, 11.00–14.00 & 17.00–21.00 Sun. This stylish, contemporary addition to the Dartmouth dining scene has been a hit since it opened. Enjoy a *Nectarini* (raspberry vodka & peach schnapps mixed with orange & pineapple juices) at the lounge/bar, & while eating on the (seasonal) patio or in the upstairs dining area, tuck in to braised Malaysian lamb shank, wonderful seared halibut with mango salsa, or perhaps fillet of beef on a 4-mushroom ragout. A treat. **$$$**

Fan's Chinese Restaurant [124 A4] Shannon Plaza, 451 Windmill Rd; 469 9165; www.fansrestaurant.com; 11.00–14.00 & 16.30–22.00 Mon–Sat, 11.00–14.30 & 16.30–21.30 Sun. The best Chinese on the Dartmouth side of the harbour, Fan's specialises in Peking cuisine. Standout dish is the ginger beef, but everything that I've tried from the 100-plus item menu has been fresh & flavourful. **$$**

MacAskill's [124 C4] 88 Alderney Dr; 466 3100; www.macaskills.ns.ca; 11.30–14.00 & 16.00–22.00 Mon–Fri, 10.00–14.00 & 16.00–22.00 Sat. On the upper floor of the Dartmouth Ferry Terminal, this is a great spot for views across the harbour, especially after dark. Panoramas apart, seafood is the focus, & it is done well. Lunch is particularly good value. Incidentally, the restaurant takes its name from a man whose story is told in the box, page 328. **$$**

Trendz Café & Wine Bar [124 C1] 15 Spectacle Lake Dr; 446 3782; www.trendzcafe.ca; 07.00–21.00 daily (wine bar until 00.30). Once again a hotel (in this case, the Best Western, see above) has a surprisingly good restaurant. Start perhaps with ginger carrot soup, then move on to pan-fried rosemary-crusted cod. The wine bar also has a good martini & beer selection. **$$**

John's Lunch [124 D1] 352 Pleasant St; 469 3074; www.johnslunch.com; 10.00–21.00 Mon–Sat, 11.00–21.00 Sun. This unpretentious fish & chip & seafood eatery opened in 1969. Try the haddock tips, or clams. $

Two if by Sea [124 C3] 66 Ochterloney St; 469 0721; www.twoifbysea.com; 07.00–18.00 Mon–Fri, 08.00–17.00 Sat/Sun. Sophisticated but casual coffee shop/bakery/café. $

ENTERTAINMENT AND NIGHTLIFE

Alderney Landing Cultural Convention Centre [124 C4] Ochterloney St; 461 4698; www.alderneylanding.com. Next to the Dartmouth ferry terminal, hosts theatre, concerts & more.

Celtic Corner Pub [124 C4] 69 Alderney Dr; 464 0764; www.celticcorner.ca; 11.00–midnight, 11.00–01.00 Fri/Sat. A good Irish pub with splendid rooftop patio, live music & Celtic brunch menu. Kitchen closes 22.00 (23.00 Fri/Sat).

Empire Dartmouth Crossing [124 C1] 145 Shubie Dr, Dartmouth Crossing; 481 3251. Multi-screen cinema.

SHOPPING The best shopping malls are the **Mic Mac Mall** [124 C1] (*466 2056; www.micmacmall.com*) and the relatively new **Dartmouth Crossing** [124 C1] (*445 8883; www.dartmouthcrossing.com*).

Books and maps

Indigo [124 C1] Mic Mac Mall, 41 Mic Mac Bd; 466 1640. Big store for new books, magazines, etc.

John W Doull [124 C1] 122 Main St; 429 1652, **t/f** 1 800 317 8613; www.doullbooks.com; 10.00–18.00 Mon–Sat. What was something of a Halifax used-book institution moved across the harbour in 2012. Almost 50,000 titles.

Land Registration Office [124 A2] 3rd floor, 780 Windmill Rd; 424 4083; www.gov.ns.ca/snsmr/maps/. Has detailed government-produced maps of the province & its regions.

SPORT

Canoeing and kayaking

See *Shubie Park*, **page 126.**

Diving

Torpedo Ray's Scuba Dartmouth [124 A2] 625 Windmill Rd; 481 0444, **t/f** 1 877 255 3483; www.torpedorays.com. Shore & boat dives from a range of sites around the HRM (PADI Open Water dive courses from CAN$349); full gear rental from CAN$46/day.

Markets

Dartmouth Farmers' Market [124 C4] Alderney Landing; www.alderneylanding.com/market/; 08.00–13.00 Sat (Jun–Oct 10.00–17.00 Wed). Located in the Alderney Landing complex on the Dartmouth waterfront next to the Ferry Terminal.

Gyms and fitness centres

Dartmouth Sportsplex [124 A3] 110 Wyse Rd; 464 2600; www.dartmouthsportsplex.com. Just by the MacDonald Bridge. Day pass CAN$11. Facilities include cardio theatre, weight room, lifestyle centre, walking & running track, swimming pool, ice rink & squash courts.

Swimming

YMCA 21 Woodlawn Rd; 469 9622; www.ymcahrm.ns.ca

Dartmouth Sportsplex See *Gyms and fitness centres*, above.

Winter sports For outdoor **ice skating**, Dartmouth maintains groomed surfaces at Lake Charles. There is no charge, but don't expect facilities or skate rental.

OTHER PRACTICALITIES

Libraries The most convenient is the **Alderney Gate Public Library** [124 C4] (*60 Alderney Dr; 490 5745; year-round 10.00–21.00 Mon–Thu, 10.00–17.00 Fri/Sat (winter only 14.00–17.00 Sun)*), on the waterfront right by the ferry terminal. All libraries offer internet-accessible computers.

WHAT TO SEE AND DO

Bedford Institute of Oceanography [124 A2] (*1 Challenger Dr; 426 4306; www.bio.gc.ca; May–Aug Mon–Fri by appointment only, free guided tour available 09.00–16.00 by appointment*) Don't be put off by the uninspiring exterior of this building in the shadow of the A Murray MacKay Bridge: a tour of Canada's largest oceanographic research centre will bring you a new understanding of what goes on in the nooks and crannies of the ocean floor. Learn about salvage work on the *Titanic*, and techniques used to find aircraft wreckage. Then get up close and personal with marine creatures in the touch tank. Relatively new are displays on Atlantic Canada's sharks and species at risk. To get there from downtown Halifax, take the MacKay Bridge, take the Shannon Park exit immediately after the toll gates, turn right at the Stop sign and then first left. From downtown Dartmouth, take Windmill Road to Shannon Park, or take bus #51 from Dartmouth's Bridge Terminal.

Black Cultural Centre for Nova Scotia [124 C1] (*1149 Main St; 434 6223, **t/f** 1 800 465 0767; www.bccns.com; Sep–May 10.00–17.00 Mon–Fri; Jun–Aug 10.00–17.00 Mon, Wed & Fri, 10.00–19.00 Tue & Thu, 10.00–14.00 Sat/Sun; admission CAN$6*) The first site of its kind in Canada, this museum, cultural and education centre preserves and promotes Nova Scotia's black history and culture. The centre represents black communities across the province and displays tell the story of the black Loyalists who fled the American Revolution, the Maroons who came from Jamaica in 1796, and the American slaves who arrived after the war of 1812. It is a fascinating experience for anyone interested in black and/or Nova Scotia history. Located in Dartmouth's eastern outskirts at the junction of Main Street and Cherry Brook Road, to get there go 6km east along Main Street (Highway 7) from Exit 6 of Highway 111. Take bus #61 or #68 from Dartmouth's Bridge Terminal.

Dartmouth Heritage Museum [124 D2] (*26 Newcastle St; ☎ 464 2300; www.dartmouthheritagemuseum.ns.ca; ⏱ year-round 10.00–17.00 Tue–Fri, 10.00–13.00 & 14.00–17.00 Sat (summer also 10.00–13.00 & 14.00–17.00 Sun); admission CAN$2*) This restored c1867 downtown building, also known as Evergreen House, was the home of Dr Helen Creighton, Nova Scotia's best-known folklorist (see page 81). A good first stop for those interested in Dartmouth's history.

Quaker House [124 C3] (*57 Ochterloney St; ☎ 464 2300; www.dartmouthheritagemuseum.ns.ca; ⏱ Jun–early Sep 10.00–13.00 & 14.00–17.00 Tue–Sun; admission CAN$2*) A charming restored c1785 house furnished in period style – one of the oldest known residences in the area – built by Quaker whalers. Your visit is enhanced by tales told by costumed guides.

Christ Church [124 C3] (*50 Wentworth St; ☎ 466 4270; www.christchurchdartmouth.ns.ca; ⏱ for services & by appointment*) This is the oldest church in Dartmouth. The weather vane atop its steeple depicts Halley's Comet. Close by is **Sullivan Pond** (*Prince Albert Rd*), a great place to see and feed ducks, geese and swans.

World Peace Pavilion [124 D4] (*Ferry Terminal Park; ☎ 490 4000; www.halifax.ca/attractions/peacepav/; ⏱ May–Oct 08.00–dusk daily; admission free*) Opened in 1995 by visiting foreign ministers at the G7 summit, every country that had representation in Canada was asked to contribute something to represent 'our planet and efforts to shape our future'. Over 70 countries responded, and artefacts inside the triangular pavilion include pieces from two walls (the Great one in China, and the old Berlin one), a plaque made from ammunition fragments from Slovakia and part of a dismantled nuclear missile silo from the US.

Shubie Park [80 C3–4] The park takes its name from the Shubie Canal (see box, below), and trails lead through the woods along the old canal banks. The stretch between Lake Micmac and Lake Charles has been restored, complete with one of the original locks. Many visitors take to the water in canoes and kayaks, paddling from the main day-use area to Lake Charles. The **Fairbanks Interpretive Centre** (*54 Locks Rd; ☎ 462 1826; ⏱ 08.30–16.30 Mon–Fri; admission free*) has visitor information and displays on the canal's history. Alongside the centre, the new **Kaynoe Rentals** (*☎ 240 3114; www.kaynoerentals.ca; ⏱ Jul/Aug 08.00–20.00 Tue–Sun; spring & autumn 08.00–18.00 Sat/Sun*) rents canoes and kayaks from CAN$13.50/hour. The park is best accessed by taking Braemar Drive north from Exit 6 off Highway 111.

AROUND DARTMOUTH

THE EASTERN PASSAGE From downtown Dartmouth, head south down Pleasant Street (Highway 322): you'll pass big oil refineries just after Woodside. If you continue following Shore Road, you leave the harbour and come to the open sea, with good views out to Devil's Island (see page 118) before the road dead-ends about 3km from Fisherman's Cove at Hartlen Point Forces Golf Club (see page 108). If you prefer birds to birdies, there are shore and water birds on the beach here year-round, and in spring and autumn Hartlen Point is one of the best areas to see migrants.

Getting there **Bus** #60 leaves Dartmouth's Bridge Terminal roughly every 30 minutes from 06.00 to 21.00 (fare CAN$2.25) and stops near the Aviation Museum and Fisherman's Cove.

Where to eat

✕ **Boondocks** 200 Government Wharf Rd, Fisherman's Cove; ☎ 465 3474; www.boondocksnovascotia.com; 🕘 11.00–20.00 daily. Located at a very popular summer tourist draw with indoor & alfresco dining & a fine view (over the Eastern Passage & McNab's Island), Boondocks should have a lot going for it. My last visit was soon after an ownership change, so maybe things have improved since. German-flavoured menu. Not so much 'Down in the boondocks' as 'A walk in the Black Forest'. $$

✕ **Emma's Eatery** 31 Cow Bay Rd, Eastern Passage; ☎ 406 0606; www.emmaseatery.ca; 🕘 08.00–15.00 daily. Tucked in amongst a row of shops a short hop from the tourists at Fisherman's Cove is this fun little diner. Bountiful, mouthwatering, comforting all-day b/fasts, good salads, & tasty sandwiches, sensible prices – oh, & serving staff wearing 'Eat Fish Cakes' T-shirts. 'What's not to like?' as the saying goes. $

What to see and do

Fisherman's Cove *(☎ 465 6093; www.fishermanscove.ns.ca; 🕘 May–Nov; admission free)* The Eastern Passage's biggest attraction is this restored 200-year-old fishing village set around a picturesque harbour. Although many residents make their living from fishing (primarily haddock, herring, tuna and lobster), the sea is less bountiful than it once was. The present-day version (which opened in 1996) is primarily a row of craft and gift shops (including pewter, fudge and souvenirs), and a café and restaurant. On my last visit, a number of shops seem to be closed. Smell

THE SHUBIE CANAL PROJECT

Soon after Halifax was founded, the idea to use the string of seven lakes and the Shubenacadie River between Dartmouth and Truro (see page 250) as the basis for a canal linking Halifax Harbour and the Bay of Fundy had been discussed. Seemingly endless feasibility studies and surveys were done, and construction began in July 1826. Within five years, the construction company went bust.

Construction started again in 1854, and despite financial problems, the project was completed in 1861. Nine locks and two inclined planes connected the lakes and river. Steam vessels hauled barges laden with goods along the 115km canal system.

Within a few years, problems arose. Gold was discovered at one of the lakes and a dispute arose over the validity of the title of the lands on which the canal was built. Somewhat unhelpfully, fixed bridges (rather than drawbridges or swing-bridges) were built across the canal at a couple of points, meaning that most canal shipping couldn't pass under them. These factors, plus the advantages offered by the newly booming railways put paid to the canal, and it closed in 1870.

Although it fell into disrepair, some parts of the canal have recently been restored for recreational pursuits, and these are best seen at Shubie Park.

TALLAHASSEE

In August 1864, during the American Civil War, the badly damaged Confederate blockade-runner, *Tallahassee*, limped into Halifax Harbour (a neutral port) for repairs.

Two enemy (Union) cruisers anchored off Chebucto Head, waiting for her to leave the sanctuary of the harbour. The *Tallahassee*'s captain's only chance of escape was to navigate a route through the Eastern Passage, long considered too shallow, narrow and dangerous a channel for a ship of the *Tallahassee*'s size.

All lights extinguished and with a skiff going ahead to check the depth and best course to follow, the *Tallahassee* set off under cover of darkness. Miraculously, the vessel reached the open seas undetected, and was well on her way to Wilmington before the enemy learnt of her escape.

the sea air, and be sure to wander the extensive seaside boardwalk. In season, boat trips leave for McNab's Island (see page 118).

Shearwater Aviation Museum (*13 Bonaventure Av, Shearwater Airport; ☎ 720 1083; www.shearwateraviationmuseum.ns.ca/; ⏲ Apr–May & Sep–Nov 10.00–17.00 Tue–Fri, 12.00–16.00 Sat; Jun–Aug 10.00–17.00 Mon–Fri, 12.00–16.00 Sat/Sun; Dec–Mar 10.00–17.00 Mon–Fri with reduced services; admission free*) Just off Highway 322 on the site of an active RCAF heliport, the museum chronicles Canadian Maritime military aviation from 1918. Highlights include an airworthy 1943 Fairey Swordfish HS469 biplane, and a Sikorsky HO4S-3 'Horse' helicopter operational between 1955 and 1970. Always popular is the flight simulator, which allows you to 'fly' one of a variety of aircraft from the Canadian, British and US armed forces. There are also scale models of an aircraft carrier and a helicopter-carrying destroyer, library, and obligatory gift shop.

BEDFORD

Bedford wraps around the head of Halifax Harbour. Sailors gravitate to the Bedford Basin Yacht Club; also on the waterfront, DeWolf Park is pleasant for a wander. A path follows much of the waterfront, and eventually joins an unpaved trail along the Sackville River. Admiral's Cove Park at the south end of Shore Drive was popular with rock climbers and hikers: in recent years it has also been popular with Lyme disease-carrying black-legged ticks, so is best avoided. The major shopping areas are the Sunnyside Mall and the Bedford Place Mall.

GETTING THERE Take the Bedford Highway from Halifax, or Windsor Road and then Dartmouth Road from Dartmouth. By **bus** from Halifax, take bus #80 from Upper Water Street or bus #82 from the Water Street terminal. The journey time is approximately 550 minutes; the fare is CAN$2.25.

WHERE TO EAT AND DRINK

Il Mercato Sunnyside Mall, 1595 Bedford Hwy; ☎ 832 4531; www.il-mercato.ca; ⏲ 11.00–22.00 Mon–Fri, 17.00–22.00 Sat. See page 100, for details. $$

Finbar's Irish Pub Sunnyside Mall, 1595 Bedford Hwy; ☎ 832 9170; www.finbars.ca; ⏲ 11.00–22.00 Mon–Thu, 11.00–01.00 Fri/Sat, 11.00–21.00 Sun. One of the most authentic Irish menus in the province, a well-chosen bunch of beers, & usually excellent live music. Kitchen closes 21.00 Sun–Tue, 22.00 Wed–Sat. $–$$

✕ The Chickenburger 1531 Bedford Hwy; www.thechickenburger.com; ⏲ 09.00–22.00 daily (to 23.00 Thu–Sat). They tell me that this place hasn't changed all that much since it opened in 1940. They come in droves for fresh, never frozen haddock & chips, burgers, milkshakes & (you guessed it) chicken burgers. Now, if you're expecting the chicken in the eponymous burger to be grilled (or breaded & fried) breast, you're in for a surprise. In the bun are chunks of chicken cooked to a secret recipe (not my cup of tea, but who am I to argue with this diner's popularity?). $

✕ Pete's Sunnyside Mall, 1595 Bedford Hwy; ☎ 835 4997; www.petes.ca; ⏲ 08.00–21.00 Mon–Fri, 08.00–18.00 Sat/Sun. A second location for the swish food emporium with a good take-out counter, Pete's To Go (see page 101 for the first). $

WHAT TO SEE AND DO

Hemlock Ravine Park (*Kent Av; ☎ 490 4000; ⏲ year-round; admission free*) This wonderful, rugged 75ha tract of dense old-growth forest (see box below) lies beside the western side of the Bedford Basin between the Bedford Highway and Highway 102. Some of the five interconnecting walking trails (see the map by the car park) lead through towering trees to the hemlock-filled ravine, and can be slippery when wet. By the car park is a heart-shaped pond. To reach the park, take the Bedford Highway and turn onto Kent Avenue 1km north of the Kearney Lake Road junction.

Scott Manor House (*15 Fort Sackville Rd; ☎ 832 2336; www.scottmanorhouse.ca; ⏲ Jul/Aug 10.00–16.00 daily; admission free*) This c1770 gambrel-roofed Dutch Colonial mansion is furnished with period antiques. The tea room (*⏲ Jul/Aug 14.00–16.00 daily*) is a bonus.

MY HEART BELONGS TO JULIE

When Edward, Duke of Kent, arrived in Halifax in 1794 to serve as commander-in-chief of the Halifax Garrison, he was accompanied by his French mistress, Julie de St Laurent. The two lived on Citadel Hill, but Julie was less than impressed with the view – which took in the military gallows in the middle of the parade ground. She demanded a residence with a more pleasant aspect, and Edward had an elaborate estate built, incorporating a magnificent wooden mansion (long gone), the delightful pathways that you see in Hemlock Ravine Park today, and something else that has survived – the heart-shaped Julie's Pond. The only remaining building from the original estate is the Rotunda, a round music room on a knoll overlooking the water. Supposedly one of Julie's favourite places, it is not open to the public. Edward and Julie left Nova Scotia in 1800.

Because of his royal position, Edward was unable to marry his mistress, though rumours persist that the couple had several children together. He tied the knot with a German princess and their only child became Queen Victoria. Julie lived for a while in a Paris convent, before marrying a Russian–Italian nobleman.

Incidentally, the park is said to be haunted by the ghost of the loser of a duel fought in 1795 between a colonel and a naval officer. The two were said to have over-imbibed at a grand reception hosted by Prince Edward. If you want to discuss what went wrong tactically with the colonel's ghost, he is said to (re)appear from time to time at the site of the fatal fight – near the cove south of the Rotunda – most commonly at 02.00.

4

South Shore

The province's beautiful South Shore coastline is deeply indented, with many long, narrow bays, once the haunt of privateers and pirates. With lovely sandy beaches, beautiful coastal provincial parks, pretty fishing villages, towns steeped in history and a mysterious treasure island, this region is also well served with plenty of good places to stay. Some of Nova Scotia's best restaurants – and some excellent low-budget eateries – will satisfy your hunger.

You can drive the 300km-length of Highway 103, linking Halifax and Yarmouth, in under four hours. Follow this motorway which cuts across the base of numerous peninsulas and you'll see a lot of forest, the odd lake, and (occasionally) the sea off in the distance. Getting the most from the South Shore is not about speeding from town to town by the fastest route, but by giving yourself plenty of time to enjoy the historic streetscapes and what lies along – and off – the countless scenic backroads.

With enough time, you can go birding on Cape Sable Island or kayak between hundreds of beautiful islands in Mahone Bay. Sip a coffee and mingle with the yachting crowd in a Chester café. Wander the hilly streets of absorbing Lunenburg,

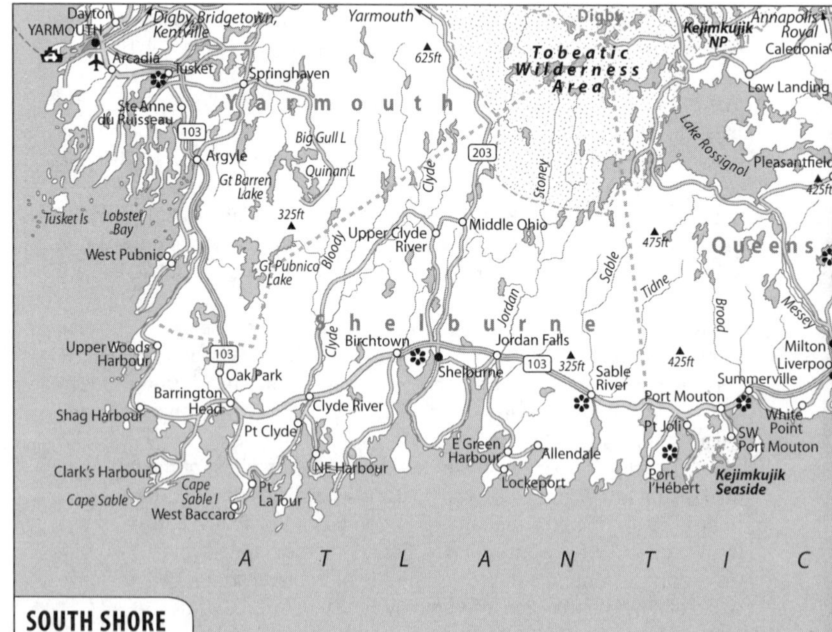

established in 1753 and the best-surviving example of a planned British colonial settlement in North America. Rent a bike to explore the surrounding forested peninsulas and inlets. Join the throngs at Peggy's Cove – or other pretty fishing villages that see virtually no visitors. Soak up the sun and breeze on magnificent sandy beaches, particularly around Liverpool, or take a ferry back in time to the Tancook Islands. Experience Acadian life past and present in the Pubnicos, and take to the dance floor at Hubbards' Shore Club. Whereas the majority of the sites and attractions are found on – or close to – the coast, heading inland on Highway 203, just west of Shelburne, leads to the huge expanse of the remote Tobeatic Wilderness Area, a dream come true for experienced back-country explorers.

Until the end of November 2012, Halifax, Yarmouth – and many of the communities in between – were connected by a daily (in each direction) coach service. At one stage, it looked as though the South Shore would be coach-less, but then Maritime Bus (see page 44) stepped in and announced a three to four day a week limited service between Halifax and Bridgewater. Those without their own transport wishing to travel between Bridgewater and Yarmouth will have to rely on shuttle services (see *Chapter 2*, page 57) or lifts from friends.

TERENCE BAY, LOWER PROSPECT AND PROSPECT

These working fishing villages have very few services and, unlike Peggy's Cove (see page 132), see very few visitors. Just before you reach Prospect, a right turn, Indian Point Road, offers parking on the left. From the end of this short road, is an old Mi'kmaq trail which leads 3km along the coast offering wonderful views.

These communities are off Highway 333 on either side of Prospect Bay, both 32km from Halifax. Terence Bay, to the east, is 17km from Prospect. No public transport serves Terence Bay and the Prospects.

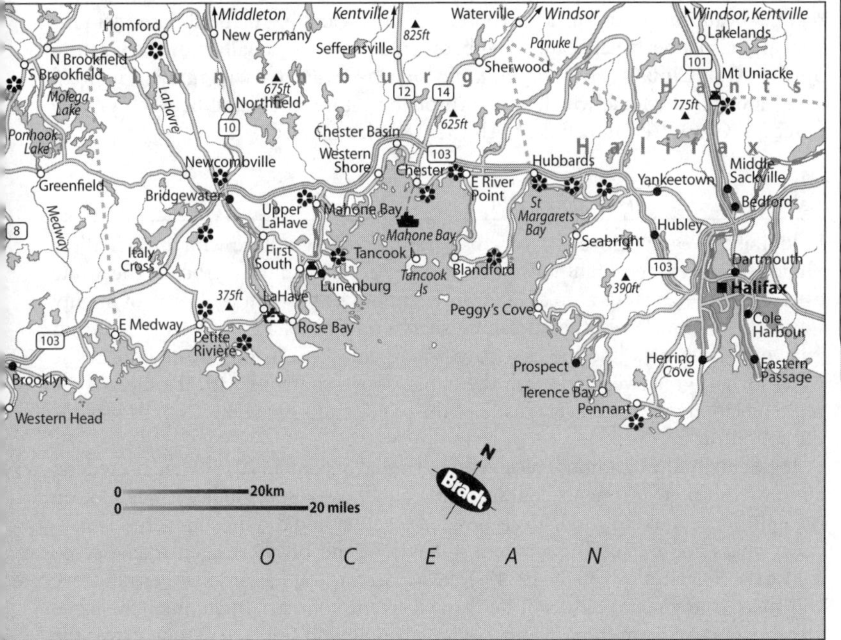

SS *ATLANTIC*

In 1873, almost 40 years before the RMS *Titanic* disaster, another White Star vessel was involved in what was at that time the greatest loss of life in a single north Atlantic tragedy. *En route* from Liverpool, England, to New York, the SS *Atlantic* ran aground on Mar's Head, just off Lower Prospect, on 1 April 1873. Although 390 of the 952 people on board survived, all but one (12-year-old John Hindley, from Lancashire) of the 156 women and 189 children on board lost their lives. At least half of the victims are believed to have been interred in a mass grave at Terence Bay.

WHAT TO SEE AND DO Set against a beautiful oceanfront backdrop, the **SS *Atlantic* Heritage Park and Interpretation Centre** (*180 Sandy Cove Rd, Terence Bay; ☎ 852 1557; www.ssatlantic.com; ⏲ (park) year-round (centre) mid May–early Oct 10.00–17.00; admission free*) mixes the rugged beauty of the local landscape with a tone of solemn remembrance for the lives lost in the SS *Atlantic* tragedy (see box, below), and the triumph of the human spirit in the rescue of the survivors. The interpretation centre includes records from the ship and recovered artefacts from the wreck, and information on other local history. In addition to a monument in memory of the victims are picnic tables, a boardwalk and a trail with interpretive panels.

It is well worth a visit to the **Suezan Aikins Studio** (*26 Cove Rd, Prospect Village; ☎ 852 3154; www.suezan-aikins.com; ⏲ by appointment*) – Suezan's work, including goldleaf/mixed media relief carvings and woodblock prints – are world class. For those interested in getting outdoors, the **East Coast Outfitters** (*2017 Lower Prospect Rd, Lower Prospect; ☎ 852 2567, **t/f** 1 877 852 2567; www.eastcoastoutfitters.com; ⏲ May–Oct*) offers guided sea kayak trips (*2hrs–multi-day*) to explore the region's beautiful coastline. They can customise a camping or B&B-based trip for you, and also offer kayak, canoe and bike rental. Golfers can all enjoy the **Granite Springs Golf Club** (*4441 Prospect Rd, Bayside; ☎ 852 4653; www.granitespringsgolf.com*), a 6,460yd course which winds through mature forest and between granite outcrops. Green fees: nine holes CAN$32, 18 holes CAN$63.

PEGGY'S COVE *(Population: 120)*

Indubitably, Peggy's Cove is a very picturesque fishing village with an incredibly photogenic octagonal lighthouse overlooking a perfect little harbour. The white c1914 lighthouse stands atop granite worn smooth by thousands of years of mighty waves. Just below it, weathered fishing shacks on stilts, stacks of lobster pots and piles of fishing nets line the tiny cove where colourful fishing boats bob in the water. Bright green vegetation on the banks above contrasts with the blue of the sea. The lapping of the waves, rustle of the wind, and squawking seagulls provide the soundtrack.

Incidentally, the lighthouse received a fresh coat of paint in 2012: when the federal and provincial governments couldn't agree on whose responsibility it was to keep the lighthouse looking good, locals bonded together and did the job themselves.

So what's not to like? The problem is that this is no 'off-the-beaten-track' secret. T Morris Longstreth wrote in 1934's *To Nova Scotia*: 'I am afraid that Peggy's Cove will meet a tragic end. She will be thrown to the tourists.' In summer the same pleasure you get from thinking how quiet, unspoilt and (relatively) tourist-free the rest of Nova Scotia is can be soured by having to share the beauty of this little village with hordes of other visitors, many of whom arrive by the busload. That doesn't mean that the place is swamped with tacky souvenir shops or rip-off bars, restaurants and hotels: on the contrary, services are limited. There's an interesting gallery, a craft shop or two, a restaurant, a couple of ice cream shops – and two car parks to cater for a lot of visitors.

You might be lucky and find that your visit doesn't coincide with the tour buses, but to escape the worst of the crowds – and perhaps take advantage of the most beautiful light – get here early, or stay late. The busiest times are between about 08.30 and 17.15. This is, of course, easier to do if you're overnighting here or nearby. Take great care if exploring the smooth granite rocks by the sea – even when things appear calm, large waves can strike without warning. It might be worthwhile bringing shoes with a good grip.

WHO WAS PEGGY?

Around 1845, a schooner *en route* from England was wrecked off the cove. Everyone was swept overboard and lost except a child who was washed ashore, taken in by a local family and given the name Margaret. Eventually she married a local and became known as 'Peggy of the Cove'. Incidentally, the couple are later said to have moved to North Dakota, USA – a long way from the sea!

GETTING THERE Peggy's Cove is approximately 45 minutes (44km/27 miles) **by car** from Halifax. Take Highway 333 (passing the turn-offs for Terence Bay, the Prospects and the Dovers), or Highway 103 to Exit 5, Highway 213 towards Tantallon, and then Highway 333. Better still: combine the two routes to make a loop.

En route to Peggy's Cove once you are out of Halifax, Highway 333 is also called Prospect Road. From Peggy's Cove to Upper Tantallon the stretch of Highway 333 which runs up the scenic west side of St Margaret's Bay is called Peggy's Cove Road.

By bus, Ambassatours/Gray Line (*423 6242,* **t/f** *1 800 565 7173; www.ambassatours.com*) run a three-hour tour between June and mid October departing from Halifax at 13.00 on Monday, Wednesday, Friday and Saturday. Note that you get no more than 90 minutes at the cove. Tickets cost CAN$52.

WHERE TO STAY Peggy's Cove B&B is in the village, and the Oceanstone within 5km (five minutes' drive).

FLIGHT 111

Over the centuries, countless lives have been lost in shipwrecks off Nova Scotia's coast. But in September 1998, it was an aircraft crashing into the Atlantic that resulted in the loss of 229 lives. There were no survivors from Swissair Flight 111 *en route* from New York to Geneva: the crash was said to have been caused as a result of a spark from a damaged wire igniting insulation material in the aircraft's in-flight entertainment system. The aircraft went down approximately 9km out to sea. Two memorials were erected. One is just off Highway 333, 2km west of Peggy's Cove (and offers a magnificent view back towards the village); the other is just off Highway 329, 100m past Bayswater Beach Provincial Park (see page 139).

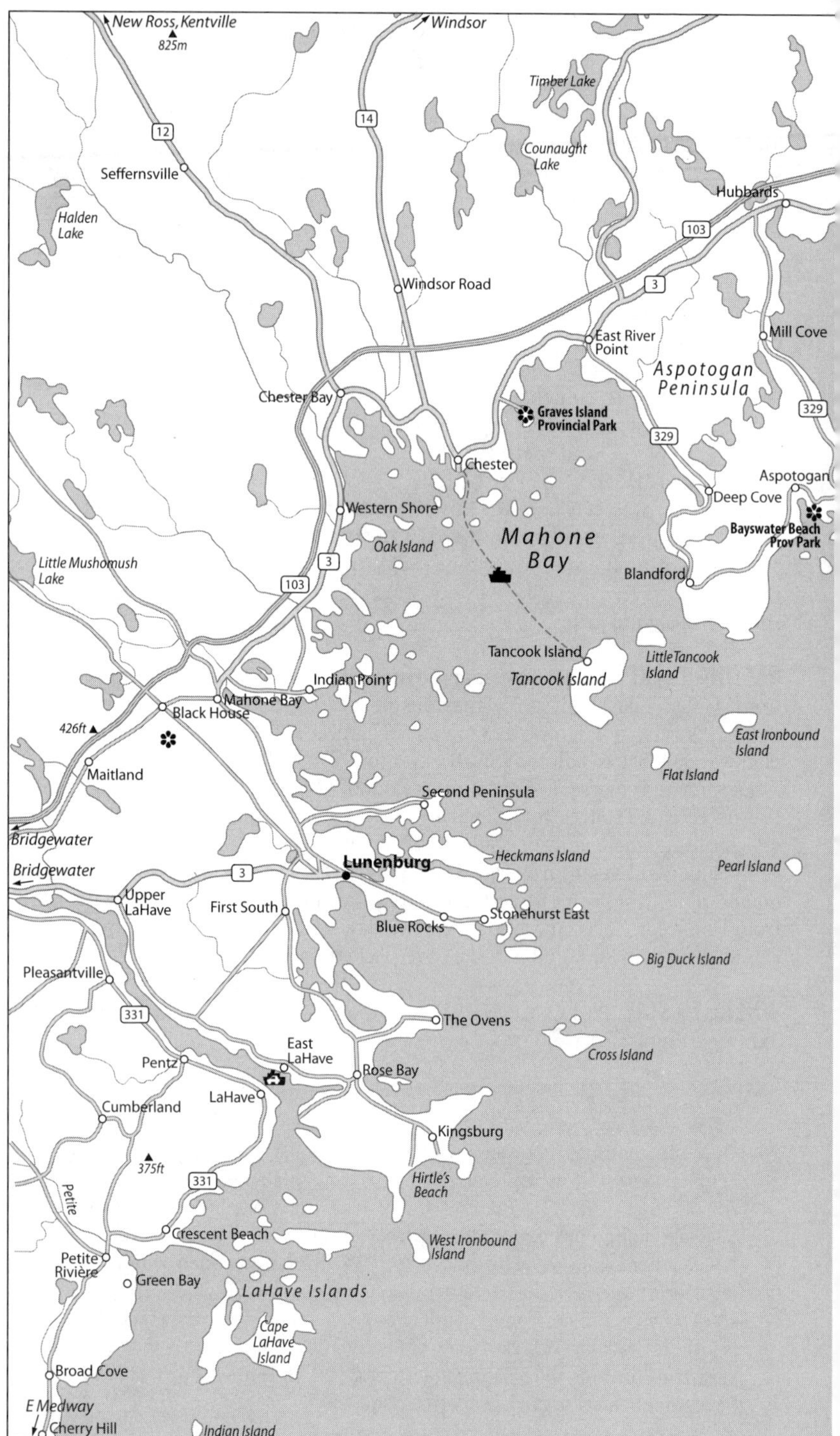
New Ross, Kentville
825m
Windsor
Timber Lake
12
14
Counaught Lake
Seffernsville
Hubbards
Halden Lake
103
3
Windsor Road
East River Point
Mill Cove
Aspotogan Peninsula
Chester Bay
Graves Island Provincial Park
329
Chester
Aspotogan
Deep Cove
Western Shore
Bayswater Beach Prov Park
Oak Island
Mahone Bay
Little Mushomush Lake
Blandford
103
Tancook Island
Little Tancook Island
Indian Point
Tancook Island
Mahone Bay
Black House
426ft
East Ironbound Island
Maitland
Flat Island
Second Peninsula
Bridgewater
Heckmans Island
Lunenburg
Pearl Island
Bridgewater
Upper LaHave
First South
Stonehurst East
Blue Rocks
Big Duck Island
Pleasantville
331
The Ovens
East LaHave
Cross Island
Pentz
Rose Bay
LaHave
Cumberland
Kingsburg
375ft
Hirtle's Beach
Petite
Crescent Beach
West Ironbound Island
Petite Rivière
Green Bay
LaHave Islands
Cape LaHave Island
Broad Cove
E Medway
Cherry Hill
Indian Island

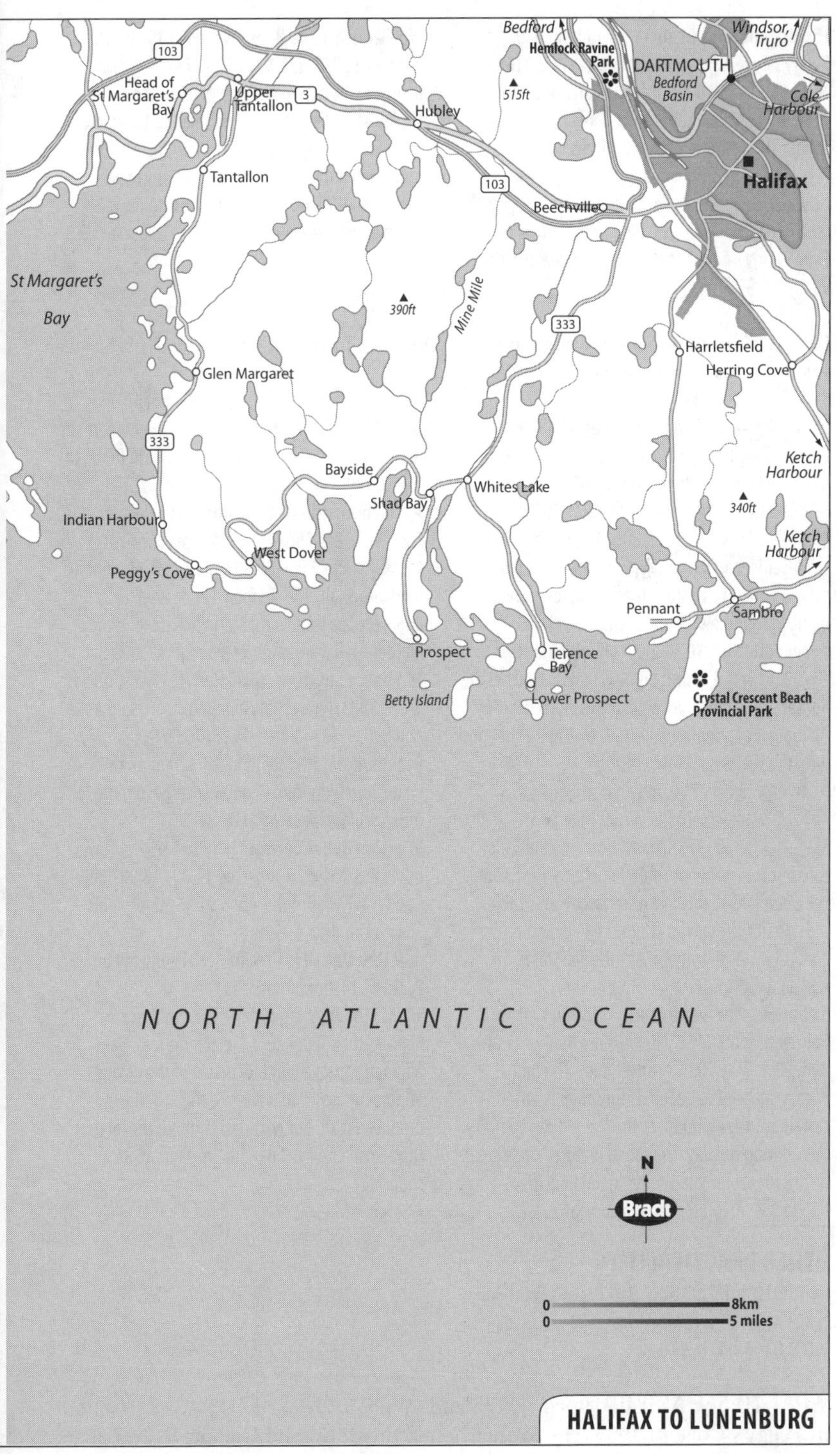

HALIFAX TO LUNENBURG

Oceanstone Resort (17 units) 8650 Peggy's Cove Rd, Indian Harbour; 823 2160, t/f 1 866 823 2160; e info@oceanstoneresort.com; www.oceanstoneresort.com; year-round. The resort – with inn rooms, 6 suites & 8 1-, 2- & 3-bedroom cottages – is located on a private beach. Good, upmarket on-site restaurant (see *Rhubarb*, opposite). Less than 5 mins' drive from Peggy's Cove – turn left when leaving the village. **$$**

Peggy's Cove B&B (5 rooms) 19 Church Rd; 823 2265, t/f 1 877 725 8732; e stay@peggyscovebb.com; www.peggyscovebb.com; Apr–Oct. Bearing in mind the fabulous picture-postcard setting, Judy & Dan's comfortable B&B, housed in a restored fisherman's home once owned by William deGarthe, offers good value. Bedrooms have private decks. Full b/fast inc. **$$**

WHERE TO EAT The Sou'wester and Dee Dee's are in the village, but within 5km – five minutes' drive – are other options:

Rhubarb at Oceanstone Resort 8650 Peggy's Cove Rd, Indian Harbour; 821 3500, 402 3163; www.oceanstoneresort.com; summer 07.30–21.00 daily; winter 17.00–21.30 Thu/Fri, 10.00–14.00 & 17.00–21.30 Sat/Sun. Fine-dining, eg: sesame-crusted chicken *paillard* (escalope) served with orzo pasta & Thai red sauce, or maple planked salmon with succotash, fennel slaw & sweet potato mash. Round it off with a slice of chocolate Grand Marnier mousse torte. Lunches are lighter – eg: lobster focaccia or seafood chowder. All main ingredients are local, & the menu changes with the seasons. **$$$**

Ryer's 5 Ryer's Rd, Indian Harbour; 823 1070; Jan–Apr 10.00–17.00 Thu–Sun; May–Dec 10.00–17.00 daily. Not a restaurant or café but somewhere to stop for lobster fresh from the pound. Available live or cooked. Picnic tables outside (for those who choose the 'cooked' option). Forget lobster thermidor, bisque, etc: this is the real deal. **$$**

Sou'wester Restaurant 178 Peggy's Point Rd; 823 2561; Jun–Sep 08.00–21.00 daily; Oct–May 10.00–sunset daily. The hordes of tourists need to be fed, & this huge licensed restaurant tries hard to do the job – it can get very busy during the day. The menu features traditional dishes (eg: Solomon Gundy), good pan-fried haddock & an interesting baked beans & fish hash. Dessert fans should try the homemade gingerbread served warm with ice cream (or go to Dee Dee's!). **$$**

Harbourside Restaurant 8369 Peggy's Cove Rd; 823 1908; www.theharbourside.ca; May–Oct 12.00–20.30 daily. Good, diner-style food, especially the seafood. For dessert, the apple pie is a stand-out. Magnificent views of St Margaret's Bay from upper-floor deck. **$–$$**

Shaw's Landing 6958 Hwy 333, West Dover; 823 1843; www.shawslanding.ca; mid Apr–mid Oct 11.00–18.00 daily (to 20.00 in season). Beautifully located seafood restaurant on the waterfront 4km from Peggy's Cove. Save room for the chocolate macaroon pie. **$–$$**

Fisherman's Corner Hwy 333 & West Dover Rd; 233 2044; Jun–Sep 11.00–18.00 daily. Good fish & chips take-out a stone's throw from Shaw's Landing. **$**

Dee Dee's Ice Cream 110 Peggy's Point Rd; 221 6614; http://deedees.ca; mid Jun–Aug 11.00–18.00 (or later) daily; May/mid Jun & Sep weather dependent. Delectable ice cream emanates from a window in one of the village's original houses. You pay more than for the mass-produced stuff, but buttered almond, chocolate, Nova Scotia berry, & banana cardamom are all superb!

OTHER PRACTICALITIES

Tourist information 109 Peggy's Point Rd; 823 2253; mid May–Oct 09.00–17.00 daily; Jul/Aug to 19.00 daily

WHAT TO SEE AND DO Born in Finland, William deGarthe (1903–83) settled in Peggy's Cove in 1955. His former home, the **deGarthe Gallery** (*823 2256;*

⌚ *mid May–mid Oct 19.00–17.00 daily; admission free*), just across the road from the tourist information office car park, now houses over 60 of his paintings and sculptures, most nautically themed. In the 1970s, he began carving a frieze on a granite outcropping on his property. Although he died before completing the project, the 30m memorial to the local fishermen and their families is still very impressive.

TANTALLON

The last of several pretty communities strung out along Peggy's Cove Road, Tantallon is 22km from Peggy's Cove **by car**, and is located 7km from Exit 5 of Highway 103.

WHERE TO EAT Grab a smoked meat deli sandwich, a (good) coffee or one of a fine selection of sweet treats – or all of the above – at **White Sails Bakery & Deli** (*12930 Peggy's Cove Rd;* ☎ *826 1966; www.whitesailsbakery.com;* ⌚ *10.00–19.00 Mon–Sat, 10.00–18.00 Sun;* **$**) and enjoy them whilst sitting at one of the café's picnic tables on the waterfront. A word of caution: drivers and cyclists should take extra care when turning into or leaving the café driveway against the traffic.

WHAT TO SEE AND DO Don't miss **ABC: Antiques, Books & Collectibles** (*12723 Peggy's Cove Rd;* ☎ *826 1128; www.abcantiques.ca*); the shop name says it all. For outdoor adventures, **Sea Sun Kayak Island Coast Adventures** (*148 Nautical Way (at Shining Waters Marine);* ☎ *850 7732,* **t/f** *1 866 775 2925; www.paddlenovascotia.com;* ⌚ *May–Oct*) offers guided sea kayak tours and overnight trips on and around the pristine waters of St Margaret's Bay. Kayak, canoe and camping equipment rentals also available as well as coastal hiking.

HUBBARDS

If you're looking for a base from which to explore Peggy's Cove, Lunenburg, and even Halifax (about a 50-minute drive away), Hubbards – 'the playground of St Margaret's Bay' – isn't a bad choice. Whilst there are no real sights here, the atmosphere is relaxed, there are good (and varied) places to stay and eat, quite a bit going on in summer, and several beaches within easy reach. By far the busiest of these is Queensland Beach: the beach at Cleveland tends to be quieter, and Hubbards itself has a large, popular, white-sand beach with relatively warm water. Accessible **by car**, Hubbards is on Highway 3, less than 2km from Highway 103 Exit 6. It is 50km from Halifax and 50km from Lunenburg.

KEEP ON DANCIN'

In August 1946, a dance was held to mark the opening of the newly built Shore Club. Was it a success? Well, dances have been held there every summer Saturday night since. Nova Scotia's last dance hall is still going strong, and is a really fun experience. The building is also the location of another Maritime institution, the Lobster Supper (see *Where to stay and eat* overleaf).

WHERE TO STAY AND EAT

Dauphinee Inn (6 rooms) 167 Shore Club Rd; ☎ 857 1790, **t/f** 1 800 567 1790; www.dauphineeinn.com; ⌚ May–Oct. In a beautiful waterfront setting, away from the main road, offering rooms decorated with period antiques. The licensed dining room (⏲ *mid Jun–early Oct 16.00–21.00 daily; Jul/Aug 10.00–14.00 Sat/Sun;* $$) is fine but the waterside deck is far better, especially for sunset. The seafood is always good, but a big draw is 'Hot Rock dining'. Super-heated granite rocks are brought to your table for you to cook your meat, poultry or fish main course. Continental b/fast inc, full b/fast at extra cost. **$$**

Hubbards Beach Campground & Cottages (16 units) 226 Shore Club Rd; ☎ 857 9460; www.hubbardsbeach.com; ⏲ mid May–Sep. Rustic but comfortable 1- to 3-bedroom cottages (many on the lagoon front). The campground has 129 sites with full-service motorhome sites & water-only tent sites. All in walking distance of one of the best sandy beaches in the region. There's a laundromat, too. **$$**

Shore Club Lobster Suppers 250 Shore Club Rd; ☎ 857 9555; www.lobstersupper.com; ⏲ mid May–mid Oct 16.00–20.00 Wed–Sun. Held in the huge, historic Shore Club Dance Hall (see box, page 137). Choose from 3 sizes of lobster, steak, chicken & a vegetarian pasta dish. Price includes salad bar, unlimited mussels, dessert & coffee/tea. Licensed. $$$–$$$$

Trellis Café 22 Main St (Hwy 3); ☎ 857 1188; www.trelliscafe.com; ⏲ year-round 08.00–21.00 daily. The seafood is fresh & very good – whether as chowder, fishcakes or pan-fried haddock – & the mile-high clubhouse sandwich is also recommended. Baked goods – such as bumbleberry crisp, coconut cream pie, or huge cinnamon buns – & bread are homemade & very tasty. Sit in or out. Licensed; regular live music. $$

FESTIVALS A **Lobster Festival** is held over a weekend in **May.** At the **Canada Day Ceilidh on the Cove** at the **beginning of July** and the beginning of August, there is music, Irish dancing, a family barbecue and fireworks at dusk. The **World Tuna Flat Races** is held at the end of July/early August. A 'tuna flat' is a cumbersome boat: teams of four rowers compete in the waters of Hubbards Cove to a backdrop of music and barbecues. At **Pumpkinfest** in October, a day of pumpkin-related activities takes place, plus competitions such as pumpkin-seed spitting.

OTHER PRACTICALITIES

$ **Bank** Scotiabank, Hubbards Shopping Centre, Hwy 3; ☎ 857 3333; ⏲ 10.00–15.00 Mon–Wed, 10.00–17.00 Thu/Fri

Library JD Shatford Memorial Library, 10353 St Margaret's Bay Rd, Hwy 3; ☎ 857 9176; ⏲ 11.00–17.00 Tue, 15.00–21.00 Wed, 18.00–21.00 Thu, 10.00–13.00 Fri, 10.00–14.00 Sat

Post office 10369 St Margaret's Bay Rd, Hwy 3; ⏲ 08.00–17.30 Mon–Fri, 08.30–12.30 Sat

Tourist information 103 Highway 3; ☎ 857 3249; ⏲ late May–mid Oct 09.00–17.00 daily. There is also a tourist office further east in Upper Tantallon (*5210 Hwy 3; ☎ 490 4000; ⏲ mid May–mid Oct 09.00–18.00 daily*) near the junction of Highways 3 & 333.

WHAT TO SEE AND DO This **farmers' market** (*Hubbards Barn & Community Park, 57 Hwy 3; ☎ 229 1717; www.hubbardsfarmersmarket.com; ⏲ May–late Oct 08.00–12.00 Sat (Jul/Aug also 10.00–12.00 Sun)*) is well worth a visit: less than 2km to the east and just off Highway 3, Bishop's Park is a good picnic spot.

Although the first visitors began to pour in when the doors first opened in 2012, the official opening of the

HIS ROYAL SAVIOUR

It is said that Prince George – later King George V, and grandfather of the Queen – nearly died in a swimming accident in 1883. Serving on the HMS *Canada*, he took some time off and went angling in Dauphinee Mill Lake, west of Hubbards. After fishing, he fell into the lake and was struggling until rescued by his guide.

Hooked Rug Museum of North America (*9849 Hwy 3; ☎ 858 3060, 275 5222; www.hookedrugmuseumnovascotia.org; ⏲ check website for opening times*) is scheduled for the summer of 2013. It aims to preserve the heritage craft of hand-hooked rugs and their evolution into fine art. Don't miss the floating gallery featuring Noah's Ark and 104 hand-hooked animals.

ASPOTOGAN PENINSULA

Just past Hubbards, consider a detour from Highway 3: Highway 329 takes you around the rugged, beautiful Aspotogan Peninsula which separates St Margaret's Bay from Mahone Bay. 'Aspotogan' derives from the Mi'kmaq language and means 'Where they block passageways for eels'. The drive around the peninsula is approximately 44km. You'll pass fishing villages (of which **Northwest Cove** is the prettiest), lovely **Bayswater Beach**, another memorial to Swissair Flight 111 (see box, page 133), and more wonderful ocean views.

Near **Blandford**, the largest community on the peninsula, and the former home of a whaling station, there are views across to East Ironbound Island (see box, below).

WHERE TO EAT Blandford's **The Deck** (*9 Firehall Rd; ☎ 228 2112; ⏲ year-round 06.00–21.00 Mon–Fri, 09.00–21.00 Sat/Sun;* **$**), a general store and licensed café (superb coconut cream pie), is your best bet for a bite to eat.

CHESTER (*Population: approx 1,200*)

On the waterfront at the northern head of beautiful island-dotted Mahone Bay, Chester enjoys a delightful setting. Whilst specific sights are limited to one museum, it's a great place to take in a performance at the theatre, enjoy the Front Harbour waterfront and browse the trendy upmarket shops, watch the yachts on the beautiful bay, play golf, wander the shady, quiet, tree-lined residential streets past elegant (and particularly expensive) mansions, admire the beautifully kept gardens, or just unwind with a coffee and pastry.

Chester has long been popular with Americans: with all the shiny, sleek yachts replacing the usual rugged fishing boats, it feels more sophisticated – and American – than most of the province's seafront communities. The town's population almost doubles during the summer months.

HISTORY Chester was first settled in 1759, predominantly by New England Planters. A blockhouse – with 20 cannons on the roof – was erected soon after to deter hostile Mi'kmaq from entering the settlement. Two of the original mid 18th-century cannons are now mounted outside the Legion Hall. It is recorded that porcupine and baked beaver were two dishes popular with early settlers.

The village prospered, initially as a result of fishing. Chester's first hotel was built in 1827, and several

ROCKBOUND

East Ironbound Island is best known as the setting for a 1928 novel by Frank Parker Day. *Rockbound* gives a wonderfully authentic picture of the lives of those farming and fishing on the island. When published, it has to be said that the islanders were far from happy with the way their lives had been portrayed.

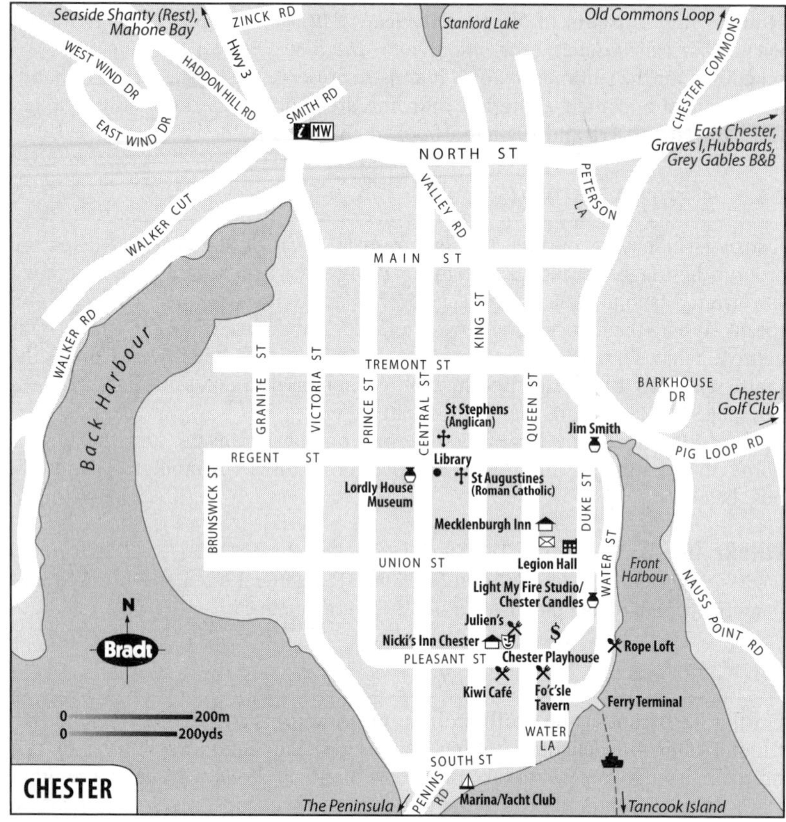

more followed. In the mid 19th century, John Wister, an American from Philadelphia, stopped here *en route* between Yarmouth and Halifax and fell in love with the place. He built a summer home and a yacht, invited his friends over, and they did the same. From such simple beginnings, Chester became known as the 'American town'.

GETTING THERE Accessible **by car**, Chester is on Highway 3, and about 5km/ 3 miles from Highway 103 Exit 8. It is 67km/42 miles from Halifax and 31km/ 19 miles from Lunenburg. **Trius Tours** (see page 44) plans to stop in Chester

SAVED BY THE BELLES

In 1782, three American privateer ships sailed into the harbour and opened fire on the settlement. Shots were exchanged. Knowing that the militia was away from the village and fearing a land attack, something had to be done. The women of the town turned their capes inside out to show their red linings (at the time, the British militia wore red coats), picked up muskets and broomsticks, and marched through the village. Watching from a distance, the privateers were fooled and decided to leave in search of easier pickings, sacking Lunenburg (see page 149) the next day.

three or four days per week *en route* between Halifax and Bridgewater. A **ferry** service connects Chester with the Tancook Islands (see page 143).

WHERE TO STAY

Gray Gables (3 rooms) 19 Graves Island Rd; 275 2000; e graygables@bellaliant.net; www.graygables.ca; year-round. Lovely, spacious house with big veranda on hillside overlooking Mahone Bay. Outdoor hot tub. Close to the golf course, approx 3.5km from 'downtown' Chester. Rate inc full b/fast (off-season continental b/fast). **$$**

Mecklenburgh Inn (4 rooms) 78 Queen St; 275 4638; www.mecklenburghinn.ca; May–Dec. A shipwright-built, eclectically decorated c1902 hillside property with fine sea views from covered balconies. Full gourmet b/fast inc (the hostess is a Cordon Bleu chef). **$$**

Nicki's Inn Chester (3 suites) 28 Pleasant St; 275 4342; www.nickisinn.com; Apr–mid Dec. 2 suites have small balconies, & the largest a double jacuzzi. Nicki Butler's restaurant (see below) is a good dinner option. **$$**

Grave's Island Provincial Park Campground (84 sites) Hwy 3; www.novascotiaparks.ca/parks/gravesisland.asp; mid May–early Oct. A pleasant campground with open & wooded sites. **$**

WHERE TO EAT AND DRINK

Nicki's Inn Chester 28 Pleasant St; 275 4342; www.nickisinn.com; Apr–mid Dec 17.00–21.00 Thu–Sun (Jul–Sep Wed–Sun). Nicki Butler's elegant but inviting restaurant offers traditional English roast dinners – on Sun evenings. On other nights, the regularly changing menu might include chargrilled beef tenderloin on truffle polenta cake, or planked Atlantic salmon on sweetcorn risotto. Well-chosen wine list. **$$$**

Rope Loft 36 Water St; 275 3430; www.ropeloft.com; May–Oct 11.30–22.00 daily (pub until midnight). Restaurant & pub with great location right by the ferry wharf on Front Harbour. Good pub food with a seafood bias (the coconut shrimp makes a great starter). **$$–$$$**

Chester Golf Club Golf Course Rd, Prescott Pt; 275 4543; www.chestergolfclub.ca; summer 08.00–21.00 Mon–Sat, 08.00–20.00 Sun; check off-season hours. Fab golf apart, it's worth coming to the course for food that is way above par. Good sandwiches & wraps, & mains such as seafood crêpes & poached salmon. Sometimes used for functions so check in advance. **$$**

Fo'c'sle Tavern 42 Queen St; 275 1408; from 11.00 Mon–Sat, from 12.00 Sun. Nova Scotia's oldest rural tavern: wood floors, upscale pub food (eg: stuffed haddock), good beer selection (try the Garrison-brewed Fo'c'sle Ale), occasional live music. Closing time varies from 19.30 on a quiet winter day to 02.00 on a summer w/end. **$$**

Seaside Shanty 5315 Hwy 3; 275 2246; www.seasideshantyrestaurant.com; May–Oct 11.30–20.00 daily (Jul–Aug until 21.00). With a shaded deck right by the water, this understated, licensed restaurant has excellent fresh seafood, including (4 kinds of) very good chowder. **$$**

Julien's 43 Queen St; 275 2324; 08.00–17.00 Tue–Sun. A French-style café very popular for pastries, desserts & fresh bread. Good brunch spot. **$–$$**

Kiwi Café 19 Pleasant St; 275 1492; www.kiwicafechester.com; year-round 08.00–17.00 daily (often later on Fri eves). Bright, welcoming, even a bit funky, this friendly licensed café has a fire for cool winter days & an outdoor eating area in warmer months. Local & natural produce used where possible. All-day b/fasts, soups, sandwiches, more substantial meals & baked (including gluten-free) goodies are all worthwhile. The lobster roll (served on a *brioche*) is a winner. **$–$$**

EVENTS Under the auspices of the Chester Yacht Club, the big event of the year is the **Chester Race Week** (*www.chesterraceweek.com*), the largest keel-boat regatta in Atlantic Canada, held in mid August. The first documented regatta was held here in 1856 and attracted crowds of over 3,000. These days, the parties and events are every bit as important as the races. A must for sailors and socialites.

OTHER PRACTICALITIES

Library Zoe Valle Library, 63 Regent St; 275 2190; www.chesterbound.com/zoevalle.htm; hours vary (see website)

$ Bank Scotiabank, 2 Pleasant St; 275 3540; 10.00–17.00 Mon–Fri

Post office 76 Queen St; 08.30–17.00 Mon–Fri, 08.00–12.00 Sat

Tourist information 3996 North St; 275 4616; Jun 10.00–17.00 daily; Jul/Aug 09.00–19.00 daily; Sep 10.00–17.00 daily; Oct–May 11.00–16.00 Thu–Sun. Housed in the old train station just off Highway 3 on the south side of town.

WHAT TO SEE AND DO The **Lordly House Museum and Park** (*133 Central St; 275 3842; www.chester-municipal-heritage-society.ca; mid Jun–mid Sep 10.00–17.00 Tue–Sat, 13.00–16.00 Sun; admission free*) is a fine, virtually unchanged, restored c1806 Georgian-style house in lovely park grounds. It was home to Charles Lordly, the district's first municipal clerk, and adjacent is a restored cottage, which was – in the late 1800s – Chester's first municipal office. It has survived virtually unchanged with many original features intact. In addition to displays on Lordly and family, there is a section on the 'butterbox babies' (see box, below). There is also a genealogy research section and children's playground.

Candle-making studio and gift store, the **Light My Fire Studio/Chester Candles** (*59 Duke St; 275 5800, t/f 1 866 739 5800; www.chestercandles.com; Jun–Sep & Dec 10.00–17.00 Mon–Sat, 11.00–16.00 Sun, rest of year 10.00–17.00 Thu–Sat, 11.00–16.00 Sun*), holds (wax) workshops and classes. Also check out the lyrical ceramics at **Jim Smith – Fine Studio Pottery** (*Cnr Water & Duke sts; 275 3272; www.jimsmithstudio.com; Jun–Sep 10.00–18.00 Mon–Sat, 12.00–18.00 Sun; Oct–May by chance or appointment*).

The **Chester Playhouse** (*22 Pleasant St; 275 3933, t/f 1 800 363 7529; www.chesterplayhouse.ca*) is a small theatre which hosts a range of music, theatre and more between early spring and late autumn.

Mainland Nova Scotia has many beautiful, scenic golf courses, and the 6,080yd **Chester Golf Course** (*Golf Course Rd, Prescott Pt; 275 4543; www.chestergolfclub.ca; May–Oct*) is one of the best. When the sun is out, magnificent views of the bay and islands will either inspire your game or make you lose concentration. Green fees: nine holes CAN$40, 18 holes CAN$70.

A pretty, often breezy park 3km east of Chester, **Grave's Island Provincial Park** (*Hwy 3; www.novascotiaparks.ca/parks/gravesisland.asp; mid May–early Oct*) can be reached by a short causeway. Good picnic spot, small beach, playground, trails and campground (see page 141).

BUTTERBOX BABIES

In the late 1920s, Lila and William Young started up a maternity home in east Chester. Most of those using their services were unwed mothers who paid the Youngs to adopt and care for their babies. The Youngs set up what was effectively a black market for babies: those who could pay thousands of dollars could have their pick of the babies in the Youngs' care.

But there was an even more disturbing twist: many babies were deemed 'undesirable', and on these, the Youngs had no desire to waste time or resources. It is thought that hundreds of tiny tragic victims were slowly starved to death and their bodies disposed of in wooden boxes used for packing butter.

TEAZER

In 1813, American privateer ships regularly threatened marine traffic off Nova Scotia's shores. One such vessel, *Young Teazer*, was chased into Mahone Bay by a British ship and was trapped. But rather than be captured, one of the crew threw a flaming brand through the magazine hatch. The resulting explosion was felt and seen by hundreds of people around the bay and most on board were killed instantly. Almost 200 years later, there are regular reports of supposed sightings of the ghost of the *Young Teazer* sailing through Mahone Bay before exploding into a ball of fire.

AROUND CHESTER

TANCOOK ISLANDS Take a trip back in time to the two Tancook Islands at the mouth of Mahone Bay, a 55-minute ferry ride from Chester. Both islands offer **walking trails**, good **birding**, and peace and quiet. You can rent bikes 200m from the ferry terminal on the larger island at **Tancook Bicycle Rentals** (*696 Big Tancook Island Rd;* **e** *tancookbikes@eastlink.ca;* ⌚ *mid May–mid Oct*). The passenger ferry makes between one and four crossings a day (⌚ *times vary: they are posted at the ferry terminal or check with the Chester tourist information office; CAN$5.25 return*). If you're thinking of visiting, www.tancook.ca is a valuable resource.

Where to stay and eat Little Tancook has no services, but the larger island (approximately 4.5km long and 1.5km wide) offers eat-in or take-out at **Carolyn's Restaurant** (*656 Tancook Island Rd;* ☎ *228 2749;* ⌚ *Jun–Oct 11.30–21.00 daily;* **$–$$**). For overnighters, accommodation choices are wilderness camping or perhaps a private rental.

NEW ROSS New Ross – located approximately 31km inland from Chester – is worth a short detour so you can visit **Ross Farm** (*4568 Hwy 12, New Ross;* **t/f** *1 877 689 2210; www.museum.gov.ns.ca/rfm/;* ⌚ *May–Oct 09.30–17.30 daily; Nov–Apr 09.30–16.30 Wed–Sun; admission CAN$6*). Located on 25ha well inland, this living museum aims to remind people that – in addition to the sea – the land played an important part in shaping Nova Scotia's past. Costumed interpreters demonstrate typical farm activities, heritage skills and crafts common 100–175 years ago. Oxen teams work the fields, there are heritage breeds of farm animals, early 19th-century buildings, a nature trail, several activities and special events throughout the year. Good for children.

Whilst you're here, if your appetite for household antiques, baskets and farm equipment from days of yore has not been satisfied, fear not. The **Hildaniel Brown House** (*1922 Forties Rd;* ☎ *689 2970;* ⌚ *Jun–mid Oct 10.00–16.30 Tue–Sun*) is close by and focuses on the years that followed those covered by Ross Farm. New Ross is on Highway 12, between Chester (31km/19 miles) and Kentville (43km/27 miles), and easy to reach **by car**. Take Exit 9 from Highway 103, or Exit 13 from Highway 101.

WESTERN SHORE This bayside community has a good low-budget seafood diner, a resort with restaurant and spa, kayak rentals, and one of the world's most storied little islands. Accessible **by car**, Western Shore is on Highway 3, 13km from Chester, 11km from Mahone Bay, and 8–10km from either Exit 9 or 10 from Highway 103.

Where to stay and eat

Atlantica Hotel & Marina Oak Island (121 units) 36 Treasure Dr; 627 2600, **t/f** 1 800 565 5075; **e** info@atlanticaoakisland.com; www.atlanticaoakisland.com; year-round. In addition to 105 guestrooms, 13 ocean-front chalets & 3 seaside villas, facilities include indoor & outdoor pools, fitness centre, minigolf, kayaking, tennis & spa. The resort is not on the famous island, but overlooks it. There's also a restaurant (*year-round 07.00–10.00, 11.00–14.00 & 17.00–20.00 daily; $$–$$$*). **$$**

Island View Family Restaurant 6301 Hwy 3; 627 2513; Mar–Dec daily (winter 11.00–20.00; summer 11.00–22.00). Right on the waterfront, this low-budget favourite known locally as the 'Green Canteen' dishes up good diner-style seafood. The fries aren't great, so it's worth paying a bit extra for the sweet potato version. $

What to see and do Offering kayak and bike rentals, **The Kayak Shack** (*75 Treasure Dr; 627 3340, 277 1182; www.kayakshack.ca; early May–mid Oct 09.00–17.00 daily (to 19.00 Fri/Sat)*) also runs a (by reservation) 'drop you off on an island for the day' service, for which you'll need a working mobile phone.

MAHONE BAY

Apart from Peggy's Cove, Mahone Bay's three churches is one of *the* iconic tourist images of Nova Scotia.

But there's far more to do in this charming and prosperous town than take a photo and move on. There are several studios and galleries to investigate, a museum to visit, the bay and its islands to explore, and some excellent eateries to try.

Behind the tourist information office is an atmospheric old cemetery, and architecture-buffs will find faithfully preserved buildings in a variety of styles including Italianate and Gothic Revival, many of these now housing B&Bs, restaurants and shops. Whilst it may not have the range of accommodation offered in Lunenburg (see page 149), it isn't a bad choice for a base from which to explore the region.

In recent decades, the beautiful setting and relaxed way of life have attracted artists, artisans and musicians, and a number of galleries and studios are dotted along Main Street. Worryingly, the first condominiums have begun to spring up and more may be on their way. Hopefully, this 'motel/box store/shopping mall-free' town won't begin to lose its character.

HISTORY Known to the Mi'kmaq as *Mushamush* and one of their favourite camping grounds, the town was founded in 1754. The majority of the early settlers were European (specifically German, French, and Swiss) Protestants, enticed by the British government's offer of free land, farm equipment, and a year's provisions. A few decades later there was a large influx of New Englanders. Mills were built at the head of the bay, and from 1850 to the early 20th century, shipbuilding thrived along the waterfront. With over 350 islands offering plenty of hiding places, the area has long been connected with pirates – a *mahone* was a low-lying craft used by buccaneers.

GETTING THERE Mahone Bay is easy to reach **by car**; it is on Highway 3 (take Exit 10 from Highway 103), 86km/54 miles from Halifax. **Trius Tours** (see *Chapter 2*, page 57) is expected to stop in Mahone Bay three or four days a week *en route* between Halifax and Bridgewater.

WHERE TO STAY

Bayview Pines Country Inn (8 rooms, 2 apts) 678 Oakland Rd, Indian Point; 624 9970, **t/f** 1 866 624 9970; www.bayviewpines.com; May–Oct; off-season by reservation. An old farmhouse

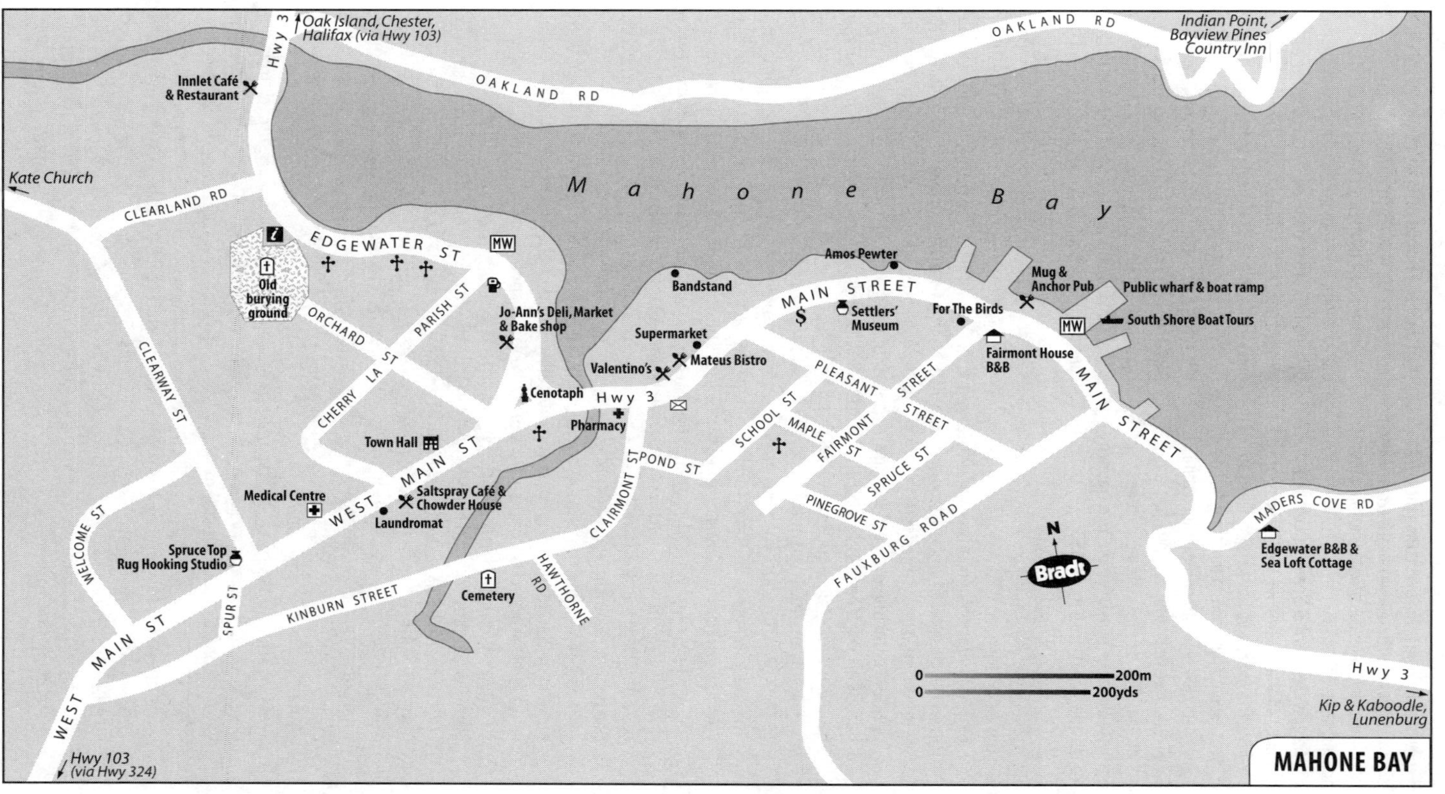
MAHONE BAY
Mahone Bay
Oak Island, Chester, Halifax (via Hwy 103)
Hwy 3
Innlet Café & Restaurant
OAKLAND RD
Indian Point, Bayview Pines Country Inn
Kate Church
CLEARLAND RD
EDGEWATER ST
MW
Old burying ground
ORCHARD ST
PARISH ST
Jo-Ann's Deli, Market & Bake shop
CLEARWAY ST
CHERRY LA
Cenotaph
Town Hall
Pharmacy
Bandstand
Supermarket
Valentino's
Mateus Bistro
Amos Pewter
MAIN STREET
Settlers' Museum
For The Birds
Mug & Anchor Pub
Public wharf & boat ramp
South Shore Boat Tours
Fairmont House B&B
PLEASANT STREET
SCHOOL ST
MAPLE ST
FAIRMONT STREET
SPRUCE ST
PINEGROVE ST
FAUXBURG ROAD
POND ST
CLAIRMONT ST
WEST MAIN ST
Medical Centre
Saltspray Café & Chowder House
Laundromat
WELCOME ST
Spruce Top Rug Hooking Studio
SPUR ST
KINBURN STREET
Cemetery
HAWTHORNE RD
MADERS COVE RD
Edgewater B&B & Sea Loft Cottage
N
Bradt
0 200m
0 200yds
Kip & Kaboodle, Lunenburg
Hwy 103 (via Hwy 324)

& converted barn on 5.7ha overlooking the bay & islands, approx 6km from town. Beach access, kayak launch, walking trails. Full b/fast inc in room (but not apt) rates. **$$**

Edgewater B&B & Sea Loft Cottage (3 rooms) 44 Mader's Cove Rd; 624 9382, **t/f** 1 866 816 8688; **e** edgewater@eastlink.ca; year-round. 2 rooms are in the lovely old house, 1 in a sweet, adjacent cottage. Beautiful setting. Susan & Paul are wonderful hosts. Washer, dryer, full kitchen, deck, balcony. Rate inc full b/fast (eg: omelette with pear, ham & Gruyère, plus cranberry scones with strawberry butter). **$$**

Fairmont House B&B (3 rooms) 654 Main St; 624 8089; www.fairmonthouse.com; year-round. Built by a shipbuilder, this outstanding c1857 Gothic Revival home still has the original curved staircase – held together with wooden pegs rather than nails or screws – in the entry hall. Cable TV, AC & heat control in rooms; free Wi-Fi. En-suite bathrooms. Full b/fast inc. **$$**

Kip & Kaboodle Tourist Accommodation 9466 Hwy 3; 531 5494, **t/f** 1 866 549 4522; www.kiwikaboodle.com; Apr–Oct. A small backpacker hostel 3km from the town centre on the road to Lunenburg, with bunk beds in 2 mixed rooms & 1

OAK ISLAND

In 1795, Daniel McGinnis rowed across to Oak Island on a hunting and fishing expedition and chanced upon a clearing at the island's eastern end. There was a lone oak tree with a branch overhanging a depression in the soil almost 4m in diameter. Putting these two things together, the youth assumed that the branch had been used to support a block and tackle pulley system which had been used to lower heavy objects into a now filled-in hole.

Having been brought up on a diet of tales of wicked pirates sailing the waters of Mahone Bay and burying treasure chests in secret places, he returned the next day with two friends – and shovels and picks. When they started to dig, the young men found a layer of flagstones just 60cm underground. Having removed these, they dug on and found three layers of oak planks at 3m intervals. They realised that this was more than three young boys could manage. They headed back to the mainland and one of the boys purchased the lot of land on which the pit was found.

It was nine years before the boys returned: at first, the pattern continued, with more oak plank layers found at 3m intervals. Some of the oak layers were covered in coconut fibre, charcoal, and a putty-like substance. A large granite stone with strange, carved markings, indecipherable to the diggers, was found at a depth of 30m. It was later taken to Halifax, and disappeared in 1919 (but that's another story).

The team took a day's break and on their return, found most of the shaft flooded. All attempts to bail or pump out the salt water failed. Tunnels were driven in from all angles, but the water menace proved impossible to conquer. Channels were then discovered leading from the sea towards the site, but even after (what looked like successful) attempts had been made to block them, the water problems continued.

Since then, despite countless groups of hopeful searchers, digging, damming, diverting, drilling and blasting haven't done the trick. Even Franklin D Roosevelt (later to become the President of the USA) was part of a 1909 expedition here.

Was 'treasure' buried here? If it was, who buried it? Almost as many theories have been put forward as attempts made to find it. The list of suspects includes Captain Kidd, Sir Francis Drake, Sir Francis Bacon, Sir Henry Morgan, Edward 'Blackbeard' Teach, Acadians uprooted from their homes, Incas who fled the Spaniards, rogue Spaniards diverting Central American booty, Knights Templar, Rosicrusians (members of a philosophical secret society originating in medieval

private double room (rooms share 2 bathrooms), communal kitchen, barbecue & common room.

Bikes to rent, biking & hiking tours offered. Linen inc. *Dorm CAN$30, private room CAN$69.* **$**

WHERE TO EAT

Mateus Bistro 533 Main St; 531 3711; www.mateusbistro.com; year-round (mid May–mid Oct 11.30–21.00 Mon–Fri, 10.00–21.00 Sat/Sun; mid Oct–mid May 11.30–20.30 daily). Bratislava-born Matthew Krizan sources fresh, local produce & prepares it with European flair. Lunch might include panko-crusted haddock, or gourmet salads & burgers: dinner pan-seared trout with mango salsa. Large deck for alfresco dining. **$$–$$$**

The Innlet Café 249 Edgewater St; 624 6363; www.innletcafe.com; year-round 11.30–21.00 daily. A 10-min waterfront walk round the bay from the town centre, this busy – sometimes too busy – licensed restaurant has an outdoor dining area with great views of the town. Stir-fries & pasta dishes are both good, & the mud cake a real treat. **$$**

Valentino's 525 Main St; 531 3666; year-round 17.00–22.00 Tue–Sun, 11.30–

Germany), and (of course) aliens. Clue-wise, in 1965, an electromagnetic search of the site by students from Massachusetts found a late 16th-century Spanish coin.

Over the years, several expedition members have reported seeing scary apparitions on the island. Two 'regulars' are said to be a man in a red frock coat who leaves no footprints in the sand, and a very large dog with red eyes that appears to stand guard at various sites on the island. More recent searches, studies and excavations suggest that an incredibly sophisticated series of tunnels and cavities connected to the sea lies underground: thus far, modern science and techniques is still losing out to the as yet unidentified engineering genius who designed and constructed it several centuries ago. By 1995, treasure hunters had managed to dig almost 60m underground: the treasure – if there is any – still has not been found.

Well over 200 years have now passed since McGinnis made his find: six treasure hunters have lost their lives, including four who died drowned after inhaling noxious fumes on a 1965 expedition. Ironically, regardless of whatever lies buried under Oak Island, literally millions of dollars have been spent trying to find it.

And what of the island in recent times? The 58ha island is now connected to the mainland by a causeway. It is owned by Oak Island Tours Inc, a somewhat secretive treasure-seeking consortium, and excavations continue (they received their current Treasure Trove Licence under the Nova Scotia government's Oak Island Treasure Act in June 2012).

The Oak Island mystery has inspired hundreds of articles, dozens of books and numerous documentaries: in more recent times two good websites, www.oakislandtreasure.co.uk and that of the Friends of Oak Island Society, www.friendsofoakislandsociety.com, keep those fascinated by the story up to date.

There's a display on Oak Island under the auspices of the Chester Municipal Heritage Society (see *www.chester-municipal-heritage-society.ca*) at Chester's old railway station (adjacent to the tourist office – see page 142).

PRACTICALITIES The Friends of Oak Island Society offers guided public tours of the island during various weekends in the summer and early autumn. Check the website for details. That apart, there are views of the island from Western Shore's Wild Rose Park, and Crandall Point Road takes you to the beginning of the causeway.

WHERE TO STAY See *Western Shore*, page 143.

THE THREE CHURCHES

The classic view of the Mahone Bay skyline – with its three churches reflected in the bay's still water – has become one of the most photographed scenes in Nova Scotia.

The white church with a tower on the right is the Trinity United Church. The oldest of the three, it dates from 1861 and was formerly Knox Presbyterian. Originally located further back, it was dragged to its present location by teams of oxen in 1885. The middle church is St John's Lutheran built in 1869, and the newest church, the high Victorian Gothic Revival-style St James Anglican Church sits on the left and was built in 1887.

Music at the Three Churches (*☎ 634 4280; www.threechurches.com*) is a series of classical concerts held fortnightly on Friday evenings between early July and early September. Tickets cost CAN$20.

14.30 Wed–Sun. Although this Italian restaurant focuses on seafood, other options are good, too. Nice atmosphere, good, relaxed service, very good homemade pasta. Fab desserts too (& I don't just mean *tiramisu!*) Delightful patio garden. $$

✕ Jo Ann's Deli 9 Edgewater St; ☎ 624 6305; www.joannsdelimarket.ca; ⌚ May–Oct 09.00–18.00 daily. There are just a couple of tables outside this tempting deli/grocery store/bakery/greengrocer. Order a salad, sandwich or grab ingredients for a gourmet picnic: the baked goods are particularly hard to resist. $

✕ Mug & Anchor 643 Main St; ☎ 624 6378; ⌚ year-round 11.30–midnight daily. Nice ambience, a deck, good pub food & regular live music. Eclectic selection of local & imported beers. $

✕ Saltspray Café 436 Main St; ☎ 624 0457; ⌚ year-round 08.00–22.00 daily. Forced to move from the waterfront after the old venue burnt down (it wasn't their fault), in its new c1860 home the Saltspray continues to offer few frills, but good-value home cooking. The pan-fried haddock, for example, is very good. $

FESTIVALS In May, there is a weekend of mussel (and wine) tasting and mussel farm tours at the **Mussel Festival**. At the end of July/early August, the **Classic Boat Festival** (*www.mahonebayclassicboatfestival.org*) is held annually (on the weekend closest to 1 August). There are workshops and demonstrations, sailing races, music and a lot more. In October, three days of music, illuminated hand-carved pumpkins, quilting workshops – not to mention scarecrows and antiques – can be enjoyed at the **Scarecrow Festival and Antique Fair**.

OTHER PRACTICALITIES

$ Bank BMO Bank of Montreal, 562 Main St; ☎ 624 8355; ⌚ 10.00–16.00 Mon–Wed, 10.00–17.00 Thu/Fri

✉ Post office 534 Main St; ⌚ 08.00–17.30 Mon–Fri, 09.00–12.00 Sat

ℹ Tourist information 165 Edgewater St; 624 6151, **t/f** 1 888 624 6151; ⌚ late May/Jun 10.00–17.00 daily; Jul/Aug 09.00–19.00 daily; Sep/early Oct 10.00–17.00 daily

WHAT TO SEE AND DO Watch and learn about the pewter-crafting process at **Amos Pewter** (*589 Main St; ☎ 624 9547, **t/f** 1 800 565 3369; www.amospewter.com; ⌚ May–Dec 09.00–17.30 Mon–Sat, 10.00–17.30 Sun; Jan–Apr 09.00–17.00 Mon–Sat*), or get interactive and finish your own piece (CAN$5). Meanwhile, artist **Kate Church** (*60 Old Clearland Rd; ☎ 624 1597; www.katechurch.com; ⌚ May–Nov by appointment*) is best known for sculptural figures made with wire, cloth and clay.

In addition to displays on the town's history (focusing – as the name suggests – on the early settlers and their backgrounds), there is a fine collection of ceramics and antiques at the **Mahone Bay Settlers' Museum** (*578 Main St; ☎ 624 6263; www.settlersmuseum.ns.ca; ⏲ Jun–early Sep 10.00–17.00 Tue–Sat, 13.00–17.00 Sun (check locally for the rest of Sep/early Oct); admission free*). The museum building is c1847.

Find just about everything those who watch our feathered friends could wish for at **For the Birds** (*647 Main St; ☎ 628 0784, t/f 1 888 660 6529; www.forthebirdsnatureshop.ca; ⏲ May–Dec 10.00–16.00 Wed–Sat, 12.00–16.00 Sun; Jan–Apr 10.00–16.00 Sat*), including equipment, gifts and advice.

South Shore Boat Tours (*☎ 543 5107; www.southshoreboattours.com/tours.html; ⏲ Jun–Oct*) runs daily two-hour tours on a 38ft boat to see dolphins, seabirds, seals, etc; four-hour trips in search of whales and Pearl Island's puffins in season (CAN$35–50).

Visit the **Spruce Top Rug Hooking Studio** (*255 West Main St; ☎ 624 9312, t/f 1 888 784 4665; www.sprucetoprughookingstudio.com; ⏲ year-round 10.00–16.00 Mon & Wed–Sat, 12.00–16.00 Sun; admission free*), which claims to have the largest collection of hooked rugs in Atlantic Canada. Regular classes are held, and you may be able to see new works being created.

LUNENBURG

Established in 1753, the original town layout has been maintained and many original wooden buildings preserved, with eight dating back to the 18th century. As the best-surviving example of a planned British colonial settlement in North America, Lunenburg's Old Town section was designated a national historic district by the Canadian government, and in 1995 it was declared a UNESCO World Heritage Site, one of only two in North America (the other is Quebec City).

The Old Town sits on a steep hillside overlooking the harbour. As you drive – or better still, walk – through you'll realise just how steep some of the narrow streets are. A guided walking tour should satisfy those wishing to dig deeper, and if walking is not for you, you can even see the sights by horse and carriage.

Many of the well-preserved brightly painted historical buildings now house inns, cafés, restaurants, shops and a seemingly ever-increasing number of galleries.

Today, the fishing industry may have dried up here, but the marine traditions and its seafaring heritage live on proudly. The Fisheries Museum of the Atlantic (see page 155) will help you understand not just Lunenburg, but coastal communities throughout the province. A dory shop on the waterfront has been making small wooden fishing boats since 1895, and traditional methods are still used. The town is the homeport of the *Bluenose II* (see box, page 153), and tall ships often grace the picturesque harbour.

Long ago, as it prospered and grew, the town spread beyond the original grid. In residential streets a few minutes' walk away are more magnificent homes, this time on much bigger plots of land. Some – with large lawns and beautiful gardens – are now B&Bs or inns.

In the Old Town area, most of the shops, museums and services are in the rectangle bounded by the waterfront, Lincoln, Cornwallis and Hopson streets.

Looking down over parts of the town is the imposing black-and-white c1894 academy, **Lunenburg Academy** [151 B1] (*97 Kaulbach St*), which most recently housed an elementary school and is open to the public on rare occasions – check with the tourist office.

Whilst Old Town Lunenburg is on a relatively steep hillside, the areas surrounding the town are relatively flat and the heavily indented coastline and peninsulas beautiful. This is an ideal area to swap four wheels for two. You can take a horse and buggy trip round the Old Town, but for a fascinating look deeper into Lunenburg's past, consider a guided walking tour. In addition to the Historic Town tour, one walk takes an in-depth look at Hillcrest Cemetery, whilst another explores Lunenburg by candlelight.

Within an easy drive or cycle ride are several beautiful small forested peninsulas and two tiny photogenic fishing villages well worth exploring. All in all, Lunenburg – roughly equidistant from Halifax and Shelburne – is one of Nova Scotia's most interesting and appealing towns.

HISTORY Early in 1753, a fleet of over a dozen ships from Halifax landed on the site of the Mi'kmaq village of *Merligueche* – 'Milky Waters'. The incomers were mostly Protestants from German-speaking parts of Europe. Land was cleared, defences built, and parcels of land dealt out. The settlement was laid out on what had become a standard plan for new coastal towns, in a compact grid with seven north–south streets intersected by nine east–west streets. It was named for King George II, Duke of Brunschweig-Lunenburg.

In the early years, the Mi'kmaq proved a threat to the settlers, several of whom were killed or taken prisoner until peace was agreed between government officials and Mi'kmaq chiefs in 1762. The next threat came from the sea. In 1782, privateer ships arrived without warning and about 100 armed men rushed ashore, plundering and burning at will.

The early settlers were far more familiar with farming than fishing, but many quickly began to take advantage of the seemingly inexhaustible bounty of the sea. As a consequence, they also became skilled shipbuilders. As the years passed, this port – on a splendid harbour protected by long peninsulas – became home to a huge fishing fleet.

At the turn of the 20th century, Lunenburg's schooner fleet sailed the Grand Banks, competing with the fleets of New England to bring home the abundance of cod. Fishing – especially in the treacherous seas around Nova Scotia – was a dangerous pursuit, and over the years hundreds lost their lives at sea.

GETTING THERE Lunenburg is on Highway 3 and 14km/9 miles from Highway 103 Exit 11, and easy to reach **by car**. It is 100km/62 miles from Halifax, 19km/12 miles from Bridgewater and 11km/7 miles from Mahone Bay. **Trius Tours** (see *Chapter*

THE BACK ROAD TO LUNENBURG

From Mahone Bay, the main route to Lunenburg is along Highway 3. A more interesting route – delightful on a sunny day – is to leave Mahone Bay towards Lunenburg on Highway 3 then turn left onto Maders Cove Road. Bear left onto Sunnybrook Road, then turn left onto Herman's Island Road. Bear left onto Princes Inlet Drive. At the fork, either bear right to rejoin Highway 3 (turn left to continue to Lunenburg) or, for another scenic side-trip, bear left along Second Peninsula Road. Go this way and you'll eventually have to turn back and retrace your steps, but you'll have passed some tranquil, delightful waters, and Second Peninsula Provincial Park. If you're doing this route in reverse, from Lunenburg, turn right from Highway 3 onto Second Peninsula Road.

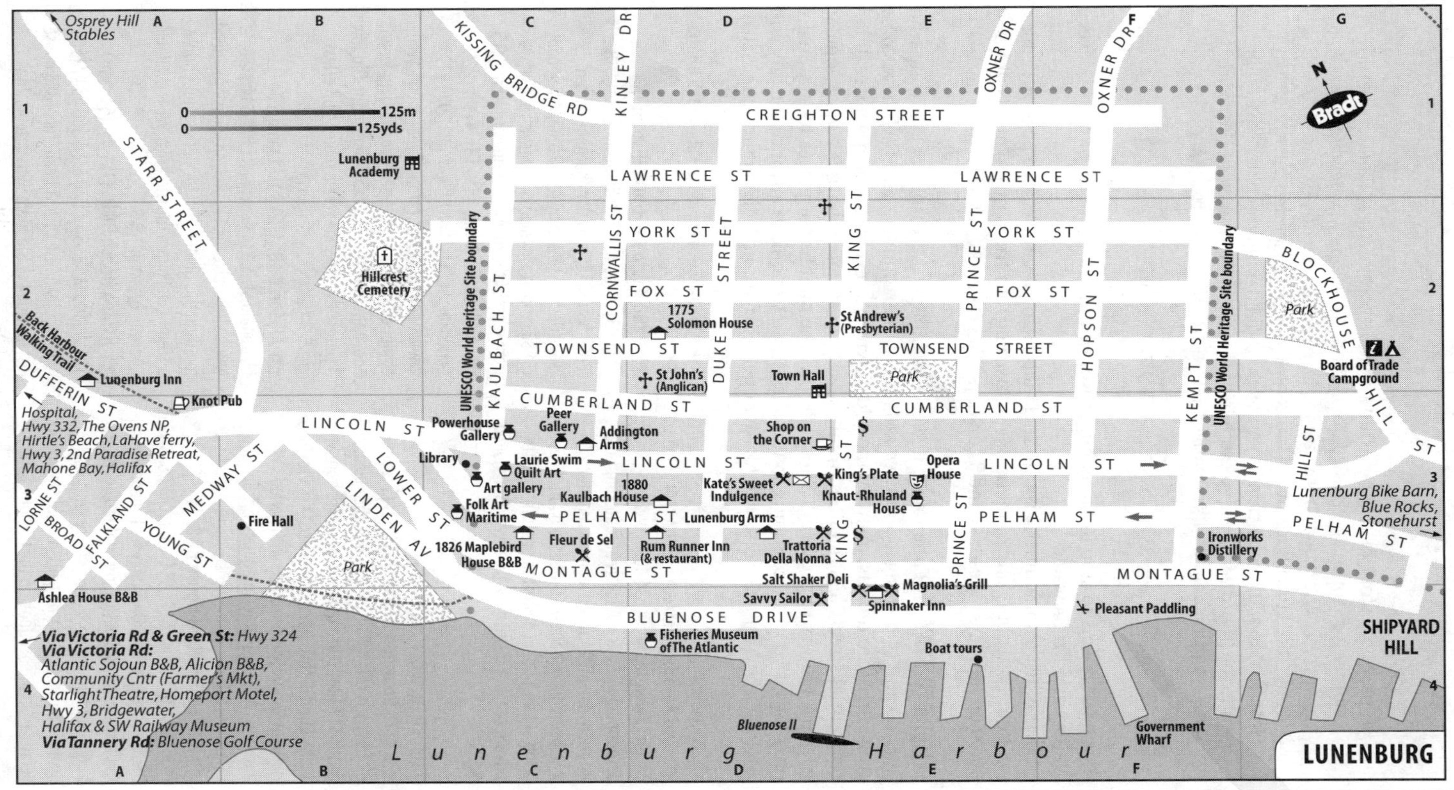
LUNENBURG
Osprey Hill Stables
Starr Street
Kissing Bridge Rd
Kinley Dr
Oxner Dr
Creighton Street
Lawrence St
York St
Fox St
Townsend St
Townsend Street
Cumberland St
Lincoln St
Pelham St
Montague St
Bluenose Drive
Cornwallis St
Duke Street
King St
Prince St
Hopson St
Kempt St
Kaulbach St
Blockhouse Hill St
Hill St
Dufferin St
Lower St
Linden Av
Medway St
Lorne St
Broad St
Falkland St
Young St
0 125m
0 125yds
Lunenburg Academy
Hillcrest Cemetery
UNESCO World Heritage Site boundary
Back Harbour Walking Trail
Lunenburg Inn
Knot Pub
Hospital, Hwy 332, The Ovens NP, Hirtle's Beach, LaHave ferry, Hwy 3, 2nd Paradise Retreat, Mahone Bay, Halifax
Powerhouse Gallery
Peer Gallery
Addington Arms
Library
Laurie Swim Quilt Art
Art gallery
Folk Art Maritime
1826 Maplebird House B&B
Fleur de Sel
1880 Kaulbach House
Rum Runner Inn (& restaurant)
Lunenburg Arms
1775 Solomon House
St John's (Anglican)
Town Hall
St Andrew's (Presbyterian)
Park
Shop on the Corner
Kate's Sweet Indulgence
King's Plate
Opera House
Knaut-Rhuland House
Trattoria Della Nonna
Salt Shaker Deli
Savvy Sailor
Magnolia's Grill
Spinnaker Inn
Fisheries Museum of The Atlantic
Boat tours
Pleasant Paddling
Government Wharf
Bluenose II
Lunenburg Harbour
Ironworks Distillery
Lunenburg Bike Barn, Blue Rocks, Stonehurst
Board of Trade Campground
Shipyard Hill
Fire Hall
Ashlea House B&B
Via Victoria Rd & Green St: Hwy 324
Via Victoria Rd: Atlantic Sojoun B&B, Alicion B&B, Community Cntr (Farmer's Mkt), Starlight Theatre, Homeport Motel, Hwy 3, Bridgewater, Halifax & SW Railway Museum
Via Tannery Rd: Bluenose Golf Course
Bradt
N

LUNENBURG BUMP

Not a ghost story or a dance, but a unique architectural feature seen in a number of forms in the Old Town, and occasionally elsewhere in the province, is the Lunenburg bump. Inspired by the five-sided Scottish dormer, the Lunenburg bump is a central dormer extended out and down from the roof, thereby creating an overhang – or 'bump' – above the main entrance. If historical architecture is one of your interests, visit the tourist office and pick up an informative architectural walking tour guide to the town.

2, page 44) plans to stop in Lunenburg three or four days a week *en route* between Halifax and Bridgewater.

If you just want a quick visit from Halifax, **Ambassatours** (see page 90) runs a six-hour Lunenburg and Mahone Bay sightseeing tour from June to mid October at 10.00 on Sundays, Tuesdays and Thursdays. Tickets cost CAN$91.

WHERE TO STAY In Lunenburg, it seems as though the wishes of everyone who ever dreamt of owning a centuries-old house and running it as a B&B have come true. There are dozens, many in the Old Town and several in the quiet tree-lined residential streets less than ten minutes' walk away. Lunenburg is a very popular base for visitors to the South Shore: despite the quantity of places to stay, many only have two or three rooms so it makes sense to book in advance for July and August. The businesses listed below are open year-round unless otherwise stated.

Upmarket

2nd Paradise Retreat [151 A2] (4 units) Second Peninsula Rd; 634 4099; www.secondparadise.ns.ca. A lovely Second Peninsula location 6km (10 mins' drive) from Lunenburg. 2, 2-bedroom cottages, a 6-bedroom farmhouse & loft set on 11ha of protected oceanfront with private beach. Eco-friendly. Reservations required. **$$$**

Mid range

1775 Solomon House [151 D2] (3 rooms) 69 Townsend St; 634 3477; www.bbcanada.com/5511.html. On a quiet street across from St John's Church, this character-filled c1775 Provincial Heritage property is furnished with period antiques. Wi-Fi available. Imaginative & delicious b/fast inc. **$$**

1826 Maplebird House B&B [151 C3] (4 rooms) 36 Pelham St; 634 3863, **t/f** 1 888 395 3863; year-round. Unusually for Lunenburg's Old Town, Susie & Barry's comfortable 'Lunenburg bump' heritage home – once a dairy farm – sits on a big plot & has a large garden, pool (seasonal), veranda & patio overlooking the harbour. Comfy living room, & reading room. Rate inc full b/fast. **$$**

1880 Kaulbach House Historic Inn [151 D3] (6 rooms) 75 Pelham St; 634 8818, **t/f** 1 800 568 8818; www.kaulbachhouse.com; May–Oct; off-season by reservation. An elegant, c1880 property in the Old Town with sea views from most of the rooms. Gourmet b/fast inc. **$$**

Addington Arms [151 C3] (4 rooms) 27 Cornwallis St; 634 4573, **t/f** 1 877 979 2727; www.addingtonarms.com; year-round. Well-equipped suites (all with sea &/or harbour view) above shops in this c1890 building in the Old Town. 3 suites have en-suite steam rooms. Full b/fast inc. **$$**

Alicion B&B [151 A4] (4 rooms) 66 McDonald St; 634 9358, **t/f** 1 877 634 9358; www.alicionbb.com. Elegant, spacious eco-friendly rooms in this quiet c1911 former senator's house a 10-min walk from the Old Town. Wi-Fi available. Gourmet b/fast inc. **$$**

Ashlea House B&B [151 A3] (6 rooms) 42 Falkland St; 634 7150, **t/f** 1 866 634 7150; www.ashleahouse.com. A beautiful c1886 house just outside the Old Town with gazebo, 2nd-floor deck & widow's walk (a railed observation platform) offering fine views. There is a family suite with interconnecting rooms. Full country-style b/fast inc. **$$**

Atlantic Sojourn B&B [151 A4] (4 rooms) 56 Victoria Rd; 634 3151, **t/f** 1 800 550 4824; **e** info@atlanticsojourn.com; www.atlanticsojourn.com; mid Apr–mid Nov; off-season by chance. In this recently redecorated very comfortable c1904 house less than 10 mins' walk to the Old Town, hostesses Sebelle & Susan pride themselves on 'thinking of everything to make your stay more enjoyable' & do a pretty good job. Full b/fast inc. **$$**

Lunenburg Arms Hotel [151 D3] (24 units) 94 Pelham St; 640 4040, **t/f** 1 800 679 4950; www.lunenburgarms.com. Good choice for those who prefer a larger hotel. Standard rooms, suites & 2-level suites, all with AC. Many overlook the harbour. Full-service Aveda spa & tanning salon is also available. **$$**

Lunenburg Inn [151 A2] (7 rooms) 26 Dufferin St; 634 3963, **t/f** 1 800 565 3963; www.lunenburginn.com; Apr–Nov. A fine c1893 building just outside the Old Town with 5 bedrooms & 2 suites, all AC. Victorian-style décor & covered veranda, sundeck & private bar. Gourmet b/fast, eg: strawberry-stuffed French toast inc. **$$**

Rum Runner Inn [151 D3] (13 rooms) 66–70 Montague St; 634 9200, **t/f** 1 888 778 6786; www.rumrunnerinn.com. Overlooking the harbour & golf course, 4 of the bright, spacious modern-looking rooms have private glassed-in verandas. See page 154 for their restaurant. Continental b/fast inc. **$$**

Spinnaker Inn [151 E4] (4 units) 126 Montague St; 634 4543, **t/f** 1 888 634 8973; www.spinnakerinn.com. 2 rooms & 2 split-level suites in this c1850 waterfront property. Bedrooms have beautiful wood floors & flat-screen TVs. Suites (with kitchenettes) ideal for families & longer stays. **$$**

Budget

Homeport Motel [151 A4] 167 Victoria Rd; 634 8234, **t/f** 1 800 616 4411; www.homeportmotel.com. A 10- to 15-min walk from the Old Town. In addition to standard motel rooms

BLUENOSE

There had long been competition between fishing fleets from Lunenburg and Gloucester, Massachusetts. So keen was their rivalry that in 1920, the *Halifax Herald* sponsored an annual race for deep-sea fishing schooners from the two fleets. When the Americans won, Canadian pride was hurt: a superior vessel had to be built in time for the next year's competition.

They came up with *Bluenose*, which not only regained the trophy, but won it for 18 years in succession until World War II loomed, and the race was suspended. New steel-hulled trawlers were rendering wooden fishing vessels redundant and in 1942, the *Bluenose* was sold to carry freight in the Caribbean. Four years later, she foundered and was lost on a Haitian reef.

For many years, this undefeated champion was featured on the back of the Canadian dime (10-cent piece): she is still remembered on Nova Scotia licence plates.

In 1963, the replica *Bluenose II* was built to the original plans by many of the original workers in the same shipyard as the original. Since 1971, she has sailed countless thousands of miles as Nova Scotia's floating ambassador.

In the last couple of years, the vessel has undergone a major restoration programme, and has been out of commission, but should now be back in the water.

If you're lucky, the *Bluenose II* will be in port, moored by the Fisheries Museum. Her schedule can be checked – and a two-hour harbour cruise booked on the website or by phoning (*634 8483*, **t/f** *1 877 441 0347; http://bluenose.novascotia.ca*).

– with fridge, microwave & toaster – there are simple 1- and 2-bedroom suites & laundry facilities on site. Most rooms newly renovated. **$**

Lunenburg Board of Trade Campground [151 G2] (55 sites) 11 Blockhouse Hill Rd; 634 8100, **t/f** 1 888 615 8305; mid May–mid Oct. Views over the front & back harbours from this open campground next to the tourist office. Serviced & tent sites. **$**

WHERE TO EAT

Food-wise, it is hard to go wrong with fresh seafood, or try local specialities such as Lunenburg pudding (a type of pork sausage) and sauerkraut.

Luxury

Fleur de Sel [151 C3] 53 Montague St; 640 2121; www.fleurdesel.net; late May–early Oct 17.00–closing daily; early/late Oct 17.00–closing Wed–Sun; off-season check availability. Housed in a beautiful old sea captain's home with a garden terrace, this award-winning restaurant offers intimate & elegant fine-dining. Try butter-poached lobster or grilled lamb saddle – or (by advance reservation) the 7-course tasting menu with wine pairings. **$$$–$$$$**

Upmarket

King's Plate at the Mariner King [151 D3] 15 King St; 634 8509, **t/f** 1 800 565 8509; www.marinerking.com; mid May/mid Jun & mid Sep–autumn from 17.00 Thu–Sat; mid Jun–mid Sep from 17.00 Wed–Mon. The German chef delivers interesting, tasty, European-influenced cuisine: starters might include an organic greens chiffonade with grilled quail, toasted pecan nuts & *Tête de Moine* cheese. A typical main course might be venison & rabbit loin served over apple red cabbage & herb *spätzle*. Last reservations at 20.00. Recommended. **$$$**

Trattoria Della Nonna [151 D3] 9 King St; 640 3112; www.trattoriadellanonna.ca; summer 11.30–14.00 & 17.00–21.00 Tue–Sat; winter 17.00–21.00 Tue–Wed & Sat, 11.30–14.00 & 17.00–21.00 Thu/Fri. Upmarket & stylish (for Nova Scotia). Pizza, pasta, seafood (eg: *passera* – tapenade-roasted halibut), & plenty of non-seafood options, such as *pollo alla mattone* (chicken cooked under a brick) or *agnello* (rack of lamb). Short but well-chosen wine list. **$$$**

Mid range

Magnolia's Grill [151 E4] 128 Montague St; 634 3287; Apr–Nov 11.00–22.00 daily. Justifiably popular, Magnolia's is laid-back & informal in terms of décor & ambience, but bright & lively in its regularly changing menu. Particular favourites include spicy peanut soup (trust me!), fishcakes & sublime (authentic) Key lime pie. The lobster linguine isn't cheap, but is worth pushing the boat out for. Reserve a table on the patio overlooking the waterfront. **$$**

Rum Runner Inn [151 D3] 66–70 Montague St; 634 8778; www.rumrunnerinn.com; May–Oct 12.00–21.00 daily. The inn's licensed restaurant highlights fresh, local ingredients & has a 'Farm-to-Fork' designation. Chef's tasting menu with wine pairings available. Reservations recommended. **$$**

Budget

Kate's Sweet Indulgence [151 D3] 242 Lincoln St; 640 3399; www.sweetindulgence.ca; 07.30–18.00 daily (from 08.30 Sat/Sun). Yes, the cakes & desserts are excellent, but don't overlook this casual café for a light lunch – the lobster roll stands out, & the soups, fishcakes, sandwiches & salads won't disappoint. Good coffee, too. **$–$$**

Knot Pub [151 A3] 4 Dufferin St; 634 3334; 12.00–21.30 daily (later in season). This dark but lively easy-to-miss pub isn't just a good spot to share a drink with the locals, but the pub grub is pretty good too. No surprises on the menu – but burgers, club sandwiches, fish & chips & the like are well made & well priced. **$**

Salt Shaker Deli [151 E4] 124 Montague St; 640 3434; www.saltshakerdeli.com; 11.00–20.00 Tue–Sat, 11.00–15.00 Sun. Nibbles, pizzas, sandwiches, plus more imaginative/eclectic choices such as *Pad Thai* or shrimp in hoisin sauce. Recommended are the smoked seafood chowder & the local mussels (choose from 8 different ways of preparation). Nice deck overlooking the harbour. **$–$$**

The Savvy Sailor [151 D4] 100 Montague St; 640 7425; www.thesavvysailor.ca; summer 07.30–16.00 daily; check for off-season hours. Licensed café (with nice little deck) offering good imaginative b/fasts (until 15.00), soups, salads, sandwiches, etc. $

Shop on the Corner [151 D3] 263 Lincoln St; 634 3434; 08.30–17.00 Mon–Sat, 12.00–17.00 Sun. A bright little corner of this 'gift shop & more' is home to a little café (wraps, bagel sandwiches, etc), which sells & serves local (roasted in the same building) Laughing Whale coffee. $

ENTERTAINMENT For live performances, check the schedules at the **Starlight Theatre** [151 A4] (*37 Hall St; 634 1987; www.pearltheatre.com*) and **Lunenburg Opera House** [151 E3] (*290 Lincoln St; 640 6500; www.lunenburgoperahouse.com*).

FESTIVALS This is a town with a full calendar of festivals and events. For more details, see www.lunenburgns.com/festivals-and-events/. Some of the best are as follows.

In June, the **Summer Opera Festival** offers performances by the Maritime Concert Opera, the province's only concert opera company. The excellent four-day **Lunenburg Folk Harbour Festival** (*634 3180; www.folkharbour.com*) in August features performances of traditional and contemporary folk and roots music at a variety of venues in the town from pubs to churches, with a main stage in a tent on **Blockhouse Hill** [151 G2]. Also in August, the **Nova Scotia Folk Art Festival** (*640 2113; www.nsfolkartfestival.com*) is a colourful event which draws the best proponents of the genre from all over the province: the downside is that – lasting just four hours – it gets too busy. The **Seafood Festival** in September is a weekend of seafood cooking demonstrations, dory boat races and live music, plus a chowder competition and beer tent. The **Once Upon a Lunenburg Christmas Market**, at the end of November/early December, is something to warm the hearts of locals and winter visitors, with dozens of decorated Christmas trees, Santa arriving by trawler and lots of jingling bells.

OTHER PRACTICALITIES

$ Banks BMO Bank of Montreal [151 E3], 12 King St; 634 8875; 09.30–16.30 Mon–Fri. TD Canada Trust [151 E3], 36 King St; 634 8809; 08.00–18.00 Mon–Wed, 08.00–20.00 Thu/Fri, 08.00–16.00 Sat

Hospital Fishermen's Memorial Hospital, 14 High St; 634 8801

Library Lunenburg Library [151 C3], 19 Pelham St; 634 8008; 10.00–17.00 Mon–Wed & Fri/Sat, 10.00–20.00 Thu, 12.00–16.00 Sun

Post office [151 D3] 242 Lincoln St; 08.30–17.00 Mon–Fri

Tourist information [151 G2] 11 Blockhouse Hill Rd; 634 8100, **t/f** 1 888 615 8305; late May–mid Oct 09.00–18.00 daily (Jun & Sep to 19.00, Jul/Aug to 20.00)

WHAT TO SEE AND DO Appropriately located on the waterfront, the **Fisheries Museum of the Atlantic** complex [151 D4] (*68 Bluenose Dr; 634 4794; http://museum.gov.ns.ca/fma/; (in season) mid May–mid Oct 09.30–17.30 daily (Jul–Aug until 19.00 Tue–Sat); admission CAN$10; (off-season) mid Oct–mid May 09.30–16.00 Mon–Fri; admission CAN$4*) includes two dockside vessels (a restored schooner and a steel-hulled trawler), an aquarium with Maritime species and touch-tank, demonstrations of marine-related skills, and three floors of exhibits. Learn about rum-running, traditional Mi'kmaq fishing methods, whales and whaling history – and much more. Absorbing. Cheaper admission is charged in the off-season when parts of the museum complex are closed.

Dating from c1793, the **Knaut-Rhuland House** [151 E3] (*125 Pelham St; 634 3498; www.lunenburgheritagesociety.ca; early Jun–Aug 11.00–17.00 Mon–Sat, 12.00–16.00 Sun; Sep 12.00–16.00 daily*) is one of the best-preserved examples of Georgian architecture in the country, with guides in period costumes.

The **Halifax and Southwestern Railway Museum** [151 A4] (*11188 Hwy 3; ☎ 634 3184; www.hswmuseum.ednet.ns.ca/; ⏲ May–Oct 10.00–17.00 Mon–Sat, 13.00–17.00 Sun; off-season by appointment only; admission CAN$6*) has the story of the H&SW with a replica 1940s' stationmaster's office, large S-gauge model railway based on the old line, old photos of stations, stock and employees, and much more. Just outside town.

Originally built in 1754, the **St John's Anglican Church** [151 D2] (*81 Cumberland St; ☎ 634 4994; www.stjohnslunenburg.org; ⏲ mid Jun–mid Sep 10.00–17.00 Mon–Sat, 12.00–19.00 Sun*) is the second-oldest Protestant church in Canada after St Paul's in Halifax. One of Canada's best examples of the 'carpenter Gothic' architectural style (wherein features traditionally rendered in stone are interpreted in wood), it was faithfully restored and reopened in 2005. There are displays on the history, fire and restoration of the church. Tours offered in summer. In addition to St John's church, look out for **St Andrew's Presbyterian** (*Townsend St*) which dates from 1828 but was 'Gothicised' in 1879. Atop the steeple, a large copper cod indicates the wind's direction.

Those who like looking at old tombstones will enjoy the **Hillcrest Cemetery** [151 B2] (*Unity Lane, off Kaulbach St*), which includes the graves of many of the German founders of the town. The cemetery is included on some of the itineraries offered by **Lunenburg Walking Tours** (*☎ 521 6867; www.lunenburgwalkingtours.com*); tours last about an hour and cost from CAN$20.

The **Bluenose Golf Course** [151 A4] (*18 Cove Rd; ☎ 634 4260; www.bluenosegolfclub.com; ⏲ late Apr–Oct*) is a short nine-hole course with stunning views over the town and harbour. Green fees are CAN$29.

Running daily guided sea kayak tours to Blue Rocks (see opposite), **Pleasant Paddling** [151 F4] (*186 Bluenose Dr; ☎ 541 9233; www.pleasantpaddling.com*) also offers other weekly tours, as well as single and double kayak rentals and shuttle service. Bikes (road and hybrids) can be rented from **Lunenburg Bike Barn** [151 G3] (*579 Blue Rocks Rd; ☎ 634 3426; www.bikelunenburg.com*); prices are from CAN$18 for up to four hours, CAN$25/day.

Definitely worth a visit is the **Lunenburg Farmers' Market** [151 A4] (*Community Centre car park, Victoria Rd & Green St; www.lunenburgfarmersmarket.ca; ⏲ May–Oct 08.00–12.00 Thu*), with plants, flowers, fresh produce, baked goods and much more. Fruit brandies and liqueurs are hand-distilled in a former blacksmith's at **Ironworks Distillery** [151 F3] (*2 Kempt St; ☎ 640 2424; www.ironworksdistillery.com; ⏲ Jan–mid May 12.00–17.00 Thu–Sun; mid May/–mid Jun & Sep–Dec 12.00–17.00 Wed–Mon; mid Jun–Aug 11.00–19.00 daily*).

Galleries The streets of the Old Town are dotted with art galleries. Some old favourites (eg: Houston North) have closed recently, but when one closes it seems two or three more open to replace it. Here are four that stand out for me.

Folk Art Maritime [151 C3] 10 Pelham St; ☎ 212 2797; www.folkartmaritime.com; ⏲ mid May–mid Oct 10.00–17.00 Tue–Sat, 12.00–17.00 Sun. Diverse collection of folk art, including paintings, carvings & more.

Laurie Swim Quilt Art [151 C3] 138 Lincoln St; **t/f** 1 877 272 2220; www.laurieswim.com; ⏲ May–Oct 11.00–17.00 daily. Subtitled 'Art Quilt Gallery of the Atlantic' – which says it all.

Peer Gallery [151 C3] 167 Lincoln St; ☎ 640 3131; www.peer-gallery.com; ⏲ mid Oct–May 12.00–16.00 Thu–Sun; Jun–mid Oct 10.30–17.30 daily. Co-operative featuring the work of a dozen contemporary Nova Scotia artists.

Power House Art Gallery [151 C3] 129 Lincoln St; ☎ 640 3363; www.powerhouseart.ca; ⏲ year-round 10.00–18.00 Tue–Sat. Nova Scotia & Inuit art, plus jewellery & handmade furniture.

Boat trips Several boat trips are offered between late spring and early autumn. The most sought after are those on *Bluenose II* (see box, page 153). Other operators include:

Heritage Fishing Tours 640 3535; www.boattour.ca. Offering the chance to fish for mackerel or pollock in the harbour.

Lunenburg Whale Watching Tours 527 7175; www.novascotiawhalewatching.com. Head out in search of whales: dolphins, seals & various seabirds are usually seen.

Star Charters 634 3535, t/f 1 877 386 3535; www.novascotiasailing.com. Sailing tours on either the little 'SPARK', or the *Eastern Star*, a 48ft wooden ketch.

Horseriding Osprey Hill Stables [151 A1] (*354 Upper First Peninsula Rd, First Peninsula; 634 7261; year-round*) If you fancy climbing into the saddle, how about a guided trail ride through quiet countryside and along beaches?

AROUND LUNENBURG

BLUE ROCKS AND STONEHURST These two photogenic fishing villages are a short drive or cycle ride from Lunenburg. Head east from Old Town Lunenburg and you'll come on to Blue Rocks Road. Follow it until you reach Blue Rocks (approximately 6km/4 miles), and turn right onto Herring Cove Road. From Blue Rocks, take Stonehurst Road and then follow signs to Stonehurst East, parking just before the wooden bridge. Stonehurst is approximately 4km from Blue Rocks.

HIRTLE'S BEACH This fine, often wild beach is over 3km long. For a wonderful (sometimes rugged) 7km coastal **wilderness hike**, walk to the right from the car park towards the end of the beach for approximately 1.5km, follow the path up into the woods, and turn left at the fork. The trail continues to Gaff Point before looping back via the west side of the peninsula. To get there, take Highway 332 from Lunenburg to Rose Bay for approximately 15km, turn left onto Kingsburg Road, then right onto Hirtle's Beach Road (approximately 8km from Highway 332).

OVENS NATURAL PARK (*Ovens Park Rd; 766 4621; www.ovenspark.com; mid May–early Oct 09.00–21.00 daily; admission CAN$8*) is a privately owned park with a cliffside hiking path giving views of the 'Ovens' – sea caves. The nearby beach was the scene of an 1861 gold rush, and you can try your hand at panning for gold.

The park is approximately 17km/11 miles from Lunenburg. To get there, take Feltzen South Road from Highway 332, then Ovens Road.

Where to stay There is a 174-site cliff-top campground (*late Jun–early Sep;* **$–$$**) with nine cabins, a swimming pool and a restaurant. The park's owners (the Chapins) had a celebrated sibling, singer/songwriter Harry Chapin (remember 'Cat's in the Cradle' and 'WOLD'?) who was killed in a car crash in 1981. Various family members and local musicians sing and play every evening in July and August.

LUNENBURG COUNTY WINERY (*813 Walburne Rd, nr Newburne; 644 2415; www.canada-wine.com; May–mid Jul & Oct–mid Dec 09.00–17.00 Mon–Fri, Aug/Sep 09.00–18.00 daily*) Nova Scotia's only winery specialising in fruit (rather than grape) wines is situated on a 40ha blueberry farm. To reach it, from Exit 11 off Highway 103 drive 24km inland to Newburne, then turn right onto Walburne Road.

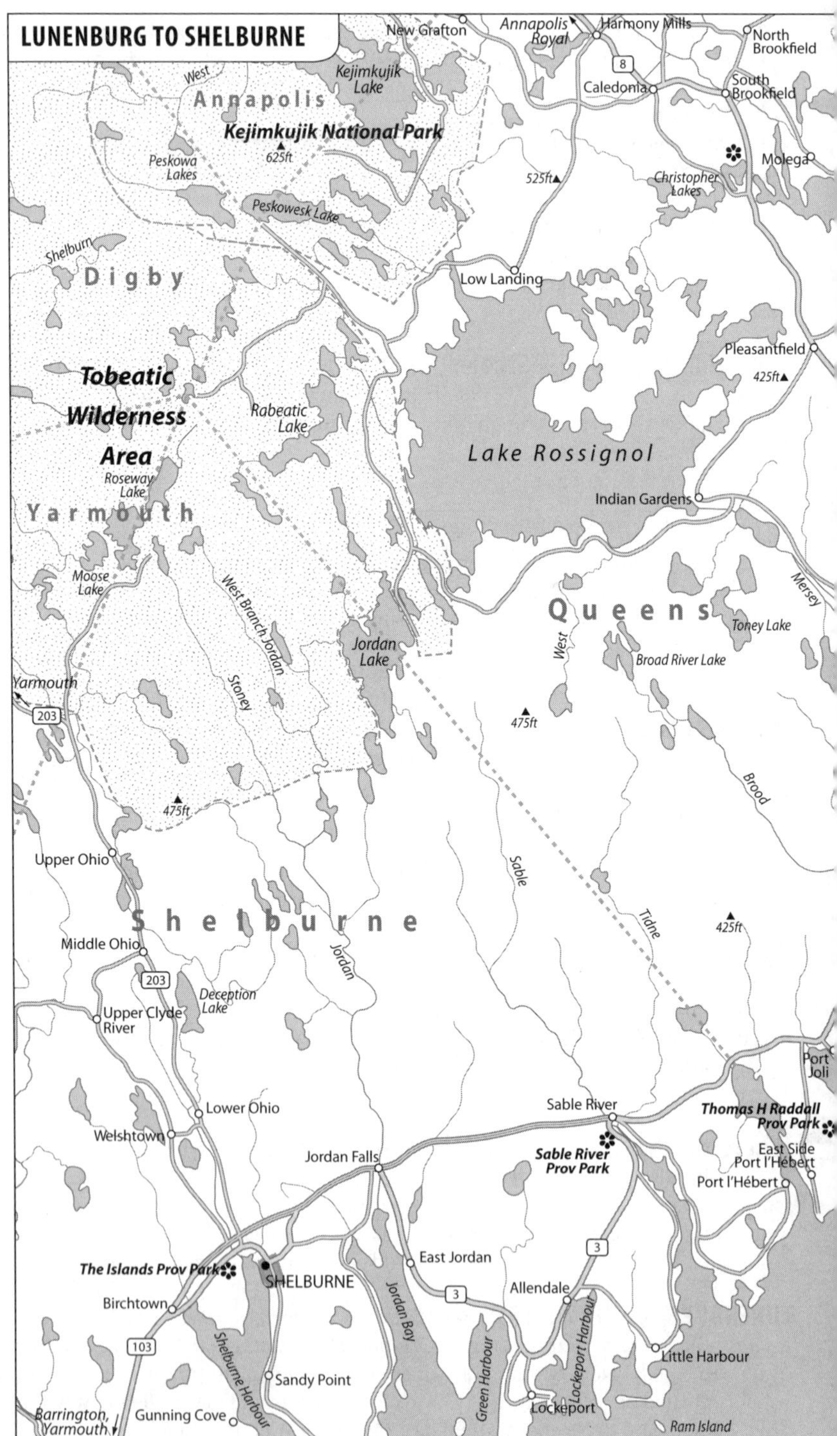
LUNENBURG TO SHELBURNE
New Grafton
Annapolis Royal
Harmony Mills
North Brookfield
8
Caledonia
South Brookfield
Kejimkujik Lake
West
Annapolis
Kejimkujik National Park
625ft
Peskowa Lakes
Molega
525ft
Christopher Lakes
Peskowesk Lake
Shelburn
Digby
Low Landing
Pleasantfield
425ft
Tobeatic Wilderness Area
Rabeatic Lake
Lake Rossignol
Roseway Lake
Yarmouth
Indian Gardens
Moose Lake
West Branch Jordan
Mersey
Queens
Toney Lake
Jordan Lake
West
Broad River Lake
Yarmouth
203
Stoney
475ft
Brood
475ft
Upper Ohio
Sable
Tidne
425ft
Shelburne
Middle Ohio
Jordan
203
Deception Lake
Upper Clyde River
Port Joli
Lower Ohio
Sable River
Thomas H Raddall Prov Park
Welshtown
Sable River Prov Park
East Side Port l'Hébert
Jordan Falls
Port l'Hébert
3
East Jordan
The Islands Prov Park
SHELBURNE
Jordan Bay
3
Allendale
Birchtown
103
Lockeport Harbour
Little Harbour
Shelburne Harbour
Sandy Point
Green Harbour
Barrington, Yarmouth
Gunning Cove
Lockeport
Ram Island

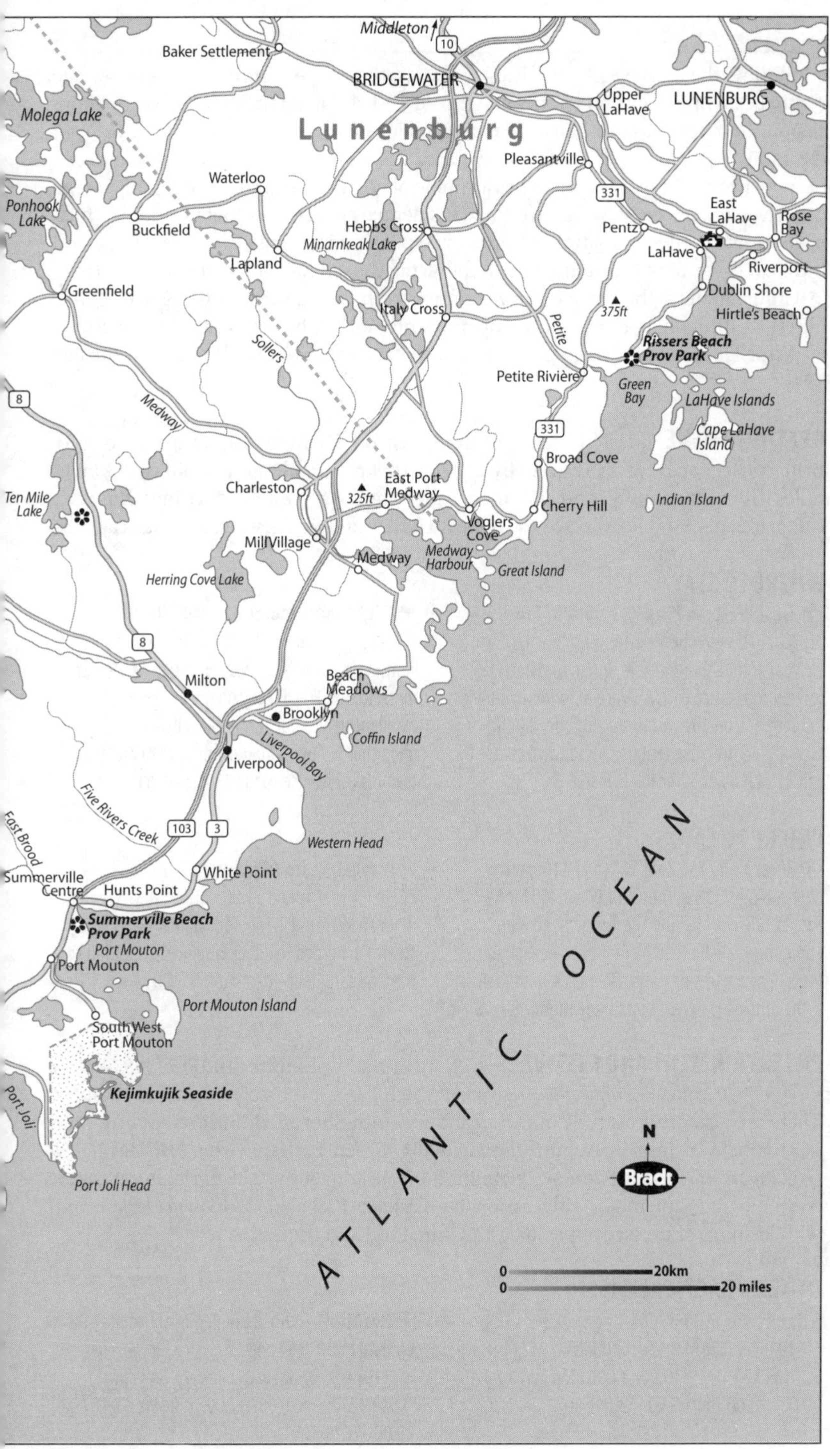
Middleton
10
Baker Settlement
BRIDGEWATER
Upper LaHave
LUNENBURG
Molega Lake
Lunenburg
Pleasantville
Waterloo
331
Ponhook Lake
East LaHave
Rose Bay
Buckfield
Hebbs Cross
Pentz
Minarnkeak Lake
LaHave
Lapland
Riverport
Greenfield
Dublin Shore
375ft
Italy Cross
Hirtle's Beach
Sollers
Petite
Rissers Beach Prov Park
Petite Rivière
8
Medway
Green Bay
LaHave Islands
331
Cape LaHave Island
Broad Cove
Ten Mile Lake
Charleston
325ft
East Port Medway
Indian Island
Voglers Cove
Cherry Hill
MillVillage
Medway
Medway Harbour
Great Island
Herring Cove Lake
8
Beach Meadows
Milton
Brooklyn
Coffin Island
Liverpool Bay
Liverpool
Five Rivers Creek
East Brood
103
3
Western Head
White Point
Summerville Centre
Hunts Point
Summerville Beach Prov Park
Port Mouton
Port Mouton
Port Mouton Island
South West Port Mouton
Kejimkujik Seaside
Port Joli
Port Joli Head
ATLANTIC OCEAN
N
Bradt
0 20km
0 20 miles

BRIDGEWATER

Straddling the LaHave River, Bridgewater is the major commercial and service centre between Halifax and Yarmouth: the largest shopping mall on the South Shore sits on the river's eastern bank. The area's major employer, Michelin, has a plant in the Industrial Park. The old downtown area was destroyed by fire in 1899 and isn't particularly attractive. The town has a couple of golf courses and museums and some nice riverside parks: on some tree-lined residential streets stand stately homes which have withstood the test of time. Outdoorsy types shouldn't miss **Riverview Park**, and the shared-use 8km **Centennial Trail** following the old rail bed is worth a wander.

Unfortunately, the town's Fairview Inn – which claimed to be Nova Scotia's oldest continually operating inn – operates no more. It burned down late in 2011.

Actor Donald Sutherland grew up and went to school in Bridgewater in the late 1940s.

GETTING THERE Located on Highway 3, just off Highway 103 (Exits 12 or 13), Bridgewater can be easily reached **by car**. It is 100km/62 miles from Halifax, 20km/12 miles from Lunenburg and 45km/28 miles from Liverpool. **Maritime Bus** (see *Chapter 2*, page 44) is expected to connect Halifax and Bridgewater four days a week.

WHERE TO STAY

Best Western Plus (63 units) 527 Hwy 10; 530 0101; www.bestwesternbridgewater.com; year-round. Comfortable, functional hotel & convention centre with a choice of rooms or suites. Indoor pool, on-site restaurant/lounge, laundry & business centre. Bike rentals. Out of town centre by Exit 12 of Hwy 103. Inc full b/fast. **$$**

Lighthouse Motel (17 units) Hwy 331, Conquerall Bank; 543 8151; www.lighthousemotel.ca; May–mid Oct. 14 pleasant motel rooms, & – directly on the riverside – 3 excellent-value larger units with kitchenettes. A good choice. Approx 10 mins' drive from Bridgewater towards LaHave (see page 164). **$–$$**

WHERE TO EAT

River Pub 750 King St; 543 1100; www.riverpub.ca; year-round 11.00–23.00 Mon–Sat, 12.00–closing Sun. The 'house beer' is an eponymous ale brewed by Propeller. Reasonable food, & nice riverside patio. The pub is hard to miss – the outside is covered by a huge mural. **$–$$**

Wayves Seafood Eastside Plaza; 543 2020; year-round 11.00–21.00 daily. Reliable diner specialising in seafood. Lighter options (eg: steamed, herbed haddock & salad) in addition to the standard deep-fried stuff. **$–$$**

ENTERTAINMENT AND FESTIVALS Catch a film at the **Empire Studio 7** (*349 LaHave St; 527 4025; www.empiretheatres.com*), which has a seven-screen cinema complex. There are also great festivals in the area. The **South Shore Exhibition** (see box, page 162) is held in July. In August, the **Growing Green Festival** (*www.bridgewater.ca/growinggreenfest*) is a two-day celebration of 'sustainability'. The agricultural theme continues in September with a four-day **Ciderfest** (*www.bridgetownciderfest.com*) with lashings of pressed apple juice and 'fun, food and friends'.

OTHER PRACTICALITIES

$ Banks Royal Bank, 565 King St; 543 0184; 10.00–17.00 Mon–Fri. Scotiabank, 421 LaHave St; 543 8155; 10.00–17.00 Mon–Wed & Fri, 10.00–20.00 Thu, 09.00–13.00 Sat

Hospital South Shore Regional Hospital, 90 Glen Allan Dr; 543 4603

Library Bridgewater Library, 547 King St; 543 9222; 10.00–17.00 Mon–Wed & Fri/Sat, 10.00–20.00 Thu

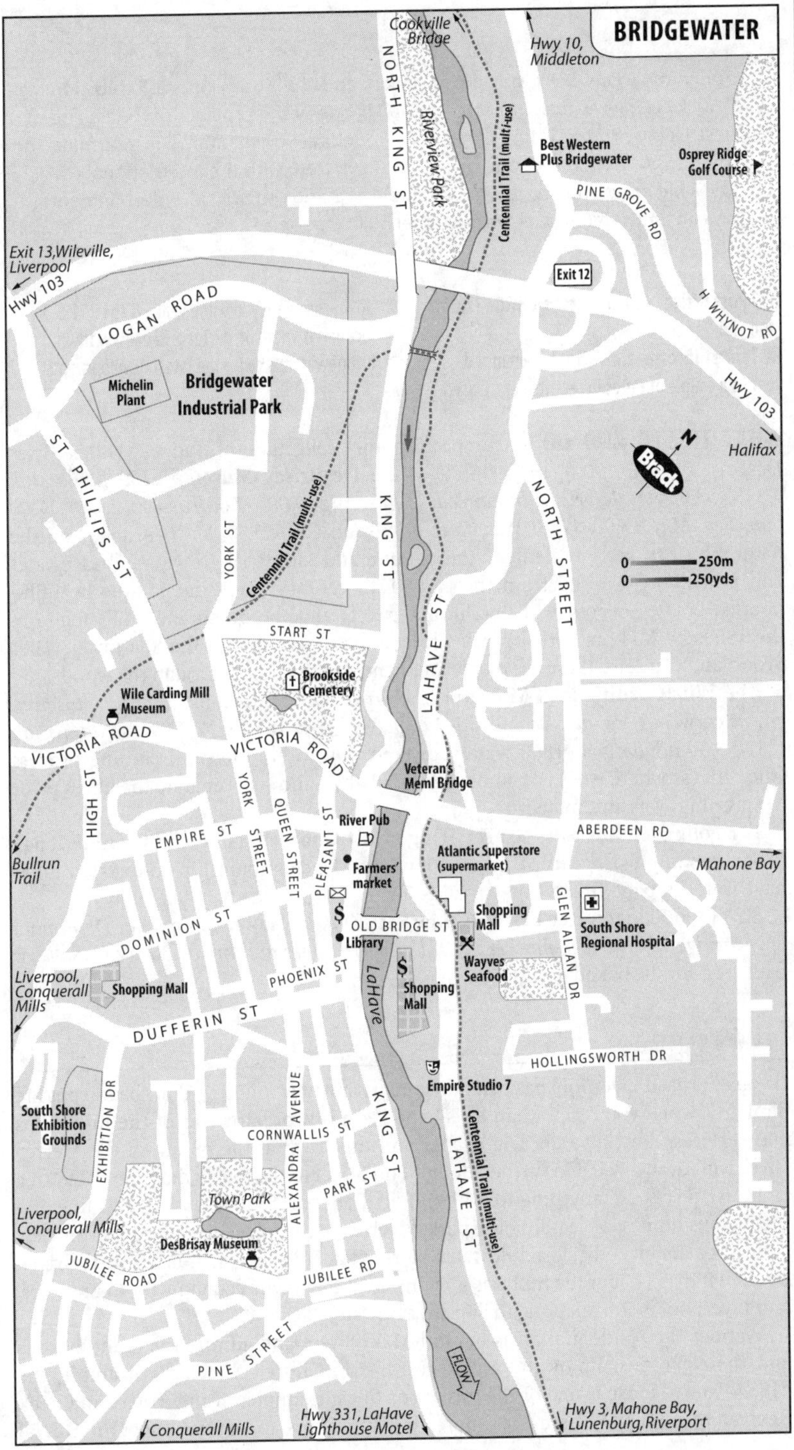

BRIDGEWATER

Cookville Bridge
Hwy 10, Middleton
NORTH KING ST
Riverview Park
Centennial Trail (multi-use)
Best Western Plus Bridgewater
Osprey Ridge Golf Course
PINE GROVE RD
Exit 13, Wileville, Liverpool
Hwy 103
Exit 12
H WHYNOT RD
LOGAN ROAD
Michelin Plant
Bridgewater Industrial Park
Hwy 103
Halifax
ST PHILLIPS ST
KING ST
NORTH STREET
0 250m
0 250yds
YORK ST
Centennial Trail (multi-use)
LAHAVE ST
START ST
Brookside Cemetery
Wile Carding Mill Museum
VICTORIA ROAD
VICTORIA ROAD
Veteran's Meml Bridge
HIGH ST
YORK STREET
QUEEN STREET
PLEASANT ST
River Pub
EMPIRE ST
ABERDEEN RD
Bullrun Trail
Farmers' market
Atlantic Superstore (supermarket)
Mahone Bay
OLD BRIDGE ST
Shopping Mall
GLEN ALLAN DR
South Shore Regional Hospital
DOMINION ST
Library
Wayves Seafood
Liverpool, Conquerall Mills
Shopping Mall
PHOENIX ST
LaHave
Shopping Mall
DUFFERIN ST
HOLLINGSWORTH DR
Empire Studio 7
South Shore Exhibition Grounds
EXHIBITION DR
AVENUE
KING ST
CORNWALLIS ST
LAHAVE ST
Centennial Trail (multi-use)
ALEXANDRA
PARK ST
Town Park
Liverpool, Conquerall Mills
DesBrisay Museum
JUBILEE ROAD
JUBILEE RD
PINE STREET
FLOW
Conquerall Mills
Hwy 331, LaHave Lighthouse Motel
Hwy 3, Mahone Bay, Lunenburg, Riverport

THE BIG EX

Agricultural fairs are big in Nova Scotia, and the **South Shore Exhibition** (*543 3341; www.thebigex.com; end Jul*) is one of the province's biggest and best. Held at Bridgewater's Exhibition Grounds at 50 Exhibition Drive, farming methods used in days gone by are not forgotten, with the International Ox-Pull a big draw. The event, which includes arts and crafts, food, entertainment and an amusement park, attracts over 50,000 people.

Post office 613 King St; 08.30–17.00 Mon–Fri

Tourist information This has changed venues a couple of times in recent years, closed down completely in some years, & the 2013 location is yet to be decided. See www.town.bridgewater.ns.ca for the latest developments.

WHAT TO SEE AND DO Encompassing the collection of Judge Mather Byles DesBrisay (1828–1900), the exhibits at the **DesBrisay Museum** (*130 Jubilee Rd; 543 4033; www.desbrisaymuseum.ca; Jun–Aug 09.00–17.00 Tue–Sat, 13.00–17.00 Sun; Sep–May 13.00–17.00 Wed–Sun; admission CAN$3.50, Sat free*) focus on the natural history, early settlement and cultural and industrial growth of Bridgewater and Lunenburg County from the early 17th century. Look out for the beautiful hooded cradle covered with birch-bark panels and the porcupine quills made in the 1860s by Mi'kmaq artist Mary Christianne Morris. Set in the 8ha Bridgewater Woodland Gardens, there are picnic areas and walking trails through the woods.

The **Wile Carding Mill Museum** (*242 Victoria Rd; 543 8233; http://museum.gov.ns.ca/wcm/; Jun–Sep 09.30–17.30 Mon–Sat, 13.00–17.30 Sun; admission CAN$3.50 adult*) is a c1860 water-powered mill where the wool-carding process (the process where wool is 'combed' – usually by hand – to separate the fibres prior to spinning) was automated.

For golfing enthusiasts, **Osprey Ridge Golf Course** (*Harold Whynot Rd; 543 6666; www.ospreyridge.ns.ca*) is a 6,607yd, par-72 championship course: ten holes have water in play. Green fees are CAN$46.

Stroll the **Bridgewater Farmers' Market** (*King St, between Empire & Dominion; www.bridgewaterfarmersmarket.ca; late spring–mid autumn 08.30–12.30 Sat*) for fruit, veg, crafts, baked goods, etc.

LIVERPOOL

If you approach Liverpool past shopping malls or heavy industry, don't be too put off. Similarly, when you reach Main Street and see a row of fairly run-of-the-mill shops and services, don't give up. Dig deeper and this town at the mouth of the Mersey River will reward you. Go further along Main Street to the town's most desirable area (if house prices are anything to go by), Fort Point, and you'll find several fine and prestigious homes, a pleasant little park, lovely water frontage, and a wonderful view – albeit of the recently closed Bowater Mersey Paper Company mill across the river. Eyesore it may be, but the mill was a mainstay of the town's economy for many years, and Liverpool is still adapting to 'life after Bowater Mersey'.

Wander the residential areas behind Main Street and admire the grand houses and their gardens. Enjoy the architecture – on Church Street, for example, the c1854 Court House is one of the province's finest examples of the American Greek Revival movement. There are interesting museums to explore, an **Old Burial**

Ground (Main Street at Old Bridge Street) to wander, a couple of good eateries, and, if you're really not in the mood for things urban, wonderful beaches nearby.

Just across the river, **Brooklyn** has a pretty marina and waterfront park which hosts many summer events. The setting is not, however, helped by the monstrous (now closed) paper mill. The area's big supermarkets and box stores are near Exit 19 off Highway 103.

HISTORY When Sieur de Mons arrived in 1604 *en route* to Port-Royal he was surprised to find a French fur trader already here. De Mons named the port after the trader, calling it Port Rossignol: the Mi'kmaq called it *Ogumkiqueok*, 'a place of departure'. A group of New Englanders, most of whom were said to be direct descendants of the Pilgrim Fathers, founded Liverpool in 1759.

A shipbuilding and shipping industry developed, but during the American Revolution several ships from the port were seized by American privateers. This stung the port's mariners who built new ships and set off to do their own privateering (see page 18).

Most of what went on in the town at that time was faithfully recorded by an early settler, Simeon Perkins, who built a fine home on the town's main street – and kept a detailed diary. Perkins records, for instance, that smallpox ravaged Liverpool until the people submitted to an ordeal called 'vaccination'. The vaccine was yet to be perfected and Perkins says that as many died of the vaccination as from smallpox.

With the cessation of hostilities, Liverpool settled into a long period of prosperity centred on shipbuilding and lumbering. Many of the downtown buildings were destroyed, however, by a great fire in 1865.

Brooklyn was originally known as Herring Cove, and the ubiquitous Nicolas Denys (see page 335) had a fishery here in 1634.

GETTING THERE Its location on Highway 3, just off Highway 103 Exit 19 makes Liverpool easy to get to **by car**. It is 147km/92 miles from Halifax and 69km/43 miles from Shelburne.

NO TROUBLE AT 'T MILL

Three minutes' drive from Exit 17 off Highway 103 is one of the province's prettiest communities. **Mill Village** – also reached by taking Port Medway Road north from Highway 103 between junctions 17 and 18 – boasts a picturesque Medway River setting, numerous beautiful century houses, and a little-known gem. Just by the bridge is the **Riverbank General Store & Café** (*8 Medway River Rd;* ☎ *677 2013;* ⏲ *08.00–21.00 Mon–Fri, 09.00–21.00 Sat/Sun*). The old beautifully located general store was bought by a 'supported living' association: staff, clients and volunteers worked to transform the space into a combination of craft shop, gift shop, grocery store and riverside café (⏲ *11.30–14.30 daily*), dishing up reasonably priced sandwiches, salads, ice cream and more. Most of the store/café staff are under the wing of the association. Worthy, and worth the detour. Incidentally, if you're heading to Kejimjukik (see page 214) or Annapolis Royal (page 208) you can continue along Medway River Road to Greenfield (approximately 25km), a lovely, riverside drive along a gravel road, from where it is 6.6km along Chapel Hill Road to Highway 8.

WHERE TO STAY AND EAT In addition to the following places listed, **Milton** (see page 168) also has a good B&B. A highly regarded local catering company, Alimento, is due to open a new restaurant in Liverpool in spring 2013. As Alimento has made a name for itself with tasty soups and gourmet burgers, you would expect the eatery to focus on fresh, local ingredients – and be worth a visit.

Best Western Plus Liverpool (65 rooms) 63 Queens Pl Dr, off Hwy 3 near Exit 19 of Hwy 103; 354 2377, t/f 1 877 354 2377; www.bestwesternliverpool.com; year-round. Well-equipped hotel with laundry, cocktail lounge, indoor pool & fitness centre. Good choice for those happy with chain hotels. Most rates inc hot b/fast. **$$**

Lanes Privateer Inn (26 rooms) 27 Bristol Av; 354 3456, t/f 1 800 794 3332; www.lanesprivateerinn.com; year-round. A Mersey River waterfront inn. Some guestrooms have

SUGGESTED DETOUR – HIGHWAY 331

From Bridgewater, Highway 331 follows the pretty, west bank of the LaHave River for about 20km to LaHave. This is the western terminus for a car ferry which makes frequent crossings of the river to East LaHave (on Highway 332). The cable ferry (CAN$5.25) runs every 30 minutes, departing LaHave on the hour and half hour, departing East LaHave on the quarter and three-quarter hour. Just past the ferry dock, a 100-plus year-old former chandlery now houses the **LaHave Crafters Co-op** (*Jun–Sep 11.00–17.00 daily*), displaying the work of numerous local artists and craftsfolk. The big draw, though, is the justifiably popular **LaHave Bakery** (*Hwy 331; 688 2908; summer 08.30–18.30 daily; winter 09.00–16.30 daily; $*). In addition to baking traditional bread made from additive-free and locally grown ingredients, and tempting cakes and squares, there are sandwiches, good coffee, soup and a couple of hot savoury items (perhaps pizza). There are only a few tables, so if the weather's nice, order 'to go' and – after a stop 150m further on at the waterfront **Westcote Bell Pottery** (*3447 Hwy 331; 693 2042; www.westcotebellpottery.com*) – walk down for a riverside picnic by the museum where Isaac de Razilly, a French nobleman and explorer, established Fort Ste-Marie-de-Grace in 1632. This was one of the first permanent European settlements in Canada, and – from 1632 to 1636 – the first capital of New France. Razilly died in 1636 and his successor decided to move his headquarters to Port-Royal (see page 185). The settlement was destroyed by fire in the early 1650s. On its site, in a former lighthouse-keeper's house, is **Fort Point Museum** (*100 Fort Point Rd; 688 1632; www.fortpointmuseum.com; Jun–Sep 10.00–17.00; off-season by appointment; park open year-round; admission free*), which presents 400 years of local history including the Mi'kmaq, early French settlement and Foreign Protestant settlers. There are fine views from a third-floor viewing platform, picnic tables and a replica lighthouse. The adjacent cemetery is also worth a wander.

Continuing on Highway 331, in less than 10km from LaHave you'll reach **Crescent Beach** where a causeway shelters a fine, long, sandy beach. Drive or cycle across the causeway to reach the LaHave Islands. The **LaHave Islands Marine Museum** (*100 LaHave Islands Rd; 688 2973; www.lahaveislandsmarinemuseum.ca; Jun–Aug 10.00–17.00 daily; admission free*) – housed in a former Methodist church – apart, there are no services for the visitor.

Back on Highway 331 it is just 1km to **Rissers Beach Provincial Park** (*Hwy 331; www.novascotiaparks.ca/parks/rissers.asp; mid May–early Oct*). In addition to a long, sand beach, a boardwalk leads across a marsh. When you reach its end,

balconies. There's a pub (🕘 *10.30–22.00 Tue–Thu, 10.00–midnight Fri/Sat, food served until 21.00*) & a very good restaurant (🕘 *07.00–20.00 daily;* **$$**) with a varied menu. In particular, the haddock cakes & bread & butter pudding with orange whisky sauce receive many plaudits. Rates inc good full b/fast. **$$**

Brooklyn Shores B&B (3 rooms) 112 Brooklyn Shore Rd, Brooklyn; ☎ 354 7171; www.brooklynshorebb.com; 🕘 year-round. The 3 rooms share 1 full bathroom & 1 wc. Good value. Pet-friendly. Rate inc full b/fast. **$**

Gallery Guest House B&B (2 rooms) 611 Shore Rd, Mersey Pt; ☎ 354 5431; www.bbcanada.com/galleryguesthouse; 🕘 year-round. Both guestrooms at this charming oceanfront B&B approximately 4km from the town centre on the same premises as the Savage Gallery (see page 167) have private entrances & decks overlooking Liverpool Bay. B/fast (cheeses, smoked salmon/cold cuts, good bread & much more) is brought to your door on a trolley at a pre-arranged time. **$**

Motel Transcotia (22 rooms) 3457 Hwy 3, Brooklyn; ☎ 354 3494; f 354 3352; 🕘 year-round.

turn left along the bank of the Petite Rivière and walk back along the beach to complete a loop. The park's two camping areas have a total of 90 open and wooded sites, some (the first to be reserved) virtually on the beach.

Again it's about 1km from the park to the village of **Petite Rivière**: cross the bridge and turn left off Highway 331 onto Green Bay Road. The community of **Green Bay** has a couple of lovely (generally sheltered) little beaches, several holiday homes and **Macleod's Canteen** (*542 Green Bay Rd;* ☎ *688 2866;* 🕘 *late Jun–early Sep 11.00–18.00 daily;* $): eat in or take your fish and chips to the beach across the road.

Retrace your steps to Petite Rivière and, at the crossroads, turn left back onto Highway 331. After about 300m, look out for the **Old Burial Ground** on the left almost opposite the Crousetown turn-off: graves date from the very early 19th century. Back at the crossroads, if you turn onto Petite Rivière Road you'll pass the **Maritime Painted Saltbox Gallery** (*265 Petite Rivière Rd;* ☎ *693 1544; www.paintedsaltbox.com;* 🕘 *May–mid Oct 10.00–17.00 daily, otherwise by chance appointment*), a fun and fascinating collection of reproduction heritage furniture and folk art. Continue on this road and follow it as it merges onto Italy Crossing Road. After less than 2km (less than 3km from the aforementioned crossroads) you'll find the **Petite Rivière Vineyards** (*1300 Italy Cross Rd;* ☎ *693 3033; www.petiterivierewines.ca;* 🕘 *summer 12.00–17.00 Sat/Sun*). Turn back on Italy Crossing Road and follow it to rejoin Highway 331. You'll see forest rather than the sea for the next 7km before reaching picturesque **Broad Cove**: on your right, sophisticated but relaxed **Best Coast Coffee** (*7070 Hwy 331;* ☎ *935 2031;* 🕘 *mid Jun–mid Oct 09.30–16.00 Tue–Sun;* $) offers not only good coffee, but gourmet sandwiches and tempting baked goodies.

Five kilometres further on at **Cherry Hill**, it's easy to miss the turn-off to another fine, long, and usually very quiet beach. Coming from Broad Cove on Highway 331, turn left onto Henry Conrad Road by the Fire Department and follow it to its end. Be aware that this beach sometimes attracts biting deer flies.

At Vogler's Cove, either continue along the coast to East Port Medway and on to Highway 103 Exit 17, from where it is 30km to Bridgewater or 17km to Liverpool. You'll have driven approximately 60km from Bridgewater.

Alternatively, turn right onto Hirtle Road. After about 9km you'll come to **Bradford Naugler's Folk Art** (*117 Hirtle Rd, Middlewood;* ☎ *543 5417; www.fromtheheartfolkart.com;* 🕘 *daily*). Bradford's wood folk-art carvings are renowned. From here it is less than 1km to Highway 103 Exit 16: Bridgewater is 19km away, Liverpool 29km.

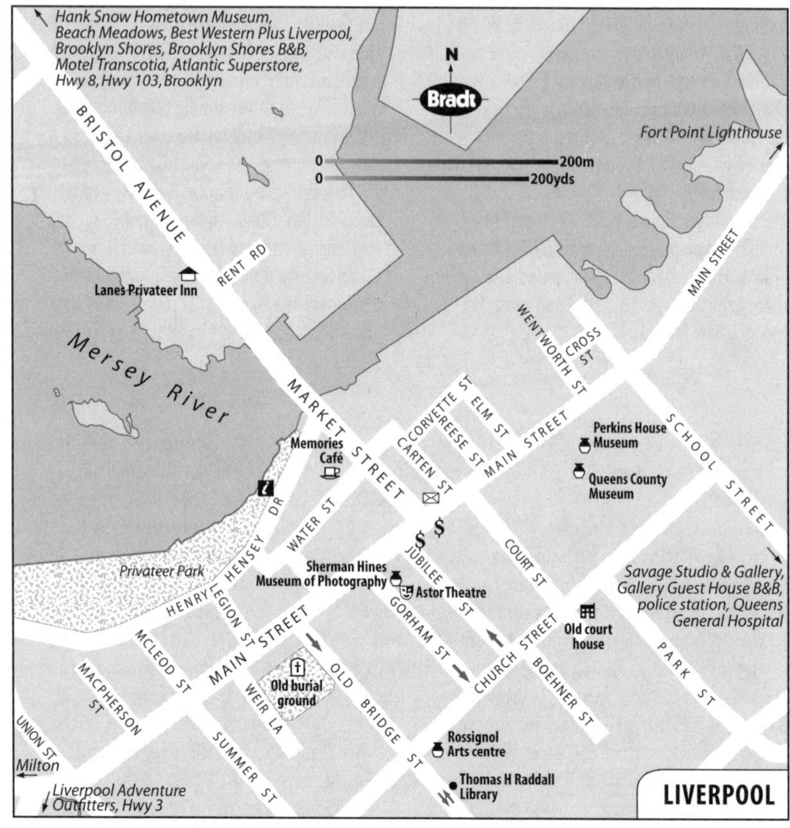

Step back a decade or 3 at this traditional-style motel. The licensed dining room (⌚ *06.00–20.00 Mon–Fri, 08.00–20.00 Sat/Sun;* **$–$$**) offers simple, good-value home cookin'. **$**

✕ **Memories Café & Eatery** 28 Water St; ☎356 3110; ⌚ year-round 08.00–16.00 Mon–Fri, 10.00–15.00 Sat. Downtown Liverpool was crying out for a decent lunch spot (especially after The Woodpile closed), & this new establishment does the job. B/fasts, soups (good haddock chowder), sandwiches, paninis, & Italian soda! **$–$$**

ENTERTAINMENT Built in 1902 as part of the Town Hall, **Astor Theatre** (*59 Gorham St;* ☎ *354 5250; www.astortheatre.ns.ca;* ⌚ *year-round*) is the province's oldest-surviving performing arts venue. Originally an opera house, as film became more popular the emphasis shifted. About 30 years ago, live performances began to regain popularity, and the Astor now has a varied calendar.

FESTIVALS In **May,** the **International Theatre Festival** (*www.litf.ca*) is a five-day amateur theatre festival held every two years (even years) at the historic Astor Theatre. **Privateer Days** (☎ *354 4500; www.privateerdays.ca*), the town's big festival (five days over the first weekend in July) is a lot of fun, with battle re-enactments, town walking tours led by guides in period costume, candlelit graveyard tours, boat races, fireworks and much more.

August sees the **Queens County SeaFest** (*www.queenscountyseafest.ca*), a three-day Brooklyn festival with a fishing competition, live entertainment, food stalls and family activities, and the **Hank Snow Tribute** (contact Hank Snow Hometown Museum for details), a three-day celebration of the Yodelling Ranger.

Ukulele concerts and workshops are held every two years (odd years) in October, at the **International Ukulele Ceilidh** (*www.ukuleleceilidh.ca*).

OTHER PRACTICALITIES

$ **Banks** Royal Bank, 209 Main St; 354 5717; 10.00–16.00 Mon–Wed, 10.00–17.00 Thu/Fri. Scotiabank, 183 Main St; 354 3431; 10.00–16.00 Mon–Wed, 10.00–17.00 Thu/Fri

Hospital Queens General Hospital, 175 School St; 354 3436

Library Thomas H Raddall Library, 145 Old Bridge St; 354 5270; 10.00–17.00 Tue/Wed & Fri, 10.00–20.00 Thu, 10.00–14.00 Sat, 12.00–16.00 Sun

Post office 176 Main St; 08.30–17.00 Mon–Fri

Tourist information 32 Henry Hensey Dr; 354 5421; mid May–Sep 10.00–18.00 daily

WHAT TO SEE AND DO Liverpool native Sherman Hines, one of Canada's most renowned landscape and portrait photographers, donated his extensive collection of photographic equipment to the **Sherman Hines Museum of Photography** (*219 Main St; 354 2667; www.shermanhinesphotographymuseum.com; mid May–mid Oct 10.00–17.00 Tue–Sat (Jul/Aug 10.00–17.00 Sun); admission CAN$4, inc free admission to Rossignol Arts Centre*), which also features work by important past and contemporary Canadian photographers. There's much more besides, including displays on holograms and camera obscura, all housed in Liverpool's c1901 former Town Hall.

Liverpool's old high school (and grounds) now house an interesting hotch-potch of exhibits as the **Rossignol Arts Centre** (*205 Church St; 354 3067; www.rossignolculturalcentre.com; mid May–mid Oct 10.00–17.30 Mon–Sat (Jul/Aug 12.00–17.30 Sun); admission CAN$4, inc free admission to Photography Museum*), including an outhouse museum, folk art, various mounted birds and animals, and an art gallery. Recently, the chance to 'stay overnight in a museum exhibit' has been offered: choose from a Mongolian tent, Indian tepee, settler's log cabin or British blockhouse. See website for details.

Art lovers who appreciate land- (and especially sea-) scapes should visit the **Savage Studio and Gallery** (*611 Shore Rd, Mersey Point; 354 5431; www.savagegallery.ca; Jul/Aug 10.00–19.00 daily; off-season by chance or appointment*), Roger Savage's gallery, which is a five-minute drive from town.

The c1766 New England-style house which is now the **Perkins House Museum** (*105 Main St; 354 4058; http://museum.gov.ns.ca/peh/; mid May–mid Oct 09.30–17.30 Mon–Sat, 13.00–17.30 Sun; admission CAN$4*) was built for Simeon Perkins, a prominent Liverpool citizen best known for the diaries which he kept. Perkins lived here until his death in 1812. There are now 'interactive ghosts' to guide you round the house.

It might look much older, and that was the idea when the interesting **Queens County Museum** (*109 Main St; 354 4058; www.queenscountymuseum.com; year-Jun–mid Oct 09.30–17.30 Mon–Sat, 13.00–17.30 Sun; mid Oct–May 09.00–17.00 Mon–Sat; admission CAN$4*) next door to the Perkins House was built in 1980. The interior is jam-packed with a whole variety of things from Mi'kmaq tools to 'privateers and pirates'. Pride of place goes to the Perkins diaries. Major improvements are planned in the form of anew Mi'kmaq-related gallery, and an interactive privateer ship. Genealogists will want to visit the research centre (fee charged).

Clarence Eugene 'Hank' Snow (1914–99) was born close by and became a country music legend, recording over 100 albums and selling over 70 million records. Check out the **Hank Snow Home Town Museum** (*148 Bristol Av;* ☎ *354 4675,* **t/f** *1 888 450 5525; www.hanksnow.com;* ⏲ *mid May–mid Oct 09.00–17.00 Mon–Sat, 12.00–17.30 Sun; mid Oct–mid May 09.00–16.00 Mon–Fri; admission CAN$3*) and see a wealth of 'Yodelling Ranger' material, including his 1947 Cadillac and his stage suits. The centre shares Liverpool's former train station with the Nova Scotia Country Music Hall of Fame.

The park on the waterfront at the end of Main Street is said to be the spot where de Mons landed in 1604: today you'll find cannon and an unusually shaped wooden lighthouse, **Fort Point Lighthouse** (*Park 21, Fort Point Lane;* ☎ *354 5741;* ⏲ *mid May–early Oct; admission free*), constructed in 1855. Shut down in 1989 with talk of demolition, Nova Scotia's fourth-oldest surviving lighthouse was saved and opened as a small museum in 1997.

Set out on foot, by bike, canoe or kayak with **Liverpool Adventure Outfitters** (*4003 Sandy Cove Rd;* ☎ *354 2702; www.liverpooladventureoutfitters.com*), who offer multi-sport tours, plus canoe, kayak, bike and rowing-boat rentals and day tours to Kejimkujik National Park (see pages 214–18).

AROUND LIVERPOOL

BEACH MEADOWS This wonderful long, sandy beach approximately 8km east of Liverpool is one of the best on the South Shore. There are two parking areas from which boardwalks lead to it through the sand dunes. There are views of **Coffin Island** (named after Peleg Coffin, one of the first settlers), with a lighthouse and abandoned fishing shanties.

MILTON Just 4km from Liverpool, either by Highway 8 or by following Main Street away from town, Milton is a pretty village on the Mersey River. There are photogenic churches, good birding and, in late spring, magnificent rhododendrons beneath the white pines at the 22ha **Pine Grove Park**. Tupper Park has a picnic area overlooking the Milton Falls. You can also visit a restored c1903 **blacksmith shop** (⏲ *mid Jun–Sep 10.00–16.00 Mon–Fri; admission CAN$1*).

Where to stay

Mersey Lodge (5 rooms) 2537 River Rd; ☎ 354 5547; **e** merseylodge@ns.sympatico.ca; www.merseylodge.com; ⏲ year-round. This rustic but comfortable lodge is well off the beaten track, approx 10km from Milton mostly on an unpaved road. Fish, swim or canoe on the river. Full b/fast inc. **$$**

Morton House Inn B&B (7 units) 147 Main St (Hwy 8); ☎ 354 2908, **t/f** 1 877 354 2908; www.mortonhouseinn.com; ⏲ year-round by

DRINKING SPIRITS

At the end of Main Street just before Fort Point, the building which is now 5 Riverside Drive was built in 1763, and operated as Dexter's Tavern. In the late 18th century, Simeon Perkins (see page 167) was a regular patron. It is said to be haunted by a tiny, uniformed, mischievous ghost. Part of another house at the opposite end of Main Street was also an 18th-century tavern and is also supposed to be haunted. Both former taverns are now private residences.

reservation. Located in the village, this c1864 Empire-style mansion with 4 B&B rooms & 3 motel-style rooms is just across the road from the river, & beautifully decorated with antiques. Full b/fast inc in B&B rate. **$–$$**

WHITE POINT Off Highway 3, 9–12km from Liverpool, visitors are drawn here for the family resort and golf course. Despite a devastating fire in November 2011 which destroyed its c1928 main lodge, White Point resort reopened a year later brighter and fresher – and with the same ambience that has been attracting holidaymakers for decades. Hunt's Point, a couple of kilometres further along Highway 3, has a popular take-away.

Where to stay and eat

White Point Beach Resort White Point; 354 2711, **t/f** 1 800 565 5068; **e** greatday@whitepoint.com; www.whitepoint.com; year-round. This long-established, popular family resort has a range of accommodation choices from standard rooms to 3-bedroom log cottages. The fire (see above) was used as an opportunity to refresh & renovate. There's a restaurant & lounge, spa, golf course (see below), 1km of private beach, indoor & outdoor (seasonal) pools & the usual resort extras – oh, & large friendly rabbits roaming the grounds. **$$**

Fisherman's Cove RV & Campground (22 sites) 6718 Hwy 3, Hunt's Point; 683 2772; www.fishermanscoverv.netfirms.com; May–Oct. Small store & laundry facilities. **$**

Seaside Seafoods 6943 Hwy 3, Hunt's Point; 683 2618; late Mar–Oct 11.00–21.00 (summer to 23.00) daily. Simple but much-loved fast-food & seafood eatery. The deep-fried clams are fantastic, plus there's the usual selection of fish & chips, burgers & soft ice cream. Picnic tables outside. **$**

What to see and do Very close to the resort, on a small peninsula with majestic ocean views, is the nine-hole **White Point Golf Club** (**t/f** *1 866 683 2485; mid Apr–early Nov*). Played as 18 holes (with separate tees for the back nine) the course is 6,200yds long. Ask about packages if staying at the resort. Green fees for 18 holes CAN$48.

Although its principal location is at Port Joli (see page 170), the **Rossignol Surf Shop** (*683 2350; www.surfnovscotia.com*) has a branch at White Point Beach Resort, and offers surfboard sales, surfing lessons and clinics, and equipment rentals.

SUMMERVILLE BEACH This long (over 1km) stretch of whitish sand is one of the best and most accessible of the South Shore beaches. Backed by sand dunes and a salt marsh, it has been designated a Provincial Park. Sunbathe, play beach volleyball, swim in the bracing waters or picnic. The beach is 17km from Liverpool, just off Highway 3, 1.5km from Exit 20 off Highway 103, and therefore easily reached **by car**.

Where to stay and eat The **Quarterdeck Beachside Villas and Grill** (*16 units; 7499 Hwy 3, Summerville Centre; 683 2998,* **t/f** *1 800 565 1119;* **e** *quarterdeck@eastlink.ca; www.quarterdeck.ns.ca; year-round;* **$$$**) is a well-equipped accommodation, with one-bedroom suites, 13 'villas' (two-storey, two-bedroom apartments) each with an oceanfront deck and balcony, two one-bedroom suites with kitchenettes and one three-bedroom cottage. Kayak, bike, surfboard rental is available. The restaurant (*May–Oct 11.30–late;* **$$–$$$**) has one of the province's best locations, especially the covered deck under which the waves lap (for which you'll need to book a table in advance). The food is good, too: lobster tails stuffed with scallops and shrimp, for example, are scrumptious. Desserts are worth leaving room for.

PORT MOUTON

This village on the bay of the same name has a couple of places to stay (including a backpackers' hostel) and a restaurant, and is well placed for exploring the region's beautiful parks and beaches. Several uninhabited islands dot the bay.

HISTORY Port Mouton was named by Champlain in 1604: when his ship was at anchor in the bay, a sheep jumped into the sea. There were a couple of attempts at settlement (by Scots in the 1620s and English around 1770) but the first lasting attempt was made in 1783 by disbanded soldiers who had served under Sir Guy Carleton. Quickly, they built over 200 houses and called their settlement Guy's Borough. The following year a fire destroyed most of their houses. This – combined with the fact that the region's soil wasn't great for farming – caused the settlers to uproot *en masse*. They headed east, and settled in what is now Guysborough (see page 379).

GETTING THERE To get to Port Mouton **by car**, it is located on Highway 103, 19km/12 miles southwest of Liverpool and 48km/30 miles from Shelburne.

WHERE TO STAY AND EAT

Port Mouton Bay Cottages & Seascape Restaurant (5 cottages) 8403 Hwy 103; 683 2020, **t/f** 1 866 933 2020; **e** pmbcottages@eastlink.ca; www.cottagesinnovascotia.com; year-round. Simple, spacious, well-equipped 2-bedroom cottages. **$$**

Port Mouton International Hostel (30 beds) 8100 Hwy 103; 947 3140; **e** pmhostel@eastlink.ca; www.wqccda.com/PMhostel; year-round. Housed in a c1961 former school, this friendly backpackers' hostel has 1 large & 4 small dorms, with most of the beds bunks. There's a big kitchen & common room, & if you don't feel like cooking, the Seascape (see below) is in walking distance. Linen/bedding inc. *Dorm CAN$30.*

Seascape Restaurant 8426 Hwy 103; 683 2626; early Apr/mid May & Sep–mid Nov 11.00–19.00 Tue–Sun; mid May–Aug 11.00–20.00 daily. Under the same ownership as Port Mouton Bay Cottages & just across the road, this restaurant ain't *haute cuisine* but the fish & chips are very good & you won't go hungry. **$$**

WHAT TO SEE AND DO The **Kejimkujik Seaside** (*St Catherine's Rd; 682 2772; www.pc.gc.ca/kejimkujik; year-round; admission free, facilities only open late May–mid Oct*) confusingly, is a separate part of Kejimkujik National Park (see page 214), which is approximately 100km inland. Kejimkujik Seaside protects 22km² of wilderness on the Port Mouton Peninsula including pristine white-sand beaches, turquoise waters, coastal bogs, an abundance of wild flowers, rich lagoon systems and coastal wildlife. Most easily reached by an 8km unpaved road from Highway 103, this is one of the least disturbed shoreline areas on the south coast of Nova Scotia. No camping is permitted.

From the car park, an easy trail (5.3km return) leads through the trees, on boardwalks over marshy areas, and on to the beach at Harbour Rocks. Here you are likely to see seals basking on the rocks or bobbing about in the water – take binoculars. You can continue along the beach before retracing your steps. A longer (8.8km return from the car park) option is to branch off the first trail and take in Port Joli Head on a coastal loop. Some sections of the beach close between late April and July to protect piping plover nesting sites. Mosquitoes may cause annoyance, even on the beach. Don't forget repellent.

BEACH BEAUTY

At the time of writing, Carters Beach is a prime contender for the 'Most Beautiful Beach in Nova Scotia' title – and, amazingly, it's still a relatively well-kept secret. It's being realistic rather than pessimistic to wonder how long it will stay unspoilt.

When you first see the beaches – there are actually three – and the island-dotted bay, you might think that you're in the Mediterranean, especially if the sun is out. The sand is golden, the crystal-clear water has a slight turquoise hue, and huge, smooth black boulders and sometimes colourful sea kayakers, give the scene depth.

Walk along the first beach and you'll find a stream blocking your way. Depending on the tide and other factors, you may be able to ford it by wading across, or it may be safer to head upstream for about ten minutes and cross there. The second beach is broad and straight, and a good place to look for sand dollars (flat, almost circular, shell-like types of urchin). The third beach is another pretty crescent which ends at high sand dunes well worth climbing for the view.

To reach Carters Beach turn onto Central Port Mouton Road from Highway 103 at Port Mouton. Continue for about 4km until you see a sign to the left to Carters Beach. There's a tiny parking area but no other facilities, and a short (less than 100m) path through the trees down to the beach.

In addition to renting surfboards and wetsuits and advising on the best surfing spots, the **Rossignol Surf Shop** (*354 7100; www.surfnovascotia.com; May, Jun & Sep 10.00–18.00 Sat/Sun; Jul–Aug 10.00–18.00 daily*) offers guided three-hour and all-day kayak tours around Port Joli and Port Mouton bays. There's another branch at the White Point Beach Resort (see page 169).

The 678ha **Thomas Raddall Provincial Park** (*East Port l'Hebert Rd, Port Joli; 683 2664; www.novascotiaparks.ca/parks/thraddall.asp; mid May–early Oct*), is 3km off Highway 103, 9km west of Port Mouton and has over 11km of trails, some multi-use, as well as an 82-site wooded campground. The best stretches of sand are Camper's Beach and Sandy Bay Beach. The park has a good selection of animal and birdlife.

LOCKEPORT

The quaint town of Lockeport is well worth exploring for its lovely old homes and fine beaches (five in all). The beautiful 1.5km-long **Crescent Beach**, not to be confused with a beach of the same name near the LaHave Islands (see page 164), is hard to miss, on the southern edge of the thin strip of land between the 'mainland' and the 'island'. Beach lovers should be aware that there are at least another dozen good beaches in the area: locals will be happy to direct you to their favourite.

Beaches apart, the town also boasts the province's only **Registered Historic Streetscape**. This comprises five houses built by descendants of town founder Jonathan Locke between 1836 and 1876. The houses offer an interesting cross-section of historical architecture with excellent examples of Colonial, Georgian and Victorian styles. A walking-tour guidebook should be available at the tourist office.

Those with children shouldn't miss the excellent marine-themed playground (*mid May–Oct*) in **Seacaps Memorial Park**.

Accessible **by car**, Lockeport is on Highway 3, 18km from Highway 103 Exit 23, 17km from Highway 103 Exit 24.

HISTORY The town was founded in 1755 by settlers from Plymouth, Massachusetts, led by a Jonathan Locke. Several other Planters followed and were joined by British settlers – and a few Icelanders.

Although in the early stages of the American Revolution residents were sympathetic to American privateers, sometimes offering them aid and even helping American prisoners who had escaped, that all changed in 1778 when whale boats from Rhode Island arrived and raided their homes for food and valuables.

Since its founding, Lockeport has been a fishing community, and shipbulding began in the 1880s.

WHERE TO STAY AND EAT

Ocean Mist Cottages (6 cottages) 1 Gull Rock Rd; 656 3200; e info@oceanmistcottages.com; www.oceanmistcottages.com; year-round. With a fabulous location less than 20m from Crescent Beach, these fully equipped & quiet 2-bedroom cottages are spacious & comfortable. Weekly rentals preferred. **$$$**

The Parrot's Pins Candlepin Café 10 Beech St; 656 2695; year-round 11.00–14.30 & 17.00–closing Tue–Sat. Housed in a 4-lane bowling alley & decorated with a range of crafts from all over the globe, the good news is that the food – 'international eclectic' – works. It helps that everything is fresh, homemade & mostly local. Try the Bluenoser Martini, a glass of scallops poached in vermouth served with pasta in a creamy vodka lemon sauce. The desserts keep up the standard. A real treat. **$$**

Lockeport Landing Café 18 Beech St; 656 3333; Jun–Sep 10.00–14.00 Wed–Mon, 17.00–20.00 Thu–Sun. New (late summer 2012) café which I am yet to visit. **$$**

FESTIVALS In August, there is a weekend fishing tournament, the **Sea Derby** (*www.lockeportseaderby.ca*).

OTHER PRACTICALITIES

$ Bank Royal Bank, 25A Beech St; 656 2212; 10.00–15.00 Mon–Wed & Fri, 10.00–17.00 Thu

Library Lillian Benham Library, 35 North St; 656 2817; see www.westerncounties.ca/library/lockeport for opening hours

Post office 30 Beech St; 08.15–17.00 Mon–Fri, 08.30–12.30 Sat

Tourist information 157 Locke St; 656 3123; late Jun–mid Sep 09.00–18.00 daily. At Crescent Beach, adjacent to the canteen (which serves good ice cream), it offers changing rooms & showers. The upstairs look-out has fine views.

SHELBURNE *(Population: 2,250)*

The town of Shelburne sits at the innermost end of what is said by many to be the third-finest harbour in the world (after Sydney, Australia, and Havana, Cuba).

A few years ago there was talk of a ferry service to connect Shelburne with Boston, USA, which gave the region's property market a brief fillip – but then the world's economic problems extinguished any such dreams.

Much of what there is to be seen lies within the area bounded by Water Street (the main street), Dock Street and King Street. Within this area are three museums and over 30 original late 18th-century Loyalist homes, most in good condition.

History aside, the waterfront is a pleasant place for a stroll. Bearing in mind that the choices for both dining and accommodation are limited, if you're visiting at the weekend and/or in peak season, it would be wise to book ahead.

HOLLYWOOD HISTORY

Much of *Scarlet Letter*, a 1990s Hollywood flop, was filmed in Shelburne. Wanting to make the location more authentic, the film company built over a dozen 'old' structures. Most were removed after filming, but some remain, including the 'historic' (c1994!) cooperage on the waterfront across from the Cooper's Inn.

HISTORY In the aftermath of the American War of Independence, the newly formed colonies were not a good place to be for those who had been loyal to the British flag. When offered passage, land under protection of the British flag, provisions and tools, many jumped at the chance. Early in 1783, 18 ships loaded with mostly aristocratic Loyalists and a large number of their black slaves sailed into Port Roseway (Shelburne's early name).

Trees were felled, land was cleared, streets were laid out and houses were built quickly. The settlement was renamed Shelburne, in honour of Lord Shelburne, Secretary of State for the Colonies. Thousands more Loyalists arrived later in the year, and Shelburne quickly (but only briefly) became the largest urban centre in British North America, having a population of over 15,000 in 1785.

Then things went sour: the government stopped providing rations and financial assistance. Race riots broke out. Many began to move away, properties were abandoned, houses were torn down for fuel and still more were allowed to fall into ruin and decay. By 1818, the population had dropped to 300.

In time, people began to move back. Shipbuilding started up again, and soon it prospered. New homes were built over the old cellars. The population tripled, and Shelburne became renowned for the building of schooners and brigantines. Late in the 19th century, when steel-hulled steam-powered ships began to replace wooden sailing vessels, Shelburne's economy fell back on fishing. Boatbuilding continued on a much smaller scale and this time yachts were the speciality.

Life continued quietly and without great incident until the 1990s when a couple of Hollywood films were shot here (see box above).

GETTING THERE Shelburne is situated on Highway 3, just off Highway 103 Exit 25 (southbound) or Exit 26 (northbound), and is therefore easy to get to **by car**. It is 210km/130 miles from Halifax, 98km/61 miles from Yarmouth and 67km/47 miles from Liverpool.

WHERE TO STAY

Boulder Cove Cottages (5 cottages) 321 Shore Rd, Churchover; 875 1542, **t/f** 1 866 732 7867; www.bouldercove.com; year-round. Lovely setting on the Birchtown Bay waterfront a 10-min drive from Shelburne. Very comfortable 1- & 2-bedroom cottages. Laundry room, walking trail, bikes & boats for guest use. Within walking distance of the Black Loyalist Heritage Site (see page 178). **$$**

Cooper's Inn (8 rooms) 36 Dock St; 875 4656, **t/f** 1 800 688 2011; www.thecoopersinn.com; Apr–Oct. Historic charm & modern convenience in a restored c1784 Loyalist home with courtyard garden across the road from the waterfront. Gourmet b/fast inc. **$$**

Water Street Lighthouse B&B (3 rooms) 263 Water St; 875 2331, **t/f** 1 888 875 2331; www.shelburnelighthouse.com; year-round. Friendly B&B a 15-min walk from the historic waterfront. Wi-Fi available. The airy guest rooms share 2 bathrooms. B/fast inc. **$**

MacKenzie's Motel & Cottages (15 units) 260 Water St; 875 2842, **t/f** 1 866 875 0740; www.mackenzies.ca; year-round.

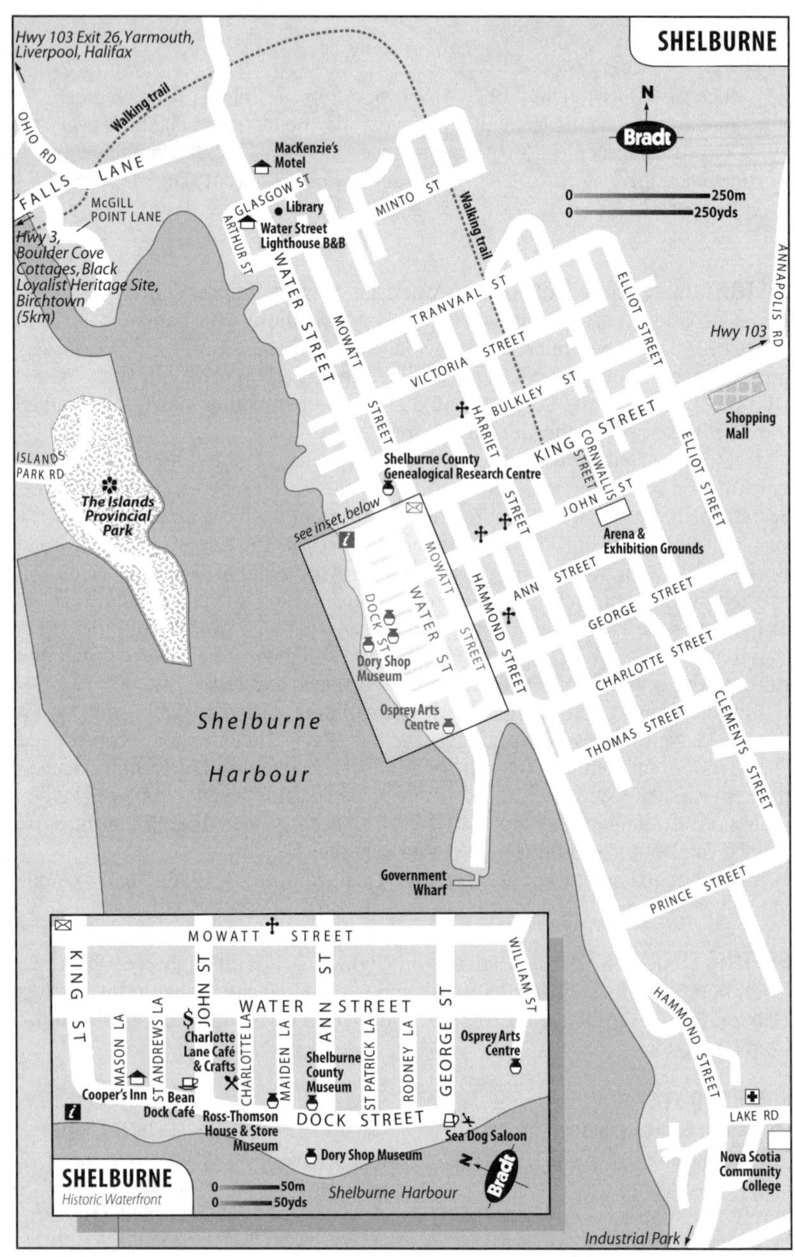

6 motel rooms, 2 suites (1 with kitchen) & 7 1- & 2-bedroom cottages. Heated outdoor pool (seasonal). Landscaped grounds. Good budget choice. Rate inc decent continental b/fast. **$**

WHERE TO EAT

Charlotte Lane Café & Crafts 13 Charlotte Lane; 875 3314; www.charlottelane.ca; early May–mid Dec 11.30–14.30 & 17.00–20.00 Tue–Sat. This is probably the most highly recommended restaurant in Nova Scotia, & – in my experience – with justification. Discerning locals & visitors travel a long way to enjoy owner-chef Roland Glauser's cooking. The menu is varied & changes seasonally: start, perhaps, with the Bluenose spinach salad. To follow, the lobster & scallop brandy gratin is superb (or try the pork tenderloin Zürich-style), & for dessert the sticky toffee pudding takes some beating. The extensive wine list includes a Nova Scotia section, & a different special cocktail is offered every evening. Although housed in a heritage building, the décor is bright, with funky local artworks. There is a small garden patio. $$

Sea Dog Saloon 1 Dock St; 875 2862; www.theseadog.com; mid Apr–Dec 11.00–21.00 daily. The pub's large outside deck is a great place for a drink or bite in the sunshine. The fish (haddock) & chips is good, & a glass of Keith's IPA makes a good accompaniment. $$

Bean Dock Café Dock St (cnr with John St); 875 1302; summer 08.30–20.00 Mon–Thu, 08.30–17.00 Fri, 10.00–16.00 Sat, 10.00–14.00 Sun; winter 08.30–16.00 Mon–Fri, 10.00–14.00 Sat. Friendly, laid-back & a good choice for coffee, light lunches & desserts. $

FESTIVALS June sees the **Shelburne County Lobster Festival**, where you can enjoy crustacean creations at various Shelburne County venues. In July, **Founders' Days** (*www.shelburnenovascotia.com/foundersdays/*) gives the opportunity to look round a Loyalist encampment occupied by volunteers in period military costume. See the waterfront festooned with brightly coloured wind-catching devices at the **Whirligig and Weathervane Festival** (*www.whirligigfestival.com*) in September.

BURCHTOWN TO FREETOWN

Amongst the Loyalists who arrived in Port Roseway (Shelburne) in 1783 were over 1,000 blacks: some were slaves, others former slaves who had sought protection under the British and served the Loyalist cause against the Americans during the War of Independence. Many of the freed were given land a few kilometres to the west of Shelburne in what became known as Burchtown (and, with time, Birchtown).

For a short while, Birchtown was the largest settlement of free blacks in North America – the population in 1784 was over 1,500 – but this was no paradise. Many blacks had been granted infertile land, there was little or no employment and poverty was commonplace. Those who could find work received about a quarter of the wage received by a white doing the same job. Nova Scotia winters were incredible shocks to systems, particularly as with no money to build houses, many lived in what were effectively roofed-over holes on hillsides. In 1791, things were so bad that an emissary was sent to raise the community's concerns with the Secretary of State in England.

As it happened, in addition to colonising Nova Scotia, the English government had similar plans for west Africa, and came up with an ironic proposal. Any adult male who wished would be given free passage to Sierra Leone where he would receive 20 acres of land (plus ten acres for his wife, and five each for any children). Many agreed to the terms, and in 1792 a fleet of 15 vessels left Halifax for west Africa. On board were over 500 from Birchtown alone.

Many of those who left had led or inspired the community: after their departure there was another exodus from Birchtown, this time to other parts of Nova Scotia. Today, fewer than 200 black Nova Scotians live in Shelburne County.

OTHER PRACTICALITIES

$ Bank CIBC, 146 Water St; 875 2388; 10.00–17.00 Mon–Fri

Hospital Roseway Hospital, 1606 Sandy Point Rd; 875 3011

Library McKay Memorial Library, 17 Glasgow St; 875 3615; 12.30–17.00 & 18.00–20.00 Tue–Thu, 10.00–17.00 Fri, 10.00–14.00 Sat

Post office 162 Mowatt St; 08.30–17.30 Mon–Fri, 08.30–12.30 Sat

Tourist information 31 Dock St; 875 4547; daily late May–Jun 10.00–17.00; Jul–Aug 10.00–19.00; Sep–late Oct 09.00–17.00

WHAT TO SEE AND DO One CAN$10 ticket (available at any of the individual museums) will gain you entry to three Shelburne museums which normally charge CAN$4 each: they are the Ross-Thomson House and Store, Dory Shop and Shelburne County Museum. Sadly, funding cuts forced the closure of a fourth – the Muir-Cox Shipbuilding Interpretive Centre.

There was something of a revolution in the Grand Banks fishing industry when someone came up with the idea of loading a schooner with small, light, stackable wooden boats (dories), sailing out to the fishing grounds, lowering them into the water and then letting fishermen try their luck. In 1983, the c1880 former dory shop, now **Dory Shop Museum** (*Dock St; 875 3219; http://museum.gov.ns.ca/dory; Jun–Sep 09.30–17.30 daily; admission CAN$4*) was opened as a museum by Prince Charles and Diana, Princess of Wales. Dories made in Shelburne were renowned for their strength.

TOBEATIC WILDERNESS AREA

The pristine Tobeatic Wilderness Area (known as 'The Tobeatic', or just 'The Toby') is vast, covering 104,000ha, and is roughly three-times the size of Kejimkujik National Park (see page 214) which borders it to the east. Spreading over five of the province's counties, this is the largest remaining wild area in the Maritimes. Within its boundaries are the headwaters of nine river systems including the Shelburne Canadian Heritage River, and Sissiboo, Roseway, Clyde and Tusket rivers. The nearest communities include Bear River to the north, Weymouth to the northwest, Caledonia to the east and Kemptville to the west.

Barrens (areas of rocky heathland with dwarf shrub and/or lichen vegetation), bogs, wetlands and remote woodland provide vast areas of diverse wildlife habitat: bear, porcupine, snowshoe hare and beaver are common. The provincially endangered mainland moose inhabits these vast wild tracts of southwest Nova Scotia. Bird species include loon, warblers, waterfowl and pileated woodpecker, and you'll likely hear the hoot of the barred owl at night. Forest wild flowers (including orchids) are plentiful in late spring and summer, and late summer and early autumn welcome an abundance of blueberries, huckleberries and cranberries. There are several pockets of old-growth forest (with some hemlock trees 400-plus years old), and the network of rivers, streams and lakes make for outstanding wilderness canoeing, camping and hiking for those with experience – there are no developed campsites and no regularly maintained trails. No motorised travel – including by ATV or motorboat – is permitted, and access vehicles should really have high clearance.

Early spring (just before mid May) and autumn are probably the best times to visit: water levels are high enough for wilderness canoeing without too many long portages, there are fewer biting insects, and daytime temperatures are more moderate – but be prepared for extreme weather at any time of year.

The **Osprey Arts Centre** (*107 Water St;* ☎ *875 2359; www.ospreyartscentre.com;* ⏲ *year-round; gallery* ⏲ *09.00–16.00 Mon–Fri*) is a performing arts centre featuring music, theatre and film, and also houses the Coastline Gallery, featuring local artists' work.

Now the **Ross-Thomson House and Store Museum** (*9 Charlotte Lane;* ☎ *875 3141; http://museum.gov.ns.ca/rth/;* ⏲ *Jun–mid Oct 09.30–17.30 daily; admission CAN$4*), this c1785 house was the workplace of brothers George and Robert Ross, from Aberdeen, Scotland. The highlight is an authentically stocked 18th-century store and chandlery. The garden is laid out and planted in late 18th-century style.

An excellent resource for genealogists, the **Shelburne County Genealogical Research Centre** (*168 Water St;* ☎ *875 4299;* ⏲ *summer 09.00–16.30 Mon–Fri (check winter hours); CAN$5/half day*) allows you to trace the roots of Loyalists and Shelburne's other early settlers.

Housed in a c1787 Loyalist building, the **Shelburne County Museum** (*20 Dock St;* ☎ *875 3219; www.historicshelburne.com;* ⏲ *Jun–mid Oct 09.30–17.30 daily; mid Oct–May 10.00–12.00 & 14.00–17.00 Mon–Fri; admission CAN$4*) is a good place to get an overview of the town's fascinating history. Be sure to see the Newsham firepumper (one of two early 'fire engines' imported from Boston in 1740) and a good exhibit on black Loyalist history.

If you're keen to **kayak**, single or double kayaks can be rented from the **Sea Dog saloon** (see *Where to eat*, page 175). They will also advise you on suggested routes and waterside attractions. What fun to arrive at a pub in a kayak!

This is true, remote wilderness, most of which has no mobile phone reception: if you overstretch yourself – and/or are unlucky – an exciting adventure could easily turn into disaster. Even if you have experience in this kind of travel, consider using the services of a guide or outfitter: local knowledge could prove crucial in planning a successful wilderness adventure.

WHERE TO STAY AND EAT If you don't like wilderness camping, there are some alternatives, such as the **Trout Point Lodge** (*189 Trout Point Rd, East Kemptville;* ☎ *482 8360, 761 2142; www.troutpoint.com;* ⏲ *May–Dec;* **$$–$$$**). The best base for exploring the western part of The Toby, riverside Trout Point Lodge has a wonderful setting right on the edge of the protected wilderness. It offers a variety of accommodation including cottages and two lodges. Part of the attraction is the remoteness (the property occupies over 40ha at the convergence of the Tusket and Napier rivers), but this also means that you'll have quite a drive if you choose not to dine on-site. In addition to woodland trails, there is river and lake swimming, canoeing, kayaking, star-gazing, mountain bikes and catch-&-release fishing. The dining room (⏲ *mid May–late Oct; 1 sitting at 19.30*) serves a creative blend of Creole and Mediterranean cuisine, and boasts an extensive wine list. The fixed-price dinner costs CAN$135 per couple. In my opinion, this is the province's best upmarket wilderness lodge.

WHAT TO SEE AND DO Weymouth-based and recommended, **Hinterland Adventures** (☎ *837 4092,* **t/f** *1 800 378 8177; www.kayakingnovascotia.com*) offers canoe tours into the Tobeatic Wilderness Area.

AROUND SHELBURNE

THE ISLANDS PROVINCIAL PARK (*Hwy 3; www.novascotiaparks.ca/parks/theislands.asp; ⌚ mid Jun–early Oct*) Huge granite boulders – left by melting glaciers 10,000 years ago – dot this pleasant park and open and wooded campground (62 sites) 5km west of Shelburne offering fine views over Shelburne Harbour. The picnic area is joined to the rest of the park by a short causeway, and there's a rocky beach.

BLACK LOYALIST HERITAGE SITE (*Old Birchtown Rd; Birchtown; ☎ 875 1310, t/f 1 888 354 0772; www.blackloyalist.com; ⌚ site year-round, museum & gift shop Jun–Aug; admission to site free, museum CAN$3*) At the time of writing, this site, 9km west of Shelburne on Highway 3, is a work in progress: construction on a new centre has begun and is due to be completed in summer 2013. The centre will highlight the Black Loyalist history and heritage, and include a gift shop. This will be in addition to the existing interpretive walking trail and old burial ground. A botanical garden and library have also been mentioned.

THE TOBY AND BEYOND One of Nova Scotia's few cross-province roads heads north from just west of Shelburne. After passing the Ohios (Lower, Middle and Upper) and crossing and re-crossing the pretty Roseway River, Route 203 skirts one edge of the vast Tobeatic Wilderness Area (see box, page 176). The road travels further inland to East Kemptville (nearby is one of the province's few luxury eco-lodges, Trout Point Lodge – see page 177), and then meets Route 340 where a left turn will take you towards Yarmouth (page 186) and a right turn towards Weymouth (page 194).

BARRINGTON

With a lovely setting at the northeast of Barrington Bay, the community has a museum complex and tourist office. Most services (supermarkets, fast food, etc) are located 8km away at **Barrington Passage**, which is also the gateway to Cape Sable Island (see page 179). Also worth visiting in the area are beautiful **Sandy Hills Beach Provincial Park** (*Hwy 309, approx 6km from Barrington*), and the lighthouse at **Baccaro Point** (*Baccaro Rd, off Hwy 309, 18km from Barrington*), a good – if breezy – spot for a picnic, and popular with birdwatchers. One of the oldest communities on the South Shore, this area (including Cape Sable Island) is one of the few parts of Nova Scotia where Quakers settled. Originally from Nantucket, they were whalers. Arriving in 1762, most moved on to Dartmouth (see page 121) in 1784 after being harassed repeatedly by American privateers. In more recent times, fishing – particularly for lobster – became the mainstay of the community.

GETTING THERE Barrington is located on Highway 103 and is easy to get to **by car**. The town is 40km/25 miles from Shelburne and 67km/42 miles from Yarmouth.

WHERE TO STAY AND EAT The following establishments are all in Barrington Passage (8km from Barrington), close to the causeway to Cape Sable Island.

Horizon Chalets & Motel (14 units) 3412 Hwy 3; ☎ 637 2242; e reservations@horizonmotels.com; www.horizonmotels.com; ⌚ year-round. 8 motel rooms & 6 larger chalet rooms. **$**

✕ **Land & Sea** 3723 Hwy 3; ☎ 637 3857; ⌚ year-round 11.00–20.00 Mon–Fri, 08.00–20.00 Sat/Sun. Standard diner-style food, hearty portions, reasonable prices & probably the best choice for a meal (rather than a snack) here. **$–$$**

✕ **Dan's Ice Cream Shoppe** 3724 Hwy 3; ☎ 637 3177; ⌚ Mar–Oct 11.00–22.30 daily. Wraps, smoothies, soup, salads – & quite good ice cream. My little daughter likes the chocolate twist covered in multi-coloured sprinkles. Fun place. **$**

FESTIVALS The **Nova Scotia Marathon** (*www.barringtonmunicipality.com/rec.htm*) offers a combination of full and half marathons run in late July.

OTHER PRACTICALITIES

$ Bank Royal Bank, 3525 Hwy 3, Barrington Passage; ☎ 637 2040; ⌚ 09.30–17.00 Mon–Fri

Library Barrington Municipal Library, 3588 Hwy 3, Barrington Passage; ☎ 637 3348; ⌚ 10.00–17.00 Tue, 12.30–17.00 & 18.00–20.00 Wed–Fri, 10.00–14.00 Sat

✉ **Post office** 2398 Hwy 3, Barrington; ⌚ 08.00–17.00 Mon–Fri, 09.00–12.00 Sat

Tourist information 2517 Hwy 3; ☎ 637 2625; ⌚ late May–late Sep 08.30–17.00 daily

WHAT TO SEE AND DO The **Barrington Museum complex** (☎ *637 2185; www.capesablehistoricalsociety.com;* ⌚ *Jun–Sep 09.30–17.30 Mon–Sat, 13.00–17.30 Sun; admission CAN$3/museum*) is a group of four museums and a genealogical centre (for which a CAN$10 research fee is charged).

Most popular is the **Seal Island Light Museum**, a half-height copy of the lighthouse that stood on remote Seal Island. There's a great view over Barrington Bay from the top. At the c1882 water-powered **Barrington Woollen Mill**, wool was washed, carded, spun, dyed and woven. The **Old Meeting House Museum** was built in 1765 by Planters. It is Canada's oldest nonconformist Protestant house of worship. Behind the building is the region's oldest cemetery.

The **Western Counties Military Museum**, houses exhibits ranging from 16th-century cannonballs to coins brought back from the Middle East by Canadian soldiers on peacekeeping duty. It shares Barrington's c1843 Old Courthouse with the **Cape Sable Historical Society Centre**.

CAPE SABLE ISLAND

Not to be confused with Sable Island (see pages 382–5), Cape Sable Island has also seen more than its fair share of shipwrecks in its time. There are few services, but ubiquitous are lobster pots and the smell of the sea. Small communities such as Centreville, Newellton, West Head – and comparatively bustling Clark's Harbour – dot the island.

The causeway to the island leads off Highway 3 at Barrington Passage, 8km/5 miles west of Barrington.

WHERE TO STAY AND EAT Self-caterers should stock up on the mainland and – with the exception of West Head (see below) – travellers should expect to go to Barrington or beyond to eat out.

Cape Sable Cottages (5 cottages) 37 Long Point Rd, Newellton; ☎ 745 0168; www.capesablecottages.com; ⌚ year-round. The décor in these well-equipped 2-bedroom cottages might not be to everyone's taste, but they are good for those looking to get away from it all. Canoes, kayaks & bikes are available. **$$**

✕ **West Head** ☎ 745 1322 ⌚ Apr–late Sep 10.00–20.00 daily. Located just by the wharf at West Head, this well-established take-out is a

BIRD ISLAND

Cape Sable Island is the most southerly accessible point in Atlantic Canada, and one of the province's best spring and autumn migration birding sites for waders. The coast around South Side Inlet and south and west of The Hawk are particularly rich viewing areas and tens of thousands of semipalmated sandpipers and short-billed dowitchers can usually be seen. In late winter and early spring thousands of Brant congregate on the flats of Hawk Channel: seeing the geese take to the skies is a highlight of the annual **Birding and Nature Festival** (*875 1542; www.discovershelburnecounty.com/birdfestival.html; late Mar*).

favourite of the local fishermen – always a good sign. In 2012, another take-out (the Route 330 Diner) set up 'shop' almost next door. I prefer the West Head. $

FESTIVALS **Island Days** at Clark's Harbour is a day of dory races held in the middle of August.

OTHER PRACTICALITIES

Tourist information 2634 Hwy 330, Clark's Harbour; 745 2586; early Jun–late Sep 10.00–17.00 Mon–Fri, 10.00–16.00 Sat/Sun

WHAT TO SEE AND DO The island has four main beaches: seals are sometimes seen at **Stoney** and **South Side** beaches, and **Northeast Point Beach** is popular with sunbathers. The wild expanse of **Hawk Beach** – named for a vessel once shipwrecked here and closest to the c1923 Cape Lighthouse, Nova Scotia's tallest – is great for solitude, proximity to nature and birding.

Named for an early 1760s' settler, the **Archelaus Smith Museum** (*915 Hwy 330; 745 3361; late Jun–end Aug 10.30–16.30 Mon–Sat, 13.30–16.30 Sun; admission free*), has displays on local history, island life, lobster fishing and shipbuilding. The most interesting exhibit is a 'wreck chair' made from wooden pieces salvaged from over 20 shipwrecks.

THE SHAG HARBOUR INCIDENT

Around a dozen residents of Shag Harbour (located on Highway 3, 9km west of Barrington Passage), witnessed a mysterious object crashing into the sea on the evening of 4 October 1967. Official investigations were carried out, and books such as *Dark Object: The World's Only Government-Documented UFO Crash* (see page 390) were written about what has been described as Canada's version of Roswell (Roswell is a town in New Mexico, USA renowned for what may have been a 'UFO incident' in 1947). The community is now home to the **Shag Harbour Incident Society Museum** (*723 0174; www.i2ce.com/shagharbour/; mid Jun–mid Sep 10.00–17.00 daily, off-season by appointment; admission free*). To find it, look out for a cream-coloured building with a flying saucer on the wall and two alien figures standing outside. Find that and you're in the right place. The society holds a UFO festival (*www.shagharbourufo.com*) in August. The local post office (*5527 Hwy 3*) has a special UFO cancellation stamp.

Colourful boats bob in **Clark's Harbour,** a busy little fishing town where the shore is lined with fish plants and boatbuilding yards. There's a petrol station, general store and a bank. A c1895 edifice constructedby shipbuilders houses the **Seaside Heritage Centre** (*2773 Main St; 745 0844, Jun–Sep*).

THE PUBNICOS

Highway 3 follows the pretty east shore of Pubnico Harbour passing Lower East, Centre East, Middle East and East Pubnico. At Pubnico, a turn onto Highway 335 takes you along the Pubnico Peninsula past Upper West, West, Middle West and Lower West Pubnico before fizzling out just before Pubnico Point. The region is well worth exploring by car or bike.

The Pubnico Peninsula is far busier and more prosperous than you might expect, and the reason is that this is the heart of one of the world's richest and most productive lobster-fishing areas. Rich too is the region's Acadian tradition, and you're more likely to hear French spoken than English. Whilst there is no official tourist information office in the Pubnicos, locals will be only too happy to try and help.

Turn off Highway 335 towards Dennis Point and follow the road all the way to the wharf area, usually buzzing with fishing boats; not surprising, seeing that this is one of Canada's largest commercial fishing ports. Around 120 boats call it home, over two-thirds of which concentrate on lobster. The others try for haddock, cod, pollock and swordfish.

At the southern end of Highway 335 is the Pubnico Point Wind Farm: the road becomes unpaved but it's worth persevering. Park and wander between the 17 immense turbines, all named after women.

HISTORY In 1653, Sieur Philippe D'Entremont was awarded the Baronnie de Pombomcoup, a region covering most of the land between modern-day Shelburne and Yarmouth. Pombomcoup (which became Pubnico) is derived from the Mi'kmaq *Pogomkook* meaning 'land cleared for cultivation'.

D'Entremont built a château here, and when he moved away transferred his title to his eldest son. Fish were plentiful, the land was good, and a prosperous settlement grew.

The Pubnico Acadians escaped deportation in 1755, but weren't so lucky three years later. The château and their buildings were destroyed, the surrounding land torched. The Acadians were exiled but eight years later began to return, and unlike those in most other places, were permitted to regain their old lands.

This is the province's oldest Acadian community still inhabited by the descendants of its founder. One 18th-century house still survives, now as a private residence, at the end of Old Church Road in West Pubnico.

GETTING THERE Pubnico is situated on Highway 3 and therefore convenient **by car**, just off Exit 31 of Highway 103, 29km/18 miles from Barrington (via Highway 103), 31km/19 miles from Shag Harbour and 4km/2 miles from West Pubnico.

WHERE TO STAY AND EAT

Argyle By The Sea B&B (3 rooms) 848 Argyle Sound Rd, Argyle Sound; 762 2759; www.bbcanada.com/8457.html; May–Oct. Rooms with private or shared bath in this quiet B&B by the ocean. Full b/fast inc. **$**

Red Cap Motel & Restaurant (6 rooms) 1034 Hwy 335, Middle West Pubnico; 762 2112; www.redcaprestaurantandmotel.com; year-round. Attractive-looking traditional motel with in-room fridges, coffee-makers,

CLAW-STOPPERS

The practice of exporting live lobsters, primarily to New England in the US, began early in the 20th century, however the buyers would only pay if the lobsters reached their destination alive. This posed a problem, as when lobsters are kept together in the same small enclosure, they use their large claws to attack each other, often fatally.

For almost a century, wooden pegs (sometimes called plugs), narrow pine wedges approximately 3cm long, pointed at one end and squared at the other, were inserted under the lobster's claw hinge joint to prevent the claws from opening. The use of pegs had an immediate impact, greatly increasing the survival rate of lobsters during shipping. As the lobster industry boomed, demand for the pegs exploded. The pegs were whittled by hand with a small homemade knife: skilled peg-makers could make a peg using just seven precise cuts. Peg-making, which started off as a cottage industry (making the pegs was a pastime which provided an extra source of money, especially after the Depression when work was scarce) turned into big business.

Finally, machines to automate parts of the peg-making process were designed, and in the late 1970s, the largest lobster-peg factory, located in West Pubnico, was producing over 30 million pegs per year. The community revelled in the title 'lobster plug capital of the world'.

To all intents and purposes, the lobster peg industry came to an end early in the 1980s when strong rubber bands became the standard way to clamp the lobster's claws closed.

high-speed internet. Surprisingly good licensed restaurant (🕘 *08.00–21.30 daily;* $$), where chef Amy Scott focuses on the freshest local produce. **$**

Yesteryear's B&B (3 rooms) 2775 Hwy 3, Pubnico; ☎ 762 2969; www.yesteryears.ca; 🕘 year-round; off-season by reservation. A Victorian heritage house with spacious bedrooms & a good craft shop (items made on the premises). Substantial b/fast inc. **$**

La Baronnie Campground (10 sites) 1207 Hwy 335, Middle West Pubnico; ☎ 762 3388; 🕘 year-round. Tent sites & 2 serviced sites near the sea, with a laundromat. **$**

Dennis Point Café Dennis Point, Lower West Pubnico; ☎ 762 1220; www.dennispointcafe.com; 🕘 year-round 05.30–21.00 daily. There's an extensive menu at this busy restaurant just across from the wharves where the latest catches are unloaded. They have a deep-fryer but fish can also be broiled or pan-fried. The seafood platters are recommended. $$

FESTIVALS Birdwatchers will be interested in the (roseate) **Tern Festival**, held over three days in late June. A big summer draw is the week-long **Festival Chez-Nous à Pombcoup** in August, celebrating all things Acadian.

OTHER PRACTICALITIES

Bank Royal Bank, 968 Hwy 335, West Pubnico; ☎ 762 2205; 🕘 10.00–15.00 Mon–Fri

Library Pubnico Branch Library, 35 Hwy 335, Pubnico; ☎ 762 2204; www.westerncounties.ca. 🕘 year-round (hours vary)

Post office 15 Church St, Middle West Pubnico; 🕘 09.00–17.30 Mon, 09.30–17.00 Tue–Fri, 09.00–11.30 Sat

WHAT TO SEE AND DO Several old Acadian buildings have been moved to the pretty 7ha **Le Village Historique Acadien (Historic Acadian Village)** (*Old Church*

Rd, West Pubnico; ☎ *762 2530,* **t/f** *1 888 381 8999; http://museum.gov.ns.ca/av/;* ⏲ *early Jun–mid Oct 09.00–17.00 daily; admission CAN$6*), which overlooks Pubnico Harbour. Costumed interpreters demonstrate traditional work methods and tell of Acadian life pre-1920, and there's an on-site café.

Occupying six rooms of a two-storey c1864 homestead furnished in traditional Acadian style and a modern annexe, the collection in the **Musée Acadien** (*898 Hwy 335, West Pubnico;* ☎ *762 3380; www.museeacadien.ca;* ⏲ *mid May–mid Oct 09.00–17.00 Mon–Sat, 12.30–16.30 Sun; admission CAN$3*) displays the history of the Acadians in Pubnico from 1653 to recent times. See a traditional Acadian garden growing plants and vegetables of the type that 17th-century Acadians would have had access to. Bonuses include a collection of over 300 cameras, and a good research centre for genealogists.

The popular 6,052yd par-72 course at **West Pubnico Golf and Country Club** (*Greenwood Rd;* ☎ *762 2007; www.pubnicogolf.ca*) has a long playing season, often opening in late March. The 15th hole is the standout. Green fees are CAN$25.

THE ROAD TO YARMOUTH

Highway 3 provides a more scenic (and slower) alternative to the motorway (Highway 103) between Pubnico and Yarmouth. There's some beautiful coastal scenery and a number of little-visited, sleepy, remote peninsulas (with few services) to explore.

By car on Highway 3, Lower Argyle is 6km/4 miles from Pubnico, Sainte-Anne-du-Ruisseau 23km/14 miles, and Tusket 28km/17 miles from Pubnico and 15km/9 miles from Yarmouth.

WHERE TO STAY AND EAT Try the comfortable Old English-style lodge right on Lobster Bay, **Ye Olde Argyler Lodge** (*6 rooms; 52 Ye Olde Argyler Rd, Lower Argyle;* ☎ *643 2500,* **t/f** *1 866 774 0400; www.argyler.com;* ⏲ *year-round;* **$$**), which has four rooms with pleasant ocean views. The licensed restaurant (⏲ *year-round 11.00–21.00 daily;* **$$$**) is housed in a modern lodge-style building and serves up gourmet 'New American' cuisine using local ingredients. Try the root beer baby back ribs or seared scallops, and for dessert, chocolate rhapsody. There is alfresco dining when the weather permits, and a full breakfast is included in the accommodation.

EEL MCMUTTON

In the days of stagecoaches, there were numerous inns between Shag Harbour and Yarmouth. The limited menu at the McDonald Inn in Clyde focused on two of the cheapest foods of that period: mutton and eels.

WHAT TO SEE AND DO On Highway 3, 19km from Pubnico, look out for the **Eel Lake Oyster Farm** (*6950 Hwy 3, Lower Eel Brook;* ☎ *648 3472; www.ruisseauoysters.com*), where Nolan D'Eon and his team farm more than three million oysters. The farm is open to visitors and boat trips to see the oyster habitat are offered for a fee. Call ahead for times, prices, etc. Continue 3km further on Highway 3 to **Sainte-Anne-du-Ruisseau**, home to the magnificent c1900 **Eglise Ste-Anne** (*Church of St Anne; Hwy 3;* ☎ *648 2315;* ⏲ *year-round*), a black-and-white Gothic-style structure with two towers, high, vaulted ceilings featuring beautiful paintings, and ornate stained glass windows. In July, the **Festival Acadien** is held in the town.

TOO MANY KNOTS UNTIE THE KNOT

Angeline Publicover was due to be married. Early in December 1868 she boarded a schooner, the *Industry*, in LaHave (see page 164), bound for Halifax: she wanted to buy her wedding dress. What should have been a simple day's sail for the seven people on board didn't turn out that way as unexpected winds came up when the ship neared Sambro. The captain tried to return to port, but the vessel was blown out to the open sea, where more gales, storms and winds blew the helpless *Industry* further and further out. Days passed with little let-up in the conditions: the crew and passengers subsisted on (rationed) water, melted hailstones and a handful of biscuits. Their Christmas Day dinner was one rotten potato divided into seven. On 29 December, a barque named *Providence* sighted the crippled schooner in the mid Atlantic: the survivors managed to transfer boats in rough seas, and just in time – the battered *Industry* sank less than an hour later. Angeline and her fellow survivors were taken on the *Providence* to London, England and then returned to Halifax on a steamer, finally arriving in Nova Scotia on 12 February, 1869.

For those who prefer happy endings, Angeline's fiancé was waiting by the dockside, and the happy couple were married a few days later. But the truth is that by the time she returned to Nova Scotia, he had changed his mind, and the wedding was not just delayed but called off.

Despite many hours of research, I could not find out if Angeline bought a wedding dress during her time in London or Halifax, or where she obtained the dress that she wore for her marriage (to a less fickle man) four years later. Plenty of other fish in the sea, as they say.

At **Tusket** you can visit the oldest standing courthouse in Canada, the (c1802) **Argyle Township Court House and Gaol** (*8168 Hwy 3; ☎ 648 2493; www.argylecourthouse.com; ⌚ May/Jun & Sep/Oct 08.30–12.00 & 13.00–16.30 Mon–Fri; Jul/Aug 09.00–17.00 daily; admission CAN$2*). Recently designated a National Historic Site, on the ground floor you can see the guards' quarters and the cells, whilst upstairs are the courtroom and judge's chambers. There is also a gift shop.

5

Yarmouth, French Shore and the Annapolis Valley

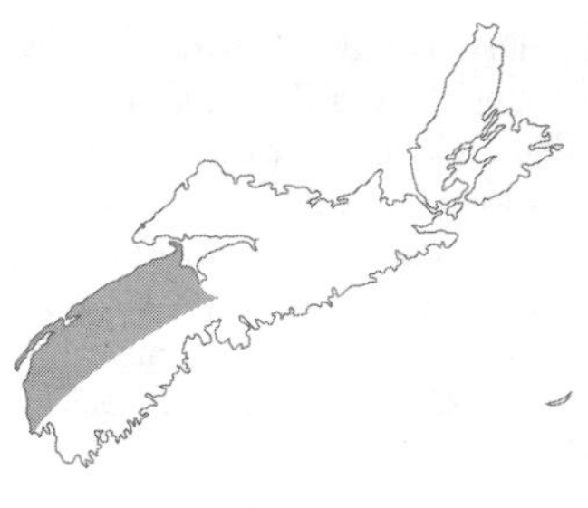

This region runs from the port of Yarmouth to Windsor, just 66km northwest of Halifax, taking in the Bay of Fundy coast and the fertile Annapolis Valley. The valley lies between two ridges, the North Mountain and South Mountain. Between Yarmouth and Digby a string of Acadian coastal communities makes up the French Shore. Close to Digby, renowned for its scallops and terminus for a year-round car ferry service to Saint John, New Brunswick, the wild and wonderful Digby Neck stretches out into the Bay of Fundy: geologically it is a continuation of the North Mountain ridge. A trip along the narrow peninsula takes you to the departure point for some of North America's best whale-watching experiences.

The Annapolis River empties into the Annapolis Basin: on the basin's north shore is the site of Port-Royal, the first permanent European settlement north of Florida. Close by is the charming historic town of Annapolis Royal, where the streets ooze history. Inland from the south shore of the basin, the funky, pretty artists' community of Bear River is worth a visit.

Highway 8, one of Nova Scotia's cross-province roads, connects Annapolis Royal with Liverpool (see page 162), and gives access to Kejimkujik National Park – perhaps the best place to explore the lakes and forests of the interior. Highway 10 connects Middleton with Bridgewater (see page 160). Having good access to the untouched back-country wilderness, and the natural wonders of Kejimkujik National Park and the Bay of Fundy, there is plenty to see, hear and do for lovers of the outdoors.

Although best known for its apple orchards, particularly beautiful when in blossom in late May, many other crops are grown in the valley, and in summer smaller roads parallel to Highways 101 and 1 are dotted with U-pick farms where (depending on the time of year) you can pick your own punnets of strawberries, raspberries, blueberries and more.

Towards its northeastern end, the valley becomes busier and more densely populated (relatively speaking). Here you'll find Kentville, the region's commercial centre, and the shopping malls of New Minas. On the Bay of Fundy coast to the north, Capes Split and Blomidon offer high cliffs and magnificent hiking.

Also close to Kentville is the lively university town of Wolfville, and just 5km further, the emotive Grand Pré National Historic Site, recently designated a UNESCO World Heritage Site.

Highway 101 is the motorway running between Yarmouth and Halifax, passing close to all the region's major communities. Highway 1 runs through the heart of many of the towns, and parallel roads such as Highways 201 and 221 provide pastoral alternatives. **Maritime Bus** (see page 44) connects Kentville with Halifax, and **Kings Transit** (see box, page 195) links communities between Weymouth and Brooklyn.

Digby and Kingston/Greenwood are the major shopping centres between Yarmouth and Kentville. There are backpacker hostels in Digby, at Brier Island on the Digby Neck, and at South Milford (between Annapolis Royal and Kejimkujik National Park).

Many festivals occur in the region, and events forming part of an apple-focused celebration are held at the **Apple Blossom Festival** (*www.appleblossom.com*) in late May/early June at various Annapolis Valley locations including Middleton (see page 222), Kentville (page 225) and Berwick (page 225).

YARMOUTH (*Population: 6,780*)

Located on the eastern side of Yarmouth Harbour, Yarmouth is the largest urban centre in western Nova Scotia and has long been one of Nova Scotia's most important ports and communities. The region's largest seaport, long the gateway for ferries to Maine, USA, suffered a huge setback in 2009 when the ferry services were terminated due to funding issues. A ferry service may be reintroduced in 2013 (see box, page 45). A few (expensive) flights a week connect Yarmouth and Portland, Maine. Shipping (primarily lumber products) and fishing (especially herring) are major contributors to present-day Yarmouth's economy, but don't compensate for the money lost when the steady flow of tourists who came in and out on the ferries was cut off.

Whilst it is no Lunenburg (see page 149) or Annapolis Royal (page 208), there are some good museums, restaurants and places to stay, a restored waterfront with pleasant waterfront park, and many beautiful Victorian mansions – particularly within the **Collins Heritage Conservation District**, which encompasses parts of

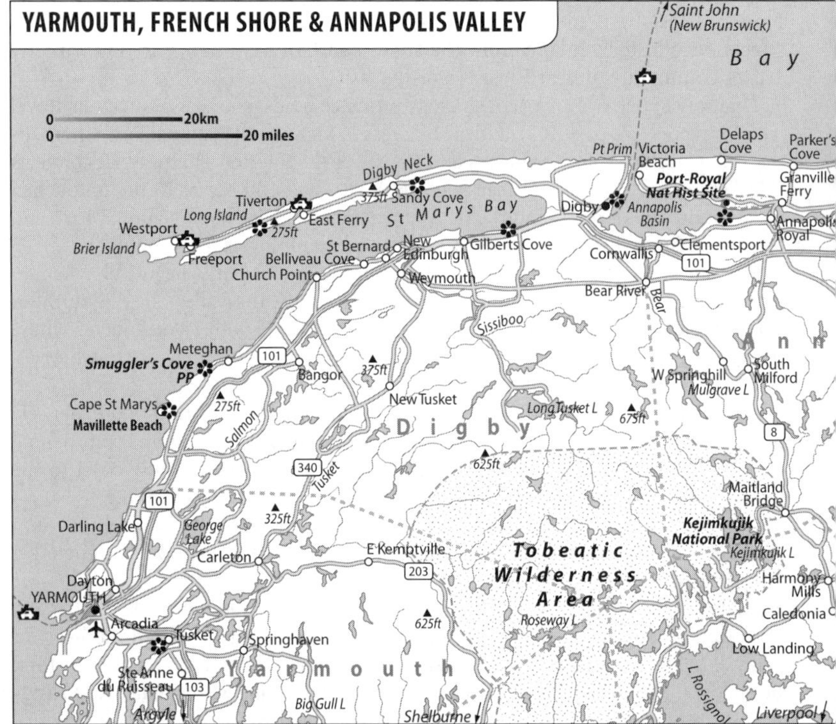

Alma, Carleton, Clements and Collins streets. Yarmouth makes a good base from which to explore the lovely peninsulas and quiet backroads – ideal for cycling – to the southwest, and the French Shore.

ORIENTATION Water Street runs along the waterfront parallel to Main Street just up the hill. The ferry terminal is at the junction of Water and Forest streets, and the airport 3.5km away at the other end of Forest Street. Highway 1 becomes Main Street and Highway 3 Starrs Road – where most of the big shopping malls are found – as they come into town: Highways 103 (from Halifax via the South Shore) and 101 (from Halifax via the Annapolis Valley) lead on to Starrs Road.

HISTORY The Mi'kmaq called the area *Kespoogwit*, meaning 'the end of the earth': Samuel de Champlain (see page 265) landed in 1604, naming it Cap Forchu (or Fourchu) for its two-pronged cape.

After Expulsion, Yarmouth's first families arrived from Cape Cod, Massachusetts, in 1762. There were no roads to connect the site with anywhere else, but wood was plentiful. Boats were needed for fishing, transportation and trade, and so Yarmouth's long history of shipbuilding began.

Peaking in the late 1870s, when Yarmouth ranked as the world's fourth-largest port of registry and possessed more tonnage per capita than any other seaport in the world, shipbuilding then began a rapid decline. From the 1850s, regular steamship services connected Boston and New York with Yarmouth. The railway arrived in the 1880s, increasing the importance of this port as one of Nova Scotia's main gateways. Yarmouth remains a significant port, fishing centre and international gateway.

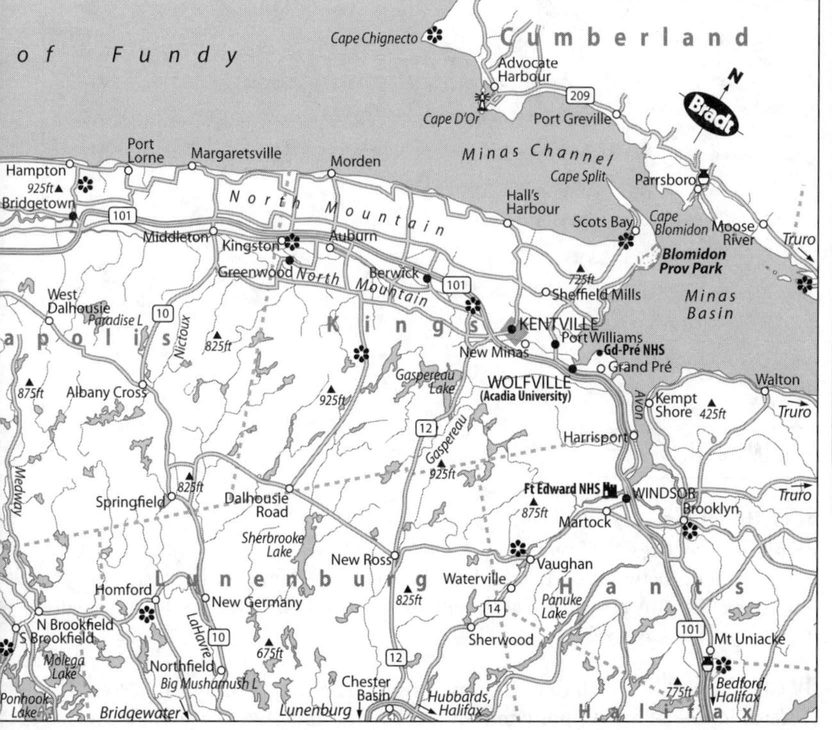

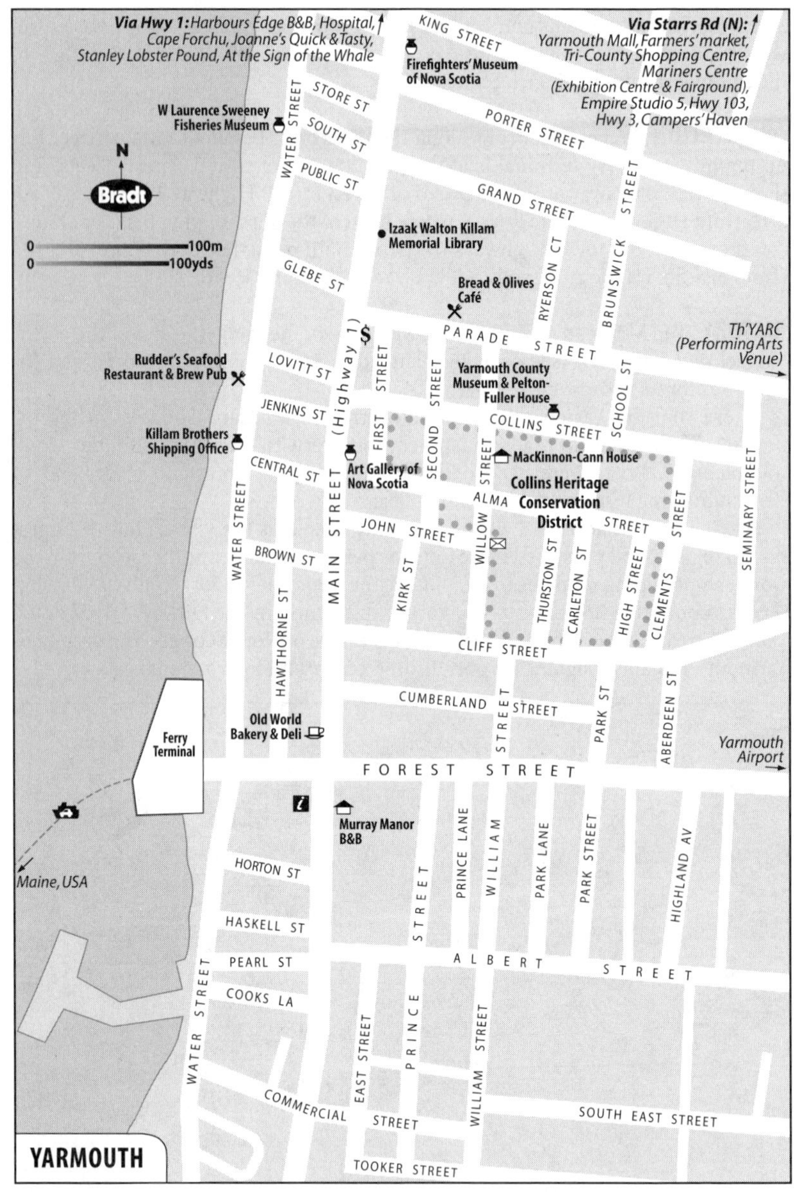

GETTING THERE

By air **Twin Cities Air Service** (**t/f** *1 800 564 3882; www.twincitiesairservice.com*) operates flights between Portland, Maine and Yarmouth three to five times a week. The airport is 3km east of town at the end of Forest Street. Taxi fares into town cost in the region of CAN$8.

By car Two of the province's major motorways, Highways 101 and 103, converge at Yarmouth. Halifax is approximately 300km/186 miles away via Highway 103 (through the South Shore), and 340km/211 miles away via Highway 101 (through the Annapolis Valley and Windsor). From Yarmouth it is 123km/76 miles to Shelburne (via Highway 103) and 105km/65 miles to Digby via Highway 101.

By shuttle Shuttle services (see *Chapter 2*, page 57) connect Yarmouth with Halifax either via the Annapolis Valley or South Shore.

By ferry The ferry terminal is very central, at the western end of Forest Street. Whether any ferries will be using it or not is another question (see box, page 45 for further details).

WHERE TO STAY

MacKinnon-Cann House Historic Inn (7 rooms) 27 Willow St; 742 9900, t/f 1 866 698 3142; http://mackinnoncanninn.com; year-round. Each guest room at this quiet, beautifully renovated c1887 Italianate mansion is decorated in the style of a different 20th-century decade: décor in the public rooms is late 19th-century Victorian. The mix works. A lovely place to stay – & eat (see below). Full b/fast inc. **$$$**

Harbour's Edge B&B (4 rooms) 12 Vancouver St; 742 2387; harboursedge.ns.ca; year-round. A c1864 house with a delightful waterfront location & friendly hosts. Great location for birdwatchers. Full b/fast inc (eg: French toast with orange & locally smoked bacon). **$$**

Murray Manor B&B (4 rooms) 225 Main St; 742 9625, t/f 1 877 742 9629; http://murraymanor.com; year-round (Nov–Apr by reservation only). Lovely Georgian Regency c1820s property in manicured garden. Brenda is a very attentive hostess with a good eye for detail. Rate inc full b/fast. **$–$$**

Campers' Haven Campground (192 sites) 9700 Hwy 3, Arcadia: 742 4848; late May–Sep. Large lakeside campground with open & wooded serviced & unserviced sites approx 6km from downtown. Heated pool (in season), hot tub, laundromat. **$**

WHERE TO EAT

Kabir's at the Inn 27 Willow St; 742 9900, t/f 1 866 698 3142; http://mackinnoncanninn.com; Jun–Sep 17.30–20.30 Wed–Sat. The elegant licensed dining room at the lovely MacKinnon-Cann Inn serves authentic northern Indian cuisine. Reservations required. **$$$**

Bread & Olives Café 11 Parade St; 881 3144; http://breadandolives.ca; year-round 11.00–14.00 Mon–Sat. New (2012) addition to Yarmouth's dining scene. On a lovely residential street. Upmarket, sophisticated, European-style with high-quality coffee & teas. Gourmet sandwiches, salads & paninis, decadent cakes & tortes. **$$**

Rudder's Seafood Restaurant & Brew Pub 96 Water St; 742 7311; http://

RUNIC RUMOURS

In 1812, what became known as the Yarmouth runic stone was brought to public notice by a retired Army surgeon. It had been found near a church between Yarmouth and Cape Forchu (see page 191), weighed around 180kg and had 13 characters carved into its flat face. Experts suggested that the characters were runes (Viking symbols), claiming this proved suggestions that Leif Ericsson visited Yarmouth in AD1007 (see page 186). However, reputable scholars have said that the visible characters were chiselled nearer 1812 than 1007, and that they are not recognisable as runic. Judge for yourself – the stone is on display at the Yarmouth County Museum (see page 191).

'YOUR FISH OR YOUR LIVES'

In August 1918, *The New York Times* reported that when on one of her regular trips out of Yarmouth in search of halibut, the *Nelson A* and her crew found themselves face to face with a German U-boat. At gunpoint, they were told to load dories with all their fish and approach the surfaced submarine.

In return for the fish, the men were given food and water – and told to row away from their boat as fast as possible. Following these instructions, moments later they heard a huge boom: both the submarine and – within minutes – the *Nelson A* disappeared beneath the surface. The crew rowed for shore, and, two days later, arrived back on dry land exhausted but alive.

ruddersbrewpub.com; ⌚ year-round 11.00–late daily. Very popular waterfront eatery, pub & microbrewery with wooden floors & beams, & large patio. Good food – start with bacon-wrapped scallops, move on to haddock fishcakes or maritime lobster sandwich, & leave room for the carrot cake or over-the-top chocolate desserts. Wash it down with a Rudder's Red or Yarmouth Town Brown. $$

Stanley Lobster Pound 1066 Overton Rd; ☎ 742 8291; http://stanleylobster.com; ⌚ mid Jun–Sep 12.00–19.00 Tue–Sat, 14.00–19.00 Sun. Forget posh restaurants & head here (it's *en route* to Cape Forchu – see page 191). Choose your lobster, then savour it in the characterful dining room on the cobble beach. You can bring your favourite tipple & enjoy your clawed meal with corn on the cob & strawberry shortcake. A fun experience for lobster lovers! $$

Joanne's Quick & Tasty Hwy 1, Dayton; ☎ 742 3467; ⌚ year-round 07.30–20.30 daily. Another of the province's nothing-to-look-at-but-good-value-food spots. Lots of deep-frying, big portions of clams, scallop, lobster & chicken. Good seafood chowder, & pies topped with mounds of whipped cream. $–$$

Old World Bakery & Deli 232 Main St; ☎ 742 2181; ⌚ year-round 07.00–1800 Tue–Fri, 08.00–16.00 Sat. Excellent sandwiches, dips, soups & baked goods at this funky little deli. Great place to grab a lunch on the go. $

FESTIVALS The **Multicultural Festival** (*http://tricountymca.com*), held in July, is a global fashion show, with concerts, films, food and more. Also in July, **Seafest** (*http://seafest.ca*) offers 11 days of varied events – many marine-related. What started out as an agricultural exhibition has developed into six days of concerts, events and activities for all the family, at the **Western Nova Scotia Exhibition** (*http://westernnovascotiaexhibition.webs.com*), held at the end of July/early August.

OTHER PRACTICALITIES

$ Bank Scotiabank, 389 Main St; ☎ 742 7116; ⌚ 10.00–17.00 Mon–Fri

Cinema Empire Studio 5, 136 Starrs Rd; ☎ 742 7489; http://empiretheatres.com

Hospital Yarmouth Regional Hospital, 60 Vancouver St; ☎ 742 3541

Library Izaak Walton Killam Memorial Library, 405 Main St; ☎ 742 5040; ⌚ 10.00–20.00 Mon–Thu, 10.00–17.00 Fri, 10.00–16.00 Sat (Sep–May 13.00–16.00 Sun)

Post office 15 Willow St; ⌚ 08.00–17.30 Mon–Fri

Tourist information 228 Main St; ☎ 742 5033; ⌚ late May–early Oct 09.00–18.00 daily, 19.00 mid Jul/Aug

Taxi Yarmouth Town Taxi; ☎ 742 7801

WHAT TO SEE AND DO With an extensive collection of fire-fighting equipment from days of yore, the **Fire-fighters' Museum of Nova Scotia** (*451 Main St; ☎ 742 5525; http://museum.gov.ns.ca/fm/; ⌚ Jun & Sep 09.00–17.00 Mon–Sat; Jul/Aug 09.00–21.00 Mon–Sat, 10.00–17.00 Sun; Oct–May 09.00–16.00 Mon–Fri, 13.00–16.00 Sat; admission CAN$3*) is much more interesting than it sounds –

and one the kids will enjoy, too. Also worth a visit are the excellent **Yarmouth County Museum and Archives and Pelton-Fuller House** (*22 & 20 Collins St; ☎ 742 5539; http://yarmouthcountymuseum.ednet.ns.ca; ⊕ Jun–mid Oct 09.00–18.00 Mon–Sat, 13.00–18.00 Sun; mid Oct–May 14.00–17.00 Mon–Sat; admission CAN$3 each or CAN$5 for both museum & Pelton-Fuller House*). The excellent museum is housed in a restored granite former c1893 church and contains one of Canada's largest collections of ship paintings and one of the province's largest costume collections. Whilst the collection focuses on Yarmouth's seafaring history and heritage, the complex also includes the largest community archives in Nova Scotia, and another wing with transportation-related exhibits and art galleries. Be sure to see the runic stone (see box, page 189), the 1860s' stagecoach and the early lens from the Cape Forchu light (see page 191). The gift shop is also one of the better ones of the genre. Next door is the antique-packed Italianate (c1895) **Pelton-Fuller House**, once the summer residence of Alfred Fuller who made a fortune in the US selling brushes and houseware, becoming known throughout North America as the *Fuller Brush Man*. The house has attractive flower gardens.

The **Art Gallery of Nova Scotia** (*Western Branch; 341 Main St; ☎ 749 2248; www.artgalleryofnovascotia.com; ⊕ year-round 12.00–17.00 Tue–Sun*) is the only branch of Halifax's Art Gallery of Nova Scotia (see page 114) and is housed in a former bank. An interesting long-established art and crafts gallery, **At the Sign of the Whale** (*543 Hwy 1, Dayton; ☎ 742 8895; http://signofthewhaleonline.com; ⊕ summer 09.00–18.00 Mon–Sat, 12.00–17.00 Sun; off-season 09.00–17.00 Mon–Sat*) showcases the work of over 150 Nova Scotia artists. **Th'YARC** (*76 Parade St; ☎ 742 8150; www.yarcplayhouse.com*), a performing arts complex, includes a 350-seat theatre and art gallery.

Killam Brothers Shipping Office (*90 Water St; ☎ 742 5539; http://yarmouthcountymuseum.ednet.ns.ca; ⊕ Jul/Aug 10.00–16.00 Mon–Sat; admission free*) is Canada's oldest shipping office and is housed in a 19th-century building: the Killam family were directly involved with many aspects of shipping for almost two centuries. A scaled-down reproduction (including a coastal freighter) of part of Yarmouth's old working waterfront, the **W Laurence Sweeney Fisheries Museum** (*112 Water St; ☎ 742 3457; http://sweeneyfisheriesmuseum.ca; ⊕ mid May–mid Oct 10.00–18.00 daily; admission CAN$3*) was built using original materials.

Adjacent to a lighthouse – one of the highest (23m) and most photogenic in the province – the original lightkeeper's quarters at **Cape Forchu** (*Hwy 304; ☎ 742 4522; http://capeforchulight.com; ⊕ May–mid Oct; admission free*) house a small museum, tea room (good sandwiches and tasty baked goods) and gift shop. Definitely worth the pretty drive. Near the car park, a trail leads down to Leif Ericsson Picnic Park. Take care on the smooth rocks which can be very slippery. To get there, follow Main Street north and turn left at the golden horse fountain onto Vancouver Street. Just past the hospital complex, turn left onto Highway 304 and follow it to its end, approximately 11km from the centre of Yarmouth. Held on Saturday mornings, the **farmers' market** (*Jul–Sep*) is held at the Canadian Tire car park (*120 Starrs Rd*).

THE FRENCH SHORE

Officially part of the Municipality of Clare, those in surrounding areas call this string of over a dozen adjoining Acadian villages The French Shore, whilst to most of the residents it is La Ville Française.

The Acadian flag (known as the *stella maris*), flies everywhere. The 'longest main street in the world' is an interesting alternative to the motorway (Highway 101).

Post-Expulsion (see page 16), returning Acadians who found their old lands taken over by others kept walking until they found land that no-one else was interested in. Despite the harsh climate and poor quality of the soil, they persevered. In time, fishing and boatbuilding developed. Mink farms were, and – rightly or wrongly – still are, another money spinner (see box, page 194).

FESTIVALS For a fortnight at the end of July/early August, residents (and many visitors) celebrate the oldest Acadian festival in Canada, the **Festival Acadien de Clare** (*http://festivalacadiendeclare.ca*), with music, food, parades, competitions and raucous fun.

MAVILLETTE The main reason for coming here is to visit **Mavillette Beach Provincial Park**, a 2km-wide gently curving stretch of sand backed by marram grass-covered dunes. Behind the dunes, a large salt marsh is home to avian year-rounders and spring and autumn migrators.

Follow Cape St Mary's Road to its end. You might see seals basking on the rocks below, and the coastal views from this point high above the sea are superb.

Where to stay

A la Maison d'Amitie (4 rooms) 197 Baseline Rd; 645 2601, **t/f** 1 888 645 2601; **e** carol@houseoffriendship.ca; http://houseoffriendship.ca; year-round. With one of the province's great settings – high on the cliffs of St Mary's Bay – & awesome views, accommodation in this modern home is up to standard, too. Full b/fast inc, & afternoon tea & home-baked goodies. **$$$**

Cape View Motel and Cottages (15 units) 124 John Doucette Rd; 645 2258, **t/f** 1 888 352 00 876 1960; http://capeviewmotel.ca; Jun–Sep. 10 motel rooms & 5, 1- & 2-bedroom cottages in a good setting & across the road from the Mavillette Beach Park. Continental b/fast inc. **$**

SMUGGLERS COVE PROVINCIAL PARK Smugglers Cove is 9km north of Mavillette. Interpretive panels tell of the rum-running past, paths lead to clifftop coastal views, and 110 steep, wooden steps descend through the trees to a sheltered cove with a pebble beach. Apparently, smugglers were attracted by a sea cave 5m high and 18m deep, but this is only accessible by water.

METEGHAN Meteghan, 3.5km past Smugglers Cove, is the French Shore's largest community, busiest port and commercial hub (though the total population is fewer

SIGOGNE

Abbé Jean Mande Sigogne (1763–1844), a French priest who fled his homeland for England during the French Revolution, arrived in Nova Scotia in the late 1790s. His mission stations extended from the Pubnicos (page 181) to Annapolis Royal (page 208) and Bear River (page 204). Much loved by his people, the Abbé was a strong influence in the education of the Acadians, and helped inspire them in their farming, fishing and trading. A terrible fire swept through the region in 1820, destroying the St Bernard Church and much else, and again the Abbé was a rock in helping rebuild both the communities' morale and their fire-destroyed buildings. He supervised the construction of many churches in southwest Nova Scotia and died in 1844: his tomb stands outside the university.

than 1,000). The port is home to several types of fishing boat and the main wharf is a hive of activity throughout the day. Meteghan River, 4.5km north of Meteghan, is Nova Scotia's largest wooden-shipbuilding centre.

Where to stay and eat

L'Auberge au Havre du Capitaine (18 rooms) 9118 Hwy 1, Meteghan River; 769 2001; http://havreducapitaine.ca; year-round. A nice inn with traditional Acadian feel (rooms have hardwood floors & are decorated with antiques – though bathrooms are modern). **$–$$**

Around the Bend Restaurant & Café 8837 Hwy 1, Meteghan River; 645 3313; year-round 05.30–20.00 daily. Prepare for a rural Nova Scotia shock: a diner where the owners have made an effort with the décor! The food is good, too, with the focus on seafood. $–$$

Other practicalities

$ **Bank** Royal Bank, Hwy 1, Meteghan; 645 2410; 10.00–17.00 Mon–Wed & Fri, 10.00–18.00 Thu

Post office 8198 Hwy 1, Meteghan; 08.00–17.00 Mon–Fri, 08.30–11.30 Sat

CHURCH POINT (POINTE DE l'ÉGLISE) A further 15km north, Church Point is the home of **Université Sainte-Anne**, founded in 1891 and Nova Scotia's only French-language university. The university is the Acadian cultural centre for the entire Clare region. On the campus is grey-shingled **Église de Sainte-Marie,** the largest wooden church in North America. Constructed between 1903 and 1905, it seats almost 1,800 people.

Where to stay

Le Manoir Samson (14 rooms) 1768 Hwy 1; 769 2526, **t/f** 1 888 769 8605; http://havreducapitaine.ca; May–Aug. Large brick building: motel-type rooms with microwave & fridge. Most rates inc light b/fast. **$**

Belle Baie Park Campground (146 sites) 2135 Hwy 1; 739 3160; www.bellbaiepark.ca; early May–late Sep. Serviced & unserviced sites at this St Mary's Bay-front campground. Heated pool (in season), laundromat. **$**

Where to eat

The consequence of the closure of the wonderful Chez Christophe (the chef/owner succumbed to cancer in 2012) and 'closed' signs on the doors of other eateries (such as the Cape View Restaurant overlooking Mavillette Beach) is a dearth of good places to eat along the French Shore. There are somewhat uninspiring seafood/diner options in Meteghan and Belliveau Cove – with the exception of Around the Bend (see above).

19th Hole Restaurant Clare Golf Club 423 Pf Comeau Rd; 769 0801; http://claregolf.ca. This restaurant in Comeauville is another possibility. $$

Beaux Vendredis 769 8618. A year or 2 ago they were 'Beaux Jeudis', so check before you set off which *beau* day it is. Good-value lobster/clams/snow crab dinners are served on Fri evenings (*Jul/Aug 18.00–21.00*) at Belliveau Cove Wharf under the Beaux Vendredis label. $$

Roadside Grill 3334 Hwy 1, Belliveau Cove; 837 5047. There's live Acadian music (*Jul–Sep 17.30–19.30 Tue*) to go with the fresh seafood, plus big portions of clams, fries & rappie pie. $$

Rapure Acadienne 1443 Hwy 1; 769 2172; year-round 08.00–17.30 daily. This is the place to try Acadian speciality rappie pie (see page 62), served – as it should be – with butter & molasses. There's 1 table inside & picnic tables outside. $

Other practicalities

Tourist information Rendez-vous de la Baie (see page 194); 769 2345; early May–early Dec 09.00–17.30 daily

What to see and do The **Rendez-vous de la Baie** complex (*23 Lighthouse Rd; ☎ 769 1234; http://rendezvousdelabaie.com; ⏰ summer 07.00–19.00 Mon–Fri, 09.00–17.00 Sat/Sun; winter 09.00–16.00 Mon–Fri, 10.00–16.00 Sat/Sun*) includes an Acadian Interpretive Centre/museum, gift shop, cinema/theatre and internet café. Those interested in genealogy won't want to miss the **Acadian Centre Archives** (*☎ 769 2114; http://centreacadien.usainteanne.ca; ⏰ 08.30–12.00 & 13.00–16.00 Mon–Fri; admission free*), a resource at the university.

BELLIVEAU COVE (L'ANSE-DES-BELLIVEAU) Belliveau Cove is 7km north of Church Point. It has a wharf, with a pretty c1889 lighthouse, and a 5km coastal interpretive trail. For accommodation/dining, see Church Point, above.

What to see and do A farmers' market (*Parc Joseph et Marie Dugas; May–Sep 09.00–12.45 Sat*) takes place in the park by the wharf. Go for the freshest local fruit, vegetables and baked goods. The **Annual Festival Joseph et Marie Dugas** is a one-day festival held in August, which features food, music, games, an arts and crafts sale and a flea market.

ST BERNARD St Bernard marks the end of the French Shore. Its **church** (*☎ 837 5687; ⏰ Jun–Sep*) has wonderful acoustics and hosts a series of classical music concerts in the summer.

WEYMOUTH

This former shipbuilding and lumber centre near the mouth of the Sissiboo River has a few services. Like many coastal communities in the province, today's Weymouth is a much quieter place than it would have been a century ago. Rumour has it that Josephine Leslie, author of the novel *The Ghost and Mrs Muir* (though she used a pseudonym), was inspired to write the book after a visit to the town.

GETTING THERE Weymouth is accessible **by car**, being on Highway 1, just off Highway 101 Exit 28. The town is 4km/2 miles from St Bernard, 76km/47 miles

MINK STINK

Around half of the mink farms in Canada are in Nova Scotia, and over 80% of those are in Digby County, particularly in the Weymouth area (see page 194). These farms have seen increasing profits in recent years: in 2011, 1.4 million pelts were produced, and global demand keeps growing. To the disappointment of environmentalists, animal lovers and prospective new neighbours, a number of produce farmers are starting to switch from raising crops to fur farming.

Those opposing the growth in mink farms complain of cruelty to animals and environmental worries – a 2012 report released by the provincial environment department said that mink farms are the most likely source of water-quality problems in nine lakes in western Nova Scotia.

The federal and provincial governments have been pouring money into the mink farm industry: the introduction of tough rules (rather than 'guidelines') to ensure tight control over waste disposal and welfare of the 'fur coats in the making' isn't exactly racing along.

DID I SEE A BUS GO BY?

The area between Weymouth and Windsor (see page 237) is relatively well served by public transport. Five connecting bus lines operated by **Kings Transit** (*678 7310,* **t/f** *1 888 546 4442; http://kingstransit.ns.ca*) stop at most of the major communities along the Annapolis Valley. Single fare is CAN$3.50 and buses don't run on Sundays or holidays. Lines and their major stops are:

Weymouth–Gilbert's Cove–Digby–Cornwallis 06.00–20.00 Mon–Fri, 08.00–18.00 Sat; every 2hrs
Cornwallis–Upper Clements–Annapolis Royal–Granville–Bridgetown 07.00–21.00 Mon–Fri, 09.00–19.00 Sat; every 2hrs
Bridgetown–Middleton–Greenwood 06.00–18.00 Mon–Fri, 08.00–16.00 Sat; every 2hrs
Greenwood–Kingston–Aylesford–Berwick–Kentville–New Minas–Wolfville 07.00–20.00 Mon–Sat; hourly Mon–Fri, every 2hrs on Sat
Wolfville–Hantsport–Falmouth–Windsor–Brooklyn 07.00–19.00 Mon–Fri, 09.00–17.00 Sat; every 2hrs

from Yarmouth and 35km/23 miles from Digby. Weymouth is also on the **bus** route to Cornwallis (see box, page 206).

WHERE TO STAY AND EAT

Baie Ste-Marie Ocean Front Cottages (3 cottages) 5–9 Riverside Rd, New Edinburgh; 769 0797, **t/f** 1 866 769 0797; http://nsoceanfrontcottages.com; year-round. 3 themed 2-bedroom cottages in a wonderful setting less than 7km from Weymouth on St May's Bay at the mouth of the Sissiboo River. Very well equipped (full-size kitchen, barbecue, washer/dryer, etc), these make an excellent base from which to visit southwest Nova Scotia. Min stay 2 nights. **$$$**

Goodwin Hotel (10 rooms) 4616 Hwy 1; 837 5120; www3.ns.sympatico.ca/goodwinhotel; year-round. Choose between a room with private or shared bath at this simple old-style hotel, an inn since 1890. Food in the licensed dining room (*summer 07.00–09.00, 11.30–13.30 & 17.00–19.00 Sun–Fri; winter same hours but Mon–Fri;* $) is dependable but won't surprise you. **$**

OTHER PRACTICALITIES

$ Bank Royal Bank, Hwy 1; 837 5136; 10.00–15.00 Mon–Fri

Library Weymouth Branch Library, 4609 Hwy 1; 837 4596; 13.30–16.30 & 18.00–20.00 Tue & Fri, 12.00–16.30 Wed/Thu, 10.00–13.00 Sat

Post office 4659 Hwy 1; 08.30–17.00 Mon–Fri, 08.30–12.30 Sat

Tourist information Sissiboo Landing, 4575 Hwy 1; 837 4715; mid May–Jun & Sep/mid Oct 10.00–17.00 Mon–Fri; Jul/Aug 09.00–18.00 Mon–Fri, 10.00–18.00 Sat, 13.00–18.00 Sun

WHAT TO SEE AND DO A cultural interpretive centre, the **Sissiboo Landing** (*details as Tourist information, see above*) tells of the Mi'kmaq, United Empire Loyalists, Black Loyalists, Acadians and the New France settlers who are seen as Weymouth's founders.

The excellent company **Hinterland Adventures** (*837 4092,* **t/f** *1 800 378 8177; http://kayakingnovascotia.com*) offers a range of canoe tours in the Tobeatic Wilderness Area (see page 176) and kayak tours along the coast. It also rents equipment.

GILBERT'S COVE

The site of interest here is the delightfully located **Gilbert's Cove Lighthouse** (*Lighthouse Rd; ☎ 837 5584; http://gilbertscovelighthouse.com; ⌚ mid Jun–mid Sep 10.00–16.00 Mon–Sat, 12.00–16.00 Sun; admission free*). Reached by a short unpaved road, the c1904 lighthouse now serves as a museum, tea room and craft shop. Climb the tower for wonderful views over the cove, St Mary's Bay and Digby Neck. There are picnic tables on the grass above the beach.

Gilbert's Cove is situated 1km off Highway 101, 11km/7 miles from Weymouth and 24km from Digby.

WHERE TO STAY AND EAT Comfortable B&B rooms (and rustic camping possibilities) are available at **The Barn at the Point** (*3 rooms; 63 Lighthouse Rd; ☎ 837 4726; http://thebarnatthepoint.ca; ⌚ year-round;* **$**) on the quiet 36ha property near the lighthouse, with woodland trails and access to the beach. It's approximately 20 minutes' drive to Digby. The licensed **café** (*⌚ seasonally, check for hours;* **$–$$**) offers all-day breakfasts, sandwiches, soup, salads, and a couple of main-course choices in the evening.

DIGBY (*Population: 2,150*)

This working town 5km from the terminal for ferries to and from Saint John, New Brunswick, has a fine setting at the south end of the vast Annapolis Basin. Since commercial scallop fishing began here late in the 1920s, the mollusc (see box, page 198) has been the mainstay of Digby's economy.

A fire in 1899 destroyed over 40 buildings in the small downtown area. Today, **Water Street** is lined with shops, cafés, and restaurants, behind which a boardwalk makes a pleasant place for a wander. It may be a major gateway, but Digby is not awash with too many tacky souvenir shops. One of the province's few resorts – with a top-class golf course – lies between the town and the ferry terminal, and the big box stores and supermarkets stretch out along the road between downtown and Highway 102.

HISTORY The Mi'kmaq name for the area is *Te'Wapskik*, meaning 'flowing between high rocks', a reference to the Digby Gut. Originally called Conway (after a former secretary of state), the current name is in honour of Admiral Robert Digby, who sailed up the Fundy on the *Atlanta* in 1783 and settled the place with 1,500 Loyalists from New England.

GETTING THERE AND AROUND **By car**, Digby is just off Highway 101 Exit 26, 105km/65 miles northeast of Yarmouth and 235km/146 miles west of Halifax. Digby is on the Weymouth–Cornwallis **bus** route (see box, above). The terminus for the **ferry** (see page 45) to Saint John, New Brunswick, is 5km from town. Walk there, or take a **taxi**. Digby Cabs (☎ *245 6162*) charge CAN$12.

WHERE TO STAY

Digby Pines Golf Resort & Spa (116 units) 103 Shore Rd; ☎ 245 2511, **t/f** 1 800 667 4637; www.digbypines.ca; ⌚ mid May–early Oct. With 79 rooms & 6 suites in the c1929 main lodge & 31 well-dispersed 1- to 3-bedroom cottages (each with a sitting room with working stone fireplace, & covered veranda), this casually elegant old-fashioned resort sits on a hillside overlooking the Annapolis Basin outside the town centre. Aveda spa, superb 18-hole golf course, heated outdoor

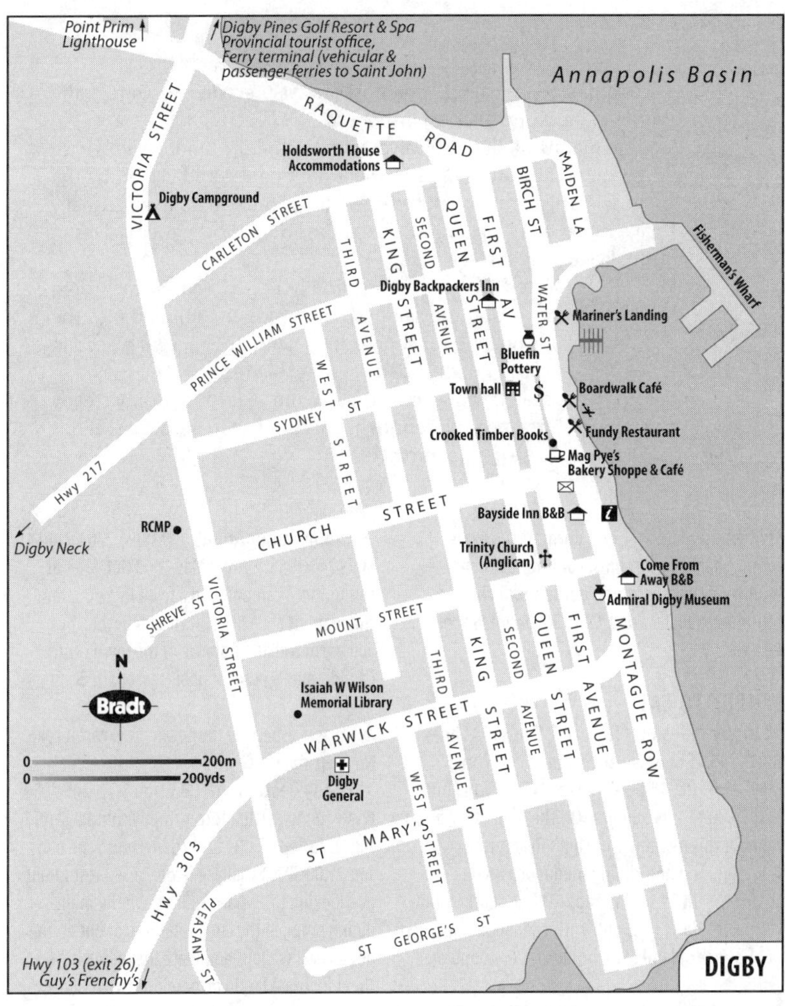

pool, tennis courts, fitness centre, children's playground, croquet, & walking/cycling trails. There are 2 bars (1 serving food & overlooking the golf course), & a main dining room (see page 198). Full b/fast inc in most rates. **$$$**

Come From Away B&B Inn (9 rooms) 98 Montague Row; 245 2413, **t/f** 1 877 392 2413; http://comefromawayinn.ca; May–Oct. 3 rooms in a c1904 main building &, tucked behind by the sea, a 2-storey modern addition with 6 more. Garden directly on waterfront. Full b/fast inc. **$$**

Bayside Inn B&B (10 rooms) 115 Montague Row; 245 2247, **t/f** 1 888 754 0555; **e** info@baysideinn.ca; http://baysideinn.ca; mid Apr–mid Oct. A c1885 building just across the road from the waterfront. Cheaper rooms have shared bathrooms. Full b/fast inc. **$–$$**

Holdsworth House Accommodations (3 rooms) 36 Carleton St; **t/f** 1 866 643 1784; www.holdsworthhousebandb.com; year-round (off-season by reservation). Friendly B&B in a beautifully restored, comfortable c1784 house (with 2 parlours & fine views) on a hillside above the town centre. Pets on premises. Rate inc full b/fast (served at Mag Pye's – see *Where to eat*, opposite). **$–$$**

Digby Backpackers Inn (12 beds) 168 Queen St; 245 4573; http://digbyhostel.com; year-round (Nov–Apr by reservation). Comfortable, friendly hostel in a Dutch Colonial-

DIGBY SCALLOPS

In Nova Scotia the word 'scallops' is almost always preceded by 'Digby': the town is home to the world's largest inshore scallop fleet.

Scallops are marine molluscs, bivalves with two hard, rounded shells with scalloped edges and a soft body. The shells are opened and closed by the adductor muscle. This is the 'meat', the only part of the scallop that is usually eaten. Unlike many other bivalve molluscs, they do not bury themselves in the sand, but live on the soft sea bed.

Scallops are harvested by 'draggers', specially rigged boats which drag huge metal mesh bags along the sea bed. The cages are emptied into the boats, and the scallops opened (or shucked) by hand. The meat is placed in containers and put on ice until the boats return to shore.

Conditions in the sea off Digby (in particular, the year-round, fairly steady cool water temperatures, and nutrient-rich sea) combine to produce scallops that – cooked well – are a gastronomic treat.

style house with 2, 4-bed dorms & a private room. Shared bathrooms, communal kitchen, laundry room, sun room, garden & deck. Bike rental for guests. *Dorm CAN$30, private room CAN$65.* **$**

Digby Campground (49 sites) 230 Victoria St; 245 1985; mid May–mid Oct. Sites at this terraced campground a few blocks up from the seafront are a little bit close together, but you are in walking distance of the town centre. Laundromat & outdoor pool (seasonal). **$**

WHERE TO EAT

Digby Pines Golf Resort & Spa 103 Shore Rd; 245 2511; www.digbypines.ca; mid May–early Oct 18.00–21.00 daily; mid Jun–mid Sep 11.00–14.00 Sun brunch. The main dining room of this resort is Churchill's Restaurant & lounge. The fine-dining menu focuses on seafood – Digby scallops appear frequently – but carnivores don't miss out, with very good roast beef & rack of lamb. Sun brunch is very popular. **$$$**

Boardwalk Café 40 Water St; 245 5497; www.boardwalkcafe.netfirms.com; Mar–May & Oct–Dec 11.00–14.00 Mon–Fri; Jun–Sep 11.00–14.00 & 17.00–20.00 Mon–Sat. An excellent, relaxed, licensed café/restaurant. A deck overlooks the wharf & Annapolis Basin. Everything is homemade: the scallops are delicious, as are the desserts – especially the pecan pie & carrot cake. No deep-fryer! **$$**

Fundy Restaurant 34 Water St; 245 4950; www.fundyrestaurant.com/fundy.shtml; mid Jun–mid Sep 07.00–22.00 daily; mid Sep–mid Jun 11.00–21.00 daily. A large, casual restaurant overlooking the wharf. Sit inside in the main dining room, in the large solarium, or out on the deck. Local scallops dominate the menu: have them for breakfast in an omelette, in chowder, with pasta – you get the idea. **$$**

Mariner's Landing 100 Water St; 245 1821; www.facebook.com/MarinersLandingRestaurant; May/Jun & Oct 11.00–19.00 daily; Jul–Sep 11.00–21.00 daily. When O'Neil Fisheries closed its unpretentious on-site restaurant, Linda Balser & her team moved around the corner

DIGBY CHICKEN

The first settlers had very little food – with one exception. Herring were plentiful and consequently were eaten at just about every meal, including on special occasions (when, in New England they would have eaten chicken). Consequently, herring became known as 'Digby chicken'. Even today, locals call herring 'Digby chicks'.

to the grander surrounds of the Digby yacht club building. The scallops & seafood are still excellent, as are the fresh fruit pies & coconut cream pie. There are fine views of the marina – albeit with a car park in the foreground – from the window tables. $$

Mag Pye's Bakery Shoppe & Café
9 Water St; 378 7937; Apr–Dec high season 08.00–17.00 daily, shorter hours off-season. Cosy, eclectically decorated café with (shock) tablecloths! Full b/fast menu, tasty sandwiches on homemade bread, nice pies (pyes?), & occasional themed dinners. Recommended. $

ENTERTAINMENT AND NIGHTLIFE Nightlife consists of the **Club 98 Lounge** in the Fundy Restaurant (see *Where to eat*, page 198), or the lounge bar at the **Digby Pines Resort** (*mid May–early Oct 17.00–22.00*).

FESTIVALS Watch 38 teams (with 'celebrity' captains) play the course at the Digby Pines Golf Resort and Spa over four days at the **East Coast Celebrity Golf Classic** (*www.eastcoastclassic.org*), held in July. In August, **Digby Scallop Days Festival** (*http://digbyscallopdays.com*) offers five days of music, races, parades and food – including, of course, Digby scallops! At the end of August/early September, the **Annual Wharf Rat Rally** (*www.wharfratrally.com*), Atlantic Canada's largest motorcycle rally, hits town for five days. Experience the smell of leather, the gleam of chrome, thousands and thousands of bikes, tattoo and piercing parlours, bandannas, paunches and more.

SHOPPING **Crooked Timber Books** (*17 Water St; 245 1283; http://crookedtimber.com; Apr–Dec 10.00–17.00 Mon–Sat*) is a good used bookstore with a special interest in Irish literature. **Bluefin Pottery** (*91 Water St; 245 5897*) has lovely pottery and a fine collection of works from over 40 local artists. Definitely worth a look. Rummage through bins of bargain used clothes at the original **Guy's Frenchy's** (*343 Hwy 303, Conway; 245 2458; www.guysfrenchys.com*) (see box, below), between Highway 101 and downtown, and enjoy the view from the car park.

OTHER PRACTICALITIES

$ **Bank** Royal Bank, 51 Water St; 245 4771; 09.30–17.00 Mon–Fri

Hospital Digby General Hospital, 75 Warwick St; 245 2501

Library Isaiah W Wilson Memorial Library, 84 Warwick St; 245 2163; 12.30–15.00 & 18.00–20.00 Tue–Thu, 10.00–17.00 Fri, 10.00–14.00 Sat

NOVA SCOTIA'S FAVOURITE SHOPS

The first **Guy's Frenchy's** opened its doors in Digby in 1972. Specialising in used clothes (but also used books, ornaments and more), there are now almost 20 Guy's Frenchy's (plus some copycat 'Frenchy's' across the province and into neighbouring New Brunswick). To many Nova Scotians, insulting Frenchy's seems to be akin to how insulting the royal family used to be in the UK.

Recently, a couple (who had bought everything that they would need for their wedding at the Digby Guy's Frenchy's) went the whole hog and got married in the store. The bins of used mens shirts, suits, sweaters, etc, were moved to one side making rummaging through them a bit awkward: however customers continued to burrow into the womens' and kids' piles as the couple made their vows.

Post office 9 Water St; 08.30–17.15 Mon–Fri
Tourist information 110 Montague Row, downtown; 245 5714, t/f 1 888 463 4429; late May–early Oct 09.00–17.00 daily (Jul–early Sep to 18.00); 237 Shore Rd, near the ferry terminal; 245 2201; 9–31 May & 18–31 Oct 09.00–17.00 daily; Jun–17 Oct 08.30–19.30 daily

WHAT TO SEE AND DO Don't miss the c1878 **Trinity Anglican Church** (*Queen St; 245 6744; www.trinitydigby.ca*), which is thought to be one of the few churches in Canada built entirely by shipwrights, and the **Admiral Digby Museum** (*95 Montague Row; 245 6322; www.admuseum.ns.ca; mid Jun–Aug 09.00–17.00 Mon–Sat; Sep/mid Oct 09.00–16.30 Tue–Fri; mid Oct–mid Dec 09.00–16.30 Wed & Fri*) housed in a mid 1800s Georgian house, with themed (eg: Marine and Costume) period rooms displaying artefacts in permanent and temporary exhibits. It has an extensive genealogy research facility (fee charged).

Take to the water in a **kayak**: single and double kayaks can be rented by the half or full day from **Dockside** (*Fundy Complex, 34 Water St; t/f 1 866 445 4950; www.fundyrestaurant.com; spring & summer*). Finish the day looking out across the water at the scallop fleet, watching the action at the wharf, then tuck in to plump, fresh, juicy scallops in one of the restaurants. Reasonably priced walking (and seafood sampling) tours of Digby are offered by **Gael Tours** (*245 4689, 247 2146; www.gaeltours.ca*): the company will also customise nature tours in the region (and offer a close-up view of life on the edge of the tide-line).

The **Point Prim Lighthouse** is worth a short drive at any time, but particularly towards sunset, as it sits on the Bay of Fundy side of **Digby Gut**, the narrow opening through which the huge Bay of Fundy tides pour into the Annapolis Basin. From here, there are fine views across the Gut to the remote wooded coastline north of **Victoria Beach** (see page 219). To get there, head towards the ferry terminal but instead of turning onto Shore Road, take the next right onto Lighthouse Road. Follow Lighthouse Road to the end (about 7.5km). Gael Tours (see above) offers a two- to three-hour Plankton, Periwinkles and Predators tour which neatly complements a whale-watching trip.

For a very challenging **golf** game, head to the 18-hole 6,222yd **Digby Pines** course on the Digby Pines Resort (see page 198), which was designed by Stanley Thompson (1894–1953), one of Canada's most celebrated golf course architects. 'Stay and play' packages are popular. Green fees CAN$79.

DIGBY NECK

Close to Digby, what looks on a map like a thin, skeletal finger (the last two 'bones' are actually islands) stretches for almost 75km and separates the Bay of Fundy from St Mary's Bay. Geologically, the Digby Neck, rarely more than 3km wide, is a continuation of North Mountain, which separates the Annapolis River valley from the Bay of Fundy. Both Brier and Long islands are made up of Jurassic basalt lava. As the lava cooled, it sometimes formed vertical polygonal columns such as Balancing Rock (see page 203).

The pace of life in Nova Scotia is generally pretty relaxed, but if you want to slow down even more, enjoy natural splendour, and take a holiday from your holiday, this beautiful area is worth some time. A line of wind turbines is a recent addition to the landscape.

There are few services, but just enough: pretty villages and good hiking, some of the province's best birding opportunities (see box, page 8) – and what may well be the best whale-watching opportunities along the entire east coast of North America.

Sunset casts a golden glow on the iconic c1914 lighthouse at Peggy's Cove

(m/S) page 132

left Tidal-bore rafting on the Shubenacadie River is an unforgettable experience – you will get wet! (NSTA) page 250

below The Three Sisters rock formations by the Bay of Fundy are popular excursion sites for sea kayaking (NSTA) page 267

bottom Fancy a wee dram? Drop by the Glenora Distillery in Glenville and sample whiskies in their tasting room or tour the whisky warehouse for a sip straight from the barrel (NSTA) pages 309–10

Sunset casts a golden glow on the iconic c1914 lighthouse at Peggy's Cove
(m/S) page 132

left Tidal-bore rafting on the Shubenacadie River is an unforgettable experience – you will get wet! (NSTA) page 250

below The Three Sisters rock formations by the Bay of Fundy are popular excursion sites for sea kayaking (NSTA) page 267

bottom Fancy a wee dram? Drop by the Glenora Distillery in Glenville and sample whiskies in their tasting room or tour the whisky warehouse for a sip straight from the barrel (NSTA) pages 309–10

above right **Birdwatchers at the annual West Pubnico Tern Festival** (NSTA) page 8

right **Cyclists along the LaHave River in Lunenburg County, near Riverport** (NTSA) page 164

below **With three national – and over 130 provincial – parks, you'll be sure to find a hiking trail to suit all levels and abilities** (NSTA) page 10

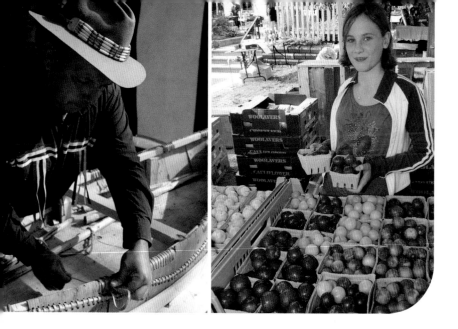

above left **Todd Labrador working on his handmade canoe: the Mi'kmaq have relied on such vessels since time immemorial** (SH) page 14

above right **Fruit seller at a farmers' market** (NSTA) page 67

below **The pews inside Eglise Sacre Coure Catholic Church in Saulnierville are covered with handmade quilts during a quilt show, part of the annual Festival Acadien de Clare** (NSTA) page 192

above left & right Nova Scotia has a rich history of artisan crafts, including rug hooking and folk art such as this painting by Maureen Newman, 'Across the marsh to Blomidon' (MN and NSTA) pages 67 and 27

right Scottish heritage lives on in modern-day Nova Scotia (NSTA) pages 28–9

below Mi'kmaq dancers at a traditional festival (Q) page 35

top left There are two moose sub-species in the province: the mainland moose and the Cape Breton moose, the latter seen here in Cape Breton Highlands National Park – approximately 5,000 individuals live on the island (NSTA) page 7

above left The only type of bear found in Nova Scotia, American black bears (*Ursus americanus*) are shy but can be seen with luck and patience (TH/FLPA) page 7

above right Seals are a common sight along the coast (NSTA) page 9

below Nova Scotia has an abundance of sea birds, such as these semi-palmated sandpipers (*Calidris pusilla*) (SS) page 9

above left Nova Scotia's provincial bird, osprey (*Pandion haliaetus*) often make their nests in the most unlikely places (MB)

above right Mayflowers (or trailing arbutus) are the provincial flower of Nova Scotia, and these fragrant blooms appear in forest glades during early spring (JR) page 4

below Often found in stands along the roadside, lupins are at their most vibrant in June (NSTA) page 4

left **A scallop-shucking competition at the Digby Scallop Days Festival in August** (NSTA) page 199

below left **Cheticamp crab fishermen unloading their catch** (NSTA) page 312

below right **Dramatic views of the lighthouse and rugged coastal scenery on the Bay of Fundy at Cape d'Or on the Glooscap Trail** (NSTA) page 264

bottom **Carters Beach is unspoilt perfection and a prime contender for the 'Most Beautiful Beach in Nova Scotia' title** (DO) page 171

Although the majority of visitors drive straight to their whale-watching trip and (when it is over) drive back again, try to allow yourself more time to explore this beautiful region.

The wild flowers are out between mid May and late June, mid July brings wild blueberries, and soon after, humpback whales. July and August can be foggy, September and October are usually beautiful, though late October can be windy.

GETTING THERE From Digby, Highway 217 runs down the centre of the peninsula for approximately 50km to East Ferry, from where a five-minute **car ferry** (*CAN$5.25 return; at half past the hour westbound*) crosses to Tiverton on Long Island. Highway 217 continues along Long Island for 18km to Freeport, from where another car ferry (*10 minutes, CAN$5.25 return*) crosses to Westport on Brier Island. Ferries are timed so that if you're going straight through, you can drive directly from one ferry to the next without too much waiting.

THE MAINLAND The first dozen kilometres along Highway 217 – a road also labelled the 'Digby Neck and Islands Scenic Drive' – is an unremarkable inland drive, but before too long there are views over St Mary's Bay and opportunities to make short side trips – for example to the Bay of Fundy shore by taking Trout Cove Road from Centreville. Gulliver's Cove-based **Fundy Adventures** (*685 Gulliver's Cove Rd; 245 4388; http://fundyadventures.com*) organises a range of customised experiences such as clam digging, dulse (edible seaweed) harvesting, or lobster fishing for those looking to learn more about the Fundy Shore.

As you continue on Highway 217 along the peninsula, a pretty provincial park on the waterfront at Lake Midway offers picnic tables and freshwater swimming. The highlight of this part of Digby Neck is the delightful Sandy Cove. Another worthwhile short detour is to turn onto Little River Road at Little River, and follow it to the St Mary's Bay shore.

The mainland ends at **East Ferry** 46km from Digby, perched atop a cliff overlooking the waters of Petite Passage, and the lighthouse on Long Island.

Where to stay and eat

Graham's Pioneer Retreat (4 cottages) 8020 Hwy 217, Centreville; t/f 1 888 839 2590; www.digbyneck.com; May–mid Oct. Come for peace & quiet on this secluded property. These 1- & 2-bedroom cottages – all with wonderful St Mary's Bay views – are comfortable with fully equipped kitchens, but don't expect TVs or phones. **$$**

The Olde Village Inn (7 units) 387 Church Hill Rd, Sandy Cove; 834 2202, 434 5544; http://theoldevillageinn.com; mid May–mid Oct. 6 B&B rooms & 1, 5-bedroom vacation home. Impressive c1830 house with sun room, views over St Mary's Bay & pool room. An inn since 1890. **$$**

Whale Cove Campground (25 sites) 50 Whale Cove Rd, Whale Cove; 834 2025; www.whalecovecampground.com; May–Oct. Located in Whale Cove, 6km south of Sandy Cove. Some sites at this open campground with laundromat overlooking the Bay of Fundy have electricity & water hook-ups. **$**

Petit Passage Café 3450 Highway 217, East Ferry; 834 2226; May–Oct 08.30–18.00 daily. A rustic café with deck overlooking Petit Passage. The seafood chowder, soups & scallop rolls are all good, as are the fruit pies. $

What to see and do

Sandy Cove Sandy Cove is located 31km from Digby and is one of the province's prettiest communities. The main part of the village is concentrated round the St Mary's Bay side of the Neck, but a short drive through the hills along Bay Road leads

JEROME

One evening in 1863, a ship was seen close to the Bay of Fundy shore at Sandy Cove. In the morning, the vessel had gone, but a strange young man sat on the sand. Although well dressed in fine linen, he was very pale: both his legs had recently been amputated above the knees. The only word he would say was 'Jerome', indicating that that was his name. Doctors, police and ministers came to question him, but he was no more loquacious. After a while, the government paid a family in Meteghan (see page 192) to take him in: Jerome spent the rest of his long life there, never uttering any other words. He died in 1912 and was buried in Meteghan parish cemetery. His story continues to fascinate.

to a long, quiet, sandy beach on the Fundy shore. This is normally a lovely beach and a fine spot from which to watch the sun set, but in 2012 a whale carcass washed ashore and for months as it rotted authorities argued over who was responsible for its removal. Hopefully, by now it'll just be the fresh sea air that you can smell.

For a magnificent view of Sandy Cove, it is worth heading up nearby **Mount Shubel** which can be reached by a relatively easy 15–20-minute trail. The trailhead is accessed by turning off Highway 217 a few hundred metres northeast of Sandy Cove onto an unpaved road (turn right if you're coming from the Digby side, left if coming from Sandy Cove itself). There's a small parking area a short distance along the unpaved road. This road isn't named or signed, so ask a local for directions if it is not immediately obvious.

WHALE WATCHING ON THE BAY OF FUNDY

The warm Gulf Stream water colliding with the cold outflow from the Bay of Fundy, combined with the tremendous tidal influence on the waters in this area, produces some of the most plankton-rich waters in the world. This attracts whales, particularly baleen whales – the largest animals on earth.

Smaller species such as finback and Minke whales and harbour porpoises are plentiful early in the season, and numbers of huge humpback whales increase as June goes on. White-sided dolphins are another possibility, and in August you might see a very rare right whale. Seals are sometimes sighted, and pelagic seabirds abundant.

Most operators offer two- to five-hour boat trips from June to mid October for approximately CAN$45–50 (many offer a 'no whales – try again free' guarantee). It's a good idea to make reservations well in advance, especially between July and early September. The main operators are:

Brier Island Whale and Seabird Cruises Westport; 839 2995, **t/f** 1 800 656 3660; www.brierislandwhalewatch.com
Freeport Whale and Seabird Tours Freeport; 839 2177, **t/f** 1 866 866 8797
Mariner Cruises Westport; 839 2346, **t/f** 1 800 239 2189; www.novascotiawhalewatching.ca
Ocean Explorations Tiverton; 839 2417, **t/f** 1 877 654 2341; www.oceanexplorations.ca. Uses small high-speed Zodiac (or similar) inflatable boats. Special trips, such as those dedicated to seabirds, on request. CAN$65.
Petit Passage Whale Watch East Ferry; 834 2226; www.ppww.ca
Pirate's Cove Whale Cruises Tiverton; 839 2242, **t/f** 1 888 480 0004; www.piratescove.ca

LONG ISLAND

Tiverton A traditional fishing village with a couple of whale-watching companies (see box on page 202). The nearby **Boar's Head Lighthouse** is a great place to gaze out over the Bay of Fundy and try to spot whales. The **tourist information** centre is located inside the Islands Museum.

What to see and do The **Islands Museum** (*Hwy 217, approx 2km from Tiverton;* ☎ *839 2853;* ⌚ *end Jun–early Sep 09.00–16.30 daily; admission free*) has exhibits detailing life on Long and Brier islands in days gone by, including display boards on Joshua Slocum (see box below).

Approximately 3.5km past Tiverton is the parking area and trailhead to **Balancing Rock**. The first part of the trail is relatively flat, with boardwalks over the wettest parts. You then descend over 200 steps on wooden staircases (slippery when wet) down to the cliffs from where there is a perfect view of a 9m pinnacle of basalt rock balanced on a seemingly far too narrow base. The route is approximately 1.5km each way.

Freeport Try and allow some time on the way or way back to explore beautiful Freeport. Although most people stay on Highway 217, instead, take the first left immediately after the church and follow Overcove Road, which eventually leads past the fishing wharves, to the end. Park and follow the trail towards Dartmouth Point. A lovely new trail leads up to a look-out and over the hill from just behind the Freeport Development Office (*243 Hwy 217*).

✕ *Where to eat*

✕ Lavena's Catch Café 15 Hwy 217; ☎ 839 2517; ⌚ mid May–early Oct 11.30–20.00 daily, off-season 11.30–18.00 usually Fri–Sun. Food at my favourite Digby Neck restaurant is freshly made: the lobster dinner, seafood chowder, scallops (pan-seared or baked) & pan-fried haddock are all excellent. The 'chicken' bit of the chickenburger is a grilled breast, & room should be saved for one of Aunt Heather's desserts! Licensed. **$–$$**

BRIER ISLAND And so to the highlight of Digby Neck. For some, whale-watching apart, there will be nothing to do on 6.5km by 2.5km Brier Island. But it won't disappoint those who enjoy the atmosphere of a community little changed by the passing decades, or are just content to watch the swirling sea and pounding waves. If you're into birdwatching, wild flowers, or even just like walking, cycling or beachcombing, you won't want to leave. Virtually everyone lives in **Westport**: though the village has paved roads, only unpaved roads and walking trails cross the rest of the island.

The squat c1965 **Grand Passage Lighthouse** can be reached via Northern Point Road. Just to the west, as the name suggests, **Seal Cove** is a

> **SOLO SAILOR**
>
> Brier Island's most famous inhabitant was Joshua Slocum who lived in Westport for a few years before taking to the high seas. In April 1895 (aged 51), he departed Boston, Massachusetts, in a tiny sloop and sailed 74,000km around the world (with Westport his first stop) single-handed, returning to Newport, Rhode Island in June 1898. In November 1909 (aged 65), he sailed off alone from Massachusetts bound for South America and was never heard from again.

good place to watch and listen to the mammals: wander down a couple of hours before (or an hour after) low tide. On the island's southwest side is the concrete **Brier Island Lighthouse**, one of the most photogenic in the province. To get there, take Wellington Street from Westport, then turn left onto Western Light Road. Or turn left onto Water Street from the ferry and follow the road just a few hundred metres to the end. Park, sit on the rocks and watch seabirds ride the swirling currents, with Peter Island and its 1909 lighthouse as a beautiful backdrop.

Relatively low-lying, the island has far less forest cover than most of the province. This sensitive ecological treasure has sedge and sphagnum bogs, and rare and unusual plants including eastern mountain aven, pitcher plant, dwarf birch, curly-grass fern and several types of orchid. Late spring and summer brings a profusion of wild flowers such as Queen Anne's lace, lady's slipper, blue iris, and many types of wild rose. And even those who couldn't tell an orchid from an Orkin will enjoy the abundance of wild strawberries.

Quite apart from anyone else, the island – on the Atlantic Flyway – is a must-visit for birdwatchers. Over 320 species have been noted here, and a wide variety of birds can be seen easily at all times of the year, including many rarities. Autumn is one of the best times, with the hawk migration a highlight.

Where to stay and eat

Brier Island Lodge and Restaurant (40 rooms) 557 Water St, Westport; 839 2300, t/f 1 800 662 8355; www.brierisland.com; May–mid Oct. 1km north of the village centre in a fine location on a bluff overlooking Westport & Grand Passage. Most of the rooms are in 2 modern 2-storey buildings, & these are better (& cost a bit more) than the rooms in the main building. The upstairs rooms have the best view! In the licensed dining room (*May–mid Oct 07.00–10.00 & 18.00–21.30 daily;* **$$**) stick to fresh local seafood. Outside mid Jun–mid Sep the menu is much more limited. **$–$$**

Brier Island Backpackers Hostel (12 beds) 225 Water St, Westport; 839 2273; www.brierislandhostel.com; year-round. 3 rooms (inc 1 family room), bunk beds, shared bathrooms, good cooking facilities & a sun deck overlooking the harbour. Comfortable, friendly, & right by the well-stocked general store which has a café (*early Jun–late Sep). Dorm CAN$20.* **$**

Dock & Doze Motel (3 units) 353 Water St; 839 2601, 247 0142; e dockanddoze@hotmail.com; May–Sep. Friendly little motel. 1 unit has a full kitchen, the other 2, microwave & fridge. **$**

BEAR RIVER

Don't take too much notice of tourist literature calling it 'The Switzerland of Nova Scotia', but this interesting little laid-back community with an inland riverside setting is well worth a visit. Pretty throughout the year, it is stunning in autumn when the hardwood trees blaze their colours.

Once a major shipbuilding centre, many of the village's riverside buildings are built on stilts – twice a day, those high Bay of Fundy tides make their way into the Annapolis Basin and up the river. Something of a cosmopolitan artists' community, a large Mi'kmaq population (see box, page 14) also calls Bear River (and environs) home.

Bear River has long been renowned for its cherries, and hosts a summer cherry festival (see opposite). It is said that cherry trees were brought over from England in the 18th century by one William Sutherland (festival cherries, by the way, are usually imported from the northwest USA).

Bear River is 17km/11miles from Digby, 29km/18 miles from Annapolis Royal and 7km/4 miles from Highway 101 Exit 24.

WHERE TO STAY AND EAT

Barnwood Inn B&B (3 rooms) 336 Chute Rd; 467 0481; www.barnwoodinn.ca; May–Oct. Well-appointed rooms in a nicely renovated heritage home on a quiet road a few mins' outside the village centre. Rate inc full b/fast. **$–$$**

Changing Tides Diner 1882 Clementsvale Rd; 467 0173; Feb–Nov 07.30–19.30. Friendly, dependable diner with daily specials & nice river views from the back room. **$–$$**

FESTIVALS Held in early/mid July, the **Cherry Carnival** is a one-day event which includes a parade, flea market, races, competitions – and lots of sweet cherries for sale. In August, the **Digby County Exhibition** is a four-day agricultural show with fairground rides, food and arts and crafts.

OTHER PRACTICALITIES

Tourist information Oakdene Centre, 1913 Clementsvale Rd; 467 3200; Jul/Aug 09.00–17.00 daily, Sep 10.00–16.00 Wed–Sun. Housed in a former school.

WHAT TO SEE AND DO Houses and churches on winding streets peer through the trees on the steep hills on both sides of the river. Be sure to stroll some of these streets to see the beautiful old houses and historic churches such as the **United Baptist Church** (*37 Pleasant St*).

Many artists and craftspeople – some very talented – now call the village home, and there are several galleries dotted all over the community including three or four on the short main street.

Longest established – and the best – is **The Flight of Fancy** (*1869 Clementsvale Rd; 467 4171,* **t/f** *1 866 467 4171; www.theflight.ca*), close to the bridge. This is one of the top craft shops in Atlantic Canada.

Across the road and a few doors up, well-priced secondhand books and a wide variety of memorabilia are housed in a former bank at **Bear River Bargains & Books** (*1886 Clementsvale Rd; 467 0334; summer 10.00–17.00 Tue–Sun; spring/autumn 11.00–17.00 Tue–Sun; winter 11.00–17.00 Fri–Sun*).

Just off the 'main drag', tucked behind a pretty little garden, is a building that is home to both **Oddacity Designs** and **The Innocent Rose** (*467 0268; www.inoutofthefog.com; mid Jun–mid Sep 10.00–17.00 daily*). Here you'll find 'wearable art', used books, vintage housewares and clothing, and more.

CLOSED DOORS

The village of Bear River and environs are home to the Bear River First Nation (in Mi'kmaq, *L'sitkuk*), one of 13 First Nation communities in the province. Archaeological evidence suggests that the L'sitkuk have been living in the area for well over 3,000 years. Until recently, you could visit the **Bear River First Nation Heritage and Cultural Centre** (*194 Reservation Rd*): on show were portraits of former Mi'kmaq chiefs and elders, local Mi'kmaq artefacts (some dating back 2,500–4,000 years), historical arts and crafts and a handmade authentic birch-bark canoe. There was also a gift shop and a 1km Medicine Trail with medicinal trees and plants. However, this was not open to the public in 2012, and future plans are up in the air. It is worth checking the website (*www.bearriverfirstnation.ca*) for updated information.

OPENING DOORS?

Seven Paddles is a brand-new (late 2012) Mi'kmaq heritage project which aims to build a link between the past and the future. The plan is to re-establish centuries-old canoe routes (with necessary portages) to reconnect the Bear River First Nation Reserve (*L'sitkuk*) with Kejimkujik National Park. Follow the project's progress at http://sevenpaddles.com.

Worth seeing, too, is the atmospheric **Old Baptist/Loyalist cemetery** up the hill on Lansdowne Road near the junction with Riverview Road.

Grapes are grown on some of the hillsides and tastings are offered at **Bear River Vineyards** (*133 Chute Rd; ☎ 467 4156; www.wine.travel; ⏲ Jun–Sep 12.00–17.00 Tue–Sun*). Less than five minutes' drive from the village, **Annapolis Highland Vineyards** (*2635 Clementsvale Rd, Bear River East; ☎ 467 0363; www.novascotiawines.com; ⏲ Jun–Oct 10.00–18.00 daily*) will be on your left. Both vineyards offer free tours and tasting.

Take River Road (passing the Fire Hall on your left), then follow the signs from the village centre to the studio/shop **Beartown Baskets** (*44 Maple Av; ☎ 467 3060; www.beartownbaskets.com; ⏲ year-round 09.00–17.00 'most days'*) to watch retired Mi'kmaq chief Greg McEwan transform ash (and wood from other deciduous trees) into beautiful traditional baskets.

The **Bear River Heritage Museum** (*1939 Clementsvale Rd; ☎ 467 0902; http://bearriverhistory.ca/; ⏲ Jul–Aug Tue–Sun; admission CAN$2*) is a local history museum in a former school (which also houses the tourist office). **Riverview Ethnographic Museum** (*18 Chute Rd; ☎ 467 4321; ⏲ year-round by chance or appointment; admission CAN$2*) is an interesting stop; it has six rooms of authentic folk costumes and artefacts from around the globe (and Bear River), and its good reference book collection adds plenty of background information.

CORNWALLIS, CLEMENTSPORT AND UPPER CLEMENTS

These three communities lie along the southern side of the Annapolis Basin between Digby and Annapolis Royal. Cornwallis was the site of a big Canadian Forces training base (and is still used as a training facility for international peacekeeping forces and Canadian naval cadets). As of summer 2012, it is also home to the **Fundy YMCA** (*1043 Hwy 1, Cornwallis; ☎ 638 9622; www.fundyymca.com*), which has a good gym, heated indoor pool and more, and is open to non-members. Clementsport was once a bustling port with hotels, shops and garages: now, activity centres around the **Moose River Rug Hooking Studio** (*14 Clementsport Rd, Clementsport; ☎ 638 3200; www.mooseriverstudio.com; ⏲ year-round 10.00–17.00 Mon–Sat*), a bright, welcoming spot, and a good place to be shown how to rug-hook or to buy supplies for the craft.

Back on Highway 1 after a studio visit, take the first right onto Old Post Road. A couple of hundred metres up the hill, look out for a church on your right. If you're passing in the summer (and if they've found a volunteer), the **Old St Edwards Loyalist Church Museum** (*34 Old Post Rd, Clementsport*) will be open. The church dates from the 1790s. You can continue along Old Post Road and then turn left to rejoin Highway 1.

As you continue on towards Annapolis Royal, look out for **2697 Highway 1** on your left. The left-hand of the two single-storey buildings (empty and forlorn at the time of writing) was last used as a garden centre. A few decades back, though, it was the Seashell, considered one of the top-ten restaurants in Canada. Patrons included actors Arthur Kennedy and James Cagney: local legend has it that the latter (who apparently 'discovered' the former) often recreated a famous scene from *The Seven Little Foys* (1955) and tap-danced on the tables. Kennedy is commemorated with a room named in his honour at the Annapolis Royal Golf Club, and is buried just south of town. Talking of movie stars, silent screen *femme fatale* Theda 'The Vamp' Bara (1885–1955) regularly visited Clementsport to see her parents – in the 1930s and 1940s many wealthy Americans had summer homes here.

Still on Highway 1 and heading towards Annapolis Royal, you then come to the area's big draws. On the left is **Upper Clements Theme Park** (*2931 Hwy 1, Upper Clements;* ☎ *532 7557,* **t/f** *1 888 248 4567; www.upperclementsparks.com;* 🕘 *mid Jun–early Sep 11.00–18.45 daily*). Disneyland it isn't, but very few come away from the province's largest theme park disappointed. There are dozens of rides and things to do and see, from minigolf and pedal go-karts to giant waterslides and a bone-shaking rollercoaster. Great for the kids, but plenty of kid-less adults go and enjoy it too. The best deal (especially if you might be returning the next day) is a CAN$28.50 Fastpass (advance purchase only).

Just across the road is the new (2012) **Upper Clements Adventure Park** (🕘 *Jun–Oct 09.00–17.00 daily; admission CAN$29*). A former wildlife park has become a giant 'aerial' adventure, a cross between an amazing take on the 'Pirates' game from school PE classes to an assault course. It's fun for anyone who is adventure-loving and fairly fit (and at least 5'2"/1.575m in footwear). The course – which takes three to four hours to complete – ends with no fewer than 14 ziplines. Both parks are on Highway 1, 7km from Annapolis Royal. The parks may close if thunderstorms are forecast.

You can stay right by the parks at **Upper Clements Cottages** (*3067 Hwy 1, Upper Clements; 7 units;* ☎ *532 0269,* **t/f** *1 800 717 6549; www.upperclementscottages.ca;* 🕘 *year-round;* **$$–$$$**). The two-bedroom cottages are comfortable and well-equipped: there's a seasonal pool, sports, and sweet bunnies all around the grounds.

GETTING THERE The three communities are on Highway 1 between Exit 23 off Highway 101 and Annapolis Royal, and hence easy to reach **by car**. Cornwallis is 17km from Digby, 16km from Annapolis Royal and 11km from Bear River (take Chute Road, then Purdy Road from Bear River). Cornwallis is the terminus for **buses**

TROUBLED BRIDGES OVER WATER

A few decades back, the province had a fine rail network, and many rue its passing (especially when you look at the current public transport situation). A few stations remain, and several stretches where the rails were taken up are now multi-use trails. Until very recently, this region also had a number of old railway bridges, but these had been allowed to fall into various states of disrepair. Rather than paying the ongoing costs of repairing and maintaining the structures for trail-users or heritage reasons, the decision was made to demolish three local bridges (those at Weymouth, over the mouth of the Bear River, and over the Moose River mouth at Clementsport). The first two were demolished in spring 2012, and – sadly – no 11th-hour pardon came in for the third. To paraphrase Steve Goodman, 'This land has got the disappearing railway (and railway bridge) blues …'

(see page 195) to Weymouth (via Digby), and to Bridgetown (via Clementsport, Upper Clements and Annapolis Royal).

ANNAPOLIS ROYAL *(Population: approx 500)*

It is hard not to like Annapolis Royal. First, it has a delightful setting on the Annapolis Basin shore – and wonderful views across the water to the pretty village of Granville Ferry from a boardwalk with benches, picnic tables and a lighthouse. The town has a tree-lined main street, one end of which is lined with gracious mansions, many of which help make up what is the largest concentration of heritage buildings in Nova Scotia, with over 120 municipally registered properties, 20 provincial heritage properties and five federally designated properties. Several of these house some of the province's best inns and B&Bs.

You'll find lovely gardens to stroll through, and waterside trails to wander. You can also visit North America's first tidal power generating plant. There are galleries and a theatre with a good year-round programme. You can visit a historical site dating back four centuries, take a candlelit graveyard tour, visit a museum housed in a 300-year-old building, and an early 18th-century cemetery. All of these can be reached easily on foot. A short drive will take you to the site of one of the earliest permanent European settlements in North America, a good golf course, a beautiful hiking trail to the Bay of Fundy shore, or Nova Scotia's biggest theme park. Despite all this, Annapolis Royal only gets really busy during some of the bigger festivals.

Don't come to 'Canada's birthplace' for the nightlife (though there is a friendly little pub), but do come to soak up the history and unique atmosphere. And note that the town doesn't end at the junction of St George Street and Drury Lane: continue just a hundred metres further on St George Street to see a couple of interesting shops (one with a café) and the O'Dell Museum.

HISTORY Although the first Port-Royal was destroyed in 1613 (see page 15), in the early 1630s, the French built a new version 11km away, this time on the south shore of the Annapolis Basin. Things were relatively calm for a couple of decades but after that the settlement changed hands backwards and forwards between the French and British.

Back under British control in 1710, the town was renamed 'Annapolis Royal' in honour of their queen, and the fort that had seen so much fighting – and had changed hands so many times – renamed 'Fort Anne'. This time – despite almost countless French attacks – the British flag was raised to stay. Annapolis Royal served as Nova Scotia's first capital until 1749 (when it was succeeded by Halifax).

Annapolis Royal prospered and during the Great Age of Sail was a bustling town with several industries and over 3,000 inhabitants. Shipbuilding reached its peak in 1874 and was centred on Hog Island, which now forms part of the causeway crossing the Annapolis River.

Its job done, Fort Anne was abandoned in the 1850s and fell into disrepair. Following a campaign by locals to have the site preserved and maintained, Fort Anne became Canada's first administered National Historic Site in 1917.

In the late 1970s Annapolis Royal was in a state of decline. The population had dwindled and the council had no money to spend on upkeep. However, a citizen-led group formed the Annapolis Royal Development Commission and lobbied both the provincial and federal governments to inject funds to preserve the town's unique heritage. Their efforts paid off, over CAN$2 million was spent

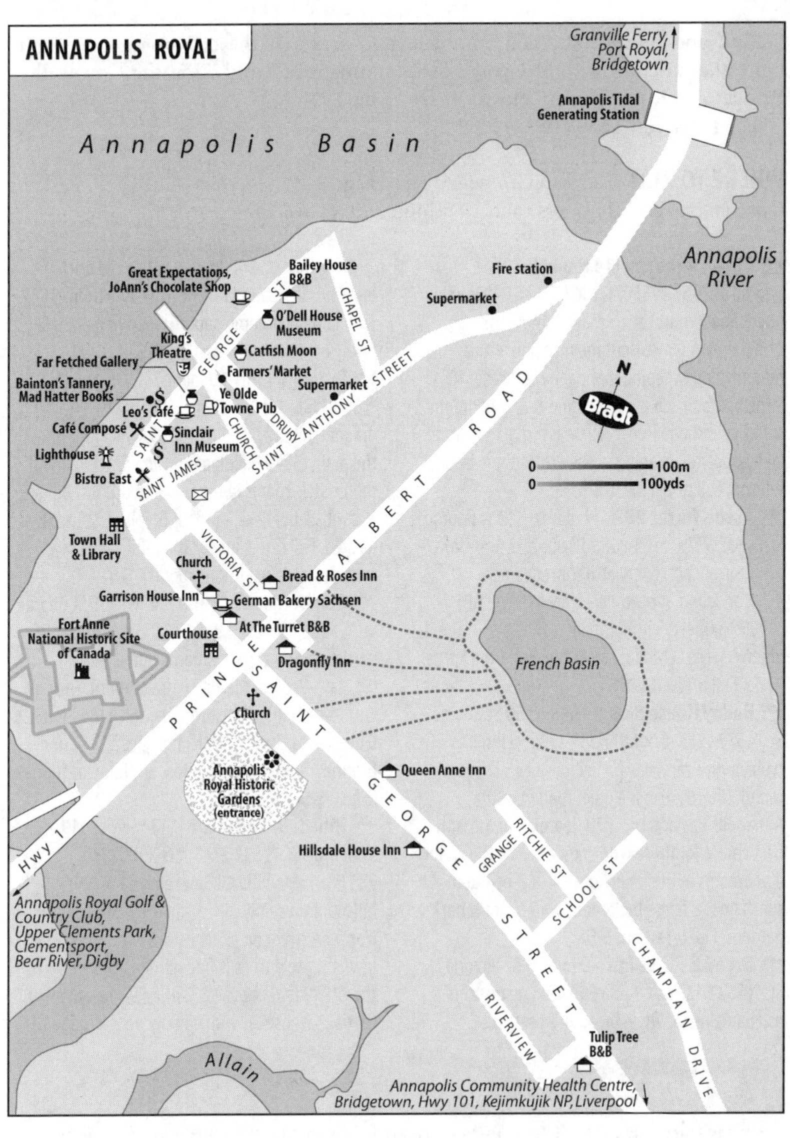

on restoration projects, and in 2004, the town was designated the 'World's Most Liveable Small Community'. The following year, the town was listed as one of five Cultural Capitals of Canada.

GETTING THERE AND AROUND If you're coming **by car** from Highway 8, which leads to town from Exit 22 of Highway 101, as it enters town the road becomes St George Street. This continues past many beautiful houses and the Historic Gardens to a traffic light and crossroads. As you continue straight (passing the old Courthouse and Fort Anne on your left, St George Street curves downhill to the shopping district and the wharf. If you're coming from Bridgetown on Highway 1, you'll cross the causeway over the Annapolis River, passing the Tidal Generating

Station and tourist office on your left, and arrive at the crossroads and traffic light, the junction with St George Street. Annapolis Royal is on the Cornwallis–Bridgetown Kings County **bus** route (see page 195).

For **taxis**, call 665 0057.

WHERE TO STAY

See also *Granville Ferry* (page 218), less than 2km away. Parker's Cove (see page 221) is less than 15 minutes' drive away.

Queen Anne Inn (14 rooms) 494 St George St; 532 7850, **t/f** 1 877 536 0403; www.queenanneinn.ns.ca; May–Nov. A striking c1865 grey & white Heritage mansion with a magnificent sweeping mahogany staircase. 10 large bedrooms in main building & 2, 2-bedroom suites in Carriage House. There is also a restaurant (see opposite). Grand, but the atmosphere is relaxed. Full b/fast inc. **$$$**

At the Turret B&B (4 rooms) 372 St George St; 532 5770, **t/f** 1 866 717 0067; **e** turretinfo@attheturret.com; www.attheturret.com; year-round. A centrally located (turreted!) c1900s' property with original woodwork, stained glass, & large veranda, across the road from Fort Anne. Full b/fast inc. **$$**

Bailey House B&B (5 units) 150 St George St; 532 1285, **t/f** 1 877 532 1285; **e** info@baileyhouse.ca; www.baileyhouse.ca; year-round. Directly across a quiet road from the Annapolis Basin, this c1770 Georgian home is the best choice for those who want to be by the water. 4 bedrooms in the main house, & a 2-bedroom coach house. Large bedrooms, waterfront & back gardens. Full b/fast inc. **$$**

Bread & Roses Inn (9 rooms) 82 Victoria St; 532 5727, **t/f** 1 888 899 0551; **e** rosesinn@ns.aliantzinc.ca; www.breadandroses.ns.ca; Apr–Nov. One of the town's few old brick buildings in Queen Anne Revival style from c1882 with large bedrooms, superb wood panelling & lovely gardens. Full b/fast inc. **$$**

Dragonfly Inn (9 rooms) 124 Victoria St; 532 7936, **t/f** 1 877 943 2378; www.dragonflyinn.ca; Apr–Nov. 3 lovely rooms in the main c1870 building (*Apr–Sep only*), with 6 motel-style rooms in the Coach House just behind. Hot tub, 2-tier deck, outdoor fireplace. Centrally located. Full b/fast inc (B&B) or, Jul–Sep only, continental b/fast (motel rooms). **$$**

Garrison House Inn (7 units) 350 St George St; 532 5750, **t/f** 1 866 532 5750; **e** info@garrisonhouse.ca; www.garrisonhouse.ca; May–Oct (off-season by reservation). Facing Fort Anne National Historic Site, this c1854 inn has 6 bedrooms, 1 suite (with large jacuzzi), period furniture & whimsical fish folk art. Rate inc full b/fast. **$$**

Hillsdale House Inn (13 rooms) 519 St George St; 532 2345, **t/f** 1 877 839 2821; **e** info@hillsdalehouseinn.ca; www.hillsdalehouseinn.ca; Apr–Oct. Set back from the street on a 5ha estate with manicured lawns, stately trees & fine gardens. 11 rooms in the c1859 main house & 2 more in the adjacent Carriage House, all individually decorated with

OF MOOSE AND MEN

It is said that in the 1790s, Prince Edward, Duke of Kent (and father of Queen Victoria), was surprised embracing an attractive serving girl at the c1708 deGannes-Cosby House at 477 George Street, now a private residence and the oldest documented wooden structure in Nova Scotia. Incidentally, the house is said to be haunted, but only by a quiet, well-mannered old lady who never bothers anyone. During the same visit the duke attended a ball held at what later became known as the Bailey House. In the 1830s, the house's owner, 'Marm' Bailey, was renowned for her 'moose muffle soup' (the muffle is the nose and the pendulous, overhanging upper lip of the moose). The Bailey House is now an elegant B&B (see above). Moose muffle soup is not on the breakfast menu.

antiques. Former guests include the then Prince of Wales (who went on to become King George V) in 1884, & author John Buchan in 1937. Licensed bar (guests only). Full b/fast inc. **$$**

Tulip Tree B&B (3 rooms) 683 St George St; 532 0151, **t/f** 1 866 532 1051; **e** reservations@tuliptree.ca; www.tuliptree.ca; year-round. Sue & Ted's gracious 100-year-old American Colonial Revival home with 3 beautifully appointed rooms is set in landscaped gardens. Full b/fast inc. **$$**

WHERE TO EAT

See also *Granville Ferry*, page 218. Only Café Composé offers waterfront dining.

Annapolis Royal Golf & Country Club 3816 Hwy 1, Allains Creek; 532 2064; www.annapolisroyalgolf.com; mid May–Sep 11.00–20.00 Mon–Sat, 11.00–18.00 Sun; Oct–May 11.00–14.00 & 17.00–19.30 Tue–Sat, 11.00–18.00 Sun. British-owned & run: in addition to scallops, haddock & the like, don't be surprised to see bangers & mash or steak pie. Choose between the casual bar/restaurant or intimate, candlelit fine-dining (reservations required). Licensed. **$$**

Bistro East 274 St George St; 532 7992; www.bistroeast.com; summer 11.00–22.00 Mon–Sat, 12.00–18.00 Sun; rest of year 11.00–20.00 Mon–Sat. Sophisticated, licensed eatery with a broad menu including seafood, gourmet pizza, pasta (handmade) & steaks, plus lighter lunches (eg: soups, salads, sandwiches). Occasionally portions can be on the small side. **$$**

Café Composé 235 St George St; 532 1251; mid May–mid Oct 11.30–14.30 & 17.00–20.00 Mon–Sat; mid Oct–mid May 11.30–14.30 Mon–Sat. This good European-style café/restaurant/bistro is stylish & centrally located in the large building next to the little lighthouse. The food is very good (schnitzels, scallops & more) & the waterside deck a delight. Pop in even if you just want a coffee & piece of strudel to keep you going. **$$**

Garrison House Inn 350 St George St; 532 5750, **t/f** 1 866 532 5750; **e** info@garrisonhouse.ca; www.garrisonhouse.ca; mid May–late Oct 17.00–21.00 daily. The restaurant has 3 intimate rooms, a screened veranda facing Fort Anne & is the best choice in the area for fine-dining. Owner/chef Patrick Redgrave's eclectic menu draws on high-quality fresh local & organic produce. Start, perhaps, with the cold applewood-smoked salmon plate before moving on to lobster risotto with shiitake mushrooms, or perhaps steamed Digby scallops with roasted tomato, feta cheese & tarragon, tossed in rotini pasta. The wine list is well chosen. Service isn't the fastest, but the food is worth waiting for. Reservations recommended. **$$**

Queen Anne Inn 494 Upper St George St; 532 7850, **t/f** 1 877 536 0403; www.queenanneinn.ns.ca; May–Oct 17.00–21.00 Wed–Sun. The licensed dining room of this heritage mansion has an exciting menu offering local fare with a global influence – lobster, scallops, free-range chicken, organic beef & more. **$$**

Ye Olde Towne Pub 9–11 Church St; 532 2244; year-round 11.00–23.00 Mon–Fri, 10.00–23.00 Sat, 12.00–20.00 Sun. This pub in a c1884 former bank has a popular outside deck. Generally, food is good & reasonably priced – particularly the daily specials. **$$**

German Bakery Sachsen Café 358 St George St; 532 1990; www.germanbakery.ca summer 08.00–20.00 Mon–Sat, 10.00–20.00 Sun (off-season probably Fri/Sat only). Good location & authentic name (Heiderose & Dieter are from Saxony), but a bit pricey for standard (albeit German) pastries & café fare. **$–$$**

JoAnn's Chocolate Shop & Café 165 St George St; 532 0120; www.this-is-the-chocolateshop.com; Mar–Dec 10.00–17.00 Mon–Sat, summer 09.00–18.00. Small café & chocolate shop featuring handmade Belgian chocolate, coffee & espresso, light lunches & baked goods. Located past the wharf next to children's playground. **$**

Leo's Café 222 St George St; 532 7424; May–Oct 09.00–16.00 Mon–Sat. Located in the c1712 Adams-Ritchie House, this is Annapolis Royal's most popular spot for a light lunch (salads, soup, wraps, gourmet sandwiches, etc), fantastic cakes & sublime cinnamon rolls. **$**

ENTERTAINMENT

King's Theatre 209 St George St; 532 7704; www.kingstheatre.ca. This c1921 theatre has an art gallery on site, & a varied programme (year-round) including theatre, films & live music.

FESTIVALS **King's Shorts** is a three-day theatre festival of ten-minute plays, staged in June. In August, **Natal Days** is a street parade with community events such as pancake breakfasts, and family activities in and around town. Some of the town's magnificent old houses (and their gardens) are decorated and illuminated for the festive season at **Victorian Christmas**, in December. There is a parade, craft market, and carol concerts.

SHOPPING

Shops and galleries

Bainton's Tannery & Mad Hatter Books (*213 St George St; 532 2070, t/f 1 800 565 2070; www.baintons.ca; year-round daily*) is one of those perfect matches: leather and new books, with a good selection of Nova Scotia/ Maritimes titles. **Catfish Moon** (*170 St George St; 532 3055, t/f 1 888 378 3899; www.catfishmoon.com; May–Oct daily*) has hand-painted ceramics (whimsical earthenware pottery), and a studio and folk art gallery. **Far Fetched** (*218 St George St; 532 0179; May–Oct daily*) has beautifully crafted *objets d'art* from around the world, especially Asia and the Far East. **Great Expectations Books & Antiques** (*165 St George St; 532 0120; Mar–Dec 10.00–17.00 Mon–Sat, summer 09.00–18.00*) has used (and some new) books, antiques and crafts. It shares a space with a café and chocolate shop.

OTHER PRACTICALITIES

$ Banks Royal Bank, 248 St George St; 532 2371; 10.00–15.00 Mon–Wed, 10.00–17.00 Thu/Fri. Scotiabank, 219 St George St; 532 2393; 10.00–17.00 Mon–Fri

Health centre Annapolis Community Health Centre, 821 St George St; 532 2381

Library Annapolis Royal Library, 285 St George St; 532 2226; 14.00–17.00 Mon, 10.00–17.00 Wed & Fri, 10.00–17.00 & 18.30–20.30 Thu, 10.00–14.00 Sat

Post office 50 Victoria St; 08.00–17.00 Mon–Fri, 09.00–12.00 Sat

Tourist information 236 Prince Albert Rd (Hwy 1); 532 5454; mid/end May & early/mid Sep 10.00–16.00 daily; Jun–Aug 09.00–19.00 daily. Located in the Annapolis Royal Visitor Information Centre in the tidal power plant on the north side of town.

WHAT TO SEE AND DO Out-of-season visitors will find many things closed, but the population is less seasonal than in some towns and there's still a little bit of life. The 7ha **Annapolis Royal Historic Gardens** (*441 St George St; 532 7018; www.historicgardens.com; mid May/Jun & Sep/mid Oct 09.00–17.00 daily; Jul/Aug 09.00–20.00 daily; admission CAN$10*) opened in 1981 and were designed to reflect the various periods of local history through a gardening perspective. The Annapolis Valley climate allows a real diversity of plants to be grown: highlights include a Victorian garden, Governor's garden, innovative garden and rose collection – with around 2,000 bushes of more than 270 cultivars. See too the replica of a 1671 Acadian house, complete with thatched roof and an Acadian garden. It is wonderful resource for heritage gardening enthusiasts, and also has an on-site café and shop. Set out for a pleasant, flat walk of approximately 25 minutes on the **French Basin Trail**, which takes you around a pretty pond often brimming with wildlife. Depending on the time of year, you might see muskrats, turtles sunning themselves, Canada geese and a lot more. There are a few access points, for example follow the path from the old railway station (which is almost opposite the entrance to the Historic Gardens), or park in the car park on Highway 1 approximately 250m from the traffic lights in Annapolis Royal heading towards Granville Ferry and the causeway. You're in the right place if you see a small skateboard park.

For both produce and crafts, head to the **farmers' market** (🕘 *year-round 08.00–13.00 Sat, & Wed afternoons Jul & Aug*). Between mid May and mid October, the market is held in the town square, and positively bustles. Off-season it downsizes significantly and moves indoors to the Historic Gardens entrance.

Situated on the causeway across the Annapolis River, the **Annapolis Tidal Generating Station** (*Hwy 1;* ☎ *532 5454;* 🕘 *mid May–mid Oct 09.00–17.00 daily (Jul/Aug to 20.00); admission free*) is one of only three tidal power plants in the world, and the only one in the western hemisphere. The plant generates over 30 million kWh of electricity per year, enough to power over 4,000 homes.

One of Canada's most important historic sites (see *History*, page 208) is the **Fort Anne National Historic Site of Canada** (*323 St George St;* ☎ *532 2397; www.pc.gc.ca/fortanne;* 🕘 *late Jun–Aug 09.00–17.30 daily; early–late Jun & Sep 09.00–17.30 Sun–Wed;* 🕘 *site & grounds year-round; admission CAN$3.90 museum, grounds free*). Beside the car park and opposite the old parade ground is the distinctive c1797 officers' quarters built by the British which now houses a museum telling the story of the fort and the Acadians in the area. Be sure to see the 2.4m x 5.5m **Heritage Tapestry**, which depicts four centuries of history and settlement in Annapolis Royal and environs. Over 100 volunteers worked on the project, and even the Queen – on a 1994 state visit to Nova Scotia – chipped in with a few stitches. Outside, see the restored c1708 French gunpowder magazine, and another gunpowder magazine which was later used as a dungeon. The fort's earthworks are the best-surviving example of a Vauban fort in North America: expansive grassy ramparts and grounds overlook the Annapolis Basin and the mouths of the Annapolis and Allain rivers, and lead right down to the water's edge. The location is magnificent: even if you're not interested in history, come for a wander, the views, a picnic, or just to let the kids roll down the slopes.

Part of the site is the **Garrison Cemetery**. Originally the St Jean Baptiste Cemetery and burial grounds for the French military forces here, it later served both the British military and the local parish. The earliest tombstone still in place dates from 1720. Between June and mid October, an entertaining candlelight graveyard tour is offered by the local Historical Association at 21.30 on Sunday, Tuesday, Wednesday and Thursday evenings.

The c1869 former home and tavern of Corey O'Dell is now the **O'Dell House Museum** (*136 Lower St George St;* ☎ *532 7754; www.annapolisheritagesociety.com;* 🕘 *year-round, hours vary*). O'Dell was once a rider on the Pony Express run (see page 220), and the downstairs rooms reflect a house of the 1870–1900 period. Upstairs you can find contemporary exhibits of community history, and the museum offers a genealogical centre and archival research facilities.

One of the most significant buildings in Canada is the **Sinclair Inn Museum** (*232 St George St;* ☎ *532 7754; www.annapolisheritagesociety.com;* 🕘 *Jun–Aug 09.00–17.00 Mon–Sat, 12.30–17.00 Sun; Sep/mid Oct 09.00–17.00 Tue–Sat; admission CAN$3*), the front part of which was built in 1710. It offers a fascinating insight into the construction techniques of the Acadians – where clay and straw were forced into the wall cavities as insulation – to the (relatively) modern. The building and town's history is brought to life by a series of ten projected 'ghosts', each representing a person who lived or worked in the building from its construction through to the 1950s.

Golfing enthusiasts can drop by the **Annapolis Royal Golf and Country Club** (*3816 Hwy 1; ☎ 532 2064; www.annapolisroyalgolf.com; ⊕ approx Apr–Oct*), a short 5,417yd course, but worth playing, not least for the wonderful views. Aside from weekends, you shouldn't need to book a tee time. Green fees CAN$37.

KEJIMKUJIK NATIONAL PARK AND NATIONAL HISTORIC SITE OF CANADA

From Annapolis Royal, Highway 8 running south presents the quickest route to visit Nova Scotia's beautiful Kejimkujik National Park and National Historic Site (*Hwy 8; ☎ 682 2772; www.pc.gc.ca/pn-np/ns/kejimkujik; ⊕ late May–early Oct; admission CAN$5.80/day*). Confusingly, the park comprises two geographically separate sections, the smaller of which, Kejimkujik Seaside, is described on page 170.

Those familiar with some of North America's national parks might not 'get' Keji, at 38,000ha the Maritimes' largest inland national park. Don't come here expecting magnificent sweeping panoramas, soaring mountains, towering waterfalls or vast canyons – this is a place of woodlands, lakes studded with islands, rivers and streams, best viewed not from a car window but on foot, from the saddle of a mountain bike, or, best of all by staying for a few nights, camping and travelling along the waterways by canoe. The modern-day visitor to Kejimkujik's back-country can retrace ancient canoe routes and experience a landscape which is very similar in appearance to that which the Mi'kmaq travelled through for so long.

HISTORY The Mi'kmaq inhabited – or at least regularly passed through – this area for thousands of years, travelling by canoe and on foot, hunting, fishing and camping. Some Mi'kmaq petroglyphs/pictographs dating from the 18th and 19th centuries have survived: these depict scenes of Mi'kmaq family life, hunting and fishing, and scenes inspired by the experience of the Mi'kmaq during the era of European contact. Their locations are closed to public access, but they can be viewed on guided tours led by Mi'kmaq interpreters.

Europeans settled in the region in the 17th century, logged most of the forests and cleared much of the land for farming. Some (largely unproductive) gold mines were also established within Kejimkujik's boundary. In the 19th and 20th centuries the site contained hunting and fishing lodges which have since been removed. The national park was established in 1967 and the National Historic Site was established in 1995.

GEOGRAPHY AND GEOLOGY The last glaciation, which began approximately 90,000 years ago and ended 11,000 years ago, was responsible for the erratics (glacier-transported rock fragments), eskers (long winding ridges deposited by meltwater from glaciers), drumlins (hills carved by receding glaciers), shallow lakes, streams and rivers seen today.

Although fresh water covers some 14% of the park, hard rock such as slate, granite and quartzite yields precious few natural minerals to the rivers and streams. River, stream and lake water in Kejimkujik is generally a tea-like brown: plants in the many wetlands contain tannin, and this colours the water.

FLORA AND FAUNA Black bears are present throughout the park, though sightings are rare. Beaver lodges and dams can be seen on many waterways, and white-tailed deer, muskrat, racoon and porcupine are common. The coyote was first sighted in the park in 1985, and is still rare, as are the American marten and southern flying squirrel (see page 6).

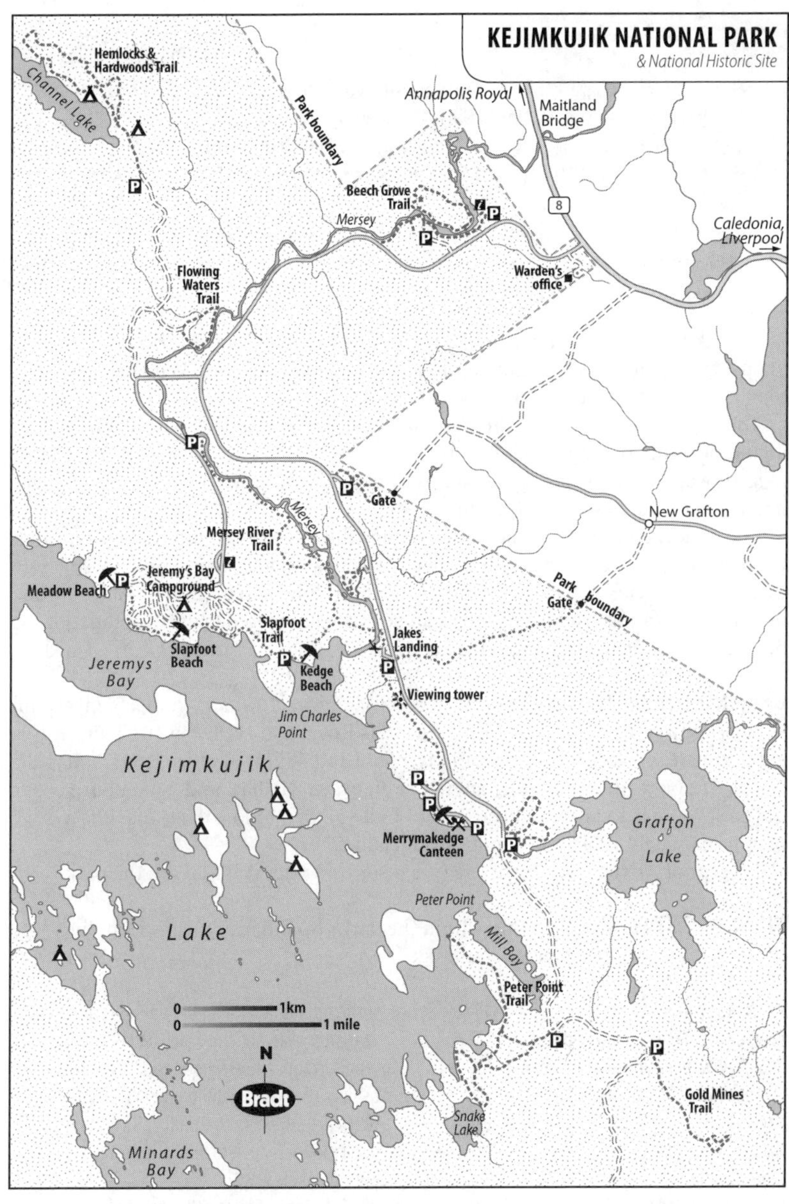

The park is home to five snake species, including the rare Eastern ribbon snake, and three turtles, one of which, the Blanding's turtle, is on the Endangered list. The chances of spotting salamanders and frogs are very good.

Six species of woodpecker, including the pileated woodpecker and the rare black-backed woodpecker, and 20 species of warbler contribute to the park's 200 or so bird species. Most common of the owls is the great barred owl, and the call of the common loon delights many campers after dark. Rarities include the scarlet tanager, great crested flycatcher and the wood thrush.

THE ROAD TO KEJI

Highway 8 leads south from Annapolis Royal, under Exit 22 off Highway 101 and on to Kejimkujik National Park 47km away, and then on to Liverpool (see page 162) 115km away. Just off Highway 8, 27km from Annapolis Royal, the **Raven Haven South Milford HI-Hostel** (*4 beds; Virginia Rd, West Springhill; 532 7320; mid–Jun–Aug;* **$**) is on the shore of Sandy Bottom Lake. There's a supervised swimming beach, canoe rentals and a canteen, and it is open to non-guests.

Kejimkujik's vascular plant count is close to 550 including 90 species of woody plants, over 20 ferns, 15 orchids, and almost 40 aquatic species. Wild flowers are at their best between late May and the end of June.

The park's forest cover is representative of the Atlantic Coast Plain region, including a mix of coniferous and deciduous species. Whilst most areas have been logged over the centuries, some stands of old growth Eastern hemlock and sugar maple-yellow birch can still be found.

The park is considered to be home to one of the healthiest populations of brook trout in Nova Scotia and possibly in all of Atlantic Canada. Kejimkujik is also home to 11 other species of fish including white and yellow perch, brown bullhead (one of the catfish family), and the American eel, which due to declining populations is now listed as a 'species of special concern'.

GETTING THERE The park's entrance is off Highway 8, which connects Liverpool – and Highway 103 Exit 19 – with Annapolis Royal and Highway 101 Exit 22. It is approximately 70km/43 miles from Liverpool and 48km/30 miles from Annapolis Royal. If you're **driving** from anywhere between Halifax and Lunenburg, your quickest route is to take Highway 103 to Exit 13, then follow the signs. It is a drive of approximately 165km/103 miles from Halifax.

Liverpool Adventure Outfitters (see page 168) offer day tours to the park.

WHERE TO STAY Overnighting within the park's boundaries means camping – the best way to truly experience Kejimkujik.

Mersey River Chalets (16 units) 315 Mersey River Chalets Rd, Maitland Bridge; **t/f** 1 877 667 2583; www.merseyriverchalets.com; year-round. These very convenient chalets have a nice setting & offer rooms in a lodge, 2 sizes of chalet (all very comfortable), & – for the more adventurous – 3 tipis (Native American-style tents), & 2 walled tents. There's a good (seasonal) restaurant (*lunch & dinner: check website for days/times;* **$$**). **$$**

Milford House Lakeside Cabins (27 cabins) 5296 Hwy 8, South Milford; 532 2617, **t/f** 1 877 532 5751; www.milfordhouse.ca; May–mid Oct. At 24km north of the park entrance, this long-established accommodation offers rustic but comfortable cabins in wooded surroundings. A number of families return here year after year. Activities include lake swimming, tennis, croquet, horseshoes, canoe rentals & fishing. The licensed dining room (*May–mid Oct high season 17.30–20.00;* **$$**) dishes up good food & is open to non-guests: reservations are a good idea. **$$**

Caledonia Country Hostel (8 beds) 9960 Hwy 8, Caledonia; 682 3266; **e** info@caledoniacountryhostel.com; www.caledoniacountryhostel.com; year-round. Camping apart, this friendly budget option in Caledonia, 15km from the park entrance, offers a 5-bed dorm, & a private dbl room. Bedding is provided, & there is a communal kitchen & deck (with barbecue), & a lounge. Bike rentals & shuttle service (including to the airport) are available for those without their own transport. *Dorm CAN$30; private room CAN$65 (discounts for longer stays)*. **$**

Whitman Inn (8 units) 12389 Hwy 8, Kempt; 682 2226, **t/f** 1 800 830 3855; http://whitmaninn.com; year-round. Outside, less than 4km from the park entrance road is this c1912 inn which has good facilities, such as a nice heated indoor pool (seasonal), & a well-regarded dining room open for b/fast (*08.00–09.30*) & dinner (*18.00–20.00, Oct–Jun by reservation only); $$*). **$**

Jeremy's Bay Campground 514 335 4813, **t/f** 1 877 737 3783; www.pccamping.ca; late May–early Oct. Over 350 sites. There are washrooms, sinks for dishwashing & a shower block (but no electrical or sewage hook-ups). Reservations are recommended. **$**

For those looking for more solitude, 46 back-country campsites are situated in beautiful wilderness settings, scattered along hiking trails and canoe routes. Each individual site has a fire box, picnic table, pit toilet, firewood, and a food storage device. For reservations for wilderness camping call 682 2772.

WHERE TO EAT

M & W Restaurant and Variety Store 644 Hwy 8, Maitland Bridge; 682 2189; mid May–mid Oct 08.00–21.00ish daily. Almost directly opposite the park entrance is this good little eatery – unpretentious, friendly & well priced. **$–$$**

Merrymakedge Canteen Jul/Aug 10.00–20.00 daily. Located at the supervised swimming beach, this is a convenient place to grab a bite to eat. **$–$$**

OTHER PRACTICALITIES Caledonia has a grocery shop, liquor store (off licence), and a couple of fast-food restaurants. There's also a **tourist office** – **Caledonia VIC** (*682 2470; http://discovercaledonia.com; early Jun–early Oct 10.00–17.00 daily*). A **farmers' market** (*May–Oct Sat*) offers local produce.

WHAT TO SEE AND DO For the day visitor, there are 15 designated **hiking trails** to explore, ranging from a 300m loop to a 3.5km each-way riverside wander. The trails are generally pretty flat, so hiking here is more about enjoying the forest, waterways, and animal, bird and plant life than gazing out over far-reaching panoramas. They might not be the giant redwoods of California, but the 300-year-old stand of towering hemlock is pretty impressive: view these and other hardwoods on the aptly named 6km **Hemlocks and Hardwoods loop**. **Mill Falls** is an easy, short (2km return) riverside wander starting at the visitor centre. The **Rogers Brook trail** is even shorter (at just 1km), but nevertheless enjoyable. The 3km return **Gold Mines Trail** leads – as you might have guessed – to an old gold mine (see *History*, page 214). For a good overview of woodlands and riverside, I would recommend combining the **Mersey River Trail** (3.5km one-way) with the 3.2km **Slapfoot Trail**.

WHAT'S IN A NAME?

Few dispute the fact that the derivation of the name 'Kejimkujik' is from a Mi'kmaq word or expression. However, many translations are bandied about, including 'swollen waters' and 'attempting to escape'. Call me juvenile, but my favourite is 'swelled private parts' – puzzlingly said to be in reference to the effort required to row across the park's largest lake. Just about everyone calls the park 'Keji'.

Mountain bikers will want to try the 4km **Peter Point Trail** and the 18km **Fire Tower Road Trail**. Bikes can be hired at **Jake's Landing** (*682 5253; e jakes@ns.sympatico.ca; www.friendsofkeji.ns.ca/jakes/; mid May–mid Oct*): this is also the place to rent canoes and kayaks (from CAN$7/hour).

Canoeing has always been the best way to explore Kejimkujik. There are spectacular routes for a wilderness camping trip, or for a day paddle: at very least rent a canoe for an hour or two. The dark, warm waters are also great for swimming. The fishing season (special licence is required) runs from April to August.

A range of interpretive activities (free with park admission) include canoe events, hikes, children's programmes, concerts, dark-sky viewing programmes, campfire programmes and guided tours of the **Mi'kmaq petroglyphs**.

GRANVILLE FERRY

Granville Ferry is a village of two parts. Coming from Annapolis Royal, turn left after crossing the causeway and you'll find fine views across the water to Annapolis Royal, especially in the afternoon (when the sun is further west). The community, which in the 1920s attracted several upper-class British families who had been living the good life in India, boasts several elegant old houses and a wonderful B&B.

If (instead of turning off) you continue along Highway 1, the other part of Granville Ferry has a campground and café, a couple of restaurants and two petrol stations. Granville Ferry is just across the causeway from Annapolis Royal. If the weather's clement, it's a pleasant walk or easy cycle ride.

GETTING THERE Granville Ferry is on Highway 1 and therefore convenient **by car**, just 1km/0.6 miles from Annapolis Royal and 22km/14 miles from Bridgetown, 9km/6 miles from Exit 22 off Highway 101. Granville Ferry is on the Cornwallis–Bridgetown **bus** route (see page 195).

WHERE TO STAY AND EAT The following are all within 2km of Annapolis Royal – less than three minutes' drive.

A Seafaring Maiden (3 rooms) 5287 Granville Rd; 532 0379, **t/f** 1 888 532 0379; www.aseafaringmaiden.com; year-round. An award-winning, beautifully decorated c1881 home with wonderful views across the water to Annapolis Royal, Fort Anne & the Annapolis River basin. A real treat. Full gourmet b/fast inc. **$$**

Dunromin Waterfront Campground (207 sites) 4618 Hwy 1; 532 2808; www.dunromincampsite.com; May–mid Oct. Open & wooded sites, serviced & unserviced, on the bank of the Annapolis River. Laundry, grocery store, café (see adjacent, pool, activities including boat rental & kayak lessons/trips. **$**

Sweet Secret Restaurant 4784 Hwy 1; 532 0909; May–Sep 17.00–20.15 daily. Another slightly unprepossessing location, but this licensed restaurant serves good seafood, salads & European cuisine (for example, schnitzel). **$$**

Stone Horse Café 4616 Hwy 1; 532 5554; May–mid Oct 08.00–14.00 Tue–Sun. Situated in the Dunromin Campground, & with no deep-fryer in sight, just good healthy, tasty homemade food at this simple unpretentious café. Soups, salads & sandwiches at lunch, & all-day b/fasts. Garden patio for warmer weather. **$**

WHAT TO SEE AND DO Having crossed the causeway, take the first left onto Granville Road toward the **North Hills Museum** (*5065 Granville Rd; 532 2168; http://museum.gov.ns.ca/nhm/; Jun–mid Oct 09.30–17.30 Mon–Sat, 15.00–17.30 Sun; admission CAN$3*). The museum is on the right, 4km past the centre of the village. Housed in a charming, superbly restored c1764 salt box-style farmhouse with Georgian décor, it has a wonderful collection of antiques including 18th-century paintings, furniture, ceramics and glassware. The museum hosts several summer events, usually on Sunday afternoons.

The **Port-Royal National Historic Site** (*Granville Rd;* ☎ *532 2898; www.pc.gc.ca/portroyal;* ⏲ *late May/late Jun & Sep/mid Oct 09.00–17.30 Sun–Thu; late Jun–Aug 09.00–17.30 daily; admission CAN$3.90*) offers a fascinating look into the life of early European settlers in the New World, and is one of the most historically important sites in not just Canada, but the whole of North America. Learn more about it in the refurbished Boulay Room and sit in the dining room and try to imagine the chatter and laughter from over five centuries ago. Accessible toilets and a picnic area are located by the car park. The site is 10km/6 miles from Granville Ferry and 12km/7 miles from Annapolis Royal.

In 1604, Sieur de Mons and Samuel de Champlain (from France) established a permanent camp, naming it 'Port-Royal': their habitation was the first permanent European settlement north of St Augustine, Florida. To keep morale high, in 1606, de Champlain set up North America's first social club, *L'Ordre de Bon Temps* (usually translated as the 'Order of Good Cheer'). Fine food and drink helped distract the settlers from the hardships of life in this remote outpost.

De Champlain established fine gardens with reservoirs and canals, and he built a summer house among trees. The gardens are marked clearly on his 1607 map, the original of which is at the Congress Library in Washington, DC.

The French settlers got on very well with the area's original residents, the Mi'kmaq, and when Sieur de Mons's monopoly was revoked in 1607, the habitation was left in the care of Mi'kmaq chief Membertou. The Mi'kmaq chief did a fine job, and when the French returned in 1610, De Mons's successor, Jean, Sieur de Poutrincourt encouraged Membertou and the Mi'kmaq to convert to Catholicism. A force commissioned to expel all Frenchmen from territory claimed by England, led by Samuel Argall from Virginia, arrived in 1613 whilst the inhabitants were away up the river. The habitation was looted and destroyed.

Between 1939 and 1940, the Canadian government built a reconstruction of the c1605 French fur-trading post based on de Champlain's drawings, using 17th-century construction techniques where possible. The buildings form a rectangle around a courtyard and are fortified by a stockade, with two cannon platforms at the southerly corners. A well dug by de Champlain is in the centre of the courtyard, and the site contains a blacksmith's shop, kitchen, communal dining room, guardroom and artisans' quarters. Costumed interpreters are on hand to provide more details.

If you feel like getting out on the water, **kayaking** introduction and tours (*2–8hrs*) exploring the Annapolis Basin are offered by Dunromin Waterfront Campground (see page 218).

VICTORIA BEACH

Rather than turning back after visiting Port-Royal (see above), if time allows consider making a side trip to Victoria Beach. Shortly after the Port-Royal site, the c1885 **Shafner's Point Lighthouse** makes a pleasant picnic spot. As you drive, there are fine views over the Annapolis Basin, and you'll pass some beautiful heritage homes in different architectural styles. As you near Victoria Beach, look out at the narrow, turbulent currents and whirlpools of the **Digby Gut**. Victoria Beach doesn't have a beach to speak of, or much to see other than a large wharf, a colourful collection of boats and a small lighthouse. It does, however, have a storied past and numerous

PONY EXPRESS

Early in 1849, six American news organisations clubbed together to finance a pony express. A steamer arrived in Halifax from England bringing newspapers from Europe. These were transported by a relay team of horseback couriers from Halifax to Digby Gut, whence they were shipped to the telegraph station at Saint John, New Brunswick. From there, the news items were relayed by telegraph to the press of the American seaboard cities. The Halifax Express covered the 232km in an average time of eight hours. Riders were changed at Kentville, but horses (not ponies) were changed every 19km. As the rider passed through Annapolis Royal, a cannon was fired to signal a steamship waiting at Victoria Beach to prepare to depart. Operating between February and November 1849, this successful system was superseded by the extension of the telegraph to Halifax. A monument to the Pony Express is found on the seaward side of the road a little before you get to the Victoria Beach wharf area.

ghost stories emanate from the community. Tales of the sounds of vessels docking but no visible signs of ships, of men dressed in clothes from bygone days who greet people on the path and then disappear into thin air, of a sailor who had died at sea returning each night to stand on the doorstep of his house leaving a puddle of seawater and seaweed, of several sightings of the Grey Lady (see page 363), and even a sea serpent with a huge head and eyes which reared up out of the water.

In the 1940s, the village was the home of historical novelist Evelyn Eaton, best known for *Quietly My Captain Waits*.

Victoria Beach is at the western end of Granville Road, 25km/16 miles from Granville Ferry and 27km/17 miles from Annapolis Royal. The road ends in uninhabited coastline at this point and you will have to go back along Granville Road to return to Port-Royal or head north towards Delap's Cove.

DELAP'S COVE

The only reason to head out to this remote area is to hike the **Delap's Cove Wilderness Trail** (see below). There's a rustic loo at the trailhead parking area, but no other services.

To reach Delap's Cove **by car**, either take Parkers Mountain Road from Highway 1, just east of Granville Ferry, or (a bit quicker) take the unpaved Hollow Mountain Road from Granville Road just east of Port-Royal. Either way, turn left at the T-junction and follow Shore Road West. Look for a sign on the left to Delap's Cove Wilderness Trail. It's approximately 17km from Granville Ferry by the shorter route.

WHAT TO SEE AND DO The **Delap's Cove Wilderness Trail** (in a remote area off Shore Road West) offers good hiking. The better (of what are actually two) trail is the 2.2km Bohaker Loop which leads from the trailhead car park through softwoods and hardwoods to the rocky Bay of Fundy shore, onto a fascinating rock cove jammed with driftwood, flotsam and a wrecked boat. The sure-footed can descend to the cove via a steep, sometimes slippery, path (watch out for the incoming tide). On the other side of the cove, Bohaker's Brook drops over the cliff edge as a 12m waterfall. There's a look-out right by the top of the cascade, from where a short extension to the trail was opened in 2012. Retrace your steps back across the bridge to rejoin the trail which follows the brook upstream before curving back to the parking area.

PARKER'S COVE

On the Bay of Fundy shore over North Mountain from Granville Ferry, less than 10km from Granville Ferry and Annapolis Royal, Parker's Cove is a working fishing village with a lobster pound where the crustacean can be purchased live or cooked. The cove can be reached **by car** by taking Parkers Mountain Road from Highway 1 just east of Granville Ferry. It is less than 15 minutes' drive from Annapolis Royal. Eat in Annapolis Royal or at Granville Ferry (see pages 208 and 218, respectively).

WHERE TO STAY

Mountain Top Cottages (17 units) 888 Parker Mountain Rd; 532 2564, **t/f** 1 877 885 1185; www.mountaintopcottages.com; May–Oct. Simple 1- & 2-bedroom cottages set in the woods overlooking a lake on an 80ha property. All cottages have a fridge, microwave & stove. Heated outdoor pool (seasonal), hiking & biking trails & watercraft for use on the lake. **$$**

Lobster Wharf Vacation Rental 4311 Shore Rd West; 532 2858, **t/f** 1 877 942 7322; www.vrbo.com/426955; year-round. On the Bay of Fundy shore, overlooking the wharf. Rent this 3- to 4-bedroom renovated c1882 house with laundry facilities, a library & solarium by the day or week.

Cove Oceanfront Campground (90 sites) 4405 Shore Rd West; 532 5166; www.oceanfront-camping.com; May–mid Oct. Open serviced & unserviced sites in a lovely Bay of Fundy shore setting, with a pool. **$**

BRIDGETOWN *(Population: 970)*

This pretty riverside town of wide tree-lined streets and grand heritage homes makes a nice wander. Pick up a **Cyprus Walk** leaflet from the tourist office, or see it at www.town.bridgetown.ns.ca. If your timing is right, you can also take to the water in a kayak.

Bridgetown is on Highway 1 and just off Highway 101 (Exits 20 and 21), 26km from Annapolis Royal and 23km from Middleton. It is easy to reach **by car**. Bridgetown is the terminus for **bus** routes west to Cornwallis and east to Greenwood (see page 224).

WHERE TO STAY AND EAT

Bridgetown Motor Inn (28 rooms) 396 Granville St East; 665 4403, **t/f** 1 888 424 4664; www.bridgetownmotorinn.ca; year-round. Dependable motel with spacious rooms, laundry facilities & outdoor pool (seasonal). Wi-Fi available. B/fast available at extra cost. **$**

Harrington House B&B (2 rooms) 325 Granville St; 665 4938, **t/f** 1 866 360 4513; www.harringtonhouse.ca; year-round (by reservation only Nov–May). A c1896 house with large gardens. 1 room has en suite, the other a private bathroom. B/fast inc. **$**

Annapolis River Campground (75 sites) 56 Queen St; 665 2801; Apr–Oct. Serviced & unserviced riverside sites; laundry service & canoe rentals. **$**

Valleyview Provincial Park Campground (30 sites) 960 Hampton Rd; 665 2559; www.novascotiaparks.ca/parks/valleyview.asp; mid Jun–early Sep. Hillside park 6km from town offering wooded sites, panoramic views over the Annapolis Valley & the province's remote forested interior. Take Hampton Mountain Rd from Granville St to get there. **$**

> **SAUPON**
>
> In days of yore, one Bridgetown hotel – now long gone – was renowned for its signature dish, *saupon*. Cornmeal was boiled in milk for several hours at an even heat. By dinner time, it had thickened, and was served with sugar.

✕ **Cool Water Café** 36 Queen St; ☎ 665 4488; ⏲ spring–autumn 07.30–16.00 Mon–Fri. Bright little café in the library building offering soups, salads, sandwiches, etc. $–$$

✕ **End of the Line Pub** 73 Queen St; ☎ 665 5277; www.endofthelinepub.com; ⏲ year-round 09.30–21.30 Mon–Fri, 09.00–21.30 Sat, 09.00–20.30 Sun. In the former train station across the road from the bookshop (see below), this pub offers over 20 types of beer & food brighter than its lighting. $–$$

OTHER PRACTICALITIES

Tourist information 232 Granville St West; ☎ 665 5150; ⏲ mid Jun–Sep 09.00–16.00 Mon–Fri

WHAT TO SEE AND DO Just over the bridge, **Endless Shores Books** (*67 Queen St; ☎ 665 2029; www.endlessshoresbooks.com*) is a friendly, used bookshop well worth browsing. Swot up on community history at the c1835 **James House Museum** (*12 Queen St; ☎ 825 1287; ⏲ Jun–Aug 09.30–16.30 Mon–Fri, off-season by appointment; admission free*). Pleasant **Jubilee Park** is on the Annapolis River. It has a good kids' playground, and hosts a **farmers' market** (*www.bridgetownfarmersmarket.com; ⏲ mid May–early Oct 11.00–15.00 Tue*). During market hours, hourly **kayak rentals** are offered (*☎ 824 0387; ⏲ mid May–Aug or later*), half- and full-day rentals at other times (same contact details): or join a group kayak trip (*☎ 824 1172; mid Jun–mid Aug 18.30 Thu*).

MIDDLETON

The self-labelled 'Heart of the Valley', Middleton has a couple of contrasting museums, and a fascinating mix of architecture, especially on Main, School and Commercial streets and Gates Avenue. One of this part of Nova Scotia's few cross-province roads, Highway 10, connects Middleton with Liverpool (see page 162).

To get to Middleton **by car**, the town is on Highways 1 and 10, and just off Highway 101 Exit 18. Middleton is on the Bridgetown–Greenwood **bus** route (see page 195).

WHERE TO STAY AND EAT

Mid Valley Motel (58 rooms) 121 Main St; ☎ 825 3433, **t/f** 1 866 332 3433; www.midvalleymotel.com; ⏲ year-round. One of the area's largest accommodations with rooms laid out in traditional motel drive-up style. $$

Century Farm Inn (4 rooms) 10 Main St; ☎ 825 6989, **t/f** 1 800 237 9896; www.centuryfarminn.com; ⏲ Jun–Sep; off-season by reservation. This c1886 farmhouse is backed by 45ha on the Annapolis River. Comfortable & welcoming. Wi-Fi available. Full b/fast inc. $

✕ **Pasta Jax** 300 Main St; ☎ 825 6099; http://pastajax.com; ⏲ year-round 11.30–14.00 & 16.30–19.30 Mon–Fri, 17.00–20.00 Sat. The awning outside just says 'restaurant' but I wouldn't worry about the name: it's the food that

WINDMILLS OF YOUR MIND

One point if – when asked who sang the Academy Award-winning 'The Windmills of Your Mind' for the 1968 film *The Thomas Crown Affair* – you say 'Noel Harrison'. A second point if you knew that Noel was a former Olympic skier, and the son of actor Sir Rex Harrison. Ten bonus points if you know that Harrison Jnr also recorded 'The Middleton Fire Brigade', dedicated to Middleton's finest who came to the rescue when Harrison's house (located between Middleton and the Bay of Fundy) caught fire in the 1970s.

A BREATH OF SEA AIR

If you feel like a stroll along the Fundy shore, or just seeing a couple of pretty coastal villages, two good choices are Margaretsville and Hampton. Both have lighthouses, little harbours, and pleasant beaches (much more cobble and pebble than sand). There's a little more going on at the former, with a tiny gallery by the wharf, a wonderful live music venue in a former church, the **Evergreen Theatre** (*1941 Stronach Mountain Rd, East Margaretsville; ☎ 825 6834; www.evergreentheatre.ca*), and a waterfall a couple of hundred metres along the beach. Hampton was once a busy resort with a very popular, cavernous dance hall near the wharf. Today's visitor will find a **lighthouse** (*www.hamptonlighthouse.com; ⏲ summer 11.00–16.00 daily*), a clifftop walk and a long stretch of beach (which is one of the best places to collect beach pebbles). For Margaretsville, take Stronach Mountain Road from Kingston. In Bridgetown, following Church Street – which becomes Hampton Mountain Road – will take you over the North Mountain to Hampton.

counts. Both cuisine & décor can best be described as 'rustic contemporary'. Start with artichoke dip or shrimp, follow perhaps with ribs or seafood pasta, & be sure to leave room for house-made dessert – especially if you're a cheesecake fan. Wash it down with a Sleeman's Honey Brown beer, or a bottle of local wine. Reservations encouraged for dinner. **$–$$**

SHOPPING **Blue Griffin Books** (*283 Main St; ☎ 363 2665; www.bluegriffinbooks.com; ⏲ year-round 09.00–18.00 Mon–Fri, 09.00–17.00 Sat*) has a good selection of used books – but not for those who like things well organised!

OTHER PRACTICALITIES

$ Bank Scotiabank, 293–301 Main St; ☎ 825 4894; ⏲ 10.00–17.00 Mon–Fri

Hospital Soldiers Memorial Hospital, 462 Main St; ☎ 825 341

Library Rosa M Harvey Middleton and Area Library, 45 Gates Av; ☎ 825 4835; ⏲ 10.00–17.00 & 18.30–20.30 Tue & Fri, 10.00–17.00 Wed/Thu, 14.00–17.00 & 18.30–20.30 Fri, 10.00–14.00 Sat

Post office 275 Main St; ⏲ 08.30–17.00 Mon–Fri

Tourist information 8 Bridge St; ☎ 825 4100; ⏲ 09.00–17.00 mid May/Jun; Sep 10.00–17.00 Thu–Mon; Jul/Aug 08.30–18.00 daily

WHAT TO SEE AND DO On Commercial Street, by the Church Street junction next to the Town Hall, see North America's first water-run **town clock**. At dusk throughout the summer months, watch out for hundreds of swifts entering the big chimney of the Middleton Regional High School at 18 Gates Avenue. The **Old Holy Trinity Church** (*49 Main St; ☎ 825 5500; ⏲ Jul/Aug or by appointment*) was consecrated in 1791 and is one of only five remaining Loyalist churches in North America.

The grand **Annapolis Valley MacDonald Museum** (*21 School St; ☎ 825 6116; http://macdonaldmuseum.ca; ⏲ mid Jun–Sep 09.00–16.30 Mon–Sat, 13.00–16.30 Sun; Oct–mid Dec & early Apr–mid Jun 10.30–16.30 Mon–Fri; admission CAN$3*) is housed in a big red-brick building from c1903 which was the first consolidated school in Canada. Varied exhibits include an old schoolroom, a recreation of a 1930s' general store, the Nova Scotia Museum's clock and watch collection, and much more.

For railway enthusiasts, the **Memory Lane Railway Museum** (*61 School St; 825 6062; http://memorylanerailwaymuseum.com; year-round 09.00–17.00 Mon–Fri, 10.00–14.30 Sat; admission free*), close to the MacDonald Museum, is a complete contrast to its neighbour but is every bit as interesting. Housed in the old railway station (in use 1917–90) is a dusty but worthwhile collection of bits and pieces from days gone by. Trains are the focus and there are both indoor and outdoor working model train tracks.

KINGSTON AND GREENWOOD

The main attractions of these two communities for visitors are a tourist office – and an Atlantic Superstore very close by – in Kingston and box stores and a huge enclosed shopping mall (and the largest air force base on Canada's east coast – with museum) in Greenwood. Self-caterers should also bear in mind that there are no other big supermarkets in the 125km between here and Digby (see page 196).

GETTING THERE Kingston is on Highway 1, 11km/7 miles east of Middleton and 40km/25 miles west of Kentville. Greenwood is 3km from Kingston: **by car**, take Bridge Street then turn left at the traffic lights. At the next lights, go straight on for the museum, or turn right for the mall. Greenwood, 2.5km from Kingston, is the terminus of **bus** routes west to Bridgetown and east to Wolfville. Kingston is on the Greenwood–Wolfville bus route (see page 195).

WHERE TO STAY AND EAT

Best Western Aurora Inn (23 units) 831 Main St, Kingston; 765 3306; www.bestwesternatlantic.com; year-round. Single-storey motel-style hotel with spacious, well-equipped rooms. 65-seat licensed restaurant (*for lunch & dinner Wed–Fri, b/fast, lunch & dinner Sat/Sun; $$*). Most rates inc b/fast. **$$**

Creekside B&B (3 rooms) 140 Hwy 221, North Kingston; 765 0346; www.creeksidebedandbreakfast.ca; May–mid Oct. Large rooms in a c1892 house on a quiet rural minor road. Library, sun room & deck overlooking vineyard. Less than 5 mins' drive to Kingston. Full b/fast (eg: salmon omelette or gingerbread waffles) inc. **$**

T.A.N. Coffee 963 Central Av, Greenwood; 242 3225; www.tancoffee.ca; 06.30–17.00 Mon–Thu, 06.30–21.00 Fri, 08.00–17.00 Sat, 10.00–17.00 Sun. Decent coffee & snacks, nice ambience. Adjoining Greenwood Mall. $

OTHER PRACTICALITES

$ Banks CIBC, 655 Main St, Kingston; 765 3351. Scotiabank, 963 Central Av, Greenwood; 765 6383; 10.00–15.00 Mon–Wed, 10.00–17.00 Thu/Fri

Library Kingston Library, 671 Main St, Kingston; 765 3631; 14.00–17.00 & 18.30–20.30 Tue, 10.00–17.00 & 18.30–20.00 Thu, 18.30–20.30 Fri, 10.00–14.00 Sat

Tourist information 510 Main St (Hwy 1), Kingston; 765 6678; mid/end May–early Oct 10.00–17.00 daily

WHAT TO SEE AND DO Well-stocked with magazines and new books, **The Inside Story** (*1016 Central Av, Greenwood; 765 6116, t/f 1 800 565 6116; www.theinsidestory.ca; year-round 09.30–21.00 Mon–Fri, 09.30–18.00 Sat, 12.00–17.00 Sun*) is across from the mall. The **Greenwood Military Aviation Museum** (*Canex Mall, Ward Rd; 765 1494 ext 5955; http://gmam.ca; Jun–Aug 09.00–17.00 daily; Sep–May 10.00–16.00 Tue–Sat; admission free*) tells the story of the World War II RAF station that went on to become Atlantic Canada's largest air base. Several aircraft are on display, and there is a gift shop and café.

BERWICK

This busy town calls itself the 'Apple Capital of Nova Scotia', the reason for the giant apple perched outside the Town Hall. Apple orchards occupy swathes of the surrounding countryside. Commercial Street – which links Highway 101 and Highway 1 – is where you'll find the majority of the shops and services. Berwick is just off Highway 101 Exit 15, 20km/12 miles west of Kentville and 21km/13 miles east of Kingston.

WHERE TO STAY AND EAT

Hidden Gardens (2 rooms) 274 Main St; 538 0813; e hiddengardens@ns.sympatico.ca; www.bbcanada.com/hiddengardens; year-round. Choose the 'Sunrise' or 'Sunset' room at this lovely old home. Seasonal outdoor pool. Rate inc enhanced continental b/fast. **$**

Kellock's 160 Commercial St; 538 5525; www.facebook.com/kellockslicensedeatery; year-round 11.30–14.30 & 16.30–closing Mon–Fri, 09.00–14.30 & 16.30–closing Sat. Located in a 135-year-old Victorian home ringed by towering elms, with stained glass windows, tin ceilings & hardwood floors. Relaxed dining. Try the applewood-smoked chicken. **$$**

Union Street Café & The Wick Pub 183 Commercial St; 538 7787; www.unionstreetcafe.ca; year-round 11.00–20.00 Sun–Thu, 11.00–22.00 Fri/Sat. Cosy, colourful & inviting café-restaurant with an eclectic menu. The chicken & roasted vegetable focaccia is a lunchtime favourite, in the evening try bacon-wrapped pork tenderloin with apple-butter sauce, followed by chocolate truffle tart. Live music (often high-quality) in the adjoining pub on Fri/Sat evenings. **$$**

KENTVILLE *(Population: 6,084)*

The largest community in – and commercial hub of – the Annapolis Valley, Kentville has some lovely old homes, a good museum in the old courthouse, and some pleasant walking trails both by the riverside and on the bed of old railway tracks. The grounds of the **Kentville Agricultural Centre** (see page 227) are beautiful in late spring.

Incidentally, **New Minas**, less than 3km east along Highway 1, is worth visiting only if you like side-by-side shopping malls, fast-food outlets and petrol stations.

THE NEW MINAS FLY OVER

New Minas was the location for what was probably the first reported sighting of UFOs over North America. An entry in the diary of Simeon Perkins (see page 167) for 12 October 1796, reads:

> A strange story comes from the Bay of Fundy that ships have been seen in the air … they were said to be seen at New Mines … by a girl about sunrise. The girl cried out and two men who were in the house came out and saw them. There were 15 ships and a man forward with his hand stretched out. They made to the eastward. They were so near people saw their sides and ports.

In our age of aircraft and space travel, UFOs are likened to flying saucers and spacecraft: in the Age of Sail over 200 years before planes were invented, UFOs looked like ships. Maybe human technology and alien technology are advancing at roughly the same rate.

FRENCH CROSS

When the Expulsion began in 1755, many Acadians living in the valley received word of what was happening further east and 50–300 community members decided to try and escape, intending to get to the coast, cross the sea and head for safety. They crossed the North Mountain but when they reached what is now Morden, they found that the winter weather had beaten them: crossing the sea would be impossible until the spring. Living mainly on shellfish – and anything the Mi'kmaq could bring them – few survived the winter. Pitifully few Acadians survived long enough to cross the water. A cross in a memorial park marks the spot: some of the shells discarded by the Acadians were used to pave the park's entrance. In good weather, this is one of the area's best coastal picnic spots. To get there, from Highway 1 at Auburn, follow Morden Road north for 12km, 14km from Highway 101 Exit 16.

GETTING THERE Kentville is accessible **by car**, being on Highways 1 and 12, the latter of which crosses the province down to Chester (see page 139), and off Highway 101 Exits 12–14, 11km from Wolfville, 74km from Chester and 105km from Annapolis Royal. Kentville is on the Greenwood–Wolfville **bus** route (see page 195) and is the terminus of the Maritime Bus route to Halifax (see *Chapter 2*, page 57).

WHERE TO STAY

Allen's Motel (12 rooms) 384 Park St; 678 2683, **t/f** 1 877 678 2683; **e** allensmotel@ns.sympatico.ca; www.allensmotel.ns.ca; Apr–Nov. What was a traditional motel set on a 1.2ha property has had renovations & additions, including 2 upstairs rooms & an accessible deluxe suite. Coin laundry. **$**

Grand Street In (5 units) 160 Main St; 679 1991, **t/f** 1 877 245 4744; http://grandstreetinn.com; year-round. 3 nice rooms in lovely, quiet c1870 Queen Anne Revival home, plus 2, 2-bedroom carriage houses, all on spacious grounds. Outdoor pool (seasonal) & hot tub. Full b/fast inc. **$**

South Mountain Park Family Camping Resort (200 sites) 3022 Hwy 12, South Alton; 678 0152, **t/f** 1 866 860 6092; http://southmountainparkcampground.com; mid May–mid Oct. A facility-packed 44ha campground 9km south of Exit 13 of Hwy 101. Open & wooded serviced & tent sites. Family activities. **$**

WHERE TO EAT

Designer Café 373 Main St; 365 3322; www.designerkentville.com; year-round 07.00–17.00 Mon–Fri, 08.00–16.00 Sat. Bright, cheery little café with good coffee & a selection of imaginative sandwiches/paninis. **$**

King's Arms Pub 390 Main St; 678 0066; http://kingsarmspub.ca; year-round 11.00–22.00 Mon–Thu, 11.00–midnight Fri/Sat, 11.00–21.00 Sun. A British-style pub with relaxing atmosphere & decent well-priced food (served until 20.00 Sun–Thu, 21.00 Fri/Sat). In summer, the patio is nice. **$**

Paddy's Brew Pub & Rosie's Restaurant 42 Aberdeen St; 678 3199; www.paddyspub.ca; year-round 11.00–midnight daily. For details, see *Wolfville*, page 229. **$**

Pizzazz Bistro 12 Webster Court; 365 3303; www.pizzazzbistro.ca; year-round 11.00–14.00 Mon–Wed, 11.00–14.00 & 17.30–21.00 Thu–Sat. New (2012) upmarket bistro serving Mediterranean-influenced cuisine. Try chorizo ravioli, or grilled lobster tail. **$$**

T.A.N. Coffee 395 Main St; 678 1225; www.tancoffee.ca; year-round 07.00–18.00 Mon–Fri, 08.00–18.00 Sat, 09.00–17.00 Sun. Good coffee & a wide selection of snacks, sandwiches, tray bakes, etc. Buzzy & usually busy. **$**

FESTIVALS The **Harvest Festival** in **October** offers wagon rides, music, food – and people dressed as pumpkins!

OTHER PRACTICALITIES

$ Banks Royal Bank, 63 Webster St; ☎ 679 3850; ⌚ 10.00–17.00 Mon–Fri. Scotiabank, 47 Aberdeen St; ☎ 678 2181; ⌚ 10.00–17.00 Mon–Fri

Hospital Valley Regional Hospital, 150 Exhibition St; ☎ 678 7381

Library Kentville Library, 95 Cornwallis St; ☎ 679 2544; ⌚ 10.00–17.00 Mon, Wed & Fri, 14.00–20.00 Tue, 10.00–20.00 Thu, 10.00–14.00 Sat

Post office 495 Main St; ⌚ 08.00–17.00 Mon–Fri

Tourist information 66 Cornwallis St; ☎ 678 4634; ⌚ late May–early Oct 09.30–15.00 Sat–Tue, 09.30–18.00 Wed–Fri; early Oct–late May 10.00–15.00 Mon–Fri

WHAT TO SEE AND DO Drop by the community theatre, **CentreStage Theatre** (*61 River St; ☎ 678 3502; http://centrestagetheatre.ca*) for a show or head to the beaches to **search for semi-precious stones** with Rob's Rocks (*677 West Main St; ☎ 678 3194; www.robsrockshop.com*).

The huge (well over 200ha) grounds of the **Kentville Agricultural Centre** (*32 Main St; ☎ 679 5333; ⌚ grounds year-round; admission free*) are a government facility, and one of the most modern and sophisticated research centres in Canada. Planted with crops and orchards, it also offers a magnificent rhododendron garden. The **Kentville Ravine Trail** leads from the car park along a river and through old growth forest.

Housed in the three-storey former c1904 courthouse – with the original courtroom on the top floor a must-see – the **Kings County Museum** (*37 Cornwallis St; ☎ 678 6237; www.okcm.ca; ⌚ Sep–Apr 09.30–16.30 Tue–Fri; May/Jun 09.30–16.00 Mon–Fri; Jul/Aug 09.30–16.30 Mon–Fri, 11.30–16.30 Sat; admission free*) has a good display on New England Planters, and a large collection of primarily Victorian textiles. Archives for genealogical research (*CAN$5 fee*).

The 6,300yd **Ken-Wo Golf Course** (*9514 Commercial St; ☎ 681 5388; http://ken-wo.com*) might sound pseudo-Japanese, but got its name because it lies halfway between Kentville and Wolfville. Course-wise, the last five holes are the toughest. Green fees CAN$59.

HALL'S HARBOUR

This pretty working fishing village is named after Captain Samuel Hall, an early 19th-century American privateer who terrorised those living in the region with frequent raids to pillage and plunder. Locals say that every seven years in winter, a phantom ship's lights are seen going up the Bay of Fundy.

Above the harbour, steep cliffs are capped with groves of hardwoods and softwoods: the cobble beach is popular for rockhounding (when the tide's out),

LOCAL BOY BECOMES BIG TURK

Hall's Harbour was the boyhood home of one Ransford D Bucknam (1866–1915). He went to the United States, came to the notice of the Sultan of Turkey, and later became Bucknam Pasha, Grand Admiral of the Ottoman Fleet. In June 1912, however, the *Illustrated London News* reported: 'Hamidiye's captain … Bucknam Pasha, has recently been noticed spending more time frequenting waterfront nightclubs than he has pacing Hamidiye's quarterdeck.'

and there's a 2km forest and river-view eco-trail. Several artists have studios in the village.

Hall's Harbour is on Highway 359, 18km/11 miles from Kentville.

WHERE TO EAT A rustic restaurant (*1157 West Hall's Harbour Rd; ☎ 679 5299; ⏲ mid May/Jun & Sep/mid Oct 12.00–19.00 daily; Jul/Aug 11.30–20.30 daily; $–$$*) is attached to the **Halls Harbour Lobster Pound** and is a popular lunch spot – choose your clawed lunch and eat it at a wharf-front table.

CAPE SPLIT AND CAPE BLOMIDON

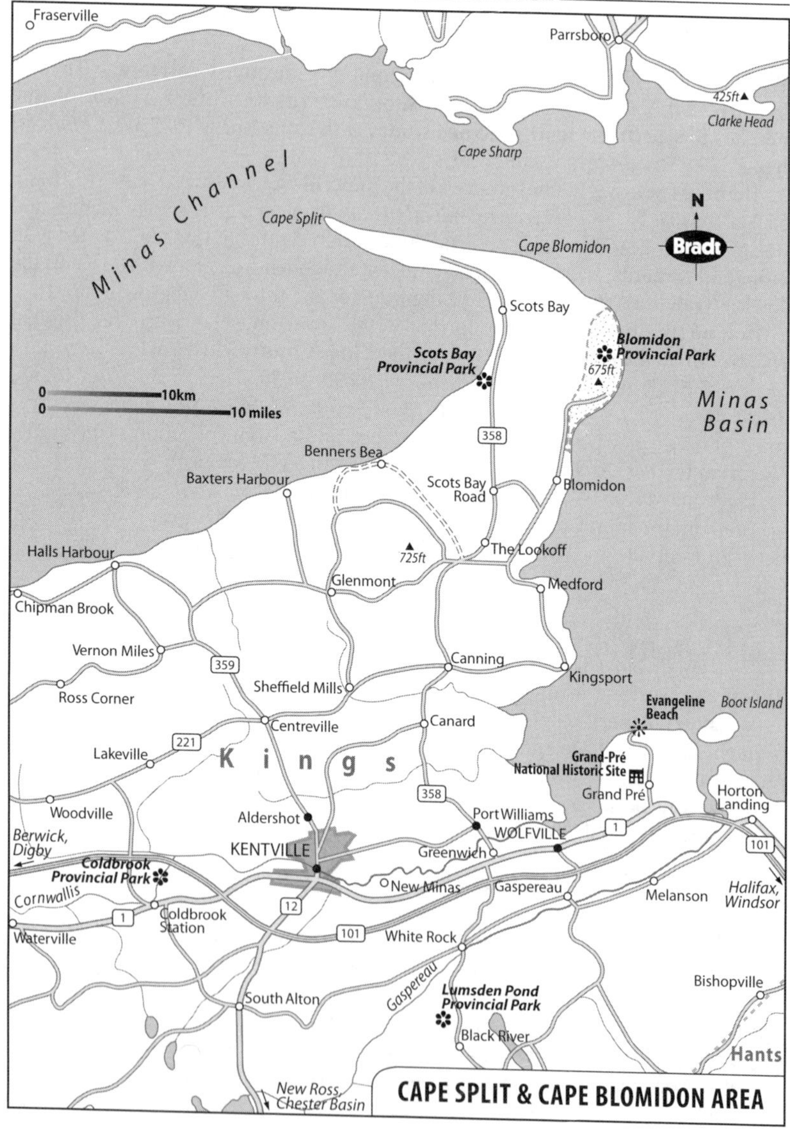

EAGLE-EYED

This part of the Annapolis Valley has the largest overwintering population of bald eagles in eastern North America with hundreds of the majestic avians in the area from late November to early March. The community of Sheffield Mills hosts a couple of annual Eagle Watch weekends (*www.eaglens.ca; late Jan/early Feb*) with food put out to attract the birds.

At almost 8km each way, the trail to **Cape Split** can be a long walk for the inexperienced hiker, but is well worth the effort. The trailhead is at the end of Scots Bay Road, approximately 30km from Exit 11 of Highway 101. Once you're on your way, you'll have to decide whether to take the more difficult coastal trail (which stays close to the clifftops and is not for those who don't like heights) or the more straightforward inland route which initially leads through mixed forest and which is easier going. Later on the trail, the forest is more deciduous: ferns cover much of the forest floor, and lichens and mosses cling to the trees. As you near the end of the cape, the trees end and you arrive at a grassy area high above the water, with the sea on three sides. If it is not misty or foggy, the views are fantastic.

Take particular care here close to the cliff edges. Allow a minimum of 4.5 hours for the return hike.

There are more spectacular views – and a network of over 14km of hiking trails – on the other (eastern) side of the peninsula at **Blomidon Provincial Park** (*Pereaux Rd; http://novascotiaparks.ca/parks/blomidon.asp;* 🕘 *mid May–early Sep*). This 759ha park, the entrance of which is 25km from Highway 101 Exit 11, is largely forested with sugar maple, beech, white spruce and yellow birch, and includes 180m-tall red sandstone cliffs and looks out over the Bay of Fundy. At low tide, wander the beaches where you might be lucky enough to find amethysts or agates. There are four official interconnecting walking trails, from the 1.6km **Look-off Trail** to the spectacular 6km **Jodrey Trail**. The 3.5km **Borden Brook Trail** leads through white spruce forest to a series of waterfalls. The park has a 70-site **campground** (🕘 *mid May–early Sep*) with open and wooded sites.

As the home of their demi-god Glooscap, the Cape Blomidon area has great spiritual significance for the Mi'kmaq.

WOLFVILLE

With a prosperous feel and a pleasant climate, Wolfville may not have the history of, say, Annapolis Royal (see page 208), but this charming town has a popular and highly regarded university, several excellent restaurants, and no shortage of beautiful heritage homes or interesting historic architecture. I mention the university because it brings a clear vitality to the town: in general, the large student population is well mannered and enhances the atmosphere, rather than overpowering it.

Highway 1 runs through town as Main Street, and (as you'd expect) this is where most shops, eateries and accommodations are found. To the east of the town centre, Main Street is lined with majestic trees.

Although not immediately obvious, Wolfville does have a waterfront, and its appropriately named Waterfront Park (which opened in 2000) hosts several outdoor events and offers fine views of Cape Blomidon. The park at the junction of Front Street and Harbourside Drive, the extension of Gaspereau Avenue offers totally

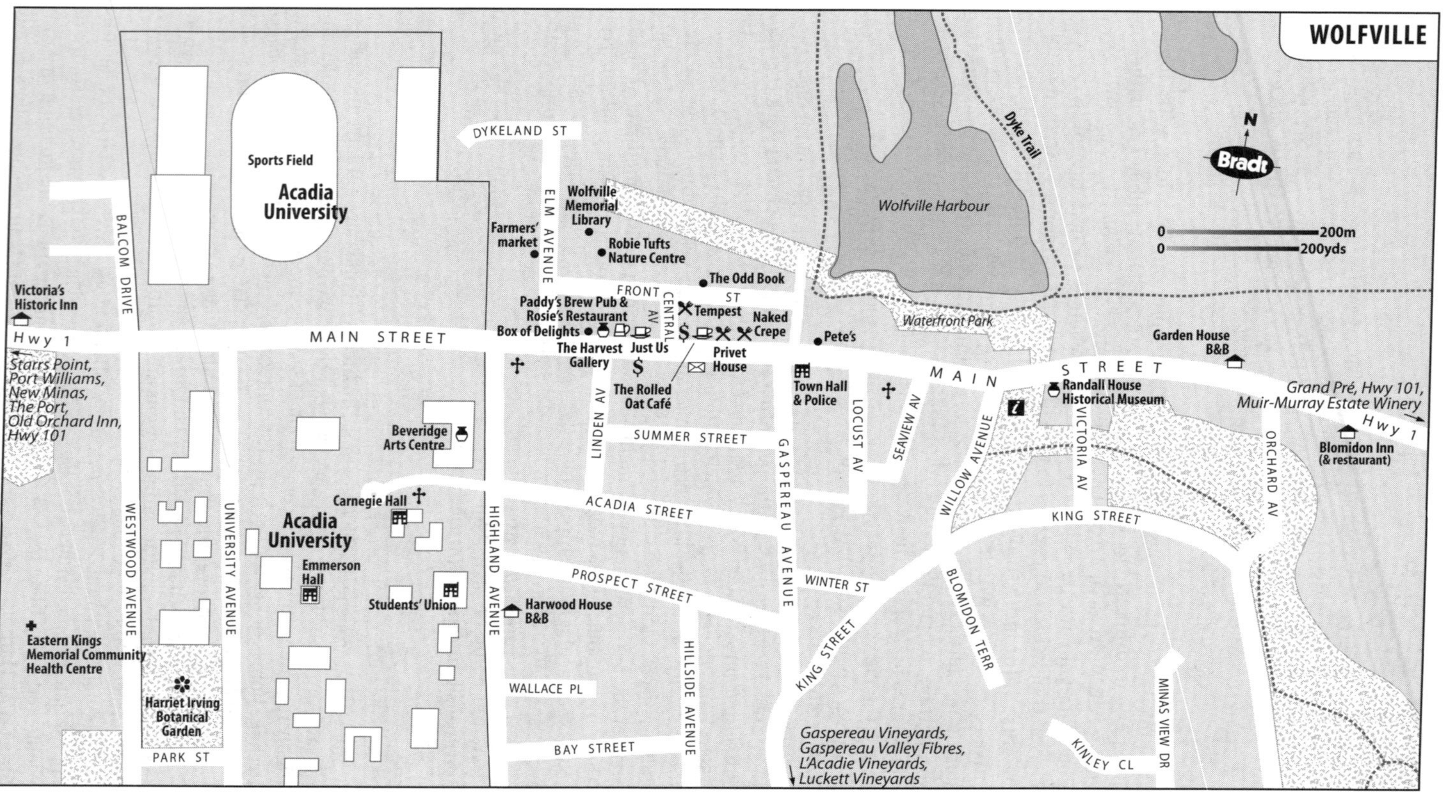

WOLFVILLE
Bradt
N
0
200m
0
200yds
Dyke Trail
Wolfville Harbour
Waterfront Park
Sports Field
Acadia University
DYKELAND ST
ELM AVENUE
Farmers' market
Wolfville Memorial Library
Robie Tufts Nature Centre
The Odd Book
FRONT ST
CENTRAL AV
Tempest
Naked Crepe
Paddy's Brew Pub & Rosie's Restaurant
Box of Delights
The Harvest Gallery
Just Us
Privet House
The Rolled Oat Café
Pete's
Town Hall & Police
Garden House B&B
Randall House Historical Museum
Grand Pré, Hwy 101, Muir-Murray Estate Winery
Hwy 1
Blomidon Inn (& restaurant)
ORCHARD AV
VICTORIA AV
KING STREET
WILLOW AVENUE
SEAVIEW AV
LOCUST AV
GASPEREAU AVENUE
SUMMER STREET
LINDEN AV
ACADIA STREET
PROSPECT STREET
WINTER ST
BLOMIDON TERR
KING STREET
HILLSIDE AVENUE
WALLACE PL
BAY STREET
MINAS VIEW DR
KINLEY CL
Gaspereau Vineyards, Gaspereau Valley Fibres, L'Acadie Vineyards, Luckett Vineyards
Harwood House B&B
HIGHLAND AVENUE
Beveridge Arts Centre
Carnegie Hall
Acadia University
Emmerson Hall
Students' Union
UNIVERSITY AVENUE
WESTWOOD AVENUE
BALCOM DRIVE
PARK ST
Harriet Irving Botanical Garden
Eastern Kings Memorial Community Health Centre
Victoria's Historic Inn
MAIN STREET
Hwy 1
Starrs Point, Port Williams, New Minas, The Port, Old Orchard Inn, Hwy 101

different views at high and low tide: interpretive panels tell of the area's history of shipping and shipbuilding. The old railway station now houses the town's library.

The land reclaimed by the 17th-century Acadian dykes is a good spot for a walk or cycle ride: hillier, the scenic hiking trail through the 12ha Reservoir Park is also a good choice. If you have a car, pop over to the pretty Gaspereau Valley for wineries, pretty riverside vistas, and more.

HISTORY Originally known to the Mi'kmaq as *mtaban* ('muddy catfish-catching place'), European settlement began with Acadians in the mid to late 17th century (some of their dykes can still be seen). After the Expulsion, New England Planters settled here, naming it 'Mud Creek' – a small harbour was connected to the Cornwallis River by a narrow, twisting stretch of water, virtually impassable at low tide. Despite problems with navigation caused by the tide and sandbars, a busy little port was established, and ships were built here.

One of the community's most important residents was Judge Elisha DeWolf (1756–1837) and it was in his honour that the town was renamed.

In 1911, Wolfville became the first town in Nova Scotia with a paved main street.

GETTING THERE Wolfville is easy to get to **by car** – it is on Highway 1 and between Exits 10 and 11 of Highway 101, 90km/56 miles from Halifax, 27km/17 miles from Windsor and 117km/73 miles from Annapolis Royal. Wolfville is on the **bus** route between Greenwood and Brooklyn (see page 195), and it is also on the Kentville–Halifax Maritime Bus route (see *Chapter 2*, page 57).

WHERE TO STAY

Blomidon Inn (29 rooms) 195 Main St; 542 2291, **t/f** 1 800 565 2291; www.theblomidon.net; year-round. The main building is a beautifully restored c1882 shipbuilder's mansion, with magnificent interior dark wood features & Italian marble fireplaces: each guest room is individually decorated. It is worth choosing a Superior or above (note that not all rooms are in the original building). Paths through landscaped themed gardens, tennis courts. The top-notch dining room is open to non-guests (see page 232). Various packages are available. Continental b/fast & afternoon tea inc. **$$**

Harwood House B&B (3 rooms) 33 Highland Av; 542 5707, **t/f** 1 877 897 0156; www.harwoodhouse.com; year-round. A tastefully renovated, quiet c1923 home with lovely garden & spacious bedrooms. Full gourmet b/fast inc – incorporating homemade bread & preserves, vegetables from the garden & local fruit. **$$**

Old Orchard Inn & Spa (130 units) 153 Greenwich Rd; Greenwich; 542 5751, **t/f** 1 800 561 8090; www.oldorchardinn.com; year-round (cabins May–Oct). Located 5km from Wolfville, just off Hwy 101 Exit 11 with over 100 well-maintained rooms & 29 cabins. Indoor pool, sauna, hot tub, spa & tennis court. Includes the excellent Acadian Room Restaurant. **$$**

Victoria's Historic Inn B&B (16 units) 600 Main St; 542 5744, **t/f** 1 800 556 5744; www.victoriashistoricinn.com; year-round. The c1893 3-storey main building contains 4 rooms & 5 suites (with jacuzzi & fireplace): 7 rooms are in the adjacent Carriage House. All are well equipped. Beautifully restored, the property blends Victorian character & modern comforts. Full b/fast inc. **$$**

Garden House B&B (3 rooms) 220 Main St; 542 1703; **e** gardenhouse@ns.sympatico.ca; www.gardenhouse.ca; year-round. Cosy, friendly B&B in a c1830 house a short walk from the town centre; rooms with shared or private bathroom & views out over the dykes. B/fast inc. **$**

WHERE TO EAT Long-term Wolfville favourite Acton's closed in 2012. The same venue reopened late in the summer as the up-market **Privet House** (*406 Main St; 542 7525; www.facebook.com/PrivetHouseRestaurant*). I didn't have the chance to

ACADIA UNIVERSITY

In term-time, over 3,000 students – plus staff – at Wolfville's Acadia University (www.acadiau.ca), one of Canada's top learning institutions, double the town's population. Beginning as Horton Academy in 1828, it became Acadia University in 1891. In addition to a gallery and botanical gardens (see page 233), the university has some magnificent buildings. The oldest is the c1878 Seminary, which displays many Second Empire features and is now home to the School of Education. The Georgian Revival-style Carnegie Hall (a science building) was built with the help of a sizeable donation by American philanthropist Andrew Carnegie. Also of note is the Italianate c1913 Emmerson Hall.

try the new incarnation, but initial reviews are (generally) positive. Another good option is **Pete's** (see *Shopping*, opposite).

✕ **Blomidon Inn** 195 Main St; ☎ 542 2291, **t/f** 1 800 565 2291; www.theblomidon.net; ⏲ year-round 11.30–14.00 & 17.00–21.30 daily. The Blomidon's restaurant is renowned, & reservations are therefore strongly recommended. The Atlantic salmon is a speciality, served in a variety of ways. Lobster, filet mignon & game feature too, & the wine list is superb. W/end brunch is another treat. $$$

✕ **Tempest** 117 Front St; ☎ 542 0588, **t/f** 1 866 542 0588; www.tempest.ca. Nova Scotia 'celebrity chef' Michael Howell made a name for the Tempest with wonderful food, beautifully presented. When he had to retire on health grounds in 2012, the restaurant was taken over by Dave Smart, his *chef de cuisine*. You would expect the tradition of high standards to live on, but I would suggest calling first to check times, type of cuisine, prices, etc. $$–$$$ (estimate)

✕ **Acadian Room at the Old Orchard Inn** 153 Greenwich Rd; Greenwich; ☎ 542 5751, **t/f** 1 800 561 8090; www.oldorchardinn.com; ⏲ 07.00–14.00 & 17.00–21.00 daily. Another fine licensed restaurant, the Acadian Room has wide windows overlooking Cape Blomidon, & a large stone fireplace. To start, the mussels & seafood chowder are both very good, followed by sautéed Digby scallops or Bay of Fundy lobster. Local poultry & pork also feature. To follow, warm apple crumble pie is a winner. $$

✕ **The Port** 980 Terry's Creek Rd, Port Williams; ☎ 542 5555; www.theportpub.com; ⏲ year-round 11.00–23.00 Sun–Thu, 11.00–midnight Fri/Sat. This stylish gastropub less than 7km from Wolfville has a beautiful deck overlooking the Cornwallis River. The lobster clubhouse & Port burger are both very popular. Sip a Planters Pale beer or a glass of one of the carefully selected wines. $$

✕ **The Naked Crepe Bistro** 402 Main St; ☎ 542 0653; www.thenakedcrepebistro.ca; ⏲ 08.00–23.00 Mon–Fri, 09.00–23.00 Sat, 10.00–23.00 Sun. With bright, modern décor, this crêperie opened in 2012 & hit the ground running. Good sweet (eg: berry parfait) & savoury (eg: Asian chicken) crêpes (many available in 2 sizes), plus a selection of 11-inch pizzas. $–$$

☕ **Just Us** 450 Main St; ☎ 542 7731; www.justuscoffee.com; ⏲ year-round 07.00–20.00 Mon–Wed, 07.00–21.00 Thu/Fri, 08.00–21.00 Sat, 09.00–20.00 Sun. A good spot for a coffee or snack in lobby of a former c1911 opera house. $

✕ **Paddy's Brew Pub & Rosie's Restaurant** 460 Main St; ☎ 542 0059; ⏲ year-round 11.00–midnight daily. Lively pub, microbrewery & restaurant. Atrium, glassed-in brewery, cosy booths, hardwood floors, patio. Food is good – seafood, pizza, pasta, burgers, etc, especially the home-smoked ribs, & desserts (eg: outrageous Irish Cream Bash Cheesecake). Beer lovers should try the house-brewed Annapolis Valley or Raven ales. Live music most nights. $

☕ **The Rolled Oat Café** 420 Main St; ☎ 542 9884; www.therolledoat.com; ⏲ year-round 09.00–15.00 Mon–Fri, 10.00–15.00 Sat. Funky, friendly little café with a wide selection of vegetarian dishes. Daily specials, such as stir-fried vegetables on quinoa. The Valley Mushroom panini is a personal favourite. Eat in or take-away. Cash only. $

FESTIVALS The **Valley Summer Theatre** (*t/f 1 877 845 1341; http://valleysummertheatre.com*) holds plays most evenings from July to mid August at the Al Whittle Theatre (*450 Main St*). In September, the **Canadian Deep Roots Music Festival** (*www.deeprootsmusic.ca*) is a three-day festival of modern roots music from across North America and around the world.

SHOPPING **Box of Delights Books** (*466 Main St; 542 9511; www.boxofdelightsbooks.com*) has a good collection of books on the province: for used books, head one street back to **The Odd Book** (*112 Front St; 542 9491; www.theoddbook.ca*). Although it specialises in out-of-print literature and academic works, the selection is varied.

Pete's (*360 Main St; 697 3331; www.petes.ca; 08.00–20.00 daily (until 21.00 Thu, until 18.00 Sun)*). Once Pete Luckett, ex-market stall trader from Nottingham, England, bought a farm and vineyard just outside Wolfville (see *Wineries*, page 234), many said that it was only a matter of time before the town became the third Nova Scotia location for his upmarket deli/food stores. Think Marks & Spencer's meets the Harrods Food Hall. Sandwiches and salads make excellent eat-in or 'to go' lunches.

Gaspereau Valley Fibres (*830 Gaspereau River Rd; 542 2656, t/f 1 877 634 2737; e brenda@gaspereauvalleyfibres.ca; www.gaspereauvalleyfibres.ca; 10.00–21.00 Tue, 10.00–17.00 Tue–Fri, 11.00–16.00 Sat/Sun*). Home-produced and 'imported' yarn, wool and wool products in a pastoral Gaspereau Valley setting less than ten minutes' drive from downtown Wolfville.

OTHER PRACTICALITIES

$ Banks Bank of Montreal, 424 Main St; 542 2214; 10.00–17.00 Mon–Fri. Royal Bank, 437 Main St; 542 2221; 10.00–17.00 Mon–Fri

Health centre Eastern Kings Memorial Community Health Centre, 23 Earnscliffe Av; 542 2266

Library Wolfville Memorial Library, 21 Elm Av; 542 5760; 10.00–20.00 Tue–Thu, 10.00–17.00 Fri/Sat, 13.00–17.00 Sun

Post office 407 Main St; 08.30–17.00 Mon–Fri

Tourist information 11 Willow St; 542 7000, t/f 1 877 999 7117; early May–late Oct 10.00–18.00 daily

WHAT TO SEE AND DO A c1800s former farmhouse, the **Randall House Historical Museum** (*259 Main St; 542 9775; www.wolfvillehs.ednet.ns.ca; Jun–mid Sep 10.00–17.00 Tue–Sat, 13.30–17.00 Sun; admission CAN$2*) houses displays and collections on the community's history. The **Acadia University Art Gallery** (*Beveridge Arts Centre, cnr of Highland Av & Main St; 585 1373; www.gallery.acadiau.ca; year-round 12.00–16.00 Tue–Sun; admission free*) has a year-round exhibition programme of contemporary and historical work, and the **Harvest Gallery** (*462 Main St; 542 7093; http://harvestgallery.ca; year-round 10.00–17.00 Tue–Sat (Jul–Oct also Mon), 12.00–17.00 Sun*) offers an interesting selection of local arts and crafts.

Despite the grand title – named for a renowned ornithologist and Wolfville resident – the **Robie Tufts Nature Centre** (*Front St*) is a roofed shelter supporting a high stack that is home to numerous chimney swifts. Around dusk on summer evenings, watch as the birds swoop down through the chimney top for the night. Nature lovers will also enjoy the **Harriet Irving Botanical Gardens** (*32 University Av; 585 5242; www.botanicalgardens.acadiau.ca; Apr–Dec dusk–dawn daily; admission free*), 2.5ha of gardens showcasing flora from the Acadian Forest Region. See a Nova Scotia take on a Victorian British walled garden, a bog area (with carnivorous plants) and a medicinal and food garden. Even for non-botanists, these

WAR HEROINE

Mona Parsons was born in Middleton (see page 222) in 1901 but studied in Wolfville. She moved to New York in 1929 to pursue an acting career and became a Ziegfield showgirl. Mona gave up dancing for nursing, then met a Dutchman and married him in Holland in 1937.

When the Nazis invaded in 1940, Mona and her husband joined the resistance, aiding downed Allied aircrews. They were arrested in 1941: Parsons was sentenced to death for treason, but was permitted to appeal and the sentence was commuted to life imprisonment. Mona Parsons is said to be the only Canadian woman to have been imprisoned by the Germans in World War II.

In 1945, she – and a Dutch lady – escaped when the Allies bombed the prison camp. The two crossed German-occupied territory on foot, Mona using her acting skills to pretend to have a speech defect. They became separated, but after several weeks she made contact with Allied forces – coincidentally, the North Nova Scotia Highlanders.

After her husband's death, she returned to Nova Scotia in 1957, remarrying and living in Chester (see page 139): her second husband died in 1964, and six years later Mona moved back to Wolfville (see page 229) where she died in 1976.

gardens make a pleasant wander. Perhaps you can pick up a picnic from the **farmers' market** (*DeWolfe Bldg, 24 Elm Av; ☎ 697 3344; www.wolfvillefarmersmarket.com; ⌚ year-round 08.30–13.00 Sat, mid Jun–Dec 16.00–19.00 Wed*). In 2011, this excellent market moved to its new permanent home, a converted former apple warehouse. In my opinion, on busy Saturdays, this new venue can get too overcrowded and is definitely not for the claustrophobic. It's still well worth a visit though, with food, produce, crafts, live music and more.

Situated 10km from Wolfville, **Prescott House** (*1633 Starr's Point Rd, Starr's Point; ☎ 542 3984; http://museum.gov.ns.ca/prh/; ⌚ Jun–mid Oct 09.30–17.30 Mon–Sat, 13.00–17.30 Sun; admission CAN$3.60*) is one of the province's best-surviving examples of Georgian architecture and was completed in 1814 by Charles Ramage Prescott, a businessman and horticulturist. In addition to period furnishings, see Prescott's granddaughter's collections of oriental rugs and hand-stitched samplers.

Paths atop the **Acadian Dykes** in and around Wolfville can be ideal for a stroll, bike ride, or long hike along the waterfront. Easiest access is either from the lower part of Gaspereau Avenue, or from the car park across from the junction of Main Street and Willow Avenue.

Wineries The Wolfville area, including the Gaspereau Valley just over the hill, is home to a growing number of wineries. Most are open to the public (at least in the form of a shop selling their products). At the other end of the scale, some have dining options, rides, tours, etc. Three of the wineries listed are in the Gaspereau Valley, easily reached by taking Gaspereau Avenue from Wolfville's Main Street up and over the hill (approximately 5km).

Between September and mid October on Saturdays and Sundays the **Wolfville Magic Winery Bus** (☎ *542 5767;* **e** *tourism@wolfville.ca; www.nsfallwinefestival.ca; fare CAN$10*) will go on a one-hour loop run to five of the region's wineries (the four shown below, and Domaine de Grand Pré (see page 237): departures are hourly between 10.30 and 15.30, allowing you to hop on and off. As this service first ran in 2012, details may well change.

L'Acadie Vineyards 310 Slayter Rd, Gaspereau; ☎542 8463; www.lacadievineyards.ca; ⏱ May–Oct 11.00–17.00 daily; Nov–Dec 12.00–17.00 Sat/Sun. Nova Scotia's top producer of sparkling wines was also the province's first certified organic winery & vineyard. The Prestige Brut is highly regarded. The winery is 6km from Wolfville, follow Gaspereau Avenue to Slayter Road.

Gaspereau Vineyards 2239 White Rock Rd, Gaspereau; ☎542 1455; www.gaspereauwine.com; ⏱ mid May–Sep 09.00–18.00 daily; Oct–Dec 10.00–17.00 daily; free tours mid May–mid Oct 12.00, 14.00 & 16.00. 14ha of vineyards overlooking the Gaspereau Valley 3km from Wolfville were planted in 1996 on a former apple orchard. Specialising in aromatic whites, Rieslings & robust reds. Snacks & food parings offered.

Luckett Vineyards 1293 Grand Pré Rd, Gaspereau; ☎542 2600; http://luckettvineyards.com; ⏱ May 10.00–17.00 daily; Jun–Oct 10.00–17.00 Mon–Thu, 10.00–20.00 Fri–Sun; Nov/late Dec 10.00–17.00 Sat/Sun. Beautifully located vineyards & farm with fabulous views over the rows of vines to Cape Blomidon & beyond, offering tours, tastings, etc. The bistro patio (⏱ *Jun–Oct 11.00–16.00 daily;* **$**) has good deli sandwiches, soups & salads; the brasserie (⏱ *Jun–Oct 17.00–20.00 Fri–Sun;* **$$**) offers tasty 'small plates'.

Muir-Murray Estate Winery 90 Dyke Rd; ☎542 0343, **t/f** 1 877 707 0343; http://muirmurraywinery.com; ⏱ Dec–Feb 10.00–16.00 daily; Mar–Jun & Oct/Nov 09.00–17.00 daily; Jul–Sep 09.00–19.00 daily. Newish winery located off Hwy 1 between Wolfville & Grand Pré. Free tours & tastings, wine library & tea room (call to check hours), where treats include lobster rolls. There are plans to add motel-type accommodation.

GRAND PRÉ

Grand Pré's pastoral landscape, dyked lands, and air of tranquillity broken only by a steady stream of tour buses give little clue as to its part in one of the most heart-rending events in Canadian history. Nearby, the **Covenanters' Church** (*1989 Grand Pré Rd*) is set on a hill. Constructed between 1804 and 1811 to replace an earlier log structure, this pretty church was built in the style of a New England Meeting House. The tower and steeple were 1818 additions. If you find it open, seize the chance: I've been by loads of times and the doors have always been locked.

Grand Pré is just off Highways 1 and 101, 1.5km/1 mile east of Wolfville, or Exit 10 from Highway 101, 21km/13 miles from Windsor.

HISTORY Grand Pré (French for 'great meadow') was first settled in the early 1680s by a couple of Acadian families from Port-Royal (see page 185). More came to join them, and through hard work and clever use of dykes to reclaim tidal marshlands, created rich farmland. Life was not problem-free: in 1704, for example, the settlement was attacked by New Englanders who broke dykes and burned crops. But the real battle occurred in the winter of 1746/47 when a French force surprised almost 500 soldiers from New England, who had arrived to establish a blockhouse at Grand Pré, and killed over 70 before a ceasefire was agreed.

By the 1750s, Grand Pré had become the largest of all the Acadian communities around the Bay of Fundy. In 1755, when the Acadians refused to sign an oath of allegiance to the British Crown, the governor ordered them to be deported (see page 16) and Grand Pré was one of the first communities selected. On 5 September 1755, a Colonel Winslow gathered the men of Grand Pré in the church and informed them that they and their families were to be deported and their lands confiscated. The village buildings were burnt to the ground, and on 29 October a fleet of a dozen ships sailed away with 2,921 Acadians on board.

In late June 2012, the Grand Pré National Historic Site and environs were designated as a UNESCO World Heritage Site.

WHERE TO STAY AND EAT

Evangeline Inn & Motel (23 rooms) 11668 Hwy 1; 542 2703, t/f 1 888 542 2703; www.evangeline.ns.ca; early May–late Oct. The 5-room inn is housed in the boyhood home of Sir Robert Borden, Prime Minister of Canada 1911–20. The 18-room motel was built in the 1950s (with a 2004 addition): rooms are spacious & pleasant. There is an indoor pool. Evangeline's Café (*early May–late Oct 07.00–19.00; $*) has a simple menu of b/fasts, salads, sandwiches & burgers. Inn rates inc b/fast. **$**

Land of Evangeline Family Camping Resort (230 sites) 84 Evangeline Beach Rd; 542 5309; May–Sep. Open & wooded sites, serviced & unserviced, with laundromat. Located near the beach with fine views. **$**

Le Caveau Restaurant at Domaine de Grand Pré Winery 11611 Hwy 1; 542 7177; www.grandprewines.com/restaurant/; May–Oct 11.30–14.00 & 17.00–21.00 daily; Nov/Dec 17.00–21.00 Tue–Sat. Bright, stylish, excellent winery restaurant with arched windows, textured walls & rich use of wood. Chef Jason Lynch uses the best seasonal local produce & cooks with a global flair. The menu changes regularly, but might include lobster risotto (made with Bay of Fundy lobster, carnaroli rice & Seyval blanc), or grilled sweetbreads with butternut squash purée & dark cumin oil. Accompanied of course by award-winning wines, this is a great dining experience. **$$$**

Just Us 11865 Hwy 1; 542 7474; year-round 07.00–18.00 Mon–Fri, 08.00–18.00 Sat/Sun. Not just a coffee shop, there's also a chocolate factory & Fair Trade museum. Bright, airy & relaxed. Close to Exit 10 of Hwy 102. **$**

WHAT TO SEE AND DO The **Tangled Garden** (*11827 Hwy 1; 542 9811; http://tangledgardenherbs.ca; Apr–late Dec 10.00–18.00 daily*) sells delicious homemade jams, chutneys, liqueurs, herb jellies and more, and its beautiful spiritually inspired herb and sculpture gardens are also worth exploring (*admission CAN$3*).

You don't need to descend to muddy **Evangeline Beach** to enjoy stunning views across the sea to Cape Blomidon. In the summer, this has long been one of the best spots to watch tens of thousands of migrating shorebirds – particularly the semipalmated sandpiper (*Calidris pusilla*), which come to gorge themselves on mud shrimp. In recent times, in addition to nature lovers, this area has also come to the notice of a number of peregrine falcons who are bigger, stronger and almost as hungry as the mud shrimp-eaters. Consequently, the sandpipers are more dispersed. It is still quite a sight, though: come a couple of hours before or an hour after high tide and you shouldn't be disappointed.

A newly designated UNESCO World Heritage Site, the **Grand Pré National Historic Site of Canada** (*2205 Grand Pré Rd; 542 3631, t/f 1 866 542 3631; www.*

EVANGELINE

Almost a century after the events of 1755, Henry Wadsworth Longfellow wrote *Evangeline: A tale of Acadie*, a poem which immortalised the tragedy that marked the lives of the Acadians. The story of his fictional heroine's search for her lost love through the trials and tribulations of the deportation from Grand Pré became an icon for the indomitable spirit of Acadians and their descendants.

Longfellow never visited Nova Scotia. In 1840, he heard a story about the Expulsion at a dinner party and decided it would make an epic poem. It was published in 1847.

grand-pre.com; ⌚ *mid May–mid Oct 09.00–18.00 daily (grounds accessible year-round – no charge); admission CAN$7.80)* is located in what was the centre of the Acadian village (see page 235), and this 5.7ha park commemorates the deportation of the Acadians in 1755. Paths lead from the modern interpretive centre (display panels, model of Grand Pré in Acadian times, multi-media theatre, gallery) to landscaped Victorian gardens and a bronze statue of Evangeline, fictional heroine of Longfellow's poem (see box opposite), and the c1922 Saint Charles Memorial church. Inside, the church paintings and stained glass windows depict the story of the Acadians. With the exception of an Acadian well, nearby dykes and a row of old willow trees, nothing physical remains from the Acadian days, but there are expansive grounds to wander, plus vegetable gardens, a blacksmith shop, orchard, and a look-out over dyked farmland. The money to buy the land for the park – and to build the church – came from the Dominion Atlantic Railway (DAR) in 1917. Taking a lead from steamship companies connecting Yarmouth (see page 186) with Boston and New York, the DAR marketed its Yarmouth–Halifax line as 'The Land of Evangeline Route'.

Approximately 3km away from the Historic Site, a cross by the sea marks the point from which the fleet carrying the expelled Acadians departed. Ironically, very close by, a monument at Horton Landing commemorates the 8,000-plus New England Planters who came in the 1760s to replace the deported Acadians.

The current owners of **Domaine de Grand Pré** *(11611 Hwy 1;* ☎ *542 1753,* **t/f** *1 866 479 4637; www.grandprewines.ns.ca;* ⌚ *Jan–mid May 11.00–17.00 Sat; mid May–mid Oct 10.00–18.00 Mon–Sat; 11.00–18.00 Sun, mid Oct–Dec Wed–Sat 11.00–17.00; 45-min winery tours mid May–Oct 3-times daily for CAN$7)*, originally from Switzerland, bought this winery (located on former Acadian farmland) in 1994 and have transformed it completely with great success – not only has it produced several award-winning wines, but it is a delightful place to visit. To round things off, there's an excellent restaurant, too (see opposite).

WINDSOR *(Population: 3,700)*

People are beginning to realise that Windsor is well located, on the Avon River, close to Wolfville and an easy run on Highway 101 to Halifax (or Highway 14 to Chester and the South Shore).

Several beautiful heritage homes are dotted about (though not in the slightly bland downtown area), efforts have been made to regenerate the waterfront, new restaurants and a hotel have opened, and there were plans to develop the huge old Nova Scotia Textiles building just outside town into flats, galleries, shops, eateries and more. But the project went bust, and Windsor remains somewhere that could be up and coming.

Some downtown walls are home to **large historical murals** (seven in total): five are by Ken Spearing, a local artist, and one each by Mi'kmaq artist Alan Syliboy and one (Acadian-themed) by Kosovo-born Nova Scotia resident Zeqirja Rexhepi.

There are several other attractions, most of which are easily reached on foot. In addition, the town is home to Canada's oldest private school, **King's-Edgehill School** (*http://kes.ns.ca*), and the **Mermaid Theatre** of Nova Scotia, renowned for children's theatre. More important for some, Windsor claims to be the birthplace of (ice) hockey.

HISTORY Situated at the confluence of the Avon and St Croix rivers, Windsor was known to the Mi'kmaq as *Piziquid* (or *Pesaquid*), 'the meeting of the waters'.

The French began to settle in significant numbers from about 1685. They ploughed fields, planted orchards and built grist mills. By 1748, well over 2,000 Acadians lived

BLUE BEACH FOSSILS

Although fossil tracks were discovered at Blue Beach over 150 years ago, this site is yet to receive the recognition of (say) Joggins (see page 268) or Arisaig (page 294). Local residents Sonja Wood and Chris Mansky have long been trying to change that, and have poured their own money and time into the **Blue Beach Fossil Museum** (*127 Blue Beach Rd, Hantsport; ☎ 684 9541; www.bluebeachfossilmuseum.com ; ⌚ mid Apr–Oct 09.30–17.00 daily*). The museum claims the largest collection of fossil bones and tracks in eastern Canada. Both museum and beach are a must for fossil fans. To get there from Wolfville or Grand Pré, take Exit 9 off Highway 101, and at the roundabout turn first onto Oak Island Road, then right onto Bluff Road. After about 3.5km, turn left onto Blue Beach Road. From Windsor, take Highway 1 through Hantsport. Shortly after Hantsport, bear right onto Bluff Road and Blue Beach Road will be on the right after approximately 4km.

in the area. When Halifax was founded in 1749, the decision was made to fortify Piziquid, and a blockhouse was constructed. In 1750, Fort Edward (see page 242) was built. Much of the planning for the Expulsion of the Acadians (see page 16) was done here, and many Acadians were held in the fort to await deportation.

After the Expulsion, new settlers began to arrive to replace the Acadians, settling on both sides of the river and renaming it the 'Avon'. In 1764, they named their settlement on the east bank 'Windsor'.

The University of King's College and its secondary school, King's Collegiate School, were founded in 1788–89 by United Empire Loyalists as Anglican academic institutions.

Shipping and shipbuilding prospered here, particularly in the second half of the 19th century. The huge Windsor Cotton Mill opened in the early 1880s, and later became Nova Scotia Textiles.

Huge fires in 1897 and 1924 accounted for much of the downtown, and a 1920 blaze destroyed the university which reopened in Halifax two years later.

With water transport made almost redundant by road and rail travel, a causeway was built across the Avon River in 1970, putting an end to shipping for Windsor.

GETTING THERE As mentioned opposite, Windsor is easy to get to **by car**. The town is 26km/16 miles from Wolfville, 66km/41 miles from Halifax (both via Highway 101 or 1), and 134km/83 miles from Truro (via Highways 14 and 102). From Windsor, **buses** (see page 195) run to Wolfville and to Brooklyn (page 245). The closest Maritime Bus (see page 57) stop (the Kentville–Halifax route) will probably be at Falmouth's Irving Mainway petrol station (*2113 Hwy 1*), a five- to ten-minute walk from Windsor's downtown.

WHERE TO STAY

Clockmaker's Inn (8 rooms) 1399 King St; ☎ 792 2573, **t/f** 1 866 778 3600; www.theclockmakersinn.com; ⌚ year-round. A beautifully restored c1894 Victorian mansion with 4 rooms & 4 suites. Original woodwork, antique furniture, stained glass windows. Full b/fast inc. **$$**

Phoenix Hollow B&B (2 rooms) 65 Chestnut St; **t/f** 1 866 900 6910; http://phoenixhollow.com; ⌚ year-round. Another B&B combining the old (the c1873 heritage house with magnificent curved staircase) with modern comforts. Comfortable, well-equipped rooms. Rate inc beverages & snacks in evening & full b/fast. **$$**

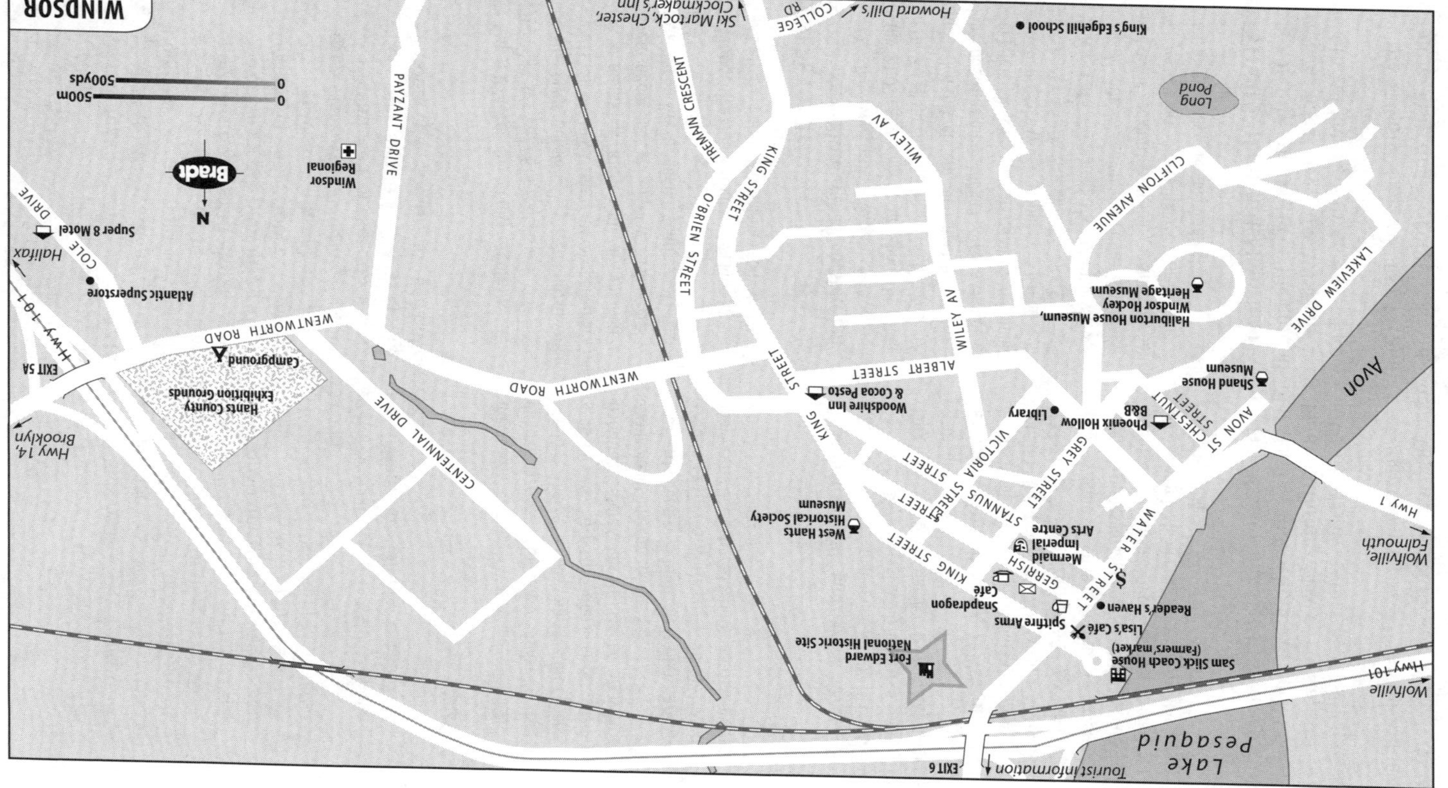
WINDSOR
Lake Pesaquid
Avon
Long Pond
Wolfville
Hwy 101
Wolfville, Falmouth
Hwy 1
Tourist Information
EXIT 6
Hwy 14, Brooklyn
EXIT 5A
Hwy 101
Halifax
Sam Slick Coach House (Farmers' market)
Lisa's Café
Reader's Haven
Spitfire Arms
Snapdragon Café
Mermaid Imperial Arts Centre
Fort Edward National Historic Site
West Hants Historical Society Museum
Woodshire Inn & Cocoa Pesto
Library
Phoenix Hollow B&B
Shand House Museum
Haliburton House Museum, Windsor Hockey Heritage Museum
King's Edgehill School
Howard Dill's
Ski Martock, Chester, Clockmaker's Inn
Hants County Exhibition Grounds
Campground
Atlantic Superstore
Super 8 Motel
Windsor Regional
WATER STREET
GERRISH
KING STREET
STREET
STANNUS STREET
VICTORIA STREET
GREY STREET
CHESTNUT STREET
AVON ST
ALBERT STREET
WILEY AV
KING STREET
O'BRIEN STREET
TREMAIN CRESCENT
COLLEGE RD
CLIFTON AVENUE
LAKEVIEW DRIVE
WENTWORTH ROAD
CENTENNIAL DRIVE
PAYZANT DRIVE
COLE DRIVE
N
Bradt
0 500m
0 500yds

GREAT GOURD ALMIGHTY

What do Halloween, Cinderella, hockey and Windsor have in common? Giant pumpkins. When you visit **Howard Dill Enterprises** (*400 College Rd; 798 2728; www.howarddill.com; year-round*), don't expect a café serving pumpkin pie or pumpkin soup: the pumpkins cultivated here are grown for size rather than taste and the operation specialises not only in growing enormous gourds but also in developing seeds for others to do the same. One of Dill's seeds grew into a (then) world-record pumpkin weighing 656kg. September and October are the best times to see the field of giants and in October, when Windsor hosts a pumpkin festival and other pumpkin-related events (see *www.worldsbiggestpumpkins.com*).

I mentioned hockey: an iced-over pond on Dill's land is said to have been where ice hockey was first played in Canada. Incidentally, cricket was introduced to Windsor in 1840 but didn't catch on.

Super 8 Motel (66 rooms) 63 Cole Dr; 792 8888, **t/f** 1 877 513 7666; www.super8motelwindsor.com; year-round. Just off Hwy 101 Exit 5A, this 3-storey motel opened in 2007. All rooms have fridge & microwave. There is a 12m indoor pool, with 25m waterslide, & a jacuzzi. No on-site restaurant. Continental b/fast inc. **$$**

Woodshire Inn (2 rooms) 494 King St; 472 3300; **e** info@thewoodshire.com; www.thewoodshire.com; year-round. This 1850s' building was one of the few to survive Windsor's great fire. The 2 luxurious suites feature cedar 4-poster beds, Egyptian cotton linen & modern bathrooms. More suites are planned. B/fast available for an extra charge. **$$**

Hants County Exhibition Trailer Park (25 sites) 237 Wentworth Rd; 798 2011; mid May–early Oct. Serviced & unserviced campsites, go-carts & minigolf. **$**

WHERE TO EAT

Cocoa Pesto Bistro at the Woodshire Inn 472 3300; www.cocoapesto.com; year-round 16.00–21.00 daily. Still not sure about the name, but the excellent cooking (using fresh, local produce) at this modern, elegant bistro hits the right spot. The home-smoked pork is a winner, the beef tenderloin lives up to its name, & the vanilla bean cheesecake won't disappoint. 3 dining rooms, & a terrace for alfresco dining. **$$–$$$**

Lisa's Café 30 Water St; 792 1986; www.lisascafe.com; year-round 11.00–20.00 daily. Good home cooking, particularly seafood; try Santa Fe-style haddock with cranberry salsa & leave room for the pies or bread pudding! **$**

Snapdragon Café and Bakery 109 Gerrish St; 798 2322; year-round 08.00–15.00 Mon–Sat. Good café/bakery dishing up snacks, soups, light lunches & baked goods – try the (very datey) date squares. **$**

Spitfire Arms Alehouse 29 Water St; 792 1460; www.spitfirearms.com; year-round 11.00–23.00 Sun–Wed (kitchen to 21.00), 11.00–late Thu–Sat (kitchen to 22.00). This English pub has a fine selection of both local & imported beers, & dishes up far better than average pub food – not just good fish & chips & bangers & mash but even a Birmingham (vegetarian) curry! Desserts are good, too. **$**

FESTIVALS **The British Motoring Festival** (*www.britishmotoringfestival.com*) takes place in July, and is held on the grounds of Kings-Edgehill School. Formerly known as 'Sam Slick Days', the **Windsor West Hants Summer Fest** (*www.samslick.ca*) is a three-day event in August, which includes theatre workshops, games, parades, concerts and fireworks.

The **Hants County Exhibition** (*www.hantscountyex.com*) is the oldest continuously run agricultural fair in North America, established in 1765. It takes place in September, with a variety of agricultural and family events – and some surprises. The 2009 exhibition included the biggest travelling reptile show in Canada while the 2012 extravaganza included a partner-carrying competition. The **Pumpkin Festival and Regatta**, Windsor's Pumpkin Festival, includes a weigh-in to find the region's heaviest gourd, and the excitement of the Pumpkin Regatta, where teams race to paddle hollowed-out and decorated giant pumpkins across a lake. It takes place in October.

SHOPPING The nearest big supermarket is the **Atlantic Superstore** (*11 Cole Dr, just off Hwy 101 Exit 5A; 798 9537; 08.00–22.00 Mon–Sat, 10.00–18.00 Sun*). In the centre of town, **Reader's Haven** (*40 Water St; 798 0133; year-round 09.00–17.00 Mon–Fri, 10.00–16.00 Sat*) is a friendly used bookshop.

OTHER PRACTICALITIES

$ **Banks** Royal Bank, 111 Water St; 798 5721; 10.00–17.00 Mon–Fri. Scotiabank, Windsor Mall, Water St; 798 5472; 10.00–17.00 Mon–Fri

Library Windsor Regional Library, 195 Albert St; 798 5424; 10.00–17.00 & 18.30–20.30 Tue–Thu, 10.00–17.00 Fri/Sat, 14.00–17.00 Sun

Hospital Hants Community Hospital, 89 Payzant Drive; 792 2000; www.cdha.nshealth.ca/

Post office 53 Gerrish St; 08.30–17.00 Mon–Fri

Tourist information 31 Colonial Rd; 798 2690; late May–early Oct 09.00–17.00 daily (Jul/Aug to 19.00)

WHAT TO SEE AND DO A c1830s' elegant wooden villa on 10ha owned by 19th-century author, humourist, and historian Thomas Haliburton (see box, below), the **Haliburton House Museum** (*414 Clifton Av; 798 2915; http://museum.gov.ns.ca/hh/; Jun–mid Oct 09.30–17.30 Mon–Sat, 13.00–17.30 Sun; admission CAN$3.60*) is much altered since Haliburton's time (he lived here 1836–56), but still worth a visit. The museum is furnished with period antiques, including Haliburton's desk. It is said that if you run around Piper's Pond within the grounds near the Clifton Gate House 13 (some say 20) times in an anti-clockwise direction, the ghost of a piper will rise up from the water and play his bagpipes. I haven't tried it.

Outlining Windsor's claim to be the birthplace of **ice hockey** (called *hockey* in Canada), the **Windsor Hockey Heritage Centre** (*Haliburton House Museum; 798 1800; www.birthplaceofhockey.com; summer hours as Haliburton House, check for mid Oct–May hours*) contains displays including old photos of players and teams, and some of the earliest ice-hockey equipment. There are also ice-hockey souvenirs. It has moved temporarily from its old location on Gerrish Street to Haliburton House Museum.

THOMAS HALIBURTON

Said to be the Father of American Humour, Thomas Chandler Haliburton was born in Windsor in 1796. His most famous creation was a fast-talking, wise-cracking American clock-seller, Sam Slick, who appeared in a regular column in the *Novascotian* newspaper. Many popular sayings are said to derive from Haliburton (via Slick) including 'quick as a wink', 'the early bird gets the worm', 'I wasn't born yesterday,' and 'barking up the wrong tree'. Although seldom read these days, in his day Haliburton was almost as popular as Charles Dickens and Mark Twain.

SPEED BONNIE BOAT

Flora MacDonald lived at Fort Edward for a few months in 1778–79. After helping save Bonnie Prince Charlie in 1746, Flora married in 1750, and shortly afterwards emigrated to North Carolina with her husband. He was an army man, and later served in the Royal Highland Emigrants Regiment in Halifax. When (as a captain) he was based at Fort Edward, Flora came to join him, but left after a few months, back over the sea (via London) to Skye, Scotland.

Still known to locals as the Imperial Theatre, the **Mermaid Imperial Performing Arts Centre** (*106 Gerrish St; www.mermaidtheatre.ns.ca*) contains a 400-seat auditorium and intimate 60-seat studio used by the Mermaid Theatre and a variety of other types of entertainment.

A fine c1890 Queen Anne-style mansion built on a hill above the Avon River for a newlywed couple, the **Shand House Museum** (*389 Avon St; ☎ 798 8213; http://museum.gov.ns.ca/sh/; ⏲ Jun–mid Oct 09.30–17.30 Mon–Sat, 13.00–17.30 Sun; admission CAN$3.60*) is beautifully furnished with wonderful interior woodwork. It was one of the first houses in the area fitted with electric lighting and indoor plumbing. There's a good view from the tower, and fascinating bike-related memorabilia – the bridegroom, Clifford Shand, was a champion cyclist (on a penny-farthing).

The **West Hants Historical Society Museum** (*281 King St; ☎ 798 4706; www.westhantshistoricalsociety.ca; ⏲ late Jun–Aug 09.30–17.30 Tue–Sat; Sep 10.00–16.00 Tue–Fri; admission free*) offers displays on Hants County history and a genealogy library in a former Methodist Church.

Built in 1750 to protect the land route from Halifax to the Annapolis Valley, the **Fort Edward National Historic Site** (*Fort Edward St; ☎ 532 2321; www.pc.gc.ca/lhn-nhs/ns/edward/index_e.asp; ⏲ grounds year-round, blockhouse late Jun–early Sep 09.00–17.00 Tue–Sat; admission free*) includes the oldest-surviving wooden blockhouse in Canada. In 1755, the fort served as a base of operations for the deportation of approximately 1,000 Acadians from the area, and it saw service during the American Revolution and War of 1812. The officers' quarters and barracks survived until 1897 when they were destroyed by fire. Between 1903 and 1973 the site was a golf course: the blockhouse offers impressive views of the Avon and St Croix rivers, and a 1km trail leads around the site's perimeter.

After a morning of sightseeing, head to the **farmers' market** (*Sam Slick Coach Hse, waterfront; ⏲ Jun–Dec 09.00–13.00 Sat*) for organic fruit and veg, baked goods, crafts and buskers – the farmers' market at Wolfville (see page 229) incidentally, is much bigger.

In winter, go downhill skiing near Windsor (and within an hour's drive of Halifax) at **Ski Martock** (*370 Martock Rd; ☎ 798 9501; www.martock.com; ⏲ in season 09.00–21.00 Sun–Wed, 09.00–22.00 Thu–Sat*), off Highway 14, approximately 9km from Windsor and 71km from Halifax (take Exit 5 from Highway 101). A quad chair and T-bar rise 183 vertical metres. It's good for beginners and families. A one-day lift pass costs CAN$40. New in 2012, the **OnTree at Ski Martock** (*☎ 798 8855; www.ontreepark.com; ⏲ May/Jun & Sep/Oct 10.00–18.00 daily; Jul/Aug 09.00–19.00 daily*) is an outdoor attraction involving climbing, obstacles and ziplining (*CAN$39*). You'll need to sign a waiver, and must arrive at least three hours before closing.

6

Minas Basin and Cobequid Bay

Twice a day, the massive tides of the Bay of Fundy pour through the Minas Channel to the Minas Basin, the eastern part of which is Cobequid Bay. Two large rivers, the Shubenacadie (pronounced 'shuben-ACK-addee') and the Salmon, empty into this bay.

In the late 1600s, Acadians settled along these shores, constructing extensive dykes to turn the tidal marshlands into fertile fields. After the deportation of the Acadians, the land was resettled, primarily by New England Planters (see page 237).

For well over a century, shipbuilding was the mainstay of the economy for just about every coastal community in this region. Particularly between 1850 and 1890, many of today's tiny, sleepy communities were bustling and prosperous, and home to a couple of shipyards. Very few traces remain.

This region divides into three main parts. One road, the 125km-long Highway 215, runs along the bay's southern shore (usually called Hants Shore) to – and along – the Shubenacadie River. From the town of Shubenacadie, one of the province's major arteries, Highway 102 (which originates in Halifax) runs north to Truro, third-largest town in Nova Scotia, set on the bank of the Salmon River. From Truro, Highway 2 runs west along the northern shore of Cobequid Bay and the Minas Basin to Parrsboro, from which Highway 209 continues west along the coast to Capes d'Or and Chignecto, before turning north along Chignecto Bay towards Amherst.

Whilst busy Truro has no shortage of services or places to stay and eat, the same cannot be said of the two shorelines, particularly the southern where there is little tourist infrastructure.

The Hants Shore is for those looking to unwind and enjoy a quiet, relaxing drive with lovely views past green fields to the red-sand shores and the water. This is the road less travelled – except perhaps by our feathered friends – and it is part of the Western Hemisphere Shorebird Reserve, and serves as a critical feeding and roosting area for huge flocks of migrating shorebirds. You can visit a couple of old lighthouses, one of which – Burntcoat Head (see page 246) – marks the spot of the world's highest tides. The region's fascinating shipbuilding history and a high concentration of wonderful heritage buildings can be seen in Maitland (see page 247). In contrast, a few kilometres away are the thrills and spills of a rather unusual pastime – tidal-bore rafting (see page 250).

Shubenacadie (see page 250) has the province's best wildlife park, and Truro one of the best city parks, plus rare (for Nova Scotia) urban treats such as a seven-screen cinema. There are also huge supermarkets where you can stock up for your onward journey.

The northern shore starts off with a couple of pleasant communities, but as you head west the coastal scenery becomes more dramatic. The Five Islands area (see page 258) is interesting and photogenic, the town of Parrsboro (page 260) has a

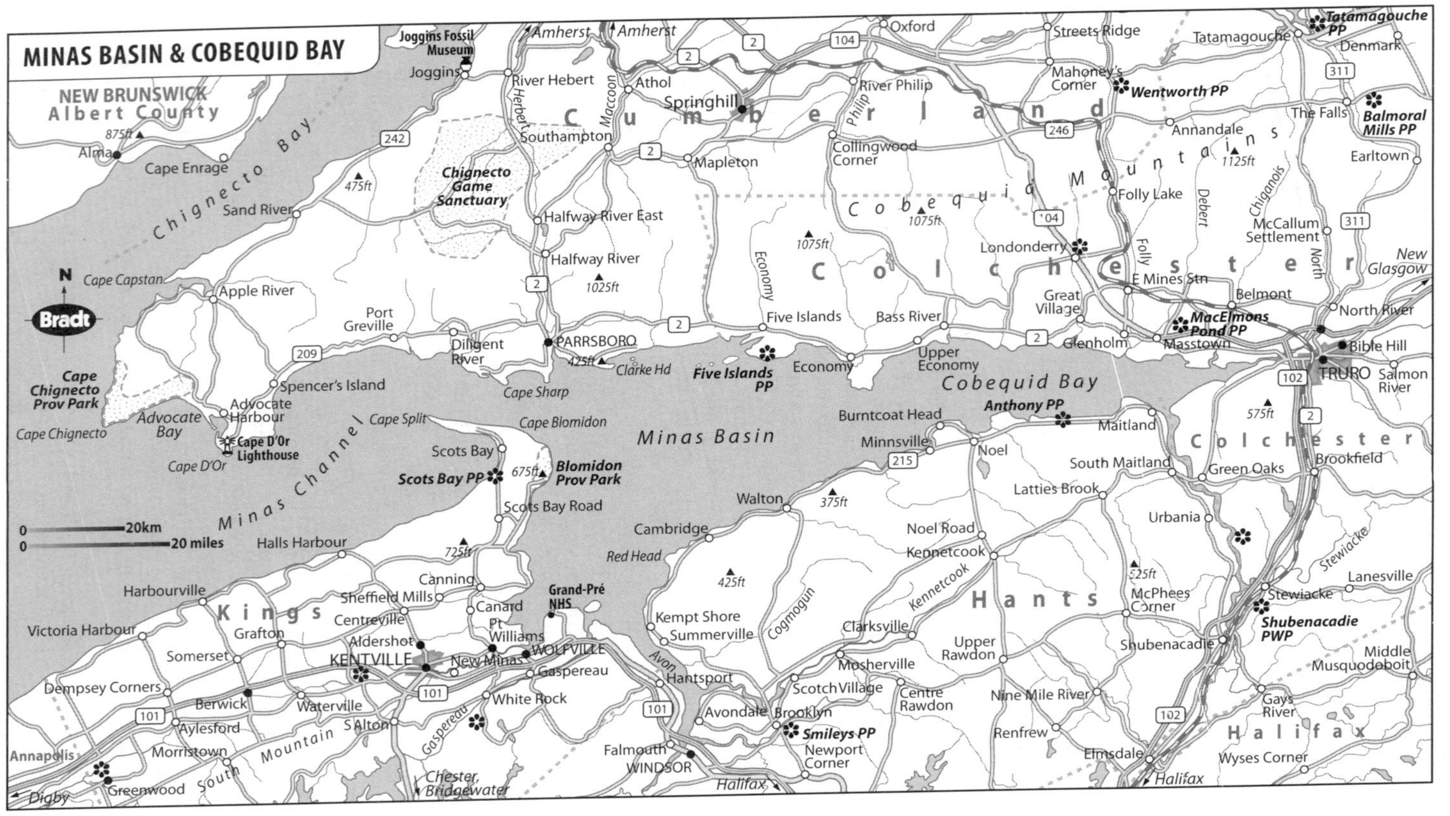

MINAS BASIN & COBEQUID BAY
NEW BRUNSWICK
Albert County
Alma
875ft
Cape Enrage
Chignecto Bay
Cape Capstan
Sand River
475ft
242
Joggins
Joggins Fossil Museum
Chignecto Game Sanctuary
River Hebert
Herbert
Amherst
Southampton
Maccoon
Athol
Springhill
Mapleton
Halfway River East
Halfway River
1025ft
PARRSBORO
425ft
Clarke Hd
Cape Sharp
Diligent River
Port Greville
Spencer's Island
209
Apple River
Advocate Harbour
Cape D'Or Lighthouse
Cape D'Or
Advocate Bay
Cape Chignecto Prov Park
Cape Chignecto
Cape Split
Scots Bay
Scots Bay PP
675ft
Blomidon Prov Park
Cape Blomidon
Scots Bay Road
Minas Channel
Minas Basin
Five Islands PP
Five Islands
Economy
1075ft
Bass River
Upper Economy
Cobequid Bay
Cobequid Mountains
Cumberland
Colchester
Hants
Kings
Halifax
Oxford
104
River Philip
Philip
Collingwood Corner
Streets Ridge
Mahoney's Corner
246
Londonderry
Great Village
Glenholm
Folly
Folly Lake
Wentworth PP
Annandale
1125ft
Debert
Tatamagouche
Tatamagouche PP
Denmark
The Falls
311
Balmoral Mills PP
Earltown
McCallum Settlement
North
Chiganois
Belmont
MacElmons Pond PP
Masstown
E Mines Stn
North River
New Glasgow
Bible Hill
TRURO
Salmon River
102
575ft
Brookfield
Green Oaks
Maitland
Anthony PP
South Maitland
Urbania
525ft
McPhees Corner
Shubenacadie
Stewiacke
Shubenacadie PWP
Lanesville
Middle Musquodoboit
Gays River
Wyses Corner
Halifax
Elmsdale
Nine Mile River
Renfrew
Latties Brook
Noel
Burntcoat Head
Minnsville
215
Noel Road
Kennetcook
Upper Rawdon
Centre Rawdon
Mosherville
Clarksville
Scotch Village
Smileys PP
Newport Corner
Brooklyn
Cogmagun
375ft
Walton
425ft
Cambridge
Kempt Shore
Summerville
Hantsport
Avon
Avondale
Falmouth
WINDSOR
101
Red Head
Grand-Pré NHS
WOLFVILLE
Gaspereau
White Rock
Canard
Pt Williams
New Minas
725ft
Canning
Sheffield Mills
Centreville
Aldershot
KENTVILLE
Alton
Waterville
Chester, Bridgewater
Halls Harbour
Grafton
Berwick
Somerset
Aylesford
Morristown
Harbourville
Victoria Harbour
Dempsey Corners
Greenwood
Annapolis
Digby
South Mountain
N
Bradt
0 20km
0 20 miles

few attractions including a good geological museum, and you can stay or eat in a lightkeeper's cottage at Cape d'Or (page 264). Talking of food, Advocate Harbour (see page 266) has one of the province's best rural restaurants. This is a region of soaring cliffs, and the provincial park at Cape Chignecto (see page 267) is nirvana for hikers and photographers when the weather is clement. The fossil-packed cliffs at Joggins (see page 268) were declared a UNESCO World Heritage Site in 2008.

You'll find a few more places to stay and eat on this side of the water, but overdeveloped it isn't. Come not for cinemas and supermarkets but for solitude and scenery.

A word of caution: the tide changes quietly but quickly and activities such as digging for clams or fossil/gemstone hunting can make you forget to keep an eye out. It is easy to get trapped with the only escape route blocked by sheer cliffs. Ignore the tides and you could pay dearly.

AROUND WINDSOR

BROOKLYN Apart from the provincial park (see below), a petrol station and a Reid's Meats & Clover Farms supermarket (*1034 Hwy 215; 757 0701; 08.00–22.00 Mon–Sat, 09.00–22.00 Sun*), there is little reason to stop in Brooklyn. Accessible **by car**, Brooklyn is just off Highway 14, 14km east of Windsor; take Exit 5 from Highway 101.

Where to stay There is a campground (**$**) in the provincial park, otherwise Windsor (see page 237) is less than 10km away.

What to see and do On the Meander River, **Smiley's Provincial Park** (*109 Clayton MacKay Rd; 757 3131; www.novascotiaparks.ca/parks/smileys.asp; mid Jun–mid Sep*) takes in forest, farmland and white gypsum cliffs. It is a good picnic spot and you can cool off with a dip in the river. There's a quiet, pleasant 86-site campground with sites in both forest and on farmland.

AVONDALE You'd never guess that this tiny, quiet community on the Avon River was once home to two thriving shipyards. Accessible **by car**, the town is 12km/7 miles off Highway 14 (the Mantua turn-off).

What to see and do Like so many museums, the **Avon River Heritage Society Museum** (*15–17 Belmont Rd; 757 1718; www.avonriver.ca; late Jun–Sep 10.00–17.00 Tue–Sun*) has been struggling to find the money to keep 'afloat'. It has exhibits on the Age of Sail and traditional shipbuilding skills, and displays on the New England Planters. There's a (surprisingly good) licensed tea room/café (check for opening hours) with an outdoor deck overlooking the Avon River.

SUMMER MUSIC

Kempt Shore, 5km from Summerville, is home to July's **Acoustic Maritime Music Festival** and August's **Annual Kempt Shore Bluegrass and Country/Folk Music Festival**: both are held at the 8ha Peterson's Festival Campground (*6055 Hwy 215; 633 2229; www.novascotiabluegrass.com*). The 29-site open campground (*Jun–mid Oct*) has 300m of beach frontage and offers views over the Avon River mouth and the Minas Basin.

The Avon River Heritage Society Museum plays home to both professional and novice artists who display and sell their work in a semi-formal environment at the **Great Little Art Show**, held in April.

SUMMERVILLE Between 1880 and 1937, Summerville was the terminus for a ferry service to Windsor. The pretty community once had a thriving shipbuilding industry. Community suppers are held throughout the year. Summerville is on Highway 215, 18km/11 miles from Brooklyn and easily accessible **by car**.

Most people stopping in Summerville these days do so to visit the **Avon Emporium** complex (*1 Wharf Rd; 633 2860; www.avonemporium.com; year-round 07.00–20.00 Mon–Sat, 10.00–16.00 Sun*) which includes a gift/craft shop.

Where to stay and eat

Shipwright Inn (4 rooms, 1 suite) 1 Wharf Rd, 633 2860; year-round. You can overnight in one of the guest rooms or the suite at this renovated c1870 shipbuilder's home. Rate inc full b/fast. **$**

Café Flower Garden Opening hours as Avon Emporium (see above). Your only eating option – but a good one – is this establishment, renowned for its seafood chowder, Sun brunch buffet (*early May–early Oct*), & Wed night music jam sessions, at the Avon Emporium. **$–$$**

ALONG COBEQUID BAY

WALTON What – at the time – was the world's largest-known barytes deposit was discovered in the area in 1941. The mineral – the main source of barium, used in industry and for X-ray imaging – was mined until 1978 when flooding halted operations. At one stage the mine accounted for 90% of Canada's barytes production. Concrete silos are the only obvious reminder that not so long ago this sleepy little harbour buzzed with cargo ships. Walton is on Highway 215, 46km/29 miles from Brooklyn and 44km/27 miles from Maitland, and convenient **by car**.

Where to stay and eat

Whale Creek Campsite (50 sites) Hwy 215; 528 2063; late May–early Sep. At the mouth of the Walton River: open & wooded sites. **$**

Walton Pub 39 Shore Rd; 528 2670; www.waltonpub.ca; 11.00–22.00 Mon–Wed, 11.00–21.00ish Thu–Sat, 12.00–20.00 Sun. Reliable pub food at sensible prices. **$**

Shopping and other practicalities The **Walton Variety Store** (*39 Hwy 215; 528 2051; 09.00–20.00 daily*) is the local general store. There is also a **post office** (*4309 Walton Wood Rd; 08.00–16.30 Mon–Fri, 09.00–13.00 Sat*).

What to see and do Inside the c1873 three-storey tower of the **Walton Lighthouse** (*Weir Rd; 528 2411; http://centralnovascotia.com/members/waltonlighthouse/; May–mid Oct 08.00–19.00 daily*) are display panels on the area's history, and a telescope. Outside, picnic tables and a short loop trail through the woods to a coastal look-out.

BURNTCOAT HEAD Many places claim the record, but most scientists – and the *Guinness Book of World Records* – concur with the claim of the Burntcoat (or is it Burncoat – the debate is ongoing) area as the actual site of the world's highest tides. The maximum tidal range (the difference between high and low tides) recorded here is an astounding 16.8m.

Burntcoat Head is easy to reach **by car**, being just off Highway 215, 60km/37 miles from Windsor, 100km/62 miles from Halifax and 50km/31 miles from Truro.

Where to stay and eat

Shangri-la Cottages (3 cottages) 619 Burntcoat Rd; 369 2050, **t/f** 1 866 977 3977; **e** reservations@shangri-lacottages.com; www.shangri-lacottages.com; year-round. Nancy & Blake's spacious, quiet, well-equipped & comfortable 1- & 2-bedroom cottages overlook Cobequid Bay & are just a stone's throw from the lighthouse park & make a good base from which to explore the region. **$$**

Deanna's Takeout 4681 Hwy 215, Noel; 369 2733; May–Sep 11.00–20.00 Thu–Sun. A great little take-out with friendly service & generous portions. Grab a club sandwich, fish & chips or just an ice cream & take it to one of the nearby parks to enjoy. **$**

What to see and do The **Burntcoat Head Park Lighthouse** (*611 Burntcoat Rd; 369 2012; mid May–mid Oct 09.00–dusk daily; lighthouse Jun–Sep 10.00–18.00 daily*) is a replica of the 1913 version. Set in a pretty picnic park, it serves as an interpretive centre. There is a panoramic view from the tower. A short **walking trail** leads to the beach which is well worth a visit when the tide is out. Walk on the ocean floor between unique flower-pot-red sandstone formations topped by trees.

MAITLAND With a lovely location on Cobequid Bay at the mouth of the Shubenacadie River, Maitland was a very important shipbuilding centre in the second half of the 19th century. While no traces of the shipyards remain, the village was designated Nova Scotia's first Heritage Conservation District for its many well-preserved 19th-century homes: styles include Second Empire, Classical Revival and Greek Revival. See, for example, the c1870 Victorian Gothic **Springhurst** (*8557 Hwy 215*), once the home of Alfred Putnam, one of Maitland's most prominent shipbuilders. Pick up a booklet with a self-guided **Historic Homes walking tour** at Lawrence House (see page 248). The village also offers a waterfront day-use park with an Acadian dyke and a reconstructed wharf. Incidentally, local town planners recently renamed a couple of Maitland's roads and re-numbered the houses thereon. Accessible **by car**, Maitland is on Highway 215, 9km/6 miles from Lower Selma, 30km from Shubenacadie and 79km/49 miles from Windsor.

History Present-day Maitland was known to the Mi'kmaq as *twitnook* – 'the tide runs out fast'. Loyalist settlers named it after Sir Peregrine Maitland, Governor of Nova Scotia from 1828 to 1834.

At one time, this was one of the busiest ports in the province, and it was here in 1874 that Canada's largest wooden ship was built by William D Lawrence. Somewhat unimaginatively, he called it the *William D Lawrence* – its nickname, 'the Great Ship', didn't show much originality either. The vessel was more than twice the size of the usual ocean-going ships of the time.

Where to stay and eat

Cresthaven by the Sea B&B (3 rooms) 19 Ferry Lane; 261 2001, **t/f** 1 866 870 2001; **e** innkeeper@cresthavenbythesea.com; www.cresthavenbythesea.com; year-round. Lovely, luxurious B&B in a c1859 former shipbuilder's house with magnificent setting. Rate inc excellent b/fast. **$$**

Foley House Inn (4 rooms) 11 Cedar Rd; 261 2844, **t/f** 1 888 989 0882; www.foleyhouse.com; mid May–mid Oct.

Accommodation in this c1830 former shipbuilder's house comprises 3 bedrooms & a suite. Bearing in mind the way places to stay & eat come & go in the village, check ahead that the licensed dining room (*currently* ⌚ *mid May–mid Oct 12.00–20.00;* $$) will be open for your visit. It specialises in seafood. Full b/fast inc. $

Millpond Campground (55 sites) 9120 Cedar St; 261 2249; www.millpondcampground.com; ⌚ May–Sep. Open & wooded campground with serviced & unserviced sites: outdoor pool. $

Tidal Life Guesthouse (3 rooms) 78 Cedar Rd; 261 2583; e info@thetidallife.ca; www.thetidallife.ca; ⌚ May–Oct. A c1870 home in over 5ha of grounds. Rooms with private & shared bathroom. Guest lounges. Friendly, good value, & nice b/fast inc. $

BING'S Eatery & Socialhouse 8913 Hwy 215; 261 3287; www.bingseatery.com; ⌚ summer for dinner Tue, lunch & dinner Wed–Sun; check for off-season hours. In the previous edition of this guide I wrote 'The village is crying out for a good eatery...' and that suggestion bore fruit. Part art gallery, part stylish but casual licensed café/bistro, part live music venue. Good views & plans to add a deck for alfresco dining. $–$$

Festivals

The **Launch Day Festival**, held on a Saturday in late September, commemorates the launch of the *William D Lawrence*, the largest wooden-hulled full-rigged vessel ever built in Canada. Expect a non-motorised procession, a launch re-enactment and a whisky barrel race. There is also a **Christmas Festival**, held in November, which includes a craft fair, Gentlemen's Tea and Christmas Tree Stroll.

Shopping

There are a few shops – antiques and bric-a-brac – and a c1839 general store with an uninspiring take-out on the north side of Highway 215, the main street.

Other practicalities

Post office 8829 Hwy 215; ⌚ 07.30–16.30 Mon–Fri, 09.00–12.00 Sat

What to see and do

The **Lawrence House Museum** (*8660 Hwy 215; 261 2628; http://museum.gov.ns.ca/lh/;* ⌚ *Jun–mid Oct 09.30–17.30 Mon–Sat, 13.00–17.30 Sun; admission CAN$3.60*), located in an elegant c1870 Classical Revival style building, was the home of William D Lawrence, one of Canada's great shipbuilders. It is here, on a hill overlooking the site of his shipyard, that he drew up the plans for construction of Canada's largest wooden ship (see *History*, opposite). Most of the furnishings are original, including furniture and exotic souvenirs collected from around the globe.

Not just for those interested in the history of shipbuilding, Lawrence House also opens a window on Victorian life in the area.

Around Maitland

Housed in a beautifully decorated c1865 former Presbyterian church 9km west of Maitland along Highway 215, the **East Hants Historical Museum** (*Hwy 215, Lower Selma; 890 7804; www.ehhs.weebly.com;* ⌚ *mid May–mid Sep 10.00–17.00 daily*) has few surprises except perhaps a small *Titanic* display.

A pretty picnic park 9km west of Maitland along Highway 215 and overlooking Cobequid Bay, **Anthony Provincial Park** (*Hwy 215, Lower Selma; 261 2947*) has wharf-side interpretive displays on the area's history and beach access at low tide.

Gallery 215 (*8247 Hwy 215, Selma; 261 2151; www.artgallery215.com;* ⌚ *late Jun–early Oct*), a former c1868 schoolhouse 2km west of Maitland along Highway 215, was built by shipbuilding carpenters and reopened in 2006 as a gallery/community centre. The work of around 50 local artists and craftspeople is displayed.

SOUTH MAITLAND

SOUTH MAITLAND Water is the focus of this small community on the Shubenacadie River, which offers rafting, wetlands birdwatching, and a good opportunity to learn about the Bay of Fundy tides.

South Maitland can be reached **by car** on Highways 215 and 236, 8km/5 miles from Maitland and 22km/14 miles from Shubenacadie. The **tourist information** centre is inside the Fundy Tidal Interpretative Centre (see below).

Where to stay and eat

Rafters Ridge Cottages (13 units) 12215 Hwy 215, Urbania; 758 4032, **t/f** 1 800 565 7238; www.raftingcanada.ca; year-round; off-season by reservation. Comfortable 1-, 2- & 5-bedroom cabins & chalets set between trees on a hillside overlooking the Shubenacadie River. Discounts are available for those rafting with the company. Even if you're not rafting, this is a pleasant place to stay, with seasonal outdoor pool & walking trails. The rustic pine & cedar licensed restaurant (*May–Oct 08.00–21.00 daily; $–$$*) doesn't have a bad menu: soups & pork dishes are usually good, as are the desserts. **$$–$$$**

What to see and do Behind the **Fundy Tidal Interpretive Centre** (*9865 Hwy 236; 261 2298; Jun–Oct 10.00–17.00 daily; admission free*), which explains the Fundy tides and the tidal bore, an observation deck high above the Shubenacadie is a good place to watch the watery action, and the rafters (see box, opposite): time your visit to coincide with the bore arrival.

Very close by, Ducks Unlimited maintains ponds which are home to a variety of waterfowl. Easy walking trails and interpretive boards enhance the birdwatching experience.

THE TIDAL BORE EXPLAINED

The Bay of Fundy sees the world's highest recorded tides. Twice daily, one hundred billion tonnes of seawater flows into the funnel-shaped bay. At the end of the bay furthest from its mouth, rivers (such as the Shubenacadie and Salmon) empty into it. The immense force and volume of the incoming tide not only halts these rivers' flows, but reverses them and sends them several kilometres backwards. The first wave caused by the incoming tide reversing the rivers' flows is called the 'tidal bore'.

The highest bores occur around the full and new moons: and although it can move at speeds over 10km/hour, sound travels a lot faster, and you're likely to hear the rush of water before you see it.

But don't be taken in by tourist brochure hype. Many see the tidal bore for the first time and say 'Is that it?' If you expect a huge tsunami-type wave, you will be very disappointed: what you are likely to see – and hear – is a wave of approximately 25cm moving steadily upriver.

In this area, South Maitland and the nearby Tidal Bore Rafting Park are excellent spots from which to view the phenomenon.

Times for the bore's arrival (generally, pretty accurate) can be found on the Rafting Park's website (see box, opposite), or obtained from local newspapers, accommodations, or tourist offices. Try to arrive at your chosen vantage point a good ten minutes early as nature doesn't always observe the timetable strictly.

On the Shubenacadie, following behind the bore are a series of rapids. These rapids are a vital factor in one of the province's most exciting water-based activities.

RIDING THE TIDE

For those seeking soaking thrills and spills, Nova Scotia offers its own unique version of white-water rafting. Things usually start with a gentle boat trip on the Shubenacadie River on which you may see bald eagles. Near its mouth, rather than a rocky bottom, the river has several sandbars. As the incoming tide rushes up the river, big – but temporary – tidal rapid waves are created over each sandbar. These rapids dissipate after ten to 15 minutes.

Skilled and experienced guides are out to thrill, and pilot motorised inflatable (zodiac-type) boats to hit the waves head-on, lifting the craft and its occupants into the air and crashing them back onto the water. Apart from the splashing and rushing water, expect shrieks and screams of laughter from your fellow passengers. The boats ride the rapid and have time to turn and do it again two or three times at each sandbar.

Some operators include a break for lunch before you return to the boats for a much calmer trip exploring upriver. Some also throw in the opportunity to slide over and through slippery, chocolate-brown mud as a (voluntary) free extra.

The rafting season runs from May to October: the moon and tides determine the expected intensity of the experience (the rafting companies' websites have tide charts to help you choose your level). Each company offers three levels of trip depending on whether regular, high or extremely high tides are expected. During lower tides, more time is spent on nature observation.

Wear old, dark clothes that you don't mind getting wet and dirty. Take a towel and extra set of clothes. Tidal-bore rafting is very popular, especially around the highest tides, so book early. Operators include:

Shubenacadie River Adventure Tours 10061 Hwy 215, South Maitland; **t/f** 1 888 878 8687; www.shubie.com; ⌚ Jun–Sep. 3-hr trips (CAN$92 inc all-you-can-eat burger/hot-dog barbecue). Mudsliding offered.

Shubenacadie River Runners 8681 Hwy 215, Maitland; **t/f** 1 800 856 5061; www.tidalborerafting.com; ⌚ May–Sep. Based in Maitland at the river's mouth, it offers longer trips. Half-day (from CAN$69) or full day (from CAN$92 inc steak barbecue).

Tidal Bore Rafting Park 12215 Hwy 215, Urbania; 758 4032, **t/f** 1 800 565 7238; www.raftingcanada.ca; ⌚ May–Oct. 2-hr (from CAN$69) & 4-hr (from CAN$81) trips. Mudsliding offered.

SHUBENACADIE

The word 'Shubenacadie' comes from the Mi'kmaq '*Segubunakade*' meaning 'place where the ground nuts grow' (these ground nuts should not be confused with peanuts – often called 'ground nuts' – but *Apios americana*, a climbing vine and member of the pea family and distantly related to the soya bean). The major attraction is the wildlife park, but it is also worth popping into the little museum.

To get to Shubenacadie **by car**, the town is on Highway 2, and just off Exit 10 of Highway 102, 66km/41 miles from Halifax and 35km/22 miles from Truro.

WHERE TO STAY AND EAT

Ⲁ Wild Nature Camping Ground (45 sites) 20961 Hwy 2; 758 1631; ⌚ late May–Sep. Open & wooded serviced & unserviced sites, 1km from Shubenacadie Wildlife Park (see opposite). **$**

✕ **Jack's Ship Diner** 2808 Main St; ☎ 758 3715; ⏱ year-round 08.00–20.00 daily. Decent diner delivering, for example, seafood, burgers, liver & onions, pan-fried haddock & pasta. $

OTHER PRACTICALITIES

$ **Bank** Royal Bank, 2824 Main St; ☎ 758 2295; ⏱ 09.30–16.30 Tue–Thu

✉ **Post office** 2770 Hwy 2; ⏱ 08.30–17.00 Mon–Fri, 08.30–12.30 Sat

WHAT TO SEE AND DO At the busiest and best of the province's wildlife parks, **Shubenacadie Wildlife Park** (*149 Creighton Rd; ☎ 758 2040; http://wildlifepark.gov.ns.ca; ⏱ mid May–mid Oct 09.00–18.30 daily; mid Oct–mid May 09.00–15.00 Sat/Sun; admission CAN$4.25 summer, CAN$2.75 winter*), 2km of largely shaded paths lead through 20ha where over 25 species of mammals and over 60 bird species (most native to Nova Scotia) can be seen. Species include black bear, moose, Sable Island horses, skunks, groundhogs, beavers and bald eagles. To see the animals out in the open, choose a cooler day or come early in the morning or in the late afternoon.

The **Tinsmith Shop Museum** (*2854 Main St; ☎ 758 2013; ⏱ mid May–mid Sep 10.00–16.00 Mon–Sat, 12.00–16.00 Sun; off-season by appointment*) was built in the 1890s and initially produced tin cans for milk, later branching out to sell all kinds of hardware. The original machinery – installed in 1896 – can still be seen. There's a craft shop and pretty garden.

AROUND SHUBENACADIE

STEWIACKE Said to be exactly halfway between the North Pole and the Equator – though some claim that the real midpoint is about 15km to the south – Stewiacke (the name comes from the Mi'kmaq meaning 'flowing out in small streams') is home to a somewhat un-Nova Scotian (more US-style) commercial attraction.

Stewiacke is about half an hour **by car** from Halifax International Airport on Highway 2, and just off Exit 11 on Highway 102, 68km/42 miles from Halifax, 30km/19 miles from Truro and 7km/4 miles north of Shubenacadie. **Maritime Bus** (see page 44) stops here *en route* between Halifax and Truro.

Where to stay and eat

Nelson House B&B (3 rooms) 138 Main St East; ☎ 639 1380, **t/f** 1 866 331 1380; www.thenelsonhousebb.com; ⏱ year-round. A stately c1905 house with a lovely veranda built for the then mayor of Stewiacke. Full b/fast inc (eg: homemade granola with yoghurt & fresh fruit or Belgian waffles with local maple syrup). **$$**

✕ **Whistler's Pub** 285 George St; ☎ 639 9221; ⏱ 11.00–22.00 daily (food until 20.00 Sun–Wed, until 21.00 Thu–Sat). The portions are generous & the standard pub food cheap & not too greasy. $

Other practicalities

$ **Bank** Heritage Credit Union, 5353 Hwy 289, Upper Stewiacke; ☎ 671 2647; ⏱ 09.30–17.00 Mon–Thu, 09.30–18.00 Fri

Library Stewiacke Branch Library, 295 George St; ☎ 639 2481; ⏱ 13.00–17.00 & 18.00–20.00 Tue, 10.00–12.00 & 13.00–17.00 & 18.00–20.00 Thu, 13.00–16.30 Fri, 13.00–17.00 Sat

✉ **Post office** 55 Riverside Av; ⏱ 08.30–17.15 Mon–Fri, 09.00–12.00 Sat

Tourist information 87 Main St West; ☎ 639 1248; ⏱ Jan–Mar & Sep–Dec 10.00–17.00 Thu–Mon; Apr–Jun 10.00–17.00 daily; Jul/Aug 09.00–19.00 daily

What to see and do The **Winding River Gallery and Complex** (*Hwy 102, Exit 11; ☎ 639 2345; www.mastodonridge.com; ⏱ late May/Jun & Sep/mid Oct 10.00–17.00*

daily; Jul/Aug 09.00–19.00 daily) is not easy to miss – a life-size replica of an 89,000-year-old mastodon, whose bones were unearthed in 1991 in a nearby gypsum quarry, stands outside in full view of Highway 102. Here (at what used to be called 'Mastodon Ridge'), you'll find a slightly eclectic mix of a gallery featuring local artists, a souvenir/ice cream shop, 18 holes of minigolf, and what is said to be the biggest KFC (formerly called Kentucky Fried Chicken) in Atlantic Canada.

TRURO

Centrally located, situated at the convergence of two of the province's major expressways, on two coach routes and served by VIA Rail, Truro has long been known as the 'Hub of Nova Scotia'. It is the province's third-largest town, with an economy based on shipping, dairy products and manufacturing. Neighbouring Bible Hill has been home to the Nova Scotia Agricultural College (Canada's third-oldest agricultural college) for over a century.

Many of those planning a trip to Nova Scotia get out a map and look for a base from which to make day trips to see all of the province's highlights. Many choose Truro. However, compared with much of the rest of the province, Truro is busy, lacks charm, and doesn't really have the same laid-back small-town feel. Railway level crossings often cause long traffic jams. But if you're happy to do a lot of driving and want somewhere with shopping, services, a good choice of accommodation and eateries from which to visit the capital, the Minas Basin shore, and perhaps the western half of the Northumberland Strait shore, then maybe Truro's for you.

HISTORY The Mi'kmaq named Truro *Cobequid* meaning 'the end of the water's flow' or 'place of rushing water' – a sure sign the tidal bore (see page 249) isn't a new phenomenon.

Pre-Expulsion, Acadian families farmed and traded in this area. A small group of New Englanders made their homes here in 1759, and in the following years, were joined by a number of Irish who Colonel McNutt (see page 17) had brought over. They dreaded the 'savage' Mi'kmaq and built a stockaded fort, retiring into it every evening. After some time passed and the Mi'kmaq had failed to display any hostility, the fort was abandoned.

GETTING THERE AND AROUND Truro is on Highway 2, very close to the junction of Highway 104 (the Trans Canada Highway – Exit 15) and Highway 102 Exit 14, and easy to reach **by car**. It is 117km/73 milesfrom Amherst, 91km/57 miles from Parrsboro and 100km/62 miles from Halifax. Two Maritime Bus **coach** routes stop here: one connects Amherst (and New Brunswick) with Halifax, and the other, Sydney with Halifax (see *Chapter 2*, page 44). Three days a week, one **train** (see page 44) in each direction connects Truro with Halifax, and Amherst (and Montreal). The **VIA Rail** (**t/f** *1 888 842 7245; www.viarail.ca*) journey between Halifax and Truro takes approximately 90 minutes. Tickets start at CAN$23 for a single.

Taxis are available from **Layton's** (*895 4471*) and **Scotia** (*883 8093*).

 **WHERE TO STAY** The places listed are open year-round unless otherwise stated.

Baker's Chest B&B (4 rooms) 53 Farnham Rd; 893 4824, **t/f** 1 877 822 5655; www.bakerschest.ca. Century home with lovely gardens, a large indoor jacuzzi, new outdoor pool (seasonal) & a fitness room. Full b/fast inc. **$$**

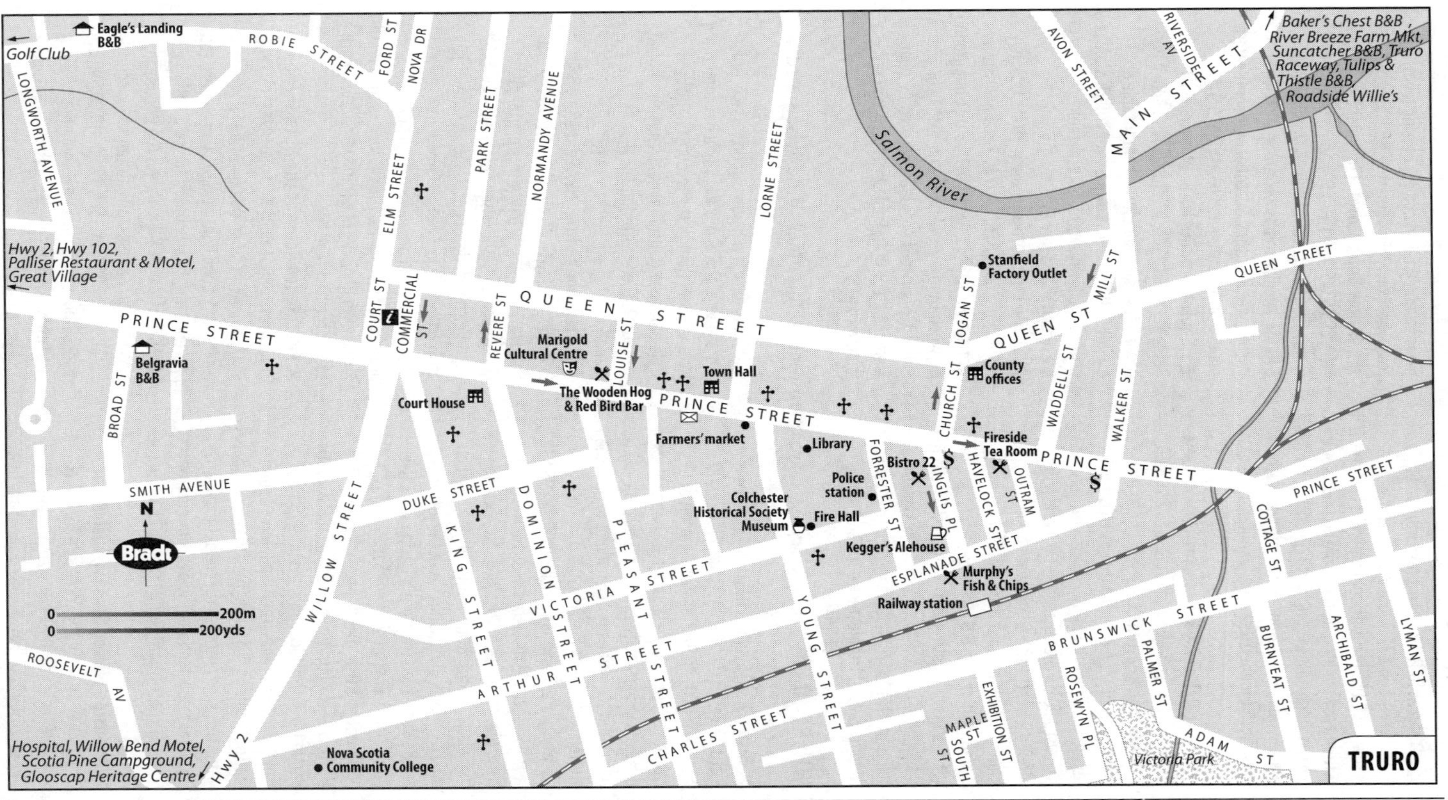
TRURO
Eagle's Landing B&B
Golf Club
ROBIE STREET
FORD ST
NOVA DR
LONGWORTH AVENUE
ELM STREET
PARK STREET
NORMANDY AVENUE
LORNE STREET
Salmon River
AVON STREET
RIVERSIDE AV
MAIN STREET
Baker's Chest B&B, River Breeze Farm Mkt, Suncatcher B&B, Truro Raceway, Tulips & Thistle B&B, Roadside Willie's
Hwy 2, Hwy 102, Palliser Restaurant & Motel, Great Village
COURT ST
COMMERCIAL ST
REVERE ST
QUEEN STREET
LOUISE ST
Stanfield Factory Outlet
MILL ST
QUEEN STREET
LOGAN ST
QUEEN ST
PRINCE STREET
Belgravia B&B
BROAD ST
Marigold Cultural Centre
The Wooden Hog & Red Bird Bar
Court House
Town Hall
PRINCE STREET
Farmers' market
Library
CHURCH ST
County offices
WADDELL ST
WALKER ST
Fireside Tea Room
PRINCE STREET
PRINCE STREET
Bistro 22
FORRESTER ST
INGLIS PL
HAVELOCK ST
OUTRAM ST
Police station
Colchester Historical Society Museum
Fire Hall
Kegger's Alehouse
ESPLANADE STREET
Murphy's Fish & Chips
Railway station
COTTAGE ST
SMITH AVENUE
N
Bradt
DUKE STREET
KING STREET
DOMINION STREET
PLEASANT STREET
VICTORIA STREET
YOUNG STREET
WILLOW STREET
0 200m
0 200yds
ROOSEVELT AV
ARTHUR STREET
BRUNSWICK STREET
PALMER ST
BURNYEAT ST
ARCHIBALD ST
LYMAN ST
ROSEWYN PL
EXHIBITION ST
MAPLE ST
SOUTH ST
CHARLES STREET
ADAM ST
Victoria Park
Hospital, Willow Bend Motel, Scotia Pine Campground, Glooscap Heritage Centre
Hwy 2
Nova Scotia Community College

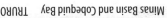

Belgravia B&B (3 rooms) 5 Broad St; 893 7100, t/f 1 866 877 9900; www.belgravia.ca. A fine c1904 house with many period features & within easy walking distance of the town centre. Hearty full b/fast inc (eg: focaccia with scrambled eggs & smoked salmon, or homemade waffles with fresh blueberry sauce & vanilla yoghurt). **$$**

Suncatcher B&B (2 rooms) 25 Wile Crest Av, North River; 893 7169, t/f 1 877 203 6032; e suncatcher@eastlink.ca; www.bbcanada.com/1853.html. A comfortable c1970s' B&B about 5km from the town centre with stained glass studio on premises (w/end workshops offered). Hosts Ruth & Gerry are friendly & knowledgeable about the area. Full b/fast & evening snack inc. **$$**

Tulips & Thistle B&B (4 rooms) 913 Pictou Rd; 895 6141, t/f 1 866 724 7796; www.tulipsandthistlebedandbreakfast.com. Very friendly & comfortable; nice deck, sun room, pleasant garden. A 9km drive outside town, off Hwy 104, Exit 17. Full gourmet b/fast inc. **$$**

Willow Bend Motel (28 units) 277 Willow St; 895 5325, t/f 1 888 594 5569; www.willowbendmotel.com. With 15 standard rooms, 6 (larger) deluxe rooms & 7 suites. All have microwaves & fridges. Seasonal outdoor (heated) pool. 'Deluxe' continental b/fast inc. **$$**

Eagle's Landing B&B (3 rooms) 401 Robie St; 893 2346, t/f 1 866 893 2346; www.bbcanada.com/10009.html. Comfortable & friendly with garden & nice balcony/deck & an easy walk to the town centre. Gourmet full b/fast & evening snacks inc. **$–$$**

Scotia Pine Campground (160 sites) Hwy 2, Hilden; 893 3666, t/f 1 877 893 3666; www.scotiapine.ca; Jun–mid Oct. Large campground between Truro & Brookfield (take Exit 12 or 13 from Hwy 102); serviced sites for motorhomes, open & wooded tent sites. Pool (in season), sauna & laundromat. **$**

WHERE TO EAT The places listed are open year-round unless otherwise stated.

Bistro 22 16 Inglis Pl; 843 4123; www.bistro22.ca; 11.00–14.00 Tue/Wed, 11.00–14.00 & 17.00–20.30 Thu–Sat. Lunches at this casual but upmarket restaurant are good salads, pizzas, gourmet sandwiches & paninis: the dinner menu might include roasted halibut, or pork chop stuffed with Gouda & spinach. **$$**

Kegger's Alehouse 72 Inglis Pl; 895 5347; www.keggersalehouse.com; 16.00–22.00 Mon/Tue, 16.00–midnight Wed–Sat. Offering a fine range of local & international ales, good pub food (eg: steak quesadillas – but the jury is still out on the deep-fried cheesecake), cocktails & lively atmosphere. Live music Wed–Sat evenings. **$$**

The Red Bird 623 Prince St; 895 0779; 16.30–closing Tue–Sat. Styled like a 1930s bar, in the late afternoon & evening there's a menu of well-done traditional Nova Scotia cuisine. Later on, 'snackier' food takes over. Wash it down with – or forget the food & just come for – the largest selection of wines, liqueurs, beers & spirits (particularly single malt whisky) in the area. **$$**

Roadside Willie's Smokehouse & Bar 27 Jennifer Dr, Bible Hill; 843 3486; www.roadsidewillies.ca; 11.30–20.00 Mon–Wed, 11.30–21.00 Thu–Sat, 16.00–21.00 Sun. Tasty pub food, decent portions, good service, fun atmosphere. The extensive menu has something for everyone, though the feature is southern-style barbecue (with the meat/chicken smoked in-house). There's often music (live or 'player piano'). **$$**

The Wooden Hog 627 Prince St; 895 0779; 09.00–15.00 Mon–Wed, 09.00–21.00 Thu/Fri, 11.00–21.00 Sat. A warm, friendly atmosphere in this licensed European-style café. Light lunch includes soups, salads & sandwiches on fresh-baked bread. Evening fare is more substantial with generally good seafood (eg: crab cakes), pasta & chicken dishes. The eatery is named for the ¾-scale wood model of a Harley Davidson which adorns the back wall. **$$**

Fireside Tea Room at the Nova Scotian Emporium 880 Prince St; 893 8285; 09.00–17.00 Mon–Thu & Sat, 09.00–21.00 Fri. Not just tea but very good light meals (salads, soups, etc), plus tempting & tasty baked treats. **$–$$**

Murphy's Fish & Chips 88 The Esplanade; 895 1275; www.murphysfishandchips.com; 11.00–19.00 Mon–Sat, 12.00–19.00 Sun. An uninspiring location in a little shopping mall, but this family-friendly eatery offers well-cooked, well-priced seafood. **$**

FESTIVALS The Provincial Exhibition Grounds in nearby Bible Hill are the new home of the **Nova Scotia Bluegrass & Oldtime Music Festival** (*www.downeastgrass.com*), a three-day festival held in July. In August, there are three days of blues music, plus a custom motorbike show, at the **Dutch Mason Blues Festival** (*www.dutchmason.com/festival/*), and drumming, dancing, Mi'kmaq food and crafts at the **Mi'kmaq PowWow**. Also in August is the province's premier agricultural and industrial fair, the **Nova Scotia Provincial Exhibition** (*www.nspe.ca*).

OTHER PRACTICALITIES

$ **Banks** Royal Bank, 940 Prince St; ☎ 893 4343; ⏲ 10.00–17.00 Mon–Wed & Fri, 10.00–19.00 Thu. Scotiabank, 7 Inglis Pl; ☎ 895 0591; ⏲ 10.00–17.00 Mon–Fri

Hospital Colchester Regional Hospital 207 Willow St; ☎ 893 4321

Library Truro Branch Library, 754 Prince St; ☎ 895 4183; ⏲ 10.00–20.00 Tue–Thu, 10.00–18.00 Fri, 10.00–17.00 Sat

Post office 664 Prince St; ⏲ 08.00–17.15 Mon–Fri

Tourist information Victoria Sq, Court St; ☎ 893 2922; ⏲ May/Jun & Sep/mid Oct 09.00–17.00 daily; Jul/Aug 08.30–19.30 daily; Glooscap Heritage Centre (see page 256) ⏲ mid May–mid Oct 08.30–19.30 Mon–Fri, 10.00–18.00 Sat/Sun; mid Oct–mid May 08.30–16.30 Mon–Fri

WHAT TO SEE AND DO In and around the downtown area is some fine architecture: Truro has three designated Heritage Conservation Districts. 'Tree sculptures' (see box below) are another interesting feature. Golf lovers can head to the **Truro Golf Club** (*86 Golf St; ☎ 893 4650; www.trurogolfclub.com*) and there are several other courses within a few minutes' drive of town. The town's *pièce de résistance*, though, is the wonderful Victoria Park.

ICH BIN EIN BERLINER

A local Truro businessman has loaned the town six sections of the Berlin Wall. These are on display at 867 Prince Street.

Occupying over 160ha, **Victoria Park** (*Brunswick St & Park Rd; ⏲ Apr–Nov; admission free*) is one of the most beautiful natural parks in eastern Canada. The grassy day-use area at the main entrance can get busy on sunny weekends. From there, choose from numerous trails through the woods of red and white spruce, ancient hemlock, and white pine. Head along a deep Triassic gorge and see two picturesque waterfalls on Lepper's Brook. Jacob's Ladder is a 175-step wooden staircase up the side of the gorge. For a fabulous view over the surrounding area and the Cobequid Basin, take the trail to the look-out at the top of Wood Street (there is also road access to Wood Street).

Truro's Salmon River is one of the most accessible places to watch the **tidal bore**, the incoming tide forcing the Salmon River back the wrong way and filling the

TREE ART

Truro's tall, beautiful elm trees were ravaged by Dutch elm disease in the 1970s but in 1999, the town commissioned an artist to carve the base of a diseased tree into a sculpture – of Sir Adams G Archibald, Truro's Father of Confederation (see box, page 20). This became the first of a series of representations of many of Truro's most prominent residents and historical figures. Dotted about town, these include an Acadian farmer and a bear carrying an ice-hockey stick. A sculpture booklet is available at the tourist office.

riverbed. Tidal-bore (see page 249) times are listed in the *Truro Daily News* and at the tourist information office. A good place to bore-watch is by the **Palliser Restaurant and Motel** (*103 Tidal Bore Rd, by Exit 14 of Hwy 102; closed & for sale at time of writing*). There's a small interpretation centre and floodlighting for nocturnal visitors.

Housed in a c1900 brick building, the **Colchester Historical Society Museum** (*29 Young St; ☎ 895 6284; www.genealogynet.com/colchester/; ⏰ Jun–Aug 10.00–17.00 Mon–Fri, 14.00–17.00 Sat; Sep–May 10.00–12.00 & 13.00–16.00 Tue–Fri, 13.00–16.00 Sat; admission CAN$2*) has displays on the town and region's heritage and natural history; the bookshop has a good selection of titles on Truro and the surrounding province.

The Marigold **Cultural Centre** (*605 Prince St; ☎ 897 4004; www.marigoldcentre.ca*) is a performing arts centre with small art gallery and 206-seat auditorium. It has good year-round theatre and live music schedule.

There's usually something going on for families at the **River Breeze Farm** (*660 Onslow Rd; ☎ 895 5138; www.riverbreeze.info*), such as U-pick (pick-your-own fruit) or (in autumn) Atlantic Canada's largest corn maze.

The UK has M&S, but for Nova Scotia and much of Canada, Truro's Stanfield's – established well over a century ago – is the company most associated with underwear. If you're keen for a browse, head over to the **Stanfield Factory Outlet** (*1 Logan St; ☎ 895 5406; www.stanfields.com; ⏰ 09.00–17.00 Tue–Sat*). The Saturday **farmers' market** (*Old Fire Hall, 15 Young St; www.trurofarmersmarket.com; ⏰ Mar–mid Dec 08.00–13.00 Sat & summer 12.00–18.00 Wed*) has over 40 stalls (Wednesday is quieter).

Outside town To find out what harness racing is all about, head out on a Sunday afternoon to the **Truro Raceway** (*Bible Hill Exhibition Grounds, Ryland Av, Bible Hill; ☎ 893 8075; www.truroraceway.ca; ⏰ year-round*), the largest of the province's three harness-racing tracks.

Just off the motorway (4km from Truro at Exit 13A off Highway 102) and guarded by a 13m statue of Glooscap, the **Glooscap Heritage Centre and Mi'kmaw Museum** (*65 Treaty Trail, Millbrook; ☎ 843 3496, **t/f** 1 800 895 1177; www.glooscapheritagecentre.com; ⏰ mid May–mid Oct 08.30–18.30 Mon–Fri, 08.30–16.30 Sat/Sun; mid Oct–mid May 08.30–16.30 Mon–Fri; admission CAN$6*) is the best of the province's few museums/centres devoted to the Mi'kmaq. There's a multi-media presentation on Mi'kmaq heritage and Glooscap legends, and displays of traditional Mi'kmaq porcupine quillwork, beadwork and clothing. Regular workshops are held; there is also a gift shop. Ask about a couple of short walking trails nearby.

Catch a film at the multi-screen **Empire Studio 7** (*20 Treaty Trail, Millbrook; ☎ 895 3456; www.empiretheatres.com*), right by the Glooscap Heritage Centre.

AROUND TRURO

GREAT VILLAGE This pretty community is associated with Pulitzer Prize-winner Elizabeth Bishop (see box opposite). Many large Victorian homes are still standing. Great Village was a major shipbuilding area: the first four-masted vessel ever built in Canada, the *John M Blaikie*, was constructed here in the 1880s.

Great Village is on Highway 2, 27km/17 miles from Truro and 62km/39 miles from Parrsboro.

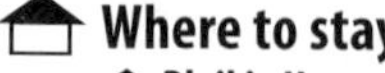

Where to stay

Blaikie House B&B (4 rooms) 8 Wharf Rd; ☎ 668 2985; www.blaikiehouse.ca; ⏰ year-round by reservation. A beautiful c1870s' Queen Anne Revival house with magnificent curved mahogany

ELIZABETH BISHOP

The father of Elizabeth Bishop (1911–79) died when she was eight months old and her mother was permanently institutionalised in 1916. Elizabeth lived with her maternal grandparents across from St James United Church in Great Village and attended the local school in 1916–17, writing: 'the school was high, bare and white clapboard, dark red-roofed and the four sided cupola has white louvers.' The building, at 8849 Highway 2, hasn't changed much since.

In 1917, her father's parents took her from her relatively happy life in Great Village to live with them back in Massachusetts, though she returned to Great Village for two months each summer.

Many of her works were inspired by her time here including the wonderful In the Village and the poignant poem *First Death in Nova Scotia.*

In 1949, Bishop became Poet Laureate of the United States.

staircase, Victorian décor & shared bathrooms. Full b/fast inc. **$**

Hidden Hilltop Family Campground (148 sites) 2600 Hwy 4, Glenholme; 662 3391, **t/f** 1 866 662 3391; www.hiddenhilltop.com; mid May–mid Oct. 6km from Great Village, the majority of sites here are serviced, many surrounding a large, open grassy play area. Lots of summer activities, decent-sized outdoor pool (seasonal) & a laundromat. **$**

What to see and do As well as offering three antique shops, the village has several galleries nearby. Contemporary art fans will want to pop into **Joy Laking Studio Gallery** (*6730 Hwy 2, Portaupique; 647 2816,* **t/f** *1 800 565 5899; www.joylakinggallery.com; Jun–Sep 10.00–17.00 Mon–Sat, 13.00–17.00 Sun, or by appointment; admission free*), 10km west of Great Village, to see watercolours and serigraphs – including works in progress – made by one of the province's top contemporary painters at this gallery. Stop by **heather lawson** (*5759 Hwy 2, Bass River; 647 2287; www.heatherlawson.ca; mid Jun–early Sep 10.00–17.00 Mon–Sat, otherwise by chance or appointment*) to see this gifted stone carver (and capital-letter disliker) at work – and perhaps pat a goat! She is based approximately 16km from Great Village towards Economy.

St James United Church (*cnr of Hwy 2 & Lornevale Rd*) dates from 1845 but was rebuilt by shipbuilders in 1883 after a fire the previous year: the ceiling resembles an inverted ship's keel. A **farmers' market** is held here on Saturday mornings (*Jun–mid Sep*).

EN ROUTE TO PARRSBORO

ECONOMY AND AROUND There are few services in the village or environs, but great natural beauty. Worth a visit is **Thomas's Cove Coastal Preserve** off Economy Point Road, an almost completely enclosed tidal estuary. Hike the three trails (the longest is 4km), explore tidal mud flats (watch out for the incoming tide) and see the effects of the Bay of Fundy tides on the sandstone coastal landscape. Look out too for blue heron, cormorants, raptors and belted kingfisher.

Several wonderful hiking trails run along and around the **Economy River**, from less than 1km (Economy Falls) to a spectacular 18km hike (Kenomee Canyon), much of it in wilderness. To reach the trailheads, turn inland from Highway 2 onto River Phillip Road. Even if you're not hiking, it's worth a drive along this road for the views from the roadside look-out.

Economy is accessible **by car**, on Highway 2, 52km/32 miles from Truro and 36km/22 miles from Parrsboro.

Where to stay

Four Seasons Retreat (11 cottages) 320 Cove Rd, Upper Economy; 647 2628, **t/f** 1 888 373 0339; www.fourseasonsretreat.ns.ca; year-round. Comfortable, well-equipped 1-, 2-, & 3-bedroom cottages are spread out & tucked between the trees. Fine views over Cobequid Bay. Beach access, (seasonal) outdoor heated pool. **$$**

Other practicalities

Post office 2676 Hwy 2; 08.00–17.00 Mon–Thu, 08.00–12.00 Fri/Sat

What to see and do If you are here in August, indulge at the **Clam Festival**, which celebrates the bivalve mollusc over three days. Epicures will also love **That Dutchman's Cheese Farm** (*132 Brown Rd, Upper Economy; 647 2751; www.thatdutchmansfarm.com; year-round 09.00–18.00 daily but Dec–Apr ring ahead to check*), a traditional Dutch-style farm making cheese off Highway 2. Gouda, both natural and flavoured, is popular, but look out for experimental varieties such as Dragon's Breath. There are also gardens, trails and farm animals to pet. A café (*mid Jun–early Sep 11.00–16.00*) serves a limited menu, offering cheese or ham rolls, apple tart, ice cream and hot drinks. Plans are afoot to expand the café and extend its opening season, and to add more attractions (and perhaps an admission charge).

Stop by the **Cobequid Interpretive Centre** (*3246 Hwy 2; 647 2600; Jun–Sep 09.00–17.00 daily*) for displays on the geology, history and culture of this stretch of Cobequid Bay coastline, and information on local hiking trails. Climb the steep stairs up the World War II coastal watchtower for fine views of the mud flats below.

FIVE ISLANDS Mi'kmaq legend has it that Glooscap (see pages 30–1) created the Five Islands when he threw pebbles at Beaver (who had built a dam and flooded Glooscap's medicine garden).

More recent tales tell of ghosts and buried treasure, though no-one has yet reported finding anything. The power of the water has worn a sea arch or tunnel through Long Island, the third in the chain.

Five Islands is on Highway 2, 24km/15 miles from Parrsboro and 67km/42 miles from Truro, convenient to reach **by car**.

MASSTOWN MARKET

There is little in the way of shopping/eating on (or near) the coast between Truro and Parrsboro (see page 260) – and (with all respect) the latter isn't exactly a New York or Paris. So before you visit Great Village and beyond, you might want to make a stop at the **Masstown Market** (*10622 Hwy 2, Masstown; 662 2816, **t/f** 1 866 273 0614; www.masstownmarket.com; year-round 09.00–21.00 daily*). This part-farmers' market/deli/café is also home to a garden centre, lighthouse interpretive centre, and a fish and chip stand. It is just off Exit 12 off Highway 104.

Incidentally, one of the first churches in Nova Scotia was built near here by the Acadians in 1705. It was burnt down by the British when the Acadians were deported in 1755.

Where to stay and eat

Five Islands Retreat (3 rooms & 3 cabins) 254 2628; www.fiveislandsretreat.com; early Apr–mid Sep. In 2003, Dick Lemon, a lawyer & winery entrepreneur, bought Long Island, 1 of the 5 islands. Although topped by a relatively flat plateau, the island is encircled by sheer cliffs. A 194-step staircase was constructed, with building supplies brought in by helicopter. The island sleeps 12 (in a 3-bedroom main house & 3 cabins – 1 a replica lighthouse & 1 boat-shaped). It is rented out in its entirety, from CAN$450 per night. **$$$$**

Gemstow B&B (2 rooms) 463 Hwy 2; 254 2924; www3.ns.sympatico.ca/gemstow; year-round; off-season by reservation. Comfortable B&B in century house with fine views. Judy, Gerry & their pets are very welcoming. Rate inc full b/fast with homemade bread & preserves. **$–$$**

Mo's at Five Island (3 rooms) 951 Hwy 2; 254 8088; www.mosatfiveislands.com; year-round; off-season by reservation. A combination of hostel (1 room with 4 bunk beds, 2 private rooms – all share 2 bathrooms), art & bookshop, & rather good café (pizzas, salads, soups & full meals; **$–$$**). Check the café is open if visiting out of season. *Dorm bed CAN$29, private room CAN$75.*

Five Islands Ocean Resort & Campground (105 sites) 482 Hwy 2, Lower Five Islands; 254 2824, **t/f** 1 866 811 3716; www.fiveislands.ca; mid May–mid Oct. Lovely coastal views, sea-view outdoor pool, laundromat, canteen, playgrounds. **$**

NOT SINCE MOSES

The owner of Five Islands Retreat (see adjacent listing) established this event consisting of 5km and 10km charity runs across the ocean floor – at low tide – between the 'mainland' beach and the five islands in July 2007, and it has already proved a runaway hit. For more, see www.notsincemoses.com.

Five Islands Provincial Park Campground (90 sites) For contact details, see below; late Jun–early Sep. Open & wooded sites. A beautiful location. **$**

Diane's Restaurant 874 Hwy 2; 254 3190; May & Oct 11.00–19.00 Fri–Sun; Jun–Sep 11.00–21.00 daily. Linked to a clam factory, so those molluscs are a good choice. So too are fishburgers, seafood chowder & more. If you're here in blueberry season, save room for dessert. B/fast served from 08.00 Sun. Licensed. **$**

Granny's 1193 Hwy 2; 728 3311; early May–mid Sep 11.00–21.00 daily. Another good (although again high cholesterol) choice. Generous portions of fish & chips or clams & chips; ice cream also available. Ask about the charity 'fish & buoy wall'. **$**

What to see and do The **Five Islands Provincial Park** (*Bentley Branch Rd, off Hwy 2; 254 2980; www.novascotiaparks.ca/parks/fiveislands.asp; late Jun–early Oct; admission free*), on the side of Economy Mountain, is a must for hikers, fossil hunters, beachcombers, geologists and those who enjoy magnificent coastal scenery.

The 637ha park lies on red sandstone deposited over 225 million years ago. Much of the sandstone and basalt was removed by erosion over the next 180 million years. When the Ice Age ended, flooding rapidly eroded more of the remaining sandstone, creating the 90m cliffs. The sea stack known as the Old Wife, and the protective caps of the five islands themselves, are examples of basalt, more resistant to erosion than the soft sandstone.

Keep your eyes open on the beach (not just for the incoming tide): not only are agate, amethyst, jasper and stilbite sometimes found, but also fossils.

Hikers can enjoy the 4km **Estuary Trail** along the shore of East River's tidal estuary, the 5km **Economy Mountain Trail**, which follows an old logging road, passing through stands of maple, birch, beech and white spruce; and the (recently modified due to erosion but still worthwhile) 2.2km each-way **Red Head Trail**. Although it is the most difficult – with a few ups and downs and a long uphill section

– of the park's trails, it gives access to look-outs, some of which are spectacular. Look out over the magnificent sandstone cliffs, rock formations and sea stacks such as the Old Wife – and, of course, the five islands. The trail can be walked in an hour or two, but allow a lot more time to enjoy the look-out side-trips.

The park has a pleasant campground and two picnic areas.

PARRSBORO *(Population: 1,400)*

Thanks to its population, Parrsboro is easily the largest community along the north shore of the Minas Basin. The town leapt into the limelight – at least for those interested in palaeontology – in the mid 1980s when two Americans unearthed one of the biggest and most important fossil finds in North America at nearby **Wasson's Bluff**. The cliffs yielded more than 100,000 fossilised bone fragments, all dating from shortly after the mass extinction some 200 million years ago that marked the end of the Triassic period and the beginning of the Jurassic.

Since then, Parrsboro has become a base for fossickers and rockhounds, and every August the town hosts the **Gem and Mineral Show** (previously called the 'Rock Hound Roundup'). But don't come expecting fossil-themed commercialisation – this is Nova Scotia!

Located at the head of a tidal river, the town has some services, a couple of modest supermarkets and some magnificent old houses – some of which are now inns – built by those who prospered during Parrsboro's glory days. In addition, there are a couple of good museums, an interesting (summer) theatre, and a golf course. It is an obvious base from which to explore the region.

In the past few years, feasibility and environmental impact studies have been carried out with regard to constructing the province's second tidal power project (the first is at Annapolis Royal – see page 208). The test site is in the sea approximately 10km west of Parrsboro, but you can learn more about the site – and tidal energy in general – at the FORCE visitor centre (see *What to see and do*, page 262).

Situated on Highway 2 and Highway 209, Parrsboro is easy to get to **by car**. The town is 65km/40 miles from Amherst, 97km/120 miles from Truro and 193km/160 miles from Halifax. **Tourist information** can be found at the Fundy Geological Museum (see page 262).

HISTORY Rockhounding is nothing new in this area: Samuel de Champlain (see page 219) was the first recorded European visitor in 1607, collecting amethysts from the beach.

Named in 1784 after Lieutenant-Colonel John Parr, Governor of Nova Scotia, from the late 18th to the early 20th centuries, Parrsboro was a busy mercantile centre, an important transport hub, and the focus of a vast shipbuilding region.

WHERE TO STAY

Gillespie House Inn (7 rooms) 358 Main St; 254 3196, **t/f** 1 877 901 3196; www.gillespiehouseinn.com; year-round; off-season by reservation. Conveniently located & housed in a gracious c1890 eco-friendly home. Peaceful, charming & tastefully decorated. Yoga studio available. Wholesome full b/fast inc. **$$**

Maple Inn (8 rooms) 2358 Western Av; 254 3735, **t/f** 1 877 627 5346; www.mapleinn.ca; May–Oct. 2 adjacent c1893 Victorian Italianate-style properties were converted to create this B&B. 6 comfortable rooms, a 1- & 2-bedroom suite & a honeymoon suite. Full b/fast & afternoon refreshments inc. **$$**

Riverview Cottages (18 cabins) 3575 Eastern Av; 254 2388, **t/f** 1 877 254 2388; www.riverviewcottages.ca; May–mid Oct. Clean cabins in a peaceful setting on the Aboiteau River.

Most cabins have simple kitchenettes but don't expect TVs, in-room phones or Wi-Fi. **$**

Glooscap Campground & RV (73 sites) 1300 Two Islands Rd; 254 2529; www.town.parrsboro.ns.ca/glooscapcampground.html; mid May–Sep. 6km from the town centre, with sea views, sandy beach & open & wooded sites. **$**

WHERE TO EAT

Bare Bones Bistro & Pizzeria 151 Main St; 254 2270; www.ghostinthekitchen.com; (bistro) mid May–early Oct 11.00–21.00 Wed–Sun (Jul/Aug Tue–Sun); (pizzeria) year-round Mon–Sat. 2 eateries at different ends of 1 location. Pizza choices are imaginative, & the standards are also handled well. Bistro lunches are gourmet salads, sandwiches, pasta & upmarket burgers: dinner in summer is unexpectedly fine-dining that wouldn't be out of place in a far bigger, more sophisticated metropolis. Pizzeria **$$**; bistro **$$$**

Harbour View Restaurant 476 Pier Rd; 254 3507; mid May–mid Oct 07.00–20.00 daily. Popular seafood restaurant by the water. The usual suspects (scallops, clams, lobster, seafood chowder, haddock), plus flounder. Deep-fried is the norm, but grilling or pan-frying may be available on request. Reasonable prices, generous portions. **$$**

ENTERTAINMENT

Ship's Company Theatre 18 Lower Main St; 254 3000, t/f 1 800 565 7469; www.shipscompany.com; Jul–Sep, main stage performances 20.00 Tue–Sun & 14.00 Sun; tickets CAN$28. A highly acclaimed & innovative professional company: the repertoire focuses on new works from Atlantic Canadian playwrights. The company staged its first production aboard the shell of a disused 1924 ferry: when a new theatre was built in 2004, the remains of the vessel were incorporated into the lobby.

FESTIVALS Held in June, **Classics By The Bay** stages three days of classical music performances. In August, the **Nova Scotia Gem and Mineral Show** is a three-day festival celebrating the province's rich mineral and fossil heritage.

OTHER PRACTICALITIES

$ Banks CIBC, 209 Main St; 254 2066; 10.00–17.00 Mon–Fri. Royal Bank, 188 Main St; 254 2051; 10.00–17.00 Mon–Fri

Health centre South Cumberland Community Care Centre, 50 Jenks Av; 254 2540

Library Parrsboro Library, 91 Queen St; 254 2046; Jun–Sep 10.00–13.00 & 14.00–17.00 Tue/Wed, 13.00–16.00 & 18.00–20.00 Thu/Fri, 10.00–15.00 Sat; Oct–May, same except 11.00–16.00 Sat.

Post office 247 Main St; 08.30–17.00 Mon–Fri, 09.00–12.30 Sat

WHAT TO SEE AND DO Those with an interest in fossils and geology – or just more beautiful coastal scenery – should drive along **Two Islands Road**. There are

FOSSIL FINDER

Eldon George was born in Parrsboro around 1930 and began collecting minerals and fossils when he was eight. A year later he put a 'Rocks For Sale' sign in the window of the family house. In 1984, he discovered the world's smallest dinosaur footprints as he sheltered from a hailstorm whilst fossicking at Wasson's Bluff.

He has been collecting, displaying and selling rocks and minerals for almost 60 years but is now in his eighties: at the time of writing, his shop/museum, house and entire collection are on the market.

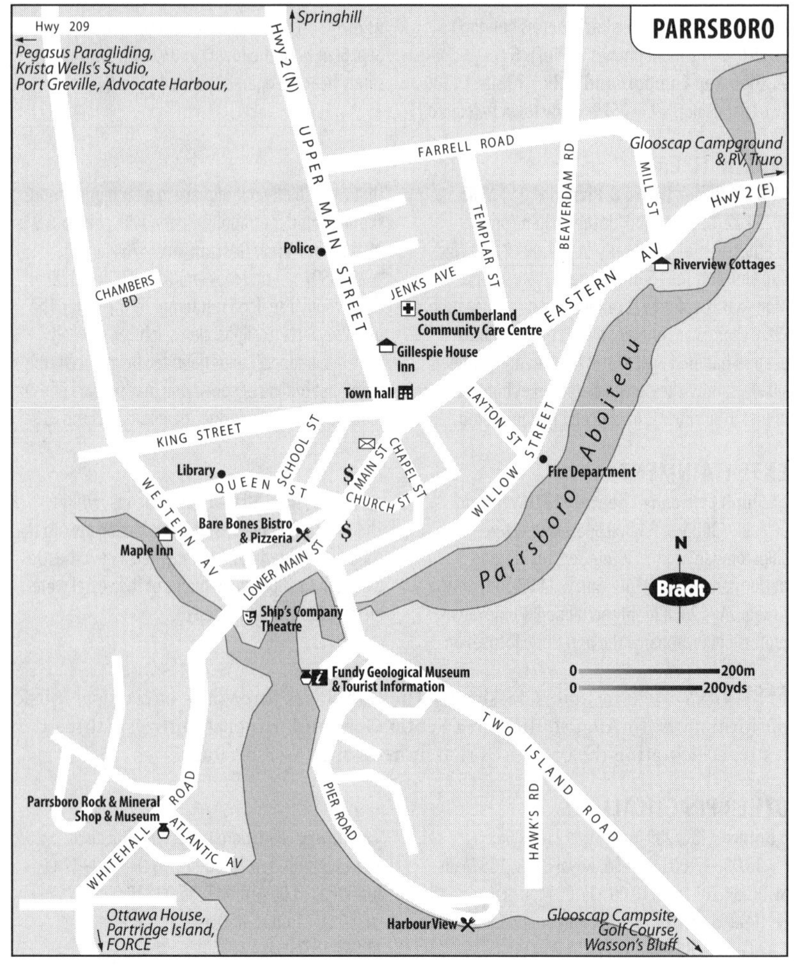

magnificent views of the rugged coastline, and about 6km from town you'll reach a car park. Interpretive panels describe the area's unique geology, and the fossil discoveries made here. A trail leads down to the beach and to **Wasson's Bluff**. This area is protected by law, and no fossil collecting is allowed, except by permit (see page 36). At the excellent award-winning **Fundy Geological Museum** (*162 Two Islands Rd; ☎ 254 3814, t/f 1 866 856 3466; museum.gov.ns.ca/fgm/; ⏲ Jun–mid Oct 09.30–17.30 daily; mid Oct–May 08.30–16.30 Mon–Fri; admission CAN$7.50*), see locally found minerals, semi-precious stones, fossils, and some of the oldest dinosaur bones ever found in Canada. Guided geological tours of the nearby beaches are offered in July and August: there's a year-round calendar of events.

Interpretive displays and interactive exhibits abound in FORCE's (the Fundy Ocean Research Center for Energy's) new **centre** (*1156 West Bay Rd; ☎ 254 2510; www.force.ca/visit; ⏲ May/Jun & Sep/Oct 11.00–16.00 Tue–Fri, 10.30–16.30 Sat/Sun; Jul/Aug 10.00–17.00 daily; admission free*) overlooking the tidal energy test site.

A wide variety of rocks and minerals can be seen in the **Parrsboro Rock and Mineral Shop and Museum** (*349 Whitehall Rd; ☎ 254 2981; ⏲ May–Oct 10.00–*

18.00 daily), plus a gallery/museum (*admission free*) of rare fossils of prehistoric dinosaurs, reptiles and amphibians: these include the world's smallest dinosaur footprint. Prospector supplies, books and maps – and some of the fossils and minerals – are on sale (see box, above).

Beautifully located by the Partridge Island causeway, parts of the huge **Ottawa House Museum By-the-Sea** (*1155 Whitehall Rd; ☎ 254 2376; www.ottawahousemuseum.ca; ⌚ late May–mid Sep 10.00–18.00 daily; admission CAN$2*) – 3km from the town centre and used as a summer home for over 30 years by Sir Charles Tupper, Canada's sixth prime minister – date back to 1765. On display are artefacts and exhibits highlighting the region's shipbuilding and commercial history, including rum running. Special events are held in summer. The museum is also a genealogical research centre.

Mi'kmaq legend has it that Glooscap created **Partridge Island** (a sandy natural causeway appeared in 1869 after freak weather, connecting it to the mainland) from a disobedient partridge. Archaeological evidence points to Mi'kmaq occupation 10,000 years ago. Various trails start from the end of the causeway, most rewarding of which is the **Look-Off Trail** which climbs to a look-out offering panoramic views in all directions. Reach the causeway by continuing on Whitehall Road past Ottawa House (see above). The island is less than 5km from Parrsboro.

Just southeast of the town centre, **Parrsboro Golf Course** (*Greenhill Rd; ☎ 254 2733; www.parrsborogolf.ca; ⌚ mid May–mid Oct*) offers a nine-hole 2,343yd clifftop course with above-par views over Minas Basin. Green fees are CAN$23 for nine holes and CAN$35 for 18 holes.

Around Parrsboro In Diligent River, about 10km west of town off Highway 209, you can stop by the delightful **Krista Wells' Studio** (*9874 Hwy 209; ☎ 254 2972; www.kristawells.ca; ⌚ by chance or appointment*) and discover whimsical paintings, mosaics, jewellery and more.

For a bird's eye view, check out **Pegasus Paragliding** (*☎ 254 2972; www.pegasusparagliding.com*), also based in Diligent River. Tandem flights are offered year-round (*advance reservations required, CAN$115*) as are courses.

GREVILLE BAY

The major points of interest along the next section of coastline are the village of Port Greville, and the tiny community of Spencer's Island.

MAIDEN'S CAVE

In the 18th century, Deno, an Italian pirate, seized a British ship with a valuable cargo. He made all but one of the ship's crew and passengers walk the plank, sparing only the beautiful daughter of the captain. Steadfastly the girl resisted the pirate's efforts to charm her. A great storm drove the pirate ship way off course, and finally it landed near Parrsboro, where – to their amazement – the pirates found a beach covered in jewels. When they'd gathered all the precious stones that they could find, Deno entombed his reluctant captive in a cave that had been found during the jewel-gathering, walling it up with stones. Some time later, passing Mi'kmaq heard strange wails and fled. They told others who were bolder and came to explore. Too late, they broke in and found the girl's skeleton. Her spirit is still said to haunt the cave.

PORT GREVILLE Another pleasant little community which would now show few indications of its ship building glory days were it not for the fascinating Age of Sail Heritage Centre.

Port Greville is 22km/14 miles from Parrsboro and 82km/51 miles from Joggins.

Where to eat The café (*early Jun & Sep 10.00–18.00, Thu–Mon & Jul/Aug daily;* $) at the **Age of Sail Heritage Centre** (see below) serves light lunches (eg: lobster rolls), soup or chowder, sandwiches and desserts (the carrot cake is a stand-out). The food is good and the prices very reasonable. You don't have to visit the centre to be able to use the café (but I'd recommend it).

What to see and do Considering Nova Scotia's worldwide importance during the 'Age of Sail', there are precious few signs left of such an important part of the province's history. The **Age of Sail Heritage Centre** (*Hwy 209; 348 2030; www.ageofsailmuseum.ca; Jun & Sep–mid Oct 10.00–18.00 Thu–Mon, Jul/Aug daily; admission CAN$3*) does a wonderful job at addressing that. Housed in a former c1854 Methodist church are audio-visual and panel displays, and thousands of artefacts which bring life to the history of shipbuilding along this shore. The centre comprises a two-storey main building, blacksmith shop, band-saw shed and a c1907 lighthouse. A new (2012) addition is a two-level building which expands on the story of the tides and winds, and where the vessels sailed. It also houses a research area. There is a good café (see above) and play area.

SPENCER'S ISLAND At the western end of Greville Bay, this isn't actually an island but takes its name from a real one just off nearby Cape Spencer. That island is said to have been formed by mythical Mi'kmaq hero Glooscap when he upturned his large stone cooking pot.

The community became another important shipbuilding centre in the second half of the 19th century: the first large vessel to be launched was the *Amazon*, built in 1861 (see box opposite). In summer, the c1904 beachfront **lighthouse** is sometimes open to the public: beside it is a picnic park.

Spencer's Island is 1.2km from Highway 209, 40km/25 miles from Parrsboro.

Where to stay and eat There has been a beachfront eatery on and off for the last few years, and it has usually been above average food-wise. It was closed in 2012, and empty and on the market at the time of writing, so its future is uncertain.

Spencer's Island B&B (3 rooms) 789 Spencer's Beach Rd; 392 2721; e spencebb@yahoo.ca; Jun–Sep. Close to the beach & well located for exploring the region: pity the season is so short. 3 guest rooms share 2 bathrooms. Full b/fast inc. $

Old Shipyard Beach Campground (26 sites) 774 Spencer's Beach Rd; 392 2487; www.oldshipyardbeachcampground.com; Jun–Sep. Open serviced & unserviced beachfront sites. Laundromat. Kayak tours available. $

ADVOCATE HARBOUR AND CAPE D'OR

Many people rush through in a hurry to get to nearby Cape Chignecto Provincial Park, but try to make time to explore this beautiful area on Advocate Bay, tucked between the towering cliffs of Cape d'Or and Cape Chignecto, and backed by forested mountains.

A 5km-long natural barrier pebble beach – always piled high with driftwood – almost closes off the harbour entrance, especially when the tide is out. Grey seals

THE MYSTERY SHIP

When the first vessel was built at Spencer's Island, few would have believed that 150 years later, she would still fascinate the world at large. Around 1860, Joshua Dewis built a brigantine designed to carry lumber as her main cargo, and named her *Amazon*.

On her maiden voyage, the captain died of a heart attack within 24 hours of setting sail. Other bumps and tangles included the *Amazon* grounding in the English Channel. After suffering severe damage in a storm off the coast of Cape Breton Island, she was sent to a New York marine scrapyard. Sold at auction and made seaworthy again, she was relaunched and renamed *Mary Celeste*. On 5 November 1872, she departed New York, bound for Genoa, Italy, with a hold full of alcohol. On board were a well-respected captain, his wife and two-year-old daughter, and a crew of seven.

A month later, she was spotted by another ship's crew floating aimlessly near the Azores. Their calls unanswered, they boarded the silent vessel finding it fully provisioned with the sails set and nothing out of place. There were hints that those on board had left in a hurry – the single lifeboat was gone, the child's toys strewn on deck. None of those who had been on board the *Mary Celeste* were ever seen again.

A board of inquiry concluded that piracy or foul play was unlikely, and, while her true fate will never be known, theories abound as to why the captain and crew abandoned ship. The most plausible of these suggests that, although very experienced, the captain had never carried crude alcohol on any of his ships. When the alcohol casks began to leak, he may have feared that the vapour might ignite and explode, and may have ordered a hasty evacuation. Their lifeboat could have drifted for days before perhaps being capsized by a big wave and sending its passengers to a watery grave.

After the inquiry she continued sailing for years, but, beset by more troubles, was sold and resold 17 times. In 1884, the *Mary Celeste* was finally scuttled off Haiti for insurance reasons and rediscovered by a team of Canadian divers in 2001.

During the late 1800s, crewless ships left to founder were not unheard of, and rarely attracted media attention. But in 1884, a budding writer penned a short story closely based on the *Mary Celeste* mystery. The author – who changed the name of the ship to the *Marie Celeste*, and added a few other bits of fiction – was Arthur Conan Doyle.

are sometimes seen (their rookery is 20km out to sea, on Isle Haute). The easiest beach access is from West Advocate. Dykes built centuries ago by the Acadians to reclaim farmland from the sea are still visible, and make for pleasant walks. The sunsets are magnificent.

Previously known only to nature lovers, sea kayakers and those looking for unusual accommodation, **Advocate Harbour** has a new attraction that is wowing gastronomes from near and far – one of the top two (with Charlotte Lane; see page 174) 'rural' restaurants in the province.

At East Advocate, signs lead you towards Cape d'Or. The road soon becomes unpaved. One Samuel de Champlain named the cape in 1604, but the metal he saw glittering in the sunlight wasn't gold – it was copper. At **Horseshoe Cove**, located down a left turn about 4.5km after the crest of the hill, a copper-mining community thrived during the late 19th century, and to this day pure copper nuggets are sometimes found on the beach, as too are agates and other semi-precious stones.

Cape d'Or provides the only opportunity in Nova Scotia to stay in a lightkeeper's cottage. The c1965 **Cape d'Or Lighthouse**, manned until 1989, is now automated, but the cottages – built late in the 1950s – now house an excellent restaurant and a guesthouse. The lighthouse and foghorn warn those at sea of the **Dory Rips**, or riptides: three separate tides converge, resulting in incredibly treacherous, turbulent waters. If the mist starts to roll in during your visit, prepare yourself: the modern-day foghorn – which sounds every 60 seconds – will make you jump.

The main unpaved road continues to a car park with interpretive boards and a replica lighthouse. Trails lead along the cliffs to spectacular viewpoints, or down to the (real) lighthouse. Going down is fine but not everyone enjoys the steep, steady 1km trek back up.

Both Cape d'Or and Advocate Harbour can be reached **by car**. Cape d'Or is off Highway 209, 44km/27 miles from Parrsboro and 59km/37 miles from Joggins. Advocate Harbour is on Highway 209, approximately 2km from the Cape d'Or turn-off at East Advocate.

WHERE TO STAY AND EAT

Driftwood Park Retreat (5 units) 49 Driftwood Lane, Advocate Harbour; 392 2008, **t/f** 1 866 810 0110; www.driftwoodparkretreat.com; Apr–Oct. Choose from 4, 2-bedroom chalets & a 1-bedroom chalet with loft. All are fully equipped, comfortable & very close to the seafront. A great get-away-from-it-all spot within a couple of kilometres of the entrance to the provincial park. **$$**

Lightkeeper's Kitchen & Guest House (4 rooms) Cape d'Or; 670 0534; www.capedor.ca; May–mid Oct. This former lighthouse provides the only opportunity to stay in a lightkeeper's cottage in Nova Scotia. It has a spectacular setting with the pounding tides on one side & basalt cliffs behind. Rooms are with en-suite, private or shared bathroom & there are fabulous views & a common room. Note that the lighthouse's foghorn is an important navigation aid: if the fog rolls in, the horn is called into action – regardless of whether or not guests might be sleeping. The attached licensed restaurant (*May–mid Oct for lunch & dinner Thu–Tue;* **$$**) has similar panoramas. Reservations are recommended & payment accepted only in cash. Light lunches (eg: salads, sandwiches, fishcakes, seafood chowder) & imaginative evening meals are served, using fresh local ingredients where possible. The guesthouse & restaurant are a few mins' walk downhill from the car park. Make the effort – it's worth it! **$**

Reid's Tourist Home (4 units) 1391 West Advocate Rd, West Advocate; 392 2592; http://reidstouristhome.ca; Jun–late Sep. 3 motel-style guest rooms & 1, 2-bedroom cottage on a working cattle farm. **$**

Wild Caraway Restaurant & Café 3721 Hwy 209, Advocate Harbour; 392 2889; www.wildcaraway.com; summer 11.00–21.00 Mon & Wed–Sat, 09.00–21.00 Sun; check off-season hours. Although only open since May 2009, word of Andrew Aitken & Sarah Griebel's restaurant has spread like wildfire. The cuisine focuses on locally sourced products: the eponymous wild caraway, for example, seeds from which are used in a Caesar salad dressing, grows just outside the building. *Ceviche* is made with locally caught flounder. Décor is contemporary, the service very professional, & the wonderful food is matched by the wine list. The lovely views are a bonus. A real foodie's delight. **$$**

OTHER PRACTICALITIES

Library Advocate Harbour Library, 93 Mills Rd; 392 2214; 10.00–12.00 & 13.00–16.00 Wed & Fri, 14.00–18.00 Thu, 09.00–13.00 Sat

Post office 3727 Hwy 209; 08.30–15.30 Mon–Fri, 09.00–13.00 Sat

What to see and do An Advocate Harbour-based sea kayaking operator, **NovaShores Adventures** (*392 2761,* **t/f** *1 866 638 4118; www.novashores.com*)

offers tours from two hours to multi-days. It's a great way to explore the region's natural splendour – such as the Three Sisters, one of the province's most iconic rock formations – and it's highly recommended. Prices start from CAN$55.

CAPE CHIGNECTO PROVINCIAL PARK

Covering 4,200ha, Cape Chignecto Provincial Park (*West Advocate Rd; 392 2085; www.capechignecto.net, www.novascotiaparks.ca/parks/capechignecto.asp; mid May–early Oct; admission CAN$5.10 day pass*) is Nova Scotia's largest provincial park and should not be missed by lovers of the wild outdoors. It is located on an arrow-shaped headland pointing into the Bay of Fundy, flanked by Chignecto Bay and the Minas Basin. Although encompassing 29km of pristine coastline, much of the park sits high above the huge tides, with some cliffs reaching 185m. In the water below, nature has created a range of natural sculptures, such as the Three Sisters, huge misshapen sea stacks.

The park has no roads, and to stay within its boundaries you'll have to camp. Partly for these reasons – and the somewhat 'out-of-the-way' location – Cape Chignecto has been something of a hidden gem. But the secret has begun to get out and the opening of a second entrance and day-use area in 2009 brought more publicity.

Ten **marked trails** give access to the natural highlights. These range from quick jaunts to the beach from the Red Rocks visitor centre, or the Three Sisters lookout from Eatonville Beach visitor centre to challenging all-day hikes which should only be attempted by experienced hikers, such as the spectacular Red Rocks visitor centre–Refugee Cove trail. The big one is a multi-day circuit of the Cape (see box, opposite). The longer hikes are all likely to involve climbing steep slopes and following vertiginous cliffside paths. The wonderful nature, magnificent scenery and spectacular views are a just reward.

Expect to see yellow birch, American beech, Eastern hemlock, balsam fir, sugar maple and white and red spruce. For much of the summer, you'll also see wild flowers. Whilst the peninsula is home to bobcats, moose and black bear, these are very rarely encountered. Far more common are whitetail deer, rabbit and hare. Grey seals can often be seen in late summer, basking on rocks in the coves.

Hiking apart, the park's stunning shoreline, secluded coves and beaches are a wonderful area for **sea kayaking** (see NovaShores Adventures, opposite).

There are two entrances to the park: the long-established entrance very close to Advocate Harbour, and the newer entrance at Eatonville, accessed via the West Apple River Road. Near both entrances are visitor centres and picnic tables.

Access to the park **by car** is via Red Rocks Road from the village of West Advocate on Highway 209, 46km/29 miles from Parrsboro, or by West Apple River Road 13km/8 miles further northwest along Highway 209.

CAPE CIRCUIT

The 49km circumnavigation of Cape Chignecto is one of Nova Scotia's – and eastern North America's – great coastal hikes. Although it can be hiked in two to three days, this is not a hike to be rushed. Accommodation is a choice of remote hike-in campsites, and two wilderness cabins near Arch Gulch and Eatonville: reservations are required. Sections of the trail are strenuous with steep ascents and descents. This is a fantastic trail, but should only be attempted by self-sufficient, experienced hikers – who have a good head for heights.

WHERE TO STAY The park has 31 well-spread walk-in **campsites** between 75m and 300m from the car park, and almost 60 beautifully located back-country hike-in sites, but no drive-up camping. There are also a couple of wilderness cabins. Reservations (**t/f** *1 888 544 3434*) are required for hike-in campsites and cabins, and recommended for walk-in campsites.

JOGGINS

Although noted for its coal mining – there are records of coal from Joggins being sold in Boston as early as 1720 – what gives Joggins a prominent position on the 21st-century map goes back much further.

At the head of the bay, Joggins's 15- to 30m-high sea cliffs stretch for 15km and – twice daily – feel the force of the Bay of Fundy's huge tides. Over time this has eroded the cliff face to reveal thousands of fossils. The exposed alternating grey and reddish-brown cliff faces date from the Carboniferous period.

These fossil cliffs were first brought to public attention in 1852 when geologists found tiny fossilised bones of *Hylonomous lyelli*, one of the world's first reptiles. This was the first evidence that land animals had lived during the Coal Age.

Since then, the cliffs – labelled the 'Coal Age Galapagos' – have revealed a wealth of other important discoveries and are recognised as a world-class palaeontology site, with many experts believing that they preserve the most complete record of life in the Pennsylvanian Period (341 to 289 million years ago) anywhere in the world. This was declared a UNESCO World Heritage Site in the summer of 2008.

Although you can access the beach below the cliffs from several points, you will gain far more from your experience if you precede your exploration with a visit to the Joggins Fossil Centre (see opposite).

You can wander the rock strewn beach at the cliff base and search for fossils which have fallen from the cliff face, but can't take any fossils away with you without a permit (see page 36). The cliff site has picnic tables and interpretive signage. Most of the rocks on the beach have fallen from the cliff face, so proceed with caution – and pay attention to the tides, which come in very quickly.

Visitor services are limited in Joggins – but at least the Fossil Centre (see opposite) has a café! It also has a **tourist information centre**.

To get there **by car**, Joggins is on Highway 242, 55km/34 miles from Advocate Harbour, 35km/22 miles from Amherst and 45km/28 miles from Parsborro.

WHERE TO EAT

Roundhouse Café Joggins Fossil Centre (see opposite); ⌚ May–Sep 10.00–16.00 daily. Fair-trade, organic coffee & tea, wholesome, homemade salads, sandwiches, cakes & cookies. $

TINY TOES

In September 2012, Gloria Melanson was walking along Joggins Beach when something caught her eye. Across the corner of a piece of rock (which measured about 10cm by 10cm) were tiny tracks. It transpired that Gloria had found the world's smallest known fossil vertebrate footprints, tiny tracks left by a fossil specimen of the ichnogenus *Batrachichnus salamandroides* approximately 315 million years ago. Gloria must have good eyes: the salamander-like creature which left the tracks was probably only about 8mm from snout to tail, and the whole trackway measures less than 5cm.

WHAT TO SEE AND DO The exhibits at the c2008 purpose-built and environmentally friendly **Joggins Fossil Centre** (*100 Main St; 251 2727, t/f 1 888 932 9766; www.jogginsfossilcliffs.net; late Apr/May & Sep/Oct 10.00–16.00 daily; Jun–Aug 09.30–17.30 daily; off-season by appointment; admission CAN$10.50 inc 30-min beach tour, or CAN$25 inc 90- to 120-min guided tour*) include interpretive displays of 300 million-year-old fossils – including insects, amphibians, plants and trees. Guided tours of Joggins Fossil Cliffs can be booked through the centre (phone or see website for schedule), and it also contains the tourist information centre, a gift shop and a café.

SPRINGHILL

Not the prettiest of towns in the province, Springhill is a coal-mining town. The mines – which brought happiness, prosperity and tragedy – are long closed, but still benefit the community. Since they were shut down, the shafts filled with water that has been heated by the surrounding earth to an average temperature of 18°C. Recently, technology has allowed businesses in Springhill's industrial park to use the heated water to reduce their winter heating bills substantially. There are plans to include a geothermal display at the Miners' Museum (see below). The town is home to the province's largest 'correctional facility'. Other than visiting inmates, there are two contrasting attractions (see below).

Springhill is accessible **by car**, on Highway 2, 7km from Exit 5 of the Trans Canada Highway (Highway 104), 25km/16 miles from Amherst and 50km/31 miles from Parrsboro.

WHERE TO EAT It's fair to say that Springhill doesn't have a reputation as a gourmet's paradise. There's a Tim Horton's and a Pizza Delight on Main Street, or mix with the locals and down a beer or two as you nosh on standard diner fare just north of the town centre at the **Lamp Cabin** (*141 Junction Rd; 597 8539; call for hours; $–$$*).

FESTIVALS The **Irish Festival** is a celebration of Irish music, with food, dancing and a street parade, held over three days in June.

OTHER PRACTICALITIES

$ Bank CIBC, 41 Main St; 597 3741; 10.00–17.00 Mon–Fri
Hospital All Saints Springhill Hospital, 10 Princess St; 597 3773
Library Springhill Library, 75 Main St; 597 2211; 12.00–18.00 Tue & Fri, 10.00–17.00 Wed/Thu
Post office 68 Main St; 08.30–17.00 Mon–Fri
Tourist information Anne Murray Centre, 36 Main St; Jul/Aug 09.00–17.00 daily

WHAT TO SEE AND DO Two years after the Syndicate Mine closed in 1970, the **Springhill Miners' Museum** (*145 Black River Rd; 597 3449; mid May–mid Oct 09.00–17.00 daily; admission CAN$6, tours CAN$3*) opened on the site. Mining artefacts, the miners' washhouse and their lamp cabin are quite interesting but the highlight is the mine tour: don overalls, hard hats and rubber boots and descend 100m underground (most guides are former coal miners). There's even a chance to dig out some coal to take back with you. Note that the tour is not for the claustrophobic or those not keen on the dark.

THE PRICE OF COAL

In 1891, an underground mine explosion claimed 125 lives, including over a dozen boys. In 1956, several railcars broke loose from a mine train and rolled backwards down into the mine, derailing and then hitting a power line. The resulting blast killed 39 miners. Rescuers with no breathing equipment were able to rescue 88 survivors.

Less than two years later, an underground earthquake (or 'bump') occurred in a mine, killing many miners instantly and trapping numerous others underground with no food and water and a dwindling air supply. Mine officials, workers, volunteers and local doctors risked their lives and rescued 104 trapped miners: 74 others were not so lucky. The dead are remembered in the Miners' Memorial Park on Main Street.

Incidentally, the disaster had been predicted by Mother Coo, a fortune teller from Pictou, who also gave advance notice of other mining tragedies including the disasters at Westville's Drummond Mine (59 dead) and Stellarton's Foord Pit (50 dead) in 1873 and 1880 respectively.

Rather than being seen as a human early-warning system, Mother Coo was regarded as a pariah and driven from the area.

Anne Murray was born in Springhill in 1945. Some 25 years later, she released a song called 'Snowbird' and this went on to become one of North America's most played songs of 1970. Over the years, she has racked up more gold and platinum albums, Grammy awards and country music awards than any other Canadian and sold more than 55 million albums. Exhibits at the **Anne Murray Centre** (*36 Main St; ☎ 597 8614; www.annemurraycentre.com; ⌚ mid May–mid Oct 09.00–17.00 daily; admission CAN$6*) range from a lock of hair from her first haircut to glittering stage costumes and her plentiful gold/platinum albums. Buy Murray-memorabilia in the gift shop, or record a duet with Anne in the centre's mini recording studio. All together now, 'Spread your tiny wings and fly away …'

BASS RIVER CHAIRS

Extra space in your luggage? Search antique shops for a real Nova Scotian heritage souvenir.

In 1860, the Fulton brothers built a sawmill near the Bass River mouth (close to Great Village – see page 256) and began making furniture. From 1885, they concentrated solely on chairs, and in 1903, the operation became the Dominion Chair Company.

What had become known as 'Bass River chairs' (though the name was never registered) are renowned throughout the province and further afield for their distinctive style and quality. Chair manufacture in Bass River ceased in 1989 when the factory burnt down.

7

Northumberland Shore

Mainland Nova Scotia's north shore fronts the Northumberland Strait and stretches from the provincial border with New Brunswick to the west, to Aulds Cove, from where the Canso Causeway leads to Cape Breton Island to the east. The shortest and quickest way to get between the two points is on Highway 104, the Trans Canada Highway (TCH), a drive of 265km. However, Highway 104 runs well inland, and just about everything of interest in the region is away from the motorway, on or within a few kilometres of the waterfront. So once again it is best not to rush things, but to take the smaller, quieter, far more scenic roads through quaint communities such as Pugwash, Oxford and Tatamagouche.

Paddle the coastal inlets in a sea kayak, enjoy a scenic round of golf, or hike beautiful trails high above Antigonish Harbour. Or go for a dip: this region of rolling hills and pastoral landscapes is renowned for its beaches, most of which are within provincial parks, and summer swimming is a pleasure – the slogan 'warmest water north of the Carolinas' is oft heard. The average sea temperature between July and late September is over 22°C. To the west, the tide recedes from the red sand beaches to expose vast mud flats: further to the east the stretches of sand at Melmerby and Pomquet beaches are not to be missed.

Scottish Heritage is a big draw for many – from 1773, Pictou was the gateway to Nova Scotia for thousands of Scottish Highlanders, and their history and culture lives on through much of the region.

Those who enjoy things urban should like the pleasant towns of Amherst, Pictou and Antigonish (home to the St Francis Xavier University) but as Amherst, the biggest of the three, has a population of just under 10,000, we're not talking about vast built-up sprawl. Stellarton's vast and impressive Museum of Industry is an ideal rainy-day choice (see page 293).

AMHERST *(Population: 9,700)*

On higher ground than the surrounding marshland and overlooking the Bay of Fundy, Amherst is the land gateway between Nova Scotia and all points west, and the largest town in Cumberland County. The historic downtown – with many magnificent well-preserved sandstone buildings and beautiful old homes on Victoria Street East – is relaxing and pleasing on the eye. Large, colourful murals bring the community's heritage to life, and more continue to be added. One of the most impressive is the **Signature Mural** on the corner of Havelock Street and Victoria Street East, depicting the downtown area during a big parade in 1910.

The c1935 Greek-temple style **Dominion Building** at 98 Victoria Street East has had different lives: originally used as a post office, and recently home (for 15

THE COMMUNIST CONNECTION

In 1916, socialist Leon Trotsky was deported to the US. The following year, when revolution overthrew Tsar Nicholas II, the door was open for him to return to Russia, and he departed New York on the SS *Kristianiafjord*. The ship docked in Halifax, where Canadian and British naval personnel arrested Trotsky, and took his wife and young sons into custody. After a short time at the Citadel in Halifax, Trotsky was transferred to an internment camp in Amherst, which contained around 800 German prisoners, many of them sailors from submarines, where he stayed for almost a month. He aired his political views to the inmates at every opportunity, and it is said that when he left, it was to the sound of the international Socialism anthem *Internationale* being sung by cheering German prisoners. The Trotsky family left Nova Scotia from Halifax a few days later, *en route* to Copenhagen.

years) to the Tantramar Theatre Society. There are no more live performances now, though: in 2012 the thespians were turfed out and municipal officials moved in.

Recently (work was completed in summer 2012), the centre of town was given a sprucing-up (roads and pavements re-paved, etc), and it is looking all the better for it.

HISTORY The town of Amherst was founded in 1764 near the site of a British fort destroyed in 1755. It was named for General Jeffrey Amherst, one of the leaders in the victory over the French at Louisbourg in 1758. Many of the early settlers originated in Yorkshire, England.

Centrally located on the only land route between Nova Scotia and the 'mainland', Amherst prospered between the mid 1800s and the early 20th century. The town became renowned for its diverse and active economy, including mining and manufacturing, and was labelled 'Busy Amherst'. Textiles, footwear and even

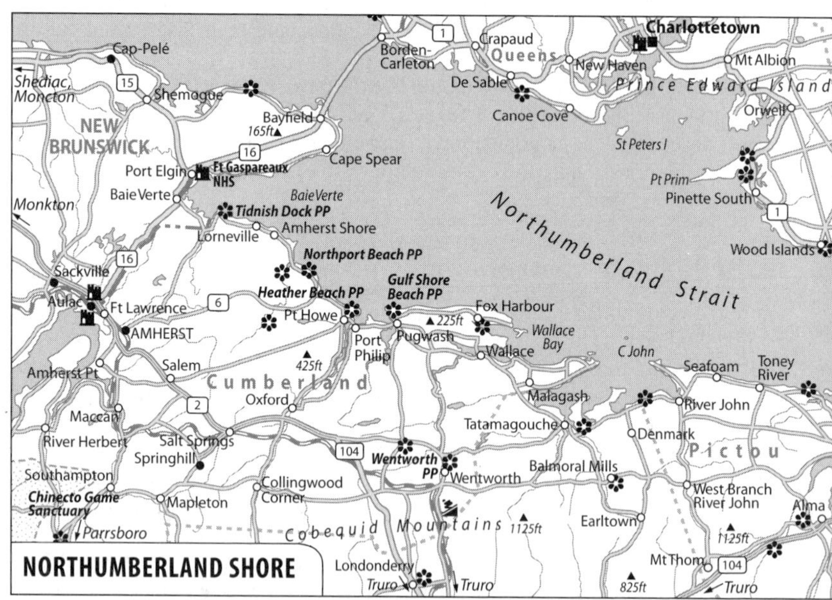

pianos were just some of the items produced here, and in 1908, no other town in the Maritimes had a higher industrial manufacturing output. It was during this period that many of the town's largest and most impressive buildings and homes – many of which still stand – were built.

GETTING THERE AND AROUND Amherst is just off Highway 104 (TCH), via Exits 2–4, and therefore very convenient to reach **by car**. It is 4km/2 miles from the New Brunswick border, 117km/73 miles from Truro, 207km/129 miles from Halifax, 183km/114 miles from Pictou and 231km/144 miles from Antigonish. Amherst is on the Maritime Bus **coach** (see *Chapter 2*, page 44) line between Moncton (New Brunswick) and Halifax: there is also a service to Charlottetown, Prince Edward Island. Amherst is also accessible **by train**, being on the VIA Rail line (see page 44) between Montreal and Halifax. Three days a week, one train a day in each direction stops *en route* at Amherst's impressive century-old sandstone station at Station Street.

Taxis are available from **D&J Taxi** (*667 8288*) and **M&J Taxi** (*661 2560*).

WHERE TO STAY Rather than overnight in Amherst, some people prefer to stay in Lorneville on the Northumberland Strait shore, where you can also camp at the Amherst Shore Provincial Park (see *Around Amherst*, page 276).

Amherst

Amherst 8 Motel (50 rooms) 40 Lord Amherst Dr; **t/f** 1 877 503 7666; www.super8amherst.com; year-round. A 2-storey c2005 motel with indoor pool lacking in character, but with decent rooms which have microwaves, mini fridges & coffee makers. Continental b/fast inc. **$$**

Regent B&B (4 rooms) 175 Victoria St East; 667 7676, **t/f** 1 866 661 2861; www.theregent.ca; year-round (Mar by reservation only). A lovely Georgian house with stained & leaded glass windows & hand-carved woodwork & sun deck in garden. Formal full b/fast served on fine china inc. **$$**

Brown's Guest Home B&B (3 rooms) 158 Victoria St East; 667 9769; **e** dnallen@eastlink.ca; www.brownsguesthome.ca; May–Oct. A c1904 house very close to the town centre with

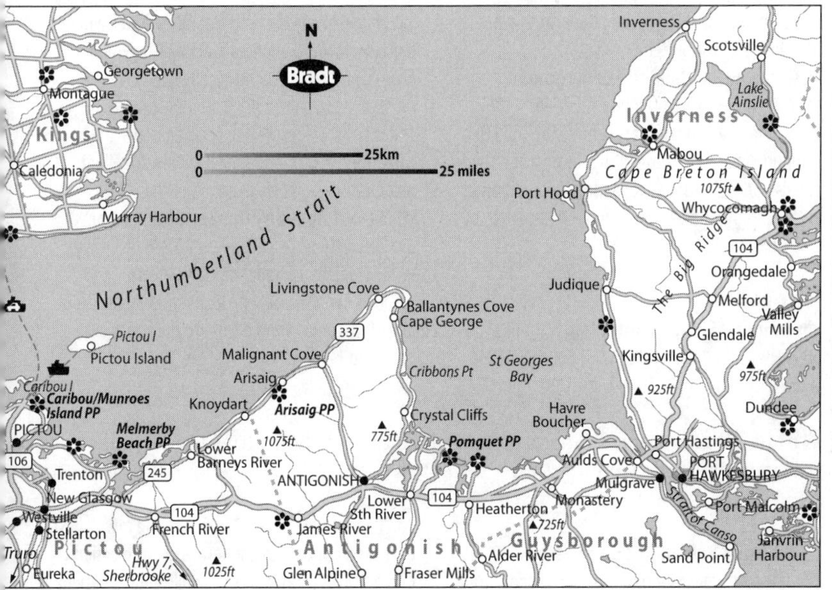

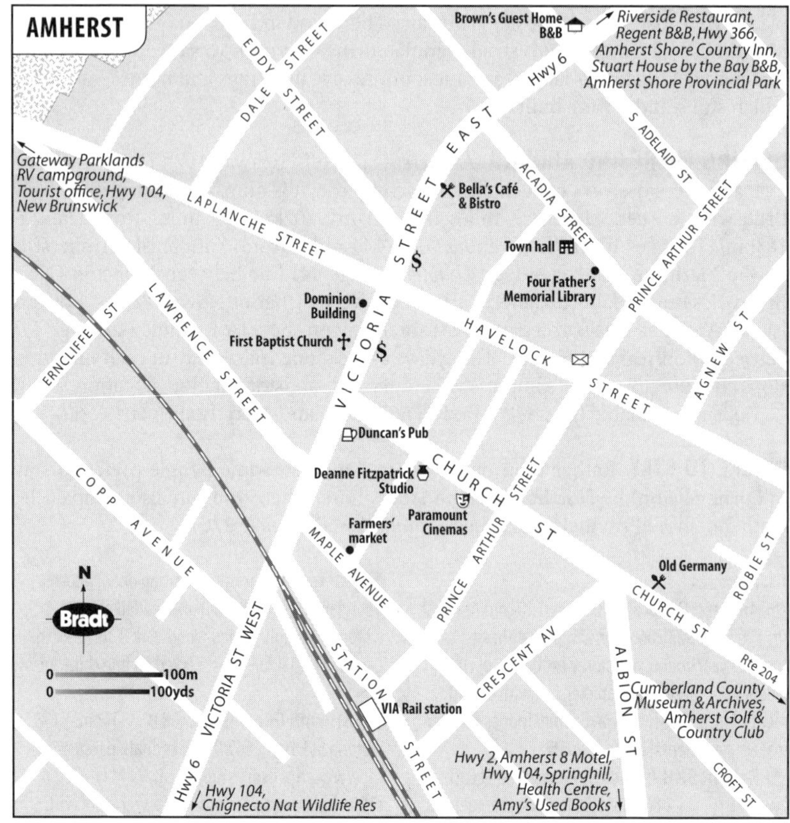

shared bathrooms. Included in the price is a 'no fried foods' b/fast buffet. $

Gateway Parklands RV Campground (127 sites) 1434 Fort Lawrence Rd; 667 1106; www.gatewayparkland.ca; mid May–mid Oct. Although geared to those with motorhomes, there are also open & wooded tent sites & a laundromat at this campground approx 5km from Amherst, by Exit 1 of Hwy 104. $

Lorneville

Amherst Shore Country Inn (11 units) 5091 Hwy 366; 661 4800, **t/f** 1 800 661 2724; www.ascinn.ns.ca; May–Oct & Dec–Apr Fri/Sat only. A lovely inn on 8 seaside hectares with gardens, lawns & a long private beach owned & run by members of the Laceby family (see *Blomidon Inn*, page 231) & offering 2 rooms, 6 suites & 3 cottages. Various packages available combining accommodation & dining. Excellent restaurant (see *Where to eat*, opposite). $$

Stuart House by the Bay B&B (3 rooms) 5472 Hwy 366; 661 0750, **t/f** 1 888 661 0750; www.stuarthousebedandbreakfast.com; Jun–Aug (May & Sep/Oct by reservation). This late 19th-century home close to the beach is a good choice. Good full b/fast inc. $

WHERE TO EAT

For a dining treat, it is worth the half-hour drive to Lorneville and the Amherst Shore Country Inn.

Amherst

Duncan's Pub 49 Victoria St West; 660 3111; www.duncanspub.ca; year-round 11.00–23.00 Mon–Sat, 12.00–22.00 Sun. The town's best pub has a relaxed atmosphere, a good selection of drinks (inc cocktails) & good live entertainment

THE AMHERST MYSTERY

Amherst made the front pages late in the 19th century when an 18-year-old local girl, Esther Cox, began experiencing strange poltergeist-like phenomena: little fires, voices, and rapping noises.

Doctors called to treat her also noted bizarre happenings: inexplicable movements under the bedclothes, inanimate objects moving about the room, and sudden banging noises.

The disturbing happenings continued unabated, and when a neighbour's barn (where Esther had been working) was destroyed by a mysterious fire, she was arrested, charged and convicted of arson. She spent a month in jail but during her trial met a man with whom she became smitten.

On her release, her fiancé took her to a Mi'kmaq medicine man who performed a type of exorcism on her. The happy couple moved to Massachusetts and she was troubled no more by evil spirits.

In 1888, a best-selling book was written about Esther's experiences. Her house on the town's Princess Street is long gone, but *The Great Amherst Mystery* lives on.

Thu/Fri evenings. The food's good, too: scallop-stuffed mushroom caps & seafood chowder stand out – & that's just for starters. Save room for the cheesecake or *tiramisu*. Book in advance if you're dining. $$

Old Germany 80 Church St; 667 2868; Feb–Dec 11.00–20.30 Wed–Sun. Homely décor & hearty food: think Goulash (& other) soup(s), *Wiener schnitzel* & German sausages – a little bit of Deutschland in Amherst. Try the *sauerbraten* (spiced, marinated roast beef) with red cabbage & potato dumplings washed down with a glass of cherry schnapps. $$

Bella's Café & Bistro 117 Victoria St East; 660 3090; year-round 09.00–18.00 Mon–Wed, 09.00–20.00 Thu–Sat. A popular, sometimes busy, spot offering tasty snacks & light meals. Good bistro-style food (eg: crabcakes with Creole tartar sauce) in the evening. Art on display. $–$$

Lorneville and *en route*

Amherst Shore Country Inn (see opposite) for dinner May–Oct daily; Dec–Apr Fri/Sat only (reservation only), dinner (set meal CAN$45) served at 19.30. Has wonderful sea views. The fixed-price menu comprises a soup, a salad, a choice of 2 entrées & choice of 2 desserts. Dinner at the inn has long been considered one of the province's gastronomic treats.

Riverside Restaurant 3636 Hwy 366, Tidnish Bridge; 661 2521; end May–Aug 11.00–19.00 daily. Good diner-style fare. Fish & chips, pan-fried haddock, club sandwiches, etc. 24km from Amherst *en route* to Lorneville. $–$$

ENTERTAINMENT

Paramount Cinemas 47 Church St; 667 7791; www.empiretheatres.com

FESTIVALS In October, the **Nova Scotia Fibre Arts Festival** (*www.fibreartsfestival.ca*) is a five-day event celebrating rug hooking, knitting, quilting, sewing and more.

OTHER PRACTICALITIES In the main, the many practicalities (services, department stores, supermarkets and shopping malls) are out of the centre along uninspiring South Albion Street.

$ Banks Royal Bank, 103 Victoria St East; 667 7275; 10.00–17.00 Mon–Fri. Scotiabank, 79 Victoria St East; 667 3328; 10.00–17.00 Mon–Fri

Health centre Cumberland Regional Health Care Centre, 19428 Hwy 2; 667 3361. Just outside town in Upper Nappan.

Library Four Fathers Memorial Library, 21 Acadia St; 667 2549; 10.00–17.00 Mon & Thu/Fri, 10.00–20.00 Tue/Wed, 10.00–13.00 Sat

Post office 38 Havelock St; 08.30–17.00 Mon–Fri

Tourist information Provincial Welcome Centre; Exit 1, Hwy 104 (TCH); 667 8429; mid Oct–Apr 09.00–16.30 daily; May–mid Oct 08.30–17.00 daily (or later, eg: 21.00 in Jul/Aug)

WHAT TO SEE AND DO For a huge selection with a particularly good maritime history section, stop by **Amy's Used Books** (*51 South Albion St; 667 7927; year-round 10.00–18.00 Mon–Thu, 10.00–21.00 Fri, 10.00–17.00 Sat*).Those interested in rug hooking shouldn't miss the **Deanne Fitzpatrick Studio** (*33 Church St; 667 0560; www.hookingrugs.com; 09.00–16.00 Mon–Fri, 10.00–15.00 Sat*) – Deanne may well be the best contemporary exponent of the genre in the province.

South of Amherst's main historic district, the **Cumberland County Museum and Archives** (*150 Church St; 667 2561; www.cumberlandcountymuseum.com; Feb–mid Dec 09.00–17.00 Tue–Fri, 12.00–17.00 Sat; admission CAN$3*) is housed in the c1838 Grove Cottage, home of Father of Confederation (see box, page 201) Robert B Dickey. See articles and documents relating to Trotsky's time in Amherst (see box, page 272), a player piano, a wonderful Victorian c1870 staircase and art gallery, plus beautiful gardens. It also has a well-stocked research library and archives.

The red sandstone **First Baptist Church** (*66 Victoria St East; 667 2001; 09.00–16.00 daily*), built in Queen Anne Revival style in 1846, is worth a visit.

Grab some fresh produce at the local **farmers' market** (*Maple Av & Electric St; May–Dec 10.00–14.00 Fri*).

Around Amherst Spend a night at the woodland campground in **Amherst Shore Provincial Park** (*42 sites; Hwy 366; mid Jun–early Oct*), close to a lovely beach (see box opposite) or go green at **Amherst Golf and Country Club** (*John Black Rd;*

TRAINS AND BOATS

Ships travelling between the Gulf of St Lawrence and New England had to make a long and arduous journey around Nova Scotia. To save well over 1,000km of sailing, the construction of a canal across the 27km Isthmus of Chignecto (which separates the Northumberland Strait from the Bay of Fundy) had long been suggested. In 1881, Henry Ketchum, a Scottish-born engineer, proposed the Chignecto Marine Transport Railway. His plan was for hydraulic lifts to be built to raise ships onto 'cradles' which would then be pulled by locomotives along a special railway track. The line was to run between Fort Lawrence on the Bay of Fundy coast and Tidnish Dock on the Northumberland Strait. After years of negotiations and feasibility studies, Canada's federal government agreed to subsidise the railway's construction in 1888 – subject to the railway's completion within an agreed timescale.

The timescale was too tight, especially considering the marshy nature of much of the land, and in 1892, when the line wasn't completed by the deadline agreed, the government withdrew its financial support.

At Tidnish Dock Provincial Park (*Hwy 366*) a few remains can still be seen, such as the railbed, a stone culvert over the Tidnish River, and remnants of the dock. The park, 25km from Amherst, has interpretive panels and a short walking trail alongside the old rail track.

BESIDE THE SEASIDE

Along Highway 366, three provincial parks – Amherst Shore, Northport Beach and Heather Beach – offer beach access and more. The beaches are visually striking, with lush green vegetation contrasting with both the red sandstone cliffs (over 10m high in many places) and the blue of the sea. At low tide, the tidal flats often extend well over 1km. The park at Amherst Shore, 36km from Amherst and 27km from Pugwash, has a campground (see opposite) and walking trails: at Northport Beach, 42km from Amherst and 21km from Pugwash, sandbars keep the sea shallow and the water even warmer, whilst Heather Beach, 50km from Amherst and 14km from Pugwash, is usually the busiest of the three.

667 1911; www.amherstgolfclub.com; Jun–late Oct), a 6,347yd course to the east of town, with lush fairways, fast greens – and, more often than not, strong winds to contend with. Green fees are CAN$48.

The 1,670ha **Chignecto National Wildlife Reserve** (*Southampton Rd; year-round 24hrs; admission free*) encompasses the Amherst Point Migratory Bird Sanctuary and is best known for its variety of waterfowl, both breeding and migratory; the wetlands are among the best waterfowl-breeding grounds in the province. Some 8km of trails wind through a diverse landscape of woodlands, fields, ponds and marshes, offering several bird-viewing sites. To get there follow Victoria Street West to the southwest, cross Highway 104, then continue for 3km.

OXFORD

The Oxford region produces over half of the country's total blueberry harvest each year, earning the town the title of 'Wild Blueberry Capital of Canada'. Approach from Highway 104 and you'll be greeted by a giant smiling blueberry. The town is also a centre for products made from the sap of the region's thousands of maple trees. Oxford's rivers are popular with anglers trying for salmon and trout, and for those with canoes. The surrounding forests are home to abundant wildlife – this attracts hunters in the autumn, so wear something bright if you're out leaf-peeping.

Situated 1.5km off Highway 104 Exit 6, Oxford is easy to get to **by car**. If you're approaching from Highway 6, take Highway 301 south for 16km/10 miles from Port Howe. The road follows the wooded banks of the river Philip and passes through verdant farmland for 16km/10 miles to Oxford. To return to Highway 6, cross the river and follow Highway 321 north. This circuit is beautiful when the autumn colours are blazing.

Oxford is on the Maritime Bus **coach** line between Amherst and Halifax (see *Chapter 2*, page 44).

The **Capitol Theatre** (*5220 Main St; 447 2068; www.town.oxford.ns.ca/visit/*) is a c1923 Art Deco-style 163-seat theatre, which hosts films, music jam sessions, etc.

WHERE TO STAY AND EAT

Blueberry In (4 rooms) 5148 Main St; 447 2760; www.blueberryin.com; year-round. Guest rooms have hardwood floors & tiled en-suite bathrooms. Antique furnishings, library. Rate inc full b/fast. **$**

Parkview Family Restaurant 4670 Main St; 447 2258; year-round 07.00–19.30 Mon–Fri, 08.00–19.30 Sat/Sun. Old-fashioned motel restaurant dishing up generous portions of diner food, such as liver & onions or fish & chips. **$**

FESTIVALS The **Cumberland County Exhibition and Blueberry Festival** (*www.cumberlandcountyexhibition.canadianwebs.com*) is a six-day agricultural festival held at the end of August–early September, which includes dances, concerts, kids' events and craft displays.

OTHER PRACTICALITIES

Post office 5152 Main St; 08.00–17.15 Mon–Fri, 08.00–12.00 Sat

Tourist information 105 Lower Main St; 447 2908; www.town.oxford.ns.ca; May/Jun & Sep/Oct 09.00–16.30 Mon–Fri; Jul/Aug 09.00–16.30 daily. Housed in a former bank.

PUGWASH

This quaint community is located on a pretty harbour at the mouth of the Pugwash River. Across the river from downtown, Pugwash's **salt mine** isn't easy to miss. Each year, the mine produces over one million tonnes of salt. No tours are offered, but you can watch vast quantities of sodium chloride being loaded onto cargo ships. Whilst this operation spoils an otherwise idyllic riverside, it brings a much-needed boost to the local economy. Having said that, summer 2012 brought news of dozens of job cuts as the mine's US owners decide whether or not to keep it open.

Scottish heritage is strong, here, and street signs are in both Gaelic and English. Durham Street, part of Highway 311, is the main street: the waterfront walkway in Eaton Park makes for a pleasant wander. Pugwash is on Highway 6, 50km/31 miles east of Amherst and 37km/23 miles west of Tatamagouche, convenient **by car**.

WHERE TO STAY AND EAT

Hillcrest View Inn (8 units) 11054 Hwy 6; 243 2727; www.hillcrestview.ca; year-round. The Hillcrest has had a makeover & has 6 motel-style rooms, a suite & a 2-bedroom cottage. Food in the on-site restaurant (*Jun–Sep 11.00–20.00 Mon–Fri, 08.00–20.00 Sat/Sun; $$*) is a cut above the usual motel dining options, & focuses on fresh, local produce. Dessert fans should try the 'raspberry chocolate brownie overload'. **$$**

Inn the Elms (4 rooms) 10340 Durham St; 243 2885; www.intheelms.com; year-round. Furnished with antiques, this lovely old house has 3 rooms with en-suite bathroom, & 1 with a shared bathroom. The new (2012) owners are planning to open an on-site restaurant. Rate inc full b/fast. **$**

Gulf Shore Provincial Park (50 sites) 2367 Gulf Shore Rd; 243 2389; www.gulfshorecampingpark.com; mid Jun–mid Sep. In the provincial park. A grassy, open campground on the seafront. **$**

Sandpiper Restaurant 8244 Hwy 6, Port Philip; 243 2859; Apr–Nov 11.00–19.00

CAPTAIN PUGWASH

The name 'Pugwash' comes from the Mi'kmaq word *pagweak*, meaning 'deep water'.

Incidentally, this Pugwash did not provide the inspiration for the surname of one of the UK's favourite cartoon characters. The late John Ryan created Captain Horatio Pugwash in 1950 when he was an art teacher in Middlesex, England. Seven years later, he was surprised to hear that a gathering of great minds (see box opposite) was being held in a previously virtually unknown Nova Scotia town which shared his captain's name.

THE BRAIN GAME

In 1955, Albert Einstein called for a conference to discuss the dangers of a nuclear war. Pugwash-born millionaire, Cyrus Eaton, offered to sponsor the event here. Part of his sales pitch was that the beauty of the Pugwash area would produce clarity of thought. And so in 1957, 13 nuclear scientists, including three from the Soviet Union, met on the Pugwash foreshore at Eaton's large but otherwise unremarkable residence (which became known as the Thinkers' Lodge).

It was the first of many such gatherings, now known as the Pugwash Conferences on Science and World Affairs (*www.pugwash.org*), which take place annually or biennially in some of the world's greatest metropolises, London, Washington, Rome, Tokyo – and, as recently as 2003 – Pugwash.

Although the lodge was designated a National Historic Site (NHS) in 2008, unlike most such sites is not under Parks Canada's jurisdiction: the lodge is owned and managed by by the Pugwash Parks Commission. In recent times, the lodge was only open sporadically (restoration work was being carried out), but it was opened to the public in July/August 2012. For the latest information, check with the Cumberland Regional Development Authority (*www.cumberlandrda.ca*).

daily (summer to 20.00). A licensed, good-value place approx 8km west of Pugwash specialising in seafood. $$

Chatterbox Café 10163 Durham St; 243 4059; Jun–Oct 09.30–18.00 daily (or later); off-season hours vary. Welcoming & relaxing with a library, secondhand books for sale, fair trade organic coffees, speciality teas, soups, salads & sandwiches. Live entertainment Fri/Sat evenings in summer. $

FESTIVALS Over the 1 July Canada Day holiday, Pugwash hosts the **Gathering of the Clans Highland Festival**, with Highland games, traditional music and dancing.

SHOPPING There is a **farmers' market** (*10222 Durham St; May–Oct 08.30–13.00 Sat*) on Saturdays, a welcome new addition to the Pugwash calendar. **Seagull Pewter** (*9926 Durham St; 243 3850,* **t/f** *1 888 955 5551; www.seagullpewter.com; Jun–Sep 09.00–17.00 Mon–Sat, 12.00–17.00 Sun; Jan–May 10.00–17.00 Thu–Sat; Oct–Dec 10.00–17.00 Mon–Sat*) is a long-established operation creating, designing and handcrafting pewter. Tours are offered in season.

OTHER PRACTICALITIES

$ **Bank** Scotiabank, Water St; 243 2541; 10.00–17.00 Mon–Fri

Library Pugwash Library, 10222 Durham St; 243 3331; Jun–Sep 14.00–19.00 Mon & Thu, 11.00–13.00 & 14.00–17.00 Tue/Wed, 13.00–18.00 Fri, closed Sat; Oct–May, same except 09.00–12.00 Sat

Post office 10154 Durham St; 08.00–17.15 Mon–Fri, 08.30–12.00 Sat

WHAT TO SEE AND DO The **Gulf Shore Provincial Park** (see opposite) has picnic areas and a nice red sand beach 4km from Pugwash. A very scenic 6,160yd links course, **Northumberland Links** (*1776 Gulf Shore Rd; 243 2808,* **t/f** *1 800 882 9661; www.northumberlandlinks.com; late Jun–mid Oct*) is 9km from Pugwash. Green fees are CAN$55.

WALLACE

For almost two centuries, this community on the shore of beautiful Wallace Bay has been renowned for its sandstone, which exists as a result of geological activity 300 million years ago. The first quarry opened in 1811, and several others followed. Wallace sandstone was used in the construction of many important buildings both in and outside Nova Scotia: these include the Nova Scotia Legislature in Halifax, the Peace Tower of the Canadian Parliament buildings in Ottawa and the Montreal Stock Exchange.

The stone is still quarried here, but this picturesque seaside village now depends primarily on fishing, farming and lumbering for its livelihood. The bay's salt marshes and tidal inlets attract a whole range of birdlife, and Wallace's public wharf is a popular spot from which to watch the sun rise and set. Accessible **by car**, the town is located on Highway 6 and Highway 307, 19km/12 miles from Tatamagouche and 17km/11 miles from Pugwash.

STAR FROM WALLACE

One of the world's greatest astronomers, Simon Newcomb (1835–1909) was born (and grew up) in Wallace.

WHERE TO STAY AND EAT

Fox Harb'r Golf Resort & Spa (72 suites) 1337 Fox Harbour Rd; 257 1801, **t/f** 1 866 257 1801; www.foxharbr.com; May–Oct. Approx 9km from Wallace, each of the 12 modern 'guesthouses' contains 6 deluxe suites. The resort has its own marina & private airstrip, & incorporates a private gated community, spa & wellness centre, golf academy & seaside tennis courts. Other activities include clay-pigeon shooting & sea kayaking. Golfing guests can take a swing at the fabulous Graham Cooke-designed private 7,253yd par-72 course. **$$$$**

Jubilee Cottage Inn (3 rooms) 13769 Hwy 6; 257 2432, **t/f** 1 800 481 9915; **e** jubileecottage@ns.sympatico.ca; www.jubileecottage.ca; year-round. Comfortable inn in a tastefully restored c1912 home with several period features. Set on 1.2ha on Wallace Bay – kayaks available for guest use. The Qi Sera Restaurant (*year-round: lunch 11.30–13.30 Mon–Fri, 10.30–14.00 Sun brunch, dinner 18.30–21.30 daily; reservations required;* **$$**, *4-course dinner CAN$40*) offers light lunches, a good set-menu Sun brunch & an innovative set-menu-themed dinner (which might include such things as butternut & coconut soup, & pan-seared maple trout with turnip-apple compote). Local organic ingredients used where possible. You can bring your own wine (corkage CAN$5 per bottle). There are plans for a new restaurant concept, so check before booking. Gourmet b/fast inc. **$$**

D&D Bayview Campground (15 sites) 3323 South Shore Rd, Malagash Centre; 257 2209; mid May–mid Oct. Delightful views over Tatamagouche Bay from the open campsites: 6km off Hwy 6. **$**

FESTIVALS Wallace is the ideal base for these Malagash festivals. In May, the new **Dandelion Festival** includes crafts stalls, photography competitions, and a lawn-mowing competition. During the **Summer Festival** in July, Malagash's Jost Vineyards plays host to a Saturday afternoon of food, music and winery tours. In August also at Jost Vineyards, enjoy all things blueberry during the **Malagash Blueberry Festival**, or spend a Saturday afternoon of music, food and displays of work by local artists at the **Art & Jazz Festival**. At the **Jost Vineyards Grape Stomp** in September, teams of four stomp grapes for charity.

SHOPPING At **Collector Canes** (*659 Ferry Rd; 257 2817; www.auracom.com/zperry/; by appointment*), Doug and Zella Perry hand-carve each cane from

Nova Scotia hardwoods. Walking sticks, hiking sticks and shepherd's crooks can be customised.

OTHER PRACTICALITIES

✉ **Post office** 3872 Hwy 307; ⌚ 08.00–17.00 Mon–Fri, 09.00–13.00 Sat

WHAT TO SEE AND DO The 585ha **Wallace Bay National Wildlife Area** (*Aboiteau Rd; ⌚ year-round 24hrs; admission free*) is a reserve just west of Wallace, encompassing a large marsh and small forest at the head of Wallace Bay. Although primarily of interest to birdwatchers – this is an important migration and breeding habitat for waterfowl – a 4km loop trail along a raised dyke makes a pleasant and easy wander. Housed in the restored c1840 home of a local shipbuilder, the **Wallace and Area Museum** (*13440 Hwy 6; ☎ 257 2191; www.wallaceandareamuseum.com; ⌚ Jun–Sep 09.00–17.00 Mon–Sat, 13.00–16.00 Sun; off-season 10.00–14.00 Mon & Thu; admission free*) offers local history, plus changing themed displays and also 4km of walking trails on the museum grounds.

Around Wallace Wallace is a good base for a visit to the **Malagash Peninsula**, where lush green farmlands roll down to the red sandy shore. Two sites are well worth a visit. **Jost Vineyards** (*☎ 257 2636,* **t/f** *1 800 565 4567; www.jostwine.com; ⌚ May–Christmas 09.00–17.00 Mon–Sat, 12.00–17.00 Sun; Christmas–Apr 09.00–16.00 Mon–Sat; free tours mid Jun–mid Sep 12.00 & 15.00*) was created by the Jost family from Germany's Rhine Valley – the first vines actually came from the agricultural research station at Kentville (see page 225). The most common grapes grown are French and German varieties (Marechal Foch, Vidal, Muscat, Baco Noir and L'Acadie). Smaller quantities of other grapes are grown on a more experimental basis. Most harvesting takes place in September and October. Pair the vineyard's produce with local cheeses and deli nibbles on the licensed terrace.

Canada's – and the British Commonwealth's – first salt mine operated here at the **Malagash Salt Miner's Museum** (*1926 North Shore Rd; ☎ 257 2407; ⌚ mid Jun–mid Sep 10.00–17.00 Tue–Sat, 12.00–17.00 Sun; admission CAN$2*) between 1918 and 1959. The salt was particularly pure owing to long slow crystallisation, and despite a large amount of unmined salt, the mine was closed as the harbour here was too shallow for larger shipping. Operations moved to Pugwash (see page 278), which has a deeper harbour.

WENTWORTH

If you feel like an inland excursion, the Wentworth Valley is a good choice. Although best known as the largest of the province's few downhill-skiing destinations, Wentworth and the Wentworth Valley are popular year-round with lovers of the outdoors – when the snow has gone, the hilly region is ideal for hiking and biking. In autumn, the high proportion of maple trees contribute to a fine display of colours.

Easily accessible **by car,** Wentworth is on Highway 4, 24km/15 miles from Exit 7 of Highway 104, 28km/17 miles from Exit 11 of Highway 104 and 22km/14 miles from Wallace (via Highway 307).

WHERE TO STAY AND EAT

Wentworth International Hostel (2 family rooms & 2 dorms) 249 Wentworth Station Rd; ☎ 548 2379; e wentworth@hihostels.ca; www.hihostels.ca; ⌚ year-round. A former c1870s'

NICE ICE WINE

Grapes are hand-picked before dawn in December or January, when the night-time temperature drops below -8°C. At these temperatures virtually all of the liquid in each grape is frozen, leaving just a tiny amount of intensely flavoured juice. Before the grapes can thaw, they are pressed to release these drops. The resulting juice then undergoes many weeks of fermentation and ageing before the final flavour-packed product emerges. It has to be said that thick, amber, sweet ice wine is not everyone's cup of tea (and isn't cheap).

farmhouse with fully equipped kitchen, shared bathrooms, common room & large patio deck. Snowshoes & cross-country skis to rent. *Dorm from CAN$25; private room from CAN$40.* **$**

Wentworth Valley Inn (15 rooms) 14962 Hwy 4; 548 2202; www.valleyinn.ca; year-round. This rustic, traditional-style motel has new owners & many changes, guest cottages & more recreation facilities are planned (& underway). Eat or have a drink at the Split Crow pub (*12.00–midnight daily*) or licensed country restaurant (*12.00–14.00 & 16.00–18.30 Wed–Sat, 12.00–17.00 Sun;* **$$**). Check the website for updates on work-in-progress, opening times, etc. **$**

FESTIVALS Take a ski-lift up a mountain to see the glory of the autumn colours at the **Fall Colours Festival**, held in October on (Canadian) Thanksgiving weekend.

WHAT TO SEE AND DO There is a network of over 25km of trails all centred on the Wentworth Hostel and nearby **Wentworth Provincial Park**, which lies about 4km off Highway 4, just past the entrance to Ski Wentworth if you're coming from Truro or Halifax. Tough but not too long – and very rewarding if it is clear – is the 2km **Look-off Trail** from the hostel. In addition, an easy, short (400m return) trail starts 0.5km south of the Wentworth Valley Inn and leads to the picturesque Wentworth Falls.

Ski Wentworth (*14595 Hwy 4; 548 2089; www.skiwentworth.ca*) has the highest vertical in the province at 250m and the largest area of downhill skiable terrain in the Maritimes.

A quad-chair, T-bar and 'magic carpet' get you to the top of the 20 trails, three of which are open for skiing after dark. Learn-to-ski or snowboard schools are offered. There are numerous packages and offers, but a basic one-day lift pass is CAN$42. There is also a rental shop, and for *pendant-*, *après-*, and *en place de-*ski, visit **Ducky's Pub & Restaurant** (*548 2404, hours vary;* **$$**) in the main lodge. Snowmobilers can purchase a trail pass to explore over 170km of groomed trails.

TATAMAGOUCHE

This pretty community at the confluence of the French and Waugh rivers has become a popular stop for visitors. Its name evolved from the Mi'kmaq *takamegoochk*, meaning 'meeting of the waters'. Some fine Victorian homes still stand and you'll also find a couple of museums (one housed in the old railway station), and interesting dining and accommodation choices.

The **Trans Canada Trail** offers a great opportunity for hiking or biking along the coast, and the old railway bed passing through the village has been converted to a trail popular with hikers, cyclists and cross-country skiers in winter. You can park on Creamery Road (off Main Street): the trail stretches from Nelson Park over the French River and along the shores of the Waugh River.

TATAMAGOUCHE CHOO-CHOO

The c1887 railway station was scheduled for demolition in the 1970s but was acquired by an enterprising teenager, Jimmie LeFresne. At first he used it to house a farmers' market, but later purchased seven (1911–78) railway carriages and converted them into comfortable suites. A 1928 dining car became the restaurant (soups, salads, sandwiches at lunch, salmon, pasta and steak for dinner). His ambition created a unique, character-packed fun place to stay and eat (see below).

Tatamagouche is on Highway 6, 84km/52 miles from Amherst and 49km/30 miles from Pictou.

WHERE TO STAY

Balmoral Motel (18 rooms) 131 Main St; 657 2000, **t/f** 1 888 383 9357; **e** stay@balmoralmotel.ca; www.balmoralmotel.ca; Apr–Oct. A traditional motel overlooking Tatamagouche Bay comprising 2 single-storey buildings. Hot b/fast, newspaper, Wi-Fi, most phone calls, guest laundry, all inc. **$$**

Train Station Inn (10 rooms & suites) 21 Station Rd; 657 3222, **t/f** 1 888 724 5233; www.trainstation.ca; Apr–Oct. See box, above, for further information. The licensed restaurant (*reservations recommended;* **$$**) is open daily for lunch & dinner. Complimentary muffins & scones, full b/fast available for a surcharge. **$$**

Poplar Grove Campground (30 sites) 758 Willow Church Rd; 657 3034; mid May–mid Oct. Open campground 6.5km from Tatamagouche. **$**

WHERE TO EAT

Big Al's Acadian Restaurant and Lounge 9 Station Rd; 657 3341; www.big-als.ca; year-round 11.00–20.00 Mon–Wed, 10.00–21.00 Thu–Sat, 10.00–20.00 Sun. Good portions of pub-style seafood (eg: breaded scallops). A 'Tata' institution for over a quarter of a century. Licensed. The kitchen closes at 20.00 Mon–Wed & Sun, at 21.00 Thu–Sat. **$**

Chowder House on Main 265 Main St; 657 2223; summer 07.00–21.00 daily; rest of year 08.00–19.00 daily. A family-style restaurant offering excellent seafood (great chowder), burgers, etc. Licensed. **$**

Green Grass Running Water Café 102 Main St; 657 9393; year-round 10.00–16.00 Mon–Thu, 10.00–20.00 Fri/Sat. Named for a 1993 novel by Thomas King, this eatery has lunch-type items, homemade soups, quiches, desserts, homemade ice cream & the like. Fishcakes are popular. The walls feature First Nations art, including work by top Mi'kmaq artist Alan Syliboy. **$**

FESTIVALS In July, the **Lavender Festival** (*Seafoam Lavender Farm; contact details on page 285*) is a new two-day aromatic fest celebrating all things lavender – lavender oat cakes, lavender ice cream … you get the picture.

Over the last weekend in September, Tatamagouche also hosts eastern Canada's largest **Oktoberfest** (*657 3030; www.nsoktoberfest.ca*), attracting over 3,000 revellers. Think beer garden, dances, polkas and oom-pah music. Food is a mix of Canadian and German, with lobster rolls, sausages and schnitzels. German and local beers are served, and there's a schnapps bar.

SHOPPING The **Raven Gallery** (*267 Main St; 657 0350; Jun–Sep 09.00–19.00 Mon–Fri, 10.00–18.00 Sat, 13.00–17.00 Sun; Sep–Jun: 09.00–17.00 Tue–Fri, 10.00–17.00 Sat*) is a charming gallery/craft shop. **Sara Bonnyman Pottery** (*326 Maple*

Av; ☎ *657 3215;* e *sara.bonnyman@ns.sympatico.ca;* ⏲ *Jul–Aug 10.00–16.00 Mon–Sat; off-season by appointment*) has a range of pottery – including unique Moss scuttles (types of jugs used in shaving) – and hooked rugs.

OTHER PRACTICALITIES

$ **Bank** Scotiabank, 243 Main St; ☎ 657 2440; ⏲ 10.00–17.00 Mon–Fri

Library Tatamagouche Branch Library, 237 Main St; ☎ 657 3064; ⏲ 11.00–17.00 & 19.00–21.00 Tue & Thu, 13.00–17.00 Fri, 09.00–13.00 Sat

Post office 236 Main St; ⏲ 08.00–17.00 Mon–Fri, 09.00–13.00 Sat

Tourist information The Fraser Cultural Centre; 362 Main St; ☎ 657 3285; ⏲ Jul–mid Sep 10.00–17.00 Mon–Sat, 10.00–16.00 Sun. This c1889 former Canadian Red Cross building also houses an art gallery.

WHAT TO SEE AND DO There are a number of attractions within the **Creamery Square** complex (*39 Creamery Rd;* ☎ *657 3500; www.creamerysquare.ca*). The **farmers' market** (*Feb–late Dec, Sat morning*) is (deservedly) one of the most popular in the region. The **Margaret Fawcett Norrie Heritage Centre** (⏲ *mid Jun–Sep 10.00–18.00 daily; off-season by appointment*) is a former c1925 creamery which now houses a fascinating interactive museum with a varied collection including exhibits on Acadian, Mi'kmaq and European settlement, butter production, and Anna Swan (see box, below). You can also see the Brule Fossils, discovered nearby in 1994, and the only example of a 29 million-year-old fossilised Walchia (primitive conifer) forest found in its original growth position. There are also local genealogical and historical archives.

The **Senator's Stage** is an open-air venue with frequent live performances in season (and views over the Waugh River estuary). You may be able to see work on the reconstruction of an 18th-century wooden boat underway in the boatshop. And scheduled to open in July 2013 is the **Centre for the Arts**: the plan is for theatrical and musical productions, dinner theatre, movies, festivals, etc.

The 23m wooden grain **Tatamagouche Grain Elevator Village** (*44 Creamery Rd;* ☎ *657 1040; www.tatagrainelevator.com;* ⏲ *Jun–Sep, check for hours; admission free*) was built in 1957 and is said to be the only prairie-style grain elevator east of the Canadian province of Manitoba. Attached warehouses are home to gift/arts and crafts shops, and the venue hosts a variety of entertainment.

BIG SWAN

The third of 13 children of (average-height) Scottish immigrants, Anna Swan was born near Tatamagouche in 1846. She was healthy at birth, but tipped the scales at 8.18kg, and measured 69cm long. By the age of seven she had outgrown her mother. When in her teens, she was offered a position at Barnum's American Museum in New York. She married in 1871 (her husband was well over 2m tall) at London's St-Martin-in-the-Fields Church, after first being introduced to Queen Victoria. The couple had two children: a daughter (stillborn) weighing over 8kg, and a son who – at the time – was the largest newborn ever recorded, at 10.6kg and 71cm tall. Sadly, he died within 24 hours. Anna died of tuberculosis in 1888, aged 41. At her height she was 2.36m tall and weighed 179kg.

Big Al's Restaurant (see page 283) has life-size wooden statues of Anna and her husband.

I TAWT I TAW A DINOSAUR

Patrick Keating was walking his dog on a beach near Tatamagouche in summer 2012 when something sticking out of the mud attracted his attention. What he saw turned out to be a sizeable fossilised part of a sail-back reptile, 300 million years old and the only one ever found in Nova Scotia (previously footsteps believed to have been made by this type of creature had been found at nearby Brule). A week later, Keating and his family returned to the beach: his wife found the reptile's head, and his son another portion of the rib cage. The sail-back creature is classified as a reptile, not a dinosaur. The specimen the Keatings found is believed to have been a juvenile, approximately 1m from head to tail. Adult sail-back reptiles are thought to have been four- or five-times larger.

Around Tatamagouche A photogenic three-storey c1874 mill off Highway 311, the **Balmoral Grist Mill** (*660 Matheson Brook Rd; 657 3016; http://museum.gov.ns.ca/bgm/; Jun–mid Oct 09.30–17.30 Mon–Sat, 13.00–17.30 Sun; admission CAN$3.60*), approximately 10km from Tatamagouche, in a delightful riverside setting. Although originally a water mill, electricity now supplies the power. That apart, wheat, oats and barley are still ground using 19th-century methods.

Wander the beautiful lavender fields overlooking the sea at the **Seafoam Lavender Farm** (*3768 Hwy 6, Seafoam; 657 1094; www.lavendercanada.com; Jun–Sep 10.00–18.00 daily*), then purchase all sorts of lavender goodies from cosmetics to brownies; located 31km from Tatamagouche, 25km from Pictou.

The **Sugar Moon Farm** (*Alex MacDonald Rd, Earltown; 657 3348,* **t/f** *1 866 816 2753; www.sugarmoon.ca; Sep–Jun 09.00–17.00 Sat/Sun; Jul/Aug 09.00–17.00 daily; admission free*) is a working sugar maple farm just off Highway 326, approximately 35km from Tatamagouche. Learn all about maple syrup production and taste the results. Buttermilk pancakes with lashings of maple syrup are served in the pancake house (last orders at 16.30) and maple products are available in the gift shop. It also has accessible hiking trails and snowshoe rentals in winter. The regular Chef's Nights featuring top guest chefs from around the province are very popular.

On Highway 326, 17km from Tatamagouche, see the workings of a c1894 lumber mill at the **Sutherland Steam Mill** (*Hwy 326; Denmark; 657 3016; www.museum.gov.ns.ca/ssm/; Jun–mid Oct 09.30–17.30 Mon–Sat, 13.00–17.30 Sun; admission CAN$3.60*), powered by steam generated from a huge boiler. Learn how wagon wheels, windows and architectural trim were manufactured before automated assembly lines, and observe many examples of resourcefulness throughout the mill. Rain barrels on the roof provided fire protection, a copper bathtub was used for soaking shingles, and a recycled cream separator was converted into a band-saw.

Based at Cape John (outside the village of River John), 8km off Highway 6, 28km from Tatamagouche and 40km from Pictou, **Coastal Spirit Expeditions** (*351 2283; www.coastalspiritexpeditions.com*) offers half- and full-day guided sea kayaking trips, sea kayaking instruction, and rentals.

PICTOU *(Population: 3,400)*

The harbour town of Pictou is one of the largest communities on the Northumberland Shore. Although just 8km from the terminal of the car ferry service (to and from Prince Edward Island), it is largely bypassed by the provincial highway system.

Only in the last ten–15 years has Pictou – derived from the Mi'kmaq name for the area, *Piwktook* ('exploding gas') – become a popular destination for visitors: the redevelopment of the waterfront, and, in particular, construction of a replica of an 18th-century ship, have been instrumental in putting the town firmly onto the tourist map.

BURNING QUESTION

If you look out across the Northumberland Strait after dark, you might be able to add yourself to the list of those who have seen a three- (some say four-) masted ship ablaze. The spectral burning vessel has also been seen from Prince Edward Island.

The principal attractions, main museum, restaurants, and historic accommodations are found on or close to the waterfront, but there are also some lovely old houses in the residential streets further back. Granite was imported from Scotland and used to build several town edifices – you'll see fine examples of Scottish vernacular, New England Colonial, Gothic and Second Empire styles.

The local paper mill, which has been known to waft unpleasant odours over the water, shipbuilding, and one of tyre-manufacturer Michelin's three factories in Nova Scotia are major employers (though tough times at the paper mill have meant many job cuts), and there's lobster fishing.

Getting there and around Pictou is accessible **by car**, situated at Exit 3 of Highway 106, 10km/6 miles from the ferry terminus to Prince Edward Island (see page 45), 75km/47 miles from Truro, 169km/105 miles from Halifax and 183km/105 miles from Amherst, and 14km/9 miles north of Exit 22 from Highway 104.

For taxis, try **Alf's** (☎ *485 5025*) or **Dime's** (☎ *485 6089*).

HISTORY In an effort to boost Nova Scotia's population, an agent named John Ross was sent to Scotland to try to attract disgruntled Highlanders (see page 17).

Ross placed a notice in the *Edinburgh Advertiser*, promising any family prepared to move to Nova Scotia (which he portrayed as a rich paradise with the most fertile of soil) free passage, their own farm land, and one year's provisions. In total, 189 Highlanders, including 71 children under eight, took up the offer.

Ross had chartered an old Dutch cargo ship, the *Hector* (said to be in poor condition), and she set sail from Loch Broom, Ross-Shire, in July 1773. It took the *Hector* 11 weeks to cross the ocean – 18 of the passengers died *en route*, most from smallpox. When she limped into Brown's Point in Pictou Harbour on 15 September, the land didn't seem to live up to the promises. Those on board were greeted by miles and miles of thick, unbroken forest right down to the shoreline and the nearest settlement several days' travel away. But the industrious new arrivals – 33 families and 25 single men – pulled together, set to work, felled trees and began to build a town on the site of an old Mi'kmaq village.

The almost ubiquitous stands of pine were put to good use, and less than a year after the *Hector*'s arrival, a ship laden with lumber sailed for England. This business boomed, and before too long shipbuilding also became established.

The *Hector*'s voyage marking the beginning of a massive wave of Scottish immigration through the port over the next century, Pictou quickly became known as the 'birthplace of New Scotland'. Many of the Scots then dispersed along the Northumberland Strait shore, or to Cape Breton Island.

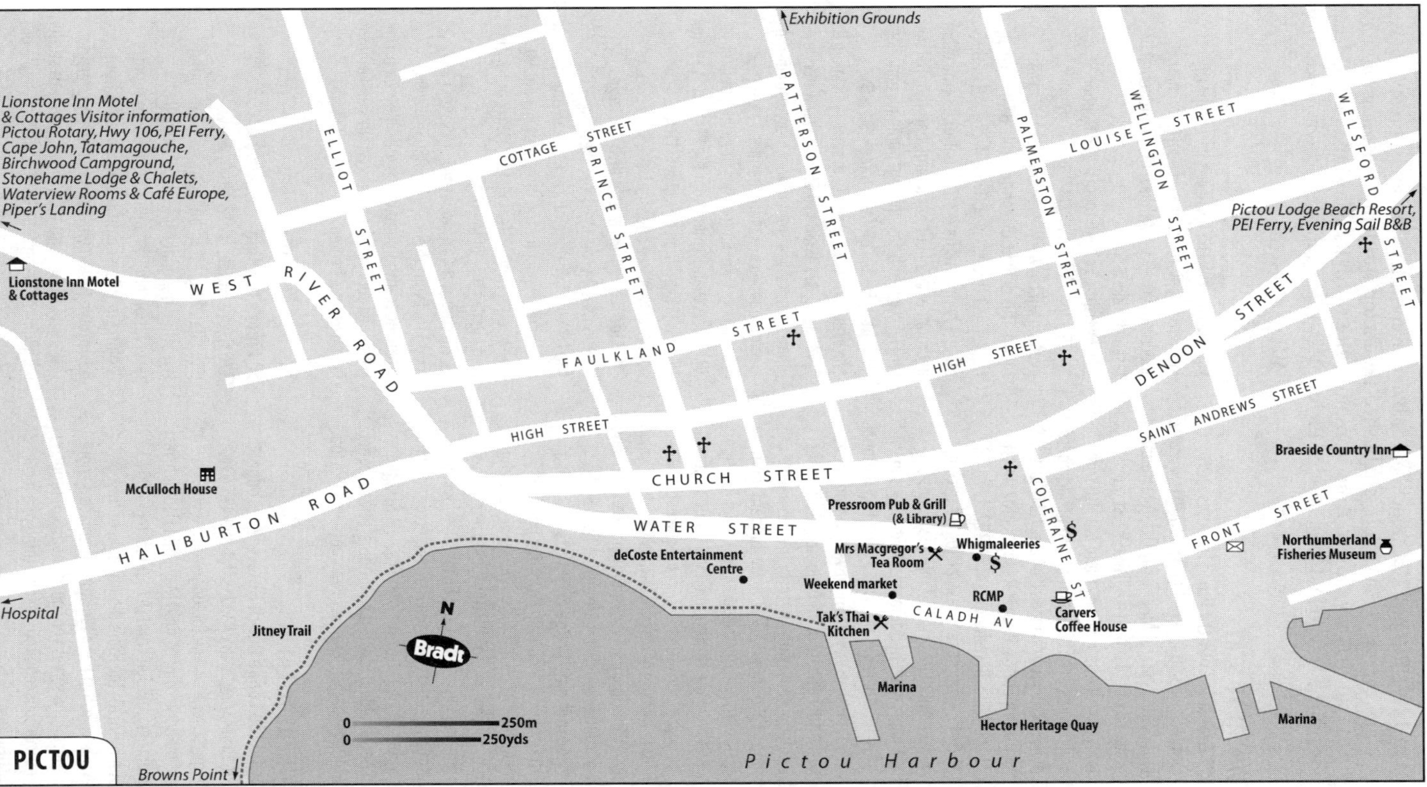
PICTOU
Lionstone Inn Motel & Cottages Visitor information, Pictou Rotary, Hwy 106, PEI Ferry, Cape John, Tatamagouche, Birchwood Campground, Stonehame Lodge & Chalets, Waterview Rooms & Café Europe, Piper's Landing
Lionstone Inn Motel & Cottages
Exhibition Grounds
Pictou Lodge Beach Resort, PEI Ferry, Evening Sail B&B
WEST RIVER ROAD
HALIBURTON ROAD
ELLIOT STREET
COTTAGE STREET
PRINCE STREET
PATTERSON STREET
PALMERSTON STREET
LOUISE STREET
WELLINGTON STREET
WELSFORD STREET
FAULKLAND STREET
HIGH STREET
DENOON STREET
SAINT ANDREWS STREET
CHURCH STREET
WATER STREET
COLERAINE ST
FRONT STREET
CALADH AV
McCulloch House
Braeside Country Inn
Pressroom Pub & Grill (& Library)
Mrs Macgregor's Tea Room
Whigmaleeries
deCoste Entertainment Centre
Weekend market
RCMP
Carvers Coffee House
Tak's Thai Kitchen
Northumberland Fisheries Museum
Jitney Trail
Hospital
Browns Point
Marina
Hector Heritage Quay
Marina
Pictou Harbour
N
Bradt
0 250m
0 250yds

In 1817, Thomas McCulloch, a Presbyterian minister who was a great believer in equal access to education, established the Pictou Academy. For many decades it was said that any eastern American university worth its salt would have at least one professor who had graduated at Pictou. The original Pictou Academy was torn down in the 1930s.

WHERE TO STAY

Braeside Country Inn (18 rooms) 126 Front St; 485 5046, **t/f** 1 800 613 7701; www.braesideinn.com; May–early Oct. A tastefully renovated c1938 inn on a hillside. Most guest rooms have harbour views. There are also some family rooms, Wi-Fi & a laundry room. Packages offered. Rate inc enhanced continental b/fast. **$$**

Pictou Lodge Beach Resort (102 units) 172 Lodge Rd, Braeshore; 485 4322, **t/f** 1 800 495 6343; **e** guest.services@pictoulodge.com; www.pictoulodge.com; mid May–mid Oct. The lodge's main building was built of logs in the 1920s: for 3 decades this was a Canadian National Railways resort, welcoming royalty & Hollywood stars. Under private ownership since 2007, thus far things are staying on track. There is a wide range of accommodation, from standard rooms to 3-bedroom executive chalets, in a quiet location overlooking the Northumberland Strait. Restaurant (see below). Private beach, & on-site activities include free use of canoes, kayaks & paddleboats, heated outdoor pool (seasonal), mini driving range & putting green. Bikes are available. **$$**

Stonehame Lodge & Chalets (22 units) 310 Fitzpatrick Mountain Rd, Scotsburn; 485 3468, **t/f** 1 877 646 3468; www.stonehamechalets.com; year-round. A lovely hilltop retreat beside a working farm 12km from Pictou. Overlooking farmland, forests & Pictou Harbour. Accommodation comprises 10, 1- to 3-bedroom chalets & 12 rooms in new building (drive-up entrances, private decks, whirlpool baths). Nearest restaurants are in Pictou. For self-caterers, chalets have fully equipped kitchens. Scenic trails, heated pool (seasonal), mountain bike & snowshoe rental. Continental b/fast available. **$$**

Evening Sail (6 rooms) 279 Denoon St; 485 5069, **t/f** 1 866 214 2669; **e** stay@eveningsail.ca; www.eveningsail.ca; year-round. This delightful, comfortable B&B is a real treat: the 3 suites have private decks, & 2 of the other 3 bedrooms have small balconies (the other bedroom is small but has a large bathroom). Free Wi-Fi. Excellent b/fast inc (eg: pumpkin pancakes, fresh fruit, freshly ground coffee). **$–$$**

Waterview Rooms (2 rooms) 1338 Shore Rd; 485 1440, **t/f** 1 888 896 6512; www.waterview-rooms.com; year-round. Very nice Austrian-run accommodation in a pretty hamlet. Large, new (2010) rooms. An outdoor hot tub is planned for 2013. Less than 10 mins from the PEI ferry & approx 15 mins (18km) from downtown Pictou. Good on-site restaurant (see opposite). **$–$$**

Lionstone Inn, Motel and Cottages (14 rooms & 14 cottages) 241 West River Rd; 485 4157; www.lionstoneinn.ca; year-round. Better than you'd expect for the price, this is a decent low-budget choice. Near Pictou Rotary but within walking distance of town. **$**

Birchwood Campground (55 sites) 2521 Hwy 376, Lyons Brook; 485 8565; www.birchwoodcampground.ca; mid May–Sep. Open & wooded serviced & unserviced sites 3.5km from Pictou Rotary, heated outdoor pool. **$**

WHERE TO EAT

Pictou Lodge Beach Resort 172 Lodge Rd, Braeshore; 485 4322, **t/f** 1 800 495 6343; **e** guest.services@pictoulodge.com; www.pictoulodge.com; mid May–mid Oct for b/fast & dinner; mid Jun–mid Oct for lunch (11.00–13.30 Sun brunch). The main dining room of this exclusive resort has a big stone fireplace & more importantly, serves very good food. Sun brunch (reservations required) is something of a local institution. **$$$**

Piper's Landing 2656 Hwy 376, Lyons Brook; 485 1200; www.piperslandingrestaurant.com; year-round (weather-dependent) from 17.00 daily by reservation only. Imaginative modern country cooking in this elegant restaurant 8km from downtown Pictou with a magnificent riverside setting. Start perhaps with mushroom caps stuffed with lobster, & continue with scallop casserole or T-bone steak. Last reservations 20.00. **$$$**

Café Europe See Waterview Rooms, opposite; ⌚ Apr–Jun & Sep–Dec from 17.30 Thu–Tue; Jul/Aug from 17.30 daily. The Bauers claim to serve the best schnitzels (pork or chicken) & *spätzle* in Nova Scotia, & most visitors are in agreement. The lobster tortellini is one of several other good choices. Well worth the drive from town. $$

Tak's Thai Kitchen 50 or 85 Caladh Av; ☎ 382 3088; ⌚ year-round 11.00–21.00 daily. Relatively authentic (Pictou isn't exactly Bangkok) tasty Thai food. On a deck overlooking the water. One of the province's better ethnic eateries, though service can sometimes be slow. $$

Mrs Macgregor's Tea Room 59 Water St; ☎ 382 1878; www.mrsmacgregors.com; ⌚ year-round 11.00–15.00 Mon–Sat (summer 17.00–20.00 Wed–Sat); check off-season dinner hours. Light lunches at this Scottish-themed tearoom include soup (eg: Scotch broth), salads, wraps, quiches & fish tacos (not everything is Scottish). Dinner menu offers more substantial fare including pan-seared haddock, meat pie, & turkey with trimmings. Desserts include traditional Scottish shortbread, maple cheesecake & sticky toffee pudding. $–$$

Pressroom Pub & Grill 50 Water St; ☎ 485 4041; www.thepressroompub.com; ⌚ year-round 11.30–22.00 daily. Cocktails, over 30 types of domestic & imported beer & generally reliable pub food (salads, steaks, sandwiches, fish & chips, pan-fried haddock). $–$$

Carvers Coffee House 41 Coleraine St; ☎ 382 3332; www.carvers.ca; ⌚ year-round 09.00–21.00 daily (Oct–May 12.00–17.00 Sun). A cheery blend of coffee house & Scottish pub: rustic décor. On warm, sunny days, the waterfront deck & patio are a delight. Tuck into a bowl of clam chowder or grab a cappuccino & lobster roll to take away. Occasional live music/trivia quizzes. $

FESTIVALS At the **Lobster Carnival** (*www.pictoulobstercarnival.ca*) in July, there is music, parades, antique cars, races, a beer garden and many other activities to mark the end of the lobster-fishing season. In August, expect parades, buskers, yacht races and more at **Natal Day**. Also in August is the **Natal Day Hector Festival** (☎ *485 8848; www.decostecentre.ca*), a five-day festival to celebrate the original *Hector*'s arrival in Pictou. Watch – or participate in – Highland dancing, attend a daily ceilidh (see page 291), and don't miss the re-enactment of the historic landing on the final day. September sees **New Scotland Days**: held over three days, the festival celebrates the pioneer spirit of the Scots who shaped Pictou County and Nova Scotia.

SHOPPING If you get a craving to buy something Scottish to take home, look no further than **Whigmaleeries** (*27 Water St; ☎ 485 2593; www.whigmaleeries.com; ⌚ year-round 10.00–17.00 Mon–Fri, 10.00–16.00 Sat*).

OTHER PRACTICALITIES

$ Banks Royal Bank, 25 Water St; ☎ 485 4352; ⌚ 10.00–17.00 Mon–Fri. Scotiabank, 70 Coleraine St; ☎ 485 4378; ⌚ 10.00–17.00 Mon–Fri

BERMUDA BETTERED BY PULCHRITUDINOUS PICTONIANS

During World War II, Lieutenant-Commander Roy B Foster DSC (b1920) was in charge of a Royal Navy submarine in the waters off Nova Scotia when orders were received to take the vessel to Pictou. He recalls being surprised to hear cries of jubilation from those on board when they heard the news. However, as they neared Pictou, another order came through instructing him to change course and head instead for the sub-tropical island of Bermuda. Whilst the commander thought that this would delight his men even more, the reverse was true. It transpired that the ladyfolk of Pictou were held in great esteem by mariners and submariners at the time (presumably for their great beauty).

Hospital Sutherland Harris Memorial Hospital, 222 Haliburton Rd; 485 4324

Library Pictou Library 40 Water St; 485 5021; 12.00–21.00 Tue & Thu, 10.00–17.00 Wed & Fri/Sat

Post office 49 Front St; 08.30–17.00 Mon–Thu, 08.30–20.30 Fri

Tourist information 350 West River Rd; 485 6213; early May–mid Oct 09.00–16.00 (later in summer, eg: Jul/Aug to 20.30 daily. Just off the Pictou Rotary, where Highways 106 & 6 meet.

WHAT TO SEE AND DO To most of the hundreds of thousands of Canadians of Scottish descent, the *Hector*'s arrival in Pictou (see *History*, page 17) was every bit as important as the Pilgrim Fathers' arrival in New England on the *Mayflower* over 150 years earlier. The story of the *Hector* is told in the three-storey interpretive centre, **Hector Heritage Quay** (*33 Caladh Av; 485 7371; www.shiphector.ca; spring–autumn 09.00–17.00 (or later) daily; guided tours offered; admission CAN$6*), which was designed to resemble an 18th-century Scottish warehouse. Costumed interpreters answer questions or tell stories to a background of bagpipe music. Rigging, blacksmithing and carpentry demonstrations relate to shipbuilding in the 18th century.

ROYAL CONNECTION?

Local legend has it that an 18th-century Pictou County resident was one of the illegitimate sons of Britain's King George IV. The resident, who died at the age of 33, was reportedly buried in Pictou's Laurel Hill cemetery. The story resurfaced as a song, 'Prince of Pictou', recorded in 2004 by local musician Dave Gunning.

But the highlight is the chance to explore the replica of the three-masted *Hector*. Go below deck and try to imagine what the voyage to a new life might have been like in the middle of the Atlantic for all those on board. The combination of the absorbing centre and the *Hector* replica – and the story they tell – make this one of Nova Scotia's most important heritage attractions.

If you feel like a wander, the 3km each way **Jitney Trail** starts at the Hector Heritage Quay and follows the abandoned rail line west along the shoreline around Norway Point and under the causeway to Browns Point.

At the c1805 brick and stone **McCulloch House** (*100 Old Haliburton Rd; 485 1150; http://museum.gov.ns.ca/mch/; Jun–mid Oct 10.00–17.00 Mon–Sat, 13.00–17.00 Sun; admission CAN$5*), built for Thomas McCulloch (see *History*, page 288), learn how one man's passion launched him on a journey to create public education in the province. Exhibits of his writings give a picture of early 19th-century Pictou life, and also include local newspapers from the period.

HECTOR #2

The replica of the *Hector* (which brought the first Scottish settlers here in 1773) towers above the Pictou waterfront. Built entirely on site by local craftspeople and volunteers, some of whom were descendants of the original *Hector* passengers, it was launched in 2000. It's a great big new old *Hector*.

The main section of the **Northumberland Fisheries Museum** (*71 Front St; 485 4972; www.northumberlandfisheriesmuseum.com; Jun & Sep 09.00–17.00 Mon–Fri; Jul/Aug 10.00–18.00 daily; adult CAN$5*) is housed in the red-brick former c1908 Canadian National Railway station, with over 2,000 exhibits on the heritage and culture of the fishing industry along the Northumberland Strait. Don't miss the live, multi-coloured, rare lobsters and other shellfish species in the tank. On the waterfront at Caladh Avenue is a fully operational lobster hatchery in a boathouse-style structure. Next door is a replica 1908-style lighthouse with information on the lighthouses of the province and Maritimes.

The **deCoste Entertainment Centre** (*85 Water St; ☎ 485 8848,* **t/f** *1 800 353 5338; www.decostecentre.ca; ⌚ Mar–Dec*) is the regional performing arts centre, housed in an excellent modern venue with a calendar of generally high-class events. In July and August on Tuesday–Thursday evenings, the centre hosts informal ceilidhs (see page 29) under the 'Summer Sounds of Nova Scotia' label.

Offering crafts, fruit and vegetables, other food and much more, the **Weekend Market** (*New Caledonia Curling Club, Waterfront; ☎ 485 6329; www.pictouweekendmarket.com; ⌚ late Jun–mid Sep 10.00–17.00 Sat/Sun*) is perfect for a stroll.

SCOTLAND THE BRAVE

In the 18th century, the Mi'kmaq who lived in the Pictou area had a particularly hostile reputation and were said to be fearless. However, they fled in terror at the sound of bagpipes.

Around Pictou From the **Caribou/Munroes Island Provincial Park** entrance (*2119 Three Brooks Rd; ☎ 485 6134; ⌚ mid Jun–early Oct*), 11km north of the junctions of Highways 6, 106 and 376, 4km east of the Caribou–Wood Islands ferry terminal (see page 45), a trail leads along 2km Little Caribou Spit to a traffic-free 100ha island. Here you'll find saltwater lagoons, salt marshes, small, secluded barrier beaches and wooded areas, good for birding, swimming, hiking or camping: choose from 95 wooded or open sites on a hillside overlooking the sea.

NEW GLASGOW, TRENTON, WESTVILLE AND STELLARTON

Across the harbour from Pictou the towns of New Glasgow, Trenton, Westville and Stellarton make up 'Industrial Pictou County'. Coal mining has been an integral part of this area's history since the first commercial mine opened in Stellarton in 1807, and since then, industry has continued to dominate. As with most of the world's industrial areas, unspoilt natural beauty is not abundant in these communities. There is one major attraction for the visitor – Atlantic Canada's biggest museum – but otherwise I would recommend sticking to the coastal corridor. New Glasgow (population: 9,550) is the region's largest community.

In summer, Westville holds what is said to be the largest **Canada Day celebration** in Atlantic Canada. Although Canada Day is 1 July, this birthday party lasts at least five days, with parades, games, barbecues, community suppers and more, climaxing in a huge firework display.

All listings are in New Glasgow and open year-round unless stated otherwise.

GETTING THERE New Glasgow is convenient to reach **by car**. The town is just off Highway 104 Exits 24–25, 2km/1.2 miles from Trenton, 4km/2.3 miles from Stellarton, 8km/5 miles from Westville, 22km/14 miles from Pictou, 69km/43 miles from Truro and 165km/103 miles from Halifax. There used to be a water taxi service to Pictou but this no longer operates: a **land taxi** to Pictou will cost approximately CAN$20. Try **Central Cabs** (☎ *755 6074*) or **K&M Taxi** (☎ *695 4040*). **By bus**, New Glasgow is on the Maritime Bus **coach** line between Halifax and Sydney (see *Chapter 2*, page 44).

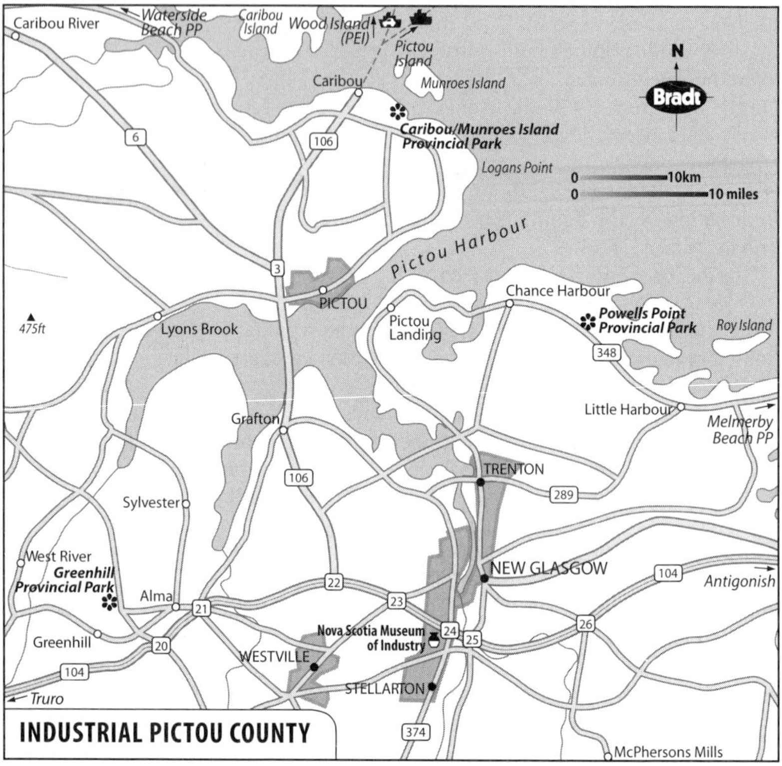

INDUSTRIAL PICTOU COUNTY

WHERE TO STAY

Country Inn and Suites By Carlson (65 units) 700 Westville Rd; t/f 1 800 830 5222; www.countryinns.com/newglasgowns. An early 1990s', 3-storey motel with decent standard rooms & 1-bedroom suites. All rooms have mini fridges; suites also have microwaves. Hot buffet b/fast inc. $$

Tara Inn Motel (33 rooms) 917 East River Rd; 752 8458, t/f 1 800 565 4312; www.taramotel.com. 32 rooms & a 2-bedroom (& kitchenette) suite. Clean, comfortable & good value. Continental b/fast inc. $

Trenton Park Campground (43 sites) Park Rd, Trenton; 752 1019; mid Jun–early Sep. Wooded & open serviced sites: pool, minigolf, fishing & laundromat. 4km from New Glasgow. $

WHERE TO EAT

Hebel's Restaurant 71 Stellarton Rd; 695 5955; www.hebelsrestaurant.ca; year-round 17.00–20.30 Tue–Sat. Housed in a mid 19th-century sea captain's house & former inn, Peter Hebel's restaurant attracts discerning foodies in the area. Start, perhaps, with almond-breaded baked brie or half-a-dozen oysters, continue with seafood Creole or braised lamb shank, & round off with the 3-coloured Belgian chocolate mousse. $$$

The Bistro 216 Archimedes St; 752 4988; www.thebistronewglasgow.com; 17.00–closing Tue–Sat. Favouring fresh, organic & locally sourced produce, this backstreet bistro (work by local artists adorns the walls) has a nice atmosphere, good service, & good food. $$–$$$

Baked Food Café 209 Provost St; 755 3107; year-round 08.00–17.00 Tue–Thu, 08.00–20.00 Fri/Sat. Great licensed bakery/café turning out not just artisan bread but good soups, sandwiches, paninis, coffee & more. $

Dine & Dash Diner 195 Main St, Trenton; 695 3300; year-round 10.00–20.00 Mon–Fri, 08.00–20.00 Sat/Sun. The name (sort of) says it all, but the D & D is a bit more than an independent fast-food joint. Chowder, fish & chips, *quesadillas*, salads & more – but with no pretence at 'fine-dining'. $

✕ **Ming's Restaurant** 211 Provost St; ☎ 752 4102; ⏲ 11.30–20.30 daily. A good place to fill up on reasonably priced Chinese food. Cheap buffet (⏲ *12.00–14.00 Sun–Fri*). $

✕ **Pantry Kitchen** 236 Foord St, Stellarton; ☎ 755 2292; ⏲ year-round 07.00–19.00 Tue–Sat, 08.00–19.00 Sun. Simple unpretentious 'home cooking' at very good prices (many seniors are regulars). The roast turkey dinner & fish & chips are popular, & the daily special is very good value. $

ENTERTAINMENT

Empire Drive-in Westville Westville Hwy; ☎ 396 5175; www.empiretheatres.com. This drive-in cinema, off Exit 21, Hwy 104, has films in Jul/Aug every evening.

Empire Studio 7 612 East River Rd; ☎ 928 3456; www.empiretheatres.com

Glasgow Square Theatre 155 Glasgow St; ☎ 752 4800, **t/f** 1 800 486 1377; www.glasgowsquare.com. A varied year-round programme of indoor & outdoor entertainment at this riverside venue.

FESTIVALS **Canada Day** is held at **Westville** (see page 291) in July. In August in New Glasgow is the **Festival of the Tartans** (*www.festivalofthetartans.ca*), a four-day celebration including a kilted golf tournament, pipe bands, ceilidhs and Highland games, and the **Riverfront Music Jubilee** (*www.jubilee.ns.ca*), with three days of good local and regional music. Events at the **Trenton Pumpkinfest** in October include a costume ball, pumpkin-carving workshops and rides for the kids.

OTHER PRACTICALITIES

Tourist information Cowan St Rest Area, 2500 Old Truro Rd, Westville; ☎ 396 2800; ⏲ spring–early Oct 09.00–16.00 daily (summer to 19.00)

WHAT TO SEE AND DO The huge **Nova Scotia Museum of Industry** (*147 North Foord St, Stellarton; ☎ 755 5425; http://museum.gov.ns.ca/moi/; ⏲ Nov–Apr 09.00–17.00 Mon–Fri; May–Oct 09.00–17.00 Mon–Sat, 13.00–17.00 Sun (from 10.00 Jul–Oct); admission CAN$8.15*) is amongst the biggest in Atlantic Canada and sits just off Exit 24 off Highway 104. It is far more interesting than the name might suggest: there are tens of thousands of artefacts to take you from the Industrial Revolution to 21st-century hi-tech. Highlights include the *Samson* (Canada's oldest steam locomotive), the *Victorian* (the first petrol-powered car built in the Maritimes), a display of much-prized Trenton glass, and there's an abundance of interactive stuff to keep kids happy.

The c1880 Victorian **Carmichael-Stewart House Museum** (*86 Temperance St, New Glasgow; ☎ 752 5583; ⏲ Jun–Sep 09.30–16.30 Mon–Sat; admission free*), with

PITFALLS

The dangers of life underground are well known to miners and their families. On 9 May 1992, after only five months in operation, the Westray Mine in nearby Plymouth was destroyed by a huge gas explosion. All 26 men working underground at the time were killed, the youngest just 22. Fifteen bodies were recovered, but 11 remain underground. A memorial – 26 rays of light emitting from a miner's lamp, each bearing the name and age of one of the miners lost – was erected a year later at what is now the Westray Miners Memorial Park. Interpretive panels give details of the tragedy. The memorial is at the east end of Park Street, New Glasgow.

NOVA SCOTIA'S ROSA PARKS?

In Montgomery, Alabama, USA in December 1955, Rosa Parks refused to surrender her bus seat to a white passenger. She was arrested and convicted of violating the laws of segregation. The incident triggered a wave of protest that swept through the country, and led to Mrs Parks being called the 'mother of the modern day civil rights movement' in America.

Nine years earlier, in New Glasgow, Nova Scotia, Viola Desmond decided to go and see a film while she was waiting for her car to be repaired. The Roseland Theatre maintained a segregated seating policy with the stalls (ground floor) reserved for 'whites only'. Ms Desmond had weak eyesight, and did not want to sit in the balcony: she took a seat in the stalls. She was forcibly removed from the cinema, arrested and thrown in jail overnight. She was not allowed counsel at her trial or to cross-examine the witnesses testifying against her. Ms Desmond was eventually found guilty of trying to avoid paying the difference between the tax on a balcony ticket and the tax on a ticket from the cinema's main floor. The amount in question? One cent. She was sentenced to 30 days in jail and was ordered to pay a total of CAN$26 in fines. Viola moved to Montreal, and died in New York in 1965 aged 50.

In 2010, 64 years after the incident, Ms Desmond was pardoned posthumously by the then Nova Scotia lieutenant-governor, Mayann Francis. Ms Desmond's niece was reported as saying of her aunt, 'She would have laughed and said, "Pardon me for what? I didn't do anything wrong".'

The Roseland Theatre at 188 Provost Street, New Glasgow, later became the Roseland Cabaret: it has been closed since late 2011.

original hardwood floors and beautiful stained glass windows, was formerly owned by the Carmichael family, prominent New Glasgow shipbuilders. In addition to local history – particularly relating to shipbuilding – the collection includes old Trenton glassware and clothing from the late 1800s to the 1920s, including wedding gowns worn by some of New Glasgow's high society.

AROUND NEW GLASGOW Nova Scotia's first zipline park, **Anchors Above Zipline Adventures** (*464 McGrath Mountain Rd, French River; ☎ 759 7403, 922 3265; www.anchorsabovezipline.ca; ⏲ late Mar–early Dec 10.00–17.00 daily; from CAN$25–30*) boasts two lines: the first is 335m long and 73m above the ground and the second is 275m long and 58m with a drop equivalent to a ten-storey building. There's a 15-minute hike to the first line and you'll need to sign a waiver. The park is 23km (*15–20 mins*) from New Glasgow: turn off Highway 104 at Exit 27, go through French River, and follow the signs.

Called 'The Merb', **Melmerby Beach Provincial Park** (*Little Harbour Rd; ⏲ mid Jun–mid Oct*) near Little Harbour, 14km from Highway 104 Exit 27A, 16km northeast of Exit 25 from Highway 104, is a popular 1.7km beach on an isthmus. The left side (as you first walk along the beach) is more sheltered, the right is open ocean. In late summer, the water can be quite warm. Changing rooms are available.

ARISAIG PROVINCIAL PARK

Around 400 million-plus years ago, this area was covered by the sea, and as the layers of sediment built up on the sea bed, various creatures were buried.

Within the boundaries of the park, the erosion of shale cliffs has exposed a continuous record of conditions here from the late Ordovician period (448 million years ago) through the entire Silurian to Early Devonian (401 million years ago) periods. This is one of the only places in the world where such a long period of time is exposed in a single layered cliff line.

Fossils of brachiopods (shellfish), nautiloids (a type of shelled squid), trilobites (extinct spider or crab-like arthropods), snail-like gastropods, and crinoids (plant-like filter feeders) are among those that have been found and continue to be unearthed here.

In addition, experts can see differences in the geology of northern and southern Nova Scotia here with a major geological fault dividing the park. Cliffs on the east side expose dark grey shale layers, but very few fossils. On the west side, the shale layers are thinner, have more sandstone and contain abundant fossils.

An interpretive kiosk explains fossil formation. There is a picnic area, and 3km of trails, one of which leads down past observation platforms to the beach and cliffs.

Remember, you're not permitted to disturb fossils embedded in the cliffs without a permit (see page 36).

The park (*http://novascotiaparks.ca*) is on Highway 245 near the village of Arisaig, 27km/17 miles north of Antigonish, and easy to reach **by car**.

ANTIGONISH *(Population: 4,300)*

With a concentration of supermarkets, shopping malls, fast-food outlets, petrol stations and light industry along Highway 104 and (to a lesser degree) along the approaches to the town centre from Exits 31–34, this is yet another town where you could be put off if approaching from this direction. However, it is worth persevering to the downtown area of this bustling university town. Here you'll find a range of good places to stay and eat, and some fine architecture. The Greek Revival-style c1855 **County Court House** (*168 Main St*), for example, survived a serious fire in the 1940s and still houses the county's Supreme Court – and the local jail.

About 20 sculptures (carved from dying elm trees) of life-size figures including a piper and a highland dancer – dot the town. Antigonish has a strong Scottish heritage and in 2013 will have been home to the popular **Antigonish Highland Games** (see page 297) for over 150 years. The town also hosts an excellent summer theatre festival (see page 298).

In addition to the urban attractions, the town has a range of good beaches and hiking trails close by: its harbour borders a large tidal marsh where ospreys and bald eagles are commonly seen. Having said all that, first and foremost this is a working regional centre, with tourism further down the list.

HISTORY The name Antigonish probably derives from the Mi'kmaq *n'alegihooneech*, 'where branches are torn off' – a reference to a place where bears came to forage for beechnuts.

Post Expulsion settlement is said to date from 1784 when Irish Loyalists, led by Captain Timothy Hierlihy, took up a large land grant surrounding Antigonish Harbour. The majority of settlers who followed were Scots from the Highlands, who were predominantly Catholic, so whereas Pictou County's churches are mainly Presbyterian, in Antigonish County the churches tend to be Roman Catholic.

GETTING THERE **By car**, Antigonish is just off Highway 104 by Exits 31–34, 55km/34 miles to the Canso Causeway, 74km/46 miles from Pictou, 123km/76

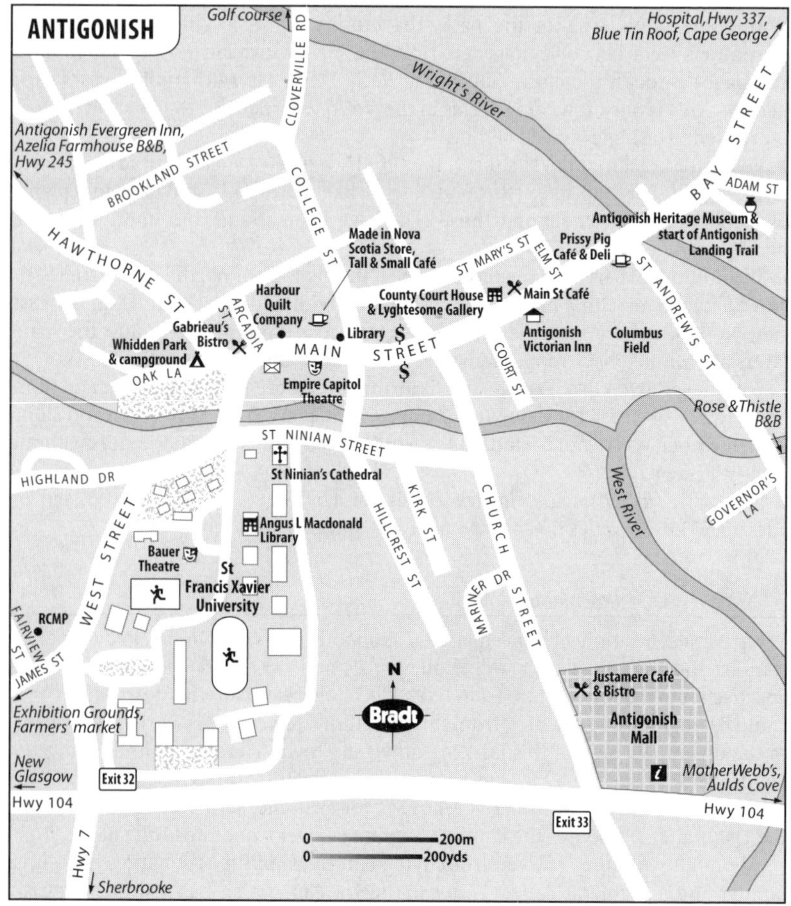

miles from Truro, 218km/135 miles from Halifax and 231km/144 miles from Amherst. Antigonish is on the Maritime Bus **coach** line between Halifax and Sydney (see *Chapter 2*, page 57).

WHERE TO STAY

The places listed are open year-round unless otherwise stated.

Antigonish Victorian Inn (13 units) 149 Main St; 863 1103, **t/f** 1 800 706 5558; **e** victorianinn@ns.sympatico.ca; www.antigonishvictorianinn.ca. In the past, this fine (c1904) house with 10 rooms, 2 apts & a modern suite in an annex was a hospital, & a bishop's residence. Set on 2ha & conveniently located, it's a good blend of old & new. Full b/fast inc. **$$**

Azelia Farmhouse B&B (2 rooms) 309 Connors Rd; 863 4262, **t/f** 1 866 309 0474; www.bbcanada.com/7409.html. Quiet & rural but just 6.5km from Antigonish, this turn-of-the-20th-century renovated farmhouse is surrounded by ash & sugar maple trees. Lovely, panoramic view from the veranda. B/fast is a highlight – it could be buckwheat pancakes with hazelnuts & maple cream served with bacon, or perhaps asparagus & crab meat omelette. **$$**

Blue Tin Roof B&B (4 rooms) 7957 Hwy 337, Livingstone's Cove; 867 3560; http://bluetinroof.com. Nice B&B in lovely – albeit somewhat isolated – surroundings, approx 30 mins' drive from downtown Antigonish. Some rooms aren't huge, but overall a good choice.

No shoes indoors & no under-11s. Rate inc full b/fast. **$$**

Rose & Thistle B&B (4 rooms) 4143 South River Rd; 735 2225, **t/f** 1 866 871 1440; **e** roseandthistle@eastlink.ca; www.roseandthistlebedandbreakfast.com. A purpose-built modern house on a hill outside the town centre with fine views over the harbour & surrounds. Guest rooms on the lower level. Large deck. Full b/fast inc. **$$**

Antigonish Evergreen Inn (8 rooms) 295 Hawthorne St; 863 0830, **t/f** 1 888 821 5566; **e** info@antigonishevergreeninn.com; www.antigonishevergreeninn.com. A pleasant, quiet single-storey motel less than 2km from downtown. Recently voted 2nd-best motel in Canada in terms of service & value. Continental b/fast inc. **$–$$**

Whidden Park & Campground (12 units & 154 campsites) 11 Hawthorne St; 863 3736; www.whiddens.com; mid May–mid Oct. These 2-bedroom well-equipped mini homes might not be for aesthetes, but provide good value for those requiring more than 1 bedroom. There are also 3 fully equipped (except bed linen) camper trailers. The campground has serviced & unserviced sites. Outdoor pools (seasonal), games & laundromat. Within walking distance of the town centre. **$$**

WHERE TO EAT

The places listed are open year-round unless otherwise stated.

Gabrieau's Bistro 350 Main St; 863 1925; www.gabrieaus.com; 10.00–21.00 Mon–Fri, 16.00–21.30 Sat. Stylish bistro with outdoor eating area. An extensive, imaginative menu, & wine list (the chef is also a certified *sommelier*). Lunch features gourmet sandwiches, flatbreads & more (perhaps vegetable *stifado*): in the evening the menu might include flambéed shrimp & escargots served on grilled polenta, or veal scallopini with marsala & mushrooms. **$$**

Justamere Café & Bistro 137 Church St; 735 3353; http://justamere.ca; 07.00–21.00 Mon–Sat (from 08.00 Sat), 08.00–15.00 Sun. Don't be put off by the corner-of-a-mall location: good atmosphere, music & art on the walls. Fresh, tasty diner-style food including good seafood chowder, all-day b/fast (eggs Benedict is a hit), & more. **$$**

Main Street Café at the Maritime Inn 158 Main St; 863 4001; www.maritimeinns.com/en/home/antigonish/; 07.00–21.00 daily (from 08.00 Sat/Sun). Tasty, well-cooked dishes such as maple whisky-soaked pork chop with green apple & cranberry salsa, & apple cinnamon *crème brûlée*. **$$**

The Prissy Pig Café & Deli 20 St Andrew's St; 863 8179; www.facebook.com/prissypigcafedeli; 07.00–16.00 daily. Bright & spacious café with art on display & a live music programme. Another popular choice for b/fast, brunch, lunch (eg: sandwiches, quiche, etc), or just a (good) coffee & wedge of cake. **$$**

Mother Webb's Hwy 104; 863 3809; www.motherwebbs.com; 11.00–22.00 daily. You'll see billboard advertising for this American roadhouse-style restaurant long before you get near to Antigonish. It manages to deliver hearty portions of reliable (if not gourmet) burgers, steaks, ribs & the like. Quick service, & very reasonable prices (if you don't add too many extras). Near Exit 35, approx 6km east of the town centre. **$–$$**

The Tall and Small Café 342 Main St; 863 4682; 07.00–18.00 Mon–Fri, 08.00–16.00 Sat. Friendly student/bohemian atmosphere, very good sandwiches, soups & coffee, & far better than usual vegetarian options. Can be very busy at lunch but you don't usually have to wait too long. **$**

ENTERTAINMENT

Empire Capitol Theatre 291 Main St; 863 4646; www.empiretheatres.com. The town's cinema.

FESTIVALS The **Antigonish Highland Games** (*863 4275; www.antigonishhighlandgames.com*), a hit since 1863 and said to be the longest-running Highland Games outside Scotland, are held in the second week of July. The 2013 Games – the 150th – promises to be extra-big. Expect to see dancing, bagpipes and caber-tossing. In late July, the three-day **Evolve** (*www.evolvefestival.com*) festival is held in Heatherton, about 25km from central Antigonish, and offers an eclectic mix of music genres. **Music on Main** (*www.antigonishmusiconmain.ca*) stages free Wednesday evening concerts between mid July and early August. Established in 1988, **Festival Antigonish** (*867 3333, t/f 1 800 563 7529; www.festivalantigonish.com*) is one of the province's biggest and best summer theatre programmes, with performances from **early July to mid September** at the wonderful Bauer Theatre on the St Francis Xavier University campus. Held over five days at the end of August/early September, the **Eastern Nova Scotia Exhibition** (*www.ense.ca*) has tug-of-wars, prize farm animals aplenty, live entertainment and much more.

SHOPPING Antigonish Mall, the town's major shopping mall, is out of the centre on Church Street by Exit 33 of Highway 104. The downtown area also has a couple of shops worth a quick browse, including the **Harbour Quilt Company** (*330a Main St; t/f 1 866 863 6801; www.harbourquiltcompany.com; 10.00–17.00 Mon–Sat, 12.00–16.00 Sun*), with gorgeous quilts and all things for quilters, along with. classes and workshops, and **The Made in Nova Scotia Store** (*324 Main St; 867 2642; www.themadeinnovascotiastore.com; 11.00–17.00 Mon, 10.00–17.00 Tue, Wed & Sat, 10.00–20.00 Fri, 12.00-16.00 Sun*), with no prizes for guessing where the crafts, preserves, cosmetics, etc, sold here were made.

OTHER PRACTICALITIES

$ Banks Royal Bank, 236 Main St; 863 0008; 10.00–17.00 Mon–Fri. Scotiabank, 255 Main St; 863 4800; 10.00–15.00 Mon–Wed, 10.00–17.00 Thu/Fri

Hospital St Martha's Regional Hospital, 25 Bay St; 863 2830

Library Antigonish Library, College St; 863 4276; 10.00–21.00 Tue & Thu, 10.00–17.00 Wed & Fri/Sat

Post office 325 Main St; 08.30–17.30 Mon–Fri

Tourist information Antigonish Mall complex, Church St; 863 4921; May–Oct 10.00–20.00 daily. The mall is just by Exit 33 of Hwy 104. The tourist office isn't in the main mall buildings, but in a small building right by the highway.

WHAT TO SEE AND DO The bells of the c1870s' **St Ninian's Cathedral** (*120 St Ninian St; 863 2338; www.antigonishdiocese.com/ninian1.htm*) were cast in Dublin, Ireland, and slate for the roof tiles was imported from Scotland. High on the cathedral's façade you can see the words *Tigh Dhe* – Gaelic for 'House of God'.

St Francis Xavier University (*University Av*), commonly known as 'St FX' or just 'X', was founded as a college by Roman Catholics in the 1850s, and gained university status in1866. Other than for prospective students, no tours are offered, but the landscaped grounds make for a pleasant wander.

Containing one of the most significant collections of Celtic culture in North America, the **Hall of the Clans** (*Angus L Macdonald Library, St Francis Xavier University; 867 2267; www.library.stfx.ca/index.php; hours vary; admission free*) comprises over 10,000 items including Scottish Gaelic, Welsh- and Irish-language resources and Celtic literature, folklore and music. Fifty coats of arms of Scottish clans adorn the walls.

Housed in the restored former c1908 railway station, the **Antigonish Heritage Museum** (*20 East Main St; 863 6160; www.heritageantigonish.ca; 10.00–12.00 & 13.00–17.00 Mon–Fri; admission free*) has two display rooms of photos and artefacts – including Mi'kmaq baskets – depicting the early days of the town and Antigonish County. There is also a genealogical resource room. The well-maintained 4.8km **Antigonish Landing Trail** leads from the museum along part of the harbour and river estuary. It's very popular with birdwatchers but just as enjoyable for walkers,

MINI CABOT TRAIL?

Lovers of lighthouses, magnificent coastal scenery and hiking should include this detour (or side trip from Antigonish) in their itineraries. The **'Cape George Scenic Drive'** also gets labelled the 'mini Cabot Trail' (for the real Cabot Trail, one of the world's great scenic drives, see page 311): that's going a bit far, but this is still a delightful and scenic little diversion. The drive begins at **Malignant Cove** on Highway 245, 8km east of Arisaig (if you are starting in Antigonish, take Highway 245 north for approximately 21km). Turn onto Highway 337. You'll pass through **Livingstone Cove**, which has an excellent B&B, the Blue Tin Roof (see page 296), and in less than 20km you'll reach Cape George Point. As you round the cape, watch for Lighthouse Road, a left turn onto a 1km unpaved road to the **lighthouse** (*www.parl.ns.ca/lighthouse/; ⌚ May–Nov hours vary*). *En route*, you'll pass **Cape George Day Park** with picnic areas and a parking area for trailheads. From this lofty setting, Prince Edward Island (over 50km away) and the highlands of Cape Breton are often clearly visible. The **Cape George Hiking Trail** comprises over 30km of loops and point-to-point trails, some reaching over 180m above sea level.

Back on the road, just past Cape George, there is a striking view of a line of cliffs, which head off into the distance towards Antigonish, with the brightly painted homes of the pretty and predominantly tuna-fishing community of **Ballantyne's Cove** directly below. Learn about bluefin tuna fishing past and present at the cove's **Tuna Interpretive Centre** (*⌚ mid Jun–mid Sep 10.00–19.00 daily; admission free*).

With indoor dining and a deck overlooking St George's Bay, **Boyd's Seafood Galley** (*Cribbons Point Wharf; ☎ 863 0279; ⌚ mid Jun–early Sep 11.00–19.300 daily; $*) is the obvious lunch spot.

You'll then pass the **Crystal Cliffs**, named for their whitish appearance (a result of their high gypsum content), and will then have a view of the narrow entrance to Antigonish Harbour.

A left turn onto Mahoney's Beach Road will lead you to a pleasant 1.8km beach trail: art aficionados will want to visit **Anna Syperek's home/studio** (*193 Mahoney's Beach Rd; ☎ 863 1394; www.annasyperek.ca; ⌚ by appointment*). Working with oils and watercolour, drawing and etching, Syperek is one of the province's top artists.

Just past **Mahoney Beach** on Highway 337, several more hiking trails ranging from 3km to 13km allow you to explore beautiful Fairmont Ridge, which overlooks the harbour. From here it is just 9km to Antigonish.

joggers and cyclists. You don't have to walk the whole way – just retrace your steps when you feel like turning round.

For those looking to bring home a piece of Antigonish, the interesting **Lyghtesome Gallery** (*166 Main St; ☎ 863 5804; www.lyghtesome.ns.ca; ⌚ Jan–Mar 10.00–17.00 Wed–Sat; Apr–Dec 10.00–17.00 Mon–Fri; admission free*) is worth a visit for a range of works by artists from Nova Scotia and the Maritimes, plus historic Scottish prints, Celtic art and more. If you're in town on a Saturday morning, pop along to the **Antigonish Farmers' Market** (*4-H barn behind the arena on James St; ☎ 867 7479; www.antigonishfarmersmarket.org; ⌚ late May–Nov 08.30–12.45 Sat*). Note that in November, the market changes venue: check the location if visiting at that time.

POMQUET You'll see many houses flying the Acadian flag in this village, established in 1774 by five families originally from St Malo, France.

Where to stay

Pomquet Beach Cottages (5 cottages) 198 Pomquet Beach Rd; 971 0314, **t/f** 1 855 240 2487; www.pomquetbeachcottages.com; year-round. 4, 2-bedroom & 1 (wheelchair-accessible), 1-bedroom comfortable fully equipped cottages (each with barbecue on deck) adjacent to the beach provincial park. Pet-friendly. **$$**

What to see and do At **Pomquet Beach Provincial Park**, the eponymous beach is backed by a series of 13 dunes stretching almost 4km. Boardwalks protect the dunes, while woods and both salt- and freshwater marshes attract a variety of wildlife: birdwatching is good, too. The park has changing rooms, loos, and interpretive panels explaining the dune formation.

AULDS COVE This community is on the mainland side of the **Canso Causeway** (see page 304). Other than seeing a disproportionately high number of larger-than-life models – a big yellow sou'wester-clad mariner manning a boatwheel stands outside the Cove Motel (see below), and dotted about town are a big iceberg, a giant puffin, and a huge lobster in an even bigger lobster trap – and, if necessary filling up with petrol, eating and/or sleeping there isn't much to delay you.

Aulds Cove is on Highways 104 and 4 and Highway 344, 5km/3 miles from Mulgrave, 10km/6 miles from Port Hawkesbury and 55km/34 miles from Antigonish **by car**.

Where to stay and eat

Cove Motel (30 units) Aulds Cove; 747 2700; **e** covemotel@ns.sympatico.ca; www.covemotel.com; May–Oct. Choose from 18 motel rooms or 12 'chalets' at this reliable motel on a small peninsula jutting out into the Strait of Canso. The large licensed restaurant (*May/Jun 11.00–21.00 daily; Jul–Oct 08.00–21.00 daily;* **$$**) can be busy with coach tours, but has a glassed-in patio with water views, an extensive menu & serves good food including lobster. **$$**

Aulds Cove Lobster Suppers 13176 Hwy 104; 747 3368; May–late Oct 11.00–19.00 daily. Despite the fact that the host is something of a loud, Acadian Basil Fawlty, the food is good. Acadian dishes are available in case you don't feel like the full lobster dinner. Just don't expect a quiet meal. **$$**

MONASTERIES AND CONVENTS

En route back to France from America in 1815, Father Vincent De Paul Merle of the Trappist Order was stranded in Halifax. He was given charge of three parishes and in 1826 his house became the Monastery of Petit du Clairvaux, North America's first Trappist monastery. He died in 1854, but the monastery continued to blossom and was 'upgraded' to an abbey by Pope Pius IX in 1876.

It later suffered a couple of devastating fires and was abandoned until 1938, when the current owners, the Order of St Augustine, purchased and rebuilt the monastery. Late in 2007, the complex – now called Our Lady of Grace Monastery (*www.ourladyofgracemonastery.com*) became home to a group of Augustinian Contemplative Nuns. To reach the monastery, take Exit 37 off Highway 104. Turn south onto Highway 16 and then right onto Monastery Road.

8

Cape Breton Island

Joined to the mainland since 1955 by the 2km-long Canso Causeway which crosses the narrow Strait of Canso, Cape Breton Island has a population of just under 150,000. Approximately 175km long and 135km wide, it covers 10,300km². At the island's core is the vast 260km² saltwater Bras d'Or Lake: to the northeast two natural passages connect the lake to the open sea, and in the southwest a short canal constructed in the 1850s and 1860s performs the same purpose. Cape Breton Island has the province's largest bald eagle population, many of which nest along the lake's shoreline.

Rugged highlands occupy much of the northern portion of Cape Breton Island: here you'll find the Cape Breton Highlands National Park, a region of deep, forested canyons, and magnificent coastal cliffs – and the best place in the province to see moose in the wild. This area of natural wonders is accessed by one of the world's great scenic drives, the 300km Cabot Trail. But don't just see it all through your car window – get out of your vehicle to hike, bike, kayak, play one of the superb golf courses, take a whale-watching trip or just relax on one of the beautiful beaches. Take a detour to remote Meat Cove, or wander the streets of the Trail's de facto capital, lakeside Baddeck, where Alexander Graham Bell was a summer resident for over 35 years.

Set on a magnificent harbour on the east coast, the port of Sydney is by far the biggest urban area: with the surrounding communities it makes up what is still called Industrial Cape Breton, a region largely built on coal mining and steel manufacturing which is home to over 70% of the island's population.

The island's major manmade attraction is in the southeast, a wonderful reconstruction of the Fortress of Louisbourg which played a major part in Nova Scotia's Anglo-French conflicts in the mid 18th century. In the southwest soak up the sleepy pastoral beauty and pretty backroads of Isle Madame.

But man has contributed another particular highlight of any visit to Cape Breton Island, part of the legacy left by the 50,000 Highland Scots who came here and settled in the late 18th and early 19th centuries – joyous Celtic music and dancing. Be sure to go to a ceilidh (see page 29) whilst in Cape Breton Island – or better still, try to time your visit to coincide with the Celtic Colours Festival (see box, page 306), a fantastic blend of traditional music, dancing and nature's splendour.

See for yourself why in 2011 *Travel & Leisure* magazine voted Cape Breton Island 'best island to visit in the continental United States and Canada' for the third time, and why in the same year *Bicycling Magazine* recognised it as one of the '50 Rides of a Lifetime'.

A century ago, Alexander Graham Bell said: 'I have travelled the globe. I have seen the Canadian and American Rockies, the Andes and the Alps and the Highlands of Scotland: But for simple beauty, Cape Breton outrivals them all.' He still has a case.

CAPE BRETON ISLAND

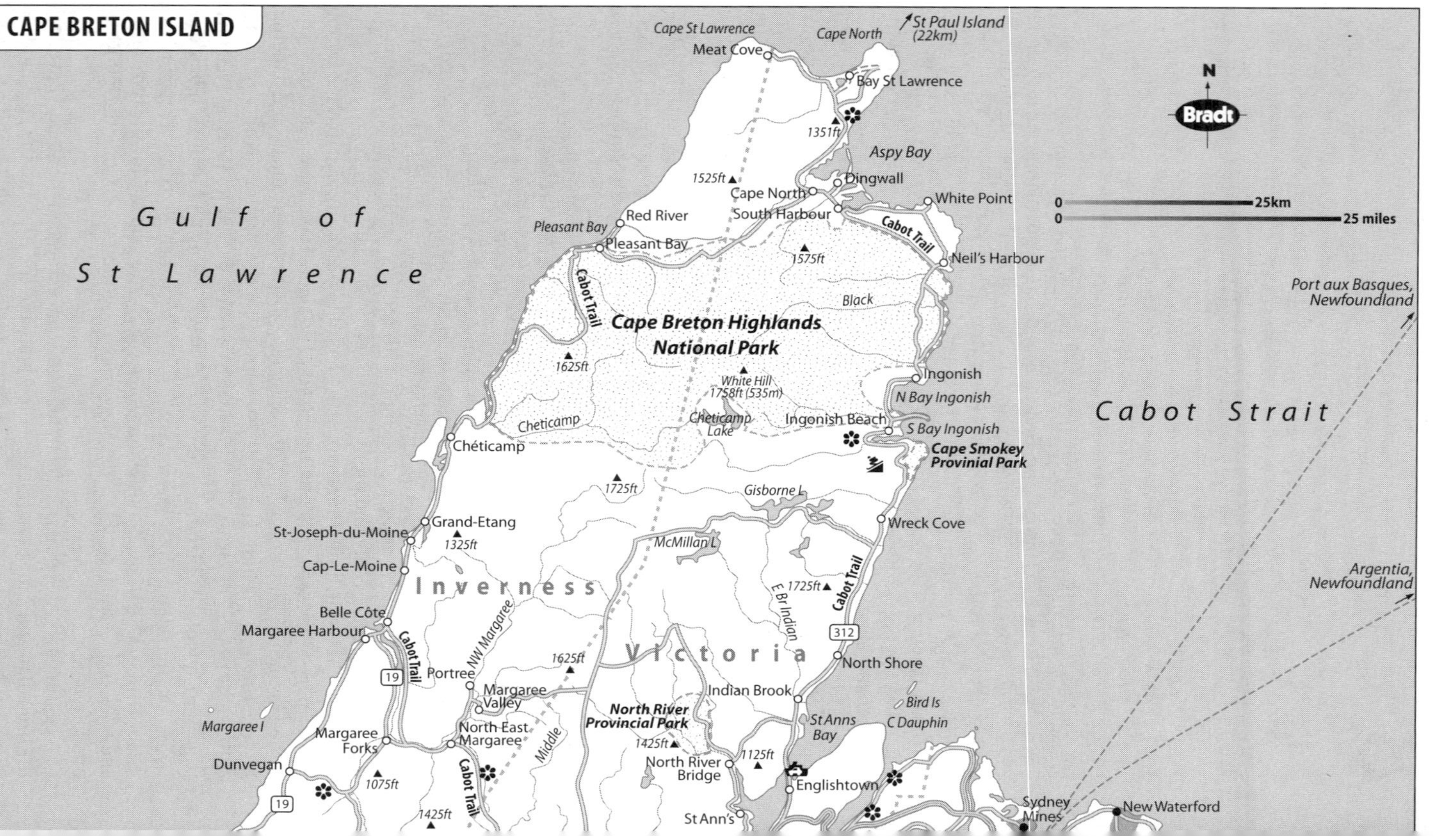

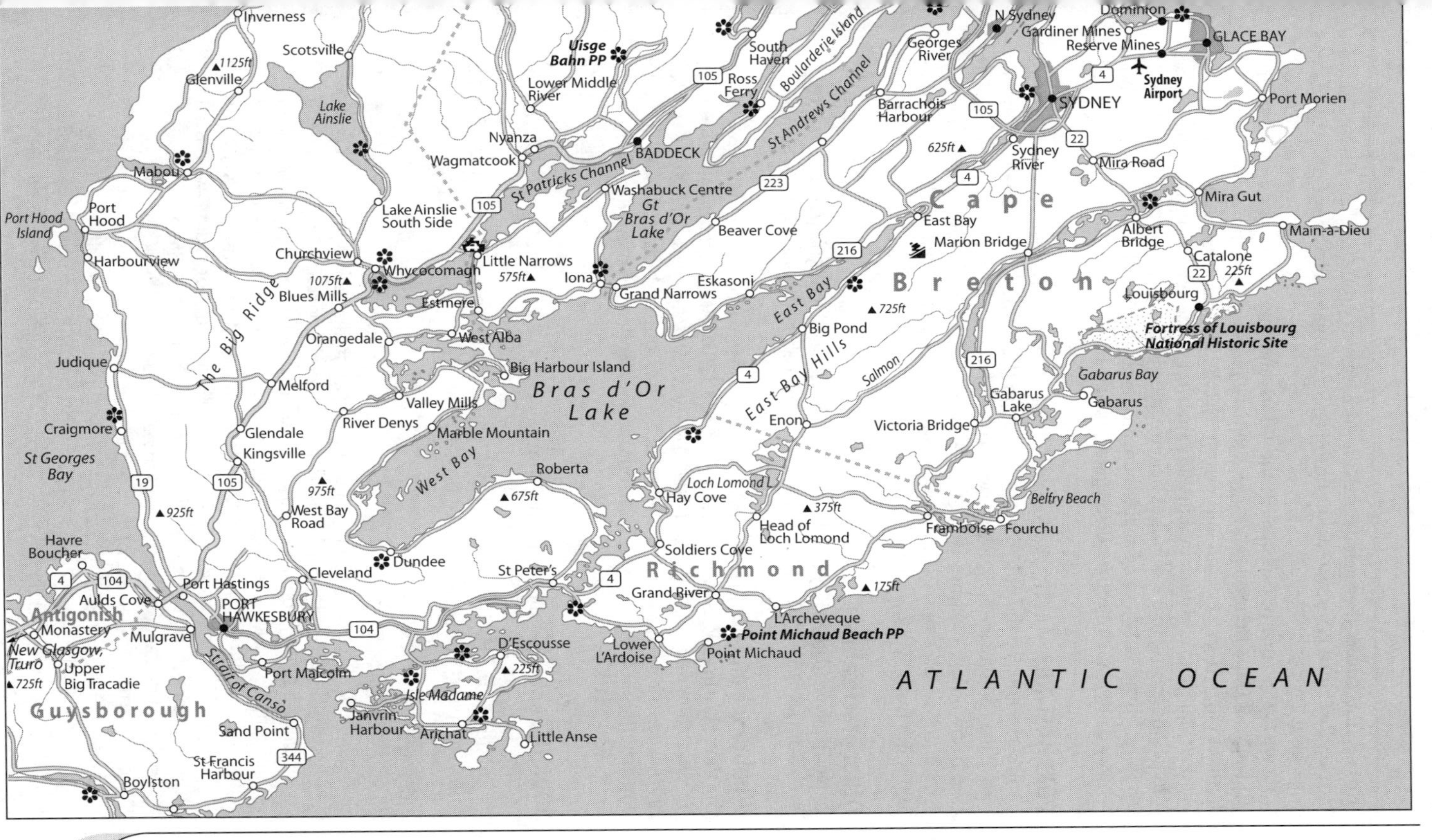
Inverness
Scotsville
1125ft
Glenville
Lake Ainslie
Uisge Bahn PP
Lower Middle River
South Haven
Boularderie Island
105
Ross Ferry
St Andrews Channel
Georges River
Barrachois Harbour
N Sydney
Gardiner Mines
Reserve Mines
Dominion
GLACE BAY
4
Sydney Airport
105
SYDNEY
Port Morien
Nyanza
Wagmatcook
BADDECK
St Patricks Channel
Mabou
625ft
Sydney River
22
Mira Road
4
223
Washabuck Centre
Gt Bras d'Or Lake
Beaver Cove
Cape
East Bay
Mira Gut
Main-à-Dieu
Albert Bridge
Marion Bridge
Catalone
225ft
22
Port Hood Island
Port Hood
Harbourview
Lake Ainslie South Side
105
Churchview
Whycocomagh
Little Narrows
575ft
Iona
Grand Narrows
Eskasoni
216
East Bay
Breton
Louisbourg
Fortress of Louisbourg National Historic Site
1075ft
Blues Mills
Estmere
West Alba
725ft
Big Pond
The Big Ridge
Orangedale
Judique
Big Harbour Island
Melford
Bras d'Or Lake
4
East Bay Hills
Salmon
216
Gabarus Bay
Gabarus
Gabarus Lake
Valley Mills
River Denys
Marble Mountain
Enon
Victoria Bridge
Craigmore
Glendale
Kingsville
St Georges Bay
19
105
975ft
West Bay
Roberta
675ft
Loch Lomond L
Hay Cove
375ft
Belfry Beach
925ft
West Bay Road
Head of Loch Lomond
Framboise
Fourchu
Havre Boucher
Dundee
Soldiers Cove
Richmond
St Peter's
4
175ft
4
104
Port Hastings
Cleveland
Aulds Cove
PORT HAWKESBURY
Grand River
Antigonish
Monastery
104
L'Archeveque
Mulgrave
Point Michaud Beach PP
Lower L'Ardoise
D'Escousse
Point Michaud
New Glasgow, Truro
Upper Big Tracadie
Port Malcolm
225ft
ATLANTIC OCEAN
725ft
Strait of Canso
Isle Madame
Guysborough
Janvrin Harbour
Sand Point
Arichat
Little Anse
St Francis Harbour
344
Boylston

THE WEST COAST

This section covers the region between Port Hastings (on the Cape Breton Island side of the Canso Causeway) and the village of Margaree Harbour 110km away on the Cabot Trail.

Scots first settled in this area in the 1770s, and their traditions are still strong. This part of Cape Breton Island seems to have produced a disproportionately high number of good dancers and musicians – Natalie MacMaster and her uncle Buddy, Ashley MacIsaac and the Rankins are amongst those who hail from the region. You get the feeling that a ceilidh is held in one community or another almost every evening. Music and dancing apart, there are some good beaches, the province's only whisky distillery, and some of Nova Scotia's best hiking.

PORT HASTINGS Port Hawkesbury (see page 356), 6km away, has accommodation and restaurants, so the only reasons to stop in this community at the Cape Breton end of the Canso Causeway are the well-stocked tourist office and the local museum (see below). Port Hastings is accessible **by car**, 51km/32 miles from Antigonish, 132km/82 miles from Cheticamp, 85km/53 miles from Baddeck and 171km/106 miles from Sydney.

Other practicalities

Tourist information 96 Hwy 4, 625 4201; May–mid Jun 09.00–17.00 daily; mid Jun–late Aug 08.00–20.30 daily; late Aug–mid Oct 09.00–19.00 daily; mid Oct–mid Dec 09.00–16.00 daily

What to see and do Briefly Canada's largest sweet shop, this building now houses the **Port Hastings Museum** (*24 Hwy 19; 625 1295; www.porthastingsmuseum.org; mid Jun–mid Oct 09.00–17.00 Mon–Fri (Jul/Aug also 12.00–16.00 Sat/Sun); admission CAN$3*); the collection focuses on life before, during and after construction of the causeway. Look out too for a collection of model ships by local craftsman Mark Boudreau.

JUDIQUE Although most visitors come here for the Celtic Music Interpretive Centre, look out too for Judique's fine stone St Andrew's Church.

Judique is on Highway 19, 27km/17 miles from Port Hastings and 18km/11 miles from Port Hood, convenient **by car**.

CANSO CAUSEWAY

The Canso Causeway connects Cape Breton with the mainland. Construction began in 1952: engineers blasted solid rock and fill from Cape Porcupine on the mainland side and dumped it into the water. Slowly the roadway-to-be began to elongate. Locks were constructed on the Cape Breton side to allow shipping to pass through the barrier. Completed in 1955, the causeway is 1.37km long with a surface width of 24m. Ten million tonnes of rock fill were used in the construction, piled to a depth of 66m. On the Cape Breton side, a 94m swing bridge allows larger vessels to pass through the locks. The causeway's construction created one of the finest ice-free harbours in the world.

Fishermen say that this wall across the strait has killed off tuna fishing in the area. On the other hand, they say lobsters are much easier to catch as the crustaceans crawl back and forth under the sea looking for a way through.

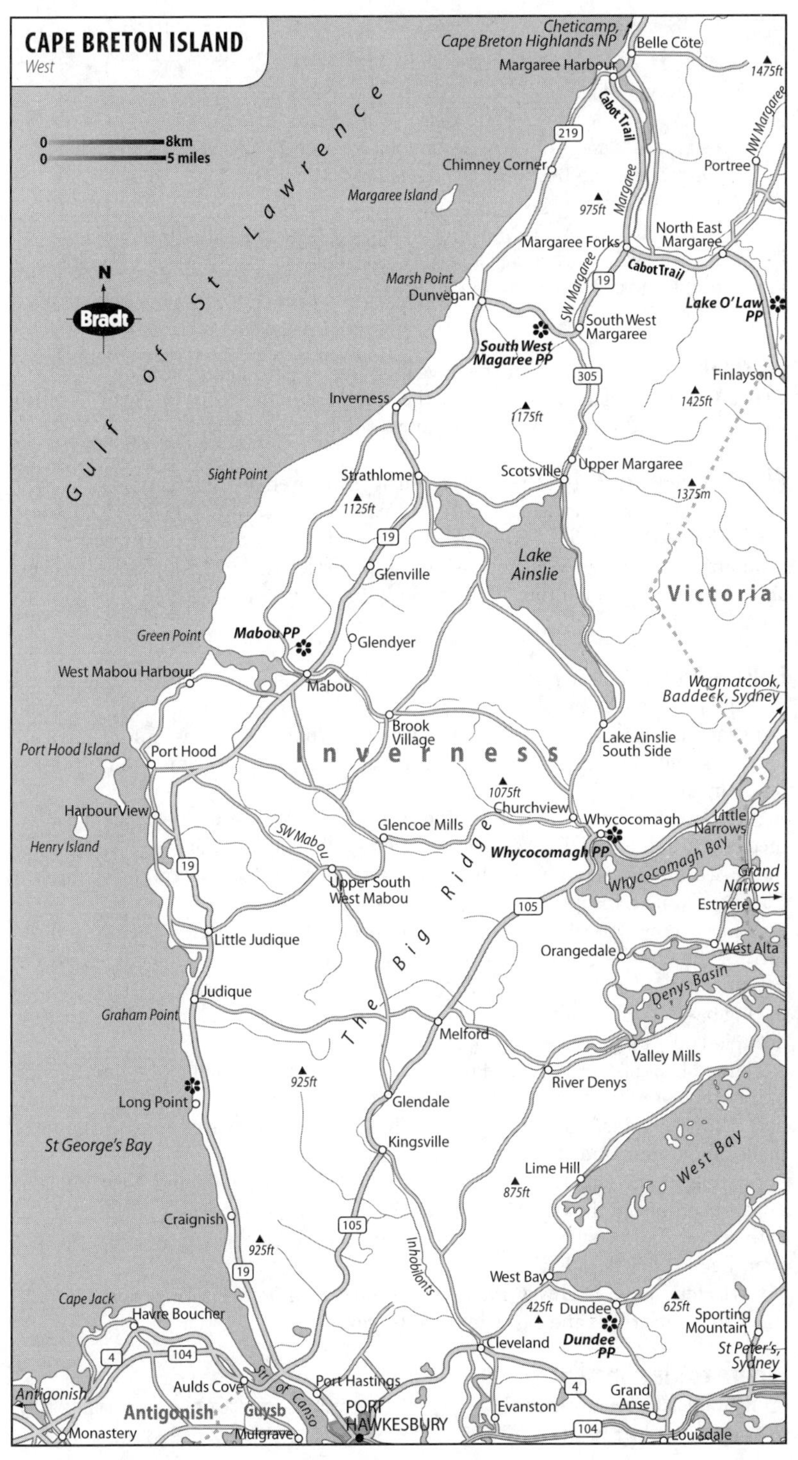
CAPE BRETON ISLAND
West
0 8km
0 5 miles
Gulf of St Lawrence
Cheticamp, Cape Breton Highlands NP
Belle Côte
Margaree Harbour
1475ft
Cabot Trail
219
NW Margaree
Chimney Corner
Portree
Margaree Island
975ft
Margaree
North East Margaree
Margaree Forks
Cabot Trail
Marsh Point
Dunvegan
SW Margaree
19
Lake O'Law PP
South West Margaree
South West Magaree PP
305
Finlayson
Inverness
1425ft
1175ft
Sight Point
Strathlome
Scotsville
Upper Margaree
1125ft
1375m
19
Lake Ainslie
Glenville
Victoria
Green Point
Mabou PP
Glendyer
West Mabou Harbour
Mabou
Wagmatcook, Baddeck, Sydney
Brook Village
Port Hood Island
Port Hood
Inverness
Lake Ainslie South Side
1075ft
Churchview
HarbourView
Henry Island
SW Mabou
Glencoe Mills
Whycocomagh
Little Narrows
Whycocomagh PP
Whycocomagh Bay
19
Upper South West Mabou
The Big Ridge
Grand Narrows
105
Estmere
Little Judique
Orangedale
West Alta
Denys Basin
Judique
Graham Point
Melford
Valley Mills
925ft
River Denys
Long Point
Glendale
St George's Bay
Kingsville
West Bay
Lime Hill
875ft
Craignish
105
925ft
Inhobilonts
19
West Bay
Cape Jack
Havre Boucher
425ft
Dundee
625ft
Sporting Mountain
Dundee PP
4
104
Cleveland
St Peter's, Sydney
Antigonish
Aulds Cove
Str of Canso
Port Hastings
4
Grand Anse
Antigonish
Guysb
PORT HAWKESBURY
Evanston
Monastery
Mulgrave
104
Louisdale

CELTIC COLOURS INTERNATIONAL FESTIVAL

This nine-day festival (☎ *562 6700*, **t/f** *1 877 285 2321; www.celtic-colours.com*) is a very good reason to delay your visit to Nova Scotia – or at least Cape Breton Island – until the second full week of October. It combines what traditionally is the best time to see nature's stunning autumn colours with Celtic music performed by the best musicians from Canada and further afield. Concerts are held each evening at venues of all sizes all around the island, there are several workshops, and numerous other events focus on Celtic heritage and culture.

Festivals Special events are held year-round – particularly during October's **Celtic Colours Festival**. In August, the town holds the **Kintyre Farm Scottish Concert**, an outdoor afternoon celebration of local music and dance.

What to see and do The **Celtic Music Interpretive Centre (CMIC)** (*5471 Hwy 19;* ☎ *787 2708; www.celticmusiccentre.com;* ⏲ *year-round 09.00–17.00 Mon–Fri, 14.00–19.00 Sun (mid Jun–Aug also 09.00–17.00 Sat)*) collects, preserves and promotes Celtic music with emphasis on Cape Breton-style. Music demonstrations are CAN$8, self-guided tour of Tom Rankin Exhibit Room CAN$6 – or do both for CAN$12.

PORT HOOD This pretty community – the self-proclaimed 'step-dancing capital of Cape Breton' – is the second largest on this route. For the non-terpsichoreal, step-dancing is a fast-paced dance which involves a lot of quick, intricate footwork, but little hand or arm movement: it is usually performed to traditional fiddle music.

There are fine views over **Port Hood Island** and if the weather is behaving, a few nice beaches to enjoy. The sea is very shallow, allowing the water to heat up early in the season and stay warm. There are days when the 'warmest water in eastern Canada' claim seems justified.

What is now Port Hood Island was connected to Cape Breton Island until the turn of the 20th century when the effects of severe winter storms cut across the isthmus and created an island. Once one of the region's most important lobster-fishing bases, the brightly coloured houses amid meadows and high bluffs are now occupied only by those who come for the summer.

Named Just-au-Corps by the French (after a garment popular at the time), much of the stone used to construct the Fortress of Louisbourg (see page 351) came from here. With time, Just-au-Corps became Chestico (this name lives on as the name of the local museum and summer festival (see opposite).

Settling in the late 18th century, Catholic Highland Scots and New England Loyalists produced the Port Hood of today. It became an important port in the mid 19th century, and coal mining which began in the 1890s helped the town prosper over the next few decades.

Port Hood is on Highway 19, 45km/28 miles from Port Hastings and 35km/22 miles from Inverness and easily reached **by car**.

Where to stay and eat

Haus Treuburg Country Inn and Cottages (6 units) 175 Main St; ☎ 787 2116; **e** kargoll@haustreuburg.com; www.haustreuburg.com; ⏲ May–Dec. 2 rooms & a suite are in the main house, but it's worth splashing out for 1 of the 3 cottages (the 2-bedroom cottage is up the hill). The dining room (*Jun–Oct 18.00–22.00 daily*) offers a set 4-course dinner for CAN$45–51 (seafood, European & traditional German dishes); reservations recommended. B/fast not inc. **$$**

Hillcrest Hall Country Inn (11 rooms) 24 Main St; 787 2211, **t/f** 1 888 434 4255; www.hillcresthall.com; mid Jun–mid Oct. Magnificent c1910 Queen Anne Revival building. 1 accessible unit, 2 suites. Fine views of harbour & beyond. Rate inc continental b/fast. **$$**

Clove Hitch Bar & Bistro 8790 Hwy 19; 787 3030; www.clovehitch.ca; year-round 11.30–21.00 (from 11.00 Sun). Nice, modern décor, friendly service, & a varied menu that is well executed. A welcome addition to the region. Food served until 21.30. **$$**

Other practicalities

$ Bank East Coast Credit Union, 138 Main St; 787 3246; 09.30–16.30 Mon–Wed, 09.30–16.00 Thu

What to see and do The **Chestico Museum and Historical Society** (*8095 Hwy 19, Harbourview; 787 2244; Jun–Aug 09.00–17.00 Mon–Fri, 12.00–16.00 Sat; admission CAN$2.50*) is a local history museum 3km south of Port Hood hosting several Chestico Days (a six-day festival in early August at Harbourview, near Port Hood) events including step-dancing demonstrations. The company **Port Hood Island View Boat Tours** (*Shore Rd, Little Judique Harbour; 787 3490; www3.ns.sympatico.ca/d_r/*) offers three-hour boat tours (CAN$30) around Port Hood Island between July and October with chances to see dolphins, whales and bald eagles.

MABOU One of the most attractive villages on Cape Breton Island's west coast, Mabou (population: 410) is the province's centre of Gaelic education (the language is taught in the local school).

In summer, the town resonates to the sound of Celtic music with a Tuesday-evening ceilidh at Mabou Community Hall, the four-day **Mabou Ceilidh** in July, music at the **Red Shoe Pub** and **Strathspey Place**, and more. The beautiful surrounding area offers wonderful hiking.

> **POSSIBLE DETOUR**
>
> For a scenic break from Highway 19, take the Colindale Road from the north end of town: unpaved for much of the way, it rejoins Highway 19 just south of Mabou.

Easy to get to **by car**, Mabou is on Highway 19, 60km/37 miles from Port Hastings, 86km/53 miles from Cheticamp and 66km/41 miles from Baddeck.

Where to stay

Ceilidh Cottages and Camping Park (10 units) 1425 New Rocky Ridge Rd, West Mabou; 945 2992; www.ceilidhcottages.ca; Jun–mid Oct. 5, 2-bedroom cottages with fireplace & deck, & a 20-site campground with tent & serviced motorhome sites. Facilities include laundromat, tennis court & heated pool (in season). **$$**

Duncreigan Country Inn (8 rooms) 11409 Hwy 19; 945 2207, **t/f** 1 800 840 2207; **e** duncreigan@ns.aliantzinc.ca; www.duncreigan.ca; year-round. A lovely, comfortable c1990 harbourside inn, a blend of traditional & modern features with 4 rooms in the main house & 4 rooms in the 1996 adjacent Spring House. Full buffet b/fast inc. **$$**

Mabou River Inn (10 units) 19 South West Ridge Rd; 945 2356, **t/f** 1888 627 9744; www.mabouriverinn.com; year-round; off-season by reservation. Choose from 7 inn rooms, or 3, 2-bedroom units with full kitchen. Good source of information & advice on fishing. Sea kayaks & mountain bikes. Rate inc deluxe continental b/fast. **$$**

HEELS STEAL SHOES

Mabou's celebrated Red Shoe Pub (see below) was named for a well-known fiddle reel. When the pub opened, the new owners were presented with a pair of red (ladies) wooden high-heeled shoes. One of these shoes disappeared without trace within the year, but the other – as prized as Cinderella's glass slipper – became the pub's emblem, and featured in the photos of many a pub patron. When not being used as a prop for souvenir snapshots, the shoe was kept on a sill in the middle of the front left-hand window. What a time we live in: after midnight one Friday night in September 2012, someone (as yet unidentified) grabbed the shoe and left the pub. A waitress gave chase, but could only watch as a car sped off. This same shoe had been purloined once before, but that time the culprit rang the pub within a day to say that he was at Halifax Airport and was couriering the stolen shoe back to Mabou. At the time of writing, no similar phone calls or ransom notes have been received.

Where to eat

The Mull Café 11630 Hwy 19; 945 2244; www.duncreigan.ca; late Jun–mid Oct 11.00–20.00 daily; mid Oct–late Jun 11.00–19.00 Sun–Thu, 11.00–20.00 Fri/Sat. Popular, unpretentious licensed restaurant: extensive menu. Eat inside or on the all-weather deck. $$

Red Shoe Pub 11573 Hwy 19; 945 2996; www.redshoepub.com; Jun–mid Oct 11.30–23.00 Mon–Wed, 11.30–02.00 Thu–Sat, 12.00–23.00 Sun. Owned since 2005 by members of local singing favourites the Rankin Family & looking like a big-city coffee house. Offers sophisticated pub food & regular (& occasional spontaneous) live music performances: you're probably paying a dollar or 2 extra for the celebrity connections. (See box, above.) Food served until 21.00. $$

Shining Waters Bakery 11497 Main St; 945 2728; call for hours. Locals value good, simple food & low prices more highly than fancy décor: they love this small place. Come for excellent sandwiches, homemade bread & baked goods. $

Entertainment

Strathspey Place 11156 Hwy 19; 945 5300; www.strathspeyplace.com; year-round. A modern 500-seat theatre with excellent acoustics & offering a varied programme.

Other practicalities

$ **Bank** East Coast Credit Union, 11627 Hwy 19; 945 2003; 09.30–16.30 Mon–Wed & Fri, 09.30–18.00 Thu

Post office 11541 Main St; 09.00–17.00 Mon–Fri

MABOU HIKING

The Mabou area offers enough excellent trails to fill a book. Over a dozen well-marked trails through the beautiful highlands have been developed (and are maintained) by the Cape Mabou Trail Club, which produces an invaluable map, sold in various places in Mabou, including the general store.

If you'd rather stay on more level ground, one of several possibilities is to walk the Rail Trail from Mabou (near the bridge over the Mabou River) to Glendyer Station, approximately 4km each way. Old railway line it may be, but the views are stunning. West Mabou Beach Provincial Park (see page 309) also has good trails.

What to see and do A shrine, **Mother of Sorrows Shrine** (*45 Southwest Ridge Rd; ☎ 945 2221; ⌚ year-round daily; admission free*) is dedicated to Our Lady of Seven Sorrows and the pioneers of the Mabou area, and enclosed in a miniature pioneer church. A (usually quiet) park, **West Mabou Beach Provincial Park** has a picnic area, good birding, ponds, sand dunes, old farm fields and marshes, and a beautiful 2km sandy beach. For walkers, the Old Ferry Road and Acarsaid (Harbour) trails are both worthwhile. To reach the park from Highway 19, take Colindale Road at Port Hood, or the West Mabou Road just before you get to Mabou Station. Housed in a c1874 former general store, ***An Drochaid* (The Bridge Museum)** (*11513 Hwy 19; ☎ 945 2311; ⌚ Jul/Aug 09.00–16.00 Wed–Sat, 13.00–16.00 Sun, 12.00–16.00 Tue; admission free*) focuses on traditional Cape Breton music and local history. Special events are held year-round.

GLENVILLE Although green hillsides flank this village on Highway 19, it was once known as Black Glen (it's a long story). These days, most people stop here for one reason: since 1990, Glenville has been home to a whisky distillery and inn (see box, below). Glenville is approximately 9km north of Mabou and 10km from Inverness.

THE BATTLE OF THE GLEN

Many have likened the straths, glens and lochs in this region to the land that lies to the north of England. One of the highlights of a holiday in bonnie Scotland is the abundance of wonderful whisky distilleries to visit. As you tour Cape Breton Island, make a stop between Mabou and Inverness at Glenville. Here you'll be rewarded with a good place to stay, eat, tap your feet – and to sample a wee dram or two. And like the province itself, the precious liquid produced at the Glenora Distillery (which opened in 1990) has a story to tell.

In 2001, the Edinburgh-based Scotch Whisky Association (SWA) filed a suit against the Glenora Distillery, arguing that the use of the word 'Glen' in the distillery's main product (Glen Breton Rare Single Malt Whisky) misled consumers to believe the spirit was a 'Scotch', a designation that can only be used for whiskies made in Scotland. Although Glenora Distillery made (and makes) no references to 'Scotch' anywhere in its marketing, in 2008, the Federal Court of Canada ruled that the company could not register a trademark including the word 'Glen' in the name of its whisky. Glenora appealed the decision, compiling 4,000 pages of documentation. A panel of three judges from the Federal Court of Appeal found in favour of the distillers.

Still the SWA would not accept defeat. It may have lost that battle, but the war was not yet over. Its last chance was to take the matter to the highest court in the land (even though there was no evidence of even one whisky-drinker being misled by the nomenclature).

In June 2009, the Supreme Court of Canada dismissed the SWA's final appeal and awarded court costs to the distillers. Over seven years of litigation finally ended, and the distillery registered the Glen Breton trademark.

In 2010, the good folk of Glenora celebrated their victory and the first anniversary of the trademark registration by releasing a 15-year-old Single Malt, appropriately named the 'Battle of the Glen™'. It is not a Scotch.

Where to stay and eat

The Glenora Inn and Distillery (15 units) 13727 Hwy 19; 258 2662, **t/f** 1 800 839 0491; www.glenoradistillery.com; early May–late Oct. Choose from 9 rooms or 6 hillside chalets. Lovely brookside setting & delightful flowered courtyard. Spacious rooms, a highly regarded restaurant ($$$) focusing on local ingredients prepared with modern flair – try, for example, the lobster & scallop fettuccini or the coffee-rubbed ribeye steak – & pub ($$) with free live Celtic music sessions twice daily. Many people choose to stay & eat here rather than in Mabou or Inverness. Buy whisky-related souvenirs & more at the gift shop. Standard (25 min) guided distillery tours (inc sample) run on the hour daily (*09.00–17.00; CAN$7*): private tours (which include a visit to the whisky warehouse where you will draw & taste a barrel sample, followed by a tutored tasting in the pub), are available by advance reservation. **$$**

INVERNESS Most visitors are attracted to the largest community (population: 1,800) along Highway 19 not by the town's mining history (coal was mined commercially here from 1890 to 1958), but by a huge, long sandy beach. An extensive boardwalk runs alongside the beach, and – compared with many other beaches further south – the sea can be quite warm. Breathing new life into the region – and drawing new visitors from afar – is Cabot Links, a fabulous links golf course and resort which opened in 2012. So successful has the course been that there is even talk of a second course (Cabot Cliffs) being added. At the wharf, depending on the season, watch fishermen unload lobster, crab or tuna.

In summer, there's a weekly ceilidh at Inverness Fire Hall on Thursday evenings.

Incidentally, Inverness is home to acclaimed author Alistair MacLeod, whose work includes the Cape Breton Island-set *No Great Mischief*.

To reach Inverness **by car**, the town is on Highway 19, 80km from Port Hastings, 57km/35 miles from Cheticamp and 153km/95 miles from Sydney.

Where to stay and eat

Cabot Links Lodge (48 rooms) 15933 Central Av; 258 4653, **t/f** 1 855 652 2268; **e** golf@cabotlinks.com; www.cabotlinks.com; mid Apr–mid Nov. The well-appointed guest rooms at this fabulous, brand-new (2012) resort have floor-to-ceiling windows with golf course & sea views. Design is contemporary, & the lodge lives up to its 'low-key luxury' billing. See opposite for details of the golf course. The Panorama Restaurant (*end Jun–mid Nov 06.00–15.00 & 17.00–22.00, reservations recommended; $$$–$$$$*) offers wonderful views, unpretentious fine-dining & a good wine list. At dinner, try for example the lobster-stuffed chive ravioli, followed by pan-seared local rainbow trout. You can also choose snacks & more substantial fare at the well-stocked Cabot Bar (*end Jun–mid Nov 11.00–22.00; $$*) adjacent to the 18th green: it also has a nice patio. Restaurant & bar are open to non-guests. **$$$–$$$$**

Inverness Beach Village (41 cottages) 50 Beach Village Rd; 258 2653; **e** village@macleods.com; www.macleods.com; Jun–mid Oct. The 1- & 2-bedroom cottages are OK: what keeps people coming back here is the magnificent beach location. There's an open & wooded 50-site campground (serviced & unserviced) on the same site, plus laundry facilities & tennis court. **$$**

Coal Miners Café 15832 Central Av; 258 3413; year-round 07.00–21.30 daily. This friendly eatery offers quite a sophisticated menu, though on occasions can't quite cope with it. Live entertainment Jul/Aug Thu evenings. $$

Tommycat Bistro 15643 Hwy 19; 258 2388; Apr–Oct 11.00–22.00 daily. Yet another Nova Scotia place where the uninspiring appearance belies a rather good eatery. Seafood, pasta, steak. Licensed. $$

Festivals The **Broad Cove Scottish Concert**, at Broad Cove, near Inverness is the largest outdoor Scottish concert on Cape Breton Island and is held on the last Sunday in July.

Other practicalities

$ **Bank** Royal Bank, 15794 Central Av; ☎ 258 2776; ⊕ 10.00–15.00 Mon–Wed & Fri, 10.00–17.00 Thu

Hospital Inverness Consolidated Memorial Hospital, 39 James St; ☎ 258 2100

Post office 16 Railway St; ⊕ 08.30–17.30 Mon–Fri

What to see and do Housed in the former c1901 railway station, the **Inverness Miners' Museum** (*62 Lower Railway St; ☎ 258 3822; ⊕ Jun–Sep 09.00–17.30 Mon–Fri, 12.00–17.00 Sat/Sun; admission CAN$2*) was saved from demolition by a noble citizen, and contains information on the region's mining history. The **Inverness County Centre for the Arts** (*16080 Hwy 19; ☎ 258 2533; www.invernessarts.com; ⊕ year-round, check for hours; admission free*) exhibition centre features a good gallery including local and international artists, and also hosts occasional live music performances. There's also a gift shop.

Watch horse-harness racing on Sunday afternoons at the **Inverness Raceway** (*Forrest St*) from May to October (*Jul–Aug Wed evenings*).

Try your hand at the famous **Cabot Links golf course** (*see contact details opposite; ⊕ end Jun–mid Nov, depending on weather*), a challenging, new seaside course (five holes play adjacent to the beach), which opened in 2012. Rod Whitman designed the 6,803yd par-70 links course, which has already established a wonderful reputation. Six yardages are offered (the shortest, 3,733yds). Green fees are CAN$130 for resort guests and CAN$110 for non-guests.

MARGAREE HARBOUR This quaint village with a cluster of shingle and clapboard houses wraps around a once-bustling harbour flanked by two c1900 lighthouses. The busy old-fashioned general store is the hub of village life.

By car, Margaree Harbour is at the junction of Highway 219 and the Cabot Trail, 112km/70 miles from Port Hastings, 27km/17 miles from Cheticamp and 60km/37 miles from Baddeck.

Where to stay and eat

Duck Cove Inn (24 rooms) 10289 Cabot Trail; ☎ 235 2658, **t/f** 1 800 565 9993; **e** info@duckcoveinn.com; www.duckcoveinn.com; ⊕ Jun–late Oct. Motel on a hillside overlooking the Margaree River, just a short walk from Margaree Harbour. Laundry facilities. The licensed dining room (⊕ *Jun–late Oct 07.30–10.00 & 17.30–20.00 daily; $$*) offers good-value family dining. **$$**

THE CABOT TRAIL

The Cabot Trail is the official name for a road which loops around northern Cape Breton Island. This region is justly renowned for its spectacular unspoilt beauty and regularly features high on lists of the world's best scenic drives.

The most spectacular stretch of the approximately 300km trail is the 115km between Cheticamp and Ingonish Beach, much of which passes through the Cape Breton Highlands National Park. From early summer well into autumn, pilot, minke, fin and humpback whales come to feed in the Gulf of St Lawrence and off the northern tip of Cape Breton Island. Whale-watching tours depart from Cheticamp, Pleasant Bay, Bay St Lawrence and the Ingonishes.

The national park apart, there are many other beautiful sections of the Cabot Trail, such as the drive through the Margaree Valley. There are also some beautiful side trips such as the one from Cape North to Meat Cove.

This is not a drive to be rushed: ideally plan to stay a couple of nights (ideally more) *en route* to have time to walk some trails, appreciate the lookouts, take a side trip or two, look round Baddeck, try your hand at sea kayaking, go whale watching, cycling, or just relax on the beach.

As no public transport operates here, you'll need your own vehicle or to join a tour.

One-day Cabot Trail tours are offered by Sydney-based **Tartan Tours** (see page 351) and Baddeck-based **Bannockburn Discovery Tours** (page 333). **Salty Bear** (see page 59) offers a three-day tour from Halifax.

A WORD OF WARNING

The first time I drove this route it was through thick fog and although I suspected that I was passing magnificent scenery, I could just make out the trees by the side of the road. I tried to make the best of it, and did a couple of 'atmospheric' forest trails, but felt quite down. Luckily, the fog lifted on the second morning, and I saw what all the fuss was about. Keep your fingers crossed!

Guided and self-guided bike tours of the entire Cabot Trail are offered by **Pedal and Sea Adventures** (see page 84) and **Sea Spray Outdoor Adventures** (page 323). There are several strenuous climbs, and some sections have no paved hard shoulders. Not for the novice! Sea Spray, in my opinion, offer the best activity tours of the northern Cabot Trail and vicinity – including possibilities to cycle some of the best sections of the Cabot Trail via shuttled day trips from accommodations based at the 'Top of the Island'. For other tour operators, see page 351.

BELLE COTE Just north of the Margaree River, the wharf at the fishing village of Belle Cote tends to be busy with fishermen returning with their catches in the middle of the day between spring and autumn. Wander the beach on the other side of the breakwater, and, in season, buy a fresh-cooked lobster at the pound.

Belle Cote is just off the Cabot Trail, less than 4km/2 miles from Margaree Harbour and 23km/14 miles from Cheticamp.

Where to stay and eat

Island Sunset Resort (18 units) 19 Beach Cove Rd; 235 2669, **t/f** 1 866 515 2900; www.islandsunset.com; mid Jun–mid Oct. The very comfortable, well-decorated cottages overlook the beach, with wonderful sea views. The licensed restaurant (*mid Jun–mid Oct 16.00–21.00;* **$$$**) serves good, fresh food: start perhaps with Cape North mussels, whilst the prime rib & snow crab are both delicious. **$$$**

Ocean Haven and Acres & Ocean (3 units) 49 Old Belle Cote Rd; 235 2329, **t/f** 1 888 280 0885; www.oceanhaven.ca; Jun–mid Oct. Choose a room with en-suite or private bathroom at this restored farmhouse B&B on 40ha overlooking the ocean. Or rent Acres & Ocean, the 2-bedroom cottage with full kitchen. Full b/fast inc (B&B only). **$$**

Festivals Held in July, **Belle Cote Days** festival includes five days of concerts, dances, barbecues and competitions, as well as a golf tournament.

CHETICAMP (*Population: 1,000*) Cheticamp – the largest Acadian village in North America – is a busy fishing village set along a protected waterway that opens to the Gulf of St Lawrence. Just 5km from the western entrance to the **Cape Breton Highlands National Park**, the community has long been regarded as a centre for the craft of **rug hooking**. It is also a departure point for **whale-watching** cruises to

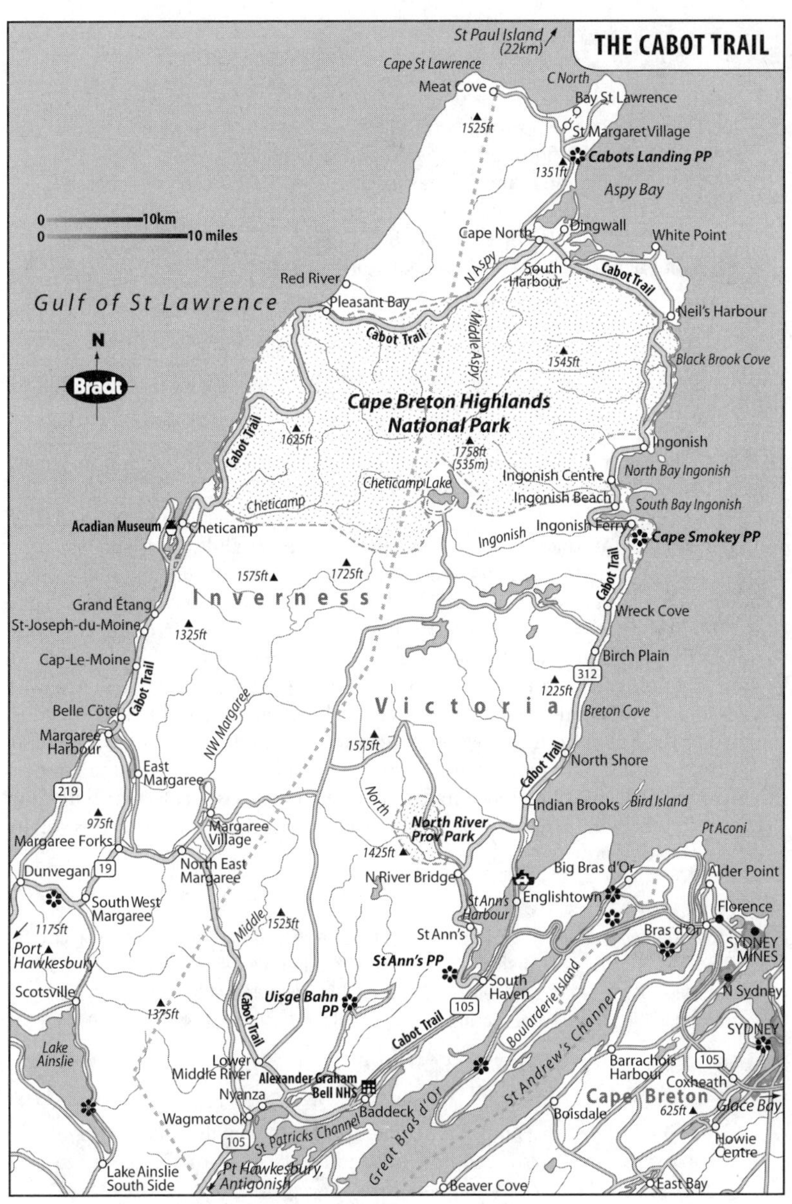

the Gulf of St Lawrence, and home to a good golf course overlooking the harbour. Virtually all attractions, places to stay and eat, and services are strung along the main road through town, the Cabot Trail.

A road along a sandbar leads to **Cheticamp Island**, where you can walk (or drive) to the Enragee Point Lighthouse. The island's large cow population probably accounts for large number of flies.

Situated on the Cabot Trail, Cheticamp is easy to get to **by car**. It is 88km/55 miles from Baddeck and 115km/71 miles from Ingonish Beach. If you continue

SCARECROWS

Nearby Cap Le Moine has an unusual attraction: Joe's Scarecrows. In 1946, Joe Delaney planted a garden and placed scarecrows in it. When tourists stopped to see the figures, he created and planted even more. He died in 1996 but his children maintain his display of over 100 scarecrows dressed and masked to represent politicians, actors and other famous personalities as well as everyday life in Cape Breton. They also run a seasonal eatery from an adjacent trailer. On the Cabot Trail, 9km north of Belle Cote.

more than a few kilometres past Cheticamp, the Cabot Trail passes through the national park (see page 317), and – even if you have no intention of stopping or using facilities – park entry fees are payable.

History The history of Cheticamp was strongly influenced by fishermen from Jersey, Channel Islands, particularly the Robin Company which came to Cheticamp in the late 1760s to exploit the fisheries. Two families settled permanently in 1782, and they were joined by 14 Acadians from St John's Island (as Prince Edward Island was then known) who became affectionately known as 'Les Quatorze Vieux', and many other Acadians who had spent the post-Expulsion years looking for somewhere new to put down roots. Formerly called Eastern Harbour, following the influx of impecunious Acadians the community was labelled *cheti camp*, or 'poor camp'.

Construction of the imposing Romanesque-style c1892 Église St-Pierre was a team effort: parishioners donated a day's work per month, and blocks of stone donated by the Robin Company were dragged across the ice from Cheticamp Island by horses. In addition to man-hours, the parishioners also donated all the lumber. The Baroque-style interior – redecorated in the late 1980s – is spectacular, with four plaster columns looking remarkably like marble: the 1904 Casavant organ is still in excellent working order.

Where to stay

Maison Fiset House (8 units) 15050 Cabot Trail; 224 1794, **t/f** 1 855 292 1794; www.maisonfisethouse.com; year-round. Friendly, new, modern inn/B&B with good view. 6 rooms, & 2 suites with whirlpool baths. All have balconies, & there's a nice patio. Rate inc full b/fast. **$$–$$$**

L'Auberge Doucet Inn (11 rooms, 2 suites) 14758 Cabot Trail; 224 3438, **t/f** 1 800 646 8668;

MASKS

In the Middle Ages, the French took a one-day respite from the rigours of Lent to enjoy themselves. Disguised from head to toe, locals went from house to house getting people to try to guess their identity: they were known as *mi-carêmers*. They then removed their masks and were offered treats. This tradition has largely died out in most French and Acadian regions but remains strong here and in Cheticamp (see page 312). Festivities take place in the third week of Lent (usually March) and last a week. The celebration has led to the revival of carnival mask-making as a folk art. A new purpose-built Centre de la Mi-Carême (*51 Harbour Rd, Grand Etang; 224 1016; www.micareme.ca; mid May–late Oct 09.00–16.00 daily; admission CAN$5*) opened in the summer of 2009, displaying over 100 masks crafted locally for the annual festival.

e doucetinn@ns.sympatico.ca; www.aubergedoucetinn.com; May–mid Nov. In pleasant grounds, the rooms feel a bit more 'motel' than 'inn', but are clean & quite spacious. Full b/fast inc. **$$**

Cheticamp Outfitters Inn B&B (6 rooms) 13938 Cabot Trail, Point Cross; 224 2776; www.cheticampns.com/cheticampoutfitters; May–Nov. Wonderful views from this modern cedar home set on a hillside approx 3km south of Cheticamp. Rooms with private or (cheaper) shared bathroom. The Acadian hosts know the area very well. Full b/fast inc. **$**

Merry's Motel & B&B (10 rooms) 15356 Cabot Trail; 224 2456; e merrysmotel@capebretonisland.com; www.capebretonisland.com/cheticamp/merrysmotel; mid May–mid Oct. 2 rooms in the main house (shared bath) & 10 traditional motel units (private bath). Clean, friendly & good value. Light b/fast inc. **$**

Cheticamp Campground (114 sites) Cape Breton Highlands National Park western entrance, Cabot Trail; t/f 1 877 737 3783 (reservations); www.pccamping.ca; late May–mid Oct: sites can be reserved for late Jun–early Sep. Open & wooded campground with flush toilets, showers & kitchen shelters, serviced & unserviced sites. Note: national park entrance fee payable (see pages 312–14 & 317). **$**

Plage St-Pierre Beach & Campground (94 sites & 50 seasonal) 653 Cheticamp Island Rd; 224 2112; www.plagestpierrebeachandcampground.com; mid May–mid Oct. Open & wooded serviced & tent sites, laundromat & canteen. On Cheticamp Island, with a long stretch of beach frontage. **$**

Where to eat

Le Gabriel 15424 Cabot Trail; 224 3685; www.legabriel.com; early May–late Oct 11.30–22.00 daily. This large licensed restaurant/sports bar (incorporating a mock lighthouse) is about as upmarket as things get in Cheticamp. The seafood (eg: shrimp & scallop kebabs, broiled fillet of haddock, or sole stuffed with scallops & crab) is good. Lounge, billiard table & a regular programme of live Acadian/Celtic music. **$$**

All Aboard Restaurant 14925 Cabot Trail; 224 2288; www.allaboardrestaurant.ca; year-round 11.00–21.00 daily. Good value, licensed Acadian family restaurant with good food (strong on seafood but carnivore options too) & regular live music. Not huge so can get very busy (worth making a reservation in high season). **$–$$**

Restaurant Acadian Contact details as Cheticamp Hooked Rugs, see page 316; mid May–late Oct 11.00–19.00 daily (mid Jun–mid Sep until 20.00). It might not look much, but – with traditionally dressed serving staff – this is a great place to try authentic Acadian dishes such as chicken fricot. The lobster salad is a good choice & the butterscotch pie divine. Licensed. **$–$$**

Seafood Stop 14803 Cabot Trail; 224 1717; www.cheticampns.com/seafoodstop/; May–mid Oct 11.00–20.00 daily. Not just an unpretentious seafood restaurant (several pan-fried options), but also a lobster pound & fish market (good for self-caterers or barbecuers). **$–$$**

Aucoin Bakery Rue Lapointe 14, Petit Etang; 224 3220; year-round 07.30–17.00 Mon–Sat. Take-away energy-boosting calorific treats between Cheticamp & the national park. **$**

Restaurant Evangeline 15150 Cabot Trail; 224 2044; year-round 06.30–21.00 daily. A simple, unsophisticated diner dishing up reliable fish & chips, pizzas & the like. **$**

Festivals The **Festival de I'Escaouette** (*www.festivallescaouette.com*) in July/August is an event-packed festival celebrating Acadian culture and heritage.

Shopping A stop that seems to be on every coach-tour itinerary is **Flora's** (*14208 Cabot Trail; 224 3139; www.floras.com; May–Oct 08.30–18.00 daily*), but this big, often-busy craft and souvenir shop isn't a tourist trap: whilst there are few real bargains, in general, prices are fair.

Other practicalities

$ Bank Royal Bank, 15374 Cabot Trail; 224 2040; 10.00–17.00 Mon–Fri

Health centre Sacred Heart Community Health Centre, 15102 Cabot Trail; 224 1500

Post office 15240 Cabot Trail; 08.45–17.15 Mon–Fri

Tourist information Les Trois Pignons Museum, 15584 Cabot Trail; 224 2642; mid May–mid Oct 08.00–19.00 daily.

What to see and do For hooked rug enthusiasts, Cheticamp is the perfect stop. Head to **Les Trois Pignons Museum of the Hooked Rug and Home Life** (*15584 Cabot Trail; 224 2642; www.lestroispignons.com; mid May–mid Oct 09.00–17.00 daily; Jul/Aug to 19.00; admission CAN$5*), whose collection links Cheticamp's history with the development of rug hooking. The **Elizabeth LeFort Gallery** has a unique collection of hooked rug masterpieces by Ms LeFort, Cheticamp's most famous daughter, and, some would say, the country's best rug hooker – her works have graced walls in Buckingham Palace, the White House and the Vatican. Starting in the 1930s as a rug-hooking co-operative, **Cheticamp Hooked Rugs** (*15067 Cabot Trail; 224 2170; www.cheticamphookedrugs.com; mid May–late Oct 09.00–17.00 daily; Jul/Aug until 18.00*) has expanded into a good craft shop (with locally made hooked rugs) and museum of local Acadian life, with hands-on demonstrations of weaving, carding and spinning. You can also contribute a loop or two on – and enter a draw to win – a hooked rug. There's also an on-site Acadian restaurant/café (see page 315).

Relax on the green at **Le Portage Golf Club** (*15580 Cabot Trail; 224 3338, t/f 1 888 618 5558; www.leportagegolfclub.com*), a 6,751yd par-72 course. Not quite up there with Cape Breton Island's very best courses, but still well worth a round. Green fees are CAN$59.

Or enjoy the view on horseback: **Little Pond Stables** (*103 LaPointe Rd, Petit Etang; 224 3858, t/f 1 888 250 6799; www.horsebackcapebreton.com*) offers wooded trail, beach and mountain rides of 90 minutes, plus short pony rides for little kids.

OMM

Turn off the Cabot Trail onto Pleasant Bay Road, and within five minutes you'll come to the remote community of Red River. As you'd expect, there are weathered houses and fishermen's shacks: less predictable is a Tibetan Buddhist Monastery. If you wish to look round **Gampo Abbey** (*224 2752; www.gampoabbey.org; tours are generally offered Jul/Aug 13.30 & 14.30 Mon–Fri*), it's best to ring ahead to check.

Whale watching Local operators offering 2.5- to three-hour boat trips two or three times a day for approximately CAN$39 include:

Love Boat Seaside Whale Cruises 224 2899, t/f 1 877 880 2899; www.loveboatwhalecruises.com. Tours mid Jun–mid Oct.

Whale Cruisers 224 3376, t/f 1 800 813 3376; www.whalecruisers.com. Tours mid May–early Oct.

PLEASANT BAY The Cabot Trail leaves the park just before Pleasant Bay, a working fishing village which bills itself 'Whale Watching Capital of Cape Breton Island'. Whales come closer to Pleasant Bay than they do to Cheticamp (see page 312), so tours from here tend to be shorter. For a list of tour operators, see opposite. Hikers should be sure to take the **Roberts Mountain Trail**: not all that long, but steep. If it is clear, you'll be rewarded with a magnificent 360° view.

Pleasant Bay is on the Cabot Trail, accessible **by car**. The village is 42km/26 miles from Cheticamp and 73km/45 miles from Ingonish Beach.

Where to stay and eat

Highland Breeze (3 rooms) 42 Harbour Rd; 224 2974, **t/f** 1 877 224 2974; **e** highlandbreezebnb@yahoo.ca; www.bbcanada.com/highlandbreeze; year-round. Moose are often seen from the deck of this modern chalet-style 3-bedroom B&B with outdoor hot-tub & seasonal pool. There's also a deluxe 1-bedroom apt. Country b/fast (continental b/fast only for apt), evening dessert, & entry to the Whale Interpretive Centre included in rate. **$$**

Midtrail Motel & Restaurant (20 rooms) 23475 Cabot Trail; 224 2529, **t/f** 1 800 215 0411; www.midtrail.com; mid May–mid Oct. Recently renovated motel rooms at this pink complex with wonderful views on 12ha on the waterfront. The licensed restaurant (*mid May–mid Oct 08.00–20.00 daily;* **$$**) isn't bad, & the seafood is recommended. **$$**

HI-Cabot Trail Hostel 23349 Cabot Trail; 224 1976; **e** cabottrailhostel@hotmail.com; May–Oct. A clean & friendly backpackers' hostel with 14 beds divided between 2 dorm rooms & 2 private rooms. Shared bathrooms, 2 kitchens. Bike friendly. *Dorm CAN$30; private room CAN$65 (discount for HI members)*. **$**

Rusty Anchor Restaurant 23197 Cabot Trail; 224 1313; May–Oct 08.00–22.00 daily. Set on a hill with a fabulous view & a deck overlooking Pleasant Bay, this is a great spot. The menu is a bit more creative than many, & once again fresh seafood the best choice. Save room for dessert, too. **$$**

What to see and do

Whale watching It's worth booking in advance for July and August trips. Operators include:

Captain Mark's 224 1316, **t/f** 1 888 754 5112; www.whaleandsealcruise.com. Both conventional boats (CAN$39) & Zodiac-type (CAN$51) offered.

Fiddlin' Whale Tours 1 866 688 2424; www.fiddlinwhaletours.com. Conventional boat, CAN$45.

Whale Interpretive Centre (*104 Harbour Rd; 224 1411; Jun–mid Oct 09.00–17.00 daily; admission CAN$5*) Ideal place to learn more about whales – and see a life-size model of a pilot whale.

CAPE BRETON HIGHLANDS NATIONAL PARK

Established in 1936, the Cape Breton Highlands National Park (CBHNP) (*224 2306; www.pc.gc.ca/pn-np/ns/cbreton; late May–mid Oct; admission CAN$7.80*) was the first national park in the Maritime Provinces. The largest protected wilderness area in the province, it encompasses 950km^2 of the Maritime Acadian Highlands, one of the 39 natural regions of Canada. In addition to the magnificent forested highlands and deep river canyons, large sections of northern Cape Breton Island's stunning coastal wilderness fall within the park's boundaries. Wildlife is plentiful, with moose top of most visitors' 'want to see' lists. If you drive the western part of the Trail in late afternoon or early evening, you're very likely to see moose standing in the roadside ditches: drive slowly and carefully. From the Trail's look-outs, you might see whales just offshore.

The Cabot Trail is the only road through the park: along the road are two-dozen scenic roadside look-outs, many with interpretive panels: if the weather is clear, enjoy magnificent breathtaking views of the Highlands, the Gulf of St Lawrence, and, on the eastern side, the Atlantic. Pass soaring cliffs, rocky

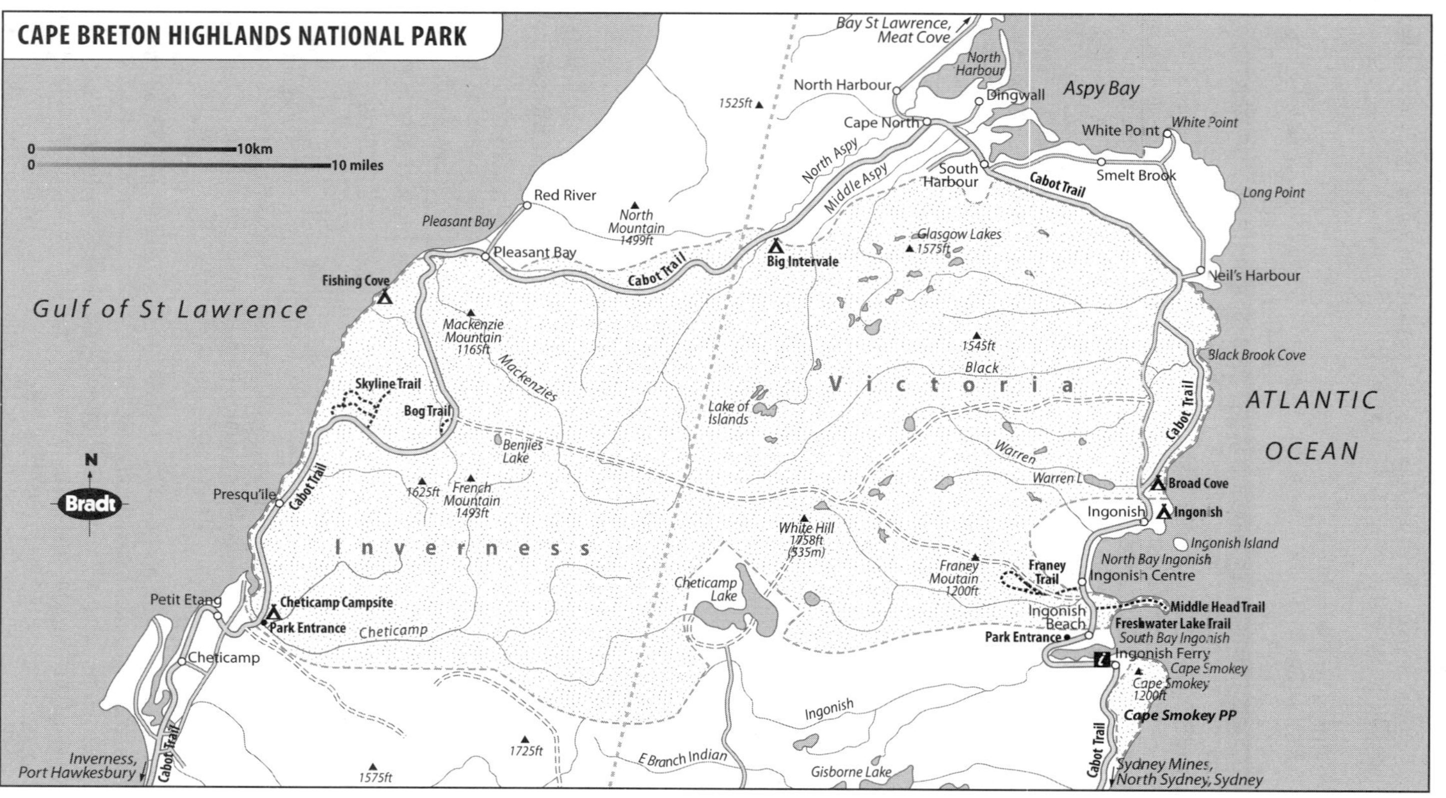
CAPE BRETON HIGHLANDS NATIONAL PARK
0 10km
0 10 miles
Gulf of St Lawrence
ATLANTIC OCEAN
Aspy Bay
Bay St Lawrence, Meat Cove
North Harbour
North Harbour
Dingwall
Cape North
White Point
White Point
Smelt Brook
South Harbour
Long Point
Neil's Harbour
North Aspy
Middle Aspy
Cabot Trail
1525ft
Red River
Pleasant Bay
Pleasant Bay
North Mountain 1499ft
Big Intervale
Glasgow Lakes
1575ft
1545ft
Black
Black Brook Cove
Victoria
Lake of Islands
Fishing Cove
Mackenzie Mountain 1165ft
Mackenzies
Skyline Trail
Bog Trail
Benjies Lake
Warren
Warren L
Broad Cove
Ingonish
Ingonish
Ingonish Island
N
Bradt
Presqu'ile
1625ft
French Mountain 1493ft
Inverness
White Hill 1758ft (535m)
Franey Moutain 1200ft
Franey Trail
North Bay Ingonish
Ingonish Centre
Middle Head Trail
Freshwater Lake Trail
Ingonish Beach
South Bay Ingonish
Park Entrance
Ingonish Ferry
Cape Smokey
Cape Smokey 1200ft
Cape Smokey PP
Cheticamp Lake
Petit Etang
Cheticamp Campsite
Park Entrance
Cheticamp
Cheticamp
Ingonish
1725ft
1575ft
E Branch Indian
Gisborne Lake
Inverness, Port Hawkesbury
Sydney Mines, North Sydney, Sydney

shorelines, fabulous beaches – and one of the world's top golf courses. Although I strongly advise you to get out of your vehicle as often as possible to walk a few trails, enjoy a picnic with an awesome view, or just wander a deserted beach, this is a park that *can* be enjoyed by those much happier doing their sightseeing without having to undo their seat belts.

With all this and sandy beaches, mountain trails, old-growth forests, waterfalls and highland barrens carpeted in rare wild flowers, this national park is one of the finest in Canada – and that's saying something.

The Cabot Trail dips in and out of the park: this means that those who do not wish to camp can stay very close to all the natural beauty, albeit just outside the park's boundaries.

GEOGRAPHY The CBHNP protects a spectacular portion of the largest remaining wild area of the Maritime Acadian Highlands. The dominant feature is the forested high plateau, which encompasses White Hill, the province's highest point at 535m. Extensive bog systems on the plateau are drained by numerous streams, stained the colour of tea by tannins leeching from the vegetation. After heavy rain, or during the spring snow melt, these in turn feed plunging waterfalls. There are also deep, forested canyons, and magnificent coastal cliffs which tend to be steeper to the west and more gently sloping on the park's eastern side.

A unique mix of Acadian, Boreal and Taiga forest regions co-exists as a result of the rugged topography and cool maritime climate.

GEOLOGY The park's plateau is part of the worn-down Appalachian mountain chain which stretches from Georgia to Newfoundland. Part of the park belongs to the Blair River inlier (an area, or formation of, older rocks completely surrounded by a more recent formation), formed 1,500 to 1,000 million years ago, and the oldest rocks in the Maritime Provinces.

FLORA AND FAUNA The most common tree species include balsam fir, white and yellow birch, white and dwarf spruce and sugar maple – there are over 750 vascular plant species, the vast majority native. These include Arctic–Alpine species such as dwarf birch (*Betula nana*) and southern temperate plants such as Dutchman's breeches (*Dicentra cucullaria*).

The park is also home to white-tailed deer, moose, black bear, beaver, mink, red fox, snow-shoe hare, Gaspe shrew, rock vole and lynx, and over 200 bird species, including eagles and red-tailed hawks. Wildlife can be seen offshore too, with pilot and minke whales, and harbour seal the most commonly seen marine mammals. Humpback whales and grey seals are spotted less frequently.

TRAILS Walkers and hikers can choose from 26 trails which range from ten minutes to six hours. A short summary of each trail is given on the park map obtainable at the information centres, or on the website (see page 317). Mountain biking is permitted on four of the trails.

Suggestions include the ten- to 15-minute **Bog Trail**, where a boardwalk – with interpretive boards – leads through a highland plateau bog: flora includes pitcher plants and wild orchids. Or try the well-hiked (and well-liked) 9km **Skyline Trail**, which despite its name, doesn't involve a huge amount of climbing: it leads to a headland clifftop high above the sea. On this trail, look carefully for moose which often lie down in the undergrowth very close to the path: the majority of walkers pass them by without noticing them. Many people visiting the park stay at the

Ingonishes (see page 323), and that area has some good and understandably popular trails, such as the 2km wander around Freshwater Lake (look for beavers towards dusk). Very hard work but worth it for the view is the 7.5km **Franey Trail**, which involves an ascent of over 300m. And despite starting behind a resort, the 4km **Middle Head Trail** is very enjoyable, with fine coastal views, and the possibility of seeing whales from the end of the peninsula.

It is definitely worth talking to the information centre staff and listening to their hiking suggestions.

TOURIST INFORMATION The park has information centres (⌚ *late May–mid Oct 09.00–17.00 daily; Jul/Aug until 19.00*) at both entrances: **Cheticamp** (📞 *224 2306*), and **Ingonish** (📞 *285 2691*). In the off-season, ask for information at the park office at the Cheticamp entrance. The information centre at Cheticamp is by far the larger and in addition to exhibits on natural history, sightseeing and hiking opportunities, also houses a well-stocked bookshop, **Les Amis du Plein Air** (📞 *224 3814*).

WHERE TO STAY The park has seven **campgrounds**, six accessible by road (and ranging from ten to 194 sites), and one hike-in. Reservations are only accepted at two: Cheticamp and Broad Cove (**t/f** *0877 737 3783 to reserve*). The campgrounds at Cheticamp, Broad Cove and Ingonish are described in the respective sections. Suggestions for non-campers are shown under the appropriate area.

FESTIVALS The **Lobsterpalooza** (*www.lobsterpalooza.ca*) festival takes place in numerous Cabot Trail coastal communities at the end of May/early June. It comprises five weeks of events which celebrate seafaring traditions – and seafood. Also held over five weeks at various Cabot Trail communities, the **Hike the Highlands Festival** (*www.hikethehighlandsfestival.com*) in September includes guided hikes in the Highlands of Cape Breton Island.

THE FAR NORTH

The Cabot Trail community of Cape North is the launching point for a beautiful side-trip to explore some of Nova Scotia's most stunning scenery and remote communities.

CAPE NORTH The small community of Cape North is about 30km from the eponymous geographic feature – which, as the name might suggest, is Nova Scotia's most northerly point.

Winter visitors may be tempted to don cross-country skis – the **North Highlands Nordic Ski Club** is based here.

Cape North is on the Cabot Trail, 71km/44 miles from Cheticamp and 44km/27 miles from Ingonish Beach. The small community is easy to get to **by car**.

Where to stay and eat

Markland Coastal Cottages (20 units) 802 Dingwall Rd; 📞 383 2246, **t/f** 1 855 872 6048; **e** info@themarkland.com; www.themarkland.com; ⌚ May–mid Oct. Close to the quaint fishing village of Dingwall, 5km from Cape North, the Markland offers log rooms & 1- & 2-bedroom chalets. A simple place to stay & enjoy the outdoors. Heated outdoor pool (seasonal), & private beach in a magnificent, scenic location. Its restaurant ($$$) is good – fresh, local ingredients, seafood, organic vegetables, etc – but not cheap. **$$$**

Oakwood Manor (4 units) 250 North Side Rd; 📞 383 2317; www.oakwoodmanorbedandbreakfast.

MEAT COVE DETOUR

Consider a beautiful, scenic side-trip from Cape North to Bay St Lawrence and Meat Cove, the province's most northerly community.

Follow Bay St Lawrence Road along the lovely Aspy Bay shore to Cabot Landing Provincial Park. This picnic park has a long red sand beach – tinged white in places by naturally occurring gypsum – facing Aspy Bay, and a cairn commemorating the supposed landfall of John Cabot in 1497 (see page 15). If the weather is clear, you'll have a good view of St Paul Island (see page 322). For those who feel like burning off some calories in return for amazing views, the park is also the starting point for a hike up the 442m **Sugar Loaf Mountain**.

St Margaret's Village has a lovely setting, and a right turn leads to **Bay St Lawrence**, another pretty fishing village (crab is a speciality). Whale-watching and other boat trips depart from the wharf with some of the province's most remote and stunning coastal scenery as a backdrop. Fin whales – the second-largest whale species after the blue whale – are often seen. Local operators include the excellent **Oshan Whale Watch** (**t/f** *1 877 383 2883; www.oshan.ca;* ⌚ *Jul–Oct*), who can also arrange birdwatching boat trips, deep-sea fishing charters, and (with notice) trips to St Paul Island. There's also **Captain Cox's Whale Watch** (📞 *383 2981,* **t/f** *1 888 346 5556; www.whalewatching-novascotia.com;* ⌚ *mid Jun–Oct*). Very fresh seafood can be purchased at the village's Victoria Co-op Fisheries, or stock up with groceries at the store. There's The Hut, a decent take-out, a simple café in the Community Centre, and an ATM.

Continue to **Capstick**, and then on a 7km unpaved road: virtually all the way, you will enjoy spectacular views from high above the sea. Whilst drivers will want to concentrate on the road, passengers can look out for pods of whales in the bays below. The road descends to (and ends at) remote **Meat Cove**. Here, you'll find a **Welcome Centre** (⌚ *Jun–early Oct 09.30–16.30 Mon–Fri*), which houses a tea room, a couple of simple places to stay – the rustic **Meat Cove Lodge** (📞 *383 2790; http://meatcovelodge.ca;* ⌚ *Jun–mid Sep*), the **Hines Ocean View Lodge** (📞 *383 2512, 383 2562; www.hinesoceanviewlodge.ca;* ⌚ *May–Oct*), and the amazingly located clifftop 26-site **Meat Cove Campground** (📞 *383 2379; www.meatcovecampground.ca;* ⌚ *mid Jun–mid Oct*), which also rents kayaks. There are some very good hikes and Meat Cove is a place for those who appreciate nature and the great coastal outdoors: ironically, this is also a popular moose-hunting area in the hunting season. For trail suggestions – and more on Meat Cove – see http://meatcove.ca.

com; ⌚ May–Oct. A c1930 manor house on a 80ha estate, with 3 rooms & a suite. If you like old wood, you'll love the beautiful interior. Full b/fast inc. **$**

⛺ Hideaway Campground, Cabins & Oyster Market (4 cabins, 37 campsites) 401 Shore Rd, South Harbour; 📞 383 2116; www.campingcapebreton.com; ⌚ mid May–mid Oct. Rustic camping cabins & well-spread open & wooded sites approx 5km from Cape North, overlooking Aspy Bay, with laundromat. Canoe & kayak rentals, & boat launch. Oysters sold. Recommended for campers. *Cabins CAN$50.* **$**

What to see and do The **North Highlands Community Museum** (*29243 Cabot Trail;* 📞 *383 2579; www.northhighlandsmuseum.ca;* ⌚ *late Jun–late Oct*

10.00–18.00 daily; admission CAN$2) houses displays which tell of pioneer days in the Cape Breton Highlands, and more recent history. See, too, artefacts from the *Auguste*, wrecked in Aspy Bay in 1761 *en route* from Quebec to France. Of the 121 on board, only seven reached the shore alive. Traditional skills – for example net mending, weaving, ropemaking, quilting and boatbuilding – are demonstrated in July and August. There is also a settlers' garden, operational forge and culture centre.

Some 2km west of Cape North village, **Arts North** (*28571 Cabot Trail;* ☎ *383 2732; www.arts-north.com;* ⊕ *Jun–Oct 09.00–19.00 daily*) displays the work of over two-dozen surprisingly gifted resident artisans, including handmade pottery, native-wood cutting boards, jewellery, prints, driftwood carvings, quilting and basketry. Meanwhile, the new **St Paul Island Museum** (*Dingwall Rd, Dingwall;* ⊕ *mid Jun–mid Oct 10.00–18.00 daily*) tells the story of St Paul Island (see box below). Alongside is a well-travelled **lighthouse**: originally the St Paul Island Southwest Lighthouse, it arrived in Dingwall in 2012 by way of Dartmouth (see box, below).

For those wishing to take to the water, **Eagle North** (*299 Shore Rd, South Harbour;* **t/f** *1 888 616 1689; www.kayakingcapebreton.ca*) is a family business that rents canoes and sea kayaks and offers 90-minute, three-hour and full-day guided sea kayaking trips exploring the region's beautiful coastal waters.

ST PAUL ISLAND The rocky shores of St Paul Island – 22km offshore between the tip of Cape North and the Ingonishes (see page 323) – have accounted for over 350 recorded shipwrecks.

The Graveyard of the Gulf lies directly in the path of marine travel to and from the Gulf of St Lawrence, and in an area prone to thick fog in the spring and early summer and squalls and snowstorms in the autumn and winter.

Very hilly, the 4.5km by 1.5km island is covered with stunted spruce. Two lakes feed several streams. In season, there are abundant wild flowers but no animal life. The only relatively safe landing areas are Atlantic Cove, and Trinity Cove on the island's opposite side.

In the early days, each year, when fishermen came to St Paul in spring, they would find the frozen bodies of shipwreck survivors who had managed to scale the island's cliffs only to perish from exposure and starvation.

For decades, demands were made for a lighthouse: in just one stormy 1835 night, four ships were wrecked on the island's shores.

Finally in 1837, construction of two lighthouses, one at each end of the island, began. A building was also put up to house shipwreck victims. Subsequently there were still occasional tragedies, but far less loss of life.

BEACON BROUGHT BACK

An iron lighthouse that stood at the southwest end of St Paul Island from 1917 was replaced with a fibreglass version in 1962. The iron tower then stood near offices at the Canadian Coast Guard Maritime base in Dartmouth. For many years, the citizens of Dingwall and the St Paul Island Historical Society campaigned to bring the iron lighthouse back close to home, and in August 2012 their dream came true. The federal government contributed CAN$108,000 towards the cost of transporting the lighthouse to Dingwall where it has become an important feature standing proudly alongside the St Paul Island Museum (see above).

Visits to the island can be arranged through Oshan Whale Watch (see box, page 321) and you'll need a permit from the Real Property: Safety and Security Department of Fisheries and Oceans Canada (*426 3550; www.dfo-mpo.gc.ca*).

The island's shipwreck-dotted waters are popular with divers – if you'd like to join them, Terry Dwyer (e *shipwrecked@ns.sympatico.ca; www.wreckhunter.ca*) may be able to help.

THE EAST COAST

Beautiful though the Cabot Trail is, at the start of the next section of the Trail, a simple detour will yield rich rewards. Further south is a popular resort area known collectively as 'The Ingonishes' at the southeastern boundary of the Cape Breton Highlands National Park. Just a few kilometres further on is magnificent Cape Smokey before the scenery eases down a gear or two from the highs further north.

For a spectacular alternative to the next stretch of the Cabot Trail, turn off at Effies Brook and follow White Point Road. *En route*, look out for the excellent **Sea Spray Outdoor Adventures** (*383 2732; www.cabot-trail-outdoors.com; year-round, hours vary*), which offers a wealth of local knowledge, cycle hire and a range of guided and self-guided tours from hiking, cycling, sea kayaking and trail running in summer, to snow-shoeing, cross-country and back-country skiing in winter.

Along White Point Road you'll pass high cliffs and a photogenic sheltered lagoon before a long descent to the picturesque and beautifully situated village of **White Point**. See the colourful fishing boats protected by the little harbour, and be sure to wander down the track towards the point (the site of the village during the Age of Sail). Watch for whales, sit in the meadow and tuck into a picnic, or just soak up the coastal scenery. Climb back up the hill and continue through the fishing villages of New Haven and Neil's Harbour to rejoin the Cabot Trail.

NEIL'S HARBOUR This busy working fishing community has a sandy beach bordered by high cliffs. On a hillock is a pyramid shaped white wooden lighthouse with a square base, topped by a red light. In the summer the lighthouse is home to an ice cream shop.

Neil's Harbour is just off the Cabot Trail, 28km/17 miles north of Ingonish Beach, and convenient to reach **by car**.

Where to eat There are two simple, unpretentious seafood-focused diner/take-outs within approximately 500m of each other.

Chowder House 336 2463; May–Sep 11.00–20.00 daily. On the point near the lighthouse. $

Sea Breeze 336 2450; mid Apr– mid Sep 11.30–18.00 daily. My preferred option, offering good, simple, fresh home-cooking in a converted old house overlooking the beach. $

THE INGONISHES On the shores of two lovely large bays (North and South), separated by the ruggedly beautiful Middle Head Peninsula, are the communities of (from north to south) Ingonish, Ingonish Centre, Ingonish Beach, Ingonish Harbour and (16km from Ingonish) Ingonish Ferry. Offshore is Ingonish Island.

Ingonish Beach is the eastern gateway to the Cape Breton Highlands National Park: within this region are a range of fine accommodations, excellent eateries, beautiful beaches (offering swimming in both fresh and salt water), and a relaxed resort atmosphere. Many will be drawn by the chance to play one of the world's best golf courses, others for the hiking. You can camp here, but it is also a good base from which non-campers can explore the national park and Cape North area.

Dotted about the Ingonishes are a couple of convenience stores, a liquor store, a bank and a laundromat.

Many people come and stay for a week or more – even if you're on a tight itinerary try to give yourself a couple of nights at least. Demand for accommodation can exceed supply in July and August, so book well ahead.

Accessible **by car**, the Ingonishes are on the Cabot Trail, 110km/68 miles east of Cheticamp and 100km/62 miles north of Baddeck.

Where to stay

Keltic Lodge Resort and Spa (82 units) Middle Head Peninsula, Ingonish Beach; 285 2880, t/f 1 800 565 0444; e keltic@signatureresorts.com; www.kelticlodge.ca; mid May–mid Oct. This Ingonish institution is in a magnificent setting on the peninsula dividing North & South bays. There are 32 rooms in the main lodge, 10, 2- to 4-bedroom cottages & 40 upmarket-motel-style rooms in the inn at Keltic (probably the best choice). For restaurants, see below). Facilities include a bar, outdoor heated pool, tennis courts & Aveda spa, but the *pièce de résistance* is the golf course (see opposite). Various packages are offered. **$$$$**

Seascape Coastal Retreat (10 cabins) 36083 Cabot Trail, Ingonish; 285 3003, t/f 1 866 385 3003; www.seascapecoastalretreat.com; May–Oct. Comfortable 1-bedroom cottages with kitchenettes in a wonderful location aimed at couples rather than families. For restaurant listing, see below. Use of kayaks & mountain bikes. Recommended. Full b/fast & snacks inc. **$$$**

Castle Rock Country Inn (17 rooms) 39339 Cabot Trail, Ingonish Ferry; 285 2700, t/f 1 888 884 7625; e castlerock@ns.sympatico.ca; www.ingonish.com/castlerock; year-round. A modern Georgian-style inn on a cliffside high above the Ingonishes with magnificent views. Rooms are on 3 levels (basement rooms are smaller but still have ocean views). For the on-site Avalon Restaurant, see below. Continental b/fast inc. **$$**

The Point Cottages by the Sea (6 cottages) 2 Point Cottages Lane, Ingonish; 285 2804; www.thepointcottages.com; Jun–mid Oct. 3, 1-bedroom, 2, 2-bedroom & 1, 3-bedroom cottage in a group of 12 in a great location virtually on the beach. A 1-week min rental applies Jul/Aug. **$$**

Broad Cove (194 sites) t/f 1 877 737 3783 (reservations); www.pccamping.ca; late May–mid Oct. A large open & wooded campground with serviced & unserviced sites, flush toilets, showers & kitchen shelters. Only a short walk to the sea, approx 5km north of Ingonish. **$**

Ingonish (590 sites) Ingonish Beach; late Jun–early Sep. Open campground, unserviced sites flush toilets, showers, kitchen shelters, 10 mins' walk to the lake or beach. **$**

Where to eat

Keltic Lodge Resort & Spa Middle Head Peninsula, Ingonish Beach; 285 2880, t/f 1 800 565 0444; e keltic@signatureresorts.com; www.kelticlodge.ca. Keltic offers 2 dining options: the modern **Atlantic Restaurant** (*early Jun–mid Sep 11.00–20.00 daily;* **$$**), offering casual family-style dining (predominantly seafood), & the fine-dining gourmet **Purple Thistle** (*mid May–mid Oct 18.00–21.00 daily;* **$$$–$$$$**). Reservations recommended; dress code – smart casual – applies.

Seascape Coastal Retreat 36083 Cabot Trail, Ingonish; 285 3003, t/f 1 866 385 3003; www.seascapecoastalretreat.com; mid Jun–late Oct, daily 11.30–14.30 & 17.00–21.00. Specialising in seafood & also very good with alfresco dining when the weather permits. **$$$**

Avalon Restaurant at Castle Rock Country Inn 39339 Cabot Trail, Ingonish Ferry; 285 2700, t/f 1 888 884 7625; e castlerock@ns.sympatico.ca; www.ingonish.com/castlerock; year-round 17.00–20.00 daily (Nov–Jun by reservation only). The on-site licensed restaurant shares the inn's views & offers alfresco dining when the weather permits. In 2012, the Avalon's menu offered Asian–Cape Breton fusion cuisine & this may change in the future. It is unlikely that standards will drop suddenly. Considering the panorama & food quality, prices are reasonable. $$

✕ **Coastal Restaurant & Pub** 36404 Cabot Trail, Ingonish; ☎ 285 2526; ⏱ May–Oct 08.00–22.00 daily. Good, dependable family dining with the emphasis on seafood. If you prefer red meat, you won't have much room for pudding after the Coastal's signature 'ringer burger'. Patio. Licensed. $$

✕ **Main Street Restaurant & Bakery** 37764 Cabot Trail, Ingonish Beach; ☎ 285 2225; ⏱ Sep–Jun 07.00–20.00 Tue–Sat; Jul/Aug 07.00–21.00 Tue–Sat. Good-size portions, well-cooked food & friendly service: another place that does superb seafood chowder – & a lot more. $$

✕ **Seagull Restaurant** 35963 Cabot Trail, Ingonish; ☎ 285 2851; ⏱ end May–early Oct 12.00–19.30 Wed–Mon. The Seagull doesn't claim to do *haute cuisine*: here the deep-fryer is king. Big portions of diner food, low prices, fabulous views from the outdoor (covered) patio. Easy to miss – look out for a single-storey white building on the waterfront. $

Other practicalities

$ **Bank** Scotiabank, 37787 Cabot Trail, Ingonish Beach; ☎ 285 2555

Library Victoria North Regional Library, 36243 Cabot Trail; ☎ 285 2544; ⏱ 12.00–17.00 & 18.00–20.00 Tue–Thu, 09.00–12.00 & 13.00–17.00 Fri, 10.00–12.00 & 13.00–17.00 Sat

✉ **Post office** 37813 Cabot Trail, Ingonish Beach; ⏱ 08.00–17.00 Mon–Fri, 10.00–14.00 Sat

What to see and do Ingonish **whale-watching** tour operators seem to come and go, but **Keltic Express Zodiac Adventures** (**t/f** *1 866 688 2424; www.capebretonwhaletours.com;* ⏱ *May–Oct*) runs a 90-minute to two-hour tour which costs CAN$55. If golf is your thing, **Highland Links Ingonish Beach** (☎ *285 2600,* **t/f** *1 800 441 1118; www.highlandslinksgolf.com*) is one of Canada's top courses. Featuring on most 'World's 100 Best Courses' lists, this 6,592yd par-72 course was designed by Stanley Thompson, who was also responsible for the Digby Pines course (see page 196). The setting is truly magnificent. Note that there are walks of up to 500m between holes. Green fees are CAN$102.

CAPE SMOKEY From Ingonish Ferry, the Cabot Trail climbs steadily to the crest of 360m Cape Smokey, named for the white cloud that often sits atop the red granite promontory. You're no longer within the national park, but nature is just as stunning here.

A turn-off leads to the **Cape Smokey Provincial Park** (⏱ *mid May–mid Oct; admission free*) which provides magnificent vistas of the mountainous coastline. There are several picnic areas, and a moderate to difficult 10km return trail leads past several look-outs to the very tip of the Cape. Bald eagles and hawks can often be seen soaring the updrafts and moose are plentiful in this area: on my last visit I saw three by the roadside between the Cabot Trail and the parking area.

From the top of old Smokey, the steep and twisting road descends, offering views of the offshore Bird Islands (see page 329).

Cape Smokey is on the Cabot Trail, 13km/8 miles south of Ingonish Beach, and 87km/54 miles from Baddeck.

WRECK COVE TO INDIAN BROOK The Cabot Trail continues along the coastal plain passing little fishing communities, a handful of studios/craft shops, and a couple of beaches.

Where to stay

Cabot Shores Wilderness Resort (9 units) 30 Buchanan Dr, Indian Brook; **t/f** 1 866 929 2584; www.cabotshores.com; ⏱ year-round. 5 rooms in the old farmhouse, & 4, 2-bedroom chalets on a 22ha lake & ocean-front property. On-site bistro (caters to vegetarians/vegans) & licensed bar (check opening times), live music. Canoes, kayaks, bikes, plus meditation, yoga, etc. Pet friendly. Cabot Shores also offers various camping options. **$$**

English Country Garden B&B (5 rooms) 45478 Cabot Trail, Indian Brook; **t/f** 1 866 929 2721; **e** ipgreen@ns.sympatico.ca; www.capebretongarden.com; year-round. Penny & Ian have created a luxurious B&B on 15 lakeside hectares. There are 4 themed beautifully decorated suites in the main house, & an open-plan private B&B cottage down the path. A 3-course set menu is offered for CAN$63 in the (reservation only) dining room (*Oct–Apr 19.00 Thu–Sat; year-round Thu–Sat by advance reservation for guests*): the main course might be maple baked salmon, or perhaps *filet mignon* with hunter sauce. Full b/fast inc. **$$**

Wreck Cove Wilderness Cabins (2 cabins) 42314 Cabot Trail, Wreck Cove; 929 2800, **t/f** 1 877 929 2800; www.capebretonsnaturecoast.com; year-round. Cosy, fully equipped 2-bedroom cabins ideal for lovers of the outdoors, just 5 mins' walk from the sea & close to highland walking trails. **$$**

Where to eat

The Dancing Moose Café 42691 Cabot Trail, Birch Plain; 929 2523; http://thedancingmoosecafe.ca; in-season 07.00–16.00 daily; check for off-season times. New (2012) addition offering Belgian waffles, Dutch pancakes, coffee, baked goods – & a wonderful sea view. **$–$$**

Clucking Hen Café & Bakery 45073 Cabot Trail, North Shore; 929 2501; May 08.00–18.00; Jun & Sep–mid Oct 07.00–19.00 daily; Jul/Aug 07.00–20.00 daily. A friendly, laid-back licensed eatery. The fish chowder is very good, & the pan-fried haddock dinner recommended. Outdoor eating area. For a calorific treat, grab a cinnamon roll, blondie or wedge of homemade pie. **$**

Wreck Cove General Store 42470 Cabot Trail, Wreck Cove; 929 2900; www.wreckcovegeneralstore.com; year-round, in summer daily. This well-stocked old-fashioned store is worth a stop: excellent lobster sandwiches in season, pizza by the slice, oatcakes, & in summer, ice cream. **$**

What to see and do If you would like a glimpse of local handiwork, stop by **Leather Works** (*45808 Cabot Trail, Indian Brook; 929 2414; www.leather-works.ca; 09.00–17.00 most days, extended by chance or appointment*). John Roberts and his team hand-make a range of beautiful leather goods including fire buckets. Also visit Barbara Longva's shop/studio **Sew Inclined** (*41819 Cabot Trail, Wreck Cove; 929 2050; www.sewinclined.ca; May–Oct 09.00–17.00 daily*) for unique hats and historic clothing.

NORTH RIVER Shortly after Indian Brook, the Cabot Trail turns inland before reaching North River. With an excellent place to stay and eat, beautiful provincial parks nearby, several artisans' shops and galleries to visit, and a good kayaking company just up the road, this is worth considering as a base from which to explore the Cabot Trail and the Bras d'Or Lake area.

Winter visitors looking to do some wilderness Telemark skiing should check out **Ski Tuonela** (*295 7694; www.skituonela.com*), between North River and St Ann's (see opposite).

North River is on the Cabot Trail, 20km/12 miles from Exit 11 of Highway 105, 55km/22 miles from Ingonish Beach and 36km from Baddeck.

Where to stay and eat

Chanterelle Country Inn (12 units) 48678 Cabot Trail; 929 2263, **t/f** 1 866 277 0577; www.chanterelleinn.com; May–Oct. 'Green' inn set on 60ha overlooking the North River estuary: 9 guest rooms & 3 well-equipped nearby cottages. Very comfortable. Don't expect TVs or AC. The menu in the rather good licensed dining room (🕘 *May–Oct 18.00–20.00;* **$$$**) changes nightly & always includes a vegetarian, non-vegetarian & seafood main course & freshly baked artisan bread. Locally sourced ingredients. Imaginative buffet b/fast inc (room, not cottage). **$$**

What to see and do Popular with anglers and hikers, **North River Provincial Park** is a small riverside picnic park that gives access to the North River Wilderness Area. A moderate–difficult (9km each way) trail leads to the 31m North River Falls. Take up a paddle with **North River Kayak** (📞 *929 2628; www.northriverkayak.com;* 🕘 *mid May–mid Oct*) for kayak rentals, lessons, courses, and guided half-, full- and multi-day trips around the region's lovely waters.

ST ANN'S At 17km further along the Cabot Trail from North River is St Ann's: home to the Gaelic College of Celtic Arts and Crafts, the community is considered the centre of Cape Breton's Gaelic culture. St Ann's Provincial Park has a picnic area and a short walking trail that leads to a vantage point overlooking the beautiful harbour. There's even a 'kayak and learn songwriting' trip.

St Ann's is on the Cabot Trail and just off Highway 105 Exit 11, 74km/46 miles south of Ingonish Beach and 17km/11 miles from Baddeck. It is 17km/11 miles from North River.

Where to stay and eat

St Ann's Motel (8 rooms) 51947 Cabot Trail; 📞 295 2876; e stannsmotel@ns.aliantzinc.ca; www.baddeck.com/stannsmotel; 🕘 May–Oct. A traditional-style motel right on the waterfront with wonderful views. Rooms are simple but perfectly comfortable. **$$**

RELOCATION, RELOCATION, RELOCATION

The Reverend Norman McLeod (or MacLeod), originally from Scotland, arrived in Pictou (see page 285) in 1817 and quickly established and ran a church there. Having earned a good reputation, he was offered a church in Ohio (USA) to minister to other Highland Scots who had settled there. He accepted on the condition that all the members of his congregation who wished to join him could come too.

McLeod and his flock sailed out from Pictou in the Ark, bound for America. As luck would have it, before the ship had lost sight of Nova Scotia's shore, the Ark was caught in (not a flood but) a big storm, and – in darkness – the ship's captain took refuge in the nearest safe water, St Ann's Bay.

When the new day dawned, the passengers cast their eyes on a landscape very similar to their old Scottish homeland, and decided that they'd done more than enough travelling. They dispensed with all thoughts of Ohio and made their new homes here. They were rewarded with severe winters and crop failures.

McLeod's son sailed off to take cargo to Glasgow, but was not heard from for eight years. Finally, word came from him in Australia, suggesting that his father (and, of course, the entire congregation) come to join him. By now, there were too many parishioners for one ship, and so between 1851 and 1858 seven shiploads of McLeod's followers sailed almost halfway across the planet.

Incidentally, McLeod was less enamoured with Australia than his son had been, and led his followers across the Tasman Sea to New Zealand instead. It was from there – in his late eighties – that he went to meet his maker.

ANOTHER TALL STORY

Angus MacAskill was one of 14 children and as a baby was so small that few thought he would survive. He was six when the family came to Nova Scotia from the island of Harris in the Scottish Hebrides, and 14 before anyone began to notice his unusual size and strength. He grew to be 2.36m tall and weighed 193kg and became known in Gaelic as *Gille Mòr St Ann's* ('The St Ann's Big Boy'). An entrepreneurial tradesman met him by chance and took him on tour to show off his size and strength. He often performed with a tiny midget, who, it is said, would dance in the palm of MacAskill's huge hand. Like all good giants from Nova Scotia, he went to England to meet Queen Victoria. Her majesty is said to have commented that he was the tallest, strongest and stoutest man ever to have entered her palace, and the *Guinness Book of World Records* listed him as 'the tallest true (non-pathological) giant'. When he tired of showbiz, he returned to a simple life as a St Ann's storekeeper, and passed away in 1863 aged 38. He is buried in the local cemetery. Learn more at the Giant MacAskill Museum (see below).

✕ **Lobster Galley** 51943 Cabot Trail, South Haven; ☎ 295 3100; ⏲ early May–late Oct 08.00–21.30 daily. Start with lobster-stuffed mushrooms, & move on to sautéed Digby scallops. Deck with water views. Licensed. Next door to St Ann's Motel. $$

Festivals The **Festival of Cape Breton Fiddling** (*www.capebretonfiddlers.com*) is a two-day event with concerts and workshops, which takes place in August.

What to see and do The **Gaelic College/*Colaside Na Gàidhlig*** (*51779 Cabot Trail;* ☎ *295 3441; www.gaeliccollege.edu*) is the only institution of its kind in North America. The college was founded in 1938 in a log cabin to encourage the study and preservation of the Gaelic language, arts and culture. Primarily an educational institution, it offers year-round programming in the study of the Cape Breton Gaelic language, music, dance, arts, and crafts. Several musical and cultural events take place during the summer; there is a craft shop with a wide range of Celtic gifts, Gaelic-language books, and music books and supplies. The **Great Hall of the Clans** (⏲ *09.00–17.00 daily; admission CAN$7*) features interactive exhibits portraying the cultural and linguistic evolution of the Gaels of Cape Breton Island, Nova Scotia and Canada. An art gallery tells the Reverend McLeod saga (see box, page 327). Daily demonstrations in kiltmaking, music, dance, and language, and a Gaelic film presentation (July/August).

ENGLISHTOWN In addition to taking a boat to the Bird Islands (see page 329), you can visit a museum commemorating another of Nova Scotia's larger-than-life characters – the **Giant MacAskill Museum** (*Hwy 312, Englishtown;* ☎ *929 2875;* ⏲ *mid Jun–mid Sep 09.00–17.00 daily; admission CAN$4*); see box above. Incidentally, there's also a Giant MacAskill Museum at Dunvegan on the Scottish Isle of Skye.

Englishtown is on Highway 312, 10km/6 miles from St Ann's.

Where to stay

⛺ **Englishtown Ridge Campground** (73 sites) 938 Englishtown Rd; ☎ 929 2598; www.englishtown-ridge.com; ⏲ mid May–mid Oct. The campground offers good facilities, serviced & tent sites, & overlooks St Ann's Bay & Harbour. $

NOVA CHINA

Cape Dauphin (which you'll pass on a Bird Island tour) was – according to Canadian architect and author Paul Chiasson – the site of a pre-Columbian Chinese community. He claimed that these Chinese settlers would have had a strong impact on Mi'kmaq culture. Few (if any) experts agree with the theories expressed in *The Island of Seven Cities: Where the Chinese Settled When They Discovered America*, but do experts always get it right?

THE BIRD ISLANDS Birdwatchers (and others) will want to take a boat trip around Hertford and Ciboux islands, much more commonly known as the Bird Islands. You won't land on either island, but the boat goes close enough to get a good view, though binoculars and/or telephoto lenses will enhance the experience of the thousands of seabirds that nest here. Depending on the time of year (June and July are probably best), expect to see black guillemots, razorbills, black-legged kittiwakes, great cormorants and Atlantic puffins. Grey seals and bald eagles are also often seen. Contact **Donelda's Puffin Boat Tours** (*1099 Hwy 312, Englishtown; ☎ 929 2563,* **t/f** *1 877 278 3346; www.puffinboattours.ca; ⏲ mid May–mid Oct; 2.5 to 3hr boat trip CAN$35–40*). *En route* are good views of Cape Dauphin: according to Mi'kmaq legend, somewhere at the cape (the exact location is kept secret to protect the site) is Glooscap's Cave – sometimes called Fairy Hole – where the man-god was supposed to have lived for several winters.

BADDECK (*Population: 1,100*) With a beautiful setting on the shores of the sparkling **Bras d'Or Lake** and well located on the Cabot Trail but in relatively easy reach of many of Cape Breton Island's highlights, Baddeck is understandably popular. There are numerous activities, ranging from ceilidhs to kayaking, within walking distance for the visitor, and one must-see museum.

Learn about the ecology of the area's lakes in a late 19th-century former post office, and be sure to get out onto the water (Baddeck's yacht club is the sailing centre of the Bras d'Or Lake). Take a trip on a sail boat, or rent a kayak. In summer, have a swim in the lake from an island beach. A top golf course and beautiful waterfall hike are in easy driving distance.

History The name Baddeck derives from the Mi'kmaq *abadak*, 'place near an island' – referring to what is now called Kidston Island (see page 333). European settlement began late in the 1830s when an Irish and a Scottish family made their homes here. Within 50 years, Baddeck was home to several hotels, a post office, a

ON THE WATER

One of the delights of a visit to Baddeck is getting out onto the water. Choose from a sail on a schooner, go self-propelled in a sea kayak, or take a dip at Kidston Island.

Amoeba Sailing Tours ☎ 295 2481; www.amoebasailingtours.com; ⏲ Jun–mid Oct. 3–4 90-min sailing trips daily on a 67ft schooner. Costs CAN$25 pp.
Paddledog Kayak Tours ☎ 295 3363; www.paddledog.ca; ⏲ Jul/Aug. 90-min beginner-friendly sea kayak tours on the waters around Baddeck & Kidston Island. Costs CAN$44 pp.

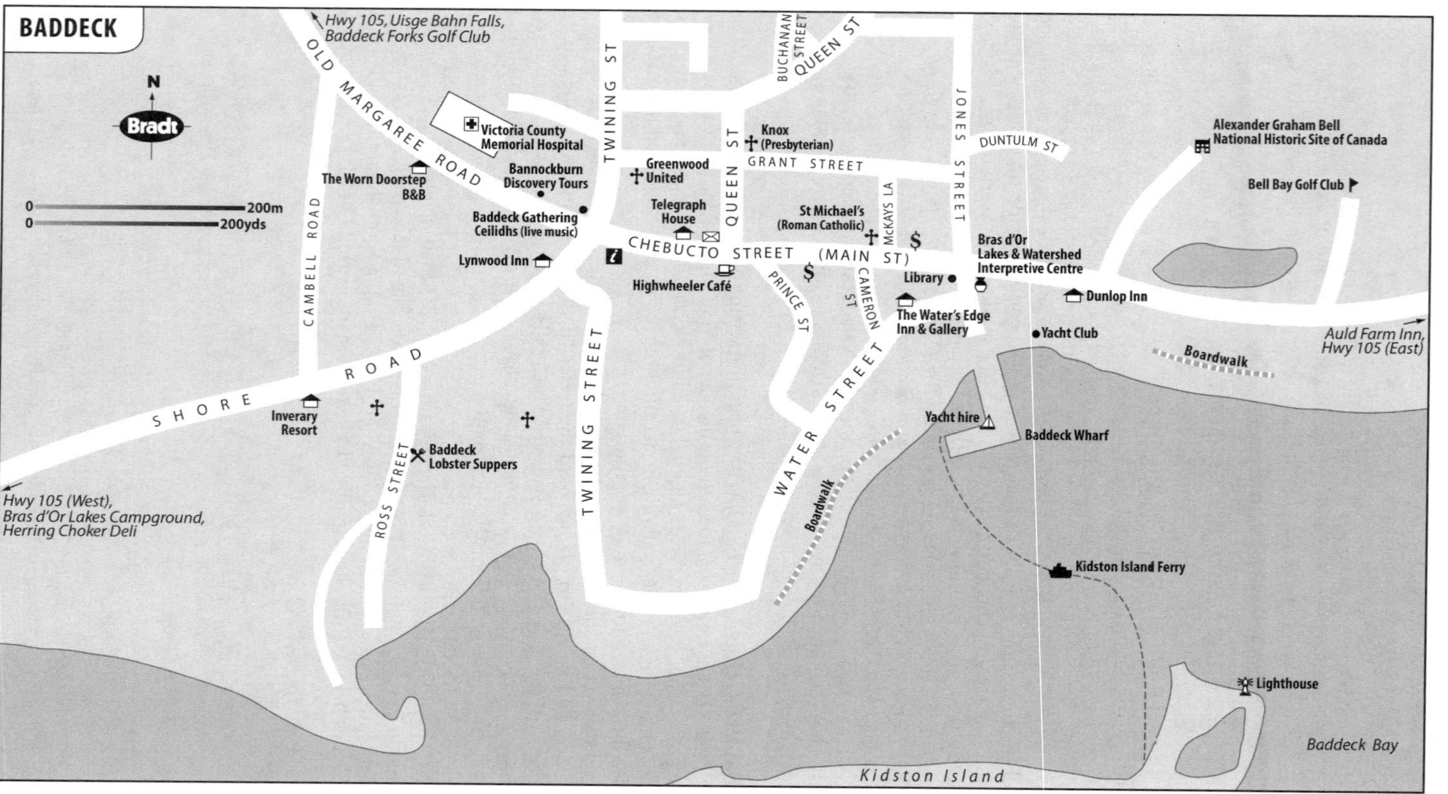
BADDECK
N
Bradt
0 200m
0 200yds
Hwy 105, Uisge Bahn Falls, Baddeck Forks Golf Club
OLD MARGAREE ROAD
Victoria County Memorial Hospital
The Worn Doorstep B&B
Bannockburn Discovery Tours
Baddeck Gathering Ceilidhs (live music)
Lynwood Inn
CAMBELL ROAD
SHORE ROAD
Inverary Resort
ROSS STREET
Baddeck Lobster Suppers
Hwy 105 (West), Bras d'Or Lakes Campground, Herring Choker Deli
TWINING ST
TWINING STREET
Greenwood United
Telegraph House
Highwheeler Café
BUCHANAN STREET
QUEEN ST
Knox (Presbyterian)
GRANT STREET
CHEBUCTO STREET (MAIN ST)
PRINCE ST
St Michael's (Roman Catholic)
McKAYS LA
CAMERON ST
WATER STREET
Boardwalk
JONES STREET
DUNTULM ST
Library
The Water's Edge Inn & Gallery
Bras d'Or Lakes & Watershed Interpretive Centre
Dunlop Inn
Yacht Club
Yacht hire
Baddeck Wharf
Alexander Graham Bell National Historic Site of Canada
Bell Bay Golf Club
Boardwalk
Auld Farm Inn, Hwy 105 (East)
Kidston Island Ferry
Lighthouse
Baddeck Bay
Kidston Island

LET'S HEAR IT FOR THE BELLS

Alexander Graham Bell (AGB) was born in Edinburgh, Scotland in 1847. By 1885, he had already invented the telephone and was living with his American wife in the US. Travelling via Nova Scotia to Newfoundland, the Bells passed through and fell in love with this area. In 1885, AGB bought land across the inlet from Baddeck and had a summer home built (Beinn Bhreagh).

Although best known for inventing the phone, Bell's major interests were flight and aerodynamics. Financed by his wife, he formed the Aerial Experiment Association. Experiments with man-carrying kites led to the creation of the *Silver Dart*, and this craft, piloted by Baddeck native Douglas McCurdy, took off from iced-up Baddeck Bay on 23 February 1909. Flying 9m in the air for a distance of about 1.4km, this was the first heavier-than-air flight in the British Empire.

In 1919, AGB (aged 72), his wife and his estate manager invented a prototype hydrofoil: the *HD-4* smashed the then world water-speed record, travelling at 114km/h.

Bell had many other interests – including the pastoral. For example, he experimented on raising multi-nippled sheep for 30 years. In addition to providing financial support and input for her husband's work, Mabel Bell was instrumental in the development of one of Cape Breton Island's traditional crafts. Rug hooking had always been popular, but Mrs Bell hired a teacher of the art to come over from Washington, and this revolutionised the colours and designs that the rug hookers used.

AGB died in 1922, and his wife the following year: both are buried at Beinn Bhreagh. Still owned by the family, the estate is not open to the public.

library, three newspapers and numerous other services. A well-known celebrity, Alexander Graham Bell, arrived to settle with his family (see box above).

In 1908, Baddeck was struck by an outbreak of cholera which claimed over 30 lives, and there was more tragedy in 1926 when fire destroyed almost two-dozen buildings along Main Street.

Getting there If you are coming **by car**, Baddeck is just off Highway 105 Exits 8 or 9, 85km/53 miles from Port Hastings, 77km/46 miles from Sydney and 111km/69 miles from Louisbourg. It is also on the Maritime Bus **coach** route between Halifax and Sydney (see *Chapter 2*, page 44).

Where to stay

Inverary Resort 368 Shore Rd; 295 3500, **t/f** 1 800 565 5660; www.inveraryresort.com; May–mid Dec. This lakeside resort on over 4ha offers a spa, various activities, & 9 types of accommodation. As you'd expect, the higher cost rooms & units are better, less popular rooms cheaper. Food at the Lakeside Restaurant (*mid Jun–Oct 11.00–22.00 daily;* **$$**) may not be spectacular, but it is above average & prices – considering the fantastic waterfront setting – reasonable. When the weather's good, dining on the deck is a delight. Licensed. **$$–$$$**

Dunlop Inn (5 rooms) 552 Chebucto St; 295 1100, **t/f** 1 888 290 1988; www.dunlopinn.com; May–Oct. A very comfortable centrally located Victorian inn with individually decorated rooms right by the water. With 2 waterside decks, sun room & private beach. Continental b/fast inc. **$$**

Lynwood Inn (32 suites) 441 Shore Rd; 295 1995, **t/f** 1 877 666 1995; **e** lynwood@baddeck.

com; www.lynwoodinn.com; ⌚ year-round; off-season by reservation. 3 rooms in this c1868 original house, 29 suites (some with balconies) in the 2002 addition. The elegant licensed Victorian-style restaurant (⌚ *mid Jun–mid Oct 07.00–21.00; daily; $$*) has a casual atmosphere, & is one of the better ones in Baddeck. Fresh, local ingredients are used where possible, the lobster platter is good value, & the desserts very good. Live local entertainment most evenings. **$$**

Telegraph House (39 units) 479 Chebucto St; 295 1100, t/f 1 888 263 9840; www.baddeck.com/telegraph; ⌚ year-round. In addition to rooms (some up a couple of flights of stairs) in the grand c1861 main building – a former telegraph office – there is also a modern motel section & 4 cabins. Alexander Graham Bell (see box, page 331) stayed here several times in the 1880s (Room 1). The dining room (⌚ *for b/fast & dinner daily; $$*) is good without being outstanding. **$$**

The Water's Edge Inn & Gallery (7 units) 18–22 Water St; 295 3600; e stay@thewatersedgeinn.com; www.thewatersedgeinn.com. Tastefully decorated, stylish & comfortable rooms – some with lake view – are on the 1st or 2nd floor, above a rather good art & crafts gallery. **$$**

The Worn Doorstep (4 suites) 43 Old Margaret Rd; 295 1997; e hunter.baddeck@ns.sympatico.ca; www.baddeck.com/worndoorstep; ⌚ year-round. Spacious, comfortable suites (all with private entrances) in friendly guesthouse. Highly recommended. **$$**

Auld Farm Inn B&B (8 rooms) 1817 Bay Rd, Hwy 205, Baddeck Bay; 295 1977; www.auldfarminn.ca; ⌚ Feb/Mar & May/Oct. Nice, characterful renovated farmhouse 7km east of Baddeck with en-suite or private bathrooms. Veranda. Rate inc full b/fast. **$**

Bras d'Or Lakes Campground (95 sites) 8885 Hwy 105, between Exits 7 & 8; 295 2329; www.brasdorlakescampground.com; ⌚ mid Jun–Sep. 5km from Baddeck, with open serviced & unserviced sites, set back from over 100m of lakeshore. Pool, store & laundromat. **$**

Where to eat

Baddeck Lobster Suppers Ross St; 295 3307; www.baddeck.com/lobstersuppers/; ⌚ Jun–Oct 16.00–21.00 daily. The lunch menu is short & simple (lobster rolls, mussels, seafood chowder, etc): dinners are the big draw. Not a good choice for an intimate, romantic meal, but fun & reasonable value. Most come for lobster served with all-you-can-eat mussels, seafood chowder, etc, but salmon or steak are possible substitutes. *Set dinner CAN$38.* **$$$$**

Herring Choker Deli 10158 Hwy 105, Nyanza; 295 2275; www.baddeck.com/herringchoker/; ⌚ Apr–Oct 08.00–18.00 daily. Good café/deli/bakery 10km west of Baddeck with deck overlooking the lake offering a range of freshly made wraps, paninis, soups, salads, sandwiches & baked goods. An ideal spot for b/fast or a light lunch. In case you're wondering, the name comes from the slang term for someone from New Brunswick. **$**

Highwheeler Café 486 Chebucto St; 295 3006; ⌚ May–mid Oct 07.00–18.00 daily. Superb coffee, friendly service, great sandwiches, snacks & baked goods. Also does a good-value packed lunch to take away. Patio deck. **$**

Another dining option is the **Baddeck Forks Golf Club** (see opposite).

Festivals Not only are events held in town during the Celtic Colours Festival (see page 306), but you can enjoy Cape Breton fiddle music and dancing every evening in July and August as part of the **Baddeck Gathering Ceilidhs** (*St Michael's Parish Hall, Main St; 295 0971; www.baddeckgathering.com; admission CAN$10*). The first full week of August sees seven days of races at the **Bras d'Or Yacht Club Regatta**.

Other practicalities

$ Bank Royal Bank 496 Chebucto St; 295 2224; ⌚ 09.30–17.00 Mon–Fri

Hospital Victoria County Memorial Hospital, 30 Old Margaree Rd; 295 2112

Library Baddeck Public Library 526 Chebucto St; 295 2055; ⌚ 13.00–17.00 Mon, 13.00–17.00 & 18.00–20.00 Tue & Fri, 17.00–20.00 Thu, 10.00–12.00 & 13.00–17.00 Sat

HIGHLAND VILLAGE/*AN CLACHAN GÀIDHEALACH*

On a 17ha hillside site with a magnificent view of the Bras d'Or Lake and surrounding countryside, the **Highland Village Museum** (*4119 Hwy 223, Iona; ☏ 725 2272, t/f 1 866 442 3542; museum.gov.ns.ca/hv/; ⏲ Jun–mid Oct 09.30–17.30 daily; admission CAN$9*) is North America's only living-history museum for Gaelic language and culture. The museum is 24km east of Highway 105 Exit 6, via the Little Narrows ferry (CAN$5.25), and 61km from Sydney. The complex includes a visitor centre and 11 historic buildings (some original, some replicas). Costumed staff, activity demonstrations, language, stories, music and song bring to life the culture and lifestyle of the Gaels who settled in Nova Scotia from the Highlands and Islands of Scotland in the late 1700s and early 1800s. Be prepared for a lot of walking.

✉ **Post office** 485 Chebucto St; ⏲ 08.00–17.00 Mon–Fri, 08.00–12.00 Sat

Tourist information 454 Chebucto St; ☏ 295 1911; ⏲ late May–mid Oct 09.00–17.00 daily (Jul/Aug to 19.00)

What to see and do An absorbing museum dedicated to Baddeck's most famous resident on a 10ha site with lovely views of the Bras d'Or Lake, **Alexander Graham Bell National Historic Site of Canada** (*Chebucto St; ☏ 295 2069; www.pc.gc.ca/lhn-nhs/ns/grahambell/; ⏲ late May/Jun, early Sep/mid Oct 09.00–17.00 Wed–Sun; Jul–early Sep 09.00–17.00 daily; admission CAN$7.80*) contains working models, photographs and multi-media exhibits on flight and much more, including several hands-on children's programmes. There is also a full-size replica of the *HD-4* hydrofoil. New in 2012 was a behind-the-scenes 'White Glove' tour (*CAN$5 extra*), allowing you to touch and feel some of AGB's personal mementos. Maybe some of his magic will rub off on you (through the gloves).

Nearby is the **Bras d'Or Lakes and Watershed Interpretive Centre** (*Chebucto St; ☏ 295 1675; www.brasdor-conservation.com; ⏲ Jun–Aug 09.00–19.00 daily (limited hours in Sep); admission free*), housed in a c1885 former post office, which has six interactive exhibits detailing the history, geography, geology and ecology of the lake.

Just 200m across the water from Baddeck, wooded **Kidston Island** has short walking trails, a beach with supervised swimming, and a lighthouse dating from 1875. Reach it by a free ferry, every 20 minutes in July and August only (*10.00–18.00 Mon–Fri, 12.00–18.00 Sat/Sun*). Those keen on walking should get in touch with **Bannockburn Discovery Tours** (*☏ 295 3310, t/f 1 888 577 4747; www.bannockburntours.com*), who run six- to eight-hour Cabot Trail tours to and from Baddeck from CAN$102.

Approximately 16km from Baddeck, **Uisge Bahn Falls Provincial Park** has a 1.5km (each way) trail to its namesake photogenic falls (*Uisge Bahn* is Gaelic for 'white water'). To reach the park, take Margaree Road from Baddeck, or Exit 9 of Highway 105, to Baddeck Bridge, then turn right towards Big Baddeck and Baddeck Forks. After 6.5km turn left onto North Branch Road.

Scenic nine-hole 3,000yd par-36 riverside **Baddeck Forks Golf Course** (*12 Extension, Baddeck Forks; ☏ 295 2174; www.baddeckforksgolf.com; ⏲ May–Oct*) has a pro-shop and decent licensed dining (*⏲ May–Oct 11.00–20.00 Mon–Fri, 08.00–21.00 Sat/Sun; $$*), 14km from Baddeck – call or see website for directions. Green fees CAN25. **Bell Bay Golf Club** (*761 Hwy 205; ☏ 295 1333, t/f 1 800 565 3077; www.bellbaygolfclub.com*) is also a good bet with excellent facilities and fabulous views over the Bras d'Or Lake. This 7,037yd par-72 course is one of Cape Breton

Island's best. Ask about play-and-stay packages (*May, Jun & mid Sep/Oct*). Green fees are CAN$94.

MARGAREE RIVER VALLEY The Margaree River is divided into two main channels: the Northeast Margaree, which rises on the plateau of the highlands, and the Southwest Margaree. The two branches tumble over rapids and waterfalls, through deep salmon pools and verdant forested floodplains before merging at Margaree Forks and then flowing into the Gulf of St Lawrence at Margaree Harbour.

The valley is peaceful, pastoral and beautiful in any season, though at its most spectacular when ablaze with autumn colours.

From Margaree Forks, choose the road on either bank of the river to reach Margaree Harbour (see page 311) or Belle Cote (page 312). The official Cabot Trail follows the west bank, but East Margaree Road also offers wonderful river views.

The Margaree River is renowned for its **fishing**, particularly salmon and trout, and the valley offers good **hiking**.

The Margaree Valley is easily reached **by car** from Inverness via Highway 19, or from Highway 104 via the Cabot Trail. Margaree Forks is 27km/17 miles from Inverness, and 50km/31 miles from Baddeck.

Where to stay and eat

Old Miller Trout Farm Guest House (1 cottage) 408 Doyles Rd, Margaree Forks; 248 2080, **t/f** 1 800 479 0220; **e** oldmiller@ns.sympatico.ca; www.oldmiller.com; mid May–Oct. A fully equipped, *gîte*-like quiet 2-bedroom cottage by a pond on a working trout farm: U-fish (rainbow & speckled trout). Approx 2km off the Cabot Trail. 2-night min stay. **$$$**

Normaway Inn (29 units) 691 Egypt Rd, Margaree Valley; 248 2987, **t/f** 1 800 565 9463; www.normaway.com; mid Jun–mid Oct. 9 inn rooms & 3, 1- & 3, 2-bedroom suites in an old-fashioned c1928 main lodge 3km off the Cabot Trail, & 17, 1- & 2-bedroom rustic cabins spread out over a peaceful 100ha estate. Guided fishing trips can be arranged. Food in the dining room (*mid Jun–mid Oct 07.30–10.00 & 18.00–21.00 daily; $$$*) is generally good & there's live entertainment in the evenings. **$$**

Scottish Crofters Campground (32 sites) 51 Acadian Rd; 248 2304; **e** scotcroft2@ns.sympatico.ca; Jun–Oct. Open serviced & tent sites & laundromat located 400m off the Cabot Trail. **$**

Dancing Goat 6335 Cabot Trail, Margaree Valley; 248 2308; year-round 10.00–17.00 Tue–Sun. Not very big, but very, very good. Excellent coffees, sandwiches & wonderful desserts. Try the cranberry almond scones. **$**

Other practicalities

Tourist information 7990 Cabot Trail, Margaree Forks; 248 2803; early Jun–early Oct 09.00–17.00 daily (Jul/Aug to 19.00)

What to see and do Angling, salmon fishing and local history are all housed in a former schoolhouse, now **The Margaree Salmon Museum** (*60 East Big Intervale Rd, Northeast Margaree; 248 2848; mid Jun–mid Oct 09.00–17.00 daily; admission CAN$2*).

AROUND BRAS D'OR LAKE

In addition to Baddeck (see pages 329–34) and apart from the ever-changing views of the beautiful bays, islands and yachts and pleasure boats on the tidal waters, the lake shores offer several other points of interest. A scenic drive (look out for signs with a bald eagle motif – the shore and surrounding areas are a major nesting area for hundreds of these majestic birds) runs all the way around the shore of this vast lake, but most people just choose a section depending on their interests and itinerary.

WAGMATCOOK The best reason to stop in Wagmatcook is to learn about the Mi'kmaq at the culture and heritage centre (see below).

Wagmatcook is on Highway 105, 15km/9 miles from Baddeck and 25km/16 miles from Whycocomagh.

What to see and do The **Mi'kmaq Interpretive Centre (Wagmatcook Culture and Heritage Centre)** (*10765 Hwy 105;* ☎ *295 2999,* **t/f** *1 866 295 2999; www.wagmatcook.com;* 🕘 *May–Oct 09.00–20.00 daily; off-season 09.00–17.00; admission free*) tells the story of the Mi'kmaq through multi-media presentations, slides and live demonstrations of crafts. An on-site restaurant is available. The centre is worthwhile, but (in my opinion) not as fascinating and informative as it could be – and more than one person has told me that they stopped by (during supposed opening hours) to find the place closed.

WHYCOCOMAGH Located just east of the Skye River, Whycocomagh's name comes from the Mi'kmaq *We'koqma'q*, 'Head of the waters'. Wrapped in mountains on three sides, the community's 'open' side fronts the Bras d'Or Lake. Its main claims to fame are the fact that Alexander Graham Bell once described it as 'the Rio de Janeiro of North America', and the view from trails in its eponymous provincial park (see *Where to stay*, page 336).

To reach Whycocomagh **by car**, it is on Highway 105, 50km/31 miles from the Canso Causeway, 30km/19 miles from Baddeck and 115km/71 miles from Sydney. Whycocomagh is on the Maritime Bus **coach** route between Halifax and Sydney (see *Chapter 2*, page 44).

NICOLAS DENYS

Born in Tours, France, in approximately 1598, Nicolas Denys's name crops up throughout Nova Scotia and Atlantic Canada's early history. Denys first came to Nova Scotia as part of an expedition led by Isaac de Razilly in 1632. He settled on the LaHave River (see page 164), and after a spell in France returned to these shores as Governor of Canso and Ile Royale (what is now Cape Breton Island). He established various settlements, including one here at Saint Pierre (St Peter's) in 1650. Trading extensively with the Mi'kmaq and other settlers at that time, he constructed a track on the isthmus between the sea and the lake to allow teams of oxen to haul boats onto skids and across the portage.

In 1654, Denys obtained a concession from Louis XIV to work all the island's minerals in return for a 10% royalty.

In the years that followed, he ran many businesses here (eg: fishing, lumber, and farming) but in 1669, his home and business were destroyed by fire. In financial ruin, he moved to Nipisiguit (now Bathurst, New Brunswick) and began writing about the lands he had lived in and visited, and their peoples. Denys wrote the first guidebook to Cape Breton, published in 1672: copies (in English and French) can be viewed at his eponymous museum (see page 338). He died in 1688 and legend has it that he is buried near what is now the 15th hole of Bathurst's Gowan Brae Golf Course.

Where to stay and eat

Bear on the Lake Guest House 10705 Hwy 105, Aberdeen; 756 2750, t/f 1 866 718 5253; www.bearonthelake.com; mid May–Oct. 7km east of Whycocomagh. 4-bed dorms & private rooms, lounge, deck overlooking the lake, fully equipped kitchen, laundry facilities, bike rentals, free Wi-Fi & more for backpackers & low-budget travellers. *Dorm CAN$30; private room CAN$75 (discount for HI members).* **$**

Fair Isle Motel (20 units) 9557 Hwy 105; 756 2291, t/f 1 877 238 8950; e fairislemotel@ns.sympatico.ca; www.fairislemotel.com; mid May–Oct. A traditional-style motel on the hill above the main road, overlooking the lake, offering standard rooms, a couple of suites & some larger rooms (all recently renovated & all with kitchenettes). Laundry facilities. **$**

Moeller's Lake View Cottage, B&B (3 units) Portage Rd, South Side Whycocomagh Bay; 756 2865, t/f 1 877 756 2865; www.capebretoncottage.com; May–Oct; off-season by reservation. With 2 ground-floor B&B rooms with private entrance in a modern house, or a well-equipped, comfortable 1-bedroom cottage close by. Bald eagles often nest on this 15ha forested lakeshore property. Full b/fast inc. **$**

Whycocomagh Provincial Park (62 sites) t/f 1 888 544 3434 (reservations); mid Jun–mid Oct. Sites on grassy slopes or tucked into the forest on a hillside less than 500m east of town. 3 short but steep & challenging trails lead up Salt Mountain, 240m above sea level. If it is clear, views from the mountaintop are sensational. **$**

Charlene's Bayside Restaurant & Café 9657 Hwy 105; 756 8004; year-round 11.00–19.00 Mon–Thu, 08.00–20.00 Fri–Sun. Come not for the décor but for the justifiably renowned seafood-packed chowder. The other options tend to be more hit than miss. **$$**

Vi's Restaurant 9381 Hwy 105; 756 2338; year-round 07.00–20.00 Mon–Sat, 08.00–20.00 Sun. This institution recently celebrated its 50th birthday. Nothing fancy or pretentious, just reliable home cooking. **$**

Other practicalities

$ Bank Royal Bank, 72 Village Rd; 756 2600; 10.00–16.00 Mon–Wed, 10.00–17.00 Thu/Fri

Post office 115 Main St; 08.30–17.00 Mon–Fri, 08.30–12.30 Sat

ORANGEDALE This little community is worth a short stop for those with an interest in railway history. Trains haven't stopped here for over two decades but the memory lives on in 'Orangedale Whistle', a song by The Rankins (see page 304).

Orangedale is just off Orangedale Road, 7km/4 miles south of Highway 105 Exit 4.

What to see and do Visit the **Orangedale Railway Museum** (*1428 Main St; 756 3384; late Jun–late Aug 10.00–17.00 Wed–Sun; Sep/mid Oct 10.00–17.00 Sat/Sun*), housed in the restored c1886 station which was in operation until 1990. There are several good displays and an interpretive centre in a replica freight shed.

DUNDEE On West Bay on the southern shore of Bras d'Or Lake, Dundee has a small provincial park with a sandy beach, and a resort with one of Cape Breton Island's highly regarded 18-hole golf courses. At **Roberta**, 12km along the shore, you can rent kayaks to explore this part of the lake.

To reach Dundee **by car**, it is 51km/32 miles from Orangedale and 24km/15 miles from St Peter's.

Where to stay and eat

Dundee Resort and Golf Club (98 units) 2750 West Bay Hwy; 345 2649, t/f 1 800 565 5660; www.capebretonresorts.com/dundee.asp; mid May–Oct. With 60 hotel rooms & 38, 1- & 2-bedroom cottages. Facilities include tennis, indoor & outdoor (seasonal) pools, spa, hiking, canoe & pedal-boat rental. This resort has been looking a bit worn recently. The restaurant serves b/fast, lunch & dinner, & there's a pub on site. You can also eat in the golf clubhouse. Various packages are offered. **$$$**

Kayak Cape Breton and Cottages (2 cottages) 5385 Dundee Rd, Roberta; 535 3060; www.kayakcapebreton.com; May–Oct. 2 well-equipped 2-bedroom cedar-log cottages are tucked between the trees by the lakeside. Min stay applies: 2 nights May/Jun & Sep/Oct; 3 nights Jul/Aug. Kayak lessons, guided trips & rentals are all offered. 12km from the Dundee Resort & 16km from St Peter's. **$**

What to see and do Located in a stunning setting, **The Dundee Resort Championship Golf Course** (*345 0420,* **t/f** *1 800 565 5660; www.dundeegolfclub.com; May–Oct*) is absolutely beautiful, but you'll really need to concentrate and play hard, particularly on the front nine. Expect a lot of hills and long par-fours! Various stay-and-play packages are available, and the course is open to non-resort guests. Green fees CAN$75.

ST PETER'S (*Population: 735*) One of Nova Scotia's oldest communities, pleasant St Peter's is situated on a narrow strip of land separating the Atlantic Ocean and the Bras d'Or Lake. The largest community on the southern part of the lake shore and the service centre for Richmond County can almost be described as bustling in summer. The eponymous canal is one of two access points for boats entering Bras d'Or Lake and there are picnic areas on the canal's grassy banks.

History Founded by Nicolas Denys (see box, page 335) as Saint Pierre in 1650, the French later built a fort on this strategically important portage between the Atlantic and the Bras d'Or Lake.

They seriously considered establishing their capital here, but that honour went to Louisbourg (see page 349). In 1745, the British attacked the fort and torched the buildings, and in 1793, built Fort Grenville on the site.

Work on the construction of an 800m canal, now the **St Peter's Canal National Historic Site** (*733 2280; www.pc.gc.ca/lhn-nhs/ns/stpeters; year-round;*

CHAPEL ISLAND

The Potlotek First Nation Reserve (PFN) is sometimes described as the Mi'kmaq 'capital'. The PFN encompasses Chapel Island itself (*Mniku* to the Mi'kmaq), and a strip of land from the lakeshore back across Highway 4 which was granted to the Mi'kmaq in the 1830s. The first missionary priest to visit this region lived among the Mi'kmaq and settled with them on Chapel Island in the 1740s: he built a church here in 1754. This is the longest continuous mission in Canada.

Held over the weekend starting on the third Friday in July, the Potlotek Pow Wow is an important social, cultural and spiritual event for the Mi'kmaq and gives an opportunity for them to share their culture and heritage with others. In addition to daily feasting, there are dancing demonstrations, story telling, traditional games, and masses. Authentic arts and crafts are sold.

There isn't a huge amount for the casual visitor to see but the island still holds great spiritual significance for the Mi'kmaq. To visit the island, turn from Highway 4 onto Chapel Island Road (10km east of St Peter's) or onto Mountain Road (1km further east along Highway 4). Ask around near the shore, and someone will probably take you across by boat (make sure that they wait around to take you back) for a few dollars.

There is also a Mi'kmaq–owned-and-operated eatery, the Bistro (*12012 Hwy 4*), but don't expect any traditional Mi'kmaq cuisine.

The PFN is approx 10km/6 miles east of St Peter's via Highway 4.

admission free), began in 1854 and was completed in 1869. Its opening saved over 120km of sailing for vessels wishing to enter or leave the southwest of the Bras d'Or Lakes. The lock system operates on some summer days – call to check dates/times.

Getting there St Peter's is accessible **by car**, being on Highway 4, 55km/34 miles from Port Hastings, 24km/15 miles from Isle Madame, 38km/24 miles from Big Pond and 87km/54 miles from Sydney.

Where to stay and eat

Bras d'Or Lakes Inn (19 rooms) 10095 Grenville St; 535 2200, **t/f** 1 800 818 5885; **e** info@brasdorlakesinn.com; www.brasdorlakesinn.com; year-round. A red cedar-log building in a lovely lakefront location. Rooms are comfortable & well equipped. Wood features strongly in the décor of the licensed restaurant & lounge (*07.30–10.00 & 17.00–20.00 daily;* **$$$**): large picture windows look out over the lake. The restaurant offers Canadian cuisine with a French influence, try crab & scallop-stuffed crêpes followed by cedar planked salmon. Dinner reservations recommended. There is a lounge with live entertainment most nights (ceilidh on Thu), a patio, exercise room, private dock. Kayaks, paddleboat, canoe & bicycles for rent. **$$$**

Canal House B&B (5 rooms) 9329 Pepperell St; 535 2049; **e** info@canal-house.com; www.canal-house.com; year-round. Rooms with private or en-suite bathrooms & a good-sized garden in this friendly B&B. Full b/fast inc. **$**

Joyce's Motel & Cottages (24 units) 10354 Grenville St; 535 2404; www.joycesmotel.com; Jun–Sep. 6 simple motel rooms & 18 basic 1- & 2-bedroom cabins/cottages (some with cooking facilities) across the main road from the lake. Laundromat & outdoor pool. **$**

Festivals At **Nicolas Denys Days** at the end of July/early August, events include auctions, a parade, ceilidhs, and chowder lunches. Get festive with a display of decorated Christmas trees at the **Festival of Trees** in November.

Other practicalities

$ Bank Royal Bank, 9955 Grenville St; 535 2001; 10.00–15.00 Mon–Fri

Post office 9981 Grenville St; 09.00–17.00 Mon–Fri, 09.00–14.00 Sat

Tourist information 10259 Granville St; 535 2185; early Jun–mid Oct 09.00–17.00 daily (Jul/Aug to 19.00)

What to see and do Walking trails in **Battery Provincial Park** (*535 3094; www.novascotiaparks.ca/parks/battery.asp; mid June–early Sep; admission free*) lead to the c1883 Jerome Point Lighthouse, and a short but steep section to the site of Fort Grenville (see *History*, page 337). Both of these offer lovely views.

The town also has the world's only museum, the **Nicolas Denys Museum** (*46 Denys St; 535 2379; Jun–Sep 09.00–17.00 daily*), dedicated to this important historical

TEA AT RITA'S

Big Pond, on Highway 4, halfway between St Peter's and Sydney, is best known as the home of Rita MacNeil, acclaimed singer, songwriter and recording artist. Rita's fans, and other hungry travellers, will want to stop at **Rita's Tea Room** (*8077 Hwy 4; 828 2667; www.ritamacneil.com; Jul–mid Oct 10.00–17.00 daily;* **$–$$**) to see a collection of Rita memorabilia, and to tuck in to soup, salads, sandwiches, sweet things and more: it is good stuff, but prices seem a few celebrity-connection dollars higher than the norm. Rita pops in sometimes and (most summers) performs a few concerts at the local community centre.

ESKASONI

Less than 4km northeast along Highway 4 from East Bay, Highway 216 leads 26km west to the Eskasoni (the name comes from the Mi'kmaq for 'still waters') First Nation, the biggest Mi'kmaq reserve in the province (in fact, in the world). The setting is scenic, and the people of Eskasoni are just beginning to realise that not only are people interested in learning about the Mi'kmaq way of life, but also that tourists can bring money to their community. **Eskasoni Cultural Journeys** (*379 2422,* **t/f** *1 855 376 2422; www.eskasoniculturaljourneys.ca*) has put together some short tours and is working with the Highland Village (see page 333) to offer a bi-cultural tour. Over 19s can gamble at the new **Eskasoni Gaming Centre** (*4716 Shore Rd; 379 1451; www.eskasoni.ca*), which boasts 60 video lottery terminals (VLTs). Eskasoni is also home to the **Unama'ki Institute of Natural Resources** (*379 2163,* **t/f** *1 888 379 8467; www.uinr.ca*), which represents Cape Breton's Mi'kmaq voice on natural resources and environmental concerns.

figure (see box, page 335). The **Wallace MacAskill Museum** (*7 MacAskill Dr; 535 2531; mid Jun–Aug 09.30–17.30 daily; Sep/Oct by appointment; admission free*) is also well worth a visit: this c1850s' house with period furnishings is the restored birthplace and childhood home of perhaps the world's best marine photographer, Wallace MacAskill (1890–1956). In addition to a good collection of his works – many in their original frames – one room is dedicated to a display of vintage cameras.

EAST BAY East Bay offers the chance to play golf between spring and late autumn, and to hit the slopes when the snow comes down. Bald eagles are often seen in this area. A new marina may have opened by the time you read this.

East Bay is on Highway 4, 27km/17 miles from Sydney and 54km/34 miles from St Peter's.

Where to stay and eat

Birches at Ben Eoin Country Inn (12 units) 5153 Hwy 4; 828 2277, **t/f** 1 866 244 8862; www.thebirchescountryinn.ca; Feb–Dec. Welcoming, comfortable 2-storey inn with 10 spacious, luxurious modern rooms & 2 suites. Outdoor jacuzzi. Bike friendly. **$$**

Malcolm's mid Jun–mid Oct 17.00–21.00 daily, mid Oct–Dec & Feb–mid Jun 17.00–21.00 Tue–Sat. The Inn's licensed restaurant offers fine-dining in elegant & intimate surroundings. The menu changes with the seasons (most ingredients are local): try, for example, lobster bisque or halibut tagliatelle. **$$$**

What to see and do A newish (2009) Graham Cooke-designed 6,973yd par-72 course, **The Lakes** (*Hwy 4; 539 6494; www.thelakesgolfclub.ca*) offers fabulous views and dramatic elevation changes. Green fees are CAN$94. Take to the snow in winter on the scenic slopes of **Ski Ben Eoin** (*Hwy 4; 828 2222; www.skibeneoin.com*), overlooking the lake. Snowshoe rentals also available.

SYDNEY

With a past in which the words 'steel' and 'coal mining' feature prominently, not to mention years of bad press about its 'tar ponds' (see box, page 340), those who are not industrial historians could be forgiven for wondering if they should include Nova Scotia's second (and Cape Breton Island's) largest urban centre in their itineraries. In fact, Sydney is no longer a city, but since 1995 has been part of the Cape Breton Regional Municipality (*Population: 104,000*), which also includes communities such as North Sydney, Sydney Mines and Glace Bay.

Like Halifax (and its namesake in Australia), Sydney lies on a magnificent harbour, and the downtown area occupies part of a peninsula jutting out into the water. Despite the setting, with the exception of a pleasant historic district and a nice waterfront boardwalk, it isn't the most attractive of places. For most visitors it is only a bit of an exaggeration to say that once you've walked along both the **Esplanade** and parallel **Charlotte Street** (just one block inland) between Townsend and Amelia streets, you've done Sydney.

There are, of course, some other attractions, including a good art gallery at **Cape Breton University** and a **casino**, and for those who like an urban base, Sydney is well placed for day trips to Louisbourg and many of the Bras d'Or Lake communities. It is blessed with good accommodation choices, and – where they once feared to tread – foodies are now spoilt for choice.

The 3km waterfront boardwalk buzzes with activity on nice summer days, and by the time you read this, work to redevelop **Wentworth Park** (established in 1785) just south of downtown back into an attractive green space – with duck ponds, walking paths and picnic areas – should have been completed.

North Sydney's former railway station, now housing offices, at 1 Station Street, is worth a look for its fine Victorian architecture.

Neighbouring **Sydney Mines** is more attractive: its red sandstone c1904 Gothic-style former post office is now used as the Town Hall, and the c1905 railway station now houses a heritage museum.

COKE IS BAD FOR YOU

Being a huge steel, coal and coke producer had its downsides for Sydney. An unwanted consequence of almost a century of coke-making was massive-scale pollution caused by waste run-off. Most of the estimated 700,000 metric tonnes of hazardous, contaminated sludge collected in two ponds, an area of approximately 31ha. In 1986, the federal and provincial governments decided it was time to think about cleaning up the Sydney Tar Ponds, and drew up a plan to try to achieve this. Coke production didn't stop until 1988. By 1994, it was clear that the intended cure for the clean-up was not going to work, and the project was abandoned a year later. The years passed with a lot of hot air and little action, the sludge sloshing about virtually untouched at Canada's most contaminated industrial site.

In 2004, a CAN$400 million ten-year clean-up plan was announced which involved incinerating almost four metric tonnes of carcinogenic toxicants, stabilising contaminated sediments by mixing them with cement, and using friendly bacteria to decontaminate soil. The area would then be covered with special materials, and later landscaped.

At the time of writing, the pungent stench common in previous decades has gone. Areas of the site now look green and lush: a stream with clear, clean water bubbles along. Industrial machinery is still at work elsewhere on the site, but you feel (and hope) that the end is in sight. Future plans for the reclaimed land (which is very close to downtown Sydney) include an outdoor concert venue, walking trails, cycle paths and sports fields.

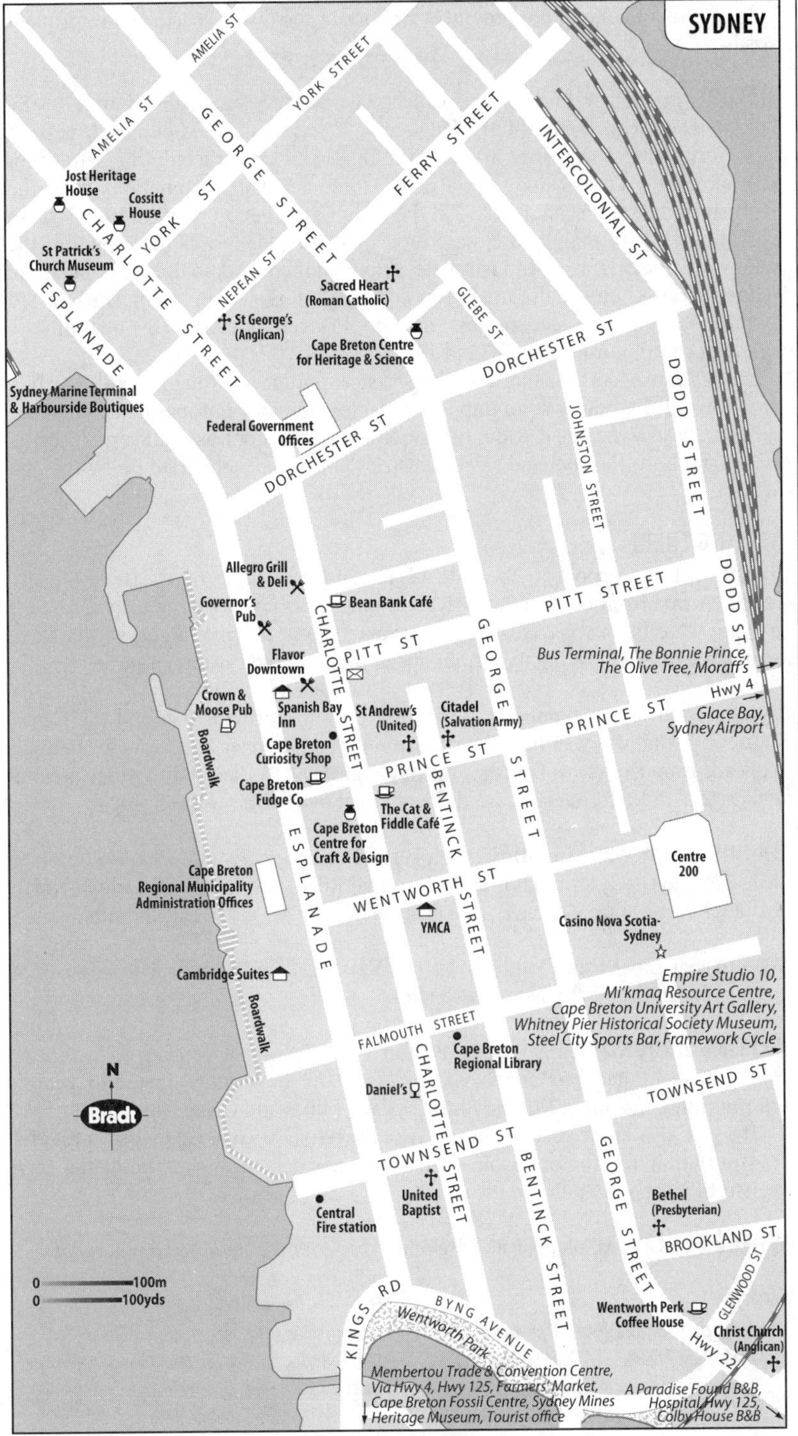
SYDNEY
AMELIA ST
AMELIA ST
YORK STREET
GEORGE STREET
FERRY STREET
INTERCOLONIAL ST
Jost Heritage House
Cossitt House
CHARLOTTE STREET
YORK ST
St Patrick's Church Museum
ESPLANADE
NEPEAN ST
Sacred Heart (Roman Catholic)
GLEBE ST
St George's (Anglican)
Cape Breton Centre for Heritage & Science
DORCHESTER ST
DODD STREET
Sydney Marine Terminal & Harbourside Boutiques
Federal Government Offices
JOHNSTON STREET
DORCHESTER ST
Allegro Grill & Deli
Bean Bank Café
PITT STREET
DODD ST
Governor's Pub
PITT ST
GEORGE STREET
Flavor Downtown
Bus Terminal, The Bonnie Prince, The Olive Tree, Moraff's
Hwy 4
Glace Bay, Sydney Airport
Crown & Moose Pub
Spanish Bay Inn
St Andrew's (United)
Citadel (Salvation Army)
PRINCE ST
Boardwalk
Cape Breton Curiosity Shop
PRINCE ST
Cape Breton Fudge Co
BENTINCK STREET
The Cat & Fiddle Café
Cape Breton Centre for Craft & Design
Centre 200
Cape Breton Regional Municipality Administration Offices
WENTWORTH ST
YMCA
Casino Nova Scotia-Sydney
Cambridge Suites
Empire Studio 10, Mi'kmaq Resource Centre, Cape Breton University Art Gallery, Whitney Pier Historical Society Museum, Steel City Sports Bar, Framework Cycle
Boardwalk
FALMOUTH STREET
Cape Breton Regional Library
N
Bradt
Daniel's
TOWNSEND ST
TOWNSEND ST
BENTINCK STREET
GEORGE STREET
United Baptist
Central Fire station
Bethel (Presbyterian)
BROOKLAND ST
GLENWOOD ST
0 100m
0 100yds
KINGS RD
BYNG AVENUE
Wentworth Park
Wentworth Perk Coffee House
Christ Church (Anglican)
Hwy 22
Membertou Trade & Convention Centre, Via Hwy 4, Hwy 125, Farmers' Market, Cape Breton Fossil Centre, Sydney Mines Heritage Museum, Tourist office
A Paradise Found B&B, Hospital, Hwy 125, Colby House B&B

Sydney Mines is one of the province's important fossil sites, particularly for plant fossils.

HISTORY Previously known as Spanish Bay, Sydney was founded in 1785 by Colonel DesBarres, a Swiss-born Huguenot. It was first settled by Loyalists from New York State: a garrison, in use until 1854, was constructed. The settlement was named for Lord Sydney, the British Home Secretary. Immigrants from the Scottish Highlands began to arrive in the early 1800s. For 35 years, until the island was reunited with mainland Nova Scotia in 1820, Sydney was the capital of the colony of Cape Breton. As industrial development increased, so did the population. Sydney became home to the largest self-contained steel plant in North America, fed by the area's numerous coal mines. One pit – Princess Colliery in Sydney Mines – operated continuously from 1875 to 1975.

Sydney ranked as Canada's third-largest steel producer through World War II, a time when its harbour was an important staging point for Europe-bound shipping convoys. Post-war came decades of economic decline, not least for Sydney's iconic mainstays: both the coal and steel industries had completely dried up by the end of 2001.

GETTING THERE

By air Sydney Airport (IATA code YQY) is 14km/9 miles northeast of the city centre. A **taxi** from outside the arrivals area to downtown Sydney costs CAN$14; try City-wide Taxi (*564 5432*) or Kings Taxi (*564 4444*). For flights within Nova Scotia, see page 53, for flights further afield, page 43, and car hire, page 56.

By car Highway 105 connects North Sydney with Port Hastings and the Canso Causeway: Highway 125 links North Sydney, Sydney River and Sydney. Highway 22 heads from Sydney to Louisbourg, and Highway 4 to Glace Bay. Sydney is some 400km/249 miles from Halifax, a drive of about five hours (without stops).

By bus/coach **Maritime Bus** coach services connect Sydney with Halifax (see page 57): the coach terminal is at 99 Terminal Road. A stop is also made in North Sydney. Several shuttle services (see *Chapter 2*, page 44) also make the run.

By sea For those travelling to and from Newfoundland, the ferry terminus (see page 45) is on the North Sydney waterfront.

GETTING AROUND **Transit Cape Breton** (*539 8124; www.cbrm.ns.ca/transit.html*) offers limited **bus** services (*Mon–Sat only*) between Sydney and nearby communities, including North Sydney, Sydney Mines and Glace Bay.

There is also an accessible **Handi-Trans service** (*539 4336*) which provides transportation for those unable to use the normal buses, but note that pre-registration is required to use the service.

WHERE TO STAY

All places listed are open year-round unless stated otherwise.

Sydney

Cambridge Suites Hotel (145 units) 380 Esplanade; 562 6500, **t/f** 1 800 565 9466; www.cambridgesuitessydney.com. Fine downtown Esplanade location, with a rooftop fitness centre. Free Wi-Fi, free local calls. These clean & comfortable modern suites are a good choice for families & those who like spacious accommodation. Overnight parking CAN$7. See opposite for on-site restaurant, Trio. Rate inc deluxe continental b/fast. **$$$**

A Paradise Found B&B (3 rooms) 62 Milton St; 539 9377, t/f 1 877 539 9377; www.paradisefoundbb.com. A lovely old house on a quiet tree-lined residential street within walking distance of downtown. Full b/fast inc. $$

Colby House B&B (4 rooms) 10 Park St; 539 4095, t/f 1 855 539 4055; www.colbyhousebb.com. Beautiful c1904 home on a tree-lined street in walking distance of downtown. Tastefully furnished with many original features including grand staircase. Comfortable, well-equipped rooms with en-suite or private bathrooms. Lovely veranda. Rate inc full b/fast. $$

Spanish Bay Inn – Premiere Executive Suites (13 suites) 10 Pitt St; 562 5747, t/f 1 866 259 6673; www.spanishbayinn.ca. Successful mix of B&B, hotel & suites: well-equipped apt-like suites (with kitchenette or full kitchen) in historic downtown waterfront building. Free parking. Rate inc deluxe continental b/fast. $$

North Sydney, Sydney Mines and beyond

Chambers' Guest House B&B (4 rooms) 64 King St, North Sydney; 794 7301, t/f 1 866 496 9453; e cheryl.chambers@ns.sympatico.ca; www.bbcapebretonisland.com; May–Oct. A lovely c1880 former sea captain's house with shared or en-suite bathrooms & a veranda, & pleasant garden. Full b/fast inc. $

WHERE TO EAT

Sydney The dining scene here has improved in recent times with the opening of some exciting bistros & excellent coffee shop/cafés.

Flavor Downtown 16 Pitt St; 562 6611; http://cbflavor.com; 08.30–20.30 Mon–Sat, 10.00–15.00 Sun. Modern, bistro-style eatery serving all-day b/fast, gourmet sandwiches & wraps, plus more substantial fare (eg: seafood, pasta, beef tenderloin). Imaginative & tasty food. Lunch $–$$; dinner $$–$$$

Governor's Pub & Eatery 233 Esplanade; 562 7646; 11.00–22.00. A fine, upmarket restaurant downstairs, & 1 floor up is a rather good Celtic gastro pub (*11.00–02.00 daily*) with regular live music. Harbour views & – if the weather permits – patio dining. $$–$$$

Allegro Grill & Deli 222 Charlotte St: 562 1623; 11.00–17.00 Mon, 11.00–21.00 Tue–Thu, 11.00–22.00 Fri/Sat. Allegro's imaginative menu, fun ambience & healthy freshly made food help liven up the downtown dining scene. $$

The Bonnie Prince 50 Reeves St; 567 1510; www.bonnieprince.com; 11.00–21.00 daily (from 12.00 Sun). Big portions of pan-fried haddock, fish & chips, steaks, burgers, pasta, etc. Quick service. A little dark, & the décor is a bit cheap film-set, but all-in-all a decent low-budget choice. $–$$

The Olive Tree 137 Victoria Rd; 539 1553; www.facebook.com/olivetreebistro; 11.00–21.00 Mon–Sat, 16.00–21.00 Sun. Friendly, licensed pizzeria/bistro. Very good pizzas (light, thin crust) & tasty Mediterranean-style cuisine (eg: Greek-style shrimp & scallop fettucine with tomato & ouzo sauce). Good-value lunch specials. $–$$

Trio at the Cambridge Suites 180 Esplanade; 563 7009; www.cambridgesuitessydney.com; 07.00–10.30 & 11.30–22.00 Mon–Sat, 07.00–10.30 & 17.00–22.00 Sun. One of the better hotel eateries. Start with lobster-stuffed portobello mushroom & move on to candied salmon with garlic mash, or chicken penne. Good choice of wine & cocktails. $–$$

All Star Grille Casino Nova Scotia (see page 346); 11.00–21.00 Mon–Thu, 07.00–00.00 Fri/Sat, 07.00–21.00 Sun. Not *haute cuisine* but there are often good meal deals to try to lure hungry passers-by into the casino … $

The Cat and Fiddle Café 319 Charlotte St; 270 3220; www.thecatandthefiddlecafe.com; 10.00–17.00 Mon–Sat. Good coffee/teas, healthy food (salads, wraps, soup, dips – including some tasty Lebanese-style dishes). Recommended. $

Bean Bank Café 243 Charlotte St; 562 5400; www.beanbank.ca; 07.30–17.00 Mon–Fri, 08.30–17.00 Sat, 09.00–15.00 Sun. Conveniently located & offering excellent coffee & good snacks, sandwiches & baked goods. $

Wentworth Perk Coffee House 697 George St; 270 3355; www.wentworthperk.com; 07.30–20.00 Mon–Sat, 11.00–17.00 Sun. Delicious wraps (the Perk wrap is a popular b/fast item) & sandwiches, decadent desserts, & great coffee. Cosy, friendly & comfortable. Outdoor deck. $

North Sydney, Sydney Mines and beyond

Black Spoon Bistro 320 Commercial St, North Sydney; 241 3300; www.blackspoonbistro.com; 11.00–20.00 Mon–Sat (to 21.00 Fri/Sat). Lunch at this great bistro includes gourmet paninis (try the chipotle chicken), soups, & salads (eg: grilled vegetable). In the evening, try the pan-fried halibut or hazelnut-crusted salmon. Save room for bananas Foster. $$–$$$

NIGHTLIFE AND ENTERTAINMENT In addition to Governor's Celtic pub (see page 343), try:

Sydney

Centre 200 481 George St; 564 6668; www.centre200.ca; year-round. Home to the Cape Breton Screaming Eagles ice-hockey team from mid Sep to mid Mar, this large modern facility (6,500 capacity as an arena, 3,000 in theatre-mode) & exhibition centre hosts big-name concerts. A CAN$5 levy (Capital Improvement Fund) is added to all tickets over CAN$5.

Crown & Moose Pub 300 Esplanade; 567 7014; 11.00–00.00 daily (until 01.00 Fri/Sat). This British-style pub at the Delta Sydney hotel is a popular spot for locals & hotel guests. Live music Fri/Sat evenings; patio in summer.

Daniel's 456 Charlotte St; 562 8586; 10.00–02.00 Mon–Sat, 12.00–02.00 Sun

Empire Studio 10 Prince St Plaza, 325 Prince St; 539 9050; www.empiretheatres.com. The cinema offers 10 film choices.

Membertou Trade and Convention Centre 50 Maillard St; 539 2300; www.membertoutcc.com. Concerts, performances, comedy shows & more.

Steel City Sports Bar 252 Townsend St; 562 4501. Almost legendary Sydney venue. Pub, restaurant, sports bar, dancing & live music.

North Sydney

Rollie's Wharf 411 Purves St; 794 7774; www.rollieswharfrestaurant.com; 10.00–02.00 daily. Popular with the younger crowd, overlooking the harbour & close to the ferry terminal. Live music on Thu evenings.

FESTIVALS Held in May, **PierScape** is a week-long eclectic arts and food festival. In August, **Action Week** (*www.actionweek.com*) includes concerts, a Busker festival, a Caribbean festival and more. The terminus for ferries to and from Newfoundland (see page 45) is around the harbour in North Sydney, where horse shows and events – the biggest of which is the **Cape Breton County Exhibition** (*www.eans.ca/CapeBretonCountyExhibition.htm*) festival – are held in the summer at the Exhibition Grounds on Regent Street.

SHOPPING Aimed at cruise-ship passengers, therefore only open when cruise ships are visiting Sydney in high season, the **Harbourside Boutiques** (*Joan Harriss Cruise Pavilion, 74 Esplanade*) is like a 'best of' for what's on offer in Sydney and the

WHERE'S THE OPERA HOUSE?

In 2002, a British couple, both 19, booked their flights on the internet and flew here via Halifax. Before too long, they realised that although there was a big harbour and the name was the same, this wasn't the Sydney they were expecting. They didn't get to climb the Harbour Bridge, sunbathe on Bondi Beach or have a drink in a Paddington bar, but a kind and sympathetic Air Canada employee took them under her wing. She drove them to see many of Cape Breton Island's delights, and invited them home for dinner. The couple were particularly impressed with the friendliness of the local people. Sydney (Nova Scotia) airport staff said that although on occasion the odd bag turned up here instead of Australia, this was the first time it had happened to humans.

island in general. For other versions of most-things-under-one-roof, head for the **Sydney Shopping Mall** (*272 Prince St*), or (further out) the larger **Mayflower Mall** (*800 Grand Lake Rd*).

In addition to the stores mentioned below, be sure to visit the shop at the **Centre for Craft and Design** (see page 346). **Cape Breton Curiosity Shop** (*296 Charlotte St; 564 4660*) is one of the better gift/souvenir shops with helpful, friendly staff. The **Cape Breton Fudge Co** (*15 Prince St; 539 9900; www.capebretonfudgeco.com; 10.00–17.00 Mon–Sat*) has loads of flavours of fudge, all made on-site, plus a tea, coffee and cake café, and occasional live music. **Moraff's Yarns & Crafts** (*752 Victoria Rd; 564 8339*) is an old-fashioned shop with old-fashioned service, selling all you need for knitting, sewing and more.

OTHER PRACTICALITIES

Bike hire Framework Cycle and Fitness, 273 Townsend St; 567 1909, **t/f** 1 866 567 1909; www.frameworkfitness.com; 10.00–17.00 Mon–Fri, 09.00–13.00 Sat. Bike hire; daily or weekly rentals.
Gym YMCA, 399 Charlotte St; 562 9622; www.cbymca.com. Day pass (pool & gym access) CAN$10.
Hospital Cape Breton Regional Hospital, 1482 George St; 567 8000
Library James McConnell Memorial Library, 50 Falmouth St; 562 3161; 10.00–21.00 Tue–Fri, 10.00–17.30 Sat
Post office 269 Charlotte St; 08.00–17.00 Mon–Fri
Tourist information 20 Keltic Dr, Sydney River; 539 9876; Jun & Sep/mid Oct 09.00–17.00 daily; Jul/Aug 08.30–18.00 daily; Marine Terminal, 74 Esplanade; kiosk open only when cruise ships are in port.

WHAT TO SEE AND DO There are two beautiful churches worth visiting in Sydney. **St Patrick's Church Museum** (*87 Esplanade; 562 8237; Jun–Aug 09.00–17.00 daily; admission CAN$2*) is a small c1828 Pioneer Gothic-style building and Cape Breton Island's oldest standing Roman Catholic church. Some stone used in the building's construction came from the ruins of Louisbourg (see page 349). Displays focus on the city's history. Much has been added to **St George's Anglican Church** (*119 Charlotte St*) since its construction (1785–91) as a garrison chapel – this was the first Anglican church on Cape Breton Island. The adjoining graveyard has several interesting sandstone and limestone grave markers.

Also on Charlotte Street, **Cossit House** (*75 Charlotte St; 539 7973; http://museum.gov.ns.ca/ch/; Jun–mid Oct 09.30–17.30 Mon–Sat, 13.00–17.30 Sun; admission CAN$2*) proudly bills itself as Sydney's oldest house: the c1787 manse was home to the town's first Anglican minister, a Rev Ranna Cossit. The house has been restored almost to its original condition, and several rooms have been furnished based on an 1815 inventory of Cossit's estate. Costumed guides give tours. **Jost Heritage House** (*54 Charlotte St; 539 0366; Jun–Aug 09.00–17.00 daily; Sep/Oct 10.00–16.00 daily; admission CAN$3.75*) is another historical house nearby. Parts of this building also date from 1787, but unlike the Cossit House, there have since been additions in several different architectural styles. Each part of the house has been furnished in keeping with the era in which it was built.

On the ground floor of a c1904 Colonial Revival-style former theatre, **The Cape Breton Centre for Heritage and Science** (*225 George St; 539 1572; www.oldsydney.com/museums/centre.html; Jun–Aug 09.00–17.00 Mon–Fri; Sep–May 10.00–16.00 Tue–Fri; admission free*) has displays focusing on the social and natural history of eastern Cape Breton.

At the University, you can find a repository of documents relating to the Mi'kmaq at the **Mi'kmaq Resource Centre** (*Beaton Institute, Cape Breton University, 1250*

Grand Lake Rd; ☎ *563 1660; www.mrc.uccb.ns.ca;* ⏲ *year-round 09.00–16.30 Tue–Fri; Mon by appointment; admission free*). While you're there, stop by Cape Breton Island's first (and only) full-time public art gallery, the **Cape Breton University Art Gallery** (*1250 Grand Lake Rd;* ☎ *563 1342; www.capebretonu.ca;* ⏲ *10.00–16.00 Mon–Fri; admission free*), which has a diverse permanent collection of historical and contemporary Canadian and international artwork. For art-lovers, **The Cape Breton Centre for Craft and Design** (*322 Charlotte St;* ☎ *270 7491; www.capebretoncraft.com;* ⏲ *10.00–16.00 Mon–Fri, 12.00–16.00 Sat; admission free*) has an overview of the work of some of Cape Breton Island's best artisans and an excellent gallery shop.

Get two (actually three) museums for the price of one at the **Cape Breton Fossil Centre and Sydney Mines Heritage Museum** (*159 Legatto St, Sydney Mines;* ☎ *544 992; www.cbfossil.org;* ⏲ *mid May–mid Oct 09.00–17.00 Tue–Sat; off-season by appointment; admission CAN$6*). Numerous 300 million-year-old fossils have been found over the years in the area's coalfields: fossil hikes are also offered three or more times weekly for an extra CAN$11. In the adjacent former railway station is a museum telling the story of the community of Sydney Mines – with emphasis of course on coal mining and steel manufacture. A recent addition is a local sport museum.

Staffed by enthusiastic volunteers and housed in a former synagogue, **Whitney Pier Historical Society Museum** (*88 Mt Pleasant St;* ☎ *564 9819; www.whitneypiermuseum.org;* ⏲ *Jun–Sep 09.00–12.00 & 13.00–16.30 Mon–Fri; off-season by appointment; admission free*) is an unusual hands-on museum that illustrates the multi-cultural (in close proximity are the Holy Ghost Ukrainian Church, Polish St Mary's Parish Church and St Phillips, the only African Orthodox Church in Canada) community which developed around the steel plant and coal piers.

If you're keen to try your luck at the tables, head over to the **Casino Nova Scotia–Sydney** (*525 George St;* ☎ *563 7777; http://sydney.casinonovascotia.com;* ⏲ *year-round 11.00–03.00 daily*). You'll find the typical assortment of slot machines and table games (*17.00–02.00 Wed–Sun*). For 19s and over only.

In season, large cruise ships are regular visitors to the **Sydney Marine Terminal** (also home to a tourist office and what is said to be the world's biggest violin – the fiddle is of course a vital part of Celtic music). Many passengers jump into waiting taxis and zoom off in the direction of Louisbourg or Baddeck.

On your way in or out of town? Drop by **Cape Breton Farmers' Market** (*340 Keltic Dr, Sydney River;* ☎ *564 9948; http://cbfarmersmarket.com;* ⏲ *year-round 08.30–13.00 Sat*) – it's well worth a visit between late spring and the end of autumn.

AROUND SYDNEY

GLACE BAY Glace Bay is the former heart of Cape Breton Island's once-flourishing coal industry. Mining apart, the town has another claim to fame as the place from which in 1902, the first west-to-east transatlantic wireless message was sent by **Guglielmo Marconi**.

Despite the death of the mining, Glace Bay is very much alive. For the visitor, in addition to the excellent mining museum (more interesting than it sounds!), there's a very good heritage museum, the beautifully renovated c1920s' **Savoy Theatre** (*116 Commercial St;* ☎ *842 1577; www.savoytheatre.com*) – a wonderful live music venue – and the Marconi site.

Accessible **by car**, Glace Bay is on Highways 4 and 28, 21km/13 miles northeast of Sydney. An hourly **bus** #1 (*Mon–Sat; CAN$2.25*) connects Glace Bay with downtown Sydney.

Where to eat

Miners' Village Restaurant early May–late Sep 11.00–20.00 daily. Located at the Miners' Museum (see below), this licensed restaurant offers a varied menu & reasonable prices. Try the seafood chowders or Atlantic halibut – & save room for old-fashioned dessert. $$

What to see and do Displays on the history of coal mining both in Cape Breton and internationally can be found at the **Cape Breton Miners' Museum** (*17 Museum St; 849 4522; www.minersmuseum.com; Jun–late Oct 10.00–18.00 daily; Nov–May 09.00–16.00 Mon–Fri; admission CAN$6*); also check out the recreation of a mining village between 1850 and 1900, with a miner's home and company store. Well worth the extra admission is the guided tour (*CAN$6, in off-season by appointment only*) of the **Ocean Deeps Colliery**, over which the museum has been built. Don a hard hat and cape to be guided deep underground by a retired miner to where the coal was extracted manually. A summer bonus is weekly concerts by the Men of the Deeps, a choir of working and retired Cape Breton Island miners (*late Jun–late Aug 20.00 most Tue; book in advance*).

The interesting **Glace Bay Heritage Museum** (*14 McKeen St; 842 5345; Feb–Jun & Sep–Dec 14.00–16.00 Tue, Thu & Sat; Jul/Aug 10.00–17.00 Tue–Sat, 13.00–18.00 Sun; admission free*) occupies two storeys of the restored c1903 former town hall. A large mural depicts both mining and another pursuit popular in Glace Bay in days gone by, sword fishing. See also the old court room and council chambers. There's also a gift shop with a good selection of books on Cape Breton Island, and a secondhand bookstore.

On the site of the **Marconi National Historic Site** (*Timmerman St, Table Head; 295 2069; www.pc.gc.ca/lhn-nhs/marconi; Jul–early Sep 10.00–18.00 daily; admission free*) in 1902, with use of a 400-wire antenna suspended from four 61m wooden towers, Guglielmo Marconi sent the first west-to-east transatlantic wireless message. In addition to displays on Marconi's life on Cape Breton Island and his experiments and achievements, there's a model of the original radio station: the foundations of the huge transmitting towers are visible outside.

THE SOUTH

By far the biggest attraction in the southeast of Cape Breton Island is the reconstruction of the fortress at Louisbourg. Much of the island's south coast is rugged, remote and sparsely populated, even by Nova Scotia standards. You won't see many people, or many (if any) shops, eateries and places to stay. Somewhat harsh – even bleak – for much of the year, it is best enjoyed in good weather by those who like pottering along on quiet roads, taking side-trips to pretty fishing villages, and soaking up an atmosphere of days gone by.

Highlights of this comparatively little-travelled trail include an opportunity to explore the beautiful coastal waters by sea kayak at Gabarus, gorgeous beaches at Belfry and Point Michaud, and the delightful Isle Madame.

Rising Tide Expeditions (see page 353) offers kayak tours of the Mira River, the waters around Louisbourg, and the Gabarus region.

PORT MORIEN This pleasant, quiet little seaside lobster-fishing village has a wide sandy barrier beach and a migratory bird sanctuary. It's not a bad choice for those who want a quiet base from which to explore the larger old industrial urban centres, and Louisbourg (see page 349), a 45-minute drive away.

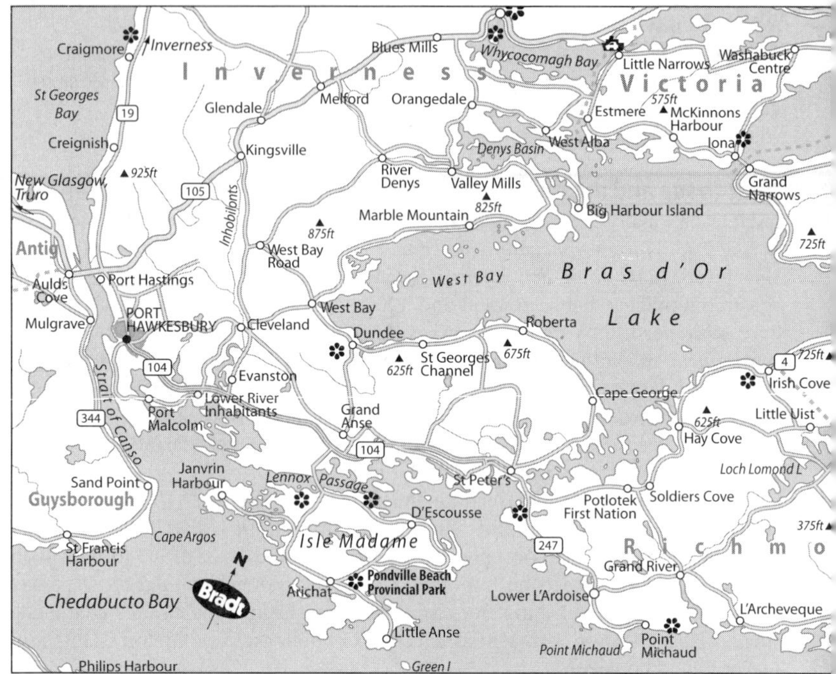

To reach Port Morien **by car**, the village is on Highway 255, 10km/6 miles from Glace Bay, 30km/19 miles from Sydney and 50km/31 miles from Louisbourg.

> **DIB DIB DIB**
>
> The first Boy Scout troop in North America was established in Port Morien in 1908.

Where to stay and eat

Port Morien Rectory B&B (2 rooms) 2652 Hwy 255; 737 1453, t/f 1 888 737 1453; e pmrectorybb@seaside.ns.ca; www.bbcanada.com/pmrectorybb; year-round. Housed in a c1885 former Anglican Church rectory, both guestrooms offer ocean views. Full b/fast inc. **$$**

Dock Y'ur Dory Restaurant & Gift Shop 2845 Hwy 255; 737 1832; May–Sep 11.00–19.00 daily. A licensed ocean-side restaurant/tea room with a large deck. The fresh ocean-caught 'catch of the day' is always good, as is pan-fried haddock. $–$$

MAIN-A-DIEU (*Population: 235*) The name Main-à-Dieu is a French corruption of the region's Mi'kmaq name, *Menadou*. This is the largest fishing village on the coast between Port Morien and Louisbourg.

To reach Main-a-Dieu from Port Morien **by car**, continue south on Highway 255 then turn left onto Main-à-Dieu Road, a total distance of approximately 28km /17 miles. The village is 17km from Louisbourg, via Main-à-Dieu Road.

What to see and do Look out for tiny **St James Cemetery**, dating from 1768. Stop off first at the **Coastal Discovery Centre** (*2886 Louisbourg–Main-à-Dieu Rd; 733 2258; www.coastaldiscoverycentre.ca; Jul/Aug 10.00–16.00 daily; Sep–Jun 09.00–17.00 daily*), which houses the Fishermen's Museum, a seasonal café and a

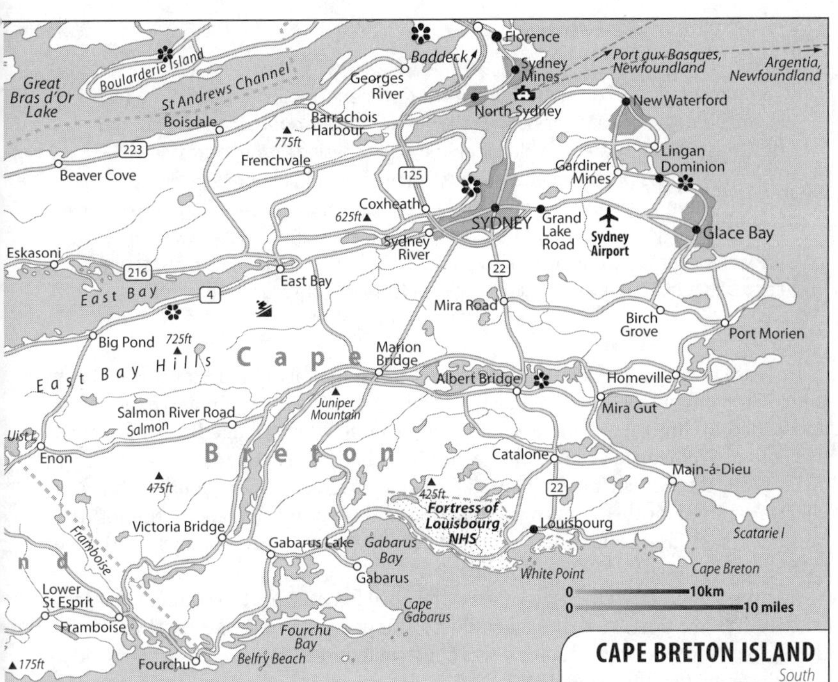

public library (☎ *733 5708*). Then wander the sandy beach or the boardwalk just behind. A short but worthwhile shoreline hike is the **Moque Head Trail**.

LOUISBOURG (*Population: 1,250*) Although best known for its wonderfully impressive reconstructed historic site (see page 352), the small fishing town of Louisbourg has a few other attractions too.

These include a lighthouse with a spectacular setting, shipwrecks in the harbour for divers to explore, a railway museum, an Elizabethan-style theatre and some good beaches a short ten-minute drive away along the unpaved Kennington Cove Road. You will see both English (Louisburg) and French (Louisbourg) spellings used, with the latter much more common.

Louisbourg is on the coast in the southeast corner of Cape Breton Island, 32km/20 miles from Sydney via Highway 22. It is 111km/69 miles from Baddeck and 207km/129 miles from the Canso Causeway. The town can only be reached **by car**, as no scheduled public transport comes this way.

History Around 1719, the French began a huge project to construct what was not to be just a military fort, but a fortified town that would be a prestigious centre for commerce, culture and government, the capital of Ile Royale (as Cape Breton Island was then known). Home to 2,000–5,000 French soldiers, fishermen, merchants and their families and children, it was just about ready when New Englanders attacked by land in 1745, supported by a large British naval force. The fortress fell in seven weeks.

The victors' success was tempered by the reality of the severe winters here: food (particularly fresh food) was scarce, shelter limited – owing to damage caused by the assault – and sanitary conditions awful. Ten times more New Englanders died of the cold, disease or starvation than had been killed in the fighting.

LIGHTHOUSE HISTORY

The second-oldest lighthouse on the North American continent, and the first in what is now Canada, was built by the French at Louisbourg in the 1730s, and destroyed (though later rebuilt) when the British besieged the fortress in 1758. The current version, on a volcanic rock outcrop, was first lit in 1924: enjoy the views! Recently developed scenic trails lead from the lighthouse along the coast in both directions. One part of the trail juts out enough to allow a panoramic view of the fortress, looking much as it would have to ships passing by over two centuries ago. To get there, follow Havenside Road from Main Street.

In 1748, the Treaty of Aix-la-Chapelle returned the fortress to France, and back under French control, it thrived again. Fortifications were repaired, strengthened and added to. But the second assault came in 1758, when a huge British force led by General Wolfe once again took the 'impregnable' fortress after a six-week siege.

In 1760, the British totally demolished the fortifications and outer works: in later years some of the stones were recycled and used in the construction of new buildings such as Halifax's Government House (1800), and Sydney's St George (1785) and St Patrick's (1828) churches.

As mines boomed in the Sydney area, the need for transport to connect that area with an ice-free port, so that coal could be shipped year-round, grew. As a result, the Sydney and Louisburg Railway was constructed in 1895.

Two centuries after the British had laid Louisbourg to waste, the Canadian government approved a plan to rebuild the fortifications and parts of the historic fortress to how they would have looked in the 1740s. Where possible, traditional French construction methods – and many of the original stones – were used in the painstaking reconstruction.

Where to stay

Cranberry Cove Inn (7 rooms) 12 Wolfe St; 733 2171, **t/f** 1 800 929 0222; www.cranberrycoveinn.com; May–Oct. A fine inn with individually themed guestrooms.Rate inc full b/fast. **$$**

Louisbourg Heritage House B&B (6 rooms) 7544 Main St; 733 3222, **t/f** 1 888 888 8466; www.louisbourgheritagehouse.com; Jun–early Oct. Each of the rooms in this centrally located c1886 former rectory have lovely wood floors & private balcony. Full b/fast inc. **$$**

Point of View Suites (& Campground) (16 units) 15 Commercial St Ext; 733 2080, **t/f** 1 888 374 8439; www.louisbourgpointofview.com; Jun–mid Oct. Bright, modern, well-designed deluxe suites & apts – many with kitchen facilities – in a great location on a 1.6ha peninsula with private beach & fortress views. Motorhome campground (no tents) with 24 full-service sites. **$$**

Wolvespack Cottage (2 rooms) 157 West Shore Rd; 733 2062; **e** wolvespackcottage@ns.sympatico.ca; Jun–Oct. Choose from a room with private or en-suite bathroom at this quiet, relaxing modern oceanfront home approx 5km from the historical site. Borrow a bike or kayak to work off the excellent b/fast (included in the room rate). **$$**

Spinning Wheel B&B (3 rooms) 5 Riverdale St; 733 3332, **t/f** 1 866 272 3222; www.spinningwheelbedandbreakfast.com; May–Oct. Don't expect big bedrooms or a grand mansion. Private or shared bathroom available. Do, however, expect a warm welcome, huge b/fast (included) & good value. **$**

Lakeview Treasures Campground & RV Park (75 sites) 5785 Louisbourg Hwy; 733 2058, **t/f** 1 866 233 2267; www.louisbourgcampground.com; Jun–Sep. Open & shaded campground 10km from the fortress with lake frontage & motorhome & serviced sites. Pool (in season), small store & take-out. **$**

Where to eat In addition to the listings below, there are also restaurants and a café inside the historic site.

Beggars Banquet Point Of View Suites, see opposite; Jul/Aug, 1 sitting at 18.00 daily. Not just dinner (soup, salad bar, choose from lobster, snow crab, halibut & chicken – plus all the trimmings – then ginger cake & tea or coffee) but musical entertainment, too. The idea comes from banquets held for the poor in days of yore, & you are encouraged to dine clad in period costumes (provided before you are seated). Reservations strongly recommended. *CAN$46.*

Grubstake Restaurant 7499 Main St; 733 2308; www.grubstake.ca; late Jun–mid Oct 12.00–20.15. Long established, but still maintaining high standards. The varied menu includes seafood & other interesting choices: steaks aren't bad, the barbecue pork has countless fans, but I'm partial to the shrimp/scallop flambée. $$

Lobster Kettle 41 Commercial St; 733 2723; www.lobsterkettle.com; Jun 16.00–20.00 daily; Jul/Aug 11.30–21.00 daily; Sep/Oct 11.30–20.00 daily. With a wonderful waterfront setting & fantastic views, generally, this licensed restaurant tends to do seafood well (especially lobster & snow crab). $$

Entertainment

Louisbourg Playhouse 11 Aberdeen St; 733 2996; www.louisbourgplayhouse.com; late Jun–mid Oct. Based on London, England's (Elizabethan) Globe Theatre, Louisbourg's version opened in 1994. The programme focuses on live theatre & Cape Breton music.

Festivals Held in August, the **Feast of St Louis** is a recreation of an 18th-century celebration honouring French monarch Louis IX, with cannon salutes, musket firings, dancing, children's games and music.

Other practicalities

$ Bank Royal Bank, 7509 Main St; 733 2012; 10.00–15.00 Mon–Wed, 10.00–17.00 Thu/Fri

Library W W Lewis Memorial Library, 10 Upper Warren St; 733 3608; 14.00–17.00 & 18.00–20.00 Tue & Thu, 14.00–17.00 Wed & Sat, 10.00–11.30 & 14.00–17.30 Fri

Post office 7529 Main St; 08.30–17.30 Mon–Fri, 09.30–13.30 Sat

Tourist information 7495 Main St; 733 2720; early Jun–early Oct 09.00–17.00 daily (Jul/Aug to 19.00)

What to see and do Appropriately housed in the former c1895 Sydney and Louisburg railway station, the **Sydney and Louisburg Railway Museum** (*Main St; 733 2720; Jun & Sep 09.00–17.00 Mon–Fri; Jul–Aug 10.00–19.00 daily; admission free*) has exhibits for train fans, including two passenger carriages from 1881 and 1914 and a working model of the line in an original freight shed.

If you're keen to get out and explore the island from above or below the water, there are a number of tour operators you can contact:

Louisbourg Scuba Services 733 2480; www.louisbourgscuba.com; year-round. Offers a range of services, including courses & charters to dive wrecks such as the Celebre, which sank in 1758.

Paradise Kayaks 200 Byrnes Lane, Catalone; 733 3244; www.paradisekayaks.com Based 8km north of Louisbourg, Paradise offers kayaking lessons. 1-hr group kayak lessons cost CAN$25 pp (min 4 people); individual lessons start at CAN$50.

Tartan Tours 578 4501; www.tartantours.guided-tours.ca Half- & full-day tours (leaving from Sydney) to destinations such as Baddeck & the Cabot Trail. Prices vary depending on numbers.

Fortress of Louisbourg (*733 3552; www.pc.gc.ca/louisbourg; late May–early Oct 09.30–17.00 daily (limited services except Jul–early Sep); early Oct–late May*

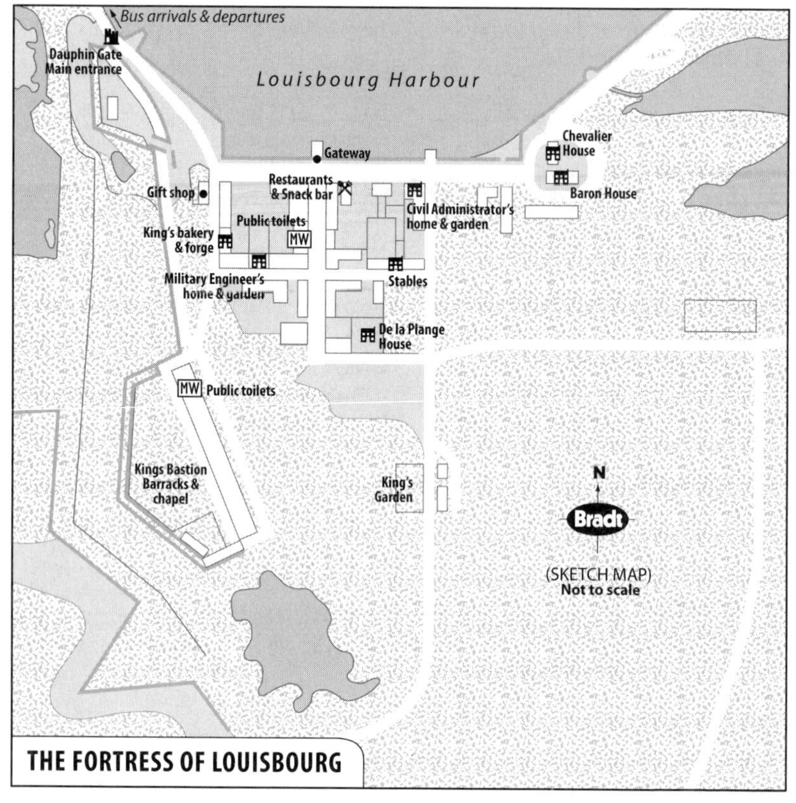

THE FORTRESS OF LOUISBOURG

09.30–16.00 Mon–Fri when buildings closed but grounds open; admission CAN$7.30; Jul–early Sep CAN$17.60) You can't miss Louisbourg's *pièce de résistance*: the **Fortress of Louisbourg National Historic Site of Canada**. To say that this site is the largest historical reconstruction in North America doesn't really begin to give an idea of the scale of the 6,700ha site.

Park (for free) at the visitor centre, buy your ticket and take the seven-minute bus ride to the fortress area. The reconstructed area alone sprawls across some 10ha, with dozens of buildings to visit and numerous activities to entertain you.

Theme centres and exhibits abound, each of which offers insight into a different part of the history and everyday life of the fortress in the 1740s. Whereas in many other living museums you'll see a few interpreters demonstrating a few traditional techniques, when everything is up and running Louisbourg seems alive with men, women and children in costume, only too prepared to interact – in character – with visitors.

See building techniques demonstrated, nail making, open-hearth cooking and lace making. Observe military exercises and musket firing. Haggle with street vendors, or watch a video on a soldier's life. Herbs and vegetables are tended in tidy back gardens.

Strikingly obvious is the class difference at the time, with both fine houses on cobbled streets for the gentry, and simple spartan dwellings for the have-not's.

Join a guided walking tour (check in advance for tour times), or use the site map to explore on your own. Be prepared for windy and/or wet weather, and a lot of walking. Allow far more time than you usually would for a 'standard' historical site or living museum. Get in the mood, and go back over two-and-a-half centuries!

In 2013, a year of celebrations will mark the 300th anniversary of the Isle Royale colony (Cape Breton Island) with Louisbourg as its capital.

Where to eat If you work up an appetite whilst exploring the site, your options include a café and a couple of restaurants, themed either for humble soldiers, or officers and gentlemen.

Grandchamp's Tavern Jul–early Oct from 10.30 daily. You are given a spoon with which to eat 18th-century-style rustic French cuisine served in a wooden bowl & prepared to authentic recipes. The menu isn't overlong but includes at least 1 fish, meat & vegetarian option each day. With period décor & waiting staff in costume, it is a fun experience. Licensed. $$

Hotel de la Marine Jul/late Aug from 11.00 daily. This 'upper class' (more formal) dining experience represents what the higher-ranks of society could expect upon a visit to Louisbourg. Your finer dining is served on china crockery – & you also get a knife & fork. Licensed. $$

L'Epee Royale Café Jul–early Oct daily from 10.00. Offers period desserts, baked goods, sandwiches & wraps. $

MARION BRIDGE This small community is named for the bridge which crosses the Mira River. Services are limited with the focus a gift shop/tea room.

Marion Bridge is convenient to reach **by car**; it is on Highway 327, 15km/9 miles from Sydney, 31km/19 miles from Louisbourg and 25km/16 miles from Gabarus.

Where to eat

Riverbank Restaurant 856 Grand Mira South Rd, Juniper Mountain, Marion Bridge; 727 2012, t/f 1 866 550 5824; www.mirarivercottages.de; summer 16.00–20.30 Wed–Sun. Swiss-German & Canadian specialities, good seafood chowder & desserts. Good value. To get there, turn onto Grand Mira South Rd from Hwy 327 approx 800m after crossing the Mira River (heading south): the restaurant is approx 5km from the junction. $–$$

What to see and do A peaceful 200ha wildlife park at the confluence of the Salmon and Mira rivers 8km west of Marion Bridge, **Two Rivers Wildlife Park** (*Grand Mira North Rd; 727 2483; www.tworiverspark.ca; mid Oct–mid May 10.00–16.00 daily; mid May–mid Oct 10.00–19.30 daily; admission CAN$6.50*) displays wildlife native to the Maritimes (with a couple of exotic extras such as emus).

GABARUS This is a truly picturesque fishing village. Before you reach the breakwater, turn left onto Harbour Point Road past the **Harbour Cemetery** which has lost several graves to the sea, to reach the c1950s' **lighthouse**. Pity that there is nowhere to stay or eat.

Gabarus is on Highway 327, 45km/28 miles from Sydney, 56km/35 miles from Louisbourg and 88km/55 miles from St Peter's.

What to see and do If you feel like a **coastal hike**, at the breakwater turn right onto Gull Cove Road, and follow it to its end. The walking trail (6km each way) leads to what was the fishing community of **Gull Cove**. After about 1km you'll reach **Harris Beach**, and have a wonderful view over Gabarus Bay.

Rising Tide Expeditions (*Hwy 327; 884 2884, t/f 1 877 884 2884; e info@risingtideexpeditions.ca; www.risingtideexpeditions.ca*) offer guided sea kayak trips (*Jun–Sep*) from half-day paddles around the beautiful Gabarus Bay to five-day trips in three different regions of Cape Breton Island, some camping, some inn-based. Rising Tide does not rent out sea kayaks.

BELFRY BEACH Don't be surprised to have this magnificent long stretch of sand – backed by Belfry Lake – to yourself. This is a remote and very sparsely populated corner of Cape Breton Island, and the beach itself is easily missed by the casual tourist. Long may it stay that way! Enjoy the solitude and natural splendour, and wander for miles. You might see harbour or grey seals in June and July, you'll definitely see a range of seabirds, and – in spring and summer in particular – migratory shorebirds.

To reach Belfry Beach **by car**, it is located at the end of Belfry Road, off Fourchu Road approximately 8.5km/5 miles south of the tiny community of Gabarus Lake.

POINT MICHAUD A fine beach justifies Point Michaud's inclusion in this book. There's not a lot else going on. Encompassing a glorious 3km curve of sand backed by marram grass-covered dunes, **Point Michaud Beach Provincial Park** makes for a stunning stop. The beach is popular (perhaps that is the wrong word to use – it rarely gets at all busy) with surfers, windsurfers and birdwatchers.

Point Michaud is 21km/13 miles from St Peter's and 67km/42 miles from Gabarus.

ISLE MADAME

Despite the name, this is actually a cluster (measuring approximately 16km by 11km) of islands separated from Cape Breton Island by the narrow Lennox Passage.

Arichat is the most significant of the main communities, and several tiny hamlets such as picturesque **Little Anse** and **Samsons Cove** fringe secluded inlets and coves. Acadian heritage is still strong here, and you will often hear French being spoken.

Once again, specific sites are few, the attraction being beautiful coastal scenery, genuinely friendly people, and a very relaxed atmosphere. With a wooded interior, relatively gentle terrain, virtually no heavy traffic, a lovely beach, a fine hiking trail and a few good places to stay and eat, this is a delightful area to motor (or better still, cycle) around, especially when the sun is out.

On the Lennox Passage waterfront, **Martinique** has a picnic park, the c1884 Grandique Point Lighthouse and a small beach, but the best beaches are on **Janvrin Island** and at Pondville, where the sandy 1km-long strand is backed by dunes and a lagoon.

Probably the best of Isle Madame's numerous trails is the **Cape Auguet Eco Trail** which begins near Boudreauville, offering over 10km of loop trails, both coastal and through hardwood forest.

Accessible **by car**, the bridge across to Isle Madame is 5km/3 miles from Exit 46 of Highway 104, 35km/22 miles from Port Hastings, 24km/15 miles from St Peter's, and 109km/68 miles from Sydney.

HISTORY European contact with Isle Madame goes at least as far back as the early 16th century, when Basque and Portuguese fishermen took refuge from storms at Petit-de-Grat, the oldest fishing village in the area. The name is a combination of French and Spanish/Basque and means 'little fishing place (station)'.

Initially, Isle Madame was named Sante Marie. The name change was in honour of Madame de Maintenon, second wife of French monarch Louis XIV.

One of the oldest communities in Nova Scotia, Arichat had strong business ties with Jersey in the Channel Islands during the mid 1700s, not least because that was

LOBSTERS

You'll see them on many menus, in tanks in restaurants and supermarkets, and the contraptions used to capture them in a multitude of fishing villages.

A lobster has a long body and five sets of legs, including two large front claws, one of which is large and flat while the other is thinner and smaller. The body, tail and claws are protected by a hard shell. Lobsters grow by moulting, or shedding their shell. After a moult (typically in summer), the lobster is soft-shelled and filled with the sea water it has absorbed in the process. Up to two months pass before the absorbed sea water is replaced by new flesh. The shell hardens again in the cold sea before the cycle repeats.

Although live lobsters range in colour from brownish-rust to greenish-brown, all lobster shells turn bright orangey-red when cooked – traditionally by being immersed in a pot of salted water that has been heated to a rolling boil. Lobsters die within moments when immersed in boiling water. They have very primitive nervous systems, and the jury is out on whether they experience anything similar to the concept of pain. Often called the 'King of Seafood', though it can be messy to extract (especially for novices), the lobster's white flesh is firm and dense with a rich flavour.

Lobster fishers use small boats to fish with baited, wooden-frame or plastic-coated steel-mesh traps which are weighted and lowered to the sea bottom. The traps are hauled by ropes attached to buoys which mark their location.

Atlantic Canada's waters are divided into specific fishing areas, each with its own season, varying in length from eight weeks to eight months. These are staggered to protect summer moults.

If you're wondering how fresh lobster manages to appear on menus year-round, the answer is lobster pounds. In the past, these were large, fenced areas of the ocean where captive lobsters lived until required, new technology has meant huge dry-land holding facilities being built. One of the biggest of these is owned by Clearwater Seafoods, and is on Isle Madame at Presqu'Ile Cove.

Here, around one million lobsters usually reside in individual containers stacked over 30 levels high. Their environment makes the crustaceans lose all inclination to moult. Lobsters caught all over the Maritime provinces are brought here, and, when required, shipped all over the world.

Although no scheduled tours are offered, in the past staff at the pound have been happy to show visitors around. If you'd like to see the facility, it might be worth phoning ahead. For various reasons, you may choose not to eat it during your time in Nova Scotia, but be prepared to be offered lobster frequently (and, more often than not, for the offerer to be surprised if you decline).

where most of its early inhabitants, many of whom were French Huguenots, had come from. The red-petalled Jersey lilies visible in many of the island's gardens were brought over three centuries ago. In the late 18th century in particular, the harbour teemed with commerce and shipbuilding. When tall ships ruled the seas, it was a booming Atlantic seaport with 17 consular representatives.

Previously connected to Cape Breton Island only by water transport, a bridge across Lennox Passage was completed in 1919.

The economy was built around fishing, and fishing and fish processing are still hugely important. Shellfish and to a lesser degree, mackerel, predominate now.

WHERE TO STAY AND EAT

L'Auberge Acadienne Inn (17 rooms) 2375 Hwy 206; Arichat; 226 2200, t/f 1 877 787 2200; e inn@acadienne.com; www.acadienne.com; year-round. Friendly, comfortable, modern – but traditional Acadian-style – country inn. There are 9 rooms in the main building & 8 roomy drive-up motel-style units. Laundry facilities. The licensed dining room (*year-round 07.30–10.00 & 17.00–20.00 daily (mid Jun–mid Oct to 20.30); $–$$*) specialises in Acadian dishes & seafood & is excellent. **$$**

Robin's Harbour View Cottages (3 cottages) Robin's Rd, Arichat; 226 9515; e robinscottages@ns.sympatico.ca; mid May–mid Oct. Overlooking the harbour, these well-equipped 2-bedroom cottages are good for those wanting extra space. **$$**

Vollmer's Island Paradise (6 units) 1489 Janvrin's Harbour Rd; 226 1507; e info@vipilodge.com; www.vipilodge.com; May–Oct. Hand-built log cabins on lovely Janvrin Island really allow you to get away from it all. Canoes available, boat trips & scuba diving offered (*Jul–Sep*). B/fast not inc. **$$**

Vina Motel (4 rooms) 2354 Hwy 206, Arichat; 226 2662; year-round. Simple, basic motel rooms with small fridge & microwave. **$**

FESTIVALS The **Acadian Festival** at Petit-de-Grat is a five-day event celebrating Acadian culture and heritage, which takes place in August.

SHOPPING Nearby, major seafood distributor **Premium Seafoods** (*449 Lower Rd; 226 3474; www.premiumseafoods.ns.ca; year-round 08.00–17.00 Mon–Sat*) has a retail outlet.

OTHER PRACTICALITIES

$ Bank East Coast Credit Union, 9 Cap La Ronde Rd, D'Escousse; 226 2722; 09.00–16.00 Mon–Wed & Fri, 09.00–18.00 Thu

Library Petit-de-Grat Branch Library, 3435 Hwy 206; 226 3534

Post office 2451 High Rd, Arichat; 08.00–17.00 Mon–Fri, 10.00–13.00 Sat

WHAT TO SEE AND DO Overlooking the harbour is the large, wooden cathedral of **Notre Dame de L'Assomption (Our Lady of the Assumption)** dating from c1837. In 1858, the then bishop imported a pipe organ – now considered to be one of very few of its kind in North America – from Philadelphia, USA. Just by the cathedral, **Cannon Look-Off** offers fine views and has interpretive displays detailing the region's history. The c1789 forge down on the waterfront, now the **LeNoir Forge Museum** (*Lower Rd; 226 9364; early Jun–Aug 10.00–17.00 daily; admission free*), was built in the French Regime style. It was used more recently as an ice house, and in 1967, restored as a working museum.

PORT HAWKESBURY

A short drive from Port Hastings (see page 304) Port Hawkesbury is a major commercial and industrial centre on the Strait of Canso. As at Mulgrave across the water, construction of the nearby Canso Causeway has created an ice-free deep-water port capable of accommodating the largest ships in the world.

In these tough economic times, the community is still reeling from the recent (2011–12) closure – and consequential job losses – of a call centre and the huge NewPage paper mill. On/off negotiations to find a prospective buyer for the mill appeared to be productive, but most of the mill workers said that they wouldn't take anything for granted until the machinery was rolling once again.

If you feel like stretching your legs, some nice walking trails head off into the woods around town.

GETTING THERE Port Hawkesbury is easy to get to **by car**. The town is on Highway 4, 6km/4 miles from Port Hastings and 7km/4.3 miles to the Canso Causeway. It is 43km/27 miles from St Peter's and 165km/103 miles from Sydney. Port Hawkesbury is on the Maritime Bus **coach** route between Halifax and Sydney (see page 44).

WHERE TO STAY

Maritime Inn Port Hawkesbury (73 rooms) 717 Reeves St; 625 0320, t/f 1 888 662 7484; www.maritimeinns.com. A comfortable mid range hotel with indoor & seasonal outdoor pools, & a fitness centre. See below for Millers Café and Millers Tap & Grill restaurant listings. **$$**

Gagnon House (3 rooms) 24 Philpott St; 625 1146; Apr–Dec. Conveniently located Cape Cod-style house. Rooms with en-suite or shared bathroom. Warm & knowledgeable hosts. Front & back decks, Strait of Canso views. Full b/fast inc. **$**

Harbourview B&B and Motel (9 units) 209 Granville St; 625 3224, t/f 1 877 676 6886; www.harbourviewbb.com; year-round. There are 3 rooms in the c1880 main house (built for a ferry captain), & 6 motel rooms with fridge & microwave. Guest laundry, Wi-Fi. Watch the modern-day water traffic from the glass-enclosed patio. Full b/fast inc. **$**

WHERE TO EAT

Millers Café 717 Reeves St; year-round 06.30–14.00 Mon–Fri, 07.00–14.00 Sat/Sun. Maritime Inn Port Hawkesbury's (see above) on-site restaurant is good for a hotel eatery. **$$**

Millers Tap & Grill 717 Reeves St; year-round 14.00–23.00 daily; food served until 21.00 (Jul–Sep until 22.00). Maritime Inn Port Hawkesbury's other on-site restaurant is licensed. The food – the closest you'll come to fine-dining in these parts – is good value. **$$**

China King 825 Reeves St; 625 7000; year-round 11.00–22.00 daily. Food from the fixed-price buffet or standard menu is well presented & tasty. The crispy calamari & hot pepper squid are both recommended. **$**

Fleur-de-Lis Tea Room and Dining Room 634 Reeves St; 625 2566; year-round 07.00–19.00 Mon–Sat, 10.00–14.00 Sun. An easy-to-miss little gem tucked away in the Causeway shopping mall. There's no deep-fryer, & very few processed ingredients are used. All-day b/fast, seafood, Scottish & Acadian cuisine & more. Start with maple nut salad, then go for Acadian fishcakes or the grilled haddock dinner. Desserts are homemade & usually very good. Recommended. **$**

Shindigs Pub 510 Granville St; 625 0263; www.shindigspub.com; year-round 11.00–late daily (from 15.00 Sat/Sun). Waterfront pub with good atmosphere. Regular live music. Food is a bit hit or miss. **$**

FESTIVALS A four-day festival in July, **Festival of the Strait** (*www.festivalofthestrait.ca*) hosts a variety of activities including sailing, canoe races, outdoor concerts and dances.

WHEN THE CIRCUS CAME TO TOWN

It was the summer of 1870. A local man was short-changed as he bought a ticket for the circus, and when one of the circus staff struck the indignant chap, all hell broke loose. One man was killed, several were badly injured, and most of the circus animals escaped. When order was finally restored, the show was cancelled and the circus limped out of town, battered and bruised – and missing two monkeys. The primates enjoyed a few days of swinging around Port Hawkesbury and frightening the townsfolk before they were shot.

CAUGHT IN THE WEB

Born in 1935 in New Brunswick, Melissa Friedrich was convicted of killing her husband in 1991: on a deserted road near Halifax, she ran him over twice with a car. She had drugged him heavily to encourage him to lie down in the road. Sentenced to six years in jail for manslaughter, she was released after serving two.

Shortly after her release, she went to Florida and met a man at a Christian retreat. The two married in Dartmouth, Nova Scotia in 2000, but a year later his family members noticed his health seemed to be deteriorating rapidly: there were unexplained fainting spells, his speech was often slurred, and he had to have frequent hospital stays. His family claimed that his money was disappearing far more rapidly than one might expect. He died of cardiac arrest in 2002: no post mortem was carried out and there were no charges over his death.

Melissa found her next husband – a divorcee in his 70s – on an internet dating site, and met him in Florida. Having enjoyed relatively good health up until the wedding, his fortune changed post nuptials. After eight hospital visits in as many weeks, he was told that he had an unwelcome drug in his system. He also discovered that his bank balance had plummeted to zero. Melissa was sentenced to five years in a Florida prison: she was released in 2009 and deported back to Canada, settling in New Glasgow.

Melissa married again in September 2012: she and her 75-year old husband Fred (it is rumoured that she met him via the internet) honeymooned in Newfoundland before stopping for the night in North Sydney. Hours later, Fred was taken ill, and rushed to hospital. After a few days, Melissa – now 77 – was arrested for attempted murder. I'm glad to say that Fred was released from hospital and seems to be recovering well.

Already labelled the 'Internet Black Widow' by the media, Melissa awaits trial. It is not known if she has access to a computer.

OTHER PRACTICALITIES

$ Bank BMO Bank of Montreal 634 Reeves St; ☎ 625 1250; ⏰ 10.00–16.00 Mon–Wed, 10.00–17.00 Thu/Fri

Hospital The Strait Richmond Hospital, 138 Hospital Rd, Evanston; ☎ 625 3100. 11km east of Port Hawkesbury at Exit 45 of Hwy 104.

Library Port Hawkesbury Branch Library, 304 Pitt St; ☎ 625 2729; ⏰ 15.00–20.00 Mon–Fri, 11.00–14.00 Sat

Post office 25 Pitt St; ⏰ 08.30–17.00 Mon–Fri, 08.30–12.30 Sat

WHAT TO SEE AND DO The **Port Hawkesbury Civic Centre** (*606 Reeves St; ☎ 625 2591; www.phcivic.com; ⏰ year-round*) is a fine facility, which houses an arena, performance space, YMCA fitness centre, art gallery and more. There are weekly ceilidhs (*Jul–late Aug Tue*), and a community market (*late May–early Oct 14.00–18.00 Thu*).

Summer evenings bring free outdoor concerts on Sundays at **Granville Green** (*Granville St; ☎ 625 2591; www.granvillegreen.com*).

9

Eastern Shore

Stretching for almost 350km from Lawrencetown to the Canso Causeway, this is the least visited of any of the mainland tourist regions of Nova Scotia.

Ask those who live in other parts of the province about the Eastern Shore and 'always foggy' or 'no infrastructure' will probably be the most common answers. They have a point in terms of infrastructure. There are no sizeable towns, and accommodation, shopping and services are limited and public transport non-existent.

So why come here? This region offers some of Nova Scotia's wildest and most scenic coastal landscapes. Along the length of much of the coast, dozens of forested finger-like peninsulas protrude out into the Atlantic. The so-called main highway – in reality, for all but the first 35km of its length just a quiet two-lane road – cuts across the base of the peninsulas but from time to time be sure to turn off onto one of the side roads to get to a small fishing village, beautiful beach or wild rocky headland with a view of a lighthouse on a nearby island.

Much of the region is forest-covered, with spruce, fir, birch, larch and maple predominant. This is also one of the province's most rewarding destinations for viewing the beauty of the autumn colours.

There aren't any luxury hotels, but the relatively few – but delightful – B&Bs and inns, a handful of motels, a new marina with an inn, some lovely campsites and one 'nature lover's' resort do the job.

The restaurants are also widely spaced, but although you may have to drive for a while there are some excellent dining opportunities, especially for lovers of seafood.

The sea is cold but the beaches are uncrowded and beautiful with the province's best surfing and windsurfing, and the hundreds of uninhabited, forested islands, many of which contain ruins of long-abandoned dwellings or fishing camps, and inlets make for ideal sea kayaking.

Birdwatchers will be in their element, and in addition, there is some wonderful riverside, forest and coastal hiking, and a history of gold mining. There's also an abundance of folklore, with seafaring traditions and legends still very much alive, and a very popular annual music festival.

There are, of course, foggy days, but wandering along a beautiful deserted beach, watching the sea mist roll in, and hearing the moan of a faraway foghorn can be very atmospheric.

Here, perhaps more than anywhere else in Nova Scotia, you'll feel like a traveller rather than a tourist. Come and enjoy the slow pace of life and the proximity to virtually untouched nature. It is no surprise that most of the Eastern Shore's manmade attractions celebrate days gone by, a life pre-electricity and pre-modern technology.

If you headed out to sea for approximately 170km from Tor Bay (see page 375), you would reach intriguing Sable Island National Park Reserve (pages 382–5) –

though virtually all of the limited number of people who visit this long, narrow, storied strip of sand fly from Halifax Airport.

ALONG THE EASTERN SHORE

LAWRENCETOWN AND SEAFORTH Lawrencetown has little to offer service-wise – **MacDonald House**, the building on the right at the top of the hill, has a gallery, antique shop, a tea room and a basement surf shop. The principal attraction is the **Lawrencetown Beach Provincial Park**, renowned for offering the province's best and most consistent wave breaks for surfers. The waves are best for surfing in the autumn and winter, in particular between September and May, but whatever time of the year people surf, wetsuits are a must – this isn't Hawaii. And the closest you'll get to a pina colada is a coke from the (summer-only) canteen.

For those who merely want to watch, the beach is well worth a (breezy) stop, look and stroll. Lifeguards are on duty in season, and the park has changing rooms, showers and toilets.

Far quieter, and usually surfer-free, is **Conrad Beach**, at the end of Conrad Road, 6km east of Lawrencetown. Here your only companions are likely to be birds – and birdwatchers. Boardwalks connect the small parking area with the (especially at low tide) huge, fine-sand beach. Seaforth is home to a wildlife rehabilitation centre.

Both Lawrencetown and Seaforth are accessible **by car**. Lawrencetown is on Highway 207, 18km/11 miles from Dartmouth, 20km/12 miles from Halifax and 24km/15 milesfrom Musquodoboit Harbour. Seaforth is also on Highway 207, 9km/6 miles east of Lawrencetown. It is 27km/17 miles from Dartmouth, and 15km/9 miles from Musquodoboit Harbour.

Where to stay and eat

Moonlight Beach Inn (3 rooms) 2 Wyndenfog Lane; 827 2712; www.moonlightbeachinn.com; year-round. In a magnificent location virtually on Lawrencetown Beach, each guest room has a sitting area, fireplace, dining nook, private entrance & a deck overlooking the ocean. Lobster dinners in season. B/fast inc (eg: eggs Benedict 'Maritime-style' with crab or smoked salmon). Reductions may be offered out of season. **$$**

Beach Niche (2 units) 5 Wyndenfog Lane; 827 4011; bettyhoughton@eastlink.ca;

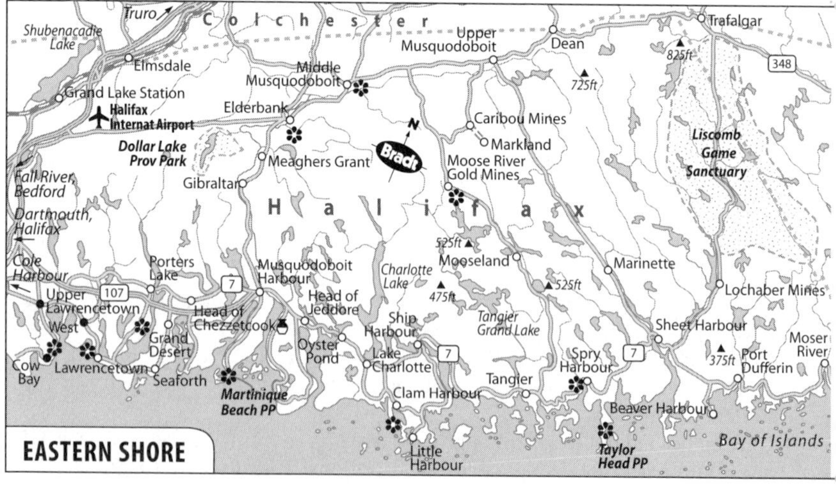

NOT JUST FOR TWITCHERS

En route between the city and Lawrencetown, nature-lovers may wish to make a detour. First get to Cole Harbour. Either follow Portland Street (Highway 207) for 7km from Dartmouth, or if you're on Highway 107, turn on to the Forest Hills Parkway (5km past Exit 14) and follow it for about 3km to Cole Harbour Road (Highway 207). Turn onto Bissett Road and after 3km you'll see the parking area and trailhead for the Salt Marsh Trail. In a few minutes you'll reach the harbour itself, and this tends to be a particularly rewarding area for watching autumn shorebirds. This is actually part of the Trans Canada Trail, and a number of footbridges lead out across the water. You don't have to do the whole 6.5km each way – just head out for a while then make your way back.

www.beachniche.ca; ⌚ year-round. Less than 100m from Lawrencetown Beach are these 2 comfortable, spacious apts, 1 with 2 bedrooms & 2 bathrooms (which can sleep up to 8), & a studio apt with dbl bed. Both have private entrances & well-equipped kitchens. Continental b/fast inc. **$–$$**

Lawrencetown Beach House (10 beds) 6 Wyndenfog Lane; 827 2345; e info@lawrencetownbeachhouse.com; www.lawrencetownbeachhouse.com; ⌚ year-round by reservation only. Hostel with 10 beds spread between 3 rooms. Private room available. Shared kitchen & bathrooms. *Dorm CAN$30; private room CAN$80.* **$**

Porter's Lake Provincial Park Campground (80 sites) 1160 West Porter's Lake Rd; 827 2250; www.novascotiaparks.ca/parks/porters.asp. Beautifully located & virtually surrounded by water, 10km from Lawrencetown. **$**

Heron's Nest Tea Room 4144 Lawrencetown Rd; 434 7895; ⌚ mid May–early Oct 11.00–17.00 Tue–Sun. Salads, soups & sandwiches & an enticing array of baked goods. **$**

Festivals At the end of August/early September is the **Kite Festival**, a one-day event with kite-flying demonstrations and competitions, and a barbecue.

Shopping Surfing shops in the area include **DaCane Beach Store** (*431 7873; www.dacanesurfshop.com; ⌚ Jun–Sep*), right in the provincial park, and **Kannon Beach** (*4144 Hwy 7; 471 0025; www.kannonbeach.com; ⌚ year-round*), at the top of the hill.

What to see and do Call in advance if you would like to visit the **Hope for Wildlife Society** (*5909 Hwy 207;* ☎ *481 2401; www.hopeforwildlife.net*), which specialises in the care, treatment and rehabilitation of injured or orphaned native mammals and birds.

THE CHEZZETCOOKS West and East Chezzetcook are pretty villages dotted along the Chezzetcook Inlet's shores.

On the eastern side of the inlet a road offering more lovely harbour views leads to East Chezzetcook. Ask local residents the best things about their community and most will mention the Acadian roots and heritage, fishing history, wild Misener's Head (further down the road), and Chad Doucette. East Chezzetcook is home to young Mr Doucette who reached the Top four in the 2006 series of reality pop talent contest *Canadian Idol*.

The neighbouring communities of Grand Desert, Gaetz Brook and Porter's Lake offer more accommodation and dining choices.

Situated on Highway 7, and between Exits 20 and 21 of Highway 107, the Chezzetcooks are convenient to reach **by car**. They are some 23km/14 miles from Dartmouth, and 14km/9 miles from Musquodoboit Harbour.

History *Chezzetcook* is a Mi'kmaq word for 'running waters divided into many channels'. The first permanent Acadian settlers arrived in 1764. They befriended the local Mi'kmaq and joined them in harvesting clams and fishing. Dykes were built to enable farming of the marshland. In the 1870s, Chezzetcook was Nova Scotia's biggest oyster producer.

West Chezzetcook's Saint Anselm Church was founded in 1740, but the current (brick) version was built in 1894. Each local family was asked to pay for 400 bricks to help meet construction costs. The church remains the major focus of the area's communities.

Where to stay

Changing Tides B&B (2 rooms) 6627 Hwy 207, Grand Desert; ☎ 827 5134; www.changingtides.ca; ⌚ year-round. A spacious, modern house 3km from West Chezzetcook with magnificent views of the ocean, wetlands & islands. Fireplace in lounge; deck & sun room. Full b/fast inc. **$$**

The IN House Musical B&B (1 room) 5315 Hwy 7, Porter's Lake; ☎ 827 2532; www.inhousemusicalbnb.com; ⌚ year-round by reservation. A Victorian-style country house less than 3km from Head of Chezzetcook, decorated with hostess's art work. Enjoy mostly original music performed by the hosts (one of whom delights in his alter-ego soubriquet, *The Cosmic Surfer)*. Sauna & Healing circle. Continental b/fast inc. **$**

Where to eat and drink

Cicero's on the Water 122 Post Office Rd, Porter's Lake; ☎ 827 3287; www.ciceros.co; ⌚ year-round 11.00–20.00 Wed, 11.00–22.00 Thu–Sat, 10.00–18.00 Sun. Italian & Canadian cuisine in a great waterside location. Start with flash-fried chili-infused calamari, & follow with roast chicken fettucine. Lovely large deck. Licensed. **$$**

Tin Roof Mercantile and Café 6321 Hwy 7, Head of Chezzetcook; ☎ 827 5313, **t/f** 1 877 827 5313; www.tinroof.ca; ⌚ summer 11.00–14.00 Wed–Sat, 12.00–14.30 Sun; winter 11.30–14.00 Thu–Sat, 12.00–14.30 Sun. Sit by the big open fire & tuck into good home cooking. Organic, local ingredients used where possible. Popular with Halifax/Dartmouth residents for w–end lunches. **$$**

Porter's Lake Pub 5228 Hwy 7, Porter's Lake; ☎ 827 3097; ⌚ year-round 10.00–21.00 Mon–Wed (pub until midnight), 10.00–21.30 Thu/Fri (pub until 02.00), 09.00–21.30 Sat (pub until

GREY LADY

Although not exclusive to this region – you hear such tales throughout the Maritimes – many of those on the Eastern Shore will tell stories about the Grey Lady, a mysterious forerunner (see page 32) seen by seafarers seemingly as a warning of impending danger.

Over the centuries (and that includes the 21st), there have been numerous sightings of a female apparition (some say veiled, some say headless) who appears to be floating on top of the water, enshrouded by a grey fog: some speculate that she is the spirit of a victim of one of the region's hundreds of shipwrecks. The vision is said to appear to those who may be heading into danger as if to warn them of the proximity of a reef, or a sudden approaching storm. The Grey Lady is not something to be scared by, but a wake-up call: see her, sharpen your senses and you could avoid danger.

02.00), 09.00–21.00 Sun (pub until midnight). This relaxed, quaint & popular pub offers a full menu – Creole linguine is a standout – & entertainment Thu–Sat evenings (plus summer Sun). $–$$

McKay's Restaurant 5191 Hwy 7, Porter's Lake; 827 5959; Mar–Dec 08.00–20.00 daily; Jan/Feb 08.0020.00 Tue–Sun. Good simple diner-style food, pleasant service & family-friendly atmosphere. Patio. $

Rose & Rooster Bakery 6502 Hwy 207, Grand Desert; 827 1042; year-round 06.00–14.00 Mon–Wed, 06.00–16.00 Thu/Fri, 08.00–16.00 Sat. New (summer 2012) place to stop for good coffee, bread, baked goods and more. $

Other practicalities

$ **Bank** Royal Bank, 5228 Hwy 7, Porter's Lake; 827 2930; 09.30–17.00 Mon–Wed & Fri, 09.30–20.00 Thu

Post office 5 Keizer Dr, Porter's Lake; 08.30–17.15Mon–Fri, 08.30–12.00 Sat

What to see and do Built in 1850, the **Acadian House Museum: L'Acadie de Chezzetcook** (*79 Hill Rd, West Chezzetcook; 827 5992; Jul/Aug 10.00–16.30 Tue–Sun; CAN$2*) retains the character of a typical Acadian home from the period. On show are clothes, documents, tools, photos and artefacts – including a mid 19th-century-style outdoor oven. There's also a sweet little tea room (*Jul/Aug 10.00–16.00 Tue–Sun; $*).

MUSQUODOBOIT HARBOUR (*Population: approx 1,000*) Musquodoboit (pronounced 'Muska-dobbit') Harbour pips Sheet Harbour (see page 370) as the largest community between Dartmouth and Canso, a distance of some 200km. Unless you're sure that you'll reach Sheet Harbour when the relevant shops or services are open, stock up here.

The Mi'kmaq name, *Moosekudoboogwek* means 'suddenly widening out after a narrow entrance at the mouth'. The harbour itself is sheltered from the Atlantic Ocean by a long barrier beach system and is an incredibly productive estuary. The varied coastal scenery includes sandy beaches, salt marshes, saline ponds, dunes, eel grass beds, mudflats and mature coastal coniferous forest.

Large numbers of birds flock to this region every year to feed and rest during their long migration, and in 1987, Musquodoboit Harbour was added to the official 'List of Wetlands of International Importance' in recognition of its importance as a habitat for diverse waterfowl populations. Birds apart, there's a railway museum and good hiking.

Musquodoboit Harbour is accessible **by car**, being on Highway 7, approximately 45km/28 miles from Halifax and 69km/43 miles from Sheet Harbour.

Where to stay and eat

Old Riverside Lodge B&B (3 rooms) 98 Riverside Av; 889 3464, t/f 1 877 859 3674; www.oldriversidelodgebnb.com; May–Oct; off-season by reservation. A c1853 lodge with original hardwood floors. Continental b/fast inc. **$$**

The Tourist Trap (3 rooms) 8384 Hwy 7; 889 3791; e info@thetouristtrap.ca; www.thetouristtrap.ca; year-round. A lovely (though less than enticingly named) guesthouse: rooms share a bathroom. There is a common room with microwave, fridge & complimentary coffee. Also on site is a café (*late Jun–mid Sep 08.00–19.00 daily; mid Sep–Dec 08.30–18.45 Wed–Sun; Jan–mid Jun 08.30–18.45 Thu–Sun;* $), specialising in province-grown organic food such as fishcakes, salads, sandwiches, good coffee & desserts, all-day b/fasts & more substantial fare). **$$**

Dobbit Bakehouse 7896 Hwy 7; 889 2919; 07.30–17.30 Mon–Fri, 08.00–17.00 Sat, 09.00–17.00 Sun. Excellent artisan bakery with 3 small tables indoors (& a picnic table outside). Turnovers, squares, delicious bakehouse cheese rolls, & good beverages – try the *choffee*! $

Harbour Fish 'N' Fries 7886 Hwy 7; 889 3366; Apr–mid Dec 11.00–19.30 daily. Again, not the most exciting of exteriors. Cheap seafood eatery with a few tables in & outside a simple building. The fried clams & fish & chips are very good but you're quite limited if deep-fried is not for you (in which case, choose the lobster roll). That aside, quality is high & prices low. $

Sher's Bear Den Café 7955 Hwy 7; 889 3003; www.accesswave.ca/~beardencafe/; summer 08.00–18.00 daily; rest of year 08.00–15.00 daily. A small yellow shack offering unpretentious standards (burgers, simple salads, sandwiches & milkshakes) plus seafood chowder, (salt cod) fishcakes & steamed mussels. $

Other practicalities

$ Bank Royal Bank, 7907 Hwy 7; 889 2626; 09.30–17.00 Mon–Fri

Library Musquodoboit Harbour Public Library, 7900 Hwy 7; 889 2227; 11.00–16.00 Tue, 17.00–20.00 Wed/Thu, 12.00–18.00 Fri, 10.00–15.00 Sat

Post office 7901 Hwy 7; 08.30–16.30 Mon–Fri, 08.30–12.00 Sat

Tourist information Main St, Musquodoboit Harbour; 889 2689; mid May–late Oct 09.00–16.00 Mon–Fri, 10.00–17.00 Sat/Sun. In the former Waiting Room of the Railway Museum complex.

What to see and do The **Musquodoboit Railway Museum** (*Main St, Musquodoboit Harbour; 889 2689; mid May–late Oct 09.00–16.00 Mon–Fri, 10.00–17.00 Sat/Sun; admission free*) is housed in the beautifully restored – and brightly painted – c1916 Canadian National Railways Station and three vintage rail cars. You don't need to be a train buff to enjoy a brief visit: there is a caboose and a huge old snowplough, and exhibits of the history of Nova Scotia's railways. Railway enthusiasts will also find photographs, maps, posters, tickets and artefacts relating to the history of the railway in the province and, in particular, this region.

The death of the province's railways (see box opposite) has brought some benefits – a section of the old line has been converted into the splendid 14.5km **Rail Trail**, part of the Musquodoboit Trailways network. Leading off the main trail are worthwhile side-trips, such as the Admiral Lake Loop, Bayer Lake Loop, and Gibraltar Loop. The trail crosses the Musquodoboit River on a long trestle bridge and then follows an old stagecoach road before reaching the shore of Bayer Lake. Access the trail from the museum car park.

The **Petpeswick Yacht Club** (*434 East Petpeswick Rd; 889 2896; www.petpeswickyachtclub.ca*) offers kayaking lessons in the summer.

BLUEBERRY EXPRESS

In 1916, the 'Dartmouth Branch Extension of the Intercolonial Railway' opened, linking Dartmouth with Musquodoboit Harbour. Prior to its construction, to reach the city people had a choice of travelling by sea, stagecoach or ox-drawn wagon over rough roads – or walking. The rail service was nicknamed the Blueberry Express: this may have been because of the copious amounts of the fruit that farmers took to the capital during the season, or perhaps because stops were so long that passengers could get off, pick their berries, and re-board the train before it moved on. There were plans to continue the line to Guysborough (see page 379) but despite some construction, the extension never came near completion. The last train ran in 1982 and the tracks were dismantled in 1985.

MARTINIQUE BEACH A worthwhile side-trip (12km each way) from Musquodoboit Harbour will take you along the shoreline of beautiful Petpeswick Inlet. You'll pass little jetties, fishing boats and neatly stacked lobster pots *en route* to the province's longest sand beach, much of which lies within the **Martinique Beach Provincial Park**. This has picnic tables and small parking areas at regular intervals along the first 1,500m from which boardwalks lead between the dunes to the stunning 5km beach.

Across the access road is a large wetland, popular with canoeists and kayakers. Part of the beach and wetland is a bird sanctuary, teeming during the spring and autumn migrations and attracting wintering Canada geese, black ducks, herons and osprey. The endangered piping plover nests on the beach and entry to sensitive areas is restricted during nesting season.

To get there **by car**, take East Petpeswick Road from Musquodoboit Harbour.

MEAGHERS GRANT Highway 357 leads north (inland) off Highway 7 along the lovely, fertile Musquodoboit Valley, one of the province's principal farming areas. The country villages, rich rolling green farmlands and forested hills make this a very pleasant drive: in the autumn, the colours are breathtaking. Among these villages is Meaghers Grant, a small community which offers a few reasons to stop.

Meaghers Grant is on Highway 357, 22km from Musquodoboit Harbour.

Where to stay and eat

River Oaks Country Lodge (8 rooms) 3856 Meaghers Grant Rd; 384 3033; www.riveroaksgolfclub.ca; mid May–mid Oct. This motel is right by the golf course: some units have kitchenettes. Deck, pool (in season), & licensed restaurant (*mid May–mid Oct 08.00–20.00 daily;* $), where the menu includes soups, pasta & seafood. **$**

Dollar Lake Provincial Park (119 sites) 5265 Old Guysborough Rd; 384 2770; www.parks.gov.ns.ca; mid Jun–early Oct. For further details, see page 366.

What to see and do Meaghers Grant is home to 18- and nine-hole courses including **River Oaks Golf Club**, whose design is one of the more successful attempts at blending fairways, greens and nature. Bird sightings (including bald eagles) are common, and you might be lucky enough to see otters, beavers, muskrats, deer or even moose. Green fees are CAN$45–50.

In addition to the Musquodoboit, both the Stewiacke and the Shubenacadie rivers are easily accessible, and all three are excellent for canoeing. **Meaghers Grant Canoe Rentals** (*384 2513*) will drive you to your chosen put-in spot so that you can paddle downstream to your vehicle. The best time of year is late spring, while the waters are still high and the weather has warmed up a bit. Be prepared – you will pass through virtual wilderness.

Just north of Meaghers Grant, a left turn onto Highway 212 will quickly bring you to the 1,200ha **Dollar Lake Provincial Park**. The eponymous lake has a white-sand beach, and the park offers picnic and camping facilities (see page 365). The park is criss-crossed with logging roads and tracks, offering a good variety of lakeside and forest walking trails.

OYSTER POND The Mi'kmaq called Oyster Pond *Pajedoobaack* – 'wave washed'. In days gone by, bivalves were abundant, hence the current name. A sawmill was built on the water's edge, a dam constructed across the 'pond's' mouth, and the water was channelled with the intention of powering the mill. The good news was that this all worked well, and the mill's owners sawed their way to prosperity. The bad news was that playing with nature prevented salt water from entering the pond at high tide. As a result, Oyster Pond had plenty of freshly cut lumber – but no more oysters. The community is now home to a small, yet fascinating museum.

Oyster Pond is on Highway 7, 68km/42 miles from Halifax, 13km/8 miles from Musquodoboit Harbour and 50km/31 miles from Sheet Harbour.

Where to stay and eat

Sea Rover Resort & Marina (9 rooms) 610 Myers Point Rd, Head of Jeddore; 889 9073; www.searover.ca; mid May–Oct. On Jeddore Harbour, this comfortable, new resort is not just for sailors. In addition to all the yacht & powerboat facilities are spacious well-equipped guest rooms, a fitness centre, & heated saltwater pool (summer only). The pub (*mid May–Oct 14.00–23.00 Fri/Sat; $–$$*) & licensed restaurant (*mid May/Oct 10.00–20.00 Sun–Wed, 10.00–21.00 Fri/Sat; $$*) are both good choices for a drink or meal. **$$**

Jeddore Lodge and Cabins (12 units) 9855 Hwy 7, Salmon River Bridge; 889 3030, **t/f** 1 888 889 3030; www.jeddorelodge.com; year-round. 2 B&B rooms (b/fast inc) & 10 1- & 2-bedroom cabins, some with fireplaces & verandas overlooking the river & harbour. Outdoor pool (seasonal). The licensed dining room (*year-round for lunch & dinner; $$*) offers salads, sandwiches & seafood. **$**

Webber Lakeside Resort (66 sites) 738 Upper Lakeville Rd; 845 2340, **t/f** 1 800 589 2282; www.webberslakesideresort.com; mid May–mid Oct. Full hook-ups, lake swimming & canoe rental; 7km from Salmon River Bridge. **$**

The Lunch Room Mitchell Cove Community Centre, 47 East Jeddore Rd; 845 2623; www.mitchellcove.ca; year-round 09.00–19.00 daily. Lisa Bedell jumped at the chance to open an eatery in part of a former school. Simple, well-cooked food at very reasonable prices. **$**

Festivals Held in September, the **Pirate Days Festival** (*www.novascotiapirates.ca*) is a day of pirate-themed fun for all the family.

What to see and do The **Black Sheep Gallery** (*1689 W Jeddore Rd, West Jeddore; 889 5012; www.blacksheepart.com; mid Jun–mid Sep 11.00–16.00 Tue–Sun; mid Sep–mid Jun by chance or appointment*) is a fascinating gallery specialising in Folk Art.

In the early 1900s, the tiny house and small farm that now make up the **Fisherman's Life Museum** (*58 Navy Pool Loop; 889 2053; http://museum.gov.ns.ca/flm/; Jun–mid Oct 09.30–17.30 Mon–Sat, 13.00–17.30 Sun; admission CAN$3.60*), comprising restored farmhouse, garden and outbuildings, were home to an inshore fisherman, his wife and 12 daughters. The Myers family lived a simple life, supplementing their meagre fishing income with a small farm operation. Inside

A SEAFARING SPECTRE

In 1817, a William Kent built a house on Kent Island, and always claimed it was haunted. The house was torn down in 1903, and a lighthouse constructed on the site in 1904. For many years, Kent's descendants operated their house adjacent to the lighthouse as a B&B, and there were several reports of supernatural activity in and around the lighthouse. A few years ago, a medium staying at the B&B announced that not only was the lighthouse haunted, but the haunter was also the ghost of Admiral Horatio Nelson. The remarks were taken with a pinch of sea salt, but a couple of years later, when researching the family history, the current Kents discovered that William, who built the house, had sailed with Nelson, serving as navigator aboard Nelson's HMS *Victory* at the Battle of Trafalgar in 1805 when Horatio met his death.

The lighthouse is not open to the public. You can see it by turning onto Ostrea Lake Road from Highway 7 at Smith Settlement 4km east of Musquodoboit Harbour and following the road along the eastern side of the water, then turning onto Kent Road. It is worth continuing to Pleasant Point for lovely views of the harbour mouth.

the house, guides in period costume hook rugs, prepare food using the old wood stove or tell stories about the land, the sea and life a century ago.

In summer, non-guests can purchase a day-pass (CAN$5) to use the fitness centre and pool at the **Sea Rover Resort & Marina** (for contact details, see *Where to Stay and eat*, opposite).

LAKE CHARLOTTE This community was named in honour of Princess Charlotte Augusta of Wales, who died in 1817 shortly after the area was settled.

Lake Charlotte is on Highway 7, 15km/9 miles from Musquodoboit Harbour and 50km/31 miles from Sheet Harbour.

Festivals See a range of antique vehicles at the Memory Lane Heritage Village (see below) at the **Antique Car Show** in June.

What to see and do The **Memory Lane Heritage Village** (*Clam Harbour Rd;* ☎ *845 1937,* **t/f** *1 877 287 0697; www.heritagevillage.ca;* ⏱ *mid Jun–mid Sep 11.00–16.00 daily; off-season by appointment; admission CAN$6*) is a community-owned attraction which takes a nostalgic look at rural coastal village life in the 1940s. Most of the 15 c1894–1949 buildings – including the two-seater outhouse – were 'rescued' from around the region, restored, and moved here. There is also a general store, homestead, barn, one-room schoolhouse, industry buildings including boat shop, fish store and gold-mining complex. Hands-on demonstrations, soundscapes and

MUSSELS SPROUT

The community of Ship Harbour (on Highway 7 between Lake Charlotte and Tangier) is home to the **AquaPrime Mussel Ranch** (*14108 Hwy 7;* ☎ *845 2993;* ⏱ *year-round 08.00–16.00 Mon–Fri, but best to call ahead to check*). Here you can learn how mussels are grown, harvested and sold: informal (free) tours are offered subject to staff availability.

guides bring the village alive. Eat in the replica 1940s' cookhouse with fresh baked bread and beans, served daily.

CLAM HARBOUR Clam Harbour boasts one of the province's prettiest beaches, which – as a result of a warmer-than-average tidal stream – is usually the best swimming beach on the Eastern Shore.

The beach park has a hiking trail, a lifeguard and canteen (weekends in season), showers and changing rooms. There is also a picnic area with tables tucked between trees: to reach it, turn right at the end of the access road. The beach is unlikely to be crowded for 364 days of the year. However, several thousand visitors (incredible considering both the Eastern Shore's population and tourist numbers) stop by for the August one-day **Clam Harbour Beach Sandcastle Sculpture Contest** (*www.halifax.ca/sandcastle/; CAN$10 to enter, free-to-enter children's competition*). Competitors enthuse about the beach's 'perfect' sand in the same way skiers rave about 'champagne' snow. Not only can designs have minute, perfect features, but the sculptures also remain in place for hours without collapsing or weathering.

This area is one reputed to have a larger than average number of foggy days, but fingers crossed that the sun will shine on the broad crescent of sand for your visit.

To get there **by car**, follow Clam Harbour Road for about 8km/5 miles from Lake Charlotte.

TANGIER *(Population: 115)* This small community once serviced several gold mines. It is now home to an excellent sea kayaking company, a factory producing arguably the province's best smoked fish, and – just off Highway 7 at Mason Point Road – the simple Prince Alfred Arch, erected to commemorate the (1861) visit to the local gold mine by Queen Victoria's son.

Tangier is easy to reach **by car** as it is located on Highway 7, 47km/29 miles from Musquodoboit Harbour and 20km/12 miles from Sheet Harbour.

Where to stay and eat

Paddler's Retreat (4 rooms) 84 Mason's Point Rd; 772 2774; e info@coastaladventures.com; www.coastaladventures.com; mid Jun–mid Oct; off-season by reservation. Under the same management as Coastal Adventures (see page 38), this laid-back c1860s' old fisherman's home is the obvious choice for anyone going on a kayaking trip. 3 rooms share a bathroom, 1 has en suite. Wi-Fi & outdoor hot tub. Full country b/fast inc. **$**

Murphy's Camping on the Ocean (40 sites) 308 Murphy's Rd, Murphy Cove; 772 2700; www.murphyscamping.ca; mid May–mid Oct. Located on a headland just off Hwy 7, 7.5km west of Tangier, with open & wooded campsites (serviced & unserviced), boat rentals, scenic boat tours & numerous other activities including a nightly campfire & mussel boil. Another great base for sea kayakers. **$**

Shopping A couple of unprepossessing buildings house **Willy Krauch and Sons** (*signposted just off Hwy 7; 772 2188, t/f 1 800 758 4412; www.willykrauch.com; year-round 08.00–17.00 Mon–Fri, 09.00–17.00 Sat/Sun*). Krauch was a Danish immigrant who settled in Tangier in the 1950s and brought with him a traditional Danish method of smoking fish: his sons continue to use this process. The smokehouse's shop stocks smoked eel and different varieties of salmon and mackerel. Pack prices range from around CAN$6.50.

Other practicalities

Post office 17276 Hwy 7; 07.30–15.00 Mon–Fri, 07.30–12.00 Sat

What to see and do One of Nova Scotia's top sea kayaking companies, **Coastal Adventures** (*84 Mason's Point Rd; ☎ 772 2774; www.coastaladventures.com*) is also one of the only places offering kayak rentals along the entire Eastern Shore. Come for expert advice, half- and full-day kayak excursions which include visits to uninhabited islands, and a range of longer (multi-day) packages.

TAYLOR HEAD PROVINCIAL PARK This beautiful park (*☎ 772 2218; www.novascotiaparks.com; ⊕ mid May–mid Oct*) occupies a narrow 6.5km peninsula, jutting into the Atlantic like a huge rocky finger. It encompasses 16km of unspoilt and virtually untouched coastline, varied habitats rich in flora and fauna, and fascinating geology.

In season, the park offers unsupervised swimming, changing rooms, several picnic areas, interpretive panels and vault toilets.

The west side of the peninsula is rugged and windswept: as a result of the salt spray and almost constant winds, white spruce and firs are stunted, almost flattened to the rocky ground. The more protected east side has sandy coves lapped by calmer waters. Several rocky barrens covered with dwarf shrubs and lichens are found in the southern portion of Taylor Head, and peat-filled open bogs are scattered throughout the park.

This is one of only a few locations in Nova Scotia where sand volcanoes (small cone-shaped geological features) are found. Other special features, called flute marks, appear as ripples in the bedrock and indicate that strong ocean currents once moved large volumes of sediment rapidly across what was the sea floor. Parallel northeast–southwest quartzite ridges that show the direction of bedrock folding can still be seen at Taylor Head, and the beach and sand dunes at Psyche Cove were formed by sand deposits from the erosion of glacial till and bedrock.

The park is home to a variety of mammals, including white-tailed deer, racoons and muskrats. Seals have been spotted on nearby rocks, and there have also been sightings of pilot whales and dolphins offshore.

For most, though, it is the park's **walking and hiking** trails that are the big draw: many people rate them among the finest coastal trail systems on North America's eastern seaboard. Possibilities include the 2km Beach Walk, and the Headland Trail, a wonderful 8km figure-of-eight hike taking in boardwalks and bogs, forest dripping with moss, and of course stretches of the shoreline.

A 5km unpaved road from Highway 7 hugs the west side of the peninsula before crossing to sheltered Psyche Cove. At the end of the road is a series of small parking areas with beach access.

The park is accessible **by car**, just off Highway 7, 14km/9 miles from Tangier and 12km/7 miles from Sheet Harbour.

GET IN WITH A LITTLE HELP FROM THE FRIENDS

The provincial government does not have the resources to keep provincial parks open for more than a relatively short season. This is not always a problem, as you can see the highlights of many parks out of season by parking outside the closed gate and walking in. Taylor Head's highlights, however, are a long way from the gated entrance. The **Friends of Taylor Head Provincial Park** (*www.friendsoftaylorhead.com*) is a non-profit society, and for the last few years its members have managed to keep the park gate open until early December – a real bonus for out-of-season visitors.

SHEET HARBOUR (*Population: 825*) Roughly halfway between Halifax and Canso, the town lies between the outflows of the West and East Sheet Harbour rivers at the head of a long narrow bay. After Musquodoboit Harbour it is the biggest community along the Eastern Shore. If you're heading east and need anything, stock up here: further along don't expect more than the sporadic general store.

Sheet Harbour was founded in 1784 by Loyalist refugees and British veterans of the American Revolution and became a prosperous centre for the lumber industry and consequently a shipbuilding centre. In recent years, the government has made an effort to make Sheet Harbour into a major port and chief supply depot for the gas platforms off Sable Island (see page 382).

Sheet Harbour is on Highway 7, 120km/75 miles east of Dartmouth and 65km/46 miles west of Sherbrooke, and therefore convenient to reach **by car**.

Where to stay and eat It's only a slight exaggeration to say that before the arrival of Henley House and Il Porto, the good burghers of Sheet Harbour hardly knew that there was more to food than fish and chips.

Back In Thyme B&B (3 rooms) 22960 Hwy 7; 885 2352; www.backinthyme.ca; year-round; off-season by reservation. A c1885 sea captain's house set on a 1.2ha riverside property with fruit trees. 1 room has a small en suite, 2 share a bathroom. Canoes & bicycle for guest use. Full b/fast inc & served in the sun room overlooking the East River. **$**

Fairwinds Motel & Restaurant (10 rooms) 22522 Hwy 7; 885 2502; www.fairwindsmotelsheetharbour.ca; year-round. A traditional single-storey motel; some rooms have sea views. The restaurant (*year-round 07.00–20.30 daily; $*) offers good service & reliable food (splendid fish & chips). Deck overlooks the sea. **$**

East River Lodge Campground (42 sites) 200 Pool Rd; 885 2864; May–Oct. Serviced & unserviced sites. **$**

Henley House Pub 22478 Hwy 7; 885 3335; www.thehenleyhousepub.ca; May–Dec 11.00–22.00 Mon–Sat, 12.00–20.00 Sun. Restaurant & pub in a c1916 former family house. Deck with lovely harbour view. Daily specials, English afternoon tea (*14.00–16.00*). The maple curry chicken penne is recommended. Live music on some w/ends. **$$**

Il Porto 22808 Hwy 7; 885 3111; year-round 11.00–19.00 daily (20.00 Fri). Mediterranean (inc Greek & Italian) dishes, plus Cajun, Creole, etc. Burgers, pizza & seafood. Small deck. **$$**

Festivals Held in August, the **Seaside Festival** is a two-week festival with a range of events including parades, Fun Day and Kids' Activity Day.

Other practicalities

$ Bank Scotiabank, 22540 Hwy 7; 885 2310; 10.00–17.00 Mon–Fri

Hospital Eastern Shore Memorial Hospital, 22637 Hwy 7; 885 2554

Post office 22526 Hwy 7; 08.00–17.00 Mon–Fri, 09.00–12.00 Sat

Tourist information Hwy 7 at the West River Bridge; 885 2595; summer 10.00–19.00 daily. In the MacPhee House Museum (see below).

What to see and do At the **MacPhee House Community Museum** (*Hwy 7 at the West River Bridge; 885 2092; late May–Sep 09.00–17.00 daily; off-season by appointment; admission free*), the *Life before Plastic* exhibit illustrates Eastern Shore life in the days before modern technology. You're unlikely to spend long here, but there are some interesting curios that may intrigue and challenge young and old alike.

PORT DUFFERIN This small community was named for the Marquis of Dufferin, Governor-General of Canada 1872–78. It offers beautiful views out to sea from the

Salmon River Bridge area. If you turn along the waterside just by the bridge, there's a small look-out: continue on this road (signposted Smiley's Point) and a 2km drive will bring you to a small jetty and parking area also offering tranquil coastal vistas.

To get there **by car**, Port Dufferin is on Highway 7, 13km/8 miles east of Sheet Harbour and 18km/11 miles west of Moser River.

Where to stay and eat

Marquis of Dufferin Seaside Inn (9 units) 25658 Hwy 7; 654 2696, **t/f** 1 877 654 2696; www.marquisofdufferinmotel.com; mid Jun–Sep (May/mid Jun & Oct by chance or reservation). A delightful historic inn. Guest rooms with private balconies & beautiful views over the fishing village, Beaver Harbour & its islands. **$$**

BAY OF ISLANDS Many of the next stretches of Highway 7 offer wonderful views of wooded peninsulas and tiny coves, and a sea dotted with dozens and dozens of uninhabited wooded islands. The region between Beaver Harbour and Ecum Secum is known as the Bay of Islands.

Small fishing communities dot the highway and in autumn the forests are ablaze with red maple and birch, the brilliant colours reflected in the rivers, lakes and coves.

Moser River Moser River's **waterfront park** on the estuary is a favourite spot for birdwatchers. Seaward, you'll see hundreds of small islands, popular with sea kayakers and yachtsmen. The Moser was once famous for its abundance of Atlantic salmon, which the old timers will tell you, could 'be scooped up in buckets' as they travelled upstream to spawn.

Moser River is on Highway 7, 18km/11 miles east of Port Dufferin and 35km/22 miles west of Liscomb.

LISCOMB MILLS This isn't a community as such, more some fine hiking trails and a resort. Accessed from the parking area and trailhead immediately east of

NECUM TEUCH AND ECUM SECUM

Necum Teuch – the name derives from the Mi'kmaq and means 'sandy river bottom' – is 5km past Moser River on Highway 7. It was home to Angella Geddes, author of several popular children's books, most famous of which is *Necum Teuch Scarecrows*, which has been translated into German and French.

In addition to writing about them, she created a large collection of articulated scarecrows – many of which represented local people – which adorned her house and garden. Sadly Geddes passed away in 2006, but her figures still live in the garden of 'Aunt Mary's House' (*29451 Hwy 7, Necum Teuch*), a simple private museum representing life in the early 1900s. It may be possible to arrange a tour of the house – it is on the left as you drive through Necum Teuch – if someone is in attendance when you visit.

If you thought that Necum Teuch was an odd name, the next community, 5km further east, is Ecum Secum (this name derives from the Mi'kmaq *Megwasaagunk*, and means 'a red house'). At Ecum Secum Bridge, turn right and follow the side road to Mitchell Bay, where there is a beautiful Anglican church and cemetery overlooking the water. Stay on this road and it will take you back to Highway 7.

LISCOMB GAME SANCTUARY

From Sheet Harbour, Highway 374 heads north for 130km to Stellarton (see page 291). For much of the way, this remote road passes through a game sanctuary established in 1928 to protect wildlife, particularly moose and woodland caribou. We are not talking safari parks here, but over 43,000ha of remote forest, logging roads, rivers and lakes and no services.

The rugged landscape is dotted with ancient drumlins (see page 214) and dips that have filled with water. The 'protected area' was cloaked in old-growth boreal forest, but sadly much of it has been logged as the legislation which created the sanctuary protected the animals themselves, with little thought for their habitat.

In recent years, environmentalists and conservationists have campaigned to extend the sanctuary's boundaries right up to the Atlantic coast and, more important, to change the designation to 'wilderness area' (see page 214). Not only has this met with little success thus far, but there have also been reports that logging activity has actually increased.

Within the sanctuary boundary, four small wilderness areas have been established, including Boggy Lake Wilderness Area, where a chain of lakes are ideal for extended canoe trips.

the Liscombe Lodge's entrance are a couple of relatively challenging hikes. The 9.6km return **Liscomb River Trail** follows the river's edge upstream to a swinging suspension bridge which spans a 20m waterfall. Near the waterfall is a fish ladder comprising 15 pools separated by concrete weirs, designed to aid salmon in their annual migration. The best time to see them 'climbing' the ladder is from early June to October (peaking in July). Return to the trailhead along the river's other bank. From the same trailhead, the rugged 2.9km loop **Mayflower Point Trail** heads to the mouth of the river opposite Rileys Island before returning along and above the riverbank.

By car, Liscomb Mills is 47km/29 miles east of Sheet Harbour, and 7km/4 miles west of Liscomb. Liscomb is 18km/11 miles east of Sherbrooke.

Where to stay and eat

Liscombe Lodge Resort & Conference Centre (67 units) 2884 Hwy 7, Liscomb Mills; 779 2307; www.liscombelodge.ca; late May–mid Oct. One of Nova Scotia's few resorts that is located not on a beach has a lovely riverside setting. Rather than 1 of the 5 cottages or 30 lodge rooms, choose a riverfront chalet & wake to the sound of birdsong. Complimentary use of good-size indoor pool & sauna, canoes & bicycles. B/fast is available in the restaurant ($$$–$$$$). Ask about packages. The lodge is famous for its 'Planked Salmon Dinner' – the fish is cooked over an open fire. Arrive early to secure a coveted window table. If prices in the lodge's restaurant are steeper than you'd like, Sherbrooke (see page 372), 24km along Hwy 7, offers cheaper dining. B/fast not inc. **$$$**

Birchill B&B & Guest House (3 units) 5254 Hwy 7, Liscomb; 779 2017; www.birchillbb.com; year-round. If resorts don't do it for you, try 1 of the B&B rooms (b/fast inc) or a 1-bedroom cottage 7km east of Liscomb Mills. Hot tub & free use of kayaks (the property is on the Liscomb Harbour waterfront): boat tours & diving trips can be arranged. **$**

SHERBROOKE This town on the St Mary's River has a hospital, a few places to stay and eat, a bank, post office, convenience store and a little supermarket. Most visitors come to see the living museum (see page 374), or **to fish**.

Every year, hundreds of fishermen come to try their luck on the river, though salmon numbers have dramatically reduced. The river was a favourite fishing spot of baseball legend Babe Ruth and many other famous celebrities and anglers.

Easy to reach **by car**, Sherbrooke is on Highway 7, 80km/50 miles from Sheet Harbour, 209km/130 miles from Halifax and 60km/37 miles from Antigonish.

History Sherbrooke was founded in the early 1800s at the farthest navigable point of the St Mary's River. Gold was discovered in the area in the late 1860s and was mined until 1890. Lumber was processed and exported, and there were shipbuilding operations.

The mines closed and shipbuilding ceased. By the late 1960s, there were few visitors apart from anglers. The town was beginning to die until ambitious locals, with help from the Nova Scotia Museum, began a big restoration project. The result is the Eastern Shore's most popular attraction.

Where to stay and eat There are also a couple of cafés on Sherbrooke's 'main drag', of which I prefer the sweet little **Village Coffee Grind** (*27 Main St*).

Sherbrooke Village Inn (19 units) 7975 Hwy 7; 522 2235, t/f 1 866 522 3818; www.sherbrookevillageinn.ca; year-round. Cottages, a family house, a B&B suite (b/fast inc) & motel-type units. The licensed dining room (*mid May–Oct 07.30–19.00 daily (summer to 20.00); $$*) focuses on seafood & most dishes are made without use of a deep-fryer. **$$**

Daysago B&B (4 units) 15 Cameron Rd; 522 2811, t/f 1 866 522 2811; www.bbcanada.com/daysago; year-round. A c1920 house in a rural setting with fine views of the St Mary's River. 3 guestrooms share 2 bathrooms, or choose the self-contained chalet Kayaks for guests' use. Full b/fast inc (B&B rooms only). **$**

St Mary's River Lodge (8 units) 21 Main St; 522 2177, t/f 1 877 497 2177; www.riverlodge.ca; Apr–Oct; off-season by reservation. Under Swiss management, the lodge itself – across the road from the river & right by the museum – has 7 guestrooms (full b/fast inc), all with private bathrooms. Across the river on a beautiful peninsula is the Lodge Residence, a 2-bedroom 2-bathroom suite with kitchen facilities & a lovely view. Pet-friendly. **$**

St Mary's Riverside Campground (24 sites) 3987 Sonora Rd; 522 2913; mid May–mid Oct. Open sites, laundromat, pool (in season). **$**

House of Jade 8164 Main St; 522 2731; Jun–Sep 11.30–19.45 Tue–Sun; Oct–May 12.00–19.00 Wed–Sun. Canadian & Chinese standards. The won ton soup is a stand-out. **$**

Festivals Tree lighting and procession, Christmas crafts, concerts, dinner theatre, Victorian tea and more can be seen at the **Old-fashioned Sherbrooke Christmas** festival, which takes place in November.

Shopping The **St Mary's River Smokehouses** shop (*8000 Hwy 7; 522 2005; www.thebestsmokedsalmon.com; 08.30–17.00 Mon–Fri*) is located at the western end of town. This shop's oven-smoked salmon strips, flavoured with pepper, maple syrup, or 'all-dressed', are particularly good.

Other practicalities

$ Bank Royal Bank, 6 Main St; 522 2800; 10.00–15.00 Mon–Fri

Hospital St Mary's Memorial Hospital, 91 Hospital Rd; 522 2882

Library Sherbrooke Library, 11 Main St; 522 2180 11.00–16.00 Mon–Tue & Thu, 09.30–14.30 Fri, 10.00–13.00 Sat

Post office 15 Main St; 08.30–17.00 Mon–Fri, 09.00–13.00 Sat

Tourist information 7975 Hwy 7; 522 2400; Jun–mid Sep 09.30–17.00 daily. At the entrance to Sherbrooke Village.

What to see and do The **St Mary's River Education and Interpretive Centre** (*8404 Hwy 7; 522 2099; www.stmarysriverassociation.com; Jun & Sep/Oct 09.00–16.00 Mon–Fri; Jul/Aug 09.00–16.30 daily; admission free*) has exhibits relating to fishing, wildlife, river enhancement and stabilisation projects, and the history of fishing. There is also a small aquarium.

An unusual living museum, **Sherbrooke Village** (*Main St; 522 2400; http://museum.gov.ns.ca/sv/; Jun–mid Oct 09.30–17.00 daily; admission CAN$10.75*) reflects Nova Scotia as it was during its industrial boom in the late 1800s/early 1900s and comprises more than 80 restored buildings, 29 of which are open to the public, and which are integrated with the town itself. It is the largest Nova Scotia Museum site and unlike (say) Memory Lane (see page 367), the buildings here are on their original sites.

Every morning at 09.30, this part of the town is closed to traffic, and the clock goes back a century. Period-costumed, knowledgeable guides help maintain the feeling that you have indeed been transported back in time as they tend to the crops, stroll through the town, staff the buildings and demonstrate such skills as pottery, weaving, candle making, blacksmithing and wood-turning.

Eat at the **Sherbrooke Hotel's tea room** – the menu is unpretentious, and – bearing in mind that it caters to something of a captive market – offers good value. Be sure to follow the Sonora Road on the east bank of the river for a few hundred metres from the main restoration area to hear the rush of water and smell the scent of lumber freshly cut by the village's authentic, photogenic water-powered **sawmill**.

Across the street in the **stamp mill**, you can see how gold ore was mined, crushed and processed during the gold rush. If you visit out of season, this is still a nice place to wander even when the village is not officially 'open'.

PORT BICKERTON Lighthouse fans will want to break their journey in this small community, just west of the Country Harbour ferry. As with much of the Eastern Shore, expect little in the way of services.

Port Bickerton is on Highway 211, 29km/18 miles from Sherbrooke and 90km/56 miles from Canso, and accessible **by car**.

GOLDEN TALES

History books state a farmer, Nelson Nickerson, found gold in 1861 while he was haymaking. The story locals tell is that a woman picking wild flowers was attracted by a shiny piece of quartz which she took home. A passing traveller later saw the quartz, recognised its significance, and casually asked the woman where she'd found it. Armed with this information, he took his leave, found himself a pick and shovel and put Goldenville (on Highway 7, 5km west of Sherbrooke) on the map. The tiny community's c1900 Presbyterian Church now houses the **Goldenville Gold Mining Interpretive Centre** (*Goldenville Rd; 522 4653; Jun–mid Oct 09.30–17.30 daily; admission free*), which tells of the history of gold mining in Nova Scotia.

SALADIN MUTINY

Just offshore from Drum Head, which is on Highway 316 between the Country Harbour ferry and Tor Bay, is Harbour Island: its southern end is named 'Saladin Point' after a vessel which ran aground here in 1844. More interesting than the fact that the *Saladin, en route* from Chile to London, was carrying a cargo of guano, copper and silver is that the vessel beached because her captain, officers and many of the crew had been butchered by mutineers who had overlooked the fact that they had not spared any skilled navigators. The four mutineers were rescued – and sent to the gallows.

What to see and do A 2km unpaved road leads to the **Nova Scotia Lighthouse Interpretive Centre** (*630 Lighthouse Rd;* ☎ *364 2000;* ⏲ *mid Jun–mid Sep 09.00–17.00 daily; admission CAN$3*): two lighthouses standing on a windswept, often fog-enshrouded bluff at the end of the headland. The newer of these is a fully automated working lighthouse dating from 1962. The older, built in 1930, is now a lighthouse museum with an original foghorn and well-laid-out display about the province's 170-plus lighthouses. A secondary building houses a collection of miniature replicas of some of the better-known lighthouses in Nova Scotia. Climb up the narrow staircase for a panoramic view of the wild and beautiful coastline and walk to a sandy beach.

For the princely sum of CAN$5.25, you and your vehicle can enjoy a pleasant – albeit just seven-minute – boat ride on the **Country Harbour Ferry** (*On Hwy 211, 7km from Port Bickerton*). The ferry operates year-round, 24 hours a day: between 08.00 and 18.00 it departs the east side (Halifax side) of the bay on the hour and half hour and the west side on the quarter and three-quarter hour. Outside those times, east-side departure is on the hour, and on the half hour from the west side. If you are going east, it is well worth checking that the ferry is running before heading this way – ask at a local tourist office. The alternate route via Country Harbour Cross Roads is longer of course, but you would also have to add on the 30km backtrack from the ferry dock.

TOR BAY Originally named 'Port Savalette' after a French fisherman, Tor Bay is worth a stop for its lovely provincial park (see page 376).

Accessible **by car**, Tor Bay is just off Highway 316, 22km/14 miles from Guysborough, 33km/21 miles from Country Harbour and 52km/32 miles from Canso.

Where to stay and eat

Seawind Landing Country Inn (13 rooms) 159 Wharf Rd, Charlos Cove; **t/f** 1 800 563 4667; www.seawindlanding.com; ⏲ year-round. On Hwy 316, about 15km east of Tor Bay, the picturesque Acadian fishing village of Charlos Cove is home to this establishment, which occupies a 8ha peninsula with over 900m of ocean frontage, including a couple of lovely secluded beaches. Most of the rooms offer sea views. Gift shop showcasing local artists & guided sea kayak tours offered. Pets welcomed. The inn has an excellent dining room open to non-guests by reservation (⏲ *summer*

CABLE HISTORY

Nova Scotia's first direct transatlantic telegraphic connection was established in 1874 when the Direct United States Telegraph Company laid a cable between Tor Bay and Ballinskelligs in Ireland's Waterville Bay. A plaque in the park's car park commemorates the event.

07.30–10.00 & 18.00–21.00 daily; off-season call to check; **$$$**), with a regularly changing menu of fresh locally sourced ingredients. Try, for example, bourbon-glazed pork tenderloin or scallops in a vermouth cream sauce. The Bailey's *crème brûlée* is a delicious dessert. **$$**

WHAT TO SEE AND DO The scenic **Tor Bay Provincial Park** (*off Hwy 316*) is situated on an isthmus along a peninsula that forms the southern boundary of the bay. Within the small day-use park, a boardwalk leads to a sandy beach, from which a short trail leads to a rocky headland where covered interpretive boards describe the geology of the region. There are other (almost always empty) beaches on the other side of the headland. The park also has picnic facilities.

CANSO Situated at the entrance to Chedabucto Bay, Canso is sheltered from the ocean by round Grassy Island (see page 378). The town is located at the extreme eastern point of mainland Nova Scotia and – were it not for a little bit of Labrador – would have the honour of being the closest point on the North American mainland to Europe. For a while Canso has been in need of a cash injection, but work to revitalise the waterfront's old Whitman Wharf is now well underway.

The surrounding waters make another great **sea kayaking destination**: however, unless your accommodation offers kayak loan or rental – and very few do – you'll need to wait until Guysborough (see page 379) or have rented one back in Tangier (page 368).

Take Union Street to its end, then follow a rugged unpaved road to **Glasgow Head**. *En route* enjoy wonderful views of the mouth of Canso Harbour, lighthouse and islands. When you reach the road end, choose between a swim in a manmade pond sheltered from the direct coastal waters by a rock barrier, and the spectacular cove on the other side of the barrier. If it's not too windy, the sandy knoll which separates the two areas is excellent for a picnic.

Two other lovely local beaches (you'll need a car or bike) are those at **Fox Island**, just off Highway 16, 11km from Canso, and at **Black Duck Cove Day Use Park** (*1609 Dover Rd;* ⌚ *mid May–mid Oct*), approximately 18km from Canso.

To reach Canso **by car**, the town is at the eastern end of Highway 16, 46km/29 miles from Guysborough, 105km/65 miles from Aulds Cove, 114km/71 miles from Antigonish and 320km/199 miles from Halifax.

History There is evidence that the French and the Basques were making annual visits to fish in the Canso area perhaps a century before 1605, the 'official' year of Canso's first permanent settlement. They built temporary shelters and came ashore to salt and dry their abundant cod catches. In any case, Canso is thought to be the oldest fishing village in the Maritimes, and one of the oldest settlements in Nova Scotia. It was one of the most coveted anchorages for the cod-fishing industry during the 16th and 17th centuries, offering shelter and a relatively ice-free harbour well positioned for markets in western Europe and the Caribbean.

From the 1680s on, New Englanders used the area for trade and fishing with increasing frequency. They decided to establish and fortify a community on Grassy Island (see page 378) in 1718. Soon after, the wood-and-earth Fort William Augustus was constructed. The settlement met its end quite suddenly in the summer of 1744 when a French expedition from Louisbourg (see page 349) attacked and burned all the buildings to the ground. The following year, New Englanders used the island as a staging point for their attack on Louisbourg. After the fall of Louisbourg, the French threat faded and Grassy Island was abandoned. It lay virtually untouched until reclaimed as a Canadian National Historic Site in 1977.

In the 18th century, there was talk that Canso, a thriving commercial centre and major fishing port, would become Nova Scotia's capital but this did not happen, partly because of its somewhat remote location.

Where to stay and eat A nice B&B, the **Whitman Wharf House** (*1309 Union St; www.whitmanwharf.com*) was closed for much of the 2012 season, but may reopen in 2013.

Last Port Motel (13 units) 10 Hwy 16; 366 2400; e hanhamsf@ns.sympatico.ca; year-round. A clean, traditional-style standard motel outside the town centre. Licensed restaurant (*summer 08.00–20.00 daily; winter 08.00–19.00 daily; $*), serving decent food including good fish & chips. **$**

Cape Canso RV Park (33 sites) 1639 Union St; 366 2937; Jun–Oct. Geared to motorhomes (sites are serviced) there are a few grassy spots on which to pitch a tent. **$**

Seabreeze Campground (74 sites) 230 Fox Island Rd; 366 2532; mid May–mid Oct. A quiet, beautifully located site overlooking Chedabucto Bay, approx 10km west of Canso. Wooded & open serviced & unserviced sites. **$**

AJ's Dining Room, Lounge & Pub 237 Main St; 366 2281; 10.00–21.00 daily, later on summer w/ends. Decent pub food, the closest Canso comes to nightlife, & occasional live music. $

Last Mermaid 14 Main St; 366 3152; www.facebook.com/lastmermaidcanso; Nov–Apr 08.00–19.00 daily; May–Oct 08.00–20.00 daily. This bright & friendly licensed eatery offers good seafood & some European dishes in summer. $

Festivals The **Stan Rogers Folk Festival** takes place in July (see box, below). At the **Canso Regatta**, boat races, dances, parades and concerts are held over an August weekend.

Other practicalities

$ **Bank** Bank of Montreal, 28 Main St 366 2654; 10.00–15.00 Mon–Fri

Hospital Eastern Memorial Hospital, 1746 Union St; 366 2794

Library Canso Branch Library, 130 School St; 366 2955; for hours, call or see www.ecrl.library.ns.ca

STANFEST

Over the first weekend in July, thousands of music fans descend on Canso for the **Stan Rogers Folk Festival** (*t/f 1 888 554 7826; www.stanfest.com*), or, more simply, Stanfest.

Born in Ontario, Stan Rogers spent many of his summers in Nova Scotia's Guysborough County when growing up. His songs often had a Celtic feel, and some were in the style of sea shanties. Following his death in an air accident in 1983, he was nominated posthumously for a Juno (the Canadian equivalent of the Grammy) Best Male Vocalist award.

Since the decision in 1997 to hold a festival in Canso in his memory, the event has been a roaring success. The ever-growing outdoor event features around 50 acts from around the world performing on seven stages. It may have 'folk' in the title, but expect to hear just about every main musical genre.

There is limited accommodation in the area, so most visitors camp at the special festival campground. In 2012, a tent camping pass cost CAN$63 (CAN$81 for an RV) and entry to the concerts CAN$115 for the entire weekend.

WHITMAN HOUSE

In 1885, wealthy merchant and businessman Clement H Whitman supervised construction of a rectory for the Baptist minister. However, the building work went so far over budget that the Baptist congregation withdrew from the project. Undeterred, Whitman poured more and more of his own money in, using the best materials he could find. When the house (one of the costliest in the province) was completed, he moved in – and generously gave his old, far more modest home to the Church for use as a rectory. The house was sold following Whitman's death in 1932, and after that resold many times. Apparently, if you'd come along at the right time, you could have picked it up for less than CAN$500. It now houses the Canso Museum.

Post office 1315 Union St; 08.00–17.00 Mon–Fri, 11.00–15.00 Sat

Tourist information Whitman Hse, 1297 Union St; 366 2170; Jun–Sep 09.00–17.00 daily. In the Canso Museum (see below).

What to see and do Housed in the magnificent three-storey Whitman House (see box, above), the **Whitman House Canso Museum** (*Whitman Hse, 1297 Union St; 366 2170; Jun–Sep 09.00–17.00 daily; admission free*) has local history exhibits covering Canso and eastern Guysborough County, including period furniture and many works by Canso folk artist Mel Schrader. There are wonderful views of the town, harbour – and fuel tanks – from the widow's walk atop the corner tower.

The waterfront **Canso Islands and Grassy Island Fort National Historic Sites of Canada** (*Union St; 295 2069; www.pc.gc.ca/lhn-nhs/ns/canso; Jul–early Sep 10.00–18.00 daily; admission & boat fare by donation*) describes the region's history: here you can see a scale model of the island before the French attack, a short video, and life-size dioramas of three island properties.

Park boats leave on demand (weather permitting) from the adjacent wharf for the 15-minute trip to Grassy Island where you can wander around, or take a self-guided (or free guided) tour of the ruins of 18th-century fortifications and remains of a colonial New England fishing station. Most traces of the church, fort, gun batteries, barracks and houses have gone, leaving just foundations and a few flattened remnants of the 18th-century fortifications. Go prepared: there are no services on the island.

There is also excellent **hiking** in the area. Follow the signs from town to take the **Chapel Gully Trail** (Chapel Gully is actually a saltwater inlet), a well-maintained easy 10km loop hike through diverse forest, over rocks and on long boardwalks. You'll find picnic tables, look-outs and numerous bird-feeders. There is also a shorter loop but offering fewer coastal views. Both loops take you across a 40m footbridge that spans the gully. This is also a popular area for birdwatchers.

HALF ISLAND COVE, QUEENSPORT AND HALFWAY COVE These three tiny communities on Highway 16 offer a couple of attractions and a good place to stay. Queensport has a beach and picnic area just off Highway 16: just offshore on Rook Island is the photogenic c1937 **Queensport Lighthouse**.

South of Highway 16 and carved by glaciers millions of years ago, the 10,000ha **Bonnet Lake Barrens Wilderness Area** is dotted with lakes, marshes, granite barrens and coastal spruce-fir forest.

You won't find a restaurant along this stretch of Highway 16 – head back to Canso, or on to Guysborough.

PRINCE HENRY SINCLAIR

Some people – many of whom are members of The Prince Henry Sinclair Society of North America – believe that Prince Henry Sinclair landed at Chedabucto Bay in 1398. In 1996, they erected a monument in the pretty picnic area at Halfway Cove to commemorate their belief. The Prince – whose other titles included 1st Earl of Orkney, Baron of Roslin, and Lord of Shetland – is thought by some to have undertaken voyages of discovery in the late 14th century to what is now Greenland, Nova Scotia and the US. Some claim that the Mi'kmaq deity Glooscap is none other than Sinclair. We do know that his grandson, William Sinclair, was the builder of Rosslyn Chapel, just outside Edinburgh, Scotland, well known to Freemasons and fans of *The Da Vinci Code*.

On Highway 16 between Canso and Guysborough, Half Island Cove is 17km/11 miles from Canso, Queensport 23km/14 miles and Halfway Cove 34km/21 miles from Canso and 15km/9 miles from Guysborough, and convenient to reach **by car**.

Where to stay

Queensport House B&B (2 rooms) 5354 Hwy 16, Queensport; 358 2402; Jun–Aug; Sep/mid Oct Sat/Sun. Overlooking Queensport lighthouse & Chedabucto Bay. Spacious, bright rooms (sgl & dbl). Substantial b/fast (inc) includes bacon & eggs, & muffins & jams (both homemade). **$**

What to see and do Lighthouse fans will want to pop in to the **Out of the Fog Lighthouse Museum** (*Hwy 16, at Half Island Cove; 358 2108; e keepers_of_the_beacon@hotmail.com; late Jun–mid Sep 10.00–18.00 Thu–Sun*). Here, a varied and extensive collection of lighthouse- and fishing-related artefacts and memorabilia can be seen. Displayed in two rooms of a former schoolhouse, exhibits include working fog horns and numerous lenses. Another must for lighthouse lovers.

GUYSBOROUGH Lying at the head of lovely Chedabucto Bay, Guysborough has a few things going on including some excellent places to eat, a brew pub, marina, golf course, kayak rentals and fine hiking/cycling trails in the area. On the main street, several businesses are located in beautifully restored historic buildings backing on to the waterfront. The **Old Court House**, which houses the tourist office and a museum, is one block up the relatively steep Queen Street from Main Street.

To get to Guysborough **by car**, it is on Highway 16, 46km/29 miles from Canso, 59km/37 miles from the Canso Causeway, 70km/43 miles from Antigonish and 281km/175 miles from Halifax.

History First European settlement dates from 1636 when Nicolas Denys (see box, page 335) established a fishing station here and called it 'Chedabouctou', after *Sedabooktook*, the Mi'kmaq name for the area, meaning 'running far back, or deep extending harbour'. Fort St Louis was built, and by 1683, the community had become home to over 150 Acadians. In 1690, the fort was sacked by privateers from New England: the last Acadians left as a result of the Expulsion (see page 16) in 1755.

Subsequently, the largest group of settlers came at the end of the American Revolution when lands were granted to Loyalists. Guysborough was named in honour of Sir Guy Carleton, commander-in-chief of the British forces in America and the Governor-General of Canada during the 1780s.

Where to stay

Des Barres Manor Inn (10 rooms) 90 Church St; 533 2099, t/f 1 888 933 2099; www.desbarresmanor.com; year-round. Built for a Supreme Court judge in 1837, this beautifully restored mansion is set in immaculate landscaped grounds. Rooms are large & furnished with antiques. All in all, this is the region's best upmarket accommodation. Full gourmet b/fast inc May–Oct, continental b/fast only Nov–Apr. **$$$**

Osprey Shores Golf Resort (10 rooms) 119 Ferry Lane; 533 3904, t/f 1 800 909 3904; www.ospreyshoresresort.com; May–mid Oct. As the name suggests, the motel-style rooms are most popular with golfers. Outdoor pool (seasonal). Ask about 'Stay & Play' packages. The licensed clubhouse lounge (*May–mid Oct 08.00–19.00 daily; $*) serves sandwiches & beverages. Continental b/fast inc. **$$**

Pepperlane Manor Bed & Breakfast (5 rooms) 22 Court St; 533 1884; www.pepperlane.ca; year-round. Wonderful views from guest rooms (3 have en-suite bathrooms, 2 share a bathroom) in Elaine & Greg's delightful, renovated c1874 house. Rate inc excellent b/fast. **$$**

Boylston Provincial Park campground (35 sites) Hwy 16; www.novascotiaparks.ca/parks/boylston.asp; mid Jun–early Sep. 5km north of Guysborough, this site offers exceptional views of the harbour & Chedabucto Bay from a hillside above the wide Milford Haven River with picnic facilities & a basic 35-site wooded campground & occasional concerts in season. Prince Henry Sinclair (see box, page 379) is once again commemorated, here by a wooden prow-shaped monument. **$**

Where to eat

Days Gone By Bakery & Restaurant 59 Main St; 533 2672; www.daysgoneby.ca; May–mid Oct 08.00–20.00 daily. Buy fresh-baked bread & pastries to take away, or sit at one of the pine tables to enjoy all-day b/fast, or healthy salads, soups & excellent-value daily specials such as pan-fried haddock or roast turkey dinner. Licensed. **$**

Des Barres Manor Inn Contact details above; year-round, reservations required. You can sit on the lovely outdoor deck when the weather is clement, or inside by the fire. The menu gives a Maritimes twist to contemporary Canadian cuisine – try the 5-course tasting menu. Excellent wine list & a true fine-dining experience. **$$$**

Rare Bird Pub 80 Main St; 533 2128; www.rarebirdpub.com; Jun–mid Oct 11.30–22.00 Wed–Sun. A tastefully restored c1866 heritage building offering good pub fare, including burgers, salads, & chowders. Patio looks out over the water. Quench your thirst with one of the pub's own Rare Bird craft beers. Occasional live music. **$**

Skipping Stone Café & Store 74 Main St; 533 2460; www.skippingstonestore.com; daily. Beautifully restored old building, patio overlooking marina & harbour. Café features light b/fasts, soups, sandwiches, locally roasted Full Steam coffee, & locally made baked goods/ice cream. **$**

Shopping There's a small Save Easy Supermarket in the **Chedabucto Centre** (*9996 Hwy 16*) on the south side of town. Both the **Days Gone By Bakery** (see above) and the **Skipping Stone Café** (see above) have a selection of gifts and crafts.

Other practicalities

Bank Royal Bank, Main St; 533 3604; 10.00–15.00 Mon–Fri

Hospital Guysborough Memorial Hospital, 10560 Hwy 16; 533 3702

Library Cyril Ward Memorial Library, 27 Pleasant St; 533 3586

Post office 120 Main St; 08.30–17.00 Mon–Fri, 10.30–16.00 Sat

Tourist information 106 Church St; 533 4008; early Jun–late Sep 09.00–17.00 Mon–Fri, 10.00–17.00 Sat/Sun. In the Old Court House Museum (see opposite).

What to see and do Paul Marcella creates beautiful leather goods in his hilltop studio, **Cobbler's Awl** (*37 Cross Rd, Boylston; 533 3054; by chance or appointment*), outside Boylston approximately 17km from Guysborough – call for directions.

It's worth checking the schedule to see if your visit to the **Chedabucto Place Performance Centre** (*27 Green St;* ☎ *533 2015; www.chedabuctoplacetheatre.com*) might tie in with a show at this excellent 300-seat venue which opened in 2007.

The c1843 church-like **Old Court House** (*106 Church St;* ☎ *533 4008; www.guysboroughhistoricalsociety.ca;* ⊕ *early Jun–late Sep 09.00–17.00 Mon–Fri, 10.00–17.00 Sat/Sun*) houses the **local museum**. Serving as both courthouse and town hall for 130 years until 1973, this is one of the country's oldest preserved courthouses. Displays include information on early Acadian and black settlements in the area, a collection of domestic tools and early photographs. There's a reading room with historical and genealogical information.

There are plans to open an artisan distillery in town in the near future.

If you're keen to go **canoeing, kayaking and cycling**, reasonably-priced rentals are available from the **Skipping Stone Café & Store** (see *Where to eat*, opposite). Whereas the entire 44km **Guysborough Nature Trail** which connects Guysborough with Cross Roads Country Harbour (on Highway 316, 25km/15 miles northwest of the eastern terminal of the Country Harbour ferry) might be too daunting for a leisurely **hike**, a walk along the first part of this trail, which follows the path of a railbed that never became a railway, is still worthwhile. Pick up the trail opposite the Fire Station on Queen Street (*Hwy 16*). The **Boylston Provincial Park** (see *Where to stay*, opposite) is also worth a visit

At the magnificently situated **Osprey Shores Golf Resort** (see *Where to stay*, opposite), green fees are CAN$32 for nine holes. There are wonderful Chedabucto Bay views from every hole, and discounts for extra rounds.

PORT SHOREHAM Between Guysborough and Mulgrave, Highway 344 follows the western bank of the Strait of Canso. At Port Shoreham, a small provincial park features a boardwalk to the 1.5km sand and pebble beach, picnic tables overlooking the sea, changing rooms and toilets.

Port Shoreham is on Highway 344, 19km/12 miles from Guysborough.

MULGRAVE Other than a tourist office, neighbouring heritage centre, library and a look-out, there is little to delay you in Mulgrave. Aulds Cove (see page 300), a five-minute drive away, has accommodation and dining options.

At the south end of town the **Scotia Ferry Look-off** offers a good vantage point from which to watch the Strait of Canso shipping. Interpretive boards tell of the pre-Causeway ferries (see below). On the north side, **Venus Cove Marine Park** has a picnic area, playground, boardwalk and floating dock on a small cove. It is also the location of the **Mulgrave Heritage Centre** (see page 382).

To get to Mulgrave **by car**, it is on Highway 344, 5km/3 miles from Aulds Cove, 54km/34 miles from Guysborough.

METAL-DETECTOR TIME

Pirate Harbour, 3km south of Mulgrave, got its name because Blackbeard is said to have wintered here, camouflaging his ship with bushes and branches to prevent it being seen from the strait. And guess what: there are rumours that he buried treasure here.

History In 1833, ferry services were established, carrying passengers from Mulgrave to Port Hawkesbury. Following the completion of the eastern extension of the Inter-Colonial Railway in 1882, passengers got off the train here to board a ferry across to Cape Breton Island. Mulgrave saw great prosperity and became one of the region's principal commercial hubs. That all changed when the Canso Causeway was completed in 1955: almost immediately, rail and much of the road traffic bypassed the town, severely hitting the social and economic life of the community.

But things have improved in recent times. One consequence of the causeway's construction was the creation of the deepest ice-free harbour on the coast of North America, and a superport has been constructed at Mulgrave.

Festivals At the **Scotia Days Festival** in July, there are five days of dances, dinners, races, music and more, culminating in a last-night firework display.

Other practicalities

Library Mulgrave Library, 390 Murray St; 747 2588; www.ecrl.library.ns.ca; see website for opening hours

Post office 433 Main St; 08.30–17.15 Mon–Fri, 08.30–13.00 Sat

Tourist information 54 Loggie St; 747 2788; early Jul/late Aug 09.00–17.00 daily. In the Mulgrave Heritage Centre building (see below).

What to see and do The **Mulgrave Heritage Centre** (*54 Loggie St; 747 2788; early Jul/late Aug 09.00–17.00 daily; admission CAN$2*) is housed in an edifice built to resemble one of the old ferries. Displays on the Canso Causeway (see box, page 304), World War memorabilia, and railway and fishing industry history can be seen here.

Highway 344 continues on to Aulds Cove (5km from Mulgrave) and ends there at the junction with Highway 104. Choose to follow Highway 104 to the west, or cross the Canso Causeway to explore Cape Breton Island.

SABLE ISLAND NATIONAL PARK RESERVE

One of Nova Scotia's most fascinating parts – and one of Canada's newest national parks – is one of the most difficult (and costly) to visit.

Not to be confused with Cape Sable Island in the southwest of the province, Sable Island is a 42km-long windswept treeless and rockless crescent of land a maximum of 1.3km wide in the Atlantic Ocean approximately 290km southeast of Halifax. The closest landfall is Canso (see page 376), and that is over 160km away.

Some of the island's many sand dunes approach 25m in height, and shift slowly towards the east. What is known as a 'freshwater lens' underlies Sable Island. It is maintained by precipitation. Where this lens is exposed to the surface, it does so in the form of freshwater ponds. These ponds (which tend to be in the west of the island) provide fresh water for the island's inhabitants. In the centre of the south side of the island was the site of brackish Lake Wallace: I say 'was' because this geographical feature has all but disappeared, having been filled in by blowing sand.

In winter and spring, the only obvious vegetation is marram grass, but in summer and autumn the island becomes almost lush with wild flowers and berries.

The island was once home to breeding colonies of the Atlantic walrus, but National Park Reserve designation came over a century too late for them. Hunted for their tusk ivory, they were last recorded here in the late 1800s. Today, Sable Island is home to the world's largest breeding colony of grey seals, which pup between late December and early February. A far smaller breeding population of harbour seals also calls the island home. However, the island's most famous inhabitants are its wild horses (see box opposite). This is also part of an important migratory flyway, and over 350 species of bird have been recorded here. Over 15 species have been recorded as breeding here in the spring and summer: one, the Ipswich sparrow, is thought to breed only on Sable Island.

Sable Island is close to one of the major shipping routes between Europe and North America. Because it lies directly in the path of most storm systems that track up the Atlantic coast, it is often hit by strange weather patterns. Being low-lying and treeless, it would have been very difficult for mariners to spot the island before it was too late – even more so in foggy conditions or after dark. The island was designated a National Park Reserve (NPR) in October 2011: the designation ensures that the island receives the highest level of protection for its natural and cultural features.

Parks Canada and Environment Canada's Meteorological Service maintain a year-round presence on the island with personnel based at Main Station. The operational hub of island activities and programmes, the station houses weather monitoring equipment, staff accommodations, workshops, emergency supplies, power generation, water treatment, and communications equipment.

HISTORY There are disputes over the 'discovery' of the island with three unsubstantiated claims by the French and Portuguese in the early and mid 16th century. In 1598, the Lieutenant-General of New France landed on Sable Island, leaving some 50 or 60 convicts with a few provisions whilst he sailed off to find a safer place to anchor. Strong winds made it impossible for him to return to the island and instead he made a brisk journey back to France. It is hard to imagine how anyone survived on the treeless windblown island without proper shelter or provisions: incredibly 11 castaways were picked up by a relief expedition in 1603.

Access to the island was first restricted in 1801 (and has been ever since) to try to stop the plunder of shipwrecks, and later to protect the island's unique environment. That year also marked the beginning of human presence on the island when Canada's first life-saving station was created. It wasn't until the 1870s that the government decided to erect a couple of lighthouses at each end of the island – it has been necessary to move these several times due to the constantly shifting shoreline. The lighthouses are no longer used for naval navigation, and the only

SABLE ISLAND'S HORSES

Seals are quite common on the beach and in the surrounding waters, and over 350 bird species have been sighted, but the island's most famous residents are equine.

There is much speculation over how the horses first came here – records suggest that a clergyman from Boston brought some here in 1737, but historians say that those would have been appropriated by fishermen or privateers (see page 18). It is thought that another Bostonian, Thomas Hancock, shipped 60 horses to the island in 1760, and that those were the ancestors of today's herds. If this is true, where Hancock obtained the horses is also unclear; one suggestion is that they had belonged to Acadians deported from Nova Scotia in 1755 (see page 16). The fact is that between 350 and 400 wild horses now run free on Sable Island.

One of the world's few truly wild horse populations is naturally controlled by the island's food and water supply. The horses fatten up on the relatively lush and plentiful summer vegetation: in winter they rely on marram grass. They supplement their diet with seaweed and kelp that washes up on the beaches.

permanent residents are four scientists, monitoring the weather and environment, and studying the wildlife.

GAS Vast reserves of offshore undersea gas were found off Sable Island in the 1990s. In 1999, the first wells were opened – the drilling platforms can be clearly seen from the island (when it is not foggy) – and the gas is transported to the mainland via a 225km pipeline. One of the many benefits of the 'National Park Reserve' designation was the introduction of a ban on any drilling within one nautical mile of the island. Park officials, scientists and environmentalists continue to keep a close watch on any unwelcome side effects from the drilling process – and keep their fingers crossed.

SHIPWRECKS AND GHOSTLY TALES The cool Labrador Current flows into the Atlantic Ocean and meets the warm Gulf Stream flowing from the southeast. Not only does this result in a far higher than average number of foggy days, but is also thought to be the cause of an immense whirlpool. The Gully, the largest undersea canyon in eastern North America, might also be a contributing factor.

Since the early 17th century, there are records of over 350 vessels which have come to grief on and immediately around Sable Island. It's impossible to estimate how many others failed to be recorded. Not without reason has it long been known as the 'Graveyard of the Atlantic'.

Today, with modern navigational equipment, few boats run aground on Sable Island: the last wreck recorded was a luxury yacht in July 1999. But remains from centuries of shipwrecks are buried in the sand, appearing and disappearing as the wind shifts the grains.

Isolated, windswept and frequently foggy, and with restricted access: not much might grow on the Graveyard of the Atlantic but it has proved fertile for those who like to tell a good yarn, and although they might not admit it, many a Maritimer believes the island to be haunted.

Stories circulated that pirates and bandits used the island as a base from which to lure ships into trouble, allowing the buccaneers to steal anything of value from the stricken vessels, and those on board. Almost as many ghost stories are told about the island as ships that have been wrecked there.

For example, it is said that a dead mother was washed ashore, clutching a baby which somehow still clung to life, albeit very weakly. The baby was taken to the nearest house, and the mother buried on the beach. No-one was surprised when the baby died a day or two later. After that there have been many reports of sightings of a sobbing female spirit wandering the beach as if looking for something.

Some survived wrecks, others were not so lucky. From time to time, bodies would be washed ashore on a strip of Sable Island's shore that became known as the 'haunted beach'. Those living on the island would regularly check the beach for bodies: if any were found, the corpse would be sewn up into a bag made from old sailcloth, and then left on the shoreline to be picked up on the supply boat's next visit – the shifting sand was too unstable for permanent burials.

In the mid 1990s, a scientist reported hearing the sound of piano music floating across the dunes. He knew that no-one else on the island would be playing a radio or CD, and also knew that although there had been pianos on the island in the past, there certainly weren't any at that time.

GETTING THERE Although Sable Island is accessible **by air** and **by sea**, that doesn't begin to tell the full story.

The most favourable travel conditions exist between August and October, since fog is often thick from late June to early August, and can impede air and boat access. Weather conditions at other times of year can make travel to Sable Island especially unpredictable.

For reasons that will become clear if you read on, visitors must be prepared for delays in transportation schedules, both in getting to the island and also when trying to depart. And we're not talking about an hour or two, or even a day or two. Significantly longer delays are not uncommon. No-one will be permitted to go to the island unless they are adequately supplied and equipped to look after themselves completely.

Anyone planning to visit the island must first register with Parks Canada. Details required include the names and number of people in the party, dates and mode of transportation to and from the island, logistical support required (aircraft landing, boat landing, accommodations, etc).

By air Air services are provided by **Maritime Air Charter** (*873 3330; www.maritimeair.com*), which operates a seven-passenger plane for the (approximately) 75-minute flight from Halifax International Airport. The company is not permitted to sell individual seats, so visitors must charter the entire aircraft. As the plane must return to Halifax the same day, most visits are day trips – or visitors will have to pay the full cost of chartering the aircraft to return to Halifax another day.

If visitors do wish to stay overnight, accommodation is extremely limited, and priority for available space is given to operational needs. In addition, the island has no permanent runway: the plane lands and takes off on the island's south beach. Island personnel must assess and mark a runway based on the condition of the beach at the appropriate time – flooding of the beach after a severe storm, for example, can interrupt air service to the island for days or weeks at a time.

Costs are likely to change, but in 2012 chartering the plane for the day and paying all the compulsory extras (including taxes) involved with the flight would cost in the region of CAN$6,250. Double that and add CAN$300 minimum per person for each night you might want to stay.

By sea The chance of dense fog, the ever-changing sandbars, and potentially rough seas around the island (not for nothing was it known as the 'Graveyard of the Atlantic') don't encourage sea arrivals. There are no wharf facilities so vessels must anchor offshore and use a Zodiac or other small boat for a beach landing. There is also a set of strict guidelines. Whilst you *may* be able to charter a boat to get you there, I am unaware of any companies offering sea travel to or from the island.

CONTACTS AND RESOURCES Since April 2012, **Parks Canada** (*www.parkscanada.gc.ca/sable/*) has been the main point of contact for co-ordinating access to the island. It has a detailed section on Sable Island National Park Reserve on its website, and produces a useful booklet (*available on request: e sable@pc.gc.ca*), entitled *Guide to Sable Island National Park Reserve*. The **Maritime Air Charter** website also has Q&A information. For further information, see also www.sabletrust.ns.ca and www.greenhorsesociety.com.

Appendix 1

BUYING PROPERTY

Many visitors come to Nova Scotia, happen to glance in an estate agent's (real estate brokerage's) window, and wonder if they are seeing things. Magnificent houses on large acreages can still be found for the sort of price you might expect for a run-down house in rural eastern Europe. People say that Nova Scotia is a Canadian version of New England, but even with the recent house-price crash in the US, prices here are still a fraction of those in Maine, New Hampshire or Connecticut. You can start house hunting long before you leave home: just go to www.realtor.ca.

If you see something you like, or – when in the province – are tempted by a 'For Sale' sign as you drive by a beautiful house on a bluff overlooking the ocean, you can contact the real estate brokerage directly (the phone number will be on the website or sign). However, I would suggest approaching another realtor (real estate broker) at a different company in the same area (for an explanation, see later in this section). You can always try more than one company until you find someone with whom you feel you have a rapport. They will work on your behalf as a purchasing agent, at no cost to you, as all the brokerage companies have access to competitors' listed properties. Give your chosen realtor a list of the properties in which you are interested and they will arrange viewing appointments. They may also suggest other properties which they feel may interest you. In general, the owners are usually out when you view a house, and your realtor is your guide through as many homes as you wish to view.

They will advise you on some of their pros and cons, and – if something interests you – will negotiate with the seller's realtor on your behalf. They act as the conduit between the buyer and the home owner. That is why I suggest avoiding the situation where your realtor is the listing realtor for the property in which you are interested: rightly or wrongly it is the perception that realtors will work harder for the seller than the buyer in such circumstances (though realtors work under a strict code of ethics, imposed by the Canadian Real Estate Association (CREA), requiring them to follow a set of guidelines when representing both buyer and seller in the same transaction). As always, remember that even if the realtor is working for you, they are in business to make a sale, not to be your friend. Rely solely on realtors' advice or opinions at your peril.

If you are considering making an offer well below the asking price, different realtors work in different ways. Some will have an informal chat with the seller's listing realtor or if it is their own listing, directly with the homeowner; whilst others will insist that you make a formal offer in writing. Either way is appropriate.

All Nova Scotia Purchase and Sale agreements now have a pre-written clause making it advisable to contact an experienced property (real estate) lawyer after signing your Agreement of Purchase and Sale and allowing them time to review the fine print and comment or recommend changes to the transaction. Any realtor should be able to point you in the direction of a good lawyer.

Your offer should include certain conditions: these will vary from purchase to purchase. They might relate to timing – don't be rushed as you are likely to need time to arrange financing (and, probably transfer of funds from the UK to Nova Scotia) before you are bound to the contract. It should be made clear that your offer is subject to a satisfactory home inspection (what is called a survey in the UK)

A NEW LIFE IN NOVA SCOTIA

Thinking of emigrating to Nova Scotia? Before you can become a Canadian citizen, you have to apply for Permanent Residence. To do this, you can be sponsored by a family member who is a Canadian citizen (or Permanent Resident) or apply under one of the following categories:

- Skilled workers and professionals
- Canadian Experience Class (if you have recent Canadian work experience)
- Investors, entrepreneurs and self-employed people

The **Citizenship and Immigration Canada** website (*www.cic.gc.ca*) has a useful self-assessment test section where you can see if you might have enough points to qualify.

Successful candidates should expect to have to wait two years or more from when they submit their initial application until they receive their Permanent Residence.

A quicker method is likely to be via the **Nova Scotia Nominee Program** (see *www.novascotiaimmigration.com*). Here you apply to the Nova Scotia Office of Immigration: if you are considered worthy, you will receive a Letter of Nomination. You then apply via the Federal scheme as above, but will hopefully have been 'fast-tracked'.

Either way, there will be fees to pay: CAN$490 for Right of Permanent Residence (PR), then CAN$475–1,050 depending on the category. You'll also have to fork out for a private medical.

Do the paperwork yourself, or engage the services of an immigration lawyer: try, for example, Lee Cohen (*423 2412; www.mleecohen.com*) or Elizabeth Wozniak Inc (446 4747; http://nsimmigration.ca/).

Moving to a foreign (albeit English-speaking) country is something of a minefield, and you may wish to seek help from a couple of commercial organisations who specialise in the field. Try **Relocation Nova Scotia** (*431 8689, (UK) +44 (0) 121 288 2682; http://relocationnovascotia.com*), or **UK2NovaScotia** (*860 0845; http://uk2novascotia.com*). Most counties in the province have offices whose brief it is to help new arrivals settle.

If you are successful, you have to 'land' in Nova Scotia within a certain amount of time (usually within a year of the date of your medical). You can then apply for a Social Insurance Number (SIN), and a Nova Scotia Health Card (benefits under the health card do not apply for six months). To maintain your PR status, you must spend at least 730 days out of five years in Canada. You can apply for Canadian citizenship if you have PR status and have spent at least three out of four years in Canada.

and, perhaps a land survey, which confirms that the home is located on the land described in the deed. If the property relies on a well for its water supply and/or a septic tank for sewage disposal – as many do outside cities and towns – I suggest that you include having those checked as a condition to be included in the agreement.

Another condition might be that the sale is dependent on your being able to obtain insurance for the property: some insurance companies will refuse to insure certain properties, or (more likely) may insist that certain changes are made before the cover that they offer will take effect.

In the vast majority of cases, either prior to making an offer to purchase or upon making the offer to purchase, you will be given a Property Condition Disclosure Statement (PCDS) which the seller has completed. In this, the seller must disclose (to the best of his or her knowledge) information about the property, even if these may be damaging to the sale. Topics covered include recent repairs, water supply, electrical services, plumbing, water leakage issues, rights of way and building restrictions. You will be allowed a certain amount of time to check this through.

It is very important that you go through the PCDS carefully, clarifying anything that is unclear, ambiguous or has been left blank. In my opinion, I think that it is worth ensuring that your home inspector has a copy of the PCDS so that they can also comment on any specific problems that have been noted thereon. Ensure also that your lawyer sees the PCDS, if available, before you go ahead with the purchase.

Once all has been settled, you pay the agreed down payment (a negotiated amount, which may be as much as 10% of the sale price) on a pre-arranged date if all the conditions have been met. Note that if you then get cold feet, you will not only lose your deposit but could be sued for damages.

Don't get carried away, and do think things through. How much will the house and grounds cost to maintain? What will happen to the property when you're not using it? Are you thinking of buying to let? Outside Halifax and Wolfville (university towns), the rental season doesn't stretch much beyond July and August. You are likely to need a property manager, or property maintenance company. Bear extra costs – such as legal fees, deed transfer tax, home inspection, adjustments (including your share of property taxes and fuel pre-paid by the seller), all plus 15% Harmonised Sales Tax (HST) – in mind. HST only applies to the purchase price of the property if you are buying a new home from a developer – but not if you are buying a home that has been owned/inhabited previously.

If you are buying a home that needs work, remember the message from all of those property programmes – repairs and renovations almost always cost far more than the amount for which one budgets.

Recommended realtors include **Tradewinds Realty Inc** (*www.tradewindsrealty.com*) and **RE/MAX** (*www.remax-oa.com*). For home inspectors, choose a member of the **Canadian Association of Home and Property Inspectors** (*www.cahpi-atl.com*).

Appendix 2

FURTHER INFORMATION

BOOKS Note that many of these titles are out of print but often pop up in (real or online) used bookshops.

Architecture

Archibald, Stephen and Stevenson, Sheila *Heritage Houses of Nova Scotia* Formac, 2003
Penney, Allen *Houses of Nova Scotia: An Illustrated Guide to Architectural Style Recognition* Nova Scotia Museum, 1989

Autobiography

Haines, Max *The Spitting Champion of the World* Penguin, Canada, 2007. Growing up in Antigonish in the 1930s–50s.
Maclean, Angus Hector *God and the Devil at Seal Cove* Petheric Press, 1976

Fiction and poetry

Bishop, Elizabeth *The Complete Poems (1927–79)* Chatto and Windus, 1983. A number relate to her time in Nova Scotia.
Buckler, Ernest *The Mountain and the Valley* New Canadian Library, 1989
Clarke, George Elliot *Whylah Falls* Raincoast Books, 2001
Eaton, Evelyn *Quietly My Captain Waits* Formac, 2001
Fitch, Sheree *The Gravesavers* Doubleday Canada, 2005. Based on the SS *Atlantic* disaster – for readers aged ten plus.
Haliburton, Thomas Chandler *The Clockmaker* BiblioLife, 2009
Joe, Rita *The Poems of Rita Joe* Abanaki Press, 1978
MacLennan, Hugh *Barometer Rising* New Canadian Library, 2007. Compelling romance set against the horrors of wartime and the Halifax Explosion.
MacLeod, Alistair *No Great Mischief* Vintage, 2001. Cape Breton Island-set Scottish family saga.
Raddall, Thomas Head *The Governor's Lady*, Nimbus, 1992

Folklore

Creighton, Helen, and others *Bluenose Ghosts, Bluenose Magic, Traditional Songs from Nova Scotia* Nimbus, 2009

History

Bradley, Michael *Holy Grail Across the Atlantic* Hounslow Press, 1988
Bruce, Harry *An Illustrated History of Nova Scotia* Nimbus, 1997
Cameron, Silver Donald *The Education of Everett Richardson: The Nova Scotia Fishermen's Strike, 1970–71* McClelland & Stewart, 1977

Campey, Lucille H *After the Hector: The Scottish Pioneers of Nova Scotia and Cape Breton 1733–1852* Dundurn Group, 2008
Choyce, Lesley *Nova Scotia: Shaped by the Sea* Pottersfield, 2007
Finnan, Mark *The Story of Sir William Alexander* Formac, 1997. The story of the first Nova Scotian.
Goodwin, William B *The Truth About Leif Ericsson and the Greenland Voyages* Kessinger, 2007
Hannay, James *The History of Acadia (1605–1763)* J&A McMillan, 1879. Very rare.
Kimber, Stephen *Sailors, Slackers & Blind Pigs: Halifax at War* Random House, 2003. The story behind Halifax's infamous VE Day riots
Kitz, Janet *Shattered City: The Halifax Explosion and the Road to Recovery* Nimbus, 2008
Ledger, Don, Style, Chris & Strieber, Whitley *Dark Object: The World's Only Government-Documented UFO Crash* Dell Publishing, 2001
MacDonald, Laura M *Curse of the Narrows* Walker & Co, 2005. The Halifax Explosion.
MacNeill, Blair H *Ferry Tales: Stories of Village Life* Pronto, 2000. Stories from Digby Neck.
Mann, William F *The Knights Templar in the New World: How Henry Sinclair Brought the Grail to Acadia* Inner Traditions Bear & Company, 2004
Perkins, Charlotte *The Romance of Old Annapolis Royal* Historical Association of Annapolis Royal, 1985
Pohl, Frederick *Prince Henry Sinclair: His Expedition to the New World in 1398* Nimbus, 1997
Raddall, Thomas Head *Halifax, Warden of the North* Nimbus, 2007
Raddall, Thomas Head *The Rover: Story of A Canadian Privateer* MacMillan, 1966

Mi'kmaq

Choyce, Lesley and May, Rita (eds) *The Mi'kmaq Anthology* Pottersfield, 1997
Knockwood, Isabelle *Out of the Depths* Fernwood Publishing, 2001. The experiences of Mi'kmaq children at school in Shubenacadie.
Lacey, Laurie *Micmac Medicines Remedies and Recollections* Nimbus, 1993
Paul, Daniel N *We Were Not The Savages* Fernwood Publishing, 2006. Nova Scotia's history from a Mi'kmaq perspective.
Spicer, Stanley T *Glooscap Legends* Nimbus, 2007. The life history of Glooscap.

Natural history

Ferguson, Laing *The Fossil Cliffs of Joggins* Nova Scotia Museum, 1988
Maybank, Blake *Birding Sites of Nova Scotia* Nimbus, 2005
O'Connor, D'Arcy *The Secret Treasure of Oak Island* The Lyons Press, 2004
Parker, Mike *Guides of the North Woods: Hunting & Fishing Tales* Nimbus, 2004
Sibley, David *The Sibley Field Guide to Birds of Eastern North America* Knopf Publishing, 2003
Thurston, Harry *Dawning of the Dinosaurs: The Story of Canada's Oldest Dinosaurs* Nimbus, 1994
Zinck, Marion (ed) *Roland's Flora of Nova Scotia* Nimbus, 1998. Two volumes.

Sports and activities

Conrod, Gary *The Nova Scotia Bicycle Book* Available from Atlantic Canada Cycling (*423 2453; www.atlanticcanadacycling.com*), 1995. Plans for a new edition in 2013. The accommodation listings are out of date but the rest of the book is still very useful.
Cuningham, Scott *Sea Kayaking in Nova Scotia* Nimbus, 2000
Dill, C *Canoe Routes of Nova Scotia* Canoe Nova Scotia Association, 1983
Haynes, Michael *Hiking Trails of Nova Scotia* Goose Lane Editions, 2012
Paine, Albert Bigelow *The Tent Dwellers* Kessinger, 2005
Smith, Andrew L *Paddling the Tobeatic: Canoe Routes of Southwestern Nova Scotia* Nimbus, 2004

Watt, Walter *Nova Scotia By Bicycle* Available from Bicycle Nova Scotia (*http://bicycle.ns.ca*), 2004

Travel writing

Bird, Will R *This Is Nova Scotia* and *Off-Trail in Nova Scotia* Ryerson Press, 1950 and 1956 respectively. Motoring around Nova Scotia in the 1950s.

Crowell, Clement W *Novascotiaman* Nova Scotia Museum, 1979

Day, Frank Parker *Rockbound* University of Toronto Press, 1998. Based on East Ironbound Island near Blandford.

Dennis, Clara *Down in Nova Scotia* and *More about Nova Scotia* Ryerson Press, 1946 and 1937 respectively. Motoring around Nova Scotia in the 1930s.

Howe, Joseph *Western and Eastern Rambles: Travel Sketches of Nova Scotia* University of Toronto Press, 1973

Richardson, Evelyn *We Keep a Light* Nimbus, 1995. Set on Bon Portage Island near Shag Harbour.

Spicer, Stanley T *Masters of Sail* Ryerson Press, 1968

WEBSITES

Driving in Nova Scotia

www.gov.ns.ca/snsmr/rmv/safe/handbook.asp Nova Scotia drivers' handbook.

www.novascotiagasprices.com Petrol costs.

Facts

www.cbc.ca/ns/ Provincial, national and international news.

http://clean.ns.ca, **www.ecologyaction.ca** and **http://nsen.ca** Environmental groups.

http://destinationhalifax.com/rainbow and **http://gay.hfxns.org** Useful information for gays.

http://nsgna.ednet.ns.ca Genealogy.

www.statcan.gc.ca Canada's official national (and provincial) statistics.

www.weatheroffice.gc.ca Five-day weather forecasts for locations all over the province.

Natural history

http://maybank.tripod.com/BSNS/BSNS.htm Birding sites of Nova Scotia.

http://nsbs.chebucto.org The Nova Scotia Bird Society.

http://nswildflora.ca Nova Scotia Wild Flora Society.

Sport and outdoor activities

www.atlanticcanadacycling.com and **http://bicycle.ns.ca** Cycling.

http://ckns.ca Canoeing and kayaking.

www.geocaching.com and **www.geocachingnovascotia.ca** Geocaching.

http://golfingns.com and **www.nsga.ns.ca** Golf.

www.novatrails.com and **www.trails.gov.ns.ca** Hiking.

www.surfns.com and **http://haliwax.com** Surfing.

Travel information and accessible travel

http://accessadvisor.ca and **www.accesstotravel.gc.ca**

www.bbcanada.com Inns and B&Bs across Nova Scotia.

www.cbsa-asfc.gc.ca Canadian Border Services Agency – customs and immigration.

www.davidorkin.info Author's updates website.

www.maritimebus.com and **www.peisland.com/triustours** Major coach operators.

www.novascotia.com Official Nova Scotia tourism site.

www.viarail.ca VIA Rail Canada schedules and prices.

Index

Entries in **bold** indicate main entries; those in *italics* indicate maps